D1337284

MASTERS
OF THE
BATTLEFIELD

MASTERS

OF THE

BATTLEFIELD

GREAT COMMANDERS
FROM THE CLASSICAL
AGE TO THE
NAPOLEONIC ERA

OXFORD
UNIVERSITY PRESS

OXFORD
UNIVERSITY PRESS

Oxford University Press is a department of the University of Oxford.
It furthers the University's objective of excellence in research,
scholarship, and education by publishing worldwide.

Oxford   New York
Auckland   Cape Town   Dar es Salaam   Hong Kong   Karachi
Kuala Lumpur   Madrid   Melbourne   Mexico City   Nairobi
New Delhi   Shanghai   Taipei   Toronto

With offices in
Argentina   Austria   Brazil   Chile   Czech Republic   France   Greece
Guatemala   Hungary   Italy   Japan   Poland   Portugal   Singapore
South Korea   Switzerland   Thailand   Turkey   Ukraine   Vietnam

Oxford is a registered trade mark of Oxford University Press
in the UK and certain other countries.

Published in the United States of America by
Oxford University Press
198 Madison Avenue, New York, NY 10016

Library of Congress Cataloging-in-Publication Data
Davis, Paul K., 1952–
Masters of the battlefield : great commanders from the classical age
to the Napoleonic era / Paul K. Davis.
p.   cm.
Includes bibliographical references and index.
ISBN 978-0-19-534235-2
1. Generals—Biography. 2. Military biography.
3. Military art and science—History. I. Title.
U51.D38   2013
355.0092'2—dc23   2012039004

1 3 5 7 9 8 6 4 2

Printed in the United States of America
on acid-free paper

For Jerri and my parents,
without whose love and continued support
this would not have been possible

CONTENTS

INTRODUCTION

One Man's Gifts

"The gods have not given all their gifts to one man. You know how
to win victory, Hannibal, you do not how to use it."

—*Maharbal, Hannibal's cavalry leader, berating him for not
following up on the decisive victory over Rome at Cannae*

TO A GREAT EXTENT THIS QUOTE, which comes from the Roman historian Livy's *History of Rome*, sums up the nature of this book. Hannibal
had proved himself a master tactician at Cannae, but he was failing as a
strategist, at least according to his cavalry leader Maharbal, when he did
not exploit that great victory and go on immediately to take Rome. There
are many who believe that the implementation of strategy is the ultimate
military accomplishment of a general. Battles do not stand alone but are
the building blocks of campaigns and of wars. Strategy means making the
battle fit into its proper place in the bigger picture.

The impetus for this book came as a suggestion from Oxford University
Press to expand on my earlier work, *100 Decisive Battles*. The original
concept was to develop a series of books that would each cover important
battles of a particular region or time. This work focuses on commanders,
offering an introduction to the nature of warfare across history and geography and expanding on key military events, such as Cannae, by looking
those in charge. Its premise is that the nature of the commanders matters
deeply.

In this respect this work follows the argument J. F. C. Fuller made in his 1936 publication *Generalship: Its Diseases and Their Cure*. Written in the wake of World War I, Fuller's work laments a general's absence from the battlefield. Soldiers need to know that whoever is sending him into harm's way understands the danger—that he realizes the gravity of the situation. As Fuller argues, the farther away from the battlefield a general stands, the more soulless he becomes. That certainly seemed to have been the case on the Western Front during World War I.

This book will focus on the great tacticians of war, those whose presence was vital to the outcome of the battle. Hannibal's victory at Cannae was no less brilliant because it did not lead to ultimate Carthaginian victory. His accomplishment (the so-called double envelopment, as we will see) became the goal of battlefield commanders from that day forward. Cannae was not a decisive battle in the strategic or grand strategic sense, but on that one day in May 216 BC Hannibal proved himself to be a great commander, one few generals dared to face in combat. Napoleon noted that a general was the "all" ("le tout") of an army: "The Gauls were not conquered by the Roman legions, but by Caesar. It was not before the Carthaginian soldiers that Rome was made to tremble, but before Hannibal. It was not the Macedonian phalanx which penetrated to India, but Alexander."[1]

Michael Grant wrote in his foreword to Liddell Hart's biography of Scipio: "Scipio Africanus offers the strongest possible argument against the hypothesis put forward by some Marxists alleging that individuals have not mattered very much in history and what matters is only a series of impersonal trends and tendencies."[2] Security experts Daniel L. Byman and Kenneth Pollack argued that they found troubling "the tendency of scholars to ignore the role of personalities in international relations." They note, "The theoretical objections raised over the years do not stand up under closer examination and should not prevent us from mining this rich ore."[3] Though their article deals with statesmen, the same concept is true in the military, where idiosyncrasies and human error undeniably affect the outcomes of battles, and even of entire campaigns and wars.

Kimberly Kagan argues for writing military history from the "eye of command" approach in her book of the same name. She notes that the contemporary "face of battle" coverage is not the proper venue for learning command lessons, as the forest is lost for the trees. The eye-of-command approach "does not prejudge at what level of the military hierarchy critical events occur. It recognizes that the morale and psychology of the soldiers on the battlefield, their physical well-being, and the weapons that they use and face all influence the course of battle and may at times be critical or decisive to its outcome. Similarly, it recognizes the potential importance of the commander's decisions and actions."[4]

This book examines those generals who made a difference in the outcome of combat—by grasping the way an enemy would think or move and acting or reacting in such a way as not only to defeat him but, in many instances, to do so in the face of forces outnumbering his own. As Kagan notes, morale and psychology matter—a sentiment echoing Napoleon's famous dictum that in war the moral is to the physical as three is to one. It is the general who provides the morale. In many cases, as we will see, a general's previous victories can be a boost to morale, but even a winning record does not qualify someone as a great tactician. Although many leading historians rank Ulysses Grant higher on the generalship scale than they do Robert E. Lee, most soldiers would have rather served under Lee than under Grant. Grant's strength as a general was his determination, not his tactical abilities. He is one of the key examples of a successful strategist who was not also a successful tactician. Given equal resources, Lee would have defeated Grant, just as he did so many other Union generals. In the end, Grant's superior firepower and manpower overwhelmed Napoleon's three-to-one ratio, but Lee's victories over superior numbers in battle after battle prove him to be the superior tactician. Grant had a habit of throwing his men into frontal attacks against defensive positions in battle after battle (as in the Wilderness campaign of 1864).

Distinctions between different levels of warfare are critical. David Chandler, in his book on the Duke of Marlborough, sets out four distinct levels:

At the apex comes "Grand Strategy," the formulation of national policy and war aims, the creation and preservation of alliances. Next comes "Strategy," the planning of campaigns and series of operations with the intention of carrying out the Grand Strategic objectives. Third are "Grand Tactics"—the devising of battle plans and the outlines of operations to profit from the situations the strategy has made possible or encouraged to develop. Fourth are "minor Tactics"—the actual fighting methods employed at the unit level to gain a local success, which, together with a dozen or more similar engagements, go to make up a victory.[5]

The "grand tactics" in modern terminology are often called the "operational" level, and most of what I cover in this book explores that level.

In each of the studies to follow, I give a brief biography of the commander, with an eye toward exploring to what degree, if any, his background shaped his leadership, and so, too, the nature of armies and warfare he had to work with. From this general overview of period warfare, I examine the course of the war in which the general fought, providing background to those particular battles that, in my view, best illustrate his ability to win. Each battle is considered both in terms of its strategic nature and actions. In the final portion of each chapter, I endeavor to show the nature of a commander's tactical skills and principles. My conclusions are based on my own views, of course, as well as those of the generals' contemporaries (if available), the works of modern biographers, and the U.S. Army Field Manual 100-5, Operations, which spells out the principles of war that have been adopted over the years. These principles are:

1. Objective—Direct every military operation toward a clearly defined, decisive, and attainable objective.

2. Offensive—Seize, retain, and exploit the initiative.

3. Mass—Mass the effects of overwhelming combat power at the decisive place and time.

4. Economy of Force—Employ all combat power available in the most effective way possible; allocate minimum essential combat power to secondary efforts.

5. Maneuver—Place the enemy in a position of disadvantage through the flexible application of combat power.

6. Unity of Command—For every objective, seek unity of command and unity of effort.

7. Security—Never permit the enemy to acquire unexpected advantage.

8. Surprise—Strike the enemy at a time or place or in a manner for which he is unprepared.

9. Simplicity—Prepare clear, uncomplicated plans and concise orders to ensure thorough understanding.

To these I have added another principle, one from the British Army's manual:

10. Morale—A positive state of mind derived from inspired leadership, a shared sense of purpose and values, well-being, perceptions of worth, and group cohesion.

THE COMMANDERS I HAVE CHOSEN reflect the nature of warfare through history. They dominated their era, or were the first to use—or best at using—the weaponry of their era. They stood out among their contemporaries in two main respects: their ability to deploy forces and their ability to motivate those forces in combat. In some cases, they revolutionized the nature of warfare with the introduction of new weapons. Though not usually ranked highly in military history, for example, the Bohemian general and Hussite leader Jan Zizka was the first effective proponent of handheld firearms on the battlefield. They also tended to be pioneers in their ways of employing the forces at their disposal, as Epaminondas did in his victories over the Spartans.

In almost every case, the commanders in this book inspired intense devotion from their soldiers. In absolutely every case, they saw what no one else saw and outthought their opponent, which in the end is the real key to success. This talent is best described as coup d'oeil, the ability to see and grasp in the blink of an eye the nature of the terrain and enemy deployment as well as how to exploit the enemy's weakness. These generals had the ability to see the limits of contemporary methods of warfare and to develop new tactics, tactics that altered the nature of warfare itself. They were great commanders.

One other thing affected the scope of this work. I selected commanders who directly commanded all or the bulk of national armies, and who controlled the battle from a central location on the battlefield, where they could see directly what was happening and react to it. After the Napoleonic wars this ability became less and less possible. While this description applies to many of the battlefields of the Civil War, the generals of that conflict who understood the nature of that style of warfare, and worked to think and act in original ways to overcome the negative aspects of that style of warfare, were subordinate generals. Had I included that war, I would have discussed Nathan Bedford Forrest, who realized the nature of warfare had changed due to the rifled musket and, rather than using the long-standing linear tactics most generals still employed, began developing an early form of fire-and-movement tactics.

MASTERS
OF THE
BATTLEFIELD

I

Epaminondas (418?–362 BC)
Beotarch of Thebes

> Everybody must praise Epaminondas for being the most famous
> Greek general, or at least consider him second to none other.
>
> *—Pausanias*

EPAMINONDAS WAS BORN to no great wealth or status. His father,
Polymnis, was of a noble but poor family. Still, through one means or
another Palymnis made sure his son received a more than ordinary education, since he "was so well educated that no Theban was more so,"
reports the first-century Roman biographer Cornelius Nepos.[1] Most
important was the instruction he received in philosophy from the well-
known student of Pythagoras, Lysis of Tarentum. Epaminondas became
so devoted to this teacher that it is said he shunned the company of those
his own age in order to learn more from the master. He also studied mathematics and music (both very important in Pythagorean thought) as well
as dancing, and as he grew older, Epaminondas engaged in gymnastics,
where he preferred speed to strength. Most of his physical training was in
the ways of the warrior.

All ancient biographers mention his personality, molded by Pythagorean teachings. These included living simply, sharing possessions com-
munally, treating all persons equally, speaking the truth in all situations,
and engaging in contemplation. Pythagoras taught that there were three
kinds of men: those who love gain, honor, or wisdom. He was also one

of the originators of the concept of transmigration of souls. All of this is reflected in Nepos's description of Epaminondas as "modest, prudent, grave, wisely availing himself of opportunities, skilled in war, brave in action, and of remarkable courage. He was so great a lover of truth that he would not tell a falsehood, even in jest; he was also a master of his passions, gentle in disposition, submitting to wrong not merely from the Theban people, but from his own friends. . . . He bore poverty so easily that he received nothing from his state save glory."[2]

Warfare of the Time

GREEK WARFARE IN THE FOURTH CENTURY BC was based on the phalanx formation, made up primarily of heavy infantry known as hoplites (from *hoplon*, the weapons and accoutrements of war). The nature of warfare went back to early Hellenic times, when communities and later *poleis* (singular *polis*, city-state) were primarily agriculturally based and not in close proximity to one another. The male citizens were true militia: farmers first and soldiers when necessary. The soldier's role depended on what weaponry and armor he could afford. Most owned a bronze helmet, breastplate, and greaves along with a round, concave wooden shield with brass or iron around the rim, which is usually described as no more than a meter in diameter. The standard weapons were a spear (some two to three meters in length) and a short sword.

Those who could not afford such array acted as peltasts, light infantry carrying the small shield called a *pelte*, whose weapons were slings or javelins and whose role was mainly skirmishing and support. John Lynn argues that the peltasts got little respect from the hoplites because they fought from a distance. The hoplite viewed such warfare as unmanly. *Real* soldiers fought their enemy face to face.[3] There was also probably some class and economic discrimination involved. Still, the peltasts were becoming a more integral part of Greek forces and at times showed themselves to be important to a battle's outcome. In 426 Athenian phalanxes at Aegitium took a severe beating from a force of Aetolian peltasts, and the Athenian general Iphicrates nearly wiped out a phalanx of Spartans near Corinth in 390. In spite of these successes, the peltasts remained a minor arm of the Greek military.

Cavalry was employed primarily as an auxiliary arm to aid the main infantry lines. When used, it was mainly for reconnaissance, screening the infantry as it deployed for battle, protecting the flanks during battle, and either pursuing a defeated enemy or covering one's own retreat.[4] The stirrup had yet to be invented, so using cavalry for shock was not yet considered. The city-state of Thebes was one of the poleis that did develop a fairly effective cavalry force. Sparta, however, fielded an inferior cavalry arm. In the Spartan military the hoplite was *the* soldier, so cavalry units were poorly trained and motivated. The wealthier Spartans raised horses but others rode them on campaign; according to Xenophon, "It was only when the ban was called out that the appointed trooper presented himself; then he would get his horse and such arms as were given him, and take the field on the moment's notice. As for the men, on the other hand, it was those who were least strong of body and least ambitious who were mounted on the horses."[5]

The standard battle formation was the phalanx, a rectangle of hoplites usually (but not always) eight ranks deep. Contemporary accounts of ancient battles described phalanxes of more than fifty ranks, but that was rare. No author of the time gave any specific reason for phalanxes being of greater or lesser depth; it was often a decision of the individual phalanx leader to make as they deployed for battle. It may have been a matter of how individual units trained in their own polis. Still, units to a depth of eight ranks are described most often.[6] Many factors would come into play when determining phalanx depth: whether the terrain covered the flanks, whether there was sufficient cavalry and light infantry to protect the flanks, the relative advantages of a narrow front for hitting power versus a wider front to prevent outflanking.

The ideal battlefield would be flat, open ground. The enemy armies approached the contest in an open formation, then tightened up as they went into battle, showing a series of almost-interlocking shields with spears protruding from above them. The troops would then break into a trot or run for shock. What happened next is a point of much scholarly debate.

The Greek word for the phalanx battle is *othismos*, meaning "shoving." What, however, does "shoving" mean? Is it a figurative "pushing the enemy back"? Is it a literal tug-of-war in reverse, where the more mass on one side usually defeats the lesser mass on the other? Is it an individual shoving: the frontline soldier using his shield as an offensive weapon along with his spear or sword, pushing the man opposite him in an attempt to make him lose his balance? All these concepts have their advocates among historians, and all have ancient sources that support or contradict them.

There has also been some argument whether the othismos was constant throughout the battle or merely a final push as the enemy began to break. If it was indeed important to have the pressure from the rear, then the side to exert it first would have an advantage; hence, it would almost certainly have been used from the initial contact. In his article on the subject, Robert Luginbill writes, "Fatigue, terrain, casualties, skill, courage, and cowardice would doubtless all play a role in varying the amount of force imparted by the leading edge of shields, but whenever two opposing phalanxes 'came to grips,' the physical pressure of othismos would normally continue until one side literally pushed the other to the breaking point."[7] Others argue that the othismos came after the front ranks had fought each other with spears and swords. When one side began to gain the momentum, the shove would be the final maneuver to force the enemy's retreat.

After reviewing the many conflicting views, Adrian Goldsworthy argues that the nature of the phalanx is as much psychological as physical. It is known that the most experienced veterans made up the front and rear ranks, putting the relative novices in the middle mass of men. After the initial violent contact, the front two rows would fight it out with their spears and, if need be, their swords. Given the weight of armor and exertion such fighting would entail, it would not be unlikely that the fighting would at times cease and the troops stop to catch their breath. The massed troops behind would give them the necessary encouragement to keep fighting (as well as block any path of retreat) while the veterans in the rear would make sure the rookies would hold their ground. Thus, to Goldsworthy's mind, othismos may not have one simple meaning. It could have been the physical contact of individuals or units, or it could be the psychological impetus necessary to hit the enemy one more time until he breaks.[8] Therefore, even if the phalanx did not smash the enemy at first contact, it could defeat them through attrition; in each case, depth of formation, combined with determination of the individuals within it, was of paramount importance. Also, if the initial contact did not result in one side breaking, the two forces could have paused to rest, replace wounded men in the front ranks, and charge again; thus, there could be multiple shoves in a battle until the side with the greater unit cohesion prevailed.

Goldsworthy also discusses a major question of practicality. Given the fact that all non-Spartan armies (less a few special units like the elite

Sacred Band of Thebes) were militia with minimal training, maintaining a close formation while on the "run to contact" is impossible. Therefore, an initial mass shove would be strongly diluted by men running faster or slower than others. Thus the Spartans, by training to keep in step and advancing more slowly, tended to win their battles by maintaining their strong front.

By the time of Epaminondas, the Greek way of war had been in existence since the second half of the seventh century BC. Many wars were fought over that span of time but, as Chester Starr notes in his text on the ancient world, "The Greek states did not press severely and continuously upon one another . . . the states of Hellas rarely pushed their wars, in view of the difficulty of sieges, to the total destruction of a defeated foe."[9] Still, there were sufficient wars for citizens of all Greek city-states to have plenty of opportunities to become veteran soldiers, even though they remained primarily civilians. Only Sparta had a standing army.

The Opponents

THE RIVAL OVER WHICH EPAMINONDAS and his Thebans gained their great victories was Sparta, a power against which Thebes should have had little success. Sparta was the dominant city-state of the Peloponnese (indeed, of all of Greece in the early fourth century BC), a region they had ruled directly or indirectly since the eighth century BC. By defeating and then intimidating neighboring populations (primarily Messenia), Sparta had developed a servant class, the helots, who did the farming necessary to keep Spartan society functional while the Spartan males spent their lives pursuing martial arts. An occasional war against the helots kept them in their subservient position and kept the army sharp when no other enemy was on hand. A "middle class" of sorts consisted of non-Spartans living in the polis that Sparta ruled, Lacedaemonia. These were the *perioikoi* (literally "dwellers about"), craftspeople who in wartime served as soldiers and support troops for the Spartan army. They served as hoplites in battle but did not have full political or social rights, and served more as the citizen militia did in other poleis. The male citizens of the city of Sparta, the Spartiates (alternatively Peers or Equals), ran the society under the direction of two kings, a twenty-eight-man council of retired soldiers and former kings (the *gerousia*), and a council of five publicly elected men known as *ephors*. All of these functioned with an *ecclesia* made up of all

Spartiates. The government thus had aspects of monarchy, oligarchy, and democracy. At most, the Spartiates numbered about 9,000, but all were trained from their youth to be the finest warriors of the Greek world. They allied with the rest of the Greeks to beat back the Persian invasions of the early fifth century, but maintained an almost continuous rivalry with Athens after that joint effort.

Thebes, located in the central part of Greece in the province of Boeotia, was a crossroads of invasion. The warfare going on constantly in its neighborhood served to keep it from ever becoming a major power, and it usually was under the sway of one of the two great powers, Athens or Sparta. A community known mostly for its "backward" farmers, it was something of a butt of jokes among the other Hellenic states. It was during one of those periods when Thebes was under the Spartan heel that circumstances began to alter, and Epaminondas was the political and military instrument of that change. He did, however, have some assistance from a close friend, Pelopidas. In 384, Pelopidas had been badly wounded while fighting in the Peloponnese, and Epaminondas had saved his life. Pelopidas became commander of the Sacred Band, the elite unit of Thebes. The unit, started earlier by Gorgidas, came into its own only under Pelopidas's command. The unit consisted of 300 full-time soldiers based in the city citadel, the Kadmeia. It was Pelopidas who motivated the forty-year-old Epaminondas to join Theban leadership.

In the wake of the Peloponnesian Wars (431–404 BC) Thebes began to grow diplomatically closer to Athens, since Sparta had emerged from the war as the major power in Greece. Also, Thebes was establishing a stronger position in the region of Boeotia, which it had long tried to control. The Boeotian Federation consisted of eleven cities that provided representatives to a sixty-man council under the leadership of *boeotarchs*, one from each city. Each city was assigned the task of providing 1,000 hoplites and 100 cavalry in time of war. Thebes's closer relationship with Athens drew Spartan ire, and in 382 Sparta launched a sneak attack on Thebes, seized the Kadmeia, and established a Spartan garrison with the aid of the local pro-Sparta faction. Leading pro-Athenian political figures, including Pelopidas, fled for Athens, where they plotted a way to take back control of Thebes. In 379 BC, the exiles staged their own surprise attack, sneaking into the city and killing the collaborators, then rousing the citizens to isolate and force the surrender of the Spartan garrison. Soon thereafter, both Pelopidas and Epaminondas (who had had no role in the overthrow) became boeotarchs.

Over the next several years Sparta failed to reimpose its will on Thebes, primarily owing to Pelopidas's engaging in some brilliant bribery and manipulation. Even more importantly, the nature of Boeotian society was changing, as Epaminondas and Peolopidas convinced the leaders of Thebes to expand the franchise to all adult males of the region, not just the city. Here we see Epaminondas's Pythagorean views coming into play. Promoting wider democracy throughout Boeotia led to a more motivated citizenry that began to feel a new sense of pride in themselves and looked to Thebes as their champion. Further, the expansion of citizenship brought the potential pool of army recruits to an all-time high. Although Thebes had in the late fifth century been able to field an army of 7,000 hoplites, by the 370s it could potentially field one of 20,000, in addition to the light infantry and peltasts.

This motivation showed itself in the years 378–374 as Theban-Boeotian forces beat back a number of Spartan invasion attempts. The high point of this conflict occurred in 375 at Tegyra, when the Sacred Band under Pelopidas won a major victory over a much larger Spartan force. Unfortunately for Thebes, while Athens enjoyed seeing Sparta humbled, it also feared Thebes's growing strength. This meant that if another Spartan invasion came, Athens was unlikely to offer aid.

As Athenian power revived in the wake of the Peloponnesian Wars, Athens's navy began threatening Persian holdings in the eastern Mediterranean. In 380 BC, the Persian king responded to a Spartan request and oversaw the negotiating of a peace treaty that granted freedom to all Greek cities in Europe in return for Persian control of all Greek settlements in Ionia. Sparta was to enforce the peace against any polis that broke the treaty. The Spartans, however, saw their privileged position as an opportunity to expand and punish Thebes for past sins. Although Sparta did not initially do so, losing at Tegyra in 375, at the time of the second renewal of the peace treaty in 371, Sparta backed Thebes into a corner. Thebes had, in the intervening years, achieved the status of leading city of Boeotia, and Thebans began to view themselves as regional overseers just as Athens led the poleis of Attica and Sparta those of the Peloponnese. The difference was that Sparta dominated subordinate states and Athens was leader of a coalition of allied states, whereas Thebes was leader of what was basically a confederation of the Boetian cities.

At the signing of the treaty, the Spartan king Aegesilaus intentionally provoked Epaminondas, who was representing Thebes. Sparta signed the treaty for the Peloponnese, then Athens signed, then the Athenian allies signed. Epaminondas signed for the Boeotian Federation. Aegesilaus demanded that the Boeoetian cities sign for themselves, and when Epaminondas refused, the Spartan king scratched Thebes off the treaty. It was a declaration of war.

The Battle of Leuctra

THE SECOND OF SPARTA'S TWO KINGS, Cleombrotus, already had an army in the field in Phocis, northwest of Boeotia, when relations were severed. Epaminondas rushed to Thebes to raise the army ahead of the Spartan arrival. He was named army commander alongside a council of six boeotarch advisors, while Pelopidas commanded the Sacred Band. Thus, Epaminondas went with a force of 6,000 infantry and 1,500 cavalry to face a Spartan army (with allies) of 10,000 infantry and 1,000 cavalry. He decided to force a battle at the pass overlooking Coroneia and seized the spot, but Cleombrotus instead marched south to enter Boeotia through Thisbae to Creusis on the Gulf of Corinth, where his forces captured the fortifications and moved inland from the coast toward Thebes. Thus, the Theban army had to rush to get back home and defend its city, but Cleombrotus was in its way at the plain of Leuctra.

Dr. Richard Andree, G. Droysens Allgemeine Historischer Handatlas, 1886

Seeing 11,000 enemy soldiers spread out before them was more than a little disheartening to the Thebans. Not only were they outnumbered almost two to one, but the omens had not been hopeful. According to Diodorous, as they had left Thebes an old blind man looking for lost slaves called out for their return and safety. Epaminondas responded with a line from Homer: "One only omen is best, to fight for the land that is ours."[10] That heartened the men, but soon thereafter a pennant from a spear flew away from its haft and landed on some Spartan graves, as if honoring or protecting them. Epaminondas told the crowd, "Do not be concerned, comrades! Destruction is foretold for the Spartans. Tombs are not decorated except for funerals."[11] Upon seeing the Spartan army, the boeotarchs with whom Epaminondas commanded demanded a vote on whether to fight or move and look for better ground; Epaminondas barely won the vote, four to three. Still, as his men faced overwhelming odds, Epaminondas thought it wise to introduce some positive omens. He secretly directed some of the newly arrived reinforcements to tell the army that weapons kept in the temple of Herakles had disappeared, meaning the ancient heroes had come to help. Another man told the troops that he had visited the cave sacred to Trophonius, son of Apollo, who had assured their victory if they would institute a festival in honor of Zeus. A turncoat, Leandrias, helped with the propaganda by relating a legend that Leuctra was an ill-chosen location for the Spartans, as it was the site of the deaths by suicide of two Theban maidens raped by Spartans, daughters of Leuctras (or Scedasus, according to Pausanias) for whom the town was named. Their curse was that Sparta would begin its decline on this plain. Epaminondas offered sacrifices and prayers for the girls and called for revenge.[12] All of these tales, true or not, rallied the Theban morale. For those who may not have been convinced, Epaminondas announced that whoever did not want to fight could leave; the contingent from Thespiae did so.

The night before the battle, Pelopidas supposedly had a dream in which he saw the long-dead maidens alive with their father. They told him the Thebans must sacrifice a maiden with chestnut hair. The next morning, as the dream was being discussed, a chestnut-colored colt ran into camp. This was deemed to be the right sacrifice and the ceremony ensued. As a final encouragement to his men, Epaminondas appealed to their patriotism. According to the ancient historian Forintinus, "In order that his soldiers might not only exercise their strength, but also be stirred by their feelings, he announced in an assembly of his men that the Spartans had resolved, in case of victory, to massacre all males, to lead the wives and children of those executed into bondage, and to raze Thebes to the ground."[13]

Across the plain things were not pleasant, either. In spite of their numerical superiority, as well as the virtually inbred tradition of winning, the Spartans were not entirely confident. At the staff meeting on the morning of the battle, subordinate commanders pushed Cleombrotus for quick action. They reminded him of some of his past failures (in two previous invasions, in 378 and 376, he had failed to bring his armies to battle) and assured him the Spartan council would not look kindly on anything that hinted at incompetence. They also (possibly owing to a religious festival) had been drinking since the morning meal. Also in many minds must have been the memory of what the Sacred Band had accomplished at Tegyra, where the smaller Sacred Band had defeated the Spartan phalanx. That certainly had been a bitter blow.[14] All of this combined to make Cleombrotus aggressive.

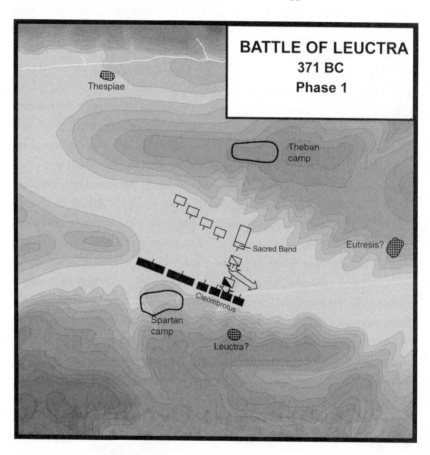

BATTLE OF LEUCTRA
371 BC
Phase 1

Thespiae

Theban camp

Sacred Band

Eutresis?

Cleombrotus

Spartan camp

Leuctra?

Epaminondas gave his men one more pep talk. He took up a live snake and then crushed its head; so too would be the fate of the enemy: kill the Spartan head and the allied body would die.[15] Even so, as Epaminondas began to form his army, he had doubts about the morale of some of his units. Thus, he needed to maximize his advantages and minimize his disadvantages. He ordered his men forward in the standard phalanx formation, but as they deployed he held back the units on the right of the line, whom he thought insufficiently motivated, thus refusing the right flank (deploying in echelon to the right rear). As Diodorus observes, "The weakest he placed on the other wing and instructed them to avoid battle and withdraw gradually during the enemy's attack."[16] Epaminondas placed his more trusted troops on the left into a formation fifty ranks deep and eighty files wide. He placed the 300 men of the Sacred Band in the front ranks, then waited to see what the Spartans would do. Cleombrotus deployed his army in the standard phalanx formation, his men in ranks twelve deep. The Spartans held the right end of their line, facing the Sacred Band and the deep phalanx; a force of mercenaries they placed in the center; the far left was held by Sparta's Peloponnesian allies.

The two armies faced each other for a time. The initial action was on the part of the cavalry. Before the infantry had fully deployed, the Spartan cavalry (after harassing Theban camp followers) rode toward the strong Theban left flank. It was met and soon routed by the Theban cavalry, superior in both numbers and quality. Xenophon writes, "Now when Cleombrotus began to lead his army against the enemy, in the first place, before the troops under him so much as perceived that he was advancing, the horsemen had already joined battle and those of the Lacedaemonians had speedily been worsted; then in their flight they had fallen foul of their own hoplites, and, besides, the companies of the Thebans were now charging upon them."[17] This is where Epaminondas demonstrated his originality. He was gambling the entire battle on one throw. His most motivated men went into battle first; if they failed, the demoralized right flank would break at the first sign of wavering. He was throwing his best troops at the more numerous Spartans, the best troops in the known world. As soon as Pelopidas and Epaminondas saw the confusion in the Spartan ranks, they began their advance.

As with the debate over the use of the "mass shove," there is also some argument over just how Epaminondas formed what has come to be called the "Theban wedge." One scholar has suggested that the Theban left was actually deployed into a point, an inverted V, with the Sacred Band at the apex. The fact that the V was hollow would not be obvious to the enemy, thus giving the impression of greater than actual numbers. All of this depends on the translation of the Greek word *embolon*, or wedge, and its use by a variety of ancient writers.[18] This theory has been answered by a different study of the word that indicates a comparison to a ram on a Greek trireme, hence the strong point of contact to break an enemy, not necessarily a literal wedge.[19] Thus, if there was a "point" to the wedge it would be at the spot at which the right wing began its refusal.

As the cavalry began to clear away and Cleombrotus saw the unbalanced formation advancing toward him, he ordered troops to shift to his right to attempt a flanking movement. Seeing this, Pelopidas ordered his Sacred Band into a run and struck the Spartans as they began their redeployment. The rest of the Theban left wing, under Epaminondas, was soon engaged and the battle was on. Harking back to the earlier discussion on othismos and the nature of a massed charge, here is my proposal as to how the initial stage of the battle was conducted. Goldsworthy argues that the narrower the formation, the easier it was to maintain cohesion. Add to that the fact that the massive Theban left flank was led by the Sacred Band. These soldiers were the nearest Theban equivalent of Spartiates, a force of men who did not farm like the normal militia, but spent their time in military training. Their defeat of a much larger Spartan force at Tegyra a few years earlier had to have built up a strong measure of confidence within their ranks. While there is no reference to their marching in step like the Spartans, these professionals must have been able to keep a tighter formation than could a standard phalanx. In Goldsworthy's opinion, "A deeper, and therefore narrower, phalanx encountered fewer obstacles and could as a result move faster and further, whilst retaining its order."[20] Add to that the timing of the charge, just as the Spartans were reorganizing from the disrupting cavalry retreat *and* trying to redeploy to take advantage of the narrower front approaching them. All of these factors should equate into a powerful initial contact that could easily have gained at least temporary momentum for the attackers. Then, the rest of the phalanx arrived for support, whether moral or physical or both. The Spartans must have been at a disadvantage from the outset.

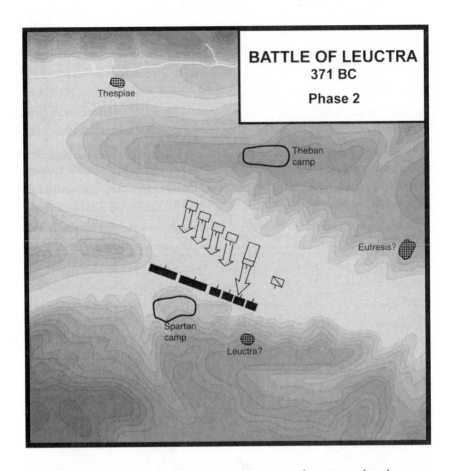

In spite of all those advantages, it was not enough to immediately sweep the field. The hand-to-hand front-rank fighting was intense. Whether Cleombrotus stood in the front rank or not, he was mortally wounded in combat. Xenophon reports that the Spartans were doing well, or "they would not have been able to take him up and carry him off still living had not those who were fighting in the front of him been holding the advantage at the time. But when Deinon, the polemarch, Sphodrias, one of the king's tent-companions, and Cleonymus, the son of Sphodiras, had been killed, then the royal bodyguard . . . [and] the others fell back before the Theban mass, while those who were on the left wing . . . gave way."[21]

The massive "ram" of the Theban left flank coupled with the speed of the attack caught the Spartans unprepared. Once their king and a number of his top men began to fall, the Spartan contingent of the battle line retreated to their camp. The mercenary and allied forces saw little or no combat because of the refused Theban flank angled backward from the front line, so they retreated just as quickly when they saw the Spartans withdraw, both from shock at the sight of such an event and fear of that "ram" striking their flank. Once in camp, established behind a ditch, the Spartans reassembled for a stand.

Epaminondas did not push his luck, for he knew he had no need to do so. Piled on the field of battle were 400 dead Spartiates out of a total of 1,000 casualties, the worst loss of Spartan life in their history, far greater than their losses at the stand against the Persians at Thermopylae in 480. Sparta also had not lost a king since that battle. Such a historic defeat was not unappreciated by Sparta's allies in the ranks. Xenophon writes that the Spartans perceived "that the allies were one and all without heart for fighting, while some of them were not even displeased at what had taken place."[22]

Epaminondas's movement to contact was an approach march, since he had a fair idea where the Spartans would be. He lost any element of strategic surprise when Cleombrotus took the long way around to approach Thebes from the west. This also cost Epaminondas the opportunity to choose the battleground. Initially, therefore, he was at a disadvantage both as to his position and his numbers. Certainly the battle itself was no surprise, since the two armies had been facing each other for a time. Epaminondas did achieve tactical surprise, however. He may or may not have known of dissension in the Spartan camp and the pressure being placed on Cleombrotus. Even if he did, he was smart enough not to underestimate his opposition.

Although facing the prime units opposite each other on the field had been done before, Cleombrotus was not ready for it. Epaminondas's deliberate attack led to a battle that he controlled as much as any commander could in a phalanx battle. The massed Theban left wing was a surprise, but Cleombrotus tried to adapt to it by shifting men to his right flank. It is possible that the Spartan cavalry was deployed as a screen once Cleombrotus saw the Theban formation and was beginning the redeployment of his own phalanx to be in an outflanking position. So the nature of the Theban deployment was unexpected and the assault began, in Xenophon's words, "before the troops under [Cleombrotus] so much as perceived that he was advancing." Although the Spartans really could not have expected their cavalry to prevail, they certainly did not expect to see it retreating into their main force. That is where the Theban control of the tempo of the battle became all important. In the midst of the turmoil and troop movement, the Sacred Band's assault came well before the Spartans were prepared.

Epaminondas's concentration of not just manpower but high-quality troops was key to his plan succeeding. The most audacious part of the plan was the refused flank, for he was chancing everything on one throw of the dice. Even though the echeloned units were the least dependable of his army, their mere presence was enough to freeze the Spartan allies.

Epaminondas neither tactically exploited his victory nor pursued his enemy; there was no need. He had inflicted sufficient casualties to not only damage the numbers of the Spartiates but more importantly to damage their reputation and morale.

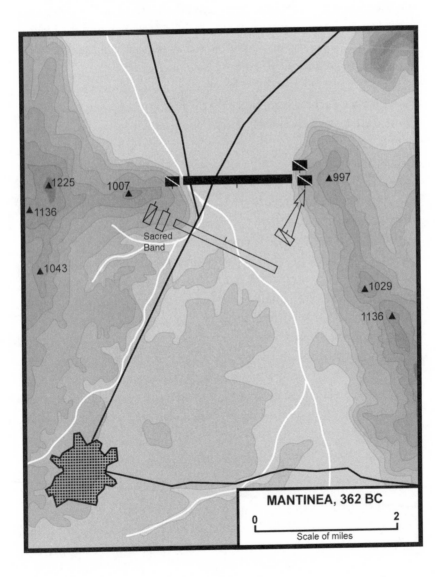

MANTINEA, 362 BC

0 — 2

Scale of miles

Epaminondas followed up the Battle of Leuctra with an invasion of the Peloponnese, where he ran rampant over Spartan-controlled territory and liberated the helots who provided the Spartiates with their agricultural sustenance. Sparta's slow decline now became precipitate. Not only beaten on the field but also humiliated before the rest of Greece, Sparta tried one last time to save its reputation and lands. The Spartans gathered one last force at Mantinea in 362, and this time it was Thebes that had the larger force. Epaminondas repeated his Leuctra maneuver at the battle with the same results. Unfortunately, he was killed in that battle. He was wounded by a spear; he asked about the progress of the battle as he was dying and learned the enemy was withdrawing. The battle was a tactical draw but a strategic victory for Thebes, since it reinforced the newly liberated peoples of Lacedaemonia and ended Spartan power once and for all.

The battle was a draw mainly because Epaminondas was killed. Until that point the Thebans were sweeping the field, according to Xenophon: "Thus, then, he made his attack, and he was not disappointed of his hope; for by gaining the mastery at the point where he struck, he caused the entire army of his adversaries to flee."[23] Victor Davis Hanson argues that had the Leuctra tactics been new and able to stand on their own, then Epaminondas's death would not have mattered. Yet ancient history is full of instances where one side gave up the fight when their leader was killed; would Leuctra have turned out differently if Cleombrotus had not died? It's impossible to say, but it is a tribute to any leader's standing that his men lose heart upon hearing of his death. The fact that the Theban wedge "caused the entire army of his adversaries to flee" sounds like a successful tactic. The Thebans around the dying general did declare victory, and that was the news that released a mortally wounded Epaminondas from this life. "I have lived long enough, for I die unconquered," he is supposed to have said.[24] Other accounts say that before the spear (or javelin) was withdrawn, Epaminondas asked after two of his chief subordinates. When informed that they had been killed, his last command was to make peace. Perhaps had he said "keep fighting" the victory would have been complete.

Epaminondas's Generalship

THE TWO MAIN PRINCIPLES OF WAR EPAMINONDAS mastered were the twin concepts of mass and economy of force. Epaminondas chose the correct center of gravity for his objective: the Spartan contingent and

King Cleombrotus. Although a deeper-than-usual phalanx had been seen in other battles, what made its deployment at Leuctra significant is that it was on the Theban left, directly facing the strength of the Spartan army. Traditionally, the place of honor in the line of battle was the far right, which meant that the best troops of opposing armies did not face each other. Historian of ancient Greece George Cawkwell writes, "Epaminondas' reversal [of tradition] at Leuctra is the mark of a revolutionary change in the conception of warfare. . . . [I]n 371 the conflict was centred on, and indeed confined to, the main antagonists."[25] As Hans Delbrück comments, "All of this is valuable only because it guarantees one's own left wing the victory over the enemy right."[26] Taking out the enemy leader as well as the strongest force on the battlefield necessarily demoralized Sparta's allied units.

Hanson in a 1998 article disputes the revolutionary nature of Epaminondas's action, primarily by taking most of the accounts by ancient historians to task.[27] While it is certainly true that every tactic Epaminondas employed at Leuctra had been used some time earlier, the question remains: how many other generals had learned any lessons from previous uses, and how many had welded them into a coherent whole? The combination of *massed* phalanx, strength versus opponent's strength, and the refused flank together took down the king and caused the vast number of Spartiate casualties.[28] It was the concentration of force at the center of gravity that is key. In his 1999 book *The Soul of Battle*, Hanson admits that the heavier left wing was "a novel tactical innovation" that "gained enormous penetrating power, as accumulated shields created greater thrust."[29]

The Theban wedge showed its other advantage in the realm of *economy of force*. In normal hoplite warfare the entire lines attacked as one, but Epaminondas attacked only with his left flank. There is some debate over whether the refusing of his right flank was intentional. Goldsworthy asserts, "It may be that later accounts of Epaminondas' echeloned advance at Leuctra described not a deliberate ploy, but the inevitably faster advance of the deep Theban phalanx compared to the rest of the army."[30]

Hanson also argues against the presence of a deliberately refused flank, taking Xenophon as the only reliable source. Not trusting Diodorus, the only ancient historian to describe the Theban formation so, he argues that if Plutarch and Diodorus mention an oblique attack by the left wing, then the right wing would trail behind, not being an intentional refusal of the flank. He asserts that "there was little tactical reason for these generally inferior troops to attempt such a complicated maneuver," what he calls "a deliberate withdrawal."[31] Refusing a flank, however, does not necessitate a withdrawal, especially on offense. While the most famous flank refusal of modern times, Joshua Chamberlain at Little Round Top at the Battle of Gettysburg, did indeed involve a deliberate withdrawal, that was the nature of being on the defense and in immediate danger of being outflanked. All Epaminondas had to do was stagger his less dependable allied forces in echelon (see map on page 15). Thus, such a move would answer Hanson's citation of Pausanias that the Spartan allies did have the opportunity to fight but would not stand their ground. The first phalanx of the echelon could, indeed, have had contact with the enemy.

Some sources refer to these forces not in the main assault as reserves, but I agree with Hanson that they were not deliberately held back for commitment at an important moment, as is the role of reserves. Held back in echelon, yes, but not as a traditional reserve to be committed as circumstances dictate.

The echelon attack and the weighted wing were introduced by Epaminondas but copied by many. The almost immediate impact came with the rise of Macedon. In his work on ancient warfare, J. E. Lendon observes that "[Philip II] lived in the house of the Theban general Pammenes, who had a formidable reputation for military cunning. In Thebes, it was said, Philip learned many lessons."[32] Philip's primary accomplishment as king of Macedon was to create a professional standing army that used the latest equipment and tactics, depending heavily on cavalry. Alexander would almost certainly not have accomplished his great deeds without the army he inherited from his father, Philip.

Epaminondas's influence was not only beneficial to Macedon in the immediate future, but was reincarnated two millennia later, as noted by Basil Liddell Hart: "He not only broke away from tactical methods established by the experience of centuries, but in tactics, strategy, and grand strategy alike laid the foundations on which subsequent masters built. Even his structural designs have survived or been revived. For in tactics the 'oblique order' which Frederick [the Great] made famous was only a slight elaboration of the method of Epaminondas."[33]

2

Alexander (356–323 BC)

King of Macedon, Leader of a Macedonian-Greek Coalition

Alexander accomplished great things in a short space of time, and by his acumen and courage surpassed in the magnitude of his achievements all kings whose memory is recorded from the beginning of time.

—Diodorus Siculus, *Library*, first century BC

UNLIKE EPAMINONDAS, the great fourth-century BC Theban general and statesman, Alexander of Macedon was born to wealth and power. He was the first and probably only child of Philip II of Macedon and his fourth wife, Olympias of Epirus. His parents were two of a kind, both intensely passionate, physically and emotionally. That mutual passion led to their marriage—and ultimately to their separation. Alexander was thus raised in a turbulent household in a turbulent time. Philip II was in the process of making Macedon the major power of southeastern Europe, and therefore spent much of his time away from his capital, home, and family in Pella. His father's absence naturally meant that Alexander became emotionally closer to his mother, but accounts of his early life, primarily from Plutarch, imply that there was no hostility between father and son in his early years.

Throughout his life, Alexander exhibited strong religious feelings, sacrificing to the gods daily and often praying for their guidance and blessing. Such practices were normal in Macedon, but certainly

Alexander's beliefs were intensified by his mother. Plutarch's biography tells this story:

> Well, then, the night before that on which the marriage was consummated, the bride dreamed that there was a peal of thunder and that a thunder-bolt fell upon her womb, and that thereby much fire was kindled, which broke into flames that travelled all about, and then was extinguished. . . . After the marriage, Philip dreamed that he was putting a seal upon his wife's womb; and the device of the seal, as he thought, was the figure of a lion. . . . Aristander of Telmessus said that the woman was pregnant, since no seal was put upon what was empty, and pregnant of a son whose nature would be bold and lion-like.[1]

Olympias claimed that this dream meant she was impregnated by Zeus, a story Alexander learned when he was in his mid-teens. He also was supposed to be descended from Herakles and Achilles. With the genealogical assertion of gods in the family line, it is no surprise Alexander took his religion and himself seriously.

In the Pellaean palace Alexander was given an education fit for a royal heir, but when he was twelve or thirteen Philip imported a special tutor, the philosopher Aristotle. Possibly thinking that Olympias was having too much influence on the boy, Philip sent Alexander and a number of other students to study at Mieza, outside the capital city. Here the teaching was much more rational than that which he had received from his mother, who was a loyal devotee of the cult of Dionysus. Historians have long debated the sway Aristotle may have had over the young Alexander. The scientific aspects of Alexander's invasion of the Persian Empire, for example, certainly demonstrate much of it. "On the other hand there is no sign that he was in the least influenced by his teacher's views on politics, limited as they were to the city-state," writes J. R. Hamilton. "Convinced of the natural inferiority of 'barbarians,' Aristotle taught Alexander that they needed a master."[2] As for his military personality, however, Aristotle had little if any influence.

Of more influence were the two military instructors who oversaw the physical aspect of Alexander's education. These were Leonidas and Lysimachus, disciplinarians who certainly instilled in him toughness of mind and body. Most of his military acumen, however, came from his father. Philip showed remarkable confidence in his son from an early age: at sixteen, Alexander was given trusteeship of the throne while his father was off campaigning. During that period, Alexander (with the assistance of one of Philip's generals, Antipater) was involved in suppressing a rebellion of the Maedi tribe in Thrace. He also established his first of many cities, Alexandropolis. In a society that valued military skills, Alexander's combat served not only to give him experience but also to show his mettle to the army, in whose ultimate control the kingship rested.

Alexander's last successful operation he shared with his father was the Battle of Chaeronea in Boeotia in 338 BC. He led the Companion cavalry (the chief Macedonian cavalry force) in the attack that destroyed the elite Sacred Band of Thebes, broke the enemy line, and as a result broke the power of Athens and Thebes. As that victory was bringing about a unification of Greece under Macedonian authority, however, a new marriage was creating division between father and son; Philip married a Macedonian princess. Olympias, long out of favor, became enraged. A son from that union would be seen by the upper classes as more fitting for the throne than one from marriage to a foreigner. For a time Alexander and Philip were estranged, and they never reestablished any sort of bond.

Successful as he had been on the battlefield, Philip was better still as a grand strategist and politician. He had manipulated potential enemies and friends with a combination of the carrot and the stick. As his army became more successful, it grew in numbers and skill so that success began to feed off itself. By the time Alexander was reaching his teens, Philip had created the finest military in the Hellenic world. He also had reached a dominant political position over the Greek city-states and created the Hellenic League, whose goal was to invade the Persian Empire and punish the Persians for their attacks on Greece a century and a half earlier. Philip therefore provided Alexander not only with a first-class military but also with a united Greece from which to draw support for implementing a generations-old dream: the invasion of Persia.

When Philip was assassinated in 336 BC, the army proclaimed Alexander king; he soon eliminated any potential rivals. After suppressing rebellions both in the north and in Greece, Alexander finally set about finishing the work his father had started.

Warfare of the Time

IT IS THE ARMY ITSELF that was Philip's greatest gift to his son. As a teenager, Philip had been a hostage in Thebes in the time between the great battles of Leuctra and Mantinea, and he undoubtedly absorbed many of his views on developing an army from the men around Epaminondas.[3] Once Philip assumed the throne in 359 BC, he began serious reforms within the Macedonian military. Macedon, like Thebes, had been a territory often crossed by passing armies, which had kept it sufficiently disorganized that it never was a serious threat to its neighbors. Philip changed that. Distancing himself from the long-standing view that military service was a duty of citizenship to be provided in times of emergency, Philip accorded it high social status. The state began providing more materiel, as well as land grants for meritorious service, and this produced eager soldiers. "Judging by results," notes military historian G. T. Griffith, "few generals ever did more to change the face of his own times and to throw a shadow over the future."[4]

The army Philip created was based on cooperation between infantry and cavalry, but his main deviation from the existing order of battle was to make the cavalry the shock troops, rather than the phalanx. While the practice of "combined arms" had been used before, Philip made it the central aspect of his army. The phalanx still existed and was still important, but it was different from what had been employed up to this time. Philip dictated lighter armor for easier maneuvering, and nearly doubled the length of the spear, making it between fifteen and eighteen feet. This new spear, the *sarissa*, made it virtually impossible for the standard Greek phalanx to close in during battle. If that happened, the longer reach of the sarissa meant that men farther back in the ranks could use it, creating a numerical advantage in a melee. It was also carried and used underhanded, rather than over the shield as was traditional. The standard Macedonian phalanx was deployed sixteen files wide and sixteen ranks deep.

By raising a standing army, Philip made sure that the men were in continuous training. Three advantages resulted from his changes. "First," writes Eugene N. Borza in an influential article, "in an age in which troops may have been expected to arm themselves, the property requirements necessary for Macedonian military service would have been relatively small, so that troops could be drawn from a broader population. Second, the longer *sarissa* enabled the Macedonian infantryman to engage in battle beyond the range of his enemy's spear. And third, the lighter shield and body armor freed both hands to manipulate his long main weapon."[5] Some military historians have seen no advantage to the adapted formation, such as Hans Delbruck, who argues it was "more cumbersome than the old one, fell more easily into disarray, and was still more sensitive on its flanks."[6] This is a minority opinion, however, given Philip's and Alexander's successes. Most have recognized the transformative evolution of the Macedonian infantry under Philip II, which got somewhat lighter, but with greater reach. As Archer Jones has noted, "The Macedonians made a virtue of the tactical innovation of the long spear and drilled their phalanx of professional soldiers so that it could function as a unit. In addition, they subdivided their troops, giving some articulation and maneuverability to an inherently unwieldy formation."[7]

Another of Philip's innovations was the *hypaspists*. There is debate over whether these soldiers were an elite infantry force (possible, considering Philip led them at Chaeronea) or a light infantry unit meant to fill the gap between the phalanx and the peltasts, the lightly armed missile-firing troops. Some argue that they were armed like the traditional Greek hoplite, with a spear rather than the sarissa, so they could be used as a more mobile force. A portion of the hypaspists have also been mentioned as acting as a personal bodyguard for Alexander.[8] Having started his military career in battles against guerrilla forces in the Illyrian hills, Philip had learned the value of light troops and incorporated them into his army. Before him the light infantry had mainly played a prebattle harassment role, but Philip expanded these troops into a part of the Macedonian army equal in value to the rest.[9]

Only in central Greece, around Thebes and Thessaly, had horse raising been possible, so cavalry to the Greeks was by necessity less important to warfare. However, by establishing cavalry (*hippeis*) as the primary force, Philip took advantage of the equine resources of Macedon. He opened up the cavalry to all comers, rewarding loyalty and ability over origins. Philip paid his horsemen with land rather than money. As his kingdom expanded the amount of land he could award grew, so the number of horsemen grew as well.[10] From the time of Philip's accession in 359 BC until his death, the Macedonian cavalry forces grew from 600 to more than 3,000.

The horsemen used a shorter sarissa, about nine feet long, with a foot-long spear point on both ends. This allowed them to stab in both directions during a melee and to continue to use the weapon even if it broke. It was also light enough to use as a throwing weapon. If the sarissa was gone, the cavalrymen still carried the curved, single-edged sword, the *kopis*. They also wore helmets and armor. Philip developed a cavalry wedge formation designed to penetrate an enemy line, then widen the break as the wedge rode deeper into the foe. The standard unit was 200 men (when made up of foreign troops, who were seen as more expendable) and 300 in the Companions. There were also light cavalry units, numbering about 400 horsemen in each, used primarily for scouting but also occasionally in combat. Their sarissa was the same length as that carried by the infantry and weighed twelve to fourteen pounds.

The use of cavalry as shock troops may seem on the surface to be obvious, but there was one major problem: the stirrup had not yet been invented. The stirrup allows horsemen to remain mounted when they hit the enemy line; without it, one has to depend on muscles in the thighs. The horse's weight as much as the man and weapon made the cavalry functional for shock. Nonetheless, Philip's formations were effective, and were the centerpiece of his combat tactics.

The Persians, Macedon's foremost enemy, also used a system of combined arms, which included a far greater number of missile weapons: bows and arrows, javelins, and slings. Owing to its massive empire, the Persians could draw on a large population with a variety of local weapons and skills. Their cavalry was mostly light and not used for shock—they used javelins or bows as their main weapon. The Persian infantryman wore no armor, just a padded uniform. His weapons were much the same as the Greek hoplite: a round shield and a nine- to ten-foot spear.

The strength of the Persian army seemed mainly to be its numbers, although its leaders had upgraded their infantry since the Greco-Persian wars of the early fifth century with the introduction of new units called *cardaces*. Modern scholarship continues to debate the exact nature of these units, about which little is known for sure.[11] Some argue that they were possibly peltasts.[12] Others say they were heavily protected heavy infantry.[13] Some have suggested that they probably had bow and arrows, and were formed in a remarkably deep phalanx.[14] One view has it is that they were Iranian youths who were undergoing military training.[15]

Greek mercenaries also played a key role in the Persian military, reflecting the Persians' openness to taking advantage of the martial skills of each nation into which they came in contact.[16] Thus, the Persian army was polyglot, but one that was multitalented and flexible. The core of the army, however, was made up of "homeland" Persians and Medes, who had a vast amount of experience in suppressing rebellions and defending the frontiers. They may not have faced great adversaries, but they were veterans nonetheless.

The Opponents

AT THE TIME OF THE MACEDONIAN INVASION of the Persian Empire in 334 BC, Darius III was on the Persian throne. He was probably born a provincial satrap in Armenia (where he may have taken the Persian name "Artašâtu"), and his rise to power has been a subject of debate. The first-century BC Greek historian Diodorus Siculus wrote that a eunuch of the royal court named Bagoas poisoned Artaxerxes III, leading to the short reign of the child Artaxerxes IV, who was also poisoned when Bagoas could not control him. (Recently translated contemporary cuneiform tablets, however, dispute Diodorus and claim that Artaxerxes III died of natural causes.)[17] Bagoas, still looking for an easy-to-manipulate king, put the possibly distant relative Artašâtu on the throne.[18] Finding him also intractable, Bagoas went for poison once again, but his plot was discovered and he was forced to drink it himself. Artašâtu rose to the throne in 336 BC and took the regal name Darius III.

Diodorus claims that Darius was well known for his bravery in battle, and therefore was acceptable to the empire's population. Egypt had revolted before Darius came to the throne, and his first order of business was to restore the empire's power in North Africa. He did so in 334 BC, but it was to be his last accomplishment; after that, he had to deal with Alexander's invasion.[19]

Alexander quickly proved himself to be his father's son. The Hellenic League that Philip had created immediately began showing signs of dissolution, with resistance led by Philip's and Alexander's constant Athenian nemesis, Demosthenes. Almost before any of Macedon's tributaries could ponder revolt, however, Alexander marched his armies throughout the region and crushed any nascent uprising. With order restored, he directed the allied forces toward Persia.[20]

Philip's best and most favored general, Parmenio, had been holding the straits at the Hellespont since the time of Philip's death. Thus, in 334 BC Alexander's army moved into Asia Minor and began liberating cities along the seaboard that were ethnically Greek. Regional satraps, unwilling to lose their authority, gathered an army—smaller than Alexander's—to oppose him. Placing themselves astride his line of march, they prepared to face Alexander at the River Granicus, near Troy.

The Granicus was probably no more than five meters wide, but had steep banks on both sides. Alexander deployed his forces in what would become the standard formation for decades to come: heavy infantry phalanxes in the center and cavalry forces on the flanks. The Persians lined up their entire cavalry force along the river bank, with their infantry force of 4,000 to 5,000 Greek mercenaries behind. No one who has studied the battle can quite fathom the rationale behind this deployment. Parmenio commanded the left while Alexander (with the Companion cavalry) was on the right. Alexander sent in a squadron of his Companion cavalry with some light infantry toward the left center of the Persian line. They were quickly beaten (possibly Alexander's intention) and in their retreat provoked the Persian left-flank units into pursuit. This exposed the rest of the Persian line: Alexander's cavalry, in an echelon formation—meaning arranged diagonally, like steps in a ladder—crossed the river and fell on the exposed flank. Alexander's own unit struck the commander's bodyguard. In hand-to-hand fighting Alexander killed a number of men and received a crashing axe blow to his helmet from which he apparently soon recovered. This first encounter with Persian troops showed that Alexander's taste for leading from the front, which he had showed at Chaeronea, had not changed.[21]

The Battle of Issus

AFTER THE GRANICUS BATTLE, Alexander continued liberating Greek cities and capturing Persian ones, establishing bases of operations and supply.[22] With Asia Minor secure, Alexander moved toward Syria. His intent was to cripple the Persian navy, which was stronger than his own, by capturing all the coastal cities and denying the enemy fleets any harbors. Meanwhile, hearing of his subordinates' defeat at the Granicus, Darius gathered his own army to fight Alexander.

Alexander stopped at Issus (now İskenderun, located near the border of modern Turkey and Syria), and left his sick to recuperate, then kept marching southward down the coast. He sent detachments into the hills to beat back guerrilla forces and to secure his flank. Alexander assumed that Darius would gather his forces in Syria in the open plains, where he could best use his cavalry and chariots. Indeed, that was Darius's original intent when he gathered his army at Sorchoi on the east side of the mountains. Here a broad plain stretched out before him, and he could employ his superior numbers. When he heard Alexander's location and the direction of his march, however, many of Darius's advisors urged him to strike rather than to wait on the Greeks. He did so, entering from the north, where he believed that there were unguarded passes, and sitting across Alexander's lines of communication and supply, forcing him to fight or starve.[23]

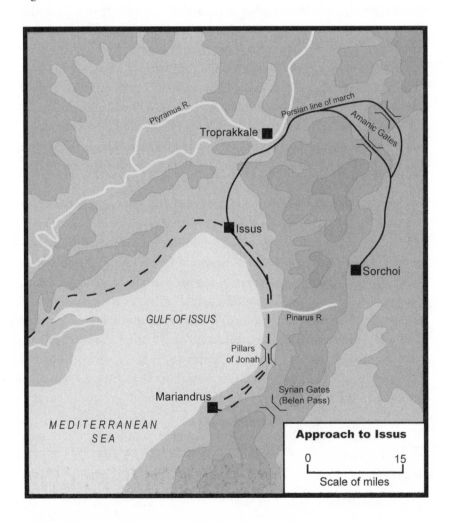

Upon occupying Issus, Darius massacred the Greek soldiers left behind.[24] He then marched southward to the Pinarus River, where he established a defensive position. This could have proven a good move; the battlefield he chose was virtually perfect for a defensive stand, with a river with steep banks in front, the ocean on the western right flank and the mountains on the left. The battlefield at Sorchoi, however, may have been far better for an offensive attack—meaning that whether he gave up a better battlefield at Sorchoi for a worse one along the Pinarus depends on his numbers, and those are greatly disputed. The source closest to the period is Arrian, a Roman historian who wrote in the second century AD. He claims that Darius had 600,000 men in his army, 30,000 of whom were Greek mercenaries. While no modern historian believes that number accurate, the implication is that the Persian numbers were large and that the total force seriously outnumbered the Greeks. If that was the case, then by placing his men along the Pinarus Darius was denying himself the ability to use his vastly superior numbers. If his army did indeed greatly outnumber Alexander's, Darius would have been far better off staying at Sorchoi or marching his army south to catch the Greeks as they emerged from the Belen Pass. If, on the other hand, Darius did not have a huge army, then establishing himself on the Pinarus and taking up the defensive was smart, given the natural strength of the position.

Estimates about the size of Alexander's army vary. Ancient-warfare historian John Warry's fall into the center: he proposes Alexander's army to consist of 22,000 infantry, 13,000 peltasts, and 5,850 cavalry (2,100 in the Companion cavalry). The Persian army consisted of as many as 10,000 Greek mercenary hoplites, along with another 20,000 cardaces, up to 65,000 light troops including tribal levies ("worse than useless against the Macedonian phalanx"[25]), and as many as 13,000 cavalry (3,000 of them Persian nobles), for a total of 108,000.[26] Another expert, Arthur Ferrill, suggests 100,000 infantry and 20,000 cavalry. Finally, Hans Delbruck avers that the Macedonian force numbered less than 30,000 and the Persians only slightly larger, though greater in cavalry strength.[27]

Even if the forces were relatively equal in number, the strength of the Persian position was key to the Persian strategy. One expert describes the upper river bed as about thirty-five meters wide with "a cliff-like right bank some three to seven meters high but with occasional breaks."[28] Another calls it invincible, with the infantry concealed within it and the cavalry ready to move forward.[29] Darius's defensive strategy stemmed from the knowledge that all he had to do was fight to a draw. If the Macedonians failed to win outright, they would be cut off from home and supplies. Since Darius did not need to win outright, he fought to not lose.

As Alexander's army had marched back northward through the Pillars of Jonah—a pass in the Nur Mountains so called because it was thought to be where was the prophet was disgorged by the whale—and onto the plain before arriving at the Pinarus, they had been on the move all day. Rather than stop and scout the battlefield (as he would do later at Gaugamela), Alexander instead marched his men straight into battle lines. They approached in phalanxes thirty-two men deep, then spread out to sixteen-man formations as they came nearer the river, and finally deployed into phalanxes eight men deep. Alexander placed his troops in their usual array: cavalry on the flanks and infantry in the center, with light infantry as a screen on the infantry flanks. The Companion cavalry deployed on the right, with the units to their left arrayed by order of performance. Alexander rated each unit after a battle and placed the best nearer him as a reward for bravery and an encouragement to the others. As they were marching onto the field, Darius quite openly shifted most of his cavalry from the hilly left side of the battlefield over to his right and massed them on the ocean flank. As the Macedonian cavalry opposite that force was small, Alexander ordered the Thessalian cavalry, some 1,500 strong, to shift to the left but to stay hidden behind the infantry on the left flank. Thus, the smaller cavalry force already deployed would serve as bait for a Persian cavalry attack, which could be stymied (if not defeated) by the hidden reserve.

The steep banks along most of the river made an infantry attack difficult, as the soldiers in the phalanxes would have to disperse to cross the water and then climb. Archers covered the riverside. The only possible place for a cavalry maneuver on the eastern, upriver side of the battlefield was a narrow ford that was no more than thirty yards wide. Alexander grasped that this single feature would prove to be the key to the battle: Darius took his cavalry away from the crossing to reinforce the western flank, but Alexander saw the ford as sufficient for his needs.

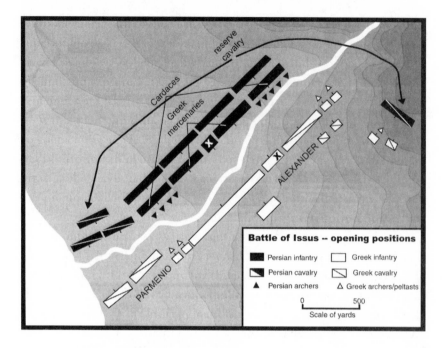

The battle took place in early November and began in middle to late afternoon. Once his men were in place, Alexander marched them ahead slowly, then finally rode across the front shouting words of encouragement. He returned to the Companion cavalry deployed on the Macedonian right, and indicated that the battle should begin. The phalanxes to his immediate left began their river crossing and found themselves faced not only with the river's steep banks, but with the Greek mercenaries as well, the best infantry Darius had to offer. Fighting uphill into a veteran force was a virtually impossible task, and all the ancient sources comment on the fierce fighting, or, as John Keegan described it, "what must have been quite a prolonged, noisy, angry, fear-smelling bout of shoving and thrusting."[30] First-century AD Roman historian Quintus Curtius Rufus writes that once the infantry made contact the fighting became desperate. "Thus, obliged to fight hand-to-hand, they swiftly drew their swords. Then the blood really flowed, for the two lines were so closely interlocked that they were striking each other's weapons with theirs and driving their blades into their opponents' faces."[31] Alexander led the Companions across the river ford against minimal resistance and turned to strike the Persian flank. On the western flank the cavalry was fighting to a standstill, though the Persians were pressing the Greek cavalry hard.

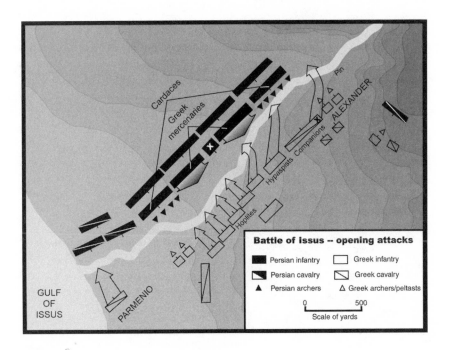

The battle at this point hung in the balance, until the Companions struck the Persian cardaces on the eastern flank. As they began to crumble, Alexander sighted Darius and drove directly for him. In hand-to-hand fighting between the two leaders, Alexander was wounded in the thigh. As Darius's bodyguards fought to protect him, the horses pulling his chariot began to panic. Darius quickly dismounted, entered another chariot, and fled the battle. Alexander intended to give immediate chase, but the cavalry engagement on the seaward flank was beginning to go badly, so he continued to roll up the Persian line and rode to help Parmenio on the far end of the battlefield. Once Darius fled, the tribal levies deployed in the rear, which had not gotten into the fight, fled as well, leaving the mercenaries and cardaces to their fate.

Darius's decision to fight only on the defensive, while strategically sound, failed as the battle unfolded. Indeed, it was the strength of the position that ultimately was its weakness. It kept them from going on the offensive and attacking the seaward flank and countering the Macedonians, a move that, given their superior numbers, might have succeeded.

There was also a psychological aspect to the Persian position. In his words to the troops before the battle, Alexander dismissed the enemy

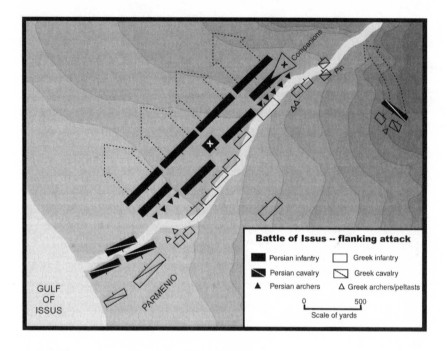

Battle of Issus -- flanking attack

■ Persian infantry   □ Greek infantry
◣ Persian cavalry   ◪ Greek cavalry
▲ Persian archers   △ Greek archers/peltasts

GULF
OF
ISSUS

PARMENIO

0   500
Scale of yards

as being weak in spirit, just as they had been at the Granicus. He also realized that the longer he took before his army charged, the more time the enemy had to see what was coming and begin to worry. According to Arian, "Alexander sought to inspire dread in the ranks of the enemy who, he once again detected, were 'trusting to the natural strength' of the position rather than to their own courage."[32] It was the same point that, centuries later, George Patton would make in World War II when exhorting his men: if they have to hide behind strong defenses, it can only be because they're scared of us.

Alexander took an approach march to the Persian army, since he knew exactly where it was. Although he did not delay in deploying his men upon arrival, the attack was deliberate rather than hasty. He took in the Persian order of battle and immediately developed a plan to engage his entire force. Since Darius had chosen the ground and watched the Macedonians march onto the field, there was no element of surprise. Darius expected to control the tempo of the battle, keeping it purely defensive and expecting superior numbers to prevail, meaning the battle would be lengthy even though Alexander arrived and deployed in midafternoon. As in all his early great battles, Alexander knew exactly how and where to concentrate his forces: the Companions aimed at the weakest part of the enemy line, then at the enemy commander. The exploitation was not complete, as most of the rear ranks of the Persian army were able to escape the battlefield. Neither was there any serious pursuit, since Alexander was obliged to give up his chase for Darius in order to assist the hard-pressed Parmenio on the left flank. Although the surviving Persian cavalry fled, the best of Darius's army, the mercenaries, were captured or killed.

The Siege of Tyre

THE VICTORY AT ISSUS WAS HARDLY the only example of Alexander's tactical abilities. His next battle was a siege at the coastal city of Tyre, built on an island roughly a half mile offshore. Instead of pursuing Darius (as he would do later after), Alexander decided to negate the power of Persia's navy by continuing to seize the ports along the eastern Mediterranean coast. With no place to land, the fleets would be ineffective and Alexander would not have to worry about maintaining a navy of his own. In the wake of the victory at Issus, some cities, such as Sidon, surrendered without a fight and were treated kindly. The first city to resist was Tyre, which had profited from an alliance with Persia. Alexander's first contact with the city elders was innocuous enough: he merely wanted to worship the local gods in Tyre's temples. When told the temples in Old Tyre on the mainland were just as good, Alexander knew the Tyrians would not be surrendering without a fight.

At this point Alexander was obliged to acquire some ships in order to keep Persian ships from resupplying Tyre. Luckily for him, his victories up to this point had convinced many naval powers to come over to his side, and he soon had more than 200 ships available to him. He also began two projects that illustrate his skill at siegecraft as clearly as the Granicus and Issus battles displayed his mastery of open-battle tactics. First, he began the construction of siege engines such as ballistae and catapults aboard his newly acquired shipping. He also began a massive construction project, building a mole, or jetty, from the shore to the island city. Recent research in the form of a sediment study has shown that this effort, while unbelievably difficult given the technology of the time, was rendered somewhat easier by the existence of a sandbar, which he used as a foundation.[33]

The rubble of Old Tyre and cedars of Lebanon from nearby forests supplied the materials needed to build the mole, which was almost five hundred feet wide. The Tyrians sent out individual divers and launched surprise naval raids that did considerable damage to the mole, but Alexander persevered; he built towers to shoot arrows down on the walls of Tyre and at any approaching ships, while having his engineers build torsion catapults larger than had been known up to this time. It may have been a new design (Phoenician and Cypriot engineers arrived with their respective navies to assist him) or it may have been a larger version of the existing arrow-shooting catapult.[34] His engineers built large cranes aboard ships to remove boulders at the base of Tyre's walls. Once they were removed, ships with battering rams could anchor alongside them and start the destruction process—the only time in history city walls have been attacked by seaborne rams.

After more than six months, the mole was completed and direct attack could commence. Direct assault against the walls, which were 150 feet high, proved impossible. Indeed, the walls around the city were so thick that rams and catapults were making little progress. Finally, a somewhat weaker section of wall was discovered along the southeastern part of the island and the siege engines began to show effect. As the bombardment

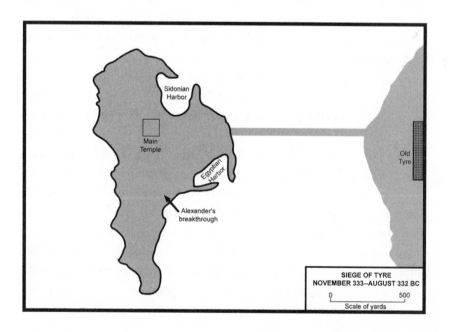

Sidonian
Harbor

Main
Temple

Egyptian Harbor

Old
Tyre

Alexander's
breakthrough

SIEGE OF TYRE
NOVEMBER 333--AUGUST 332 BC

0   500
Scale of yards

continued, Alexander's engineers built landing ramps so his soldiers could get direct access into the breach once it was created. On the day chosen for the assault, ships carrying infantry were sent all around the city, while other ships attempted to break into the two harbors on the island. Spreading the defense thin, Alexander faced a smaller (though still very determined) force when he led his men through the breach and into the city. Success in seizing the northern harbor also granted his forces access into the city, and soon the defenders were in a fighting withdrawal. Many women and children had taken refuge in the city's temples, but Curtius wrote that "the men all stood in the vestibules of their own homes ready to face the fury of the enemy. . . . The extent of the bloodshed can be judged from the fact that 6,000 fighting-men were slaughtered within the city's fortifications."[35]

The fall of Tyre had taken seven months, but solidified Alexander's reputation. Henceforth no city would be considered safe from his army. This was not his first siege, for Alexander had captured the city of Thebes early in his consolidation of power and later had taken Miletus and Halicarnassus in Asia Minor. Here, however, he marshaled all resources and used many strategems. Alexander showed himself an inventive and adaptive tactician through his unprecedented use of ship-based battering rams, mechanical devices for building and defending the mole, and new or improved-upon catapults. He launched the first amphibious assault against fortifications in history, executed masterfully coordination and leadership of naval action, and displayed personal leadership once again at the forefront of the fighting, proving himself to be a truly great captain.

Alexander's Generalship

THE MACEDONIAN KING WENT ON TO AN UNDEFEATED CAREER, leading his men to a decisive victory at the Battle of Gaugamela (also called the Battle of Arbela) over a Persian army hugely superior in numbers. His grand tactics at that battle mirrored what he had done at the Granicus and Pinaurus Rivers: find or create a hole in the enemy line near one flank, and punch his Companion cavalry through the hole with the enemy commander as his target. His infantry were there, as in the previous battles, to maintain control of the bulk of the enemy force in the front while he struck for his target behind the line he had just broken through. The Battle of Gaugamela secured his possession of the Persian Empire, and, seeking to expand his empire yet further, he marched his men into and through the Hindu Kush to India. There, he and his men faced an entirely new weapon, the war elephant, but Alexander defeated the Indian forces nonetheless. Although he failed in his ultimate personal goal of reaching the ends of the earth—such as they were known to him—and likewise failed in establishing either a Macedonian empire in the East or an Oriental-Greek society and government to last after his death, he certainly earned "the Great" that has followed his name for millennia for his battlefield exploits. In analyzing the Battle of Issus and the siege of Tyre, one can see Alexander's mastery of many principles of war, particularly in the areas of objective, offensive, economy of force, and unity of command.

At the Battle of Issus, although Darius outmaneuvered Alexander in the approach to the River Pinaurus, the position of the two armies relative to the lines of supply (while strategically significant) became secondary once the battle lines were forming. For Alexander, the *objectives* were the capture or killing of King Darius and the submission or destruction of Darius's army. Although he failed in his first objective, he secured the second. This restored the strategic situation by reopening the line of communication.

At Tyre, the objective was a weak point in the enemy walls. As with any attack on a fortified position, a commander has to find a point at which he can break through. The weakest point was not readily apparent at Tyre as it had been in Alexander's set-piece battles, but once it was created he led the initial attack through it. Once he had his troops in the city, even though they could not use the phalanx for battle, the enemy's lack of an avenue for escape spelled their doom.

When it comes to the principle of seizing the *offensive*, Alexander excels. Although Alexander was obliged to retrace his steps to respond to the Persian seizure of Issus, once the two armies deployed at the Pinarus he initiated and dictated the pace of the battle. This is only logical, since Darius was in the great defensive position and would have been unwise to come out from behind it. Having located to his satisfaction the ford toward his right flank as the attack point, Alexander sent his infantry forward. This was not so much to break the Persian center as to keep it occupied while he led the cavalry to its rear.

In the battle for Tyre, the Tyrians were obliged to play defense since they had nowhere to go, but they did conduct, as we have seen, an extremely active defense. This meant that while Alexander was building the mole and gathering a naval force, he, too, had to play defense to keep up the construction. He ultimately broke into the city and pushed the defenders through the streets and to their death. Alexander's offense was constant.

In neither of the battles, however, did Alexander employ the principle of *mass* in the traditional fashion. Normally, generals tried to hold down as much of the opposition army as possible with the fewest troops possible, in order to mass the bulk of their forces at the decisive point. For Alexander, the mass of his army was for a holding force rather than the arm of decision. Of the approximately 30,000 men he had at the Pinaurus River, the key to victory was the 2,500-man Companion cavalry, just as it had been at the Granicus. Alexander correctly divined the center of gravity as Darius, and forcing his flight from the battlefield was the key to victory. The rest of Alexander's army was subservient to the Companions' movement.

The bulk of his force was committed to the final assault at Tyre, but against the entire length of the walls rather than at the point of attack in order to spread the Tyrian defense as much as possible. His force struck every section of the defense at once in order to allow him and his personally led infantry force to exploit the weak point in the city wall. That breakthrough, coupled with the secondary entrance into the city from the northern harbor, broke the will of the defense.

Finally, Alexander's *unity of command* was critical to his success. He seemed to know from the first look at the battlefield how exactly to deploy his men, how the enemy would move their men, and how to seize the opportunity the enemy would give him. From that initial grasp of the battlefield, he would lay out the plans for his subordinates, confident that they would perform their assigned roles. They had to, for once the battle began and the Companion cavalry went forward, it would have been possible for him to lead only those near him. Hence it was critical that the soldiers maintain discipline in their ranks, as well as their belief in Alexander's plan of battle.

The same could be said concerning the entrance into and the battle for Tyre. However, during the siege, while Alexander had the vision to see what had to be done, it can certainly be assumed that many of his tactical actions had to have been made with input from his engineers. Without them, his ideas could not have been manifested in weaponry and invention. He told them what he needed, they told him if it could be done, then they did it.

ALEXANDER BROUGHT TO ALL his victories an uncanny ability to see from the outset of the battle exactly where the enemy's weakness lay. By striking that point with his strongest unit, the Companion cavalry, his initial success caused a psychological as well as physical break in the enemy force. Once the panic set in, it was impossible to stop. Although Alexander was unable to capture Darius at Issus or Gaugamela, the fact was that Alexander chose him as his ultimate target—the breakthrough elsewhere was but a preliminary. While Darius certainly made some very good strategic moves, and his reputation for bravery before becoming king was exemplary, seeing his own massive army broken by a smaller one was too much for him to face.

Alexander kept his army honed to a fine edge by drawing on a national pastime of one-upmanship. In his book *Soldiers and Ghosts*, J. E. Lendon describes how Alexander kept all the units in the army in competition with one another by placing them in ranks, from right (the commander's position of honor) to left, based on their performance in battle. He knew how intent his soldiers were on gaining not just victory but glory, so his prebattle addresses pointed out individuals for their past bravery. This singling out of valor in front of the entire army was the highest possible honor in a time before the awarding of medals for heroism. As king and commander, of course, he had to show himself the most valorous.

Few generals in history put themselves in harm's way as often as did Alexander. He was in the thick of the fighting from his first major battle at Chaeronea under his father's command, and he never backed down. Probably no example of his bravery outdoes his action at the siege of Multan in India. Believing his men to be too slow in scaling the walls, he seized a ladder himself and climbed to the ramparts. His aides were close behind him but no sooner had they reached the top than their ladder broke, leaving Alexander and just a few men alone in the midst of the city garrison. Alexander never stopped swinging his sword until brought down by an arrow. Luckily for him, his men followed his example and swarmed over the walls in time to save him and ultimately capture the town. Soldiers in any time or place will follow a man who shows he would not ask of them anything he would not also ask of himself.

So why would Alexander risk his life so often? Certainly his ego played a part in refusing to allow anyone else to outdo him in bravery. One Alexander biographer, J. R. Hamilton, argues, "Perhaps it was an inevitable consequence of leading from the front, but we may suspect that for a general he liked the thrill of battle too much."[36] Lendon argues that it was his obsession with Homer's tales of the Trojan War: "Alexander fought in rivalry with this ancestor Achilles, seeking out the heroes of the enemy to slay in single combat."[37] There was also the weighty legacy he had carried since childhood, the belief that his forebears included Achilles and Herakles, and that his own mother thought him the son of Zeus. That belief seems to have been reinforced when he visited the temple to Amon at the oasis of Siwa in Egypt, although no one knows what was said during Alexander's meeting with the priests there. While Alexander never claimed divinity for himself, after that experience he never stopped anyone else from claiming it for him. It has long been debated whether this was a true belief on his part or a clever bit of public relations to appeal to the populations of the East that viewed their rulers as divine. Given his apparent conviction that he would not be killed in battle, it would not be hard to extrapolate that he assumed a divine protection. As Curtius put it, however, he simply lacked normal human proportions. Alexander had a "continuous disregard for death, which frightens others out of their minds; a lust for glory and fame reaching a degree which exceeded due proportion but was yet pardonable in view of his youth and great achievements."[38]

In all his battles, Alexander's primary talent was, as we have seen, his ability to see what needed to be done to win, whether that involved maneuver or brute force. He never lacked for imagination to adapt to whatever problem faced him. The sieges at Tyre and Multan exemplified his ability to overcome physical obstacles by direct action. At the Hydaspes River in India, he showed his ability to outmaneuver his opponent by constantly feinting river crossings to keep his enemy's attention, while the real crossing was taking place more than a mile upstream. At that battle he also faced, as noted earlier, elephants for the first time, but offset their effect by doing what he did best: bypassing the animals fronting the enemy line and crashing a flank, forcing the enemy commander to surrender.

Alexander was most fortunate in possessing the army that he led, built for him by his father. No more disciplined force existed in the world at that time, and both the common soldiers and the noble officers were proud of their martial abilities and demanded the same in their commander. Alexander provided sufficient brains and brawn to satisfy them. Historian Eugene Borza offers a nice summation:

> Alexander was above all else a military genius, soldier, general, psychologist. Each battle was different. Each was fought as he wished. Each was decisive. Alexander never faltered or made mistakes. He won by manoeuvre, by the application of overwhelming force at the decisive point, by deception. Not only his own troops but the enemy too seem to have done precisely as he wished.[39]

The battlefield manipulation of both his own army and that of his enemy brought him victory in every battle he fought. Following Alexander's death, a void in leadership and skill on the battlefield emerged. As John Drogo Montagu has noted in *Greek and Roman Warfare*, "In the Hellenistic period (after Alexander) warfare failed to retain his subtlety and gloss."[40] The innate ability to lead with courage and tactical genius was not something Alexander could pass on, and his successors failed to keep the empire he gained.

3

Han Xin (?–196 BC)

General under Liu Bang, Emperor of the Western Han Dynasty

Generals are easy to get, but when it comes to a man like Han Xin, there is not his equal among the officers in the country. If you really want to contend for the empire, except for Han Xin there is no one who can plan it for you.

—Xiao He, chief advisor to Emperor Liu Bang

VERY LITTLE IS KNOWN of Han Xin's early years other than that he was of common birth and lived in poverty in his late adolescence and early adulthood. The primary source for Han Xin's life and career is the *Shih-chi* of Sima Qian, known in the West as *Records of the Grand Historian*. Sima Qian tells stories of Han Xin begging for food just to survive. In another, Han Xin apparently was acting tough and was challenged by a "butcher" (probably another term for bully). "You are tall and big and like to carry a sword. . . . If you can face death, try to stab me. If you cannot face death, crawl between my legs," the bully is supposed to have said. "Then Han Hsin, after looking him over carefully, bent down and crawled between his legs on his hands and knees."[1]

This humbling experience had a great effect on him and later in life, after he had achieved success, he rewarded the bully as well as those who had fed him.

Han Xin joined the army of Xiang Liang, founder of the Western Chu Kingdom, in March 208 BC, early in the dynastic rebellions against the Qin Dynasty. After Xiang Liang was defeated and killed, Han Xin shifted his allegiance to Liang's nephew and successor, Xiang Yu. Here he took his first very small step toward greatness when he was named a "palace gentleman," which was probably just a palace door guard. He must have had regular access to Xiang Yu, however, for he suggested several strategies to his master, all of which were rejected. In March or April 206 BC, the war against Qin was over and as Xiang Yu was the dominant general, he began assigning kingdoms to his generals. Liu Bang, one of his most successful generals, was given the province of Han, roughly corresponding to modern southern Henan and northern Hubei. At this point Han Xin left Xiang Yu's army for Liu Bang's, hoping a new commander might be more appreciative of his talents. One can only ponder on how these talents were acquired; it is known that Han Xin had studied the writings of Sun Tzu, but that was hardly unusual for military men of that day.

Soon thereafter, Han Xin violated some law and, with a number of others, was sentenced to death. When his turn came before the executioner, he noticed Liu Bang's chief advisor, Xiao He, and called out to him, "Does not the emperor [Liu Bang] want to go after the empire? Why should he have a valiant fighter beheaded?"[2] Intrigued, Xiao He freed Han Xin and talked with him at length. During these discussions it became clear to him that Han Xin indeed had a brilliant military mind. Xiao He mentioned his discovery to Liu Bang, who in turn appointed Han Xin head of the commissariat, something along the lines of quartermaster general. Further discussions convinced Xiao He of Han Xin's talents, but Liu Bang was uninterested.

That changed a couple of months later when a number of Liu Bang's generals deserted him. Han Xin, thinking that commissary general was as high as he would rise and not believing it to be a position in which he could employ his talents, deserted as well. Hearing of this, Xiao He pursued him. It was reported to Liu Bang that Xiao He had deserted as well. Liu was greatly pained at the loss of his chief lieutenant and was even more greatly surprised when Xiao He returned to court a few days later. Xiao He explained that he had chased down Han Xin and convinced him to return to the emperor's service. This finally convinced Liu Bang that Han Xin was a man to be trusted and taken seriously, and on Xiao He's advice he promoted him to general-in-chief.[3] It was now June 206 BC.

Warfare of the Time

THE TERRA COTTA WARRIORS OF XIAN, protecting the grave of Emperor Qin Shihuangdi, are perfect examples of how a warrior would have been accoutered in the time of the Chu-Han Conflict. The primary military arm was the infantry, which by the end of the third century BC would have been wearing scale armor made of iron, bronze, or leather strips sewn together with leather thongs. The terra cotta soldiers almost certainly represent an elite imperial guard force, but even the regular soldiers probably had at least leather armor.

The standard weapons were the halberd and the bow. The *ge*, a dagger-axe in use for almost a thousand years, vaguely resembles the European halberd or poleax. It had a point extending at right angles to the shaft, which would be used by swinging the weapon. It was originally made of bronze or jade, but by the end of the third century iron weapons were becoming somewhat more common. Some have suggested that the dagger blade could be used against charioteers, which may be one reason why chariots had become used mainly for officer transport or ceremonial purposes by the end of the third century. The head of the dagger grew wider and heavier by the same time period. The *ji*, another common weapon, was much like the ge but with a spear point extending from the shaft. Both were about ten feet long. Spears ranging from five to twelve feet were used as thrusting weapons.

The infantry was also well manned with archers. A standard five-man squad would usually be made up of three spearmen and two archers, who used both the longbow, made of bamboo, and the crossbow, which had been invented in the sixth century BC and first been used in a pitched battle (as opposed to a siege) in 341 BC. Crossbows reportedly had a range of six hundred paces—roughly the same as six hundred yards. By the time of the Chu-Han conflict, they might have become light enough (and easily enough drawn) to be used by cavalry, but those most likely came a few decades later.

Cavalry was also an important military component by this time. In previous eras the Chinese had shunned the use of horses as too barbarian. Experience fighting against the Hu on the northwestern frontier began to change some attitudes by the late fourth century, however. Wu Ling of Chao created a cavalry force and obliged his men not only to learn to fight like the barbarians but to dress like them as well. At first only peasants and Hu mercenaries were cavalrymen, but by the time of the Qin dynasty all social classes were involved. Cavalry was used mainly for harassment and pursuit rather than shock. The primary weapon for the cavalry was the bow, but horsemen also carried swords, which most infantrymen carried as well—the *jian*, a straight, double-edged blade roughly three feet long.[4]

The Opponents

DURING THE CLOSING STAGES OF THE REBELLION against the Qin, Xiang Liang invited Liu Bang to aid him in selecting a new king of Chu. The only descendent they could find, a grandson of King Huaiwang, was a shepherd, but he was named the new king of Chu and given the same name as his grandfather. After Xiang Liang was killed in battle, the shepherd king announced that whoever conquered the Qin capital of Chang'an would be the new king of that principality. Liu Bang and Xiang Yu both asked for the honor. According to contemporary histo-riographer Sima Qian, the goal was the "region within the passes."[5] This describes the Guanzhong Plain area around Chang'an, which is bordered by the Wei River to the north and mountain passes to the west, south, and east. Although both generals yearned for the glory the conquest would bring, Xiang Yu instead marched northward to the Zhou principality to relieve the prince there from an attack by Qin general Zhang Han, who had killed Xiang Liang.

Liu Bang's army therefore marched against Qin. He captured Luoyang and Nanyang, then marched westward through the Wuguan Pass (modern Danfeng) and up the Dan River to Chang'an. The Qin prime minister tried to bargain with Liu, offering to divide the kingdom with him equally; the offer was rejected. The grandson of the emperor Qin Shihuangdi killed the prime minister and took the throne. He voluntarily surrendered his kingdom to Liu in January 206 BC after serving as emperor a mere forty-six days.

In his campaign in Zhou, Xiang Yu negotiated the surrender of his rival Zhang Han and captured 200,000 soldiers in the process. Although this would have brought his army up to a reported 600,000, Xiang instead decided to kill his prisoners—by burying them alive. (He spared Zhang Han, later naming him king of Yong.) He then marched his army to Chang'an to claim it as his own. Liu Bang met Xiang Yu at the Wuguan Pass and found himself outnumbered four to one. Deciding discretion was the better part of valor, he informed Xiang Yu that he had been holding the capital in trust, awaiting his arrival: "I did not presume to take possession of the tiniest thing I came upon. I registered the officials and people, I sealed up the treasuries, and I waited for the general. . . . Day and night I was expecting the general to arrive, so how would I go against him!"[6] Xiang Yu further illustrated his brutality as he proceeded to occupy Chang'an, kill the Qin emperor and all his family, and burn the palace. He afterward invited Liu Bang to a celebratory dinner during which he planned to assassinate him, but Liu Bang escaped.

With the rebellion now officially over, Xiang named Chu king Huai-hang to be the new emperor, Yidi. He made himself king of Western Chu and named eighteen other generals and advisors to principalities across China. Instead of receiving the valuable and prestigious land of Qin, therefore, Liu Bang received the state of Han, on the southwest rim of "civilized" China. This "reward" seemed to him and most others to be a slap in the face. It was at this time that Liu Bang finally promoted Han Xin, who immediately proposed a strategy for Liu Bang to unseat Xiang Yu and claim the title of emperor for himself. Han Xin argued that Xiang was an able general but a poor leader. His execution of 200,000 Qin soldiers—while sparing their generals—had unnerved Qin's population, especially since those same generals were now the kings of the three parts of Qin: Yong, Sai, and Di. Further, when Liu had occupied the Guan-zhong area he had treated the people leniently and cancelled the Qin emperor's harsh law code, replacing it with one of only three rules. Thus, Liu had the Qin people's support and they would welcome him as their king and even as their emperor. All Liu Bang needed was an opportunity. "The conflict between them was more than a question of personalities; it was a battle between old and new, between the aristocrat and the peasant, the former kingdoms and the unified state," writes Ann Paludan, in her major book on the Chinese emperors.[7]

Upon withdrawing to his mountain capital in Han, Liu Bang had destroyed the *zhan dao*, wooden-plank roads (alternately described merely as wooden bridges) along cliffs on the way to Chang'an. This was designed both to protect himself from attack and to assure Xiang Yu that he would not be attacking the capital city. Luckily for Liu Bang, he was not the only unhappy king—the king of Qi was assassinated by one of his generals, and Xiang Yu gathered his forces from their capital in his home territory at Pencheng (modern Xuzhou) to suppress that rebellion.

This was Liu Bang's chance; with Xiang Yu occupied far to the east, he could now follow up on Han Xin's plan to unseat Xian Yu and claim for himself the title of emperor. First, Liu placed soldiers to work repairing the zhan dao. This alerted King Zhang Han of Yong, who placed troops in a blocking position for Liu Bang's outbreak.

Liu Bang and Han Xin, meanwhile, led an army westward through Hanzhong (modern Nancheng), then marched northward to Chencang (modern Baoji) on the Wei River, just upstream from Chang'an. The three kings of Qin were taken by surprise and surrendered to the Han army, and Liu Bang ruled the region—within a "few months," according to Chinese military historian Sun Haichen.[8] Whether that "few months" in the autumn and winter of 206 BC included the preliminary actions before Chencang, a battle against all three kings at once, or defeating the kings in turn is not clear. To this day in China, "advancing by way of Chencang" is an idiom for a secret move or an illicit rendezvous.

Xiang Yu could do nothing about Liu Bang's conquest, because the conflict in Qi dragged on. Liu thus seized the opportunity to expand territory under his control. He sent a column north to take control of two commanderies, Shang and Beiji, west of the Yellow River. He also sent a column toward Xiang Yu's capital at Pengcheng, where his wife and his father were being kept hostage. Xiang Yu's army turned them away. Seeing a potential threat toward his capital, Xiang Yu ordered that Emperor Yi leave the city; continuing his ruthless ways, he quickly thereafter ordered the king of Jiujiang to assassinate the expendable monarch. Liu Bang and Han Xin, in the meantime, captured Luoyang and forced the surrender of the king of Henan in February 205 BC, then took over the principality of Wei, just across the Yellow River, seven months later. This success

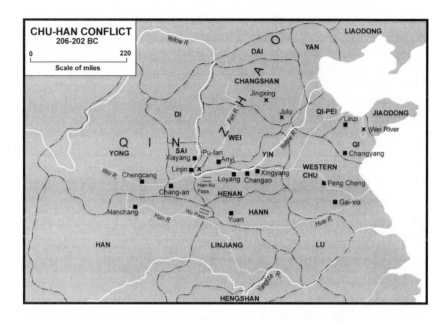

brought defections from Xiang's camp into Liu Bang's, including the king of Hann. The king of Yin, Sima Mao, resisted but was defeated; he fled to Chaoge, which Han Xin soon besieged. A feigned withdrawal drew Sima Mao out of the city and he was ambushed and captured. His submission to Liu Bang followed.

Now in possession of the city of Luoyang, Liu Bang was succeeding in Han Xin's measured strategy to strangle Xiang Yu's home province of Chu. Two things changed his mind against this course of action, however. A deserter from Xiang Yu, Chen Ping, advised Liu to march on Pengcheng, Xiang's capital city, now relatively undefended since Xiang was fighting in Chi. Liu also met Dong-gong, a longtime member of the ruling clique in Luoyang, who suggested that Liu Bang rally the kings around Emperor Yi's assassination. This brought in pledges of loyalty from the kings of Wei and Dai. Now with an army reportedly of a half-million[9] soldiers from his own kingdom as well as Sai, Di, Hann, Wei, Yin, Dai, and Henan, Liu Bang marched for and captured Pengcheng in the spring of 205 BC. Unfortunately, he did nothing to secure his victory: "Drunk with victory and puffed with pride, Liu Bang seized the treasures and women in Xiang Yu's palace for himself and indulged in drinking parties and various other dissipations every day."[10] He was thus surprised when Xiang Yu returned with a mere 30,000 men, catching the Han army unaware and defeating them so badly that "more than 100,000 of the Han troops all went into the Sui River, which ceased to flow because of this."[11] Liu Bang managed to withdraw to Xingyang on the Yellow River.

Conquest of Wei and Battle of Jingxing

HAN XIN GATHERED AN ARMY AND MARCHED to his emperor's rescue, driving back Chu forces sufficiently for the Han army to dig in at Xingyang. In the face of this turn of fortune, all of Han's recent allies hastened to swear loyalty to Xiang Yu. In Xingyang, the king of Wei asked permission to travel home to take care of his ailing parents. Once there, he courted Chu support. Liu Bang sent an ambassador on a futile mission to negotiate. Then, feeling himself strong enough in Xingyang, he detached Han Xin with an army of unknown size to recover Wei.

Bao, the king of Wei, prepared for such an eventuality. He fortified the Yellow River crossing at Pu-fan and stationed a force at Linjin (Lin-chin) to block a river crossing. When Han Xin arrived in the autumn of 205 BC, he proceeded to follow Sun Tzu's cardinal rule: all warfare is based on deception. Han Xin gave the impression of establishing a large camp by displaying many banners and gathering a large number of boats to launch an amphibious assault. As this was happening, he secretly led the bulk of his army several miles northward to the town of Xiayang. There, they constructed a fleet of pontoon crafts (reportedly made of wooden planks lashed to earthenware jugs)[12] and crossed the river. With the Wei forces still facing the diversionary force at Linjin, Han Xin marched his forces far to the east and attacked the Wei capital city at Anyi (Yuncheng). Learning of this flanking movement, King Bao marched his army away from the river back to Anyi. He was defeated outside the city and captured, after which he once again swore allegiance to Liu Bang. At this point, Han Xin's plan was to march north to Dai, then east through Zhao, which would put him in a position to strike Xiang Yu's army from the rear.

Han Xin proceeded northeast to confront the king of Dai; along the way Liu Bang sent him some reinforcements under Zhang Er. When he was dividing up the realm in 206 BC, Xiang Yu had named Zhang Er king of Changshan inside the kingdom of Zhao, alongside Chen Yu. Chen Yu, jealous of his supporting role, overthrew Zhang Er and reinstated the previous king of Zhao. In gratitude, the king named Chen Yu

king of Dai. Chen Yu appointed a subordinate, Xia Yue, to act as regent
while he stayed in Zhao. Thus, Zhang Er proved to be a valuable asset
to Han Xin, for Zhang had both a knowledge of their opponents and
a desire for vengeance. In the autumn of 205 BC, Han Xin and Zhang
Er defeated Dai forces at Yanyu and captured Regent Xia Yue. Meanwhile, Xiang Yu had been exerting pressure against the Han position at
Xingyang, so Liu Bang ordered most of Han Xin's best troops to reinforce his position, leaving Han Xin and Zhang Er with some 30,000
less-experienced soldiers. Still, they continued their march to confront
the next enemy, the forces of Zhao.

Han Xin's troops marched through mountain passes until they reached
Jingxing (the Jing gorge) sometime late in 205 BC. They entered this
extremely narrow pass heading eastward; at the far end waited 200,000
Zhao troops in a fortified encampment. They were under the command

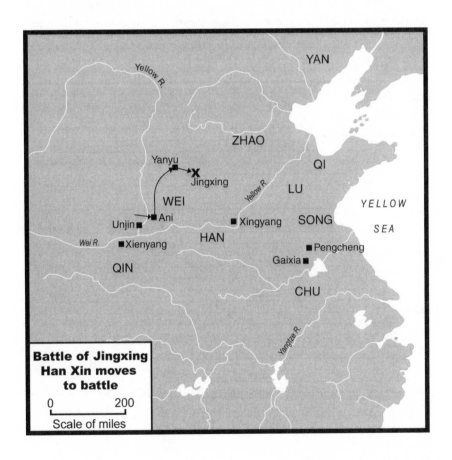

**Battle of Jingxing
Han Xin moves
to battle**

0   200

Scale of miles

of Chen Yu, the lord of Cheng'an, whose second-in-command was Li Zuoche, lord of Guangwu. Li Zuoche advised Chen Yu to send him with 30,000 men around to cut off the lines of communication, bottle the Han forces up in the pass, and starve them out. Meeting them on open ground would not be wise: "An army such as his, riding the crest of victory and fighting far from home, cannot be opposed." If contained in the gorge, however, the Han army would be unable to live off the land and too far from a supply base to last very long; "before ten days are out I will bring the heads of their two commanders and lay them beneath your banners!" Li Zuoche promised his general. "I beg you to give heed to my plan, for, if you do not, you will most certainly find yourself their prisoner."[13]

Chen Yu, a strict Confucianist, disagreed. To send forces around Han Xin's rear would not be something an honest follower of Confucius would do. Besides, he thought the number of Han troops was closer to 3,000 or 4,000 rather than the reported 20,000 to 30,000; if he did not directly confront a force he greatly outnumbered, none of his subordinates would respect him: "The other nobles would call me coward and think nothing of coming to attack me!"[14]

Han Xin sent spies ahead to learn what the Zhao forces intended, and they discovered Li's advice and Chen's rejection of it. This, coupled with advice from Zhang Er concerning Chen Yu's nature, motivated Han Xin to proceed. Having taken the measure of his opponent, Han Xin continued his march into the gorge. Some ten miles from the mouth, he encamped. That evening he sent 2,000 light cavalry, each man carrying a red Han banner, into the mountains to circle around behind the Zhao camp. Their orders were to stay hidden in the hills until they saw the Zhao camp abandoned. He also sent out a 10,000-man vanguard to deploy opposite the Zhao camp with orders to dig in with their backs to the river. This foolish deployment sent the Zhao army into peals of laughter.

At dawn the next morning, having given his men a light meal, Han Xin confided to his subordinates that they would be dining in the Zhao fort that night. None believed him, but they followed his orders nonetheless. Han Xin led the remainder of his army to the front of his vanguard, deploying with his banners and drums, the signs of his command. At that, Chen Yu sent his first wave into battle. Han Xin's men fought hard but gradually withdrew into the main body, abandoning their banners and drums. As Han Xin had foreseen, that brought the rest of the Zhao

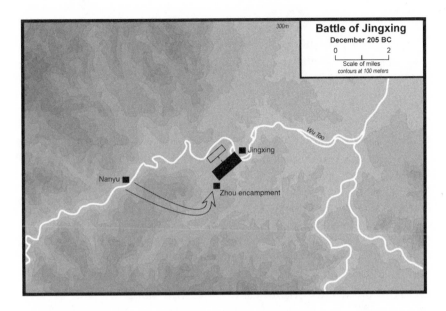

army out of their camp, eager to take part in the rout. Still, the Han forces fought so desperately they could not be destroyed. As the battle raged, the light cavalry force, hidden in the hills, emerged and entered the Zhao fort, killing the few remaining defenders. They then proceeded to take down all Zhao flags and replace them with Han banners. In the face of Han Xin's desperate fighting, Chen Yu ordered his men to withdraw and regroup for another attack. His men, now seeing the Han banners in their own camp, became panic stricken. They assumed their commanders were now dead or captured, so their morale collapsed and they began to flee. Although their commanders beheaded a few to halt the retreat, this act was fruitless.[15] As the Zhao army began to break, Han Xin ordered the attack, routing the enemy and killing Chen Yu. Chen's advisor Li Zuoche was taken captive and brought before Han Xin, who ordered him unbound and treated with utmost respect. He proceeded to question Li on the best strategy to pursue, now that Chen Yu was dead and the king of Zhao was in captivity.

That evening, as they were dining in the Zhao camp as he had predicted, Han Xin's subordinates questioned his tactics. After all, they pointed out to him, Sun Tzu's directives called for a river to be on the flank or in front, not to the rear. Han Xin replied, "Does not the book say, 'Put them at a fatal position and they will survive?' Besides, I did not have the chance to get acquainted with the troops at my disposal. . . . Therefore, I was compelled to plunge them into a desperate position where everyone would have to fight for his own life. If I had provided them with a route of escape, they would all have run away."[16]

Han Xin's movement to contact was an approach march, since his spies had given him exact details of the Zhao position. He had launched a deliberate attack that had some of the aspects of a feint. The main difference was that the bulk of his force was the feint and his small light cavalry force proved to be the decisive attack; at the same time, the use of flags in the Zhao fort to give the impression of a larger force was a feint in itself, followed by a counterattack from the main body. The key to the entire battle was audacity. Few battles in history better define the word: Han Xin risked more than 20,000 men in a position with no retreat in order to lure a massively larger force out of its position and then depended on a deception in the enemy rear to break their morale.

Battle of the Wei River

LIU BANG AND XIANG YU HAD SPENT months in 204 BC facing each other in the area east of Luoyang, between the Yellow River and the upper reaches of the Huai River, blocking each other's path toward the other's territory.[17] Cities were won and lost, with Xingyang and Changgao as the two major points of contention. Liu Bang was able to leave the combat area periodically to recruit forces in the area around Chang'an. In the summer of 204 BC, one of his advisors suggested that he not return directly to the battlefields but march south and recruit even more forces with the aid of Qing Bu, king of Linjiang, and then station their forces in the city of Yuan. This activity drew Xiang Yu southward, away from the Luoyang region, in hopes of catching Liu Bang in the open, but the Han king and his new army stayed within Yuan's walls. Peng Yue, king of Liang, meanwhile harried Chu forces in the east. When Xiang Yu turned to chastise Peng Yue, Liu Bang led his army to reinforce Changgao. Once done driving off Peng Yue, Xiang Yu returned to confront Liu Bang and quickly captured both Xingyang and Changgao, but not before Liu Bang made a hasty escape. This was sometime in the early autumn of 204 BC. He fled north across the Yellow River to Xiuwu, where Han Xin and Zhang Er were camped.

Liu Bang awarded Zhang Er military command over Zhao and sent Han Xin to attack eastward into Qi. He meanwhile fortified his position at Xiuwu and sent some cavalry to reinforce Peng Yue, who was once again harassing Chu supply lines. As Han Xin was marching toward the Pingyuan Ford across the Yellow River into Qi, Liu Bang sent an ambassador, Li Yiji, to negotiate an accord with Tian Guang, king of Qi. He succeeded in this mission: "As a result, Tian Guang revolted against Chu and joined in alliance with Han, agreeing to participate in an attack on Xiang Yu."[18] While on the march Han Xin learned of this new alliance, but continued onward. After all, he had not received royal orders to stop the invasion. Trusting to his new alliance, Tian Guang dispersed his armies and continued to entertain Li Yiji. Han Xin therefore had no trouble capturing Lixia and marching on the Qi capital of Linxi. Before making his escape, Tian Guang boiled Li Yiji alive for supposedly deceiving him. Tian Guang fled and sent a request for aid to Xiang Yu, who "accordingly sent Long Ju to go and smite him [Han Xin]."[19] Long Ju's army of 200,000, together with those rallied by Tian Guang, marched to intercept Han Xin's army. The two forces met each other on opposite sides of the Wei River, probably at the end of 204 BC.

Once again, Han Xin's opponent underestimated him. One of Long Ju's subordinates advised him to dig in and postpone battle; once the people of Qi learned that their king was still alive they would rally around him and the Han army would be isolated in hostile territory. Long Ju scoffed at the notion of avoiding a fight: "I have always felt Han Hsin to be inconsequential. He relied on a washer woman for food, so he never had any plans to support himself; he was insulted by having to crawl between a man's legs, so he lacks the courage to confront people. He is not worth worrying about."[20]

When night fell, Han Xin sent a number of his men upriver with orders to fill 10,000 sandbags and dam the river. This done, the river fell considerably but continued to run. The next morning Han Xin led his 70,000 soldiers across the river to assault Long Ju's army. After some indecisive combat, Han Xin withdrew his army back across the river. Long Ju, "truly elated, exclaimed: 'I knew Han Hsin was a coward!' Thereupon he ordered his army to ford the river and pursue Han Hsin's forces."[21] Seeing this, Han Xin gave the signal for the sandbag dam to be opened, and the rush of water drowned a large portion of the Chu troops. Long Ju was left with only a handful of men across the river, pinned against it by the now superior Han force. As the remainder of his army watched from across the river, Long Ju was killed. Tian Guang of Qi fled and was finally chased to ground and captured at Che'ng-yang. Han Xin proceeded to pacify the remainder of Qi.

While Han Xin did engage in an approach march for his movement to contact, it is unclear whether he chose the battleground. Many of the details around the battle are unrecorded. He engaged in a deliberate attack, followed by a deceptive withdrawal, using his knowledge of Long Ju's prejudice. Although Long Ju should have noticed and investigated the radical difference in river level, Han Xin's interruption of the flow was a complete surprise. With his entire force on his own side of the river and Long Ju's force now both weakened and divided, Han Xin was easily able to concentrate his army for the purpose of Long Ju's destruction. The exploitation of the trapped army was complete, although the remainder across the river fled without pursuit. Only Tian Guang was chased; with him captured rather than killed another Qi uprising was probably averted.

Over the next several months Han Xin was named king of Qi and spent his time consolidating the province. Liu Bang seemed to be growing wary of Han Xin's potential political ambitions, but Han Xin proved his loyalty by rejecting an offer from one of Xiang Yu's emissaries. One of his own advisors, seeing how powerful and talented Han Xin was, advised him to support neither Han nor Chu, but to establish himself as a third power and propose a three-way rule; thus, no one power would be able to overcome the other two: "if you choose to follow Chu, the men of Chu would never trust you, and should you choose to follow Han, the men of Han would quake with fear. With gifts such as these, whom should you follow?"[22] Even after extended arguments along these lines, Han Xin refused to abandon his fealty to Liu Bang.

Meanwhile, Xiang Yu alternated between fighting Liu Bang's forces near the Yellow River and securing his lines of communication from Peng Yue's harassment. He finally proposed to Liu Bang that they split China between them, an offer he had rejected when Liu Bang suggested it after his defeat at Pengcheng. Liu Bang accepted the offer, but as Xiang Yu was withdrawing back to Chu, the Han forces followed. Liu Bang called all his generals to meet him at Guling, but Han Xin and

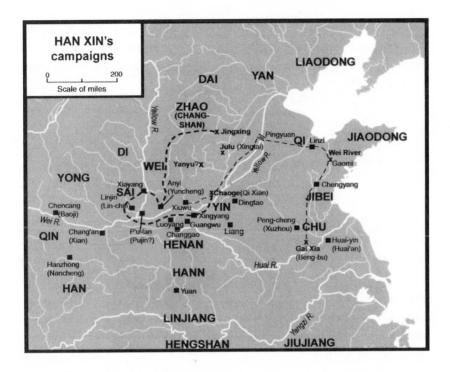

Peng Yue did not arrive. Thus, Liu Bang was forced to retreat once again to his defenses. After promises of increased land rewards for his generals (including Han Xin), Liu Bang's generals gathered together for a final battle against the Chu forces at Gaixia (modern Beng-bu). This time the Han forces were overwhelming: Han Xin commanded 300,000 in the center, with forces on each flank and two more in reserve. Xiang Yu's army numbered but 100,000. "Han Xin advanced and joined in combat but, failing to gain the advantage, retired and allowed General Kong and General Bi to close in from the sides," Sima Qian relates. "When the Chu forces began to falter, Han Xin took advantage of their weakness to inflict a great defeat."[23]

A handful of troops apparently remained under Xiang Yu's command after the battle, but were soon surrounded by Han Xin's force. Han Xin had his men sing local Chu folk songs, "so King Xiang said in great astonishment: 'Has Han already got the whole of Chu? How many men of Chu there are!'"[24] Thus was Xiang Yu deceived into believing the worst about his position. He fled with a handful of cavalry and made a last stand against pursuing Han cavalry, inflicting considerable casualties, before fleeing alone. Given an opportunity to escape across the River Wu, he chose instead to face his pursuers one last time, reportedly killing several hundred Han soldiers and receiving ten wounds himself. He then committed suicide.[25]

Han Xin's Generalship

BEING OUTNUMBERED IN EVERY BATTLE EXCEPT GAIXIA, Han Xin had to be a master of the principle of *economy of force* first and foremost. At the outflanking movement against the king of Wei, he depended on a small force appearing to be a much larger one preparing to cross the Yellow River at Linjin. Using a holding force outnumbered ten to one at the Jingxing pass allowed his strike force of 2,000 cavalry to initiate the deception in the enemy fortifications, breaking the enemy's will. Both of these operations employed sufficient manpower to hold the enemy in place while a flanking force delivered the main blow, whether physically against the king of Wei's army or psychologically at Jingxing.

For Han Xin, the two principles of *maneuver* and *surprise* were effectively inseparable. Sun Tzu's dictum concerning deception dominated all his tactics. Though the sources mention the siege of Chaoge only in passing, they describe the victory as based on the tactic of the feigned retreat. The Yellow River crossing into Wei was a classic example of "hold 'em by the nose and kick 'em in the pants" in which Han Xin used his smaller wing to pin down a superior enemy, then crossed with his larger wing upriver and swung around the enemy rear.

At Jingxing and the Wei River, Han Xin also demonstrated a characteristic that marks the truly great tacticians: knowing when to break the rules. If one can depend on his opponent to know the same rules, one can predict his actions and take advantage. After Jingxing, Han Xin's generals questioned his decision to place his men with a river at their back. Sun Tzu advises not to "array your forces near the river to confront the invader but look for tenable ground and occupy the heights."[26] The Zhao soldiers all knew that dictum, hence their breaking out in laughter as Han Xin's forces deployed. His response: Sun Tzu also says to put men in an untenable position and they will fight like cornered animals since there is no escape.

At the Wei River Han Xin also broke Sun Tzu's rules about river crossings. "After crossing rivers you must distance yourself from them. If the enemy is fording a river to advance, do not confront them in the water. When half their forces have crossed, it will be advantageous to strike them. . . . Do not confront the current's flow."[27] By blocking the river with sandbags, Han Xin did more than "confront" the current's flow. He employed the feigned retreat tactic again, and followed the dictum of striking when half the enemy had crossed the river. In all his battles, Han Xin engaged in at least one maneuver that his enemy never suspected. Only at Gaixia did the battle seem to be a fairly straightforward affair: attack with the center, withdraw, strike with the flank units. Whether he accomplished a double envelopment is not recorded, but that is the maneuver to do so.

The key to Han Xin's victories, however, lay in his manipulation of the principle of *morale*. Unlike Alexander, Han Xin depended not so much on maintaining his own army's morale as in breaking that of the enemy. Because Han Xin seems rarely to have been in command of men who stayed with him for a long period, he could depend only on his reputation to retain his troops' loyalty and keep their morale up. That didn't always work, as shown before the battle at Jingxing when he promised his men they would dine in the Zhao encampment that night. "None of his generals believed that the plan would work," Sima Qian writes, "but they feigned agreement and answered, 'Very well.'"[28] When Han Xin's light cavalry force struck from behind and planted Han flags throughout the Zhao camp, however, the vastly more numerous Zhao army lost heart and fled.

Both in Jinxing and at the Wei River, Han Xin also played on the mind of his opposing commander. Aware that neither Chen Yu nor Long Ju took him seriously, Han Xin opened his battles with what seemed to be a foolish move in order to confirm his enemies' opinions of him in their own minds. This made his deceptions all the more effective, for both opponents overcommitted their forces. When disaster struck, the soldiers of both the Zhao and Chu armies panicked, allowing the smaller Han force to turn their defeat into a rout.

AFTER GAIXIA, LIU BANG became the recognized ruler of China and established the Han Dynasty. He was later given the title Gaotzu, or

"Supreme Ancestor." Liu Bang ruled from the end of February 202 BC through the beginning of June 195 BC. In that time span he did have some trouble with the frontier barbarians, but Han Xin did not fight them. Liu Bang's opinion of Han Xin's trustworthiness waxed and waned, alternately leading Liu Bang to deprive him of his army and name him to a high-ranking position, Marquis of Huai-yin. Liu Bang's primary wife, Empress Lu, did not trust Han Xin and gathered evidence that he plotted rebellion. Invited to the imperial court, he was taken prisoner and executed. In Chinese history, only Cao Cao of the later Han Dynasty is considered near Han Xin's equal.

4

Hannibal (247–182 BC)

General of Carthage

> He was fearless in undertaking dangerous enterprises, he was prudent in discharging them. Toil could not weary his body or subdue his spirit. Heat and cold he endured alike.
>
> —Livy, *History of Rome*

HANNIBAL WAS BORN THE SON of one of Carthage's outstanding generals, Hamilcar Barca (whose surname was an epithet meaning "thunderbolt," or possibly the "flash" of a sword stroke). Hamilcar was head of the clan known in Carthage as the Barcids and rose to prominence in the waning years of the First Punic War. As the Romans were gaining the upper hand in Sicily, the main battleground of the war, Hamilcar led an expedition of mercenaries whom he had personally chosen and paid to the northeastern corner of the island, where he established a stronghold at Hercte. From there he harassed the Romans for three years, avoiding a major battle against them. He then stole away from the position to seize a Roman position on the western coast at Eryx, just north of the town of Drepana. Hamilcar continued the same harassment for a few more years, until eventually a peace treaty ended the war.

Some sources suggest that Hannibal, who would have been five, was with his father at Eyrx. If so, he was virtually born and raised at war with Rome. By the time Hannibal was nine, the war was over and Hamilcar was sent to establish a Carthaginian presence in Spain. He again led a force of mercenaries on the expedition and assembled them for a religious ceremony prior to departure. According to the first-century Roman history by Polybius, they met at the temple to Zeus. Having "poured a libation to the gods and performed the customary ceremonies," Hamilcar summoned his young son and asked if he wanted to follow his father to Spain. "Hannibal was overjoyed to accept and, like a boy, begged to be allowed to go. His father then took him by the hand, led him up to the altar and commanded him to lay his hand upon the victim and swear that he would never become a friend to the Romans."[1] This has been taken by many sources as the root of Hannibal's hatred for Rome, the so-called Barcid Rage. Polybius portrays this oath as creating a man "with a burning desire for power and seeing only one way to it, that is, by living surrounded by weapons and legions, and following one war with another."[2]

Hamilcar then left for Spain, where he succeeded in establishing Carthaginian hegemony. He died as the result of an ambush by a hostile Spanish tribe in 228 BC and was succeeded by his son-in-law, Hasdrubal. Whereas Hamilcar had been known for his military prowess as well as his diplomatic ability, Hasdrubal was more the diplomat. He solidified the hold that Hamilcar had established, ruling in Spain for eight years and establishing the city of New Carthage, modern Cartagena. During his reign, Hasdrubal made Spain extremely profitable for his homeland, but by establishing a major port and ship-building facilities he also drew the attention of Rome, whose nearest outpost was at Marseilles.

It has been debated whether Hannibal was in Spain throughout Hasdrubal's reign or had returned to Carthage for a time (as Livy relates).[3] Either way, he seems to have gained quite a bit of military experience. Although very little is known of Hannibal's upbringing, it can reasonably be assumed that his constant exposure to military men, through his father and the mercenaries that fought for him, had educated him in the ways of combat as well in the physical arts. He probably learned generalship from his father and diplomacy from Hasdrubal. He would therefore have known the importance of bravery in battle as a spur to the men under one's command, as well as the psychological importance of dealing with populations that one needs to ally with—or fight. Although some contemporary Roman accounts portray him as bloodthirsty, a more balanced look at the sources shows a man who knew the value of clemency. Still, we can only draw conclusions from his actions. As Adrian Goldworthy writes, "The true character of Hannibal eludes us. . . . We can say a good deal about what Hannibal did during his career, and often understand how he did it, but we can say virtually nothing with any certainty about what sort of man he was."[4]

Carthage came into existence as a colony of Phoenicia, the major sea power of the ancient world; the city was established in what is today Tunisia, while other Phoenician ports of call were established in Sicily, Corsica, Sardinia, the Balearic Islands, and Italy. Carthage grew into a trading power in its own right, dominating the western Mediterranean as the eastern became a battleground for Greek and Persian navies.

As Carthage spread its influence across northern Africa, wealth and status based on land came to rival that based on trade. As Carthage gained a more stable food supply, the population grew and colonies (not just trade centers) were needed to siphon off excess population. More land was therefore required, and Sicily became one of Carthage's primary settlement grounds.

Without its own military tradition to build upon, Carthage depended for the most part on mercenary troops. By the third century BC, however, the citizenry began to become more involved. They had always provided the oarsmen for the naval battles, but now they began to organize and train in hoplite-style warfare. They used chariots until the mid-third century BC; when they encountered war elephants while fighting the Greek general Pyrrhus in Sicily, the Carthaginians chose that new weapon for their shock forces.

As Carthage was establishing its sphere of influence, the citizens of Rome were doing the same. By the middle of the third century BC, they had come to dominate most of the Italian Peninsula, whether directly or indirectly. Although they showed little interest outside the peninsula, Romans came to see Carthaginian interest in Sicily as a potential threat to the southernmost regions of Rome's control. Overlapping spheres of influence thus led to military conflict when Sicily became the battleground between Carthage and Rome in the First Punic War (264–241 BC). One of the most important results of the war was that nascent Roman naval power grew into a force, one powerful enough to destroy Carthage's fleets. This obliged Carthage to spend even more time building up an army, which still depended on mercenaries to a great extent. The end of the war brought Hamilcar Barca and his family to the pinnacle of Carthaginian society and government, and it was thus Hamilcar who led an army to Spain to reestablish an economic base that had been lost with the Roman takeover of Sicily.

Warfare of the Time

WHEN HE ROSE TO THE LEADERSHIP OF CARTHAGINIAN SPAIN, Hannibal commanded a polyglot army with a variety of weapons, backgrounds, talents, and languages. Like his brother-in-law and father, he had not forced these people into service: they fought for pay and for their leader. They had followed Hamilcar and Hasdrubal and they followed Hannibal, not just because he was his father's son but because he had earned their respect in combat. He seems to have been schooled in the military arts from a young age and had the environment from which to learn a variety of the tricks of the trade from the multiethnic mercenary forces and the Iberian tribes. The government in Carthage readily named him to succeed Hasdrubal.

The mercenary infantry troops from Africa were either Carthaginian or Libyan, and they began the Second Punic War closely resembling the traditional Greek hoplites. After campaigning in Italy, however, they soon began wearing captured Roman mail and using Roman weapons, primarily the short stabbing sword known as the *gladius*. They did not, however, use the Roman shield, probably to maintain quick identification in the midst of battle. The African cavalry forces were primarily from the Kingdom of Numidia, modern Algeria. They were excellent horsemen and reputedly rode without saddle or bridle, armed with shields and long javelins. The Spanish cavalry was heavier, used more for shock than scouting or harassment. Thus Hannibal's Spanish cavalry accepted and delivered head-on charges; the Numidian light cavalry were used for harassment.[5]

Hannibal's Spanish and Gallic-Celtic infantry was made up of both heavy and light varieties, with slingers from the Balearic Islands acting as skirmishers. The light infantry (*caetrati*) carried a buckler and short sword; the heavies (*scutarii*) carried a large, flat, oval shield and were armed with short sword, stabbing spear, and javelins. The ancient Roman historian Polybius notes, "The shields used by the Spaniards and Celts [northern Iberian tribes were of Celtic/Gaulish ethnicity] were very similar to one another, but their swords were quite different. The point of the Spanish sword was no less effective for wounding than the edge.... [T]he troops were drawn up in alternate companies, the Celts naked [probably to the waist], the Spanish with their short linen tunics bordered with purple—their national dress—so their line presented a strange and terrifying appearance."[6] Like Alexander's army, the Carthaginians employed combined arms, but Hannibal depended on cavalry as the primary arm of decision. Even so, cavalry under Hannibal did not hold the special status it had had with Alexander's Companions.

The Romans also had cavalry, but the strength of their army was their infantry. Like the Greeks, the Roman Republic employed citizen-soldiers who fought for short enlistments and spent most of their lives tending their farms. Thus, whenever the Roman army took the field there was a mixture of veterans and new recruits. It was that mixture that led the Roman military to move away from the traditional phalanx formation of the ancient world. Instead of one long, continuous line, the troops were formed into "maniples"—smaller units made up of two sixty-man units called centuries, lining up twelve men wide and ten deep. The maniples deployed with gaps between them. In the second rank, another set of maniples deployed behind the gaps created in the first line. This allowed the front units space to retreat, if necessary, into the second line or the second line to advance into the first. A third line of maniples, made up of single rather than double centuries, lined up behind the second rank's gaps.

In front of the army came the *velites*, the youngest and poorest recruits who formed the skirmish line. They were armed with javelins, gladius, and a hide-covered wicker shield. In the leading line of the phalanx were the *hastati*, young men who could provide some armor for themselves. They carried two throwing spears, called *pila*, made of a long metal shaft extending from a wooden haft. This metal was tempered only about halfway back from the point, making the entire *pilum* bend on impact and rendering it temporarily useless, so that it could not be used by the enemy. The hastati also carried a short sword based on a Spanish design, the *gladius hispaniensis*, as well as a large oval shield, the *scutum*. The second line of maniples were made up of *principes*, veterans in their twenties and thirties, armed like the hastati. The third line were the *triarii*, older veterans who acted as reserves and who were armed mainly with the Greek-style spear in order to form a last line of defense. John Warry describes the Roman army going into combat:

At about 150 yards both sides charge. The front ranks of *hastati* throw their light *pila* at about 35 yards from the enemy, quickly followed by their heavy *pila*. They draw swords and close up on the run and hit the enemy with as much impact as possible. Succeeding ranks throw *pila* over the front ranks. The battle is a succession of furious combats with both sides drawing apart to recover. This might go on for several hours.[7]

Just how the separated maniples worked in battle is a question of some debate. Did they remain separated in battle? "An area of significant dispute is the lateral spacing between these dueling front rankers," Philip Sabin notes. "Polybius claims that there was only one legionary in the front rank for every six feet of unit frontage, whereas Vegetius states that legionaries fought on a frontage of just three feet."[8] Some scholars also argue that the gaps were only there during the approach. Once the velites had accomplished their skirmishing, they would withdraw through the gaps. Once they did so, the rear century would slide over the forward to fill the gap.[9] Thus, a solid line made the assault. Another possibility is that the maniples were deployed for battle (while the velites were skirmishing) in separated units, with each man having Vegetius's three-foot frontage. Then, as the velites retreated through the gaps and the maniples started forward, the men began to spread apart to Polybius's six-foot frontage. Well before physical contact with the enemy, the gaps between units would disappear and each man would have the individual fighting room he needed. As the lines drew back, the men would then close back up into a more defensive posture of a three-foot frontage. This seems a much simpler process and explanation than shifting units.

How did a battle play out? Most sources believe the hastati, once in a full line, broke into a run, with each man throwing his pilum at about thirty yards' distance from the enemy, before they hit full force with their shields and swords. If that did not cause the enemy's line to break, it became a matter of positioning legionaries in a line, thrusting at whatever enemy soldier came within reach. After a time, exhaustion would begin to set in and the opposing lines would draw apart. The dead and wounded would be replaced by soldiers advancing from the rear of the maniple. More pila would be thrown, and the assault would begin again when the soldiers had caught their breath. Periodically, if the clashes of front lines did not cause a full retreat, the hastati may have been relieved by the second line of principes. This would not only bring in fresh troops but more experienced ones to renew the fighting. At some point, one side or the other would sense defeat and begin to fall apart. Most believe that the rigorous discipline of the Roman troops was their primary advantage in the overall decision, allowing them to pound away with infantry until the other side was too tired or too broken in spirit to fight any longer.[10]

The Opponents

THE INITIAL CAUSE OF HANNIBAL'S INVASION of Italy was a treaty negotiated by his brother-in-law Hasdrubal, wherein he agreed to limit Carthaginian occupation of Spain to the south bank of the River Ebro. North of that line, Roman allies held sway. The problem arose when Hannibal, who took power after Hasdrubal's death, laid siege to the town of Saguntum, an ally of Rome that lay about a hundred miles south of the Ebro. The Roman government sent a delegation to Carthage, demanding that Hannibal be surrendered to them for punishment. The Carthaginian government argued that the Ebro agreement was made by Hasdrubal and not ratified by the government; hence, it was not bound by it. When Carthaginian leaders would not give the Roman emissaries satisfaction, war became the only option. Hannibal indeed set out for Rome, but at the head of an army rather than as a prisoner.

The Roman system of government and military command rotated annually with the election of two consuls, who had civil duties but also commanded legions in the field. Thus, Hannibal never faced the same general twice. The presumption of the system was that sooner or later an elected consul would have the talent to win battles. The primary drawback was that with no consistent leadership, little or no esprit de corps developed. Coupled with the annual draft of manpower that mixed together citizens from all across the peninsula rather than retaining local or regional units (where some knowledge of one's comrades already existed), and the fact that there was a war on and training time was therefore limited, the unit cohesion in the Roman army was negligible.

The Romans assumed they could pin Hannibal down in Spain with one force while landing another in North Africa and threatening Carthage itself. Hannibal was too fast for them, however. In March 218 BC he started out on one of the great marches in all of military history, leading some 50,000 infantry, 6,000 cavalry, and 37 elephants. He had just over seven months to cross the Pyrenees, get through southern Transalpine Gaul (modern France), cross the Rhone River, and get through the Alps into Italy before the snow fell. By the time the Romans had their first army embarked for Spain and stopped for supplies as Massilia (Marseilles), Hannibal was already past them, headed east. One of the consuls, Publius Cornelius Scipio, sent his army on to Spain under command of his brother, then left Massilia and quickly returned to the Po River valley to recruit new forces and meet Hannibal's army as it emerged from the Alps. Scipio had to pick up what manpower he could as he headed up the Italian Peninsula, and incorporated garrison forces recently beaten back by Gallic forces and therefore not the cream of the crop. Scipio therefore had an army of raw recruits and defeated veterans—a poor mix militarily and psychologically.[11]

When Hannibal entered Cisalpine Gaul (northern Italy) in November, his infantry force was down to about 20,000 and he had only a few elephants left, the rest having been lost to desertion or, in the case of the elephants and some of the soldiers, accidental deaths in the crossing. He was, however, in a region full of people who chafed under Roman dominance and were looking for a chance to gain freedom. Thus, he recruited Gauls of the Boii and Insubres tribes to refill his ranks. When the Taurini rejected his offer of peace because of their enmity toward the Insubres, Hanibal besieged, captured, and sacked their town to impress the other Gauls of the area. Pledges of support quickly began to arrive.

Scipio awaited Hannibal's troops with two legions at the Ticino River, near the modern town of Pavia. The opening battle was primarily a cavalry skirmish, with both Scipio and Hannibal leading reconnaissance parties that stumbled into each other. Scipio deployed his light infantry and held his cavalry in reserve. Hannibal charged with his heavy cavalry and engaged the Roman center, while his light Numidian cavalry rode around the Roman flanks and struck from the rear. At this, the Roman force fell apart and a wounded Scipio barely escaped with his life, rescued (according to Livy) by his eighteen-year-old-son. He wisely decided to withdraw his army southward to Placentia (Piacenza) and await two more legions that were on the march. As the reinforcements paraded through Rome, according to Polybius, "the people still believed that these troops had only to appear on the field to decide the battle."[12]

The battle at the Ticino River was a meeting engagement resulting in a hasty attack. Both sides had sufficient time to deploy their troops, but not to develop any sort of battle plan. Hannibal's key to success was concentrating cavalry on the flanks, which enveloped the Romans but did not annihilate them. As is the nature of a hasty attack, neither side had opportunity to control the tempo. The Carthaginian pursuit was directed primarily at Scipio's light infantry while the cavalry, with their wounded commander, were able to withdraw to the Roman camp.

Battle of the Trebia River

IN EARLY DECEMBER SCIPIO WAS ENCAMPED near the eastern bank of the Trebia River, south of Placentia. He had been reinforced by Tiberius Sempronius Longus, who assumed command as a result of Scipio's injury. The Romans found themselves in a difficult position, with many of their own Gallic troops defecting to Hannibal. Still, having a camp on the high ground, they were in a strong position. Unfortunately for the Romans, Sempronius was eager for glory and not content to stand his ground. Scipio had warned Sempronius to avoid battle; a winter of training would improve his own force while months of inaction would send many Gauls home from boredom. Waiting months to attack, however, would also mean sharing the glory with a recovered Scipio. "And so," writes Polybius, "since the time he chose of the engagement was not dictated by the facts of the situation but by his personal motives, his judgment was bound to be at fault."[13]

Capitalizing on the rash judgment of his enemy, Hannibal laid a trap for Sempronius. He placed his brother Mago with 1,000 infantry and 1,000 cavalry out of sight in the brush-covered valley with steep sides. He then sent a force of cavalry across the Trebia at dawn to harass the Romans and provoke an attack. When Sempronius ordered his men to chase the Numidians, the Romans formed their ranks in blowing snow and without the benefit of breakfast. Hannibal, on the other hand, had made sure his men were warm and fed. Sempronius pursued after the feigned retreat of Hannibal's cavalry and crossed the cold river, swollen from recent rains, onto open ground. Typically, Roman armies approached battlefields in column, and deployed by wheeling the column to the right until it was parallel to the enemy. This took a lot of time, especially with troops who had not had a lot of time to train. Hannibal held his men back at their campfires, and they watched the Roman lines form up across a two-mile frontage, 36,000 men strong, with some 4,000 cavalry divided on the flanks. Finally, Hannibal deployed his 8,000 slingers and light pikemen to the front, leading 20,000 mixed Gauls, Spaniards, and Africans in a long line of infantry. His elephants were placed in front of each infantry wing, with his 10,000 cavalry split evenly on the far ends.

The infantry battle started as Sempronius had hoped—with the Roman infantry making consistent headway against the Gauls in Hannibal's center. But the stronger Carthaginian cavalry gained control of the flanks. Hannibal's light infantry, after assaulting the Roman lines, had moved to the flanks, and the Roman cavalry were, according to Livy, "buried under a virtual cloud of missiles hurled by the Balearic forces. In addition to this, the elephants standing at the extremities of the wings

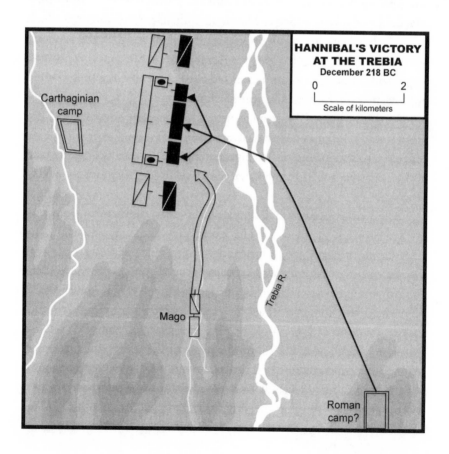

HANNIBAL'S VICTORY AT THE TREBIA
December 218 BC

0   2

Scale of kilometers

Carthaginian camp

Mago

Trebia R.

Roman camp?

caused widespread panic, especially among the horses, which were ter-rified not just by the sight but also by their unfamiliar smell."[14] Still, the Roman infantry seemed to be holding up well. The ancient Roman his-torian Appian writes that the "foot-soldiers, although suffering much and weakened by cold, wet clothes, and want of sleep, nevertheless boldly attacked these beasts, wounded them, and cut the hamstrings of some, and were already pushing back the enemy's infantry."[15]

Suddenly, Mago's hidden force struck the Roman rear. Some 10,000 of the Romans managed to break through the Gauls in the Carthaginian center and flee north to Placentia, but the bulk of the army was either slaughtered or captured. Hannibal lost some 5,000 men, but soon made up those numbers with even greater local recruiting and more desertions from the Roman army.

"Outnumbered by the Romans, Hannibal had used the weather, the terrain, psychology and superior tactics to devastate a numerically superior enemy," John Prevas writes.[16] He had used the Roman disdain for "barbarians"—for so they considered the Gauls—to his advantage. Sempronius did everything wrong, following his emotions and ambition into a sleet storm, across a freezing river, and onto ground perfectly suited for Hannibal's cavalry. Had Hannibal's Gallic allies stood their ground, eight Roman and allied legions would have been destroyed. Still, it was bad enough.

Hannibal initiated the movement to contact with the raid by his Numidian light cavalry. Knowing Sempronius's temperament, Hannibal succeeded in provoking a hasty attack, while his plan was well thought out. Using the terrain and weather, Hannibal also controlled the tempo of the engagement, forcing the Romans (because of their slow approach through the river and slow deployment) to fight while freezing, drenched, and hungry. Mean-while, the Carthaginian force was well fed, rested, and better prepared for the cold (by oiling their bodies). Initially, the only surprise was the elephants' effects on the Roman cavalry. However, once the armies were fully engaged, Mago's unexpected attack at the Roman rear was devastating. That attack, coupled with the victory of Hannibal's cavalry on both flanks, completed the envelopment. As mentioned, only the weakness of the Gallic infantry, and the Roman heavy infantry's breaking through their lines, denied Hannibal a complete exploitation of the Roman force. No pursuit of the fleeing Roman soldiers ensued owing to the rapid deterioration of the weather.

Hannibal spent the winter resting his men and establishing an intelligence network to educate himself on the enemy geography and armies. The Roman government and people steeled themselves for another campaign. According to Polybius, "It is when the Romans stand in real danger that they are most to be feared, and this principle applies both to their public and to their private life."[17] By the spring of 217 BC, two more armies were in the field against Hannibal, one of 40,000, under Gaius Flaminius Nepos at Arretium (Arezzo), and a second of 20,000, commanded by Cnaeus Servilius Geminus on the Adriatic coast at Ariminum (Rimini). They blocked the two main roads southward and were close enough to support each other if one should contact the invaders.

However, Hannibal had won two victories with flanking moves on the battlefield, and he now launched yet another strategic flanking movement. The Carthaginian troops crossed over the Apennines well away from the two waiting armies. As in the march through the Alps, what route they took through the Apennines is not exactly known, though it is likely they followed the Trebia toward its source. Local legend has Hannibal's armies camping in the region of some of the towns high in the Trebia Valley. Marching over the crest of the Italian Alps, they would have emerged near Genoa and then headed south. By this time Hannibal was down to but one elephant, the others having perished (depending on one's source) at the Battle of the Trebia, or during an extremely cold winter.

This northerly mountain crossing did not unduly concern Flaminius, however, for the Carthaginians would have to come to him anyway; they could not possibly cross the swamps north of the lower stretches of the Arno during the spring floods. Hannibal proceeded to do exactly that, as apparently his crossing of the Alps had failed to educate Flaminius as to the depth of Hannibal's skill and daring.[18] Four days and three nights in a sucking morass cost him more soldiers and his final elephant. The soldiers underwent unbearable suffering, as the trailing troops would be obliged to cross swampland already disturbed by the previous soldiers. This resulted in loud complaining and could possibly have even ended in mass desertion but for Mago's cavalry bringing up the rear and blocking any such attempt. The horses themselves suffered distemper in their hooves and collapsed in massive numbers. The soldiers also were victim to such diseases are found in swamps, with Hannibal himself losing an eye to an infection.[19] They emerged to the west of Flaminius and with an open road to Rome, to the disbelief of the opposing forces.

The Battle of Lake Trasimene

HAVING DRIED OUT, Hannibal attacked east instead of south, raiding Faesulae, near modern Florence. He was learning about the mind of his enemy. As Livy put it, "He thereupon proceeded with a very thorough and detailed enquiry into the consul's strategy and way of thinking, into geography and routes of the area and its capability of providing supplies, and into everything else that it was valuable for him to know."[20] None of the Roman writers, on the other hand, are complimentary about Flaminius. Although he had led an unspectacular foray against the Gauls several years earlier, Appian describes him as "inexperienced in war (for he had been wafted into power on a popular breeze)." Polybius describes him as "a mere mob-orator and demagogue, with no ability for the actual conduct of military affairs, and was moreover unreasonably confident in his resources."[21] According to Livy, "It was therefore perfectly clear that Flaminius would have no regard for god or man, and that his conduct would be characterized throughout by arrogance and lack of caution."[22]

Having taken the measure of his opponent, Hannibal led his army southward past Arretium toward Cortona. The Carthaginian troops set fire to the countryside, burning lands near enough to the Roman camp that Flaminius could not help but see the smoke. The Roman commander was infuriated. His officers advised him to await Servillius's 20,000 men before launching an attack, but Flaminius would have none of it. So sure was he of victory that he ignored not only advice but common sense. His promises motivated the civilians, however, if not his officers. "Indeed, he had even created such over-confidence among the populace that the soldiers were outnumbered by crowds of camp-followers who accompanied his march in the hope of finding plunder," wrote Polybius, "and carried chains, fetters and other such gear with them."[23]

Hannibal's scouts, meanwhile, had found one of the most perfect ambush sites in Italy, if not the world—on the north shore of Lake Trasimene, south of Cortona. Overlooking the northwestern part of the lake, at the site of modern Tuoro, is a chain of hills in a semicircle with the ends of the range almost touching the lake shore. Livy is enthusiastic about the choice: "Between the two there is no more than a narrow pathway, almost as if just enough space had been deliberately left for Hannibal's purpose!"[24] Upon these hills Hannibal stationed his army, and waited for Flaminius to march his men along the road by the lakeshore. On the morning of 21 June 217 BC, the Roman army marched into the defile, the hilltops covered with Hannibal's men hidden by the morning mist. Once the Romans were stretched out along the road, the onslaught from the hills was unstoppable. Polybius reports that Flaminius died quickly and without credit to himself.[25] Livy's description makes his last stand heroic.[26] Without time to deploy and in limited visibility, a credible defense was impossible. Some 6,000 men of the advanced guard did fight their way through the light infantry at the eastern end of the valley, but the remainder were lost. Some 15,000 were killed in battle or drowned in the lake and a similar number taken captive. Hannibal's loss was roughly 2,500 men.

For the movement to contact, Hannibal first engaged in an approach march since he knew exactly where Flaminius was located. Not wanting to fight on ground the enemy had chosen, Hannibal bypassed Arretium and launched raids across the area that destroyed enemy resources and provoked their commander. Flaminius followed the billows of smoke to the very ground Hannibal had chosen. Livy describes the Roman approach: "Flaminius had reached the lake at the sunset of one day, and,

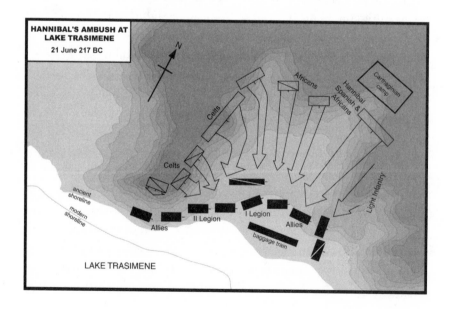

HANNIBAL'S AMBUSH AT
LAKE TRASIMENE
21 June 217 BC

when it was barely light on that which followed, he went through the defile without reconnoitering."[27] Thus was Hannibal's surprise complete. The attack concentrated every element of his force on a narrow target. He had chosen the terrain perfectly, and the weather once again was on his side. There was no need to regulate the tempo of the battle: speed was everything. The Roman army, unready for battle and unable to even see their attackers until too late to respond, was completely vulnerable. Hannibal's one failing was allowing the 6,000-man Roman vanguard to bull their way through his light infantry at the eastern end of the battlefield. Though they could hardly be expected to stand an assault of heavy infantry, it is difficult to know where else he could have placed them. Nevertheless, Hannibal made good the loss in the pursuit, and the vanguard were surrounded and captured the following day.

To complete the rout, Hannibal sent his cavalry eastward to scout the approach of Servillius's force, and they ambushed and destroyed the Roman cavalry advance guard. News of this double defeat was yet another shock to Roman hopes, and Polybius's comment on their reaction is rather different from his view after the Trebia battle, when he valorized Roman toughness: "In times of danger the Romans will go to astonishing lengths to propitiate both gods and men, and there is no ceremony of this kind which they regard as unbecoming or beneath their dignity."[28]

The Battle of Cannae

WITH THREE VICTORIES UNDER HIS BELT, Hannibal proceeded to implement his grand strategy for the campaign: promoting disaffection among those Italian states Rome dominated. Only by weakening the Roman hold on its homeland could he hope to save his own. He marched eastward to the Adriatic and rested his men and horses, moving camp from time to time as an area's resources diminished. Despite Hannibal's successes, he found himself in an undesirable situation: his victories had not broken the spirit of the Romans nor the ties to their client populations. Not only did he and his men have to live off the land, but they had to be brutal about it to demoralize Rome's allies and undercut its authority. At the same time, he could not afford to be too destructive and alienate the people he was trying to win over. He needed his own allies as Roman control of the seas meant few reinforcements from Carthage.

Through the remainder of 217 BC Hannibal and his troops moved down the eastern coast, then turned inland to meet their next opponent.

Back in Rome the politicians argued and raised more troops. The new consul, Quintus Fabius Maximus, was named dictator and given six months' unlimited power to defeat the invaders. He wisely avoided any combat while his armies were being trained, on the assumption that Rome's allies would not side with Hannibal in any serious numbers. Indeed, Roman allies remained steadfast, either through loyalty, fear of Roman retribution, or distaste at the thought of allying themselves with (or being under the authority of) the Gauls fighting with Hannibal. Fabius launched harassing raids against Hannibal and his men to let the peninsula's population know the government had not surrendered. While this "Fabian" strategy maintained the army, it wore on the public's patience. Hannibal marched back across the Apennines into Campania while Fabius led his army along just behind. With the autumn weather, Hannibal crossed back over the mountains and encamped at Gerunium. He skirmished with Fabius's second-in-command (and for a time codictator) Menucius, but no decisive battles were fought. When Fabius's consular year ended, more vigorous leaders came to power.

The year 216 BC saw the rise of two new consuls, Terentius Varro and Aemilius Paulus, the first perhaps too aggressive and the second perhaps too cautious. The Roman army now stood at 80,000 infantry and 7,000 cavalry, and the government and people wanted a quick end to the war. The new consuls followed Hannibal's army east and south toward the Adriatic and caught up to him at the Aufidus (Ofanto) River, located just inland from modern Barletta. There lay a small citadel at the village of Cannae, which the Romans used as a supply center. Hannibal had led his army there in early summer and seized the food for his troops, then awaited the Roman army's approach. For a few days the two sides jockeyed for position, establishing camps first on one side of the Aufidus then on the other.

There has been much discussion as to which side of the river the fighting actually took place on. The Aufidus meanders in a northeasterly direction to the sea three miles away, and all we know from the contemporary sources is how the two armies deployed. Polybius says the Romans faced south and the Carthaginians faced north so that the sun's rays would not be in the eyes of either. Yet the deployment took up most of the morning, rendering the sun's location fairly unimportant, and there is no spot near the battle's location where the two armies could rest a flank on the river and face directly north and south. Whether Polybius is being very general in his directions or the course of the river has significantly changed over the intervening two millennia is open to question. Appian claims Hannibal deployed with an easterly wind at his back, which rose about noon every day, so dust would blow into the Romans' faces.[29] Livy also comments on the wind, called the Volturnus, but implies the direction was fortuitous for Hannibal rather than planned, especially considering that it was the Romans who deployed first. While some maps show the battle fought on the northern bank with the river at the Carthaginians' back, most sources agree the southern side was the more likely battleground: "It is probably quite simple: on the left [northern] bank the ground is very flat, not rising above the 20-metre contour for about ten kilometres from the coast—perfect cavalry country. . . . But on the right bank the ground rises steadily from the sea, with a ridge along the river bank. . . . Thus, although it was still suitable country for cavalry, it provided more hope for the infantry than the terrain on the left bank, and Varro deserves credit for spotting it."[30]

The local food supply was running low for both armies, so, after a few days of skirmishing, battle was inevitable. Paulus and Varro alternated

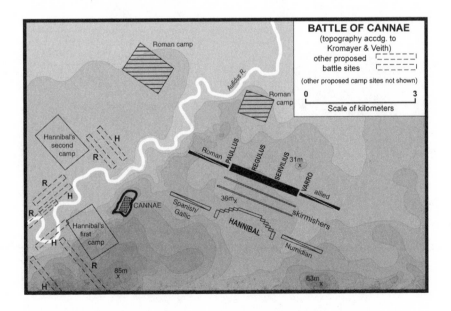

days in command, and Varro was in charge on the day of battle. Livy and Appian describe tension between the two commanders, but the more dependable Polybius makes no mention of it. In any case, the Roman army marched to the south bank of the river and formed up in its usual fashion, with infantry in the center and 3,000 cavalry on each wing. The primary difference from Roman protocol was that the men were deployed in maniples deeper than they were wide, possibly to facilitate keeping formation and possibly for extra power at contact. "The price was a loss of flexibility," writes Adrian Goldsworthy, "for the reduction in the gaps between maniples made it virtually impossible for these to change formation or wheel to face another direction."[31] Apparently, the Romans had learned nothing from the Battle of the Trebia, as they sacrificed maneuverability for power. Given that a Roman infantryman needed a six-foot frontage to properly use his gladius, a massed formation denies him that necessity. The formation would have better served a phalanx of pikemen.[32] Still, the massed Roman heavy infantry had broken the Carthaginian center at Trebia, so Varro decided to try it again with more men.

Hannibal also arranged his infantry in the center and cavalry on the wings—4,000 light horses on his right and 6,000 heavy on his left. He was outnumbered in infantry; each side had about 8,000 skirmishers, but Hannibal's heavy infantry probably numbered around 20,000 in the

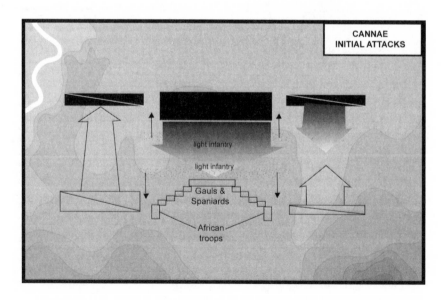

center compared with three times that (estimates go as high as to 70,000) for the Romans. Hannibal deployed his Spaniards and Gauls in the center and forward, in echelon back on both sides. His African infantry, in two columns of 6,000 each, trailed on the flanks. He had also learned the lesson of the Trebia, so his convex formation offered bait to the Roman commander, whom he was tempting to attack his center. It also was a way of buying time. As J. F. Lazenby points out, "This move would tempt the Romans into the center but also buy some time, tiring out the Romans as they moved forward, robbing them of their momentum and squeezing their formations."[33] The longer the infantry held, the more time Hannibal's cavalry forces would have to do their job.

Once the forces were in place, the skirmishers withdrew through the ranks and the battle began. The initial cavalry contest on the river side of the field quickly turned into dismounted combat. This gave the Romans little advantage, apparently, for, according to Polybius, "although the Romans resisted with desperate courage, most of them were killed in the hand-to-hand fighting. Their opponents drove the rest remorselessly along the river bank."[34] The Romans had hoped the cavalry could hold on just long enough for the infantry to prevail, but such was not to be. Hannibal's brother Hasdrubal's Spanish cavalry then rode to the opposite end of the field to assist the Numidians, engaging the larger allied cavalry force under Varro, who fled the field rather than be surrounded, with the Numidians close behind.

The stronger Roman infantry advanced on the convex Carthaginian line while two cavalry battles started on the flanks. The Roman infantry made good progress against the enemy center, pushing it back into a concave position. Goldsworthy argues that the Spaniards and especially the Gauls probably had reached the point where they were no longer the "literary cliche of the fickle and easily tired barbarian."[35] Two years under Hannibal's influence must have stiffened them. The intermingling of Spaniards and Gauls showed that the Carthaginian force was by this time more unified, and indeed gave them more incentive to prove their worth. Putting together soldiers of two warrior societies created competition to see which could fight hardest. Add to all of that the fact that Hannibal himself was with them, shouting encouragement throughout the fighting until he finally joined in it himself. These were not the same soldiers who failed to hold the line at the Trebia.

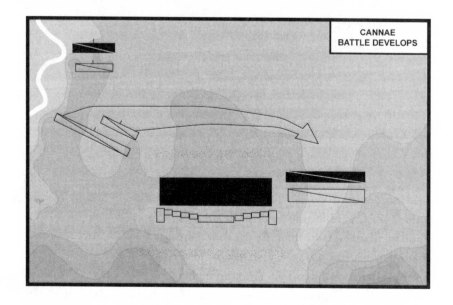

CANNAE
BATTLE DEVELOPS

Free from their initial responsibilities, the Carthaginian cavalry now turned and struck the Roman rear, creating what Bevin Alexander calls "a cauldron battle."[36] It is a tribute to the discipline of Hasdrubal and his men that they refrained, twice, from chasing the broken enemy in order to fulfill Hannibal's plan. This has been called a high-water mark of cavalry achievement in ancient times. To have two cavalry forces cease their pursuit to such an extent that most of them would turn around and assist in the main conflict was virtually unheard of.[37] The Romans found their advance halted and their retreat cut off as the Carthaginian army slowly tightened the circle. Eventually the Romans could barely move, much less fight. Hannibal's skirmishers, now on the outside of the ring, pelted the mass of men inside while the front ranks did their work hand to hand. As the great German military historian Hans Delbruck remarks, "It was impossible for any missile hurled into the mass of Romans to miss, and the more the terrified Romans allowed themselves to be pressed together, the less capable they were of using their weapons and the more certain was the harvest reaped by the enemy swords."[38] By day's end, between 48,000 and 60,000 Romans lay dead; the Carthaginian losses were about 6,000. Livy describes the disaster by saying, "The fleeing consul had with him barely 50 men, and almost the entire army shared the fate of the other consul who died there."[39] As Goldsworthy notes, this was a devastating

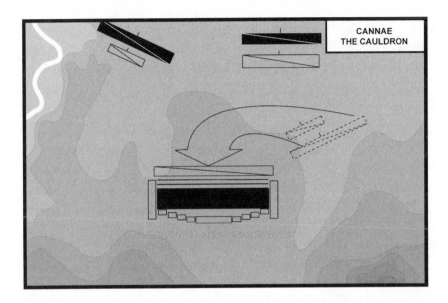

loss. "These figures need to be put into perspective. On 1 July 1916, the British Army began its offensive on the Somme, suffering an appalling 60,000 casualties on this first day. It was a disaster which still haunts the national psyche, much as Cannae was to remain a powerful image to the Romans for the remainder of their history."[40]

IN THE EARLY TWENTIETH CENTURY, German field marshall Alfred von Schlieffen published his study of the battle as a background for his massive plan of attack against France in World War I. Pointing out that Clausewitz had argued that "concentric action" didn't favor the weaker force, and that Napoleon had advised against turning both wings simultaneously, he noted that Hannibal had done both. "The weaker Hannibal had, in fact, acted concentrically, though in an unseemly way, and turned not only both wings but even the rear of the enemy."[41]

HANNIBAL SET UP THE BATTLE at Cannae by capturing the citadel and storehouse and awaiting the Roman army. Although the Romans chose which side of the river on which to fight, either bank, as Hannibal knew perfectly well, was well suited for him to employ his cavalry, making his enemy's selection of little importance. He therefore took the operational defensive to set the battle up and then switched to the offensive. Varro engaged in a deliberate attack, assuming he would be able to depend on Roman discipline and mass to break the enemy center. While Hannibal probably did not have the time or opportunity to learn as much about his opposing generals as he had prior to Trasimene, he knew that neither of them was Fabius; they were there to fight, so he could assume they would fight in the traditional Roman fashion—which they did.

When the two armies deployed and faced each other, the arrangement of troops in a cavalry-infantry-cavalry line was standard. It was the bowed-out center that was different—and the first of Hannibal's surprises. Varro apparently took no special actions when he saw the enemy center bowed toward him, a very unorthodox formation.[42] As noted earlier, the Carthaginian center probably wasn't weak at all, and as a result Hannibal could manipulate the Roman concentration of forces to his own ends. The arrival of the cavalry just as the African infantry were attacking the flanks presented yet another surprise to the Romans: fresh troops to face as they were becoming exhausted.

Everything about the course of the Battle of Cannae indicates Hannibal's total control of the tempo of the fighting, from the speed of the cavalry to the slow withdrawal of the infantry. As Clauswitz argued, small forces aren't supposed to surround larger ones. With the Romans engulfed and pressed from all sides (and pelted from above by the skirmishers using slings and spears), exploitation was total. The only survivors were the cavalry, which fled early in the battle, and the men left behind to guard the camps. Cannae is described by many historians as the greatest tactical masterpiece in history.

In the wake of this disaster, the Roman government wisely returned to the Fabian strategy—waiting Hannibal out. Many of Rome's allied provinces remained loyal, and Hannibal could not be everywhere at once. He still managed to campaign throughout the peninsula for a decade and a half but was never able to gain the upper hand and, without sufficient siege equipment or supplies, could never besiege and capture Rome. He finally left Italy to rescue Carthage from attack in 202 BC. There, he faced the Roman hero of the Spanish campaigns, Scipio, who defeated him at the Battle of Zama. Scipio's tactics bore a striking resemblance to those Hannibal used at Cannae, where Scipio had been one of the few survivors of the Roman debacle.

Hannibal's Generalship

A LIFE LIVED AROUND MILITARY MEN had prepared Hannibal for his career. Like Alexander, he suffered the same privations that he asked his men to endure. "On campaign he shared the physical hardships of his men," as Adrian Goldsworthy has it, "sleeping in the open wrapped only in a military cloak, and wearing the same clothes as the ordinary soldiers."[43] Thus, the first and most important characteristic of Hannibal's leadership was his ability to raise and then maintain *morale*. This was extremely difficult at first, as much of his army was composed of Gauls who did not know him and tended to want quick payoffs. His early battles were fought primarily to impress the Gauls into joining his struggle against Rome. The men he brought from Spain knew his strengths and qualities, and the Gauls learned soon enough. By the time of Cannae, Hannibal had gained their loyalty and trust—a fact that became evident as they held the Carthaginian line and crushed the advancing Roman forces.

Maintaining morale among troops who were enjoying successive victories was one thing, however. It was far more difficult for Hannibal to maintain morale while campaigning around Italy for another dozen years after his grand strategy had failed. He had to hold his army together by mere force of will, as neither victory nor spoils would change the situation. Still, Hannibal managed to keep an army of ragtag mercenaries functioning. In his classic work *The Great Captains*, Theodore Dodge comments, "His troops had often neither pay nor clothing; rations were scant; their arms were far from good; they must have foreseen eventual disaster, as did Hannibal. And yet the tie between leader and men never ceased to hold."[44] Perhaps of greatest use to Carthage was that he kept Rome afraid. Even as the number and quality of his forces dwindled, no Roman general would fight Hannibal head-to-head. As Dodge notes, "Weak as he was, no Roman consul dared come within reach of his arm. His patience and constancy under these trials, and the dread his name inspired, show him up in far greater measure than any of his triumphs."[45]

Another significant aspect to Hannibal's generalship was his use of *maneuver*. In his three major battles, he brought the Romans to ground he had chosen. Scipio chose the region near the Trebia River by establishing his camp, but Hannibal found and used the best ground in the neighborhood. The feigned retreat before that battle coupled with the hidden ambush force put the Roman troops at his mercy. The devastation of the countryside to lure Flaminius to Trasimene played on his opponents' vanity. The Romans came to him at Cannae when he seized a local center of gravity, a supply dump. The deployment at Cannae to entice and surround the Roman infantry showed that a feigned retreat can take place even in a restricted environment.

Additionally, all three major victories involved elements of *surprise*. Though Hannibal was famous for his use of elephants, in fact elephants played a relatively minor role at the Trebia. The battle was won because Sempronius never considered Mago's force hidden off the battlefield. Everything about the battle at Lake Trasimene, of course, was a surprise, it being one of the greatest ambushes in all of military history. And finally, the Carthaginian deployment, quality of infantry, and speed of cavalry all were unexpected at Cannae. In other more minor battles throughout his career, Hannibal showed himself again and again to be masterful when it came to using surprise to catch his enemies off guard. In one battle he duped Fabius's troops with torches tied to bulls' horns, and in another skirmish used broken terrain to hide a number of units that popped up all around Menucius's troops outside Gerunium. No wonder Roman generals were afraid to attack him even years after Cannae.

Nonetheless, massive and humiliating defeats on the battlefield hurt but never completely broke Roman morale, and ultimately time was their key ally. Hannibal's inability to conduct siege warfare saved Rome, and Fabian tactics kept the allies leery of embracing Hannibal's crusade. He kept his army together for more than a decade and a half, but could not attract the local support he ultimately needed to overthrow Rome. Meanwhile, Carthage was being hurt in its extremities and finally threatened at home, which was ultimately what forced Hannibal to abandon Italy.

5

Publius Cornelius Scipio Africanus (235–183 BC)

Roman General

> The art of generalship does not age, and it is because Scipio's battles are richer in stratagems and ruses—many still feasible today—than those of any other commander in history that they are an unfailing object-lesson to soldiers.
>
> —B. H. Liddell Hart

AS WITH HANNIBAL, details of Scipio's early years are extremely sketchy. He was born into Rome's upper crust, descended on both his father's and mother's side from the Cornellii, a family from whom consuls had been elected for 150 years. Other than that, little can be confirmed. Even Polybius, who wrote at length on Scipio's military career, glossed over his youth. He was well educated and admired Greek culture, which in his day was not a respectable characteristic, as the Greeks were viewed as a declining and somewhat profligate society; he must, however, have absorbed some of the Greek rationality in thinking, given the innovations he brought to the battlefield.

Also as with Hannibal, the first anecdote of Scipio's life concerns his relationship with his father, also named Publius Cornelius Scipio. At age seventeen or eighteen, Scipio the younger accompanied his father into northern Italy to confront Hannibal's invasion in 218 BC. At the Ticinus River, Carthaginian and Roman cavalry units unexpectedly collided. Scipio the elder led the charge, leaving his son in the care of a unit of veteran cavalry. As the battle began to turn against the Romans, Polybius tells of the younger Scipio rushing to his father's aid when the elder was wounded and surrounded: "[H]e at first endeavoured to urge those with him to go to the rescue, but when they hung back for a time owing to the large numbers of the enemy round them, he is said with reckless daring to have charged the encircling force alone. Upon the rest being now forced to attack, the enemy were terror-struck and broke up, and Publius Scipio, thus unexpectedly delivered, was the first to salute his son in the hearing of all as his preserver."[1] This episode may have proved his bravery but it was likely not his only combat experience. He may have been at the Battle of the Trebia and was almost certainly at Cannae, after which he rallied many of the disheartened officers. He therefore had firsthand knowledge of how Hannibal fought.

There is also some debate on Scipio's religious views. Livy recounts a story strongly reminiscent of Alexander. Since the age of fourteen Scipio had gone to the temple daily and stayed there in seclusion for some time, "and it generated the belief in the story—perhaps deliberately put out, perhaps spontaneous—that Scipio was a man of divine origin. It also brought back into currency the rumor that earlier circulated about Alexander the Great, a rumor as fatuous as it was presumptuous. It was said that his conception was the result of sexual union with a snake."[2] Livy also quotes Scipio's prayer to the gods prior to his expedition to Africa. Before the Roman attack on Novo Carthago, on Spain's southeastern coast, Scipio told his men that he had had a dream assuring the army of Neptune's aid in the upcoming operation.

Polybius, writing a century earlier, dismisses such notions. "As for all other writers, they represent him as a man favored by fortune, who always owed the most part of his success to the unexpected and to mere chance . . . whereas what is praiseworthy belongs alone to men of sound judgment and mental ability, whom we should consider to be the most divine and most beloved by the gods."[3] It has also been suggested that the story is false because a Roman temple was not a place for prayer and meditation but for sacrifice. Hence, the regular worship is implausible, though not impossible.[4]

Thus the same question regarding Alexander arises concerning Scipio: did he believe himself of divine heritage, or at least divine inspiration? Basil Liddell Hart supposes that Scipio, like Alexander, used such beliefs among his men to his own advantage: "Such supernatural claims only appear occasionally in Scipio's recorded utterances, and he, a supreme artist in handling human nature, would realise the value of reserving them for critical moments."[5] Appian takes Scipio's acceptance of divinity as a given. After Scipio's quick victory at Nova Carthago, Appian says, "He himself thought this, and said so both then and throughout the rest of his life, beginning from this moment."[6] Why not be both religious and practical? After all, it is no more or less likely that he combined rational calculation with religious conviction than did Stonewall Jackson.[7]

Whatever his parentage, it was saving his father at the Ticino River battle that first brought young Scipio fame; it was his father's death that led him to his destiny. After recovering from his wounds at the Ticino, the elder Scipio joined his brother Gnaeus in Spain to carry on the war against the Carthaginians in their supply base. The brothers enjoyed some success in battle and in gaining allies among the Spanish tribes, but they were both killed in separate battles in 212 BC. The remnants of their army retreated to the north bank of the Ebro, where they regrouped under the leadership of Lucius Marcius. He was soon superseded by C. Claudius Nero, who arrived with reinforcements late in 211. Nero seemed to be regarded as a temporary commander, for the Roman government was soon looking for his successor. They found him in Publius Cornelius Scipio, the younger.

Too young at twenty-four to officially hold a command rank, Scipio had it bestowed on him by public acclamation, which the Senate confirmed. There has been much debate why this occurred. Certainly there were men with more combat experience, but the government might have deemed them too valuable to spare while Hannibal was rampaging through northeast Italy. Possibly, they hoped the Scipio name, which had been so valuable in gaining allies in Spain, would generate loyalty. Scipio certainly had support within the Senate through his family connections. He seemed to have it all: family, political connections, bravery, ambition, and the charisma with which to sway the crowd.[8]

Perhaps the Senate withheld the names of other candidates, to give the public the impression they were confirming the only man who would actually volunteer for the job. It certainly would have deflected later criticism had Scipio failed in his mission. What seems most likely, however, is that the Senate recalled Nero because of the need for experienced commanders at home. Had the there been a greater number of qualified men, it would probably have sent someone else instead. Scipio was thus the best of the second string.[9] No matter the political circumstances involved, Scipio certainly wanted the job in order to avenge the deaths of his father and uncle.

Warfare of the Time

THE ROMAN ARMY FIGHTING IN SPAIN was organized along the same lines as the forces in Italy. The infantry was deployed in three ranks according to age and experience. The front rank, the hastati, consisted of the youngest recruits, usually late teens through twenties. The principes in the center rank were veterans, usually in their thirties. The first two ranks carried shield, short sword, and javelins (pila). The rear rank, the triarii, was made up of the oldest veterans who acted primarily as a reserve and were armed along the lines of Greek hoplites, with long pikes. Light infantry or skirmishers, the velites, used missile weapons such as slings and light spears in a harassing role prior to the battle's commencement. Cavalry forces remained secondary, but Scipio would begin to integrate them more thoroughly. In Roman legions they numbered 300, but in the more cavalry-oriented allied legions they usually numbered 600. They usually deployed on the flanks and were primarily for scouting, pursuit, and flank security.

Once in command in Spain, Scipio began altering the standard army format. After his capture of Nova Carthago, he began training his men with intensity. He had them make long marches in full armor and pay close attention to keeping their weapons and equipment in good repair. He also trained them in the use of the *gladius hispaniensus*, the Spanish sword.

Historians have long debated whether this weapon was first introduced by Scipio or had been used by the Roman army (at least partially) since the Gallic Wars in the 220s BC. In his biography of Scipio, H. H. Scullard argues that a lost passage from Polybius indicates that the Romans had adopted this "excellent Celtiperian sword," which was "well-pointed and suitable for cutting with either edge" at the time of the Hannibalic War.[10] The original Roman gladius was almost exclusively a stabbing weapon—used in thrusting—whereas the Spanish sword could also be used for slashing, making it much more functional in hand-to-hand combat. Probably a sword based on the Spanish style was in use by some Romans, but the high-quality iron and forging techniques were exclusively Spanish. Not until Scipio's time (primarily after the capture of Novo Carthago) would these have been widely available.

Once the velites were expended, combat did not immediately go hand-to-hand. Each legionary carried two pila, in most cases thrown during the assault before the clash of shields. The Roman throwing spear, the pilum, was a long pointed rod of iron implanted in a wooden shaft. The base of the rod was untempered, and, as noted in the previous chapter, it would bend on impact, making it useless to the enemy. The Romans, however, would reuse enemy javelins. Some have suggested that Roman battles actually involved more long-range fighting, but given that each regular soldier carried but two pila this is hard to accept.[11] If the velites were expanded in their numbers, this might seem more plausible.

More innovative than the weapons was Scipio's rearrangement of the army's formation. The velites became more important in his army, just as they were about to become throughout the Roman forces. In the wake of the massive losses in the battles against Hannibal, the Roman government was obliged to open the recruiting to greater numbers of the population. Traditionally, the soldiers provided their own weapons and armor and therefore had to be people of some means; the poor were not allowed to join the army. That changed in the years 214–212, when the proletarii became eligible. They were used as velites since they could afford no armor. The government, however, could provide each of them with a small shield and five pila.

In earlier days, the velites were harassing troops—used and then quickly withdrawn as the two armies neared each other. As the numbers of velites grew, so did their role. When Fabius was overseeing the war against Hannibal, skirmishing and harassment were the order of the day, so the use of missile-armed troops became more important. Scipio, by giving velites more training (and therefore discipline), began to grant them a greater role in battle. The Roman army was changing. Allowing the poor to join the army, coupled with wars that grew longer and farther away from Rome, was laying the groundwork for the professional army, very different from the one made up of citizen-soldiers, which had been Rome's traditional means of defense.[12]

The Carthaginian army that Scipio went up against in Spain strongly resembled that commanded by Hannibal in Italy, but grew increasingly dependent on Spanish recruits. As we saw with Hannibal, the Carthaginians depended hugely on allied forces as well as mercenaries. The Carthaginian forces were truly multiethnic and multifunctional. They included infantry from northern Africa, Spain, and Gaul, cavalry from Spain or Numidia, slingers from the Balearic Islands, and a leavening of Greek mercenaries.[13] The Spanish fielded both heavy and light infantry, based on their shield. The heavy infantry, or *scutati*, carried the long oval Celtic *scutum* while the light infantry, the *caetrati*, carried the *caetra*, a smaller and lighter buckler. The caetra was wooden, one to two feet across with a central metal boss, and was used for both parrying and attack.

The primary infantry weapons were sword and shield. There were two main sword types. The Iberians used the *falcata*, with a slightly curving blade that was sharpened hilt to tip on the outer edge, and occasionally on the final third of the blade on the inner curve. This gave it increased parrying ability. Very likely a local adaptation of the Greek *kopis* or *machaera*, it was a fearsome weapon. The blade was somewhat wider near the point than at the hilt, moving the center of gravity and increasing the kinetic energy when swung. Diodorus comments that these swords were of such quality that no helmet, shield, or bones could resist their strokes.[14] The Celt-Iberians of northern Spain used the straight, double-edged sword that the Romans soon copied. The Spanish smiths creating these were reportedly so good, and the quality of the metal so high, that the blade could be bent almost double then spring back to its original shape. Stabbing spears and javelins rounded out the Carthaginian armory.

The Opponents

WHEN SCIPIO THE ELDER AND HIS BROTHER GNAEUS campaigned in Spain, the Romans had gained two major successes. In 217 they defeated the Carthaginian navy, which hampered any reinforcement from North Africa to Spain. Second, the brothers established strong ties with many of the tribes of the peninsula, although mainly above the Ebro in traditionally Roman-dominated territory. Though one of the tribes turned coat in the middle of two battles in 211—a retreat that led to the brothers' deaths—and though some tribes drifted toward the Carthaginian cause afterward, most of the alliances they had established continued to lean in Rome's direction.

In the wake of the defeats in 211, the Roman army retreated north of the Ebro and established a defense. The troops elected Lucius Marcius Septimus as their new commander and sent word of their situation back to Rome. Luckily for them, the three Carthaginian generals fell into immediate squabbling about which was in charge, so Septimus was able to breathe easy. In 211 C. Claudius Nero arrived with reinforcements of 14,000 infantry and 1,100 cavalry and orders to play defense. Nero, as a protege of Fabius, was comfortable with a passive role. With Hannibal still active in Italy, the government viewed Spain as a sideshow—hence, very likely, why Scipio was sent there to begin with. However, when he was elected consul and sent to Spain in 210, Scipio had different ideas.

As for the Punic generals—there were three of them—we know little other than their names. One was Hasdrubal Barca, Hannibal's brother, who at Scipio's arrival was in central Spain besieging a town of the Carpetani tribe. Hasdrubal, the son of Gisgo, was on the Atlantic coast at the mouth of the Tagus River in what today would be the central Portuguese coast. The third, the youngest Barca brother, Mago, was among the Conii tribes around the Pillars of Hercules (Gibraltar). Unlike Hannibal,

who went to great lengths to learn about the personalities of his opposing generals, Scipio apparently had little chance to do so with these three, or at least there is no record that he did. From Scipio's perspective, the important thing was that the three armies were separated too far from each other to provide immediate mutual support. Even more important was the fact that none of these armies was within a ten-day march of his first target, Novo Carthago.

When Scipio arrived in northeastern Spain late in 210 he brought with him an additional 10,000 infantry and 1,000 cavalry. He landed at Emporiae, sent the fleet further down the coast to the main Roman base at Tarraco, and marched along the coastline southward toward Novo Carthago. This gave time for his arrival to be announced through the area, and those tribes that held ties to his father and uncle could (and in many cases did) renew them. Thus, when he reached Tarraco he had not only brought the Roman forces up to about 28,000 infantry and 3,000 cavalry but he also had laid the foundation for supplementing his army even further with local troops.

Novo Carthago

SCIPIO SPENT THE WINTER OF 210–209 BCE strengthening ties with the local tribes and gathering intelligence on his intended target. Novo Carthago was the primary port of entry for whatever assistance came from Carthage: it held the treasury, it contained a massive armory, and it was where the hostages held to assure the cooperation of the Spanish tribes were kept. Further, it was the primary manufacturing center, especially for weapons. On the surface, Scipio's attacking the main Carthaginian base seemed rather foolish given his relatively small force. The city was encircled with walls and surrounded by water on three sides—by a harbor and a lagoon. In reality it made perfect sense—as long as it could be captured quickly. Scipio had learned that the garrison numbered a mere 1,000 soldiers. The key was to make sure that the assault did not turn into a long siege, for that would give one or both of the Barcas the chance to march to the city's relief. Why would the Carthaginians leave their main port and supply base so lightly defended? According to Polybius, it was their rivalry. "Each went his own way in pursuit of personal ambitions, which would hardly have been fulfilled by electing to remain at New Carthage and ensure its security."[15]

The key to a successful attack lay in the nature of the lagoon on the city's northern side. After questioning local fishermen who had navigated it, he learned that in many places the lagoon was not very deep; according to Appian, it was chest high at the water's crest and knee-high when the water ebbed, which it did every afternoon, when strong north winds blew the waters through the canal and into the harbor. If he could hold the defenders' attention on a landward assault, a small force would be able to sneak across the lagoon and attack an undefended portion of wall.

He divulged none of his plans to any of his subordinates save one, his longtime friend and co-commander Gaius Laelius. Rumors, on the other hand, ran rampant throughout the army and the population, for which Scipio was grateful; the clot of stories would cloud the single one that was true. In the spring of 209 he led 25,000 infantry and 2,500 cavalry down the coast, leaving 3,000 infantry and 500 cavalry to hold his base at Tarraco. According to both Polybius and Livy, Scipio's army made the march of roughly 300 miles (2,600 Greek *stadia*) in a week. An army marching 20–25 miles in a day in the nineteenth century was considered to be making good time. Both sources say that the fleet moved along the coast at the same speed. His arrival was certainly a surprise to the citizens and garrison of the city.

The lagoon (which no longer exists) was located on the north side, and the harbor to the south. The peninsula itself was reportedly only 300 yards wide, and Polybius asserts that the circumference of the walls was 22 miles. The city was built on five hills with a sixth outside the city at the base of the peninsula. That was where Scipio established his camp, building defenses on the side not facing the city just in case a relief force should appear and to give his army maneuvering room on the side nearest the city gates. The 1,000 soldiers inside were commanded by Mago (not the same Mago as Hannibal's brother, who was in another part of Spain), who quickly drafted 2,000 citizens and armed them. When dawn broke and he saw the Romans preparing for an assault and Laelius bringing the Roman ships into the harbor armed with missile-throwing weaponry, Mago assigned his civilians to cover the walls while he placed half his soldiers on a hill near the harbor. The other half he kept in the citadel. As it turns out, the two veteran units were not designated to act as mobile reserves, which would have been the proper assignment, but to be in place for a last stand. This implies that Mago all but conceded the front gates and walls to the Romans.[16]

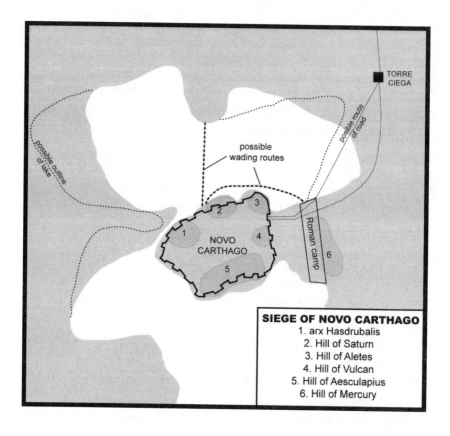

SIEGE OF NOVO CARTHAGO
1. arx Hasdrubalis
2. Hill of Saturn
3. Hill of Aletes
4. Hill of Vulcan
5. Hill of Aesculapius
6. Hill of Mercury

Before the attack began, Scipio addressed his troops, reassuring them that there was no relief force readily available, that the garrison was small, that they would be acquiring great wealth at the expense of the enemy, and (best of all) that he had been informed in a dream that the god Neptune had promised assistance. He, of course, knew of the nature of the lagoon's fluctuating waters, but, according to Livy, "made it out to be a miracle and a case of divine intervention" on behalf of the Romans.[17] Polybius uses this as an illustration of Scipio's genius: "This shrewd combination of accurate calculation with the promise of gold crowns and the assurance of the help of Providence created great enthusiasm among the young soldiers and raised their spirits."[18]

Just as the Romans were preparing for their assault, Mago launched a spoiling attack using the civilians, who came pouring out of the city gate. They gave a good account of themselves, but ultimately were both outnumbered and outclassed. When they finally broke and ran back for the city, they were barely able to get the gates closed behind them before the Romans broke through. Scipio quickly sent in 2,000 men with ladders to scale the walls, which, unfortunately for the Romans, were taller than the ladders. Again the civilians proved themselves surprisingly capable by keeping the Romans from reaching the crest; further, overloaded ladders broke and tumbled soldiers to the ground. By midafternoon Scipio called a halt. The defenders were catching their breath and hoping this signaled the beginning of a more traditional siege when the Romans started the assault again. The actions of the first attack were repeated in the second, but neither the Romans nor the defenders showed weakness or hesitation. At this point, defenders from around the walls were called to the land-ward defenses to aid in that quarter.

That was what Scipio had been waiting for. As the afternoon drew toward evening, his knowledge of the lagoon waters came into play. He led 500 men across the lagoon in the shallow areas and scaled the now-undefended walls on the north side of the city. Once inside they made their way to the gates and hit the defenders from the rear. Roman soldiers were hacking at the gates from the outside when they were opened from within. The civilians broke for their homes, pursued by the Romans who also attacked the 500 soldiers on the harbor-side hill, which had been dodging missile fire and assaults. Butchery of civilians began, stopped only when Mago surrendered the citadel, which he quickly did.

Within a day's fighting Scipio had seized the major prize of all Iberia. Scipio had made a deliberate attack using all of his forces but the cavalry. The infantry assault at the gates coupled with the pounding from the ships and the assault of marines from that quarter made his march a complete surprise. The frontal assault, pressed hard, was key to the entire action. Had he relied on merely the lagoon crossing he would have been met by stout resistance on the walls, which, according to Polybius, were manned at all points. By launching his main attack at the gates he would probably have broken through sooner or later, but that was what caused the abandoning of the defense from the lagoon side.[19]

Perhaps just as important as capturing the city and its assets—as well as freeing the hostages the Carthaginians had held—was what Scipio did after the battle was over and the spoils divided. He immediately began training his men in a new style of fighting, along the lines of what he had learned in action against Hannibal. The Roman way of fighting was unimaginative, in his view; Scipio trained the legions to employ tactics more flexible than the traditional Roman frontal attack, which depended entirely on the sheer weight of manpower. He had seen that fail at Cannae.[20] To most senior Romans, the traditional way of fighting exhibited the hallowed concept of *virtus*, virtue, and the belief that deception was dishonest. Perhaps this was a variant on the Greek hoplite attitude, as we saw in the chapter on Alexander: that real men only fought face to face.

The youthful Scipio was willing to break with the old ways. Bitter experience from facing Hannibal had already convinced him that learning from the victors was the key to beating them at their own game. With Novo Carthago he had come into possession not only of a huge arsenal but also the sword makers who specialized in crafting the Spanish sword. With a steady supply of the new weapons he began training his men.

Not many details as to how he did this are available. Nonetheless we do know that he kept the maniples but reorganized them into cohorts. The maniples consisted of two centuries of 80 men each and the cohorts became the next larger unit, containing three maniples, numbering 480 men. Ten cohorts constituted a legion. The result was that the basic tactical unit remained the same, but the cohort was made more flexible, so that it could be moved around the battlefield more easily than the legion. As Goldsworthy observes, "The old lines of the manipular legion were not effective tactical units for independent operations. The cohort, with its own command structure and with men used to working together, may well have fulfilled a need for forces smaller than a legion."[21] Movement on the battlefield—in a direction other than straight ahead—was one of Scipio's significant contributions to the Roman army's organization and behavior.

The Battle of Baecula

SCIPIO LEFT A GARRISON IN NOVO CARTHAGO and removed the rest of his men north, to their previous base at Tarraco. Inexplicably, none of the three Punic generals did anything to threaten him or try to regain their capital city. They did, however, watch a number of their allies desert and go over to Scipio. By the spring of 208 Scipio was ready to take the field again. The three Punic armies remained divided, and he was determined to fight them before they united. The closest army was that of Hasdrubal Barca, who had spent the winter in Baecula (modern Bailen) near what is today the Guadalquivir River. He was ready for action when he learned of Scipio's approach, placing himself in a strong position atop a hill with steep sides. The topmost part was fairly flat; there he placed his camp. From there the land sloped down to another shelf where he placed his skirmishers. That shelf was atop yet another, with steep slopes on three sides, so that any assault would involve strenuous climbing. Scipio's army marched toward the position ready for battle. A good look at the hill brought them up short.

For two days Scipio pondered how to attack. Fearful of the possible arrival of one or both of the other armies, he decided to start the battle. As usual he started with his velites in front, as a skirmish line. Backed with some heavier infantry, they began climbing the hill in front of the Carthaginians, who showered them with javelins and rocks. The Romans nonetheless made steady progress and Scipio sent in some more infantry for support. Hasdrubal at this point decided that the main Roman effort would come at him head-on; that was the way they had always fought. Polybius writes that Scipio "led out his troops and drew them up along the brow of the hill," taking his time. At this point Scipio launched his surprise: he divided the heavy infantry into two units; he led the right wing and Laelius the left. They worked their way up the base of the hill on both sides, then charged up to the flanks of the shelf. "While the manoeuvre was in progress," writes Polybius, "Hasdrubal was still engaged in leading his troops out of the camp. Up to this moment he had waited there, trusting to the natural strength of the position and feeling confident that the enemy would never venture to attack him."[22]

Pressured from the front and surprised on the flanks, the Carthaginian forces panicked. Hasdrubal made a hasty exit, his heavy infantry covering his retreat as he left his camp with the war chest and elephants. He waited for those who escaped to join him, then marched north for the Pyrenees to join his brother Hannibal in Italy. Scipio, unsure of the location of Mago Barca and Hasdrubal Gisgo, decided against pursuing the defeated Carthaginians. Instead, he once again divided the spoils of the captured camp and entertained the new stream of Spanish chieftains who came to pledge their support. Livy describes a meeting between the fleeing Hasdrubal and the other two generals, in which they exchanged

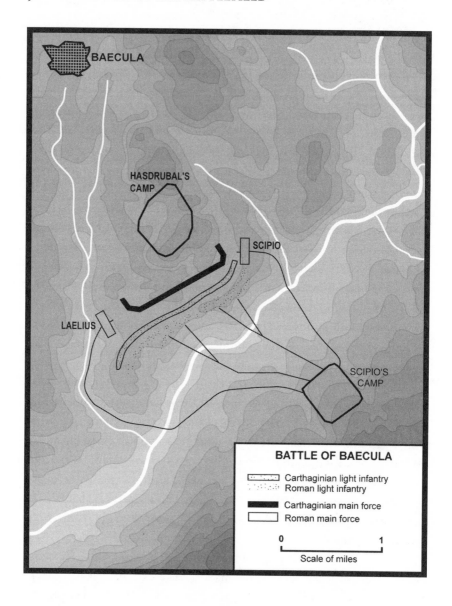

intelligence and laid out potential actions. Hasdrubal marched for Italy to join Hannibal. He never reached him, however, as he was defeated and killed at the Metaurus River in northern Italy by Gaius Nero, whom Scipio had replaced in Spain.

Scipio introduced two new aspects to Roman warfare at Baecula. First, he held the center with light troops and a relative handful of supporting infantry; the heavy infantry had always held the center. This shows that the

Romans had at last trained their lightly armed troops properly. Scipio gets the credit for using them for the first time effectively in battle.[23] Second, he engaged in maneuver, striking both enemy flanks with heavy infantry. Hasdrubal was certainly surprised at the arrival and the make-up of the flanking units, which hit him before he could properly deploy his main force.

Nonetheless, the Battle of Baecula falls well short of being decisive. The two flanking movements were not coordinated (not surprising given the broken terrain and the novelty of the maneuver). Further, once the Romans reached the plateau there was no quick reestablishment of control over the units, thus giving Hasdrubal the opportunity to make an orderly withdrawal.[24] Thus, Scipio failed to properly concentrate his forces; he did not exploit the victory, since so many of Hasdrubal's troops escaped; and he did not engage in pursuit. Though it was not a complete victory, the battle was a major accomplishment, for Scipio had to dislodge an enemy from such a strong position. This gave the Romans the momentum to go on to bigger and better things as their training and execution matured over time.[25]

Scipio's army had been the larger of the two (35,000 to Hasdrubal's 25,000) but the numbers were negated by the strength of the Carthaginian position. Livy says Hasdrubal lost 8,000 in the battle and agrees with Polybius's report of Scipio capturing 10,000 infantry and 2,000 cavalry. Most modern historians find those numbers exaggerated. Some think the numbers must include Spaniards who quit in the middle of the battle or changed sides. Others say that the numbers given by the ancient historians would be correct were the population of Baecula itself included.[26] If Hasdrubal's plan in 208 had been to assist Hannibal in Italy, then he risked being unable to reinforce his brother if he fought Scipio and lost. Had Hasdrubal won, of course, facing Scipio would have been the wise decision as he would have regained Spain for Carthage.

Whether or not Livy is correct concerning Hasdrubal's conference with his compatriots, the other two armies made no attempt to counter Scipio's victory and the resulting local alliances his victory gave him. According to Livy's account, the three decided thus: Hasdrubal Barca would proceed to Italy with as many Spanish troops as he could gather in order to keep them away from Scipio's influence. Mago should give his army to Hasdrubal Gisgo, then travel to the Balearic Islands to recruit more mercenaries, particularly slingers, their specialty troops.

Gisgo would take the Carthaginian forces to the far west coast—away from Scipio's area of rumored largesse with the Spanish tribes. Last, the Numidian cavalry general Massanissa should take 3,000 cavalry and harass pro-Roman towns along the frontier. In short, the Carthaginians would initiate no action that year. Scipio gave them little choice, anyway. Having won at Baecula, he withdrew to his base at Tarraco again and spent the remainder of the year there.

The following year, 207, the two sides did little more than spar with each other. Hasdrubal Barca's replacement, Hanno, tried to keep up recruiting among the Celt-Iberian tribes of Spain's central region and lost a small battle with Scipio's brother Lucius, while Hasdrubal Gisgo redeployed in the area around Baecula but refused battle with the Romans, retreating into a number of fortified towns. It almost seems as if the strategic situation in Italy was seeing its mirror image in Spain, with the Carthaginians engaging in Fabian tactics. Scipio, unable to maintain his army in the countryside too far away from his bases, did not press.

The Battle of Ilipa

IN 206, HOWEVER, HASDRUBAL GISGO was back on the move—into the Baetis River region west of Baecula. He'd reportedly gathered 70,000 infantry, 4,000 cavalry, and 32 elephants and seemed to be throwing down the gauntlet to Scipio. Livy asserts that the Carthaginians numbered only 50,000. Whatever the case, given the nature of Scipio's battlefield maneuvers, as we shall see, he seems to have been heavily outnumbered. The Roman leader responded by sending out subordinates to round up Spanish allies. He eventually fielded an army of about 45,000 infantry and 3,000 cavalry. About half Scipio's force was Roman or Latin, the other half locally recruited, including the tribes that had turned against his father and uncle and caused their deaths. "For without their allies the Roman forces were not strong enough to risk a battle," as Polybius observed. "Yet to do so, in dependence upon the allies for his hopes of ultimate success, appeared to him to be dangerous and too venturesome. In spite however of his perplexity, he was obliged to yield to the force of circumstances so far as to employ the Iberians."[27] The loyalty of Spanish tribes, or their perceived loyalty, figured into his battle plan.

The exact location of what came to be called the Battle of Ilipa is subject to debate. The best guess is that it took place somewhere in the neighborhood of modern Alcala del Rio, north of Seville. An alternate location is nearer the site of the Battle of Baecula. There is also an "Ilipa" near the river south of Castulo, much further east, which is another possibility. Both Polybius and Livy locate the battle there, and there is some independent evidence for such a town.[28] The description of the ground is fairly generic: Polybius says Hasdrubal's army dug their "entrenchment at the foot of the mountains, with a plain in front of him well suited for a contest and battle" while Scipio "pitched his camp on some low hills exactly opposite the enemy."[29]

Mago Barca, subordinate it seems to Hasdrubal Gisgo at this battle, launched a spoiling attack with his cavalry (accompanied by some Numidians under Massanissa) just as the Romans were setting up their camp. In his study of Scipio, Basil Liddell Hart writes that the Roman general was, "as usual, imbued with the principle of security," and had foreseen such a possibility by hiding his cavalry in the shelter of a hill and keeping them prepared.[30] The Romans put up a good fight (dismounted at times) and through surprise and toughness repulsed the Carthaginians, then pursued them. Though there is no written evidence for this, it seems as if Scipio had trained his cavalry in new tactics along with his infantry. They were now vastly better than the cavalry forces the Romans had fielded before. This action had an impact on the morale of both sides.

After the initial skirmish, both sides proceeded to a battle of nerves. Every afternoon Hasdrubal deployed his men for battle: African infantry in the center, Spanish infantry on the wings, fronted by elephants and flanked by cavalry. Every day, later in the afternoon, Scipio deployed his men: Roman infantry in the center, Spanish infantry on the wings flanked by cavalry. As Livy writes, "The Carthaginians would always be the first to lead their troops from camp, and the first to sound recall when they were weary of being on their feet. There was no charge, no spear thrown, and no battle-cry raised on either side."[31] This went on for several days. Finally, when Scipio was sure everyone knew what to expect, he shook things up. One evening after withdrawing from the field he sent word quietly around the camp: get up early and eat, then prepare to deploy at first light.

The next morning the Romans were up early, fed, and ready to go. Scipio had been at his father's side, if not in actual combat, at the Battle of the Trebia River in 218 when Hannibal had done precisely the same thing on a freezing December morning. When the Carthaginians awoke and found themselves facing a Roman army ready for battle, they rushed to deploy. As they did so, they came under fire from the Roman velites, which kept them focused on their own protection. Scipio, meanwhile, had deployed his Spaniards in the center, not his Romans, who were now on the flanks with the cavalry. When the Carthaginians had arrayed themselves for battle and seen the unexpected formation, it was too late to shift their own. The battle did not begin, however. The opposing skirmishers (with the two main forces perhaps half a mile apart) kept up their respective fire, pelting the enemy with javelins and stones. The hour drew toward noon, and the Carthaginian soldiers began to feel the heat of the sun and the hunger in their bellies.

Scipio's next move is what makes the Battle of Ilipa unique in the annals of combat, and so complex that even Polybius can't do it justice. Indeed, illustrated depictions of what happened vary from historian to historian. It seems that the Roman skirmishers, having been withdrawn in normal fashion through maniples, reformed at the rear flanks so the flanking units were three lines deep—a line of heavy infantry maniples in front, a line of light infantry second, a line of cavalry third. The entire army then proceeded to move forward, line abreast. Keeping the Spanish infantry in the center, marching forward at half time, Scipio ordered his Roman cohorts on either flank to face outward. Scipio's actions on the right flank were mirrored by Marcus Junius Silvanus and Lucius Marcius on the left. Having executed a right-flank march, they proceeded until they were even with the ends of the Carthaginian lines. Scipio then ordered a column-left march. (Some historians say the movement up to this point was actually done in echelon or in two moves, half-right march then half-left march, to end up at this point.) His unit was now perpendicular to the enemy (heavy infantry maniples on the left, velites in the center, cavalry on the right) and moving in column much more quickly than the Spaniards. At one *stade* (600 feet) from the enemy the column halted. The columns then faced outward, heavy infantry facing left, light infantry and cavalry facing right. At this point Sciopio had each line wheel toward the enemy (heavy infantry right-wheel march, light infantry and cavalry left-wheel march). When it was all over, he had his heavy infantry in line facing Hasdrubal's Spanish infantry and the light infantry and cavalry continuing the line past the enemy flanks.

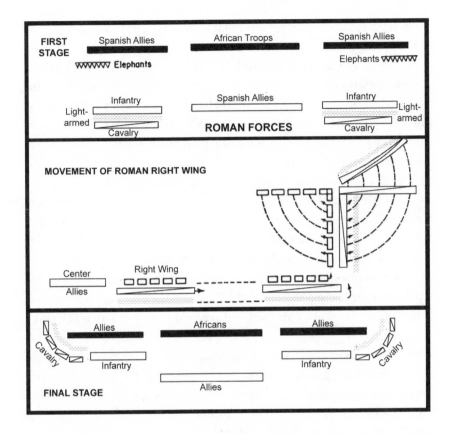

Now the actual fighting started. The velites and cavalry continued to wheel until they struck the Carthaginian flank and rear. "When these troops were at close quarters the elephants were severely handled," writes Polybius, "being wounded and harassed on every side by the *velites* and cavalry, and did as much harm to their friends as to their foes; for they rushed about promiscuously and killed every one that fell in their way on either side alike."[32] Scipio's infantry struck at the same time Hasdrubal's Spanish allies were collapsing. The Carthaginians in the center could do nothing; to turn and assist their Spanish allies would expose their flanks to Scipio's oncoming Spaniards; to charge forward would open their flanks and then rear to the Roman-Latin troops. The Carthaginian force at first stood firm and began to withdraw in order, but as the Spanish troops on the wings began to buckle the units in the center collapsed and fled. Polybius noted that had not "Providence interfered to save them, they would promptly have been driven from their camp too. A sudden storm erupted, and it was so heavy that it forced the Romans back to their own camp."[33]

Polybius leaves off his description of the battle at this point, but Livy continues with a description of the Carthaginian troubles. Hasdrubal watched while Spanish tribes fled, and he soon learned of garrisons in the area surrendering to the Romans. The following night he led the rest of his men westward but could not make good his escape to Gades (Cadiz), since the pursuing Roman cavalry and light infantry blocked his crossing of the Baetis River. The retreat, says Livy, became flight, and only got worse as the rest of the Roman army began to catch up to the pursuit. "After that it was no longer a battle; it was more like animals being slaughtered—until their leader authorized flight by personally making off to the nearest hills with approximately 6,000 poorly armed men. The rest were cut down or taken prisoner."[34] The 6,000 fugitives tried to defend themselves at a hastily built fort, but were easily surrounded. Hasdrubal abandoned his men and reached Gades, where he caught a ship for home.

Much had changed. Mago's initial spoiling attack probably would have done some damage had the battle taken place a few years earlier, but the Roman cavalry had honed their skills under Scipio's command and their counterattack drove the enemy from the field. Both sides demonstrated for a number of days before the actual fighting began, an action of which Scipio took advantage by a deployment employing surprise both in timing and in alignment of his forces. Next, his deliberate drawing out of the initial skirmishing in order to use heat, hunger, and thirst to weaken the Carthaginian troops exhibited his control of tempo. Whether at Trebia or elsewhere, he had somehow absorbed the lesson of subjecting his opponent to hunger, fatigue, and temperature.[35] Indeed, the U.S. Army's definition of "concentration" is almost a description of Scipio's maneuvers: "Attacking commanders manipulate their own and the enemy's concentration of forces by some combination of dispersion, concentration, deception, and attack."[36] And although unable to exploit the victory owing to the heavy rain (also reminiscent of Trebia), he made up for it with relentless pursuit. Liddell Hart comments that the pursuit had "no parallel in military history until Napoleon," who saw it as "one of the supreme tests of generalship."[37]

Scipio took a major risk in using these maneuvers at Ilipa. Could his men perform the complicated marching and wheeling he asked them to do in the face of the enemy? Livy's description of the maneuvers is much shorter and simpler and says nothing about an attack in column. He says merely that Scipio ordered the commanders on the opposite wing to follow his lead by extending their units outward, to engage the enemy with their light infantry and cavalry before the centers could meet, "and with these they advanced swiftly, the rest of the troops following at an angle."[38] Except for his comment about the "angle" it would appear (to Livy) that the wings marched line abreast across the field, but simply did so more quickly than the Spanish mercenaries, creating a refused center. It is possible that the advance in column was done in the interests of speed, for a column can advance more quickly than a line, and Scipio was anxious to initiate contact with his Romans before there was any possibility of his potentially unreliable Spanish allies being engaged in the center by Hasdrubal's more reliable Africans.[39] As Goldsworthy notes, "The details of the manoevre performed by the Roman army has, like so many other aspects of the war, been endlessly debated by scholars."[40] His illustration shows the two Roman wings attacking line abreast at about a thirty degree angle toward the Carthaginian flanks.

Whatever the truth of the matter, it was an extremely complicated move, one that depended on the enemy doing nothing but watch it unfold. As Liddell Hart says, "The only defence is that Scipio managed to carry it off. . . . Scipio ran the risk, hoping Hasdrubal would hesitate, which, in fact, he did."[41]

So why did the Carthaginians do nothing? Livy describes Hasdrubal as "the greatest and most famous general of the Carthaginians after the Barcas."[42] His most recent translator, J. C. Yardley, however, blames Hasdrubal, asking why he simply stood in position and allowed all this to be done in front of him. All the fancy maneuvering had left gaps in the Roman line, and exposed their flanks to the Carthaginians. "But on all the evidence Hasdrubal son of Gisgo was a hopeless general."[43] Just the fact that his army had been wrong-footed by the early Roman deployment may have paralyzed Hasdrubal, as possibly he feared some other deception and simply bided his time when he should have been launching an attack of his own.[44]

Scipio's Generalship

SPACE DOES NOT ALLOW ANY FURTHER DESCRIPTION of Scipio's actions in other battles, though he continued to show originality in battles around Carthage in 204–202. The epitome of his career was his confrontation with the master, Hannibal himself, at Zama, not far from Carthage. The student won, perhaps fittingly, with a double envelopment of Hannibal's army, though some sources opine that had the two armies been of equal quality the outcome may have been different. He fought in Gaul after that and spent much time in Roman politics. Politics proved his ultimate undoing. As Goldsworthy recounts, "Africanus was a poor politician who had difficulty achieving his objectives in the Senate quietly and without confrontation. . . . Depressed by the ingratitude of the State he had served so well, [he] went into voluntary exile in his villa in Liternum, where he died soon afterwards in 187."[45]

Scipio fulfills so many of the eleven principles of war that it is very difficult to pick two or three as examples. Perhaps one of the most important is his focus on the *objective*. When he arrived in Spain, many in Rome may have been expecting him to do little more than engage in a holding action to keep supplies and reinforcements from reaching Hannibal in Italy. If so, he disappointed them. He grasped two major concepts about how to fight in Spain. First, he knew that he could not win without a strong and secure base to maintain his lines of communication with Rome. Second, he knew that he could not defeat a united Carthaginian army. Object number one was accomplished with the capture of Novo Carthago. To achieve the second objective, he made sure he fought only separated armies: Hasdrubal Barca at Baecula and Hasdrubal Gisgo at Ilipa. After both victories he withdrew to the east coast rather than try to stretch his logistics by operating in the countryside at too great a distance from his base. Winning a series of limited objectives added up to the expulsion of the Carthaginians from Spain.

In addition, Scipio mastered the art of the *maneuver*. By breaking with traditional Roman tactics he caught the enemy unaware of what a new Roman army could do. The Battle of Ilipa was a tactical masterpiece, showing how a small army can defeat a larger one by shaking things up and using maneuver to keep it off balance, a capability he developed by introducing a more flexible formation.[46] Though the capture of Novo

Carthago did not involve innovation, the surprise attack across the lagoon was at the time a most un-Roman thing to have done. Still, all three of the battles discussed here show a single theme, as described by Liddell Hart: "In the sphere of tactics there is a lesson in his consummate blending of the principles of surprise and security."[47]

That brings us to *security*. Scipio illustrated from the beginning that he understood this concept fully. It was almost certainly driven home for him by the father's and uncle's deaths by desertion. So before the march on Novo Carthago he shared his plan with no one but Laelius, his chief of staff, who happened to be a childhood friend. Even as he accepted the pledges of tribe after tribe in the months and years following, he never fully trusted them. This is best shown at Ilipa, where he needed the Spaniards but determined not to depend on them. As Polybius observes, "He was obliged to yield to the force of circumstances so far as to employ the Iberians; but he resolved to do so only to make a show of numbers to the enemy, while he really fought the action with his own legions."[48] Also, by withdrawing to his base after his victories, he made it much more difficult for the Carthaginians to gather intelligence on Roman actions or plans.

SCIPIO'S SUCCESS WITH his new tactics proved to be vital to the overall change in the Roman military. The fighting style Hannibal introduced was embraced by Scipio's generation. By the end of the Second Punic War, the Roman army had developed from an unwieldy hoplite-style phalanx into a highly mobile force in which even heavy infantry were capable of rapid and independent maneuvers. The Romans learned the use of lightly armed troops and cavalry, and, above all, the concept and practice of combined arms.[49] Not just fighting style but the craft of generalship itself blossomed, and Scipio was the first to illustrate its advantages. Scipio learned well, so well that he never became predictable. Polybius said it best: "For while a general ought to be quite alive to what is taking place, and rightly so, he ought to use whatever movements suit the circumstances."[50]

6

Gaius Julius Caesar (100–48 BC)

Roman General

'Why, man, he doth bestride the narrow world
Like a Colossus, and we petty men
Walk under his huge legs and peep about
To find ourselves dishonourable graves.'

—*Julius Caesar*, 1.2.134–37
William Shakespeare

JULIUS CAESAR WAS BORN IN 100 BC into a politically prominent family. His uncle Marius had recently made a name for himself by organizing a new kind of Roman army and defeating an invasion of Gauls. Early in Caesar's life, his father was elected praetor, a judicial magistrate; a year later he was appointed to a governorship in Asia Minor. In 91 BC, a number of Latin provinces revolted against Rome, complaining of poor treatment after all their support over the years of Rome's growing power. This Social War lasted until 88 BC, and Marius, one of the primary figures involved, enjoyed the support of the common people, the *populares*. During the war, however, another general performed well: Lucius Sulla, a favorite of the upper classes, the *optimates*. A rivalry began between the two men, one that reflected the rivalry of the two social classes. An attempt by both to lead an expedition to suppress a rebellion in Asia Minor (the so-called Mithradatic War) resulted in a civil war in Italy, with Marius forced to flee. While Sulla went to fight in Asia Minor, Marius returned to Rome and killed his enemies, but died of natural causes soon thereafter. This political violence left Marius's supporters and family in serious danger.

When Sulla returned from victory in the East, he had himself named dictator and proceeded to use his position to severely limit the political role of the populares. He considered having Caesar killed since he was a part of Marius's extended family, but, admiring the young man's spirit, let him live. He did so reluctantly. When some assured him that Caesar, at only eighteen, could do no harm, "he declared that they had no sense if they did not see in this boy many Mariuses."[1]

Fearful for his life, however, Caesar fled Rome to the region of the Sabines (modern Umbria), then further to the Adriatic, from whence he sailed to Bithynia (north-central Asia Minor). In the two years he was there, he served with the Roman governor and fought in the siege of Miletus, where he was decorated for bravery. He had other adventures (including being held for ransom by pirates and later killing them) and then went to Rhodes to study oratory. Plutarch says he was naturally gifted and could have been famous for that skill alone (like his fellow student Cicero), but that instead he pursued politics and military affairs.[2]

With Sulla's influence gradually declining, Caesar returned to Rome in 78 BC to practice law, a profession often used as an avenue to enter politics.[3] He did not, however, ignore potential military glory. In 74 BC he raised a force to travel to Asia Minor for the Second Mithradatic War. His troops defended various Roman towns and gave the local governor time to raise a full army. Caesar returned to Rome a full-fledged war hero. Now well known, he began dabbling in political affairs.

In 68 BC, Caesar became a *quaestor* (comptroller) in the Spanish province of Baetica. In 65 he was named an *aedile* in Rome, a kind of a city manager. Responsible for taking care of the temples and overseeing the games, Caesar ingratiated himself to the populares; he planned to succeed his uncle Marius as their champion. He was elected high priest (*pontifex maximus*) two years later and continued to curry influence with the common people. A year later he was elected *praetor*, a high judge. By this point, the optimate party had started to become concerned by his stature. An accusation was leveled against him for conspiracy to commit sacrilege while he had been high priest, and it took a sizable number of bribes to make that problem disappear. Indeed, by 61 BC Caesar was broke; he had spent lavishly to acquire each of his elected positions, for his ultimate goal was the top office, that of consul, and the path to higher office was often determined by one's display of extravagance while an aedile.[4]

At this point, however, Caesar's fortunes changed. Marcus Licinius Crassus, the richest man in Rome, paid his debts. Crassus was sure it was an investment that would pay off in the future—and he was right. Caesar quickly left Italy and went back to Baetica, where he got himself appointed governor. There he seized the opportunity to suppress several rebellious towns, which he looted for the immense profit of himself and his troops. He returned to Rome a very wealthy man. He repaid Crassus and, with his wealth and popularity with the people, was able to get himself elected consul.

Caesar was in constant dispute with his co-consul, Marcus Calpurnius Bibulus, and, after using his bodyguard to rough up his opponents, decided to strengthen his position by allying himself with the two leading lights of Rome. Crassus he had already befriended; he now gained the favor of the greatest living war hero, Cnaeus Pompeius Magnus—Pompey the Great. Caesar mediated a disagreement between the two (who had been coconsuls in 70–69 BC), and then forced a land law through the Senate that favored Pompey's retired veterans. Caesar also married off his daughter to Pompey, making a son-in-law of a man six years his elder. Together, Caesar, Pompey, and Crassus became the first Triumvirate, a three-headed political beast that exercised enormous political influence over the Roman political scene. For Caesar this was a master stroke.[5]

Caesar's term as consul was marked by a mixture of reform and intimidation. He made sure that all records of the Senate and Popular Assemblies were made public, and he strengthened a law against extortion in the provinces. When he ran into opposition on other bills, he did not hesitate to use physical force to frighten or remove those voting against him. He also enriched himself with bribes. Most importantly, he secured a five-year appointment to govern Cisapline Gaul, followed soon thereafter with the addition of a one-year term as governor of Transalpine Gaul. At age forty-three, Caesar was ready to assume the highest political position. Although he had enriched himself in Spain, in Rome he had been a busy yet relatively unmemorable political player. His ambition now demanded new challenges and new frontiers in order to fulfill what he believed was his destiny.[6] What he had learned in battle and in politics were both put to good use in the next ten years.

Warfare of the Time

ALTHOUGH THE WEAPONRY OF THE ROMAN SOLDIERS had not changed significantly since the time of Scipio Africanus and the Punic Wars, the organization of the army had. The manipular legion of the third and second centuries BC gave way to the legions made up of cohorts, a unit organization attributed to Marius around the turn of the first century BC. The previously divided lines of hastati, principes, and triarii were consolidated into a single unit. Historian of the Roman army Lawrence Keppie writes, "[The cohort] was a convenient subdivision of the legion, capable of independent action. The idea seems likely to derive from the organization of the allied contingents which were provided annually to serve with the legion."[7] The legion came to consist of ten cohorts made up of three maniples of two centuries of around 80 men, giving a total of roughly 4,800 men.[8] Legions could, as in the days of the Punic Wars, number as many as 6,000 men under emergency conditions. With aspects both of the phalanx and the maniple, the legion made of cohorts could work both in mass and in parts, making it able to both meet large enemy formations and to respond to an attack from any direction.[9] The auxiliary troops, like skirmishers and cavalry, fast were becoming exclusively foreign mercenaries or allies.

Cohorts, unlike maniples, were not divided into three ranks based on age or experience. The reason for this stemmed from two major changes to the Roman military during Marius's time. First, extended enlistments became common as more distant conflicts made single-season campaigns impossible. This coincided with a renewed use of the urban poor rather than landowners as recruits. Without the necessary income for the city dweller to purchase his own equipment, the state began to provide arms and armor, which promoted standardization. Thus, all soldiers got the same gear: the pilum (throwing spear), the oval scutum (shield), and short gladius (sword), along with a helmet and mail shirt.[10] With all infantrymen armed alike, as noted earlier, this necessitated getting auxiliaries from foreign populations that specialized in archery, cavalry, and so on. Additionally, Marius is credited with introducing the practice of having each soldier carry a large amount of supplies in order to cut down on the baggage train, as well as the requirement that soldiers undergo intense training and drill. Keppie argues that this was not original with Marius, but a return to traditional Roman toughness.[11]

In addition to changes in the organization of the army, warfare in Caesar's time involved more technological complexity. Caesar was a great advocate of engineers and looked to them to provide additional support to the army of Rome. Since he often fought enemies far superior in numbers, he depended on not just the standard daily Roman entrenched camps but also on field fortifications. In his work on ancient warfare, John Warry observes that in Caesar's battle against the Belgic confederacy, the battle front was coextensive with the adjacent wall of his camp, and he protected his flanks with an earthwork on either side. "Caesar was able to develop their use on account of the astounding speed and efficiency with which his technical arm did its work. . . . Caesar himself says that the siege of Alesia could not have been undertaken without recourse to elaborate fortifications."[12]

In the Social War of 91–89 BC, the Latin provinces fought for and achieved recognition as Roman citizens. Once their citizenship went into effect, legions became even more heterogeneous in their makeup, since units were no longer "allies" bound by loyalty to a particular region. The number of legions also rose to the point that there were usually at least a dozen in existence at all times. The longer service coupled with the standardized training that came with the standardized weaponry translated into an increased professionalism, which flew in the face of Roman citizen-soldier traditions. Further, and more dangerous to the state, the more time spent away from the center of power meant a closer bond with one's comrades and commander. Adrian Goldsworthy notes, "The army ceased to represent the whole Roman people under arms and became more and more separate from the rest of society, their loyalty focusing more on their legion than on Rome. . . . This added an increasingly violent dimension to Rome's competitive politics."[13]

In the first half of the first century BC there was plenty of opportunity for combat experience. Not only was the northern Gallic frontier often lively, but civil wars in both Italy and in Spain (as well as the major slave revolt under Spartacus) and regular confrontations against Mithradates VI of Pontus in Asia Minor meant that war was more the rule than the exception.

Romans had fought Gauls (or Celts) for centuries. The Gauls were technologically much the same as in the days of Scipio. Spiritually they had not changed much either: they still seemed to love a good war, although many had settled lives and were engaged in trade. All the northern tribes, whether Gauls, Belgians, Germans, or British, varied only in their chosen weaponry, but not in their will to fight. The principal weapon of the Germans was the long spear, as was that of the Helvetii, who entered Gaul by way of modern Switzerland.[14] As Dando-Collins notes, "Their men-at-arms joined their traditional clans and formed into solid phalanxes of spearmen many men deep, each wearing a Gallic-style helmet with a plume like a horse's tail, a small breastplate, and carrying a spear up to twelve feet long. The Helvetii were Celts, larger men than the Romans, brave, and well versed in the arts of war."[15] Both also had excellent cavalry; indeed, Germans became the primary cavalrymen of the Roman army for centuries. Gallic warriors, like the traditional Roman soldier, were typically people of some means. Equipment and weaponry thus reflected one's place in society, with helmets and mail probably being worn only by the wealthiest.[16] For common warriors a long slashing sword and an elongated rectangular wooden shield would have been standard equipment. Without the means to afford armor, the regular infantryman wore anything or, in some reported cases, literally nothing. When massed armies were raised, poorer people would have been raised as a militia to act as slingers or archers.

The Gauls maintained a warrior mentality, which rarely stood them in good stead when they faced the more disciplined Romans. According to historian of the Celts David Rankin, "There can be little doubt that the military technology of the Celts was inferior to that of the Romans. It was still moulded and guided by the cultural assumptions of the Bronze Age. Their tactics were also too much affected by heroic and traditional ideas to give them good chance of success against the Romans."[17] Although the phalanx formation sometimes employed by Gauls required training and organization, they usually tended to seek glory in individual combat. The constant tribal conflicts may have kept them militarily sharp, but it guaranteed an inability to work together in large numbers.[18] This meant that tactically the tight Roman formations would hold together both on the advance and the retreat; it also meant that strategically and politically the Romans could divide and conquer.

The Opponents

THE CHANCE TO FIGHT AND GOVERN THE GAULS would provide Caesar with fame and fortune, both of which he would need to reach the top politically.[19] Caesar believed these things stood to be gained in Illyria, a province along the northeastern Adriatic Sea under the authority of Cisalpine Gaul. Defeating barbarians and spreading Roman control into the Balkans would have been sufficient to advance his goals in Rome; however, his last-minute appointment to the governorship of Transalpine Gaul would prove to be even more profitable. Things had been relatively quiet north of the Alps for some time. The stretch of land connecting Italy and Spain, Narbonensis, was occupied to protect the connection between the two major areas of Roman interest; anything to the north was barbarian country, which a Roman governor could often influence by being an unbiased judge in tribal disputes.

Being a mere arbitrator would not bring Caesar wealth or notoriety, so in 58 BC he had to manufacture a reason to launch an expedition into Gaul. The migrating Helvetii gave him that excuse. Caesar claimed that a third of a million people were invading Transalpine Gaul, though in reality they were more likely aiming at relocation to the Atlantic coast for their growing population and because of harassment from Germanic tribes (though Caesar averred that they, too, were Germanic). Caesar refused the Helvetii request for permission to cross the region peacefully, and proceeded to bar their way with troops. When the Helvetii bypassed Roman territory and entered Gaul farther north, passing through the lands of the Aedui, Roman allies, Caesar provoked a battle at Bibracte (Mt. Beuvrey in Burgundy). The Roman army crushed its opponents and captured the Helvetian camp; Caesar claimed that of the original 368,000 Helvetians and allies, only 110,000 returned to Switzerland. The Helvetii had thought of themselves as one of the superior Gallic tribes, but after their defeat at Caesar's hands they faded into history.[20]

With his forces now about 150 miles outside Roman Gaul in the neighborhood of the allied Aedui, Caesar responded to the Aedui citizens' request for protection from Germanic raids by the Suevi (or Suebi) under Ariovistus. Caesar now had little trouble gaining permission from the Senate for more military action. By classifying the Helvetii as Germans and then defeating them, he made all Germans seem to be potential threats.[21] Ariovistus, however, was an official Roman ally. A meeting between Caesar and Ariovistus accomplished nothing, as neither was willing to back away. The ensuing battle was another Roman victory, with a reported 80,000 Germans killed.

Rather than remove his troops southward for winter quarters, Caesar left most of them on-site in Aedui. By going into winter quarters on the German frontier, he virtually annexed the lands of the Aedui and Sequani; rather than emerging as their champion against the Suevi, he instead became their new master.[22]

In 57 BC Caesar's allies in the Senate secured an extension of his term in Transalpine Gaul, so he continued his conquests by meeting the challenge of the Belgae. The Belgae gathered in a mass near the Aisne River but soon found they could not keep such a large army supplied, forcing them to disperse. Caesar followed the now-separated tribes and proceeded to defeat them piecemeal. The Nervii, however, gave him a scare at the Sambre River. Sixty thousand Nervii men ambushed the Romans and took over their camp, creating chaos among Caesar's men. Scattered and unprepared, the Roman legionaries formed themselves up alongside whatever soldiers were nearby, ignoring unit designation. Caesar ordered the men into two large defensive squares, and remained in the middle of the action, helping his men's morale until the 10th Legion, Caesar's favorite, marched up to provide support. This proved sufficient reinforcement to turn the tide of battle and vanquish the Nervii.[23]

Caesar's legions traveled west in 56 BC. He fought the Venetii in a naval battle off the Brittany coast, employing the boarding tactics Romans had used since the Punic Wars. Leaving subordinates to march south and pacify the Aquitani (Aquitaine), he marched back to Belgium. The following year, however, political troubles arose at home. Caesar's fellow triumvirs and coconsuls were gaining a lot of public recognition while he was away from the capital, and Caesar realized that he needed to stay in the headlines if he was to maintain popular support. He organized a march east against the Germanic Usipi and Tecteri tribes, who had been fleeing the Suevi and crossed the Rhine into Gaul. Using a skirmish between the tribes and a Roman cavalry detachment as an excuse, Caesar and his men slaughtered the fleeing Usipi and Tecteri in their camps. He followed this up with a quick excursion across the Rhine, becoming the first Roman general to enter German territory after his engineers performed a minor miracle by throwing a bridge across the river in ten days. Caesar marched his legions across for a reconnaissance in force for eighteen days, but there was no fighting, and in the end the Romans withdrew back across the Rhine and destroyed the bridge behind them. The Roman general did, however, manage to impress both allies and enemies with the operation, as had been his intention.[24]

Caesar followed this up by another Roman first. Ramon Jimenez, in his biography of Caesar, describes his most spectacular effort to win public acclaim, an ill-advised and dangerous expedition across the English Channel to Britannia. "Even though Caesar managed to land two legions on the Kentish coast in the face of furious opposition by the Britons, a late summer storm wrecked his ships and blew his cavalry transports back to Gaul. He repaired his ships, but without his cavalry he was unwilling to advance inland."[25] A second, rather more successful invasion took place the following year, but nothing permanent was established other than a target for future Roman expansion.

Caesar spent the campaign season of 53 BC punishing tribes who had ambushed some 5,000 Romans outside modern Liege, as well as some remnant Nervii who attacked another garrison. His retribution was almost as cruel as his treatment of the Usipi and Tecteri. It seems that Caesar's blend of justice and mercy was showing too little of the latter, and the Gallic tribes began to grow angry and restless—and, eventually, smart. Intertribal squabbling had made them easy targets for too long, so the Gauls finally began to rally around a single leader, Vercingetorix of the Arvernii (modern Auvergne). Almost nothing is known of his background, other than that his father had been executed for trying to unite the tribes. Celtic historian Gerhard Herm describes him: "He was called Vercingetorix and as a man was just that: *ver* (over)–*cinget* (warrior)—*rix* (king); a man who could lead, persuade, and motivate men to great deeds. . . . Vercingetorix sought not only to regain freedom but to defend his house's claim to hegemony over the whole country."[26] Although initially expelled from his own people, Vercingetorix appealed to other tribes who realized a new approach was needed in order to fight the Romans. Vercingetorix demanded hostages from each tribe that joined him and killed the kings who refused to provide them. In this chieftain the Gauls had a worthy opponent for Caesar and his legions.[27]

Vercingetorix at once saw that the main weakness of the Roman military in Gaul was its lack of supplies. When not fighting, Caesar spent most of his time worrying about how to keep his troops fed. The first Gallic target was therefore a major Roman supply dump, Cenabum (Orleans). Vercingetorix led a successful attack, capturing Cenabum and all of the Roman inhabitants there. This news reached Caesar in Cisalpine Gaul, where he had spent the winter and had recently raised two new legions. Most of his veterans, however, were in the north. Caesar marched with his two legions westward into Transalpine Gaul to Narbo (Narbonne), heartening the subject Helvii and Ruteni tribes. He then went on the offensive.

With his handful of men (but with the veterans under his chief lieutenant Labienus marching from Belgium to his aid), Caesar surprised Vercingetorix by heading through mountain passes still covered with snow and emerging in the Rhone valley. While Vercingetorix was besieging

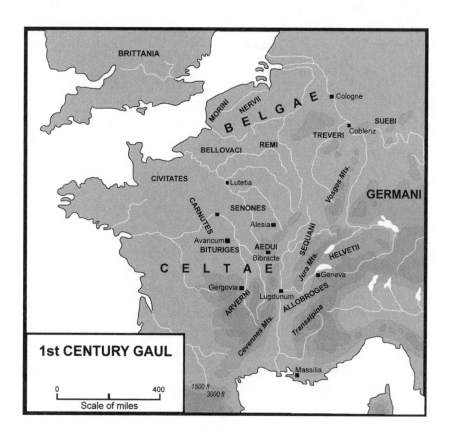

Roman allies in Gorgobina, Caesar distracted him by moving north-ward and then turning west to recapture Cenabum and seize a number of *oppida* (hill forts-towns) to scare the Gauls as well as to replenish his food supply. In response, Vercingetorix implemented a scorched earth policy as he withdrew southward. He decided against burning the oppidum of Avaricum (Bourges), however, when the inhabitants convinced him their walls could keep the Romans out. Vercingetorix moved on, and Caesar laid siege to the town. Although he had traveled with siege engines through much of his Gallic campaign, Caesar rarely seems to have been obliged to use them. At Avaricum, however, he quickly proved his mastery of siegecraft, and the Roman soldiers proved to be master excavators. In less than a month, often in downpours, they built two mobile siege towers and a 330-foot-wide, 225-foot-long, 80-foot-high ramp up to Avaricum's walls. Out of food, in a severe rainstorm, the Romans finally scaled the walls, slaughtered the population, and ate well.

Vercingetorix withdrew further southward into his home territory of the Avernii in south central Gaul and awaited Caesar's legions at his hometown of Gergovia. Caesar sent Labienus, who had joined him from Belgium, with four legions to subdue the area around modern Paris while he marched in pursuit of Vercingetorix with six legions. Here Caesar suf-fered one of his few defeats in Gaul. The town of Gergovia was atop a steep hill, making direct assault an impossibility. Caesar hoped to lay a successful siege, but doing so in the midst of the enemy's homeland was a difficult task. He managed to secure a strong position and build a fortified camp that limited the Gauls' ability to gather water and forage. However, the defection of Rome's long-time allies, the Aedui (owing to false reports of massacres by Romans), obliged him to leave about a third of his force in place while he marched away to placate the disaf-fected tribe. Although he succeeded in reconverting a column that had been marching to join Vercingetorix's cause, word of the "massacres" was sowing dissension across the region. In Caesar's absence, the Gauls at Gergovia had pressed his remaining two legions almost to the breaking point.

Caesar needed to get to a more secure location, join Labienus, and decide on his next move. However, a precipitous withdrawal would result in bad publicity. He could make no move that implied any weakness, for fear that even more tribes might arise against him.[28] He therefore decided to launch a last raid on the outer defenses and gain a quick though minor victory, in order to make the withdrawal appear voluntary rather than forced. He cleverly diverted the bulk of the defenders to the far side of town by disguising mule drivers as cavalry, allowing the Romans to capture the first wall. The speedy capture, however, encouraged the Roman troops to force a passage into Gergovia—against orders, according to Caesar.[29] Many Romans were caught inside the town; hundreds were lost. Caesar withdrew, and his fears were realized as many wavering tribes sided with Vercingetorix.[30]

The Siege of Alesia

CAESAR MARCHED TO LINK UP WITH LABIENUS and to replace his locally raised cavalry with Germans. He recruited a good force and provided them with more serviceable local horses. As he was doing so, word arrived of Vercingetorix attacking Gallia Narbonensis in the south. Caesar had no choice but to march to defend Roman territory.[31] In a battle in the homeland of the Allobroges, the newly arrived German cavalry proved decisive in defeating the Gauls. In response, Vercingetorix banked on the growing support of tribes across Gaul and retreated into the interior, finally coming to a halt at the oppidum of Alesia (Alise-Ste.-Reine),[32] which sat on a flat-topped mesa.[33] Vercingetorix's retreat to this interior location has been seen variously as both foolish and tactical; in their history of Rome, M. Cary and H. H. Scullard call it "the fatal mistake," while in her work on the Gallic Wars, Kate Gilliver's view is that Vercingetorix "allowed himself to be hemmed in . . . to catch the Roman army in a pincer movement." Hans Delbrück says it was a refuge to stem the flight of the Gauls after their most recent defeat, while Warry suggests Vercingetorix was trying to repeat his victory at Gergovia,[34] for Alesia was also impossible to assault directly. Whatever the reason behind Vercingetorix's move, when Caesar arrived at Alesia he began an encirclement, setting the stage for what would become the greatest siege since Alexander at Tyre.

Caesar asserts that Vercingetorix went into the fortress with 80,000 soldiers. Like all numbers Caesar gives in his writings, one has to take it with a few grains of salt. Delbrück agrees with Napoleon III (who idolized Vercingetorix as a French hero) that keeping 80,000 men inside Alesia made no sense, for maintaining that number in addition to the civilian population for more than a month would be impossible. Napoleon surmised that had he had that many men, Vercingetorix would have either sent out 60,000 to harass the Romans and keep them from their construction and foraging, or else would have encamped them below the city to launch sallies prior to, or even after, being encircled. Military historian Richard Gabriel believes it more likely that Vercingetorix started the siege with 10,000–15,000 cavalry on hand. Plutarch, however, goes even further in his estimate than does Caesar, claiming 170,000 inside Alesia.[35]

The number Caesar had under his command also is the subject of discussion. Delbrück writes that "Caesar had 11 legions, Numidian and Cretan sharpshooters and German cavalry and light infantry, for a total of perhaps 70,000 men." All other modern sources report ten legions. How many auxiliaries (especially German cavalry and light infantry) were on hand is undisclosed, though there were enough to beat back occasional Gallic raids during the siege and be the arm of decision against a reported 8,000 relieving cavalry.[36]

The most important thing about the siege was the engineering. Caesar may not have introduced new technology as Alexander did at Tyre, but he made the best use of what was known at the time, as well as of the physical labor abilities of the Roman infantryman. The Alesia mesa was extremely difficult to reach; it was bounded north and south by the Ose and Oserain Rivers and the walls of the mesa fell steeply to the banks, and to the east a saddle stretched over to Mt. Penneville, which was covered by Roman earthworks. Only to the west was there a plain and thus an area for a sally from the hilltop. The initial Roman works were constructed on the west face of the oppidum, where the Romans dug a ditch connecting the two rivers. It was six meters wide with sheer sides six meters deep. The start of the main defense line was 400 paces (just under 600 meters) further west. Warry describes the western defenses: "Here, there were two trenches each 15 [Roman] feet (4.4m) wide and 8 feet (2.4m) deep; the river was diverted to carry water into the inner trench wherever possible. Behind the trenches was a 12-foot (3.6m) earthwork and palisade, with antlered prongs projecting from it. Breastworks and battlements were overlooked by turrets at intervals of 80 feet (23.6m)."[37]

The earthworks encircled the mesa, a process known as contravallation, to a length of 11 Roman miles (10.1 mi. or 16.3 km). To make a sally even more difficult, the Romans placed booby traps in the approaches, "all having names that indicate the black humour with which soldiers often look at their profession. There were five rows of sharpened stakes woven together so that they could not be uprooted, which were called *cippi* ('tombstones'); then several rows of V-shaped pits that concealed fire-hardened stakes referred to as *lilia* ('lilies'); and in front of these were 30 cm (11 in) stakes embedded diagonally in the ground with iron barbs protruding from the top, known as *stimuli* ('stingers')."[38]

Vercingetorix, after launching an early and unsuccessful sally against the Romans, had his cavalry sneak out before the encirclement was complete. They were to rally the tribes to march to relieve the siege. Time was of the essence, as there was only a thirty-day supply of grain and limited cattle. Why Vercingetorix did not immediately burn the fields after having gathered in the supplies is hard to fathom, since he had previously and successfully used scorched earth tactics. When Caesar learned from deserters that a relief effort was being mounted, he put his soldiers back to work digging yet another wall to encircle the encirclement—known as circumvallation. This wall mirrored the first in style and stretched 14 Roman miles (12.9 mi. or 20.7 km). Lilia and stimuli were strewn outside this wall as well, but not to the extent that the interior was prepared. Caesar ordered his men to gather food and forage for thirty days.

As the food in Alesia began running out, a Gallic council of war met to decide the next step, should the relief force arrive too late or not at all. Critognatus, one of the chief officers, suggested cannibalism. Vercingetorix vetoed that idea, at least temporarily and, according to Cassius Dio, instead "thrust out the children and the women and the most useless among the rest."[39] Those poor souls, whose number is unrecorded, had to huddle between the stone walls of Alesia and the wooden walls of the Romans, watching the battle and starving since neither side would or could afford to feed them.

Soon thereafter the Gallic relief force arrived. Caesar recorded, "All march to Alesia, sanguine and full of confidence: nor was there a single individual who imagined that the Romans could withstand the sight of such an immense host: especially in an action carried on both in front and rear."[40] Forty-two tribes numbering 8,000 cavalry and a quarter million infantry came to Alesia's aid, or so Caesar claimed; as usual this provokes much debate. Delbrück argues that such a number could have been rallied, but most of the men would have been untrained militia. "If a Gallic commander had been capable of operating with an army of 250,000 men, it would remain an unpardonable, completely incomprehensible error on the part of Vercingetorix not to have assembled this army from the start and with such superiority to have sought an open battle."[41] While most commentators agree that this number is exaggerated, the advancing army was undoubtedly large; perhaps more than 100,000 strong.

The Gauls established themselves on a hillside about a mile to the southwest and wasted little time getting into action. With shouts of encouragement from the walls of Alesia, they launched an attack of mixed cavalry and light infantry, a tactic they had learned from the Germans. Rather than await them behind the walls, Caesar deployed his cavalry, and the ensuing battle lasted much of the day. Those in Alesia came out of their defenses and prepared to attack the inner wall when the time seemed appropriate. After a back-and-forth contest lasting all afternoon, the German cavalry finally settled the issue by massing on a flank and driving the Gallic cavalry from the field. The light infantry archers were left exposed and were run down. Meanwhile, the Gauls who had come from Alesia "returned into the town dejected and almost despairing of success."[42]

The next day the relief force spent their time preparing for a direct assault on the Roman walls, making ladders and grappling hooks. They waited until midnight to begin their attack. Caesar does not mention

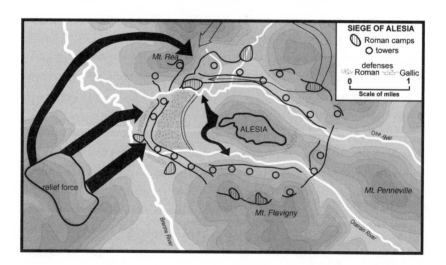

any moonlight, but does remark that the Gallic arrows did considerable damage to his men. The return fire was equally deadly, and the attackers also found themselves badly hurt by the booby traps across the Roman front. By dawn the Gauls had made little headway against the wall, and Vercingetorix's sally from Alesia was too late to assist.

With time quickly running out, the relief force developed a plan for a final assault. Scouts had observed a weak spot in the Roman wall of circumvallation to the northwest, where the steepness of Mt. Rea made it impossible to maintain a continuous encirclement. Sixty thousand picked men would be committed to that point, while the remainder of the relief force would attack across the plain from the southwest. Vercingetorix massed his men, according to Caesar, with "long hooks, movable penthouses, mural hooks, and other things, which he had prepared for the purpose of making a sally."[43] The flanking force left just after midnight and was in place on the far side of Mt. Rea by dawn. At noon the assault by the main force began, and this time the sally from Alesia was well coordinated.

Caesar placed himself on high ground, probably on Mt. Flavigny to the south. Pressure was intense from inside and out. The attack from Mt. Rea was the most successful: the Gauls came in waves, covered by their shields in a Roman *testudo* ("turtle") defense. Part of the attackers began digging to fill in the trenches and traps while others maintained a steady arrow and sling fire to keep the defenders' heads down. Vercingetorix and his men kept the interior forces busy by changing the focus of their attack away from the dangerous flat area to one of its edges, where the mesa fell most steeply to the contravallation. Although Caesar doesn't specify which edge they attacked, Theodore Dodge indicates that it may have been the southern wall, as it provided the most direct aid to the attackers from the southwest; however, the wall at the north end of the Romans' first ditch would have given the most direct aid to the attack from Mt. Rea. Whichever point they struck, it soon succeeded: "they fill the ditches with clay and hurdles, then clear the way; they tear down the rampart and breast-work with hooks."[44]

Caesar sent his trusted lieutenant Labienus (according to Dodge, from the northeastern corner of the walls)[45] to support the Mt. Rea defenses, with orders to attempt a sally if the defenses looked like they would break. Caesar strode through his lines, shouting encouragement to the defenders. As Vercingetorix's men began to break through the inner wall, Caesar met them with six cohorts under Marcus Brutus, followed by seven more under Caius Fabius; they held. With the Gauls about to break through in the northwest, Labienus sent word to Caesar that he could no longer hold and would launch his sally. Clad in his red cloak, Caesar called in reserves (presumably from the northern and eastern sections) and hastened to Labienus's aid himself. He also ordered "part of the cavalry to follow him, and part to make the circuit of the external fortifications and attack the enemy in the rear."[46] A cavalry camp existed in a flat area to the north of the walls, but Dodge argues they came from the camp atop Mt. Bussy, where Labienus had been stationed.

Once again, it was the Germans who saved the day. Struck simultaneously from both front and rear and with walls to either side, the Gauls were hemmed in and slaughtered. The repulse of Verceingetorix's attack must have broken the spirits of those inside the contravallation for, seeing the defeat, they withdrew back into Alesia. Caesar recounted that "[a] flight of the Gauls from their camp immediately ensues on hearing of this disaster,"[47] suggesting that the bulk of the forces attacking the southwest had been making little headway. The relief force soon fled their camp with fresh Roman cavalry in pursuit. Inside Alesia, Vercingetorix, succumbing to the reality of his defeat at the hands of the Romans, told his followers they could either kill him or turn him over to Caesar. They did the latter.

STARTING OFF ON DEFENSE, Caesar could implement none of the rules of the offense. Once the time came for shifting away from the defensive, however, the key characteristic of his actions at Alesia was concentration. Apparently confident in his forces facing the southwest, Caesar assumed that the key to victory was to strike the same point the enemy thought was their key. With the use of fresh reserves against a tiring enemy, Caesar struck at just the right time. With the Gauls about to penetrate the outer defenses, they must have thought that victory was in their grasp. Suddenly meeting fresh infantry to the front and cavalry from the rear, they quickly found themselves in a position from which they could neither advance nor retreat. Their surprise attack had been well planned and executed, and there was no reason for the Gauls to expect their plan to fail. When it did, however, the entire army fell apart.

Caesar then moved to exploit the sudden change in fortunes. Although his men were too tired to immediately begin a pursuit, the cavalry began within a few hours. They were easily able to catch the fleeing infantry and killed thousands more, while the remainder scattered and hurried to their respective homelands. Lacking organization, leadership, morale, or a defensible position, the Gallic army in flight was unable to do anything to hinder the pursuit. Dodge describes the siege of Alesia as "one of the most wonderful in antiquity. It equals Alexander's siege of Tyre or Demetrius' siege of Rhodes. The works Caesar erected were marvellous in their extent and intricacy.... [It] was a brilliant exhibition of Caesar's ability in engineering, strategy, tactics, logistics."[48]

Civil War

CAESAR ACCEPTED VERCINGETORIX'S SURRENDER and had him sent to prison in Rome, where he was executed during Caesar's triumph some time later. The victory at Alesia broke the main resistance to Roman rule, and it required but one more season's campaigning to quell it for good. These exhibitions of military dominance swelled Caesar's reputation and wealth. As Michael Grant notes, "What could not be denied ... was that the conquest of Gaul was a marvellous, portentous, feat of arms."[49] Caesar's political future, however, soon faced a major challenge. Pompey was the only consul left in Rome; Crassus had gone to the East to gain some martial glory for himself, but found only disaster and a grave in fighting the Parthian army at Carrhae (53 BC). With the Triumvirate effectively dissolved, Caesar faced his own disaster if he returned to Rome: his position as governor in Gaul had kept him from prosecution for highly questionable activities he had undertaken during his political career, but his political opponents would almost certainly revive those charges if he returned to the capital. Roman law forbade him bringing his legions out of Cisalpine Gaul, yet without them, he would soon find himself in jail, or worse.

This, however, seemed the moment toward which Caesar's entire career had pointed. Knowing a civil war would ensue when he brought his troops with him back to Italy, he announced, "The die is cast" and marched his men across the Rubicon River, the official northern boundary of Italy. Cary and Scullard write, "Caesar in 49 [BC], like Sulla in 83, was offered the choice between self-defence and political extinction. That he would put his head into a noose was hardly to be expected."[50] Despite the apparent rashness of his move, Caesar did have some initial advantages. His army had more veterans than any other legions in Rome's territories; additionally, Pompey had but two legions on hand with which to face Caesar's eight (once they all arrived from Gaul). Caesar also had an audacious spirit that none in the Senate could match. If they had conceived of his treasonous invasion, they certainly were not ready for it to begin in January. Yet Caesar marched in midwinter and soon held key passes into central Italy. Pompey had no choice but to head south with what forces he could muster. In a race to Brundisium (Brindisi), the major port at the southeastern tip of the Italian Peninsula, Pompey arrived first, embarked with his forces, and sailed across the Adriatic with all available ships.

Albert Nofi argues that Pompey had no real alternative other than flight, but to go to Greece was not the wisest move. Hispania, he argues, would have been better:

> He was technically proconsul of the Spanish provinces, had campaigned there for several years in the past, and had the favor of the populace, both Roman and native. From Spain, Pompey would be able to threaten Caesar's recent conquests in Gaul, and possibly fall upon Italy from the Alps, for he had strong allies in the romanized southern portions of Gaul, where the city of Massilia had declared for him against Caesar. More importantly, there were six seasoned legions in Spain plus many auxiliary troops, all under commanders loyal to Pompey. . . . Finally, Spanish financial resources were considerable.[51]

Even Africa was preferable to Greece, for some of the same reasons in addition to the fact that it was centrally located, making it easier for Pompey to respond to any of Caesar's moves. Though Greece was wealthy, it had a dearth of military resources. The troops Pompey was able to amass, while more numerous than Caesar's, were without much experience. The populace was reasonably friendly, but they would prove fickle depending on which way the wind blew. Further, even though Pompey was able to acquire a promise from the Persians—most of his troops were moved from Persia—to remain passive, such a vow was hardly set in stone given the traditional Persian-Roman hostility.

After a brief stop in Rome to get his political affairs in order, Caesar was quickly on his way to Hispania to deal with Pompey's forces there.

Basil Liddell Hart observes, "For thus concentrating against the 'junior partner' he has been much criticised. But his estimate of Pompey's inactivity was justified by the event."[52] Caesar arrived by April of 49 BC and marched to face his opponents based at Ilerda. His campaign there was swift and successful; it ended in August in victory with minimal bloodshed, and Caesar incorporated a number of Pompey's troops into several new legions. Caesar correctly assumed that Pompey would not return to Rome, and the Spanish expedition proved brilliant in not only robbing his enemy of his resources but enriching himself militarily at the same time.[53] Caesar proceeded to send troops to Sicily and Africa, as well as leaving a garrison in Hispania. With Pompey controlling the sea, Caesar needed a port and a supply of ships; Caesarian forces and ships had been besieging Massilia (Marseilles) while he was in Hispania and had forced the city's surrender in September. Still, his "fleet" was badly outnumbered and too small to ferry his entire army from Italy to Greece.

It would seem at this point, while Caesar's ships sailed from Gaul to Brundisium, that Pompey would have been wise to seek a naval action (particularly considering that defeating pirates had been one of the first great actions of his career), but he did not. Neither did he return to Italy, as troops were still arriving from the eastern frontier. Caesar thus marched back to Italy with the remainder of his troops and proceeded to Brundisium. Although he had twelve legions on hand, he only had sufficient shipping to embark seven understrength legions and 500 cavalry, which set sail at the beginning of the year 48 BC. They crossed unopposed, as Pompey's admiral assumed no one would try a winter crossing. Caesar and his men arrived in Greece without incident, but found themselves badly outnumbered and short on supplies.

Pompey was a lifelong soldier, having served in his father's command at the age of seventeen. In his younger days he had a reputation for aggressiveness and brutality, even earning the nickname "Butcher Boy." He seems to have become "Great" as a result of showing up at the end of several conflicts and grabbing public acclaim. After a successful war in the East, he had retired from military life and spent his time in politics. Thus, when he engaged in war with Caesar he had not commanded in the field in some time, and it showed. He had had the better part of a year to expand his forces, which at this point numbered nine legions, 7,000 cavalry, and 5,000 light infantry.[54] Pompey missed an opportunity to use his superior numbers, however, choosing instead to wait out the winter and engage in desultory negotiations. The remainder of Caesar's troops arrived in April, ferried over by Mark Antony, and again Pompey's fleet did not catch them. Liddell Hart notes that "even when Antony landed on the other side of Dyrrachium, Pompey, though centrally placed, failed to prevent Caesar and Antony effecting a junction at Tirana."[55]

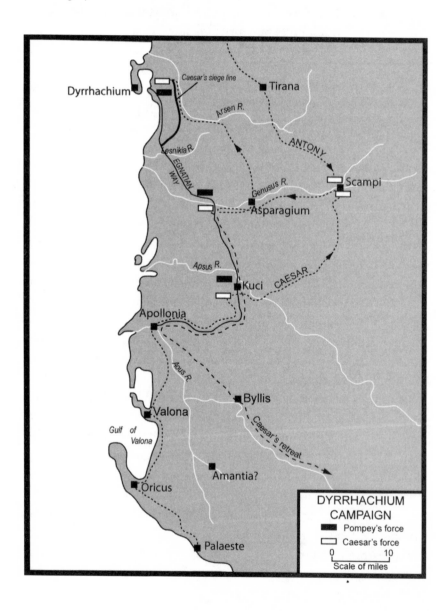

Caesar and Antony joined forces on the Genusus River, some thirty miles southeast of Pompey's main base at Dyrrhachium (modern Durres, Albania). Still short of supplies, Caesar received news that Pompey's navy had finally gone into action and captured or destroyed his entire fleet. He was now completely cut off from Italy, a vulnerability that he could not allow Pompey to exploit. Caesar sent out men to gather supplies and intercept reinforcements bound for Pompey, and then made a dash for Dyrrhachium. Although he arrived slightly ahead of Pompey's army, he did not have sufficient time to seize the town. Pompey's forces encamped on high ground near the harbor.

Caesar returned to his engineering ways. His men quickly began building a line of contravallation to hem Pompey's forces against the coast (described by Liddell Hart as "original but singularly profitless"[56] because the line could not cover the entire enemy line). Pompey would remain in control of the harbor, but would be unable to gather forage for his horses. Pompey's men immediately began construction of a defensive line facing Caesar's and both armies settled into siege warfare, extending their respective lines and engaging in frequent skirmishing. Dodge observes, "This extraordinary spectacle of Caesar bottling up Pompey, who had twice his force, by lines of circumvallation sixteen miles long, borders on the ridiculous." Indeed, the engineering feat was too bold for even Caesar to pull off: "Caesar's position and plan had been so eccentric that it was from the beginning doomed to failure. It was one of those cases where his enterprise outran his discretion."[57]

Initially, however, Caesar's plan to diminish Pompey's forage was successful. Pompey therefore planned a strike against the southern flank of the lines. Learning from deserters exactly how Caesar's works were constructed (and that at the southern end they were not yet completed), he launched an amphibious attack of three columns against the end of Caesar's line. "In short, Caesar's left flank was simultaneously to be attacked in front, in rear and in flank. In every way it was an admirably planned operation," in J. F. C. Fuller's view.[58] It was also admirably executed. Caesar's forces, attacked at dawn, were driven two miles up their lines, only to be saved by Antony's counterattack. Pompey had been quickly fortifying a captured camp and building a new one in order to establish himself outside Caesar's lines. Caesar launched a quick assault against this position, but was beaten back. Appian wrote, "It is probable that Pompey might then have captured [Caesar's camp] and brought the war to an end by that one engagement had not Labienus [now on Pompey's side], in some heaven-sent lunacy, persuaded him to pursue the fugitives instead." He did so, to his detriment; as Caesar reportedly said, "The war would have been ended to-day in the enemy's favour if they had had a commander who knew how to make use of victory."[59]

Failing to capture Pompey's camp, Caesar decided to forgo the siege and withdraw into the interior, looking for more supplies and hoping to locate a good spot to bring Pompey's army into open battle. Both Caesar and Pompey were looking to be reinforced by detachments in Macedonia: Pompey's father-in-law, Quintus Metellus Scipio, commanded two legions on the way from Syria, and Caesar was to combine with similar numbers under Domitius Calvinus, who had been sent to delay or stop Scipio. Pompey now faced the choice of whether to leave Greece and make his way back to Rome, or stay and fight Caesar's reinforced troops. Since Pompey had fled from Caesar once before, his pride may have prevented his departure; additionally, he knew that to bring the war to a decisive end he would have to pursue and soundly defeat Caesar's troops. He may also have been unwilling to abandon his allies in the East, who likely would have seen their wealth confiscated and cities sacked.[60]

When an immediate pursuit after the battle at Dyrrhachium failed to catch Caesar, Pompey began to engage in a Fabian strategy, wearing down Caesar's troops by keeping them on the move and unable to gather sufficient supplies. As Plutarch puts it, "For Pompey himself was cautious about hazarding a battle for so great a stake, and since he was most excellently provided with everything necessary for a long war, he thought it best to wear out and quench the vigour of the enemy, which must be short-lived."[61] Pompey thus followed, rather than pursued, Caesar. Unfortunately, he was accompanied by far too many politicians who failed to see past the immediate. They assumed that Caesar on the run was Caesar defeated, and the less they knew of warfare the more positive they were.[62] They kept up an incessant demand for a quick end to the war, demands Pompey would not ignore.

Caesar, meanwhile, had to find a way to feed his men. The summer had arrived and grain was plentiful, but the Greek populace hesitated to voluntarily give him aid in the wake of the recent battle. The first town to openly refuse was Gomphi in Thessaly; Caesar responded by storming the town and slaughtering the inhabitants. As is so often the case in the wake of such an action, other towns became more cooperative.

The Battle of Pharsalus

THE LONGED-FOR BATTLE CAME SOON THEREAFTER, at Palaepharsalus, outside modern Pharsala, Greece. Like Cannae, the exact location of the battlefield is disputed because of a river bisecting a plain; whether they fought on the northern or southern side is unclear. All that the contemporary sources clearly state is that the armies lined up perpendicular to the river with the water on their immediate flanks. Again, multiple sites have been proposed, but the bulk of modern research favors the north side, with Caesar's forces facing westward on level ground while Pompey's forces encamped on rising ground facing east. That assumes, as most modern interpreters do, that the actual battle site was near Palaepharsalus rather than Pharsalus. If the latter, then the armies would have been south of the river facing the opposite direction.[63]

At the beginning of August 48 BC, Pompey's army arrived and established camp on a rise just west of Palaepharsalus. Now that he had met Caesar's army, as his advisors had pressed him to do, however, Pompey seemed to be in no hurry to actually fight. Caesar writes that he "decided to test Pompey's intention, or willingness, to fight" by bringing his army out of camp and forming them up for battle, at first on his home ground at a good distance from Pompey's camp, but as the days went by progressing steadily closer to the hills where the Pompeians were.[64] In response, Pompey's army formed up each day at the base of the hill on more favorable terrain, daring Caesar to attack. Beginning to run out of food, as well as running out of patience with Pompey, on 9 August Caesar began to gather his forces to move on to a new supply center. As they were preparing to break camp, Pompey's army descended from the hillside onto the plain. Caesar was quick to respond; ever since the defeat at Dyrrhachium, his troops had longed for a fight in order to regain both their self-respect and that of their commander.

Both Roman armies deployed in traditional fashion: three units wide and three lines deep. According to Caesar, Pompey's army was made up of three groups: Cilicians (from southern Asia Minor) and Spaniards brought over by Lucius Afrianus on the right wing anchored on the

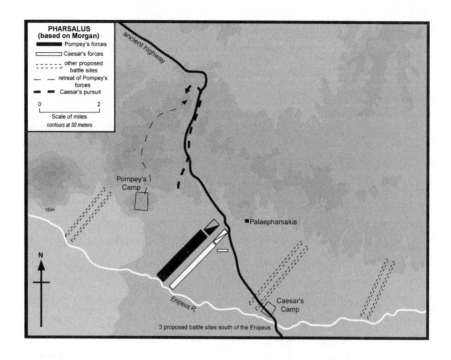

Epineus River, implying but not specifically stating they were under the command of Afrianus; Syrians in the center under the command of Scipio; and two Roman legions Caesar had turned over to Pompey upon entering Italy after the Gallic War, now under Pompey's direct command on the right. Plutarch and Appian describe them differently. Plutarch's *Caesar* and *Pompey* place Pompey on the right flank, with Scipio in the center and Domitius [Ahenobarbus] on the left. Appian mostly agrees with this, but places Lentalus on the right while Pompey and Afrianus guarded the camp.[65] Caesar claims that Pompey trusted his Cilician-Spanish troops the most, but they did not face Caesar's favorite 10th Legion on the right. Caesar also asserts that he was opposite Pompey. Left to right Caesar's three contingents were commanded by Antony, Domitius Calvinus, and Publius Sulla while Caesar stationed himself on his own right flank. Once the battle began, as we shall see, where Pompey may have been positioned would prove of little consequence.

The difference in their respective numbers is, as usual, a subject of debate. Caesar claims he had only 22,000 infantry and about 1,000 cavalry. He again neglects to mention any numbers for auxiliaries. He puts Pompey's force at 45,000 infantry and 7,000 cavalry, with about 2,000 reenlisted veterans whom he sprinkled throughout the lines and about 3,000 guarding the camp. Warry agrees with Caesar's count, but adds a further 5,000–10,000 auxiliaries and allies. Cary and Scullard agree with the number of Caesarians, but place the Pompeian force at 40,000, following Appian. David Boose and Richard Gabriel prefer Delbrück's count of 30,000 for Caesar and 40,000 for Pompey, with cavalry numbers of 2,000 and 3,000 respectively. Additionally, Pompey had a large group of archers and slingers (Warry claims 4,200) supporting his cavalry.[66] Pompey proposed the cavalry as his arm of decision. He concentrated his horse forces on his far left, placing them under the command of Labienus, Caesar's one-time chief lieutenant in Gaul. Pompey explained to his subordinates that would "outflank [Caesar's] line, take it in rear, throw his army into confusion, and rout it before a single weapon of ours is hurled at the enemy. In this way we shall finish off the war without any danger to our legions and virtually without bloodshed. This is really not difficult, as we are so strong in cavalry."[67]

Seeing Pompey's massed cavalry, Caesar responded with his customary unconventionality. He withdrew eight cohorts (one-tenth of his force) from the rear lines and placed them at a forty-five degree angle from the 10th Legion, behind his own cavalry, which was facing Pompey's. He also implemented a lesson he had learned in Gaul, taught him by his enemies as well as by his Germanic allies: mingle light infantry among the cavalry for harassing purposes. These two moves proved decisive in the battle.

Caesar, after giving his normal prebattle speech, ordered the trumpets sounded and the attack to begin. He sent forward the first two of his three lines, maintaining a reserve. As was typical, his men raised a battle cry and plunged forward, but quickly noticed Pompey's army standing still. Pompey had ordered his infantry to stand fast rather than close with Caesar's troops. This would husband their energy, while Caesar's men exhausted themselves charging across no-man's-land. At this point, one sees the advantage of a veteran army. Rather than play into Pompey's hands, Caesar's men stopped halfway across the battlefield, dressed their lines and caught their breath, out of the range of any missile attack. Then, having recovered themselves, they charged again into the enemy lines. Just seeing this calm, parade-ground sort of action on the part of the enemy must have had a dispiriting effect on those less experienced soldiers in

Pompey's army. At the point of contact, normal hand-to-hand Roman warfare began.

Pompey then ordered his cavalry charge. His plan was sound, and got off to a good start. His assault was soon forcing back Caesar's horsemen, though the charging cavalrymen were not prepared for the stones and arrows emerging from the skirmishers among their enemy. Caesar's horse troops slowed the charge somewhat before withdrawing from the field. Ready to resume full speed, Pompey's charging cavalry were not prepared to find themselves immediately facing a line of heavy infantry. The missile attacks had broken up the formation somewhat, and it now became hopelessly bunched as the horses at the front began pulling up before the advancing infantry's spear points. Here Caesar played another trick that depended on the inexperience of Pompey's cavalry: he ordered the men in the refused flank not to throw their pila but to stab at the riders' faces with them. As in modern bayonet training, the goal was to unnerve their opponent by stabbing at the most exposed and vulnerable part of his body.[68] According to Plutarch, Pompey's cavalry "numbered seven thousand, the flower of Rome and Italy, preëminent in lineage, wealth, and courage." Citizen cavalry was virtually a thing of the past by this time, and these young horsemen proved less than preeminent in courage. Caesar "expected that men little conversant with wars or wounds, but young, and pluming themselves on their youthful beauty, would dread such wounds especially, and would not stand their ground, fearing not only their present danger, but also their future disfigurement.... [T]hey could not endure the upward thrust of the javelins, nor did they even venture to look the weapon in the face, but turned their heads away and covered them up to spare their faces."[69] Thus, fleeing horsemen from the front not only broke the charge of those following, but spread fear in the rear ranks. Pompey's cavalry fled while Caesar's heavy infantry and recovered cavalry pursued.

The flight of Pompey's cavalry ruined his battle plan. The light infantry arrayed behind them were quickly cut down, and Caesar's refused flank now became a swinging gate pivoting onto Pompey's infantry flank and rear. At this point two things happened that sealed Caesar's victory. First, Pompey realized that his plan had failed, and he fled the field for his camp. Plutarch recounts: "After his infantry was thus routed, and when, from the cloud of dust which he saw, Pompey conjectured the fate of his cavalry,

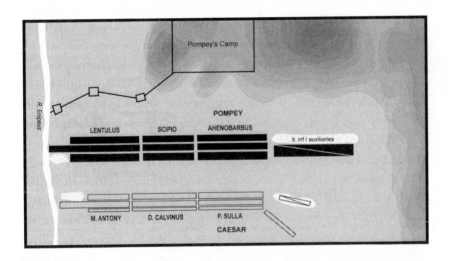

what thoughts passed through his mind it were difficult to say; but he was most like a man bereft of sense and crazed, who had utterly forgotten that he was Pompey the Great, and without a word to any one, he walked slowly off to his camp."[70] Simultaneously, Caesar ordered in his third line, the reserves. The fresh troops relieving the front two lines provided a burst of energy that broke Pompey's line. With their supposedly unstoppable cavalry and their commander in flight, the infantry turned and fled as well.

Caesar's troops followed closely as he urged them on. The heat of the day was coming on, and he did not want them to allow the fugitives any rest. Pompey rode away unpursued to the coast and caught a boat for Egypt, where Ptolemy had him executed. In his wake, he left behind a shattered army. Caesar claims that 15,000 enemy troops were killed and 24,000 captured, compared with a loss to his own army of but 200. Appian gives somewhat greater numbers:

> The losses of Italians on each side—for there was no report of the losses of auxiliaries, either because of their multitude or because they were despised—were as follows: in Caesar's army, thirty centurions and 200 legionaries, or, as some authorities have it, 1200; on Pompey's side ten senators . . . and about forty distinguished knights. Some exaggerating writers put the loss in the remainder of [Pompey's] forces at 25,000, but Asinius Pollio, who was one of Caesar's officers in this battle, records the number of dead Pompeians found as 6000.[71]

Most modern scholars are more in agreement with this count than that of the usually exaggerating Caesar.

Appian also describes in detail Caesar's quick action to assure Pompey's legionaries they would not be harmed and that only the auxiliaries would suffer. Many legionaries therefore surrendered on the battlefield or near Pompey's camp, though many fled to the hills behind the camp where they were surrounded and surrendered the following day.

Pharsalus was the result of an approach march by both armies, resulting in a pitched battle. Both sides were satisfied with the battlefield and spent a week in challenging each other to fight. Once the battle began, Pompey launched a deliberate attack with concentrated forces, but had no answer for Caesar's counterattack once the cavalry fled the field. Neither commander really controlled the tempo of the battle. Caesar displayed audacity, as usual, in his decision to weaken his already inferior numbers to create a hidden refused flank, which clearly surprised Pompey's cavalry and proved the key to the victory. With momentum on his side, Caesar exploited the situation psychologically by offering immediate terms to Italian soldiers, breaking their will to fight or flee. He further exploited the situation by slaughtering the foreigners who had aided Pompey. The pursuit was rapid and effective, gaining yet more surrendered (and pardoned) legionaries.

Caesar's Leadership

CAESAR FOLLOWED HIS BRILLIANT VICTORY at Pharsalus with a foolish pursuit of Pompey, chasing him to Egypt with a mere 3,000 soldiers. He found himself cut off in the face of far superior numbers of Egyptian troops and required rescue by Mithradates. The months he spent in isolation in Egypt gave Pompey's supporters in Italy, Africa, and Spain time to organize themselves and continue the war. Caesar was thus obliged to spend even more time fighting and defeating them before he could return to Rome and assume leadership of the government in person. His assassination in 44 BC led to even further civil war, which was finally settled by Caesar's adopted son, Octavian, with the aid of Caesar's lieutenant Mark Antony.

Even though Pompey had been nicknamed "the Great," it was Caesar who earned the reputation. Regarded by many as Alexander's equal and by others as the greatest general in history, Caesar certainly mastered many of the principles of operations.

Looking at Caesar's two campaigns, one sees that he was able to pursue two completely different *objectives*. In Gaul, each year provided a new target for Caesar to aim at. With his ultimate grand strategic goal of subduing all of Gaul, he proceeded in a very long campaign, but one that maintained organization and focus. His objectives were always particular tribes, starting with the Helvetii in his first campaign. Each fighting season thereafter took him to a new enemy, whether it be the Belgae, the British, or the Germans—whichever target needed subduing or offered a chance for political gain. Only in 51 BC did a concentration of enemies gather against him; at this point, his objective became the leader of the opposition, and capturing towns mattered only insofar as they provided supplies or bases: Vercingetorix, wherever he was, became the objective. Caesar had already proved to Gaul that his army could defeat any single tribe, but defeating the coalition under a single commander finally convinced the population to end serious resistance.

In the Civil War, the individual was again the objective: Pompey, his former ally. Even Caesar's failure to follow Pompey to Greece but instead campaign in Spain was designed to weaken Pompey's power and reputation. Only Caesar seemed to realize that Pompey was past his prime, that "the Great" had become "the Politician" and "the Hesitator." Defeating Pompey's generals in Spain was a reflection of his enemy's decreasing stature. So, too, was besieging a force much larger than his own at Dyrrhachium. Every time Caesar acted and Pompey reacted, it was a diminishing of Pompey's prestige and his self-confidence. At Pharsalus, Pompey, for all his brave talk to his sycophants, seemed to know in advance that he would not win.

Caesar was also master of the *offensive*. He showed time and again in Gaul that he would attack, and do so quickly. Strategic speed became operational advantage, a tactic Napoleon mastered again eighteen centuries later. Caesar's major operational advantage was speed. He regularly moved his army faster than his enemies moved theirs, concentrating and striking before they could act or react. That allowed Caesar to defeat larger armies. For him, speed was a "force multiplier," increasing the effectiveness of his legions and allowing him to use his army more effectively.[72] Michael Grant notes, "He could do everything with extraordinary speed. The orator Cicero, who hated him utterly, described his rapidity at the beginning of the Civil War as something horrifying and monstrous. Caesar lived at a faster tempo than the people who had to contend with him, and this gave him an enormous advantage."[73] Only during sieges did this characteristic lag, but given the rapid construction of Caesar's siege lines, perhaps it *does* apply.

In his campaigns, Caesar seemed to always be in movement to contact, even when he should not have been, as in his Egyptian troubles after Pharsalus. Dodge describes Caesar as "over-daring and over-cautious by turns," suggesting that "had not Fortune on many occasions rushed to the rescue Caesar would never have lived to be Caesar."[74] Goldsworthy also notes the problems of being overdaring: "Caesar was a great improviser rather than a great planner, a man who was bold to the point of recklessness, so that his most brilliant achievements often involved extricating his army from a crisis created by his own rashness."[75]

Both Alesia and Pharsalus are terrific examples of Caesar's use of *economy of force*. How does one hold a position, even with strong defenses on both sides, from an enemy many times one's own strength? Caesar showed at Alesia how to use just enough manpower for the job at hand. He depended on the strength of his walls and booby traps to hold the bulk of the Gallic relief force at bay and keep Vercingetorix within the contravallation. But when the last big assault took place, it was Caesar's judicious assignment of troops that won the day. Even under attack by tens of thousands, from the west and southwest, he held troops in reserve. When the sally from Alesia looked like it might break through the inner walls, he committed six cohorts, then seven, just enough to beat back the immediate threat. When Labienus was about to be overwhelmed, he led the last of the infantry reserves himself and threw in his Germanic cavalry to break the assault and win the day.

At Pharsalus, again facing superior numbers, Caesar weakened his main line to create both a reserve and a defensive-counterattacking fourth line. To do this requires not only courage but a confidence in one's knowledge of both the enemy and one's own men. Caesar knew his infantry would hold Pompey's main line; he knew his enemy cavalry's lack of combat experience would work against them. Perhaps no better example of how to know and use your own men while manipulating superior opposing numbers exists until Lee's victory at Chancellorsville.

One sees in all of Caesar's battles (perhaps because his writings make it so) a distinct *unity of command*: there is one commander, one brain, one leader. There are subordinates who have their duties, and even some freedom of action, but in battle Caesar dominates. At Alesia, given the nature of the battlefield, Gallic unity of command was impossible. In the Roman lines, there was much individual effort and bravery, but no action without Caesar's orders. Even when he could not control the whole battle when he went into action himself, the rest of the army stood fast and defended their assigned posts. At Pharsalus, the difference between Caesar and Pompey clearly illustrates this point. Pompey listened to advisors, despite the fact that few had any military experience at all, and allowed himself to be forced into action. As Dodge observes, "The great weakness in Pompey's army was the lack of one head, one purpose to control and direct events. Caesar, on the other hand, *was* his army. The whole body was instinct with his purpose."[76]

Morale, too, is a principle Caesar used to his advantage. Like Hannibal, Caesar did not just command his men, but led them. He did not come out of secure, luxurious quarters to fight among his men, as Alexander often did. Although he was raised in wealth, he did not seem to need it. He slept in a chariot at times, marched bareheaded in column with his men, and was with them in the heat of battle. How often Caesar got his own blade bloody is a matter of conjecture but, like Wellington, he always seemed to be where the fighting was most intense. In Goldsworthy's assessment, "Caesar commanded a battle from close behind the fighting line, moving to wherever he thought the next crisis would develop and judging how the fighting was going from close quarters. . . . Roman soldiers fought better [Caesar writes] when they believed that their commander was a witness to their actions."[77] His men knew he was quick to reward bravery, with both rank and riches. "In success he was brilliant, in disaster strong and elastic, and he never weakened in morale. It is adversity which proves the man. . . . To his personality his soldiers owed all they knew and all they were," says Dodge.[78] This is best illustrated after Dyrrachium, when almost immediately after their retreat, Caesar's men were clamoring for the opportunity to fight again and restore his faith in them.

THE PAST HUNDRED YEARS have produced three major commentators on Caesar and Roman warfare, whose works have been quoted throughout this chapter. Their conclusions about the Roman general are worth considering, as each holds a different view of Caesar's ultimate contribution to military history. Late in the nineteenth century, Theodore Dodge classified Caesar as one of the three great generals of antiquity along with Alexander and Hannibal, describing his abilities in almost all areas of command to be in the middle ground between the two. "What has Caesar done for the art of war? Nothing beyond what Alexander and Hannibal had done before him. But it has needed, in the history of war, that ever and anon there should come a master who could point the world to the right path of methodical war from which it is so easy to stray. Nothing shows this better than the fact that, for seventeen centuries succeeding Caesar, there was no great captain."[79] This book, of course, contends with that statement.

In the middle of the twentieth century, J. F. C. Fuller wrote extensively on historic and contemporary military affairs, so had a depth of knowledge on which to base his comparisons. While he did not fail to criticize Caesar in his work subtitled *Man, Soldier and Tyrant*, his analysis in *Military History of the Western World* gives credit where it is due. He writes that as a commander, Caesar excelled in three main respects:

> He was a marvellous organiser and his faith in his genius was unshakable. Secondly, he grasped the nature of war in his age. It was national: not merely the contending of armies, but the struggle of an entire people yearning for something new. . . . Lastly, his amazing boldness and seeming rashness were founded on his grasping of the secret that in war, as in peace, most difficulties are self-suggested—that, generally speaking, because opponents are equally fearful of each other, he who first brushes the terrors of the moment aside is the first to set his foot on the high road to victory. Caesar, like Alexander, possessed that spirit of audacity which raises generalship to its highest level.[80]

At the beginning of the twenty-first century, Adrian Goldsworthy is one of the most serious students and writers on Caesar and Roman warfare. As stated earlier, he disagrees with Fuller's assessment that Caesar was a "marvellous organiser." Like Dodge, he finds him to be no innovator. "Caesar, Pompey, and many other commanders of the late republic were especially aggressive even by Roman standards, but the difference among them was more one of degree than anything more substantial. . . . All our evidence, suggests that Caesar's command style was absolutely typical of Roman generals in this or other periods."[81]

GIVEN THESE DIVERSE VIEWS, why is Caesar included in this work? It is Caesar's embodiment of all three of these claims. Like the other battlefield commanders included here, Ceasar had the ability to see what no one else of his age could. Caesar was not an innovator; he inherited the Roman army (as did Pompey) from Marius's reforms half a century earlier. But going into war he took that army and fashioned it into an instrument of war which fitted his own genius. It was *his* army fighting *his* way. Had he and Pompey changed armies at Pharsalus, the situation would have been what Caesar described prior to his initial Spanish campaign of the Civil War, an army without a leader and a leader without an army. As Goldsworthy observes, "the difference is one of greater ability rather than differing methods." The greater ability? "He divined his enemy's intentions and he set aside his own fears." As the remainder of this work makes clear, I cannot agree with Dodge that there were no more great captains until Gustavus, but Caesar certainly dominated the age between Scipio and Belisarius.

7

Belisarius (505?–568)

General in the Service of the Emperor Justinian I of the Eastern Roman Empire

[A] most winning character, was bold to the verge of rashness, resourceful and of an inventive mind, a general always ready to make the most of the inadequate means allotted him by his parsimonious master.

—J. F. C. Fuller, *Military History of the Western World*

BELISARIUS'S BIRTH DATE is a matter of speculation, as is his upbringing. In his classic nineteenth-century biography of the general, Philip Henry Stanhope, Lord Mahon, argues that the description offered by Procopius of a "lately bearded stripling" should make him about twenty years old when he first appears in history as a member of General Justinian's private guard, a couple of years before Justinian assumed the throne in 527.[1] Procopius, who was Belisarius's secretary and contemporary, and a historian of Justinian's wars, writes that Belisarius came from the same town as Justinian, Germania in Illyria.[2] Most sources claim a humble birth, but Mahon argues for one much higher, pointing out his possession of estates at an age when he could not possibly have achieved sufficient glory and wealth from his wars to have afforded them.[3] Further, Belisarius's parents are not denigrated in Procopius's *Secret History*, as are those of his wife, Antonina, the Emperor Justinian, and Empress Theodora.

Since Justinian was born in 483, it is highly unlikely that the two knew each other until Belisarius joined the bodyguard. Procopius gives us the most complete story of his career but no hint how a member of the guard came to Justinian's attention. According to Edward Gibbon in his *Decline and Fall of the Roman Empire*, "He served, most assuredly with valour and reputation, among the private guards of Justinian; and, when his patron became emperor, the domestic was promoted to military command."[4] His first assignment was as cocommander with Sittas, about his age and brother-in-law to Theodora. Assuming the two were friends in the guard, this could well have been how he came to the attention of the man who would be emperor. Belisarius and Sittas were sent on a raid in 526 into Persarmenia, a region long disputed between Romans and Persians, where they succeeded in extensive pillaging and capturing numerous prisoners to obtain slaves.[5] On a second raid they were not so lucky, losing what appears to be a skirmish to the Persian commanders Narses and Aratius, both of whom soon defected to Justinian. Procopius certainly downplayed the encounter, saying merely that the Persians "joined battle with the forces of Sittas and Belisarius and gained the advantage over them."[6] Soon after these engagements Justinian assumed the throne in Constantinople (1 April 527) upon the death of his uncle Justin.

As emperor, Justinian inherited a long-running conflict between his empire and that of Sassanid Persia. In the wake of Alexander's defeat of the Achaemenid Empire, the Persians absorbed some Hellenistic culture while under the sway of the Successors. As the descendants of the great Macedonians began to fade in the wake of the rising Roman Empire, the Persians found themselves under the rule of the Arsacid Dynasty of Parthians, horsemen from the north. The Parthians began to restore some unity to the region and eventually faced off against the expanding Roman Empire. With a frontier generally regarded as the Euphrates River, Parthians and Romans engaged in decades of territorial give and take, although the Parthians tended to be the lesser of the two powers. In the early third century AD, the Parthian power had declined sufficiently that the Persians themselves rose up and defeated them. This led to the establishment of the house of Sassan, or Sassanid Dynasty. They reestablished the old Achaemenid titles and ambitions, which included reoccupying lands ceded to Rome. Although Eastern Roman troops kept the Persians at bay, they could not reimpose their will. Emperors Valerian and Julian the Apostate lost their lives trying, and in 363 Emperor Jovian signed a necessary but humiliating treaty with Persia that obliged the Romans to

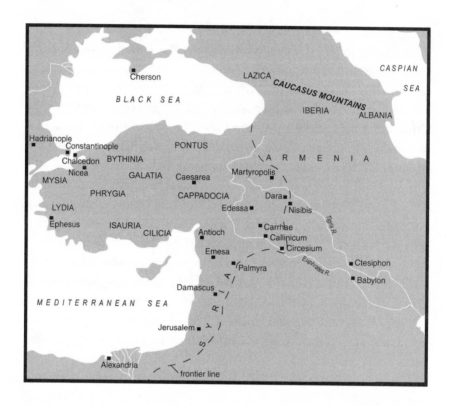

grant some territorial concessions. From this point forward, the Eastern Roman Empire gave up trying to conquer Persia.[7]

From 363 until the reign of Justinian, the relationship remained a balance of power. In 387 Rome and Persia divided Armenia between the two empires and in 422 signed a treaty that came to be called the Hundred Years' Peace. During that time, the Persians dealt with internal religious difficulties when Zoroastrian magi tried to exert significant influence in the government, as well as countering threats from the White Huns invading from the northeast. The Huns also threatened to invade via the Caucasus between the Black and Caspian Seas. This area had originally been jointly defended, but gradual Roman withdrawal had led to Roman subsidies to hold up Rome's end of the defense agreement.

Those payments laid the foundation for the Roman-Persian conflict in Justinian's reign. The Persian failure in 483 to turn over the frontier city of Nisibis (as called for in the treaty of 363) led to Roman refusal to pay its share for the Caucasus defense. The Roman emperor Anastasius

I (r. 491–518) built up defenses in Mesopotamia and Armenia, in particular the city of Dara on the Euphrates, not far from Nisibis. Between 502 and 504 the two sides engaged in serious warfare, with the Persian king Cavadh gaining early, temporary victories in Byzantine lands. A few setbacks in 504, coupled with a major Hun invasion, forced him to sue for peace in 505. A seven-year truce followed, which was never renewed, but never abrogated. During the Hunnic-Persian war, the Byzantines further irritated the Persians by allying themselves with the Caucasus kingdoms of Lazica and Iberia.

Warfare of the Time

TWO MAJOR FACTORS WERE INVOLVED in radically changing the Eastern Roman army by the early sixth century. First, the nature of the Roman citizen was vastly different than it had been in the days of the republic. Previously, military service had been a duty that adult males engaged in as an aspect of citizenship—any threat to the government and people had to be met, no questions asked. Usually no more than a season or a year of service was necessary to beat back most threats. By the end of the republic, the army was a long-service career followed mainly by the urban poor. A few centuries into the empire, however, and the attitude had changed again. Few adult Roman males answered the call to duty, for military service now involved years in foreign lands. Citizens in many trades were exempt from being drafted, and military service was so unpopular that it was not unknown for men to mutilate themselves to avoid being drafted into service.[8] Thus, the army became increasingly dependent on troops recruited from the hinterlands or even from former enemies. Decreased manpower across extended frontiers required more defense than offense, so the empire relied on *limes*, a cordon defense, or string of forts and fortified cities. These protected citizens and trade routes where there were no natural obstacles. Justinian built limes in amazing numbers and size.[9] Backing this line were mobile fighting forces designed to relieve the strong points and pursue enemies.

The second factor was the nature of the enemies themselves. Both the eastern and western empires were pressured by Asian or Eurasian "barbarian" forces that depended on mobility. Invading armies increasingly were mounted rather than made up of foot soldiers. Although the traditional Roman legion could stand up to cavalry, those troops had been heavy infantry trained by years of service. Less motivated and smaller forces (especially those raised on the frontier with no strong bond to Rome) were less likely to embrace the discipline necessary to stand fast against charging horsemen. Hence, both halves of the empire needed veteran forces that could rapidly respond to fast-moving threats and inflict damage on armies made up of soldiers who were often raised in the saddle. The influx of frontier manpower into the army meant the incorporation of peoples who had the same cavalry-oriented upbringing and experience and somewhat less dependence on the traditional infantry.

Thus, the Eastern Roman Empire in particular began to build its army around heavy cavalry and light infantry, which could move faster than loot-laden raiders on foot. The speed of the cavalry and light infantry replaced the traditional power of the Roman heavy infantry with even more flexibility than Caesar's maniples.[10] The heavy cavalry *cataphracti* wore chain mail to the knee or longer and were armed mainly with lances and bows. This allowed them to withstand enemy arrows while attacking either infantry with their lances or cavalry with their bows. In some cases the horse was armored as well. Given the difficulty of training and the expense to equip a soldier with both weapons, it is likely that the Byzantine horseman had his greatest use in shock action. Thus, the lance was primary and the bows provided versatility if necessary.[11]

Most of the cavalry was recruited from the fringes of the empire. Once the Hunnish empire collapsed not long after Attila's death, Hun horsemen joined the Roman service, as did Alans from the Iranian steppes and Germanic Goths. Southeastern Europe also became a breeding ground for horses and horsemen, as in the days of Philip and Alexander.[12] Although most of the "barbarian" troops had been expunged from the army in 400 owing to fear of disloyalty, Justinian had no such qualms in his desire to build an army large enough to reestablish the Mediterranean empire. These "federates" (*foederati*) of foreign (and ultimately domestic) troops were recruited and led by their own commander, who swore loyalty to Justinian. Such a semiprivate army was called a *comitatus*. The troops were loyal to their commander, requiring Justinian to be certain that the commanders were loyal to him, often a problem in Byzantine history.[13] The horse archers possessed the long-range effectiveness of Hunnic warriors with their famous compound bows, but could also fight well at close quarters.[14] Also at this time, aristocrats raised units of elite bodyguards (*bucellarii*), whether federate or Byzantine, that could be available to the emperor on the same terms as the federates.[15] For example, Belisarius's bodyguard numbered as many as 7,000.

The light infantry carried small shields for protection and swords or axes for close combat, but their primary weapon was the bow. The leading ranks at least were well armored and supplied with large shields to protect against enemy arrows and javelins. All soldiers were instructed in the use of the bow, making long-range warfare the primary method of opening a battle, with the heavy cavalry breaking through whatever weakened areas appeared.[16] Although some enemies were extremely effective horse archers, the standing Byzantine archer had the stability to use stronger bows and therefore engage at greater ranges. Often consisting of *limitani* (frontier militia), the light infantry were of irregular quality. Romano-Byzantine heavy infantry were fewer in number, but equipped with heavier armor, sword or axe, and a spear. They played the traditional role of breaking enemy assaults and protecting the archers. Although these forces comprised a much smaller percentage than earlier Roman armies, many authors comment on their continued importance in sixth-century battles. During Justinian's reign, the basic tactical unit remained the phalanx, although it was a more flexible unit than that of the classical Greeks. The standard formation was described as 512 men wide and likely twelve ranks deep. That would make 6,144 soldiers, a bit larger than the traditional Roman legion.[17] Contemporary authors are of the opinion that a well-trained and disciplined infantry was key to Roman warfare no matter the ratio to the other arms,[18] and they were valuable as protection for the cavalry as well as the light infantry.[19]

The army generally deployed with infantry in the center and cavalry on the flanks, with light infantry slingers in front if an enemy cavalry charge appeared imminent. After long experience against Eurasian cavalry armies, the Byzantine cavalry developed their own method of deployment. Two-thirds of the unit would be deployed forward in ranks eight deep in the center and four deep on the wings. A second line would form up 400 meters to the rear. The horses along the front line were armored. Each division consisted of *cursores* armed with bows for the offense, protected by *defensores* who closely followed up their attacks. Such tactics remained in use around the Mediterranean for almost a thousand years.[20]

The Sassanian Persian army had undergone some serious reforms in the wake of defeats at the hands of the Hephthalite (White) Huns in the 480s. By the turn of the sixth century, it was little different in makeup from the Romano-Byzantine forces. The dominant arm was cavalry, made up from the "free" citizens, the minor aristocracy. It was lighter than the Byzantine cataphracts but made up about the same percentage of the army. Horse archers were incorporated from frontier societies like the Huns and Armenians. Mercenaries and subject peoples would have furnished auxiliary cavalry in some numbers. Three thousand Sabir Huns are said to have been recruited for the attack on Satala in 530, while the Kadishaye (Kadiseni) were the primary unit of the Persian right wing at the Battle of Dara against Belisarius that same year.[21] This lighter cavalry provided archery support for the heavy cavalry, known to the Romans as the *clibanarii*[22] and to the Sassanians as the Savaran,[23] which were armored almost exactly like the cataphracts. The Parthian heavy cavalry had a larger scale-armor blanket for their horses, but by Sassanian times this seems to have been reduced to cover just the front half of the animal's body. The heavy cavalry used the lance as their main weapon, although they also carried multiple hand weapons for close-in fighting should circumstances dictate. By the reigns of Khavad and Khusrow, who were contemporaries of Justinian and Belisarius, the Savaran had abandoned the bow altogether. The elite of the Sassanian army were, as in ancient days, called the Immortals and have been regarded as being as good as or better than the Roman troops.[24]

The Persian infantry was the weakest arm. It was scorned by the Romans. Procopius quotes Belisarius in his prebattle speech before Dara: "For their whole infantry is nothing more than a crowd of pitiable peasants who come into battle for no other purpose than to dig through walls and to despoil the slain and in general to serve the soldiers. For this reason they have no weapons at all with which they might trouble their opponents, and they only hold before themselves those enormous shields in order that they may not possibly be hit by the enemy."[25] Modern historians echo that attitude, pointing to the performance at the Battle of Dara, when the *paighan* (infantry) dropped their shields and abandoned the field after the Savaran (heavy cavalry) were defeated.[26] These were peasant conscripts with neither training nor motivation, forming a rear guard and regarded as next to useless.[27]

Without a contemporary Persian historian like Procopius, exact details of Persian tactics have to be pieced together from Romano-Byzantine and later Muslim sources. It appears that they did not alter their fighting methods in the wake of defeats at Hunnic hands. Roman sources describe the typical Sassanian battle deployment as dividing an army into a center, ideally on a hill, with two wings, with spare horses being kept at the rear.[28] Some sources describe a cavalry front with infantry archers on the left wing. In some cases elephants are mentioned, though not in any battle in which Belisarius fought. Later sources describe an infantry center with cavalry wings and a force of elite reserves, or an arc of troops in the center flanked by cavalry protecting the herds on one side and the baggage on the other, with a hospital in the center rear. Combat was straightforward, dominated by the heavy cavalry, with little in the way of flanking movements or deception.

The Opponents

IN A MOVE TOWARD RECONCILIATION with the Byzantines, the Persian king Cavadh in 523 or 524 offered his fourth and favorite son, Chosroes, to Emperor Justin for adoption in order to protect him from jealous older brothers at Cavadh's death. The Romans seriously considered the offer, but ultimately rejected it as a potential threat to imperial succession; Cavadh took the refusal personally. In 524 he launched a campaign that conquered Iberia, provoking Roman counteroffensives in Persian Armenia; these were the previously mentioned attacks led by Sittas and Belisarius. Their defeat at the hands of Narses and Aratius in 526 apparently had no ill effects on Justinian's opinion, and he was the power behind Justin's throne. As Lord Mahon argues, "We may conclude that the personal conduct of Belisarius, on the last occasion, was not only free from blame, but even entitled to praise, since we find him, immediately afterwards [527], promoted to the post of Governor of Dara."[29] It is not recorded how Belisarius performed personally in that battle, but another in 528 had no better result. This was an attack in support of a Byzantine fort being erected at Thannuris, on the frontier of the southern front.[30] Procopius writes merely that "a fierce battle took place in which the Romans were defeated, and there was a great slaughter of them."[31] A contemporary account by Zachariah of Mitylene is somewhat less terse but more unflattering: when the Persians learned of the Roman approach, "they devised a stratagem, and dug several ditches among their trenches, and concealed them all round outside by triangular stakes of wood, and left several openings. . . . They did not perceive the Persians' deceitful stratagem in time, but the generals entered the Persian entrenchment at full speed. . . . Of the Roman army those who were mounted turned back and returned in flight to Dara with Belisarius; but the infantry, who did not escape, were killed and taken captive."[32]

In spite of this setback, in 529 or 530 Belisarius was named master of the soldiers in the East (*Magister Militum per Orientem*), in command of one of the empire's five field armies. (He also at this point took on Procopius as his secretary-aide, leading to the firsthand accounts of Belisarius's campaigns.) The flash point for conflict was on the upper reaches of the Tigris at the Byzantine city of Dara, not far from the Persian stronghold at Nisibis. He made his headquarters at Dara, where he was ordered to repair the city's defenses as a counterbalance to the nearby Persian stronghold at Nisibis.

In the wake of these recent military reverses, Justinian was of a mind to negotiate with King Cavadh, who had threatened war if the gold for the northern frontier defense he had long demanded was not forthcoming: "But, as pious Christians, spare lives and bodies and give us part of your gold. If you do not do this, prepare yourselves for war. For this you have a whole year's notice, so that we should not be thought to have stolen our victory or to have won the war by trickery," wrote the contemporary chronicler John Malalas.[33] Cavadh, however, did not wait a year. When Justinian's envoy was on his return trip to the Persian capital, he stopped at Dara. A Persian army was already approaching.

The Battle of Dara

BELISARIUS COMMANDED 25,000 MEN AT DARA, probably about one-third of them cavalry. Fearing the potential conflict, he had scoured the countryside for manpower to reach that number, but the discipline of the force was hurt, and their spirit broken by their former setbacks.[34] The cavalry were in finer fettle, with at least 1,200 Huns and 300 Herules (a tribe of Scandinavian descent). Belisarius had sufficient time before the Persian approach to prepare the battlefield. Perhaps remembering his own disaster against Persian trenches near Thannuris two years earlier, he had a trench dug parallel to the city walls. According to Procopius, it was "a stone's throw" away from the city wall. The trench was neither straight nor continuous, but had several crossings left for troops to advance or retreat across it. "In the middle there was a rather short portion straight, and at either end of this there were dug two cross trenches at right angles to the first; and starting from the extremities of the two cross trenches, they continued two straight trenches in the original direction to a very great distance."[35]

To the left flank were an unknown number of heavy cavalry behind a hill under Bouzes accompanied by the 300 Herules commanded by Pharas. To their right, stationed at the trench's right angle, were 600 Hun light cavalry under Sunicas and Aigan. On the other side of the trench cutout, the formation was a mirror image, less the flanking hill. Another unidentified number of heavy cavalry were deployed on the Roman right led by a number of cocommanders under the overall command of John, son of Nicetas. The infantry lined up behind the ditch, with Belisarius and his cocommander Hermogenes behind them, almost certainly leading their respective bucellarii, which could have numbered a few thousand. Procopius does not mention any light infantry deployed as skirmishers along the front.

The inset section of the trench, in the center, is described only as at right angles to the lengthy main trench; Procopius does not make it clear if that section is set forward or to the rear. Oman, *Art of War in the Middle Ages* (pp. 28–29), says the line was refused, and most maps show it set back, toward the city, but the Harvard edition of Procopius (p. 103), as well as Goldsworthy (*Name of Rome*, p. 412) and Greatrex (*Rome and Persia*, p. 172), shows it extending toward the Persian lines. Given that the main section of line was "a stone's throw" from the city walls, it seems unlikely that the entire body of infantry as well as Belisarius's bodyguard cavalry could have fit in the area if the trench section were refused. To do so would most certainly have obliged the infantry and possibly the cavalry to form up in two sections, which one would assume Procopius would have noted.

The Persian force initially numbered 40,000 under the command of Peroz Mihran.[36] He marched to Dara with such confidence that he "immediately sent to Belisarius bidding him make ready the bath: for he wished to bathe there on the following day."[37] He apparently had second thoughts as he came within site of the Roman force and found them formed up, ready for battle. Like the Romans, he placed his infantry in the center and his cavalry on the flanks. Again, specific numbers are unknown, but the Immortals[38] were placed in reserve. The others were stationed in two ranks so the rear units could rotate into battle as the leading units lost manpower or ran out of arrows. As it grew later in the day, Peroz probed the Roman left with a cavalry squadron. They enjoyed quick success until they discovered too late that the Romans were engaging in the Parthian tactic of the feigned retreat—apparently the Persians had not considered they could be beaten at their own game. Rather than follow this up with a major assault, the Persians tried another, more psychological ploy: the single combat, in which an individual soldier from either side met and fought with no intervention from their respective armies. This, too, failed the Persians when a Roman volunteer, a wrestling instructor who was not even a part of the army but an attendant to the cavalry commander Bouzes, handily defeated two Persian warriors. Peroz would have to bathe outside the city. The Persians withdrew to their camp at Ammodius, just over two miles away.

The next day was taken up in an exchange of messages, as well as a Persian reinforcement of a further 10,000 troops from Nisibis. Belisarius and Hermogenes, the civilian governor in Dara, offered a peaceful resolution to the confrontation, arguing that since both kings desired peace and negotiators were at hand, Peroz should not be seeking battle. Asserting that the greatest of blessings was peace, Belisarius insisted that Peroz should avoid a fight "lest at some time you be held responsible by the Persians, as is probable, for the disasters which will come to pass."[39] Peroz's return missive doubted Roman sincerity. Two more messages invoked God on the Roman side and the Persian gods in return. Again, Peroz alerted Belisarius that a bath, as well as dinner, was expected inside the city.

On the third day, each commander gave his troops a suitably inspiring motivational address before the armies once more formed up outside Dara's walls as they had at their first meeting. As the deployment was taking place, Pharas, the Herule commander, suggested to Belisarius that he detach his unit and station his 300 cavalry behind a hill on the far left wing. This would give the opportunity for a surprise attack on the advancing Persian cavalry flank where they could do them the greatest harm.[40] Belisarius quickly agreed. Once the armies faced each other, however, nothing happened. As Goldsworthy observes, the "Roman formation was geared to receiving a frontal attack and, with the wall of Dara so close behind them, such an attack was the only viable option open to Peroz if he wished to take the city."[41] Hence, Belisarius was not about to do anything other than await the attack. Peroz wanted to delay the battle until at least noon, hoping to force the Romans to miss their midday meal and weaken them. (The Persians normally ate later in the day.) This delay apparently did not have the desired effect.

The battle started with an exchange of arrows, but apparently only on the flanks. Procopius makes no mention of any fighting taking place in the center. The Persians had the advantage in numbers, as well as the rotation of fresh archers to the front; harking back to Thermopylae, Procopius claims the arrows darkened the sky. Unfortunately for Peroz, the Romans had a strong wind at their back, so the effect of the barrage was minimized. The Persians had been advancing while firing, for Procopius writes that as the arrows ran out, "they began to use their spears against each other, and the battle had come still more to close quarters."[42] The Roman left soon found themselves under severe pressure, for their opponents were not Persians; instead, they were up against the Kadishaye, a warlike tribe from Beth Arabaye,[43] a region some 100 kilometers south of the Dara-Nisibis area.

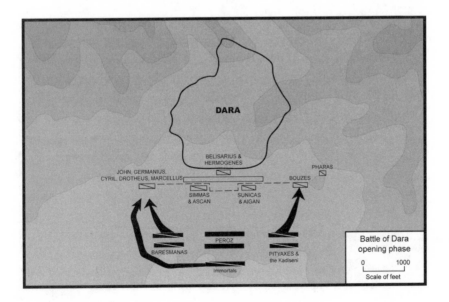

This early Persian advance, however, was exactly what Pharas the Herule had apparently been counting on, for his men "got in the rear of the enemy and made a wonderful display of valorous deeds," according to Procopius.[44] The leftward Hun unit also joined in the fray, and the Kadishaye found themselves surrounded and slaughtered. Three thousand died and the remainder fled to the safety of the Persian infantry lines.

In the meantime, Peroz had been shifting his Immortals out of reserve and to his left. Belisarius saw this and ordered the Huns under Sunicas and Aigan to cease their action on the left and rush to the opposite side of the battlefield. They joined with the right-hand Hun force under Simmas and Ascan. As his initial attack was being driven back, Peroz ordered his left-flank cavalry forward with the Immortals in support. As did the other assault, this too gained some early success and forced the Roman cavalry back. Focused on the retreating cavalry, the Sassanids were unprepared for the Huns to strike their flank. The Hunnic cavalry drove not only into but through the charging Sassanids, separating them into two forces. At this point the retreating Romans stopped before the rapidly rising ground and turned to meet their attackers, now weaker by half.

The combat turned into melee, made more chaotic as Belisarius and Hermogenes lent the weight of their reserve cavalry. Sunicas killed both the Immortals' standard bearer and their commander, Barasamas. "As a

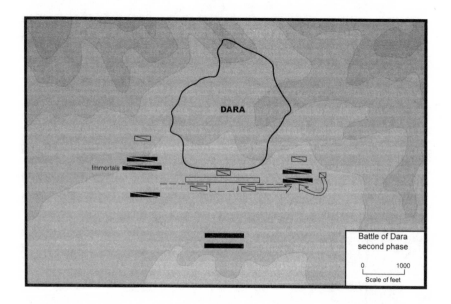

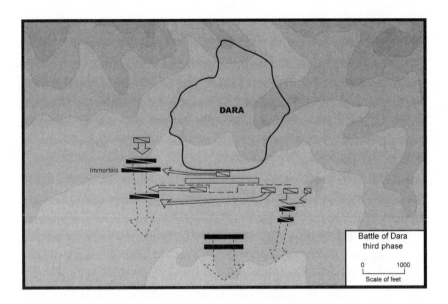

result of this the barbarians were seized with great fear and thought no longer of resistance, but fled in utter confusion," Procopius writes. "And the Romans, having made a circle as it were around them, killed about five thousand."[45] Struck from multiple angles and leaderless, the Sassanid cavalry broke. With the cavalry streaming to the rear, the infantry also broke and ran. The pursuit was on, but Belisarius halted it rather than attempt an annihilation. He knew that a cornered army could fight desperately and snatch victory from defeat, a prospect he was not willing to face. Instead, Belisarius was content to win a clear-cut victory and enjoy the benefits to his troops' morale.

All the battles discussed to this point have been won by the offense, but at Dara the defense prevailed. Belisarius had used the time during the peace talks not only to gather forces but also to prepare his position. The extended ditch across his front discouraged a frontal attack, encouraging Peroz to split his force and attack the flanks with fewer troops. Since the Persians had twice as many men, the division of forces apparently did not affect Peroz as it should have. The trench provided an artificial obstacle by which Belisarius was able to channel the Sassanian avenues of attack; it also provided security for his lesser-quality infantry and disrupted any plan for a massed assault. Belisarius's uses of mass and concentration were most notable; he quickly moved his central Hunnic horse to either flank as necessary to counter the Sassanian cavalry charges. His one use of concealment and cover, the Herules behind the hill on his far left flank, also proved effective. Being on slightly higher ground than the attackers, Belisarius also had the advantage in observation; his sighting of the Immortals shifting into position for the attack gave him time to shift his own Hun cavalry completely across the battlefield while preparing his personal bucellari reserve for the final counterattack. The positioning of his force so close to the city gates, as well as the rapidly rising ground behind his forces and the city, kept his line of communication secure and severely restricted any chance of the Sassanian cavalry succeeding in a flanking attack or move to the rear.

The loss of as much as half his army shocked Peroz and Cavadh. To make matters worse, a subsidiary offensive to the north was also defeated. Temporarily, at least, the Romans had the upper hand in this section of the frontier. After several months, Cavadh took the advice of an Arab ally named Almondar, as Mahon describes, to "avoid the beaten track of Amida or Nisibis, and to invade the Roman territories for the first time on the side of Syria. Here his approach would be unexpected, and therefore his progress easy, and he might hope to reduce the city of Antioch, which its luxury rendered both alluring and defenseless."[46] Early in 531 Cavadh sent 15,000 cavalry on a sweep to the west, the force being commanded by Azarethes. When they reached Gabbula, some 100 miles south of Antioch, the alarm was raised. Belisarius reacted swiftly by leading 20,000 men to cut off the Sassanian approach. His army included 2,000 local recruits and a number of less-than-experienced forces, for he had been obliged to leave veterans behind to guard the frontier posts if this attack proved to be a diversion for a larger Sassanian attack elsewhere.

As soon as Azarethes learned of Belisarius's approach, he began a withdrawal. Belisarius shadowed them a day's march behind. He viewed an expulsion of the enemy without a battle to be better than the risk of combat with his potentially untrustworthy troops. According to Procopius, however, Belisarius allowed himself to be swayed by aggressive subordinates and the urging of the army as a whole. After he addressed them on the folly of fighting in the wake of an extended Easter fast, the troops "began to insult him, not in silence nor with any concealment, but they came shouting into his presence, and called him weak and a destroyer of their zeal; and even some of the officers joined with the soldiers in this offence, thus displaying the extent of their daring."[47] Belisarius eventually gave in to their demands and deployed along the right bank of the Euphrates, opposite the town of Callinicum.

Procopius describes the battle as hard and closely fought, with much damage inflicted on both armies by archers. Then, late in the day a Persian attack on the allied Saracen cavalry broke through the Roman right flank, cutting off a Roman retreat. Belisarius led the infantry as long as he could, but as the Persians made more progress on both flanks he finally led the remnants of his men into and across the river to safety. John Malalas, however, gives a different account. He claims that as the right flank collapsed and many of the new recruits "saw the Saracens fleeing, they threw themselves into the Euphrates thinking they could get across. When Belisarios [sic] saw what was happening, he took his standard with him and got into a boat; he crossed the Euphrates and came to Kallinikon. The army followed him. Some used boats, others tried to swim with their horses, and they filled the river with corpses."[48] Malalas asserts that two subordinates led the fight to cover the escaping army, and they held the Persians at bay until dark.

Wherever the truth lay, the battle was a Roman defeat. However, it had little major consequence in the overall scheme of things, for Cavadh soon died and his heir, Chosroes, took the throne and initiated peace talks. Zachariah of Mitylene reports that "Belisarius, being held culpable by the king on account of the rout which had been inflicted on the Roman army by the Persians at Thannuris and on the Euphrates, had been dismissed from his command and went up to the king."[49] He was recalled to Constantinople, either as punishment for his defeat or in preparation for the invasion of Vandal-held North Africa (depending on which author one believes). The battle did, however, prove to be Belisarius's last defeat.

In Constantinople, Belisarius ingratiated (or reingratiated) himself with Justinian by suppressing a major domestic revolt, the Nika riots, in 532. The following year he led an expedition to Carthage to challenge Vandal dominance and begin Justinian's master plan to establish his rule in as much of the old Roman Empire as possible. Two major battles, Ad Decimum and Tricameron, were both Roman victories with cavalry; infantry were nearby for the battles but not directly involved in them. Neither will be discussed here, for they were as much Vandal defeats owing to their King Gelimer's poor leadership as they were Belisarius's victories won through persistence and hard fighting. They certainly aided in reinvigorating his reputation, although this wasn't necessarily a blessing. While Belisarius gained the confidence of his men by winning a campaign far from home with a smaller army than the one he faced, he also came to the attention of Justinian, who knew the fate of emperors with too-successful generals: they often found themselves overthrown. From this point forward, Justinian gave Belisarius more and more difficult tasks but with smaller and smaller forces. It is to Belisarius's credit that he not only succeeded in making bricks with very little straw but he also never let his emperor's paranoia become a self-fulfilling prophecy.

The Gothic War

THE BYZANTINES HAD FOR SOME TIME been on good terms with the Ostrogoths, branch of the Eastern Germanic Goths located in Italy. The eastern empire had supported the Gothic king Theodoric when he invaded Italy to defeat Odovacer in 493. Once established in Ravenna, Theodoric ruled not only as king of the Ostrogoths but as the eastern emperor's viceroy. A minority population in Italy, the Goths worked successfully with the existing Roman bureaucracy. Theodoric maintained a clear distinction between his own people and his Roman subjects, but he hoped that the Ostrogoths could elevate themselves to a level with the people they ruled.[50] The "viceroyalty" extended throughout Italy and into Pannonia.

All was well as long as Theodoric lived. Unfortunately, the successors of a great king rarely match his talents. Theodoric left behind but one child, a daughter named Amalasuntha. Her first husband died, leaving behind a son, Athalaric. Amalasuntha seems to have been quite capable in her own right and served as regent to her young son, but Gothic tradition would not allow a queen to be supreme ruler. Early in Justinian's reign, he had sought to strengthen relations with Theodoric, but soon he began to persecute Christian heresies, which included the Arianism practiced by the Goths. When Theodoric died in 526, the combination of religious persecution and the question of royal succession disturbed the Gothic population. Amalasuntha sought cordial relations with Justinian and aided him in his war against the North African Vandals by allowing free use of Sicilian bases. Her regency ended, however, when Athalaric died. Amalasuntha offered to marry Vandal chieftain Theodahad on the presumption that she would remain the power behind the throne. He agreed to the marriage, but afterward subverted her authority and within a few months had her killed (April 535). Justinian used the murder as his justification for committing troops to Italy. Theodahad could step down as king and swear fealty to Justinian, but anything less than that meant war.

The Gothic Military

THE OSTROGOTHS AND VISIGOTHS THAT FOUGHT together and defeated the eastern Romans at the Battle of Adrianople in 376 apparently were so satisfied with their weapons and tactics that very little had changed by the time Belisarius invaded Italy. The cavalry made up the bulk of the army and could be classified as heavy. A Gothic horseman wore a helmet with protection for his neck and cheeks and a flexible suit of armor, of metal or leather, which reached down at least to his knees. He wielded the extralong thrusting lance, the *contus*, to which a pennant was affixed, and he carried a sword and small shield as secondary weapons for close combat on horseback or when dismounted. The warriors rode armored horses and charged at the gallop with long lances held in close formation.[51]

Theodoric had begun expanding the role of infantry, but it still remained very minor. What archers the Ostrogoths used were infantry. They had greater range with their bows than did mounted archers, but were not as strong on the defensive as heavy infantry. Although the cavalry did depend on them as a line behind which to retreat, it was for the shield of arrows rather than the physically solid defense heavy infantry could provide.

Little had changed in the nature of Gothic tactics, attitudes, or armament since the days of their first appearance in Europe, nor had the basic technological aspects of warfare changed.[52] The Ostrogoths used swords produced in Roman shops or with very similar techniques.[53] Exposure to the Romans had altered their order of battle structure, however, primarily during Theodoric's reign. The Ostrogoths achieved a reputation of strength against other barbarians by building on their own traditions, but they also adapted some Roman organizational and support systems.[54] Their tactics relied primarily on mass, with only basic maneuvers included.

The principal elements of Gothic tactics were lightning-quick attacks launched from ambush and accompanied by loud war cries, outflanking maneuvers to attack the enemy's infantry, the hard and fast cavalry charge in the hope of dealing a decisive blow before the horses were exhausted, quick retreat behind the lines of their infantry in case the attack failed, and gathering new forces for follow-up attack, reinforced by reserves.[55] Unfortunately for the Goths, ambushes were difficult to set up during a siege. Therefore, they had to depend on infantry (their secondary arm) for scaling walls, for which they had little skill or experience, or await a Byzantine sally in order to bring their cavalry into play.

The Siege of Rome

JUSTINIAN SENT BELISARIUS TO SICILY in 536 with some 4,000 Byzantine soldiers and foederati, 3,000 Isaurians, 200 Huns, and 300 Moors, as well as Belisarius's bucellarii in unknown numbers. While this is a small force with which to capture all of Italy, Justinian did send a force to threaten the Goths' northern border: Mundas, commanding Byzantine forces in Illyricum (along the eastern Adriatic coast), was ordered to invade Dalmatia.

Those two forces in conjunction with an alliance with the Franks in Gaul gave the Goths three threats to face. While those were sufficient to strike fear in the Gothic king's heart, Belisarius's quick capture of Sicily sent him into a panic. Gibbon writes that although Theodahad "descended from a race of heroes, he was ignorant of the art, and averse to the dangers, of war."[56] He quickly entered into negotiations with Justinian's envoy, signing a treaty that would make Italy subservient to the empire in return for his retention of the throne. A second treaty, to be offered if the first was rejected, was to retire from the throne in return for a sizable pension. Justinian rejected the first, demanding abdication; he gladly agreed to the second. Theodahad, however, refused to abdicate upon learning that the Byzantine force approaching through Dalmatia had been defeated. He should have taken the money and run. Instead, he bribed the Franks sufficiently to keep them at bay and now had only one army to face.

By the spring of 536 Belisarius had not only conquered Sicily but had made a quick punitive expedition to Carthage as well. Leaving a small garrison in Palermo, he crossed the strait of Messina into the toe of Italy and began his march northward. His first challenge came at Naples. The citizens negotiated with Belisarius; unfortunately, they could not decide with which power their security lay, the Goths or Romans. The Goths had ruled fairly for decades and done little to restrict the habits of the Italians. The Byzantines, on the other hand, were painted by the Goths to be more Greek than Roman and with no real interest in taking care of the citizenry. The Neapolitans suggested Belisarius just move on toward Rome, but he could not leave a major city and Gothic garrison behind him. A twenty-day siege ensued that cost Belisarius men as well as time, but finally a secret entrance into the city was discovered and Naples fell. Only after significant pillage, looting, and rapine did Belisarius restrain his troops. Leaving another garrison behind depleted his forces even further, and he marched for Rome with perhaps 5,000 soldiers.

With Naples lost and a renewed Byzantine offensive in Dalmatia, Theodahad ran. The Goths had had too much of his self-serving dithering. In November 536 a gathering of Gothic warriors declared Theodahad dethroned and, as there were no more male members of the royal family, elected a man of obscure birth but of some military experience named Vittigis. In retrospect, the choice could have been better, but he was an improvement over Theodahad, who was captured and executed.[57] In Rome, Vittigis made a smart political move rather than a smart military one. He left a 4,000-man garrison in Rome and marched the rest of his army to the capital at Ravenna, where he forced Theodoric's granddaughter Matasuntha into marriage, thus giving his kingship some measure of legitimacy. Meanwhile, Rome was changing hands. Fearing a repeat of the Neapolitan experience, the citizens of the Eternal City opened their gates to Belisarius on 9 December 536. Without local support, the Gothic garrison fled.

However, the Roman citizens were not too enthused about facing a siege by their erstwhile overseers. As Lord Mahon describes, "With all the eloquence of cowardice, they attempted to dissuade Belisarius from his project of fortifying Rome, and represented, in glowing colors, the inadequate store of provisions for its maintenance, and the vast and untenable extent of its walls. They urged that its inland position cut off all maritime supplies, and that its level site presented no natural advantage for defense."[58] Belisarius politely took note, but restored the walls, emptied ships from Sicily of their grain, obliged the locals to bring him the harvest,

and sent out troops. Some spread around the southern and eastern countryside, gathering in more supplies from cities the Goths had left either
lightly garrisoned or undefended. He also sent forces northward to seize
key fortresses, hoping to delay Vittigis's advance.

Vittigis was soon on his way. With his forces making little headway
against the Byzantines in Dalmatia, he decided to attack Rome. News of
the size of Belisarius's army encouraged him and he sped for the city. The
troops Belisarius had sent north either fled back to Rome or closed themselves up in the fortresses they had captured, there to be isolated by small
Gothic forces. Procopius numbers the Gothic army at 150,000, but modern
historians disagree.[59] Fifteen thousand seems the more likely number,
though Ernest Dupuy and Trevor Dupuy propose 50,000.[60] Suffice it to say,
Belisarius was outnumbered. The Gothic numbers must have been relatively
low, however, for they only besieged the northern half of the city.

By seizing the towns of Spolento, Narni, and Perugia, Belisairus did
oblige Vittigis to slow his rush for Rome. Belisarius put the time to
good use, not only strengthening the walls but digging a wide trench
outside them. He also built a tower to guard a bridge the Goths would
be crossing. Generally described as the Milivian Bridge, it may have been
another bridge across the Anio River, today known as the Teverone, and
Procopius describes both that river and the Tiber by the same name. The
fort was certainly stout enough to defend the bridge, but the fortitude of
the defenders was not. They fled rather than fight, and a few more days of
preparation were lost.

Combat occurred quickly. Apparently in ignorance of the fall of his
bridge fort, Belisarius led 1,000 cavalry out on a reconnaissance mission.
They were surprised by a large Gothic force and obliged to stage a fighting
withdrawal. One of the fort's deserters identified Belisarius to the Goths
as riding a distinctively white-faced horse. That meant the bulk of the
Gothic army aimed toward the Roman commander in order to reap
immense glory. Belisarius and his bodyguard had an intense melee on
their hands, and they retreated back to the gate—only to find it closed
against them. Rumor had spread inside the walls that Belisarius was dead,
and the citizens were not about to let an angry horde of Goths into the
city, no matter how many Romans may have been left outside. Faced
with an unenviable situation, Belisarius did the unexpected: he ordered
a charge. The turnabout was so sudden and violent the Goths assumed

a fresh force must have sallied from the gates, so they retreated to their camps in fear. The remaining Romans and their commander (not only alive but completely unharmed) then beat their own retreat into the city.

Vittigis sent a representative to vocally harass the citizens of Rome for their betrayal and then ordered the siege to begin. The Goths established six camps, positioned to cover at least one gate each, stretching from the east bank of the Tiber at the Porta Flaminia around to the easternmost gates of Tiburtina and Praenastina. Later, one was set up west of the Tiber on the Plains of Nero (Campus Neronis) near Vatican Hill. Procopius writes that "the Goths dug deep trenches about all their camps, and heaped up the earth, which they took out from them, on the inner side of the trenches, making this bank exceedingly high, and they planted great numbers of sharp stakes on the top, thus making all their camps in no way inferior to fortified strongholds."[61]

Vittigis also ordered that the aqueducts supplying the city be destroyed. The besieged were still able to to draw water from the Tiber and from wells, so water was never in short supply, but the flow from the aqueducts had powered the mills. The Tiber therefore became the site for new mills and the grinding continued as long as there was grain. Belisarius had already stationed men at each gate and now drafted townsmen into the

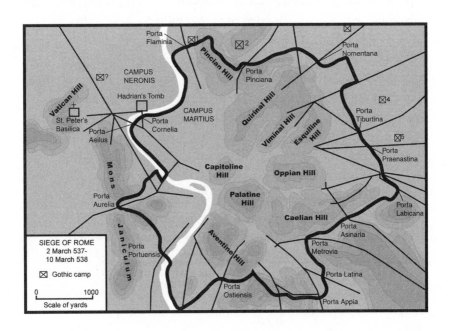

ranks to spread his forces a bit farther and give the Romans a stake in their own defense. He also ordered the commanders at each gate to disregard any report of breakthroughs in other parts of the city; they should continue to man their posts and not fly to aid others, since such alerts may have been nothing but rumors.

Learning from deserters of discontent within the city, Vittigis sent envoys to offer the Byzantines safe passage out of Rome. Belisarius was brusque (and prescient) in his reply: "I say to you that there will come a time when you will want to hide your heads under the thistles but will find no shelter anywhere. . . . And whoever of you has hopes of setting foot in Rome without a fight is mistaken in his judgment. For as long as Belisarius lives, it is impossible for him to relinquish this city."[62] Vittigis, however, was determined to make short work of the siege and began building assault engines. Three weeks into the siege, the assault weapons, wheeled towers protecting battering rams, were built and ready for use. Vittigis also had large numbers of scaling ladders built and fascines bundled to fill in the ditch outside the walls.

Belisarius had also been using his time placing his own engines for defense. Along the walls were placed a number of *ballistae*, catapults firing bolts shorter but thicker than arrows to a range roughly twice that of a bow. Inside and protected by the walls were onagers, consisting of an arm affixed at the bottom by braided rope that built torsion as the arm was pulled backward and downward; the opposite end of the arm comprised a sling holding a rock. When the arm was released the rock soared high and far. (The trebuchet of later centuries used a pivot and counterweight to accomplish the same action.) The accuracy of the onager was minimal, but the ballista could and did wreak great havoc.

Vittigis brought his engines forward on 21 March. Many of the defenders (mainly the civilians) were fearful, but Belisarius laughed. Many thought it was bravado, but he soon showed them the cause of his humor. Ordering the archers to hold their fire until he gave the signal, Belisarius allowed the rams to be hauled by their ox teams into arrow range. He then nocked an arrow and shot it through the throat of one of the Goth officers. Another followed with identical results. At that, masses of arrows flew into the advancing army. Belisarius had the archers closest to him concentrate their fire on the oxen, which soon left the rams immobile far from the city walls.

Vittigis left a force of archers behind with orders to keep up a steady fire on the defenders while he led an attack on the city gate called the Porta Praenestina to the east. Meanwhile, a third force attacked across the Plain of Nero to Hadrian's Tomb. The walls there seemed so formidable that Belisarius had stationed only a small force guarding the tomb and the Porta Cornelia. The Goths rushed the walls with large shields protecting them from arrows and were soon at the walls with scaling ladders. The defenders could not shoot down on the advancing Goths without exposing themselves, so found themselves in dire straits. One soldier, looking about, noticed the large number of marble statues around the tomb. He began breaking them into pieces and hurling the marble blocks onto the attackers. Soon all the defenders were pelting the Goths, who were forced away from the walls and then became exposed to arrow fire. Thus, the handful of defenders repelled the assault. Belisarius ordered sallies from various gates to attack the Goths while they were spread out; they abandoned their assaults and fled back to their camps. "Then Belisarius gave the order to burn the enemy's engines, and the flames, rising to a great height, naturally increased the consternation of the fugitives," Procopius writes.[63]

"Such was the loss and consternation of the Goths that, from this day, the siege of Rome degenerated into a tedious and indolent blockade," writes Gibbon.[64] At this point Belisarius wrote to Justinian, begging for reinforcement. While detailing his successes, he subtly applied some pressure on the emperor to act if he wished their victory to continue. He reminded Justinian that "it has never been possible even for many times ten thousand men to guard Rome for any considerable length of time.... And although at the present time the Romans are well disposed toward us, yet when their troubles are prolonged, they will probably not hesitate to choose the course which is better for their own interests.... [N]o man will ever be able to remove me from this city while I live; but I beg thee to consider what kind of a fame such an end of Belisarius would bring thee."[65] Upon receiving this letter, Justinian responded, but the reinforcements he sent were obliged by bad weather to stop and winter in Greece.

At this point Belisarius sent nonessential personnel out of Rome to Naples, something he probably should have done earlier in order to stretch his supplies. Luckily, they were not attacked as they fled south. He also kept supplementing the food supply by sending out his Moorish soldiers at night, when the Goths did nothing but post guards at their camps. The Moors gathered supplies and ambushed the occasional Goth soldier or patrol. This served not only to supplement the food supply, but to bolster Roman morale while harming that of the Goths. In response, Vittigis sent a large force to capture the city and harbor at Portus, which denied the besieged any succor by ship. Belisarius knew the loss of the harbor would be important, but he simply did not have the manpower to spare in order to protect it. The nearest port available to Belisarius was now Antium, a day's travel to the south. It was from there that, three weeks after the Goths captured Portus, he received a reinforcement of 1,600 cavalry dispatched from Constantinople before the siege began.

With the extra manpower now available, Belisarius was not about to let his men stand idle. He sent cavalry units out to nearby hills. When the Goths massed to charge them, the Byzantine arrows caused great damage while the attackers were at some distance. Procopius writes that "since their shafts fell among a dense throng, they were for the most part successful in hitting a man or a horse." When the cavalry had expended their arrows, they rode for the city gates with the Goths in pursuit. "But when they came near the fortifications, the operators of the engines began to shoot arrows from them, and the barbarians became terrified and abandoned the pursuit."[66] All of this encouraged the citizenry to get in on the action. They begged Belisarius to let them participate in battle. Procopius tells how Belisarius finally relented to their entreaties, as he had done against his better judgment at Callinicum against the Persians. The disaster was much the same. After early success with his cavalry, Belisarius allowed a phalanx of civilians to sweep the outnumbered Goths from their position on the Plain of Nero. Unfortunately, the loot of the camp became more interesting than the pursuit of a defeated enemy; the Goths re-formed and recaptured their camp. The untrained civilians dropped everything and fled for the city, only to find the gates closed to them and the hotly pursuing Goths. Belisarius and the cavalry saved the day, but the battle could be called nothing better than a draw.

In midsummer an envoy arrived from Constantinople with a large sum of money to pay the troops. Belisarius launched a diversionary attack out of two northern gates while a bodyguard escorted the money into the city from the south. That raised morale temporarily, but soon the citizens were once again complaining; the best Belisarius could do was promise (and

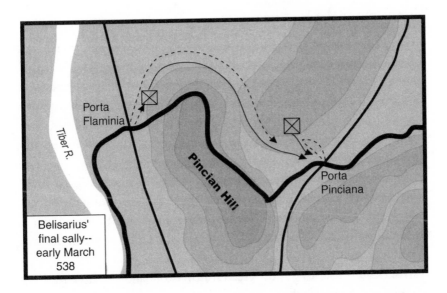

Porta
Flaminia

Tiber R.

Pincian Hill

Porta
Pinciana

Belisarius'
final sally--
early March
538

hope) that reinforcements were on their way. In the fall he sent Procopius to Naples to recruit more soldiers, then sent his wife, Antonina (who had traveled with him on this campaign), to use her organizational abilities to work on supplying ships and food. Meanwhile, he gambled that the Goths would be feeling the pressure of short rations as well. Belisarius sent raiding parties into the countryside to attack Gothic supply trains and threaten towns along the lines of communication. By intercepting enemy supplies he would not only alleviate the situation in Rome, "the barbarians might seem to be besieged rather than to be themselves besieging the Romans."[67]

Indeed, the promised reinforcements did arrive: 3,000 Isaurians, 800 Thracians, and 1,000 Byzantine cavalry, plus 500 soldiers Procopius had recruited or relieved from garrison duty. Antonina had gathered a fleet of ships and a large store of grain. The supplies and cavalry started for Rome, with the ships intending to land at the port of Ostia, across the Tiber from the harbor at Pontus that the Goths had captured. It was now late February or early March 538. Learning that both men and supplies were approaching, Belisarius planned one more major diversion. Throughout the siege the Porta Flaminia had been walled up with stone; Belisarius had done this to make the gate assault-proof from the Goths' camp just outside. During one night in March, he had the stones quietly removed until the gate was passable. The next morning he ordered a thousand men to sally from the

Porta Pinciana, the next gate to the east from the Porta Flaminia. They were ordered to charge the nearest Gothic camp, then "flee" when counterattacked. This they did. As the Goths were in hot pursuit, Belisairus ordered another force to burst through the Porta Flaminia and strike the pursuing Goths in the rear. The Goth's ensuing confusion was compounded by the Romans turning from their flight and attacking, as well as the addition of fresh troops from just inside the Porta Pinciana. The few Goths who survived fled to their camps and feared to emerge.

This brought the defense of Rome to a successful end. Vittigis offered a three-month truce, which allowed free passage of food and reinforcements into the city. Belisarius also sent more forays into the countryside to harass the Goths. Ultimately Vittigis abandoned the siege and fled for Ravenna.

Although Belisarius was the greatest field commander of his day, most at home in the open pitched battle, of which he was the master, the siege of Rome proved he was hardly one-dimensional and may have been the highlight of his career.[68] Indeed, Belisarius seemed to do everything right. He spent the three months prior to the Goths' arrival repairing the city walls and placing his engines of war. The Goths, by encamping only on one side of the city, allowed Belisarius to maintain the bulk of his forces in one area. His use of local citizenry intermixed with his troops gave increased security by expanding his numbers while still allowing the soldiers to keep a close eye on the civilians. Thus, while there were deserters, there was no serious attempt by the locals to collaborate with the besiegers. Further security was maintained later in the siege by Belisarius's decision to have the Moors patrol outside the walls at night, both scavenging and ambushing unwary Goths.

The strongest aspect of the defense was its activity. Belisarius carried the fight to the Goths more often than they attacked the city. This use of attack and feigned retreat worked over and over. Only the attack using the Roman civilians was not a success, When attacked, Belisarius was able to shift men to various portions of the wall when hard-pressed, and by holding that redeployment authority solely in his own hands he maintained unity of command. Finally, Belisarius's flexibility showed constantly, as he used raiding parties against Gothic supply lines and lured attacking Gothic forces into ambushes either by secondary sallies or by luring them into range of the defenders' fire from the walls.

Belisarius's Generalship

ECONOMY OF FORCE WAS EASILY BELISARIUS'S greatest strength, primarily because it was forced upon him by his parsimonious and suspicious emperor. He was outnumbered in every battle he fought, and as his career progressed he was given fewer and fewer men to accomplish his missions. (He commanded 25,000 at Dara, 15,000 against the Vandals in North Africa, and 7,500 in his invasion of Italy.) In the Battle of Dara he placed sufficient forces on either flank for defense, but used his mobile Hunnic cavalry in the center as the deciding factor on both flanks. At Rome, he focused his manpower at the gates and spread his force along the walls only when under attack. His infantry archers could man the walls while his cavalry could launch raids outside. In the greatest show of this principle, Belisarius intentionally depleted his defending force in order to send multiple columns into the countryside to disrupt the Gothic supply lines. He thus focused enemy attention away from the city and depleted their food supply while supplementing his own. His deployment of small cavalry forces to hilltops to draw Gothic attacks into missile fire always inflicted many more casualties than he suffered. His only violation of this principle came when he included the citizenry in an attack outside the city. Although the day was a setback, it could have been disaster.

The best example of Belisarius's mastery of *unity of command* came early in the siege of Rome, when a false report spread through the city of an enemy break-in. Belisarius responded by ordering each contingent to man its designated area and ignore any such report. He made sure that his subordinates knew that the moving of reserves from point to point was his responsibility, not theirs. All the planning for offense and defense came from him. At Dara he was technically a cocommander, but since Procopius mentions Hermogenes only in passing we can assume that Belisarius, though the younger man, was in command and that the deployment and movement of forces was in his control. He did show his ability to take suggestions, however, when he agreed with the Herulian commander's idea of hiding his force behind a hill in order to take advantage of the cover for an attack on the Persian cavalry's rear.

Unfortunately, Belisarius failed to exercise this principle in his two defeats. At Calliculum and in the major attack at Rome, Procopius tells us that Belisarius submitted against his better judgment to entreaties from his soldiers at the former and the civilians at the latter. While open-mindedness is certainly a virtue, a leader has to know his mission and give orders that fulfill it, no matter what his men or subordinates may think. Chasing the Persians out of Byzantine territory was his mission, and at Callinicum there was no need to engage an enemy that was voluntarily disengaging through a strategic withdrawal. At Rome, Belisarius's mission was to use minimal manpower to defend the huge stretch of Rome's city walls, and an assault with a large and untrained force of locals could have little advantage other than for morale purposes. In both cases Belisarius forsook unity of command and risked major disaster.

The principle of *maneuver* was undoubtedly one of Belisarius's strengths. It is a tribute to his ability to maneuver that in both the battles discussed (as well as his first victory in North Africa), he won against attacking armies. At Dara, his use of cavalry created ambushes against superior forces on both flanks. At Rome, he displayed more ability to maneuver on the defense than did Vittigis on the offense. He consistently placed the Goths at a disadvantage by forcing them into no-win situations. During the main Goth assault on the walls, he not only shifted manpower as necessary within the city to meet attacks from various points but also followed up the Gothic assault with one of his own to chase the retreating enemy and destroy their siege engines. These actions always took place from the gates facing the enemy, for quick striking and quick withdrawal. Belisarius's deployment of relatively small cavalry forces on hilltops to draw Gothic cavalry into long-range arrow fire worked every time he tried it.

Using the unguarded gates, his dispatch of night patrols not only strengthened security but also brought in much-needed food and obliged the Goths to stay in their camps. Strategically, his dispatch of cavalry forces to harass the enemy supply line and attack enemy towns created far more discomfort for the besiegers than for the besieged. Basil Liddell Hart writes, "Though the strain on the defenders was severe, the strength of the besiegers was shrinking much faster, especially through sickness. Belisarius boldly took the risk of sending two detachments from his slender force to seize by surprise the towns of Tivoli and Terracina, which dominated the roads by which the besiegers received their supplies."[69] Even in the one major mistake of the siege, his attack with the civilian infantry, Belisarius's quick action with his cavalry saved the bulk of the citizens by covering their retreat into the city.

Liddell Hart describes Belisarius as being a master of the defensive-offensive strategy. "Belisarius had developed a new-style tactical instrument with which he knew that he might count on beating much superior numbers, provided that he could induce his opponents to attack him under conditions that suited his tactics. For that purpose his lack of numbers, when not too marked, was an asset, especially when coupled with an audaciously direct strategic offensive."[70] Thus, Belisarius would advance strategically to a point where he would provoke an enemy response, and then on the battlefield would stand on the defensive until his enemy made a mistake or retreated, upon which he would turn to the offensive. Centuries later, Clausewitz would restate this very principle: "Once the defender has gained an important advantage, defense as such has done its work. . . . A sudden powerful transition to the offensive— the flashing of the sword of vengeance—is the greatest moment of the defense."[71]

Belisarius knew the strengths and weaknesses of his troops and their weaponry, and maximized what he had to take advantage of his opponents' weaknesses. This is best shown at Rome, where his horse archers repeatedly bested the Gothic heavy cavalry armed only with lances and swords. They could, however, fight toe-to-toe if necessary, as they did at the beginning of the siege at the abandoned river fort. His personal leadership in the midst of combat was a major influence in maintaining morale. His actions were always well planned; he always spent as much time as possible gauging the situation before committing his men to action.

Belisarius also developed into a master of deception. As his career progressed, deceptive operations became increasingly important in his plans. Capitalizing on his trenchworks at Dara and thereby obliging the Persians to divide their cavalry, as he wanted them to, showed great talent for a young commander, but also the ability to learn from his enemies. He also was able to consistently lure the Goths into ambushes outside the Roman walls with feints in one area that opened another area for a lightning attack. Belisarius's practice of the art of deception reflects his imagination and intellect.[72]

After the siege of Rome was lifted, Belisarius swept up the Italian Peninsula all the way to Ravenna, aided with more reinforcements led by

Justinian's other favorite, Narses. He accepted the Gothic surrender in 540 and was then transferred back to Persia to deal with the breaking of the "Everlasting Peace" that had been signed after his last campaign there. In 544 he was back in Italy suppressing a Gothic uprising. He was besieging Ravenna when the Goths offered the throne of Italy to him, rather than to the Byzantine Empire. Belisarius played along with the offer until he was inside the city; then he took it captive and signed the surrender in the name of Justinian and the empire. The mere offer, however, was enough to spark Justinian's paranoia, and Belisarius was recalled to Constantinople in 548. After some time in disgrace and forced retirement, he was the only one the emperor could call on when the capital city was threatened by a force of Huns in 559. Now in what would be considered old age, he led a few hundred men against a force of 8,000 and won a miraculous victory.

Like many generals, Belisarius was at times lucky when it came to the ability (or lack thereof) of his opposing commander. Still, given his long string of victories with minimal forces, it is difficult to find fault with his generalship: how many leaders could make such a virtue of necessity, fashioning tactics to suit his smaller armies in order to inflict such a long string of defeats on such a wide variety of opposing generals and armies with superior numbers?

8

The Two-Headed General: Chinggis Khan (1162?–1227) and Subedei (1176?–1248)

Mongol Emperor and Mongol Chief of Staff

When Chingiz-Khan rose from the grade of childhood to the degree of manhood, he became in the onslaught like a roaring lion and in the melee like a trenchant sword; in the subjugation of his foes his rigour and severity had the taste of poison, and in the humbling of the pride of each lord of fortune his harshness and ferocity did the work of Fate.

—Ata-malik Juvaini, *Genghis Khan:*
The History of the World Conqueror

If they sprout wings and fly up toward Heaven, you, Subetei, become a falcon and seize them in mid-air. If they become marmots and claw into the Earth with their nails, you become an iron rod and bore through the Earth to catch them. If they become fish and dive into the depths of the Sea, you, Subetei, become a net, casting yourself over them and dragging them back.

—*The Secret History of the Mongols*

MOST EMPIRE BUILDERS have unusual births, or at least claim such is the case. Alexander was said to have come from a line of gods and heroes and, according to his mother, was sired by Zeus. According to almost all the translations of *The Secret History of the Mongols*, the oldest-surviving Mongolian work of literature, published shortly after Chinggis Khan's death,[1] Chinggis traced his lineage to the union of a blue-gray wolf and a fallow doe.[2] Also along the line was a woman who was impregnated three

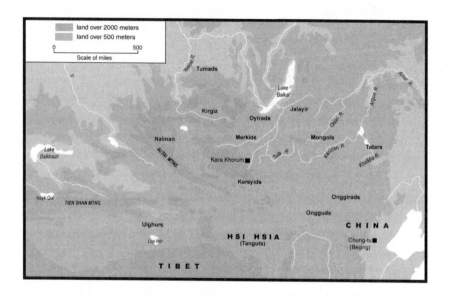

times by a man who appeared through her tent's smoke hole, rubbed her belly with heavenly light, and left on sunbeams. Most notable, perhaps, about Chinggis's birth was the story that "he emerged clenching a blood clot the size of a knuckle-bone die in his right hand,"[3] although the meaning of that sign is disputed. Born to Yesugei the Brave and Hogelun Ujin, the baby was named Temuchin. Yesugei was a minor chieftain of the Mongols, a tribe living between the Onon and Kerulen Rivers near Lake Baikal. Chinggis Khan's mother, Hogelun, of the Onggud tribe was newly married to a young man from the Merkid tribe to the west, when Yesugei kidnapped her, an act that would provoke a revenge attack years later.

When Temuchin reached age nine, his father took him to visit the Ongguds in order to arrange a marriage. Along the way they met Dei the Wise of the Onggirad tribe, who offered one of his daughters for Temuchin; Dei had just had a prophetic dream about this chance meeting and betrothed his ten-year-old daughter Borte to Yesugei's eldest son. Temuchin was left with Dei for a year. Unfortunately, Yesugei encountered a Tatar camp on his way home. They extended the traditional hospitality, but once they recognized him as a Mongol warrior against whom they had fought, the Tartars poisoned him. Yesugei reached home but died within a few days. One of his last orders was to send for Temuchin, who arrived after his father's death.[4] Temuchin did not inherit his father's followers. Mongol society was fluid, and a tribe depended on the strength of its leader for stability and protection. Steppe nomads willingly joined other leaders they regarded as accomplished warriors, and Yesugei's followers were unwilling to remain with the young Temuchin. After all, he could offer nothing in the way of protection or loot.[5] Abandoned by his father's followers, Temuchin was left with only his mother, Hogelun, his three brothers, and a sister. Because of bad blood between Yesugei and some of his relatives, Hogelun and the children were shunned by the tribe, even though according to tribal law she could have become the wife of Yesugei's youngest brother.

Left with nothing, Temuchin experienced several lean years during which he developed a number of traits that would fashion future actions. He spent some time in captivity, held prisoner by his father's former followers. Other sources claim he was held captive on more than one occasion, possibly for up to a decade, by the Chinese. These experiences certainly made it easier for him to look outside traditional tribal ties to establish his future following. In another incident, Temuchin's two half brothers had been bullying him and his brother for some time. After a quarrel over dividing the limited food supply, Temuchin and his brother ambushed and killed one of their half brothers. Though their mother abused them soundly for this offense, Temuchin never expressed regret or guilt for the bloody act of fratricide. As he was to show frequently later in life, Temuchin was not a man to suffer lightly any affronts; those who challenged him or impeded his path to power were always made to pay a heavy penalty for their behavior.[6]

Conversely, and perhaps surprisingly, Temuchin showed a remarkable capacity for gaining and keeping lifelong friends and followers. When he was a teenager, a raiding party stole his family's string of ponies. When he returned from a hunt and found out what had happened, he immediately set out in pursuit. Along the way he stopped at a campsite to ask those surrounding the fire if they had seen his lost horses. A young man in the group not only had seen them but volunteered to go along and help. The two recovered the horses, whereupon the young man, Bogorchun, offered himself to Temuchin as *noker*, "the tie of friendship [that] held Chinggis' followers to him in a relationship rather like that between Europe's medieval lord and liegeman," according to Onon in *The Secret History of the Mongols*.[7] Such people became lifelong adherents to Chinggis and his goals, and he rewarded them with similar loyalty by placing them in command positions. None of these people were from his tribe; that, too, became a foreshadowing of his unification of the multiple steppe tribes into one nation. Chinggis is perhaps the best example of Roman statesman Lucius Sulla's comment: "No friend ever served me, and no enemy ever wronged me, whom I have not repaid in full."

After the return of his ponies, Temuchin began to tread the path that would take him to power. First, to establish his own clan he returned to Dei and claimed Borte as his bride. With a valuable sable coat given as a wedding present, Temuchin went to Togoril (later to be known as Ong Khan) of the Kereyids. Togoril had been a blood brother (*anda*) to Temuchin's father, Yesugei. Temuchin used this tie (and the sable coat) to claim virtual membership in Togoril's family. Temuchin thus acquired a powerful ally and, as he was now officially an adult (fifteen being the age of majority),[8] some of his father's followers began to return.

A test of the new relationship between Temuchin and Togoril came quickly. Upon returning from his trip to the Kereyids, Temuchin found that Merkid raiders had attacked and kidnaped Borte. Temuchin called on Togoril for assistance, and it was immediate. Togoril also suggested asking help from Temuchin's boyhood anda, Jemugha, from another Mongol clan. In 1184 the forces gathered and launched a surprise raid on the Merkids, quickly defeating them and recovering Borte. She had been in captivity for roughly nine months and soon gave birth to a son, but Temuchin always treated the boy as his own.

The cooperative effort reestablished the childhood relationship between Temuchin and Jemugha. For a year and a half their clans traveled together and the bonds of anda were reinforced. Or so it seemed. One evening Jamugha suggested the two clans camp in different spots, a proposition that may have troubled Temuchin. As biographer John Man comments, "If the two were not as one, what then? If they part, they cannot be companions; if they are not companions, then they are rivals; if rivals, then one or the other must dominate; and Temuchin is surely not prepared to be a mere follower."[9] As Temuchin moved on, not only to a new camp but off on his own, large numbers of Jemugha's followers broke away and joined him. Some who followed were relatives, including a great-grandson of Borjigin, the first khan (Khabul Khan). Many were senior to him in the family but seemed to see in him the mark of greatness.[10]

Now, in 1187 or 1189, Temuchin and his followers camped at Koko Naur (the Blue Lake) and a *khuriltai*, or clan meeting, was held. According to some sources, Temuchin was named Chinggis Khan at this point. Although the term "Chinggis" is widely debated, the general consensus is that it means "oceanic" or "limitless." Other sources say he was named *gurkhan*, a position held also by Jamugha, making him the highest clan leader rather than leader of the universe (or at least of "all those who dwell in felt tents") and the title Chinggis was actually given during the larger khuriltai of 1206, when all steppe tribes swore their loyalty. Either way, it is at this point Chinggis Khan began to implement his organizational scheme for the future Mongol nation. He named his closest followers to key positions and to his noker he gave supervisory roles. His household and its staff tended to the new khan's personal needs and economic interests and became the core around which the imperial guard and administration later formed.[11]

Between his elevation to leadership status and 1196, little is known of Chinggis's activities. He emerges again as an ally of Togoril, who had spent the previous several years in exile in China. The Tatars to the east, long subject to the Chinese Chin Dynasty, were becoming too independent for Chin tastes, and Togoril had been requested to bring them back in line. Along with Temuchin's newly enlarged clan, the two defeated the Tatars, gaining revenge for Yesugei's murder and recognition from the Chin: Togoril was given the title of wang, or king, thus taking on the Mongol title of Ong Khan. Temuchin received a lesser title, but it was not important; he had received more experience and a greater reputation. Capitalizing on their strengthened bond, Chinggis soon convinced Ong Khan to name him as heir, upsetting Ong Khan's natural sons. From this point forward, the relationship between Ong Khan and Chinggis Khan was strained and inconsistent, with Ong Khan often fighting alongside Chinggis, but occasionally listening to slander and plotting against him.

Realizing the reputation Chinggis had established, the other steppe tribes decided to work together to crush his growing power. Unfortunately, he struck first. Between 1197 and 1204 he defeated the Merkids and the Naimans, both of whom had conspired with Jamugha or Ong Khan. Chinggis defeated both of those leaders, killing Jamugha and driving Ong Khan to his death in a foreign land. The survivors of these tribes were either exterminated or incorporated into units of Temuchin's army. This uninterrupted series of victories and the complete defeats of the hostile tribes raised Chinggis in the course of a decade to the position of absolute sovereign of Mongolia, and gave him a power over his own people such as no previous Mongol tribal ruler had ever come close to achieving.[12] Having total control over the steppes, Chinggis began reorganizing the population into one nation, and the army became the vehicle for that transformation.

Subedai

SUBEDAI WAS A LATECOMER TO CHINGGIS'S new nation. His brother preceded him by a few years, brought to Chinggis by their father, a blacksmith from the forest-dwelling Uriangkhai, or Reindeer Peoples, along the western shore of Lake Baikal. This settled tribe lived by hunting and trading, and they provided furs and some manufactured goods to the steppe dwellers. The blacksmith apparently held Yesugei, Temuchin's father, in high esteem, for he offered his firstborn son to Yesugei the same year that Temuchin was born. Yesugei accepted the offer, but asked for him to bring him the boy as an adult. Around 1187, when Temuchin was first allying himself with Togoril and beginning his own rise in life, the blacksmith returned and fulfilled his promise, giving his own son to Yesugei's son. This was Jelme, who stayed with Temuchin through the earliest days of his adulthood and earned his position as noker.

Jelme's younger brother was Subedei, then ten years old.[13] His mother had died in childbirth and as the only remaining son, he was to take over his father's trade. Subedei seems to have been no more interested in blacksmithing than Jelme had been, and at age fourteen he left his father to join his brother. At his age, every boy of the steppe would already be trained to ride, shoot, fight, and live off the land; Subedei could do none of those things. Apparently, however, he had a good mind and learned quickly. As Jelme's brother, he was allowed to protect the tent flap when the Mongol leadership held their planning meetings. By watching and listening, as well as learning the practical talents necessary to engage in Mongol warfare, he absorbed the finer points of strategy and tactics.

Subedei arrived in Temuchin's camp on the occasion of the separation from Jamugha. The clan leaders swore allegiance to Temuchin and gave him the title of Chinggis; at the same time he picked out Jelme and Bogorchun as his two oldest and closest companions and gave them the most authority.[14] At this point Subedei swore his fealty as well, in a way that perhaps only a boy who is eager to please might do, as described in Paul Kahn's translation in the *Secret History*: "I'll be like a rat and gather up others, I'll be like a black crow and gather great flocks, like the felt blanket that covers a horse, I'll gather up soldiers to cover you. Like the felt blanket that guards a tent from the wind, I'll assemble great armies to shelter your tent."[15] As Subedei's main biographer, Richard Gabriel, notes, "Although of no military status whatsoever, Subotai was permitted to pledge his loyalty to Temuchin along with the other clan leaders as if, somehow, he was already one of them."[16]

Throughout the following several years the details of Chinggis's life are unknown, but one can assume that Subedei learned the soldiering trade on the training field and battlefield, as well as by listening in on the staff meetings held in Chinggis's tent. Subedei next appears in the sources in 1197 before the Battle of the Tchen River against the Merkids, by which time he was in command of a *jaghun* (company) of a hundred men. He volunteered to be the point unit for the attack, a mission he undertook with unusual style. He refused Chinggis's offer of a hundred elite troops; instead, he left alone. He went to the Merkid camp and "turned traitor." The Merkids were so thrilled with this development that they failed to take the usual precautions and found themselves the victims of a surprise attack. Thus, Subedei illustrated what would become his trademarks: deception and boldness.

In 1203, Chinggis fought Jamugha and Ong Khan to a draw at the Battle of Red Willows. With a severely depleted force he withdrew to Lake Baljuna. It is indicative of Chinggis's personality that those who retreated with him did not abandon him, as was traditional steppe practice. Those who stuck with him, including the brothers Jelme and Subedei, received intense loyalty and rewards in return. The following year, with a rebuilt army, Chinggis defeated his two former allies for good. He also reorganized his army and launched a campaign against his last major enemy, the Naimans. By this point Subedei commanded a *minghan* of 1,000 men. In the Battle of Chakirmagud he is described as one of Chinggis's top commanders, whom he called his Four Dogs. Jamugha offers a powerful description in *The Secret History of the Mongols*:

> [Chinggis] fed four dogs with human flesh, then held them back with iron chains. . . . These four dogs have helmets of copper, snouts like chisels, tongues like awls, hearts of iron, whips sharp as swords. These four dogs feed on the dew and ride on the winds. These four, when they fight an enemy, feed on his flesh. These four take human flesh as their spoils. Now he's cast off their chains and set them on us. He's let them loose and they charge at us, mad with joy, their hungry mouths foaming.[17]

The Naimans were defeated after an all-day battle, with many dying by falling off mountain cliffs while retreating during the night. In 1205 Chinggis and his armies defeated the Merkids for the final time, but their chieftain escaped. Subedei was given his first independent command: hunt down the escaped Merkid leaders. Again, the *Secret History* has Chinggis wax poetic in his orders. "If they sprout wings and fly upward to Heaven, you, Subetei, become a falcon and seize them in mid-air. If they become marmots and claw into the Earth with their nails, you become an iron rod and bore through the Earth to catch them. If they become fish and dive into the depths of the Sea, you, Subetei, become a net, casting yourself over them and dragging them back."[18] The sources do not tell how long the pursuit lasted, but it was ultimately successful.

Warfare of the Mongols

WITH ALL THE MAJOR STEPPE TRIBES defeated and under his control, Chinggis transformed many tribes into one nation. For the Mongols, military training was almost as much a way of life as hunting and tending herds. What was necessary for survival, primarily use of stealth and weaponry, was necessary for warfare.[19] With such a built-in military base, Chinggis did not introduce new tactics, but instead focused on organization and discipline. He maintained the traditional method of dividing up the Mongol forces by tens. The smallest unit was an *arban*. Ten arbans made up a jaghun of 100 men. Ten jaghuns made up a minghan, and ten minghans made up a *tumen* of 10,000. The tumen was the primary striking force. The major commanders in campaigns would be assigned one or more tumens with which to operate, one of which Chinggis would command.

It is at this point that Chinggis altered the nature of steppe society. Survivors of defeated enemies were incorporated into his army by being distributed among the various units. This way, his Mongol faithful oversaw and indoctrinated the new men. Proven warriors such as Subedei were given command of regiments comprising men they themselves had captured. Additionally, Chinggis lessened the potential for an organized revolt from the newly incorporated men by allowing previous tribal attachments to remain only rarely, when Chinggis was positive of their loyalty.[20] This was supplemented with intense discipline; the least violation could be punishable by death. Chinggis also codified and supplemented traditional steppe law to create a new set of established rules, codes, and laws known as the Great Yasa. He incorporated new codes of conduct designed to bury tribal differences. For instance, there would be no more kidnapping of brides, or kidnapping of anyone for slavery. Theft of animals was also banned, and any lost property tht was found had to be returned to its owner.

All of this was formalized at the second major khuriltai, or military council, which convened in 1206. From that date forward there was but one people and one leader. If (as some sources say) he had received the title Chinggis almost two decades earlier, it was confirmed here by Teb Teghri, the shaman closest to Chinggis. Alternatively, the title was bestowed here. Either way, the blessing came from the representative of heaven, the creator god worshiped by the animist Mongols. With this act, what had started as the Mongol tribe was transformed into the Mongol nation. Chinggis took on an almost supernatural reputation, giving his commands a spiritual and almost divine authority.[21]

The army that developed on the steppes consisted exclusively of cavalry. Chinggis's army probably numbered roughly two-thirds light cavalry and one-third heavy. The light troops wore a helmet of bronze or iron with leather flaps protecting the neck and ears. If armor was worn it was lamellar, layers of leather strengthened with pitch and laced together in the same fashion as scale armor. In some cases horses wore similar covering. If no armor was worn, or during travel rather than combat, the traditional long felt jacket or skin coat was worn, with the fur on the inside for insulation. All soldiers wore a silk shirt under their clothes. This was as an aid for tending wounds. If a soldier was struck by an arrow, the silk would wrap itself around the arrowhead as it entered the body. This made removal much easier and less damaging. The heavy cavalry carried a twelve-foot lance, with a hook near the point for unhorsing enemy riders. The Mongols also carried lassoes, in this case long poles with looped rope at the end; there is some discussion as to whether these were used in combat.

All the soldiers carried compound bows, with which they were trained from childhood. Two or three bows were carried, as were two quivers with thirty arrows each. Arrows and arrowheads were designed for different uses: long range, short range, armor piercing, fire arrows, and whistling arrows for signaling. This weapon gave the Mongols their major advantage when campaigning to the west, since nothing in the armies of the Middle East or Europe could match that range: more than 300 meters for the compound bow versus 75 meters for the crossbow. The Welsh longbow was still a century away from being used outside the British Isles. The only drawback to the compound bow was that it could not be used in wet weather.

None of this could have been done without the Mongol horses, a tough breed able to operate over long distances with little food. They were fairly fast, and their speed and endurance were the finishing touch for the well-trained Mongol horseman.[22] The nomadic tribesmen lived much of their lives on horseback, treating their animals almost as extensions of themselves. The horse gave them mobility on a continental scale, for as the steppe grew a limitless store of grass the animals could always eat and the grasslands were the Mongols' highways into what would become their empire.[23] The steppe ponies would look laughably small and scrawny to the European knight, but they provided everything the steppe warrior needed, especially since they traveled on campaign with a string of three or four remounts. The horse's ability to survive on minimally nourishing grass and its resistance to cold made it the perfect mount for long-distance travel over almost any terrain. The animal also provided a source of milk as well as emergency nourishment for its rider in the form of blood.

The primary difference between the Mongol army and that of other steppe nomads was its discipline. Orders were followed immediately and to the letter, or the offender was executed. Acting without orders also brought punishment. Throughout history, one can see a major weakness in victorious armies, especially mounted troops. Many a defeat was snatched from victory when winning troops stopped to loot. Many a cavalry charge pursued the enemy so far away from the battlefield that they made themselves useless when needed. Neither of these things occurred in the Mongol armies. Chinggis realized, as few commanders have, that stopping to plunder is pointless. There was always plenty of time after the victory for that, and an equitable distribution of spoils made getting an early start in the looting just as pointless.

Other than the normal weapons training, the army trained annually in the autumn hunt, or *nerge*. Thousands of men would deploy in a massive circle, moving one way or another in response to signal flags. Once in place, they would all ride toward the center, herding all living creatures before them. Allowing an animal to escape, or killing it before the order, meant punishment. Once the circle was sufficiently small, Chinggis would take the first shot and then the slaughter would begin. This not only provided a huge store of supplies for the population, it simulated battle, just as Roman army training was described as bloodless war and war as bloody training. In his discussion of the Asian nomads, Edward Gibbon describes the hunt as "the image and as the school of war. . . . They acquire the habit of directing their eye, and their steps, to a remote object; of preserving their intervals; of suspending, or accelerating, their pace, according to the motions of the troops on their right and left; and of watching and repeating the signals of their leaders. Their leaders study, in this practical school, the most important lesson of military art: the prompt and accurate judgment of ground, of distance, and of time."[24] Although the mass hunt was not peculiar to the Mongols, Chinggis seems to have perfected it as a training operation. It seems to be one of the main reasons why the Mongol were able to engage in such organized and effective campaigning.[25] Other than the hunt, the Mongols developed sixteen tactical maneuvers that they used to defeat enemy after enemy. A few examples are listed here:

WEARING DOWN TACTIC. IF the enemy is entrenched behind a palisade that makes a cavalry charge impossible, leave a few units to keep an eye on the enemy and maintain harassment. When the enemy has to break camp to secure new supplies of food and water, then strike. In what was called the "dog fight" tactic, the Mongols feigned a withdrawal, leaving behind much of their equipment and supplies as if they had fled in haste. The city officials would send soldiers out to gather up the booty, which quickly clogged the open city gates with carts. With the soldiers on the open field, and the city gates opened, the Mongols returned and raced through the open doors to capture the city.[26]

Luring into Ambush. This is the trademark steppe tactic, the feigned retreat. Nobody did it better than the Mongols. In his work *How Wars Are Won*, Bevin Alexander writes, "They created a special unit, the *mangudai*, that would charge the enemy alone. . . . All light cavalry learned this technique, so if a large mangudai was needed, it could be formed quickly. As had happened for a millennium and a half, unsuspecting enemy units would usually be convinced that they were on the verge of victory, and would spring after the fleeing Mongols. Unseen in the rear, Mongol archers waited."[27]

Lightning and Surprise Attacks. The surprise attack is self-explanatory, but it was often a result of the "lightning" attack, which came by covering great distances more quickly than the opponent expected. The emphasis therefore was on speed to the engagement and speed in the assault. A Mongol army, being lighter in weight, could move faster from the mobilization point to the logistics base, thereby reducing the enemy's reaction time. In what was an incredible feat not matched until the introduction of railroads, a Mongol army could move as much as 600 miles in five days.[28]

Bush Clump (or Moving Bush) Tactic. This is a variation on what was called the "crow soldier" or "scattered star" tactic, the Mongols' primary method of harassment. It was usually used at night or on days with poor visibility and involved small units harassing the enemy but without the intent to encircle. It was perfect for keeping an enemy on edge.[29]

ANOTHER UNIT CHINGGIS EXPANDED was his personal guard. Originally a few hundred, it came to number 10,000. This served multiple purposes. It was the bureaucracy that ran the ever-expanding empire. It also contained elite troops Chinggis would command in battle. It further served as something like a staff school. All of Chinggis's commanders were in this personal guard and all young men with promise were brought in for training. He also kept hostages of captured leaders here, both to keep an eye on them and to indoctrinate them into the new Mongol system. Chinggis's intelligence staff also composed part of the guard, another aspect that distinguished him as a commander. Sometimes a year in advance he would send out spies to gather and disseminate disinformation. He closely questioned travelers and merchants, and had maps made during reconnoitering. When his army went on campaign it was better prepared than any military of its day.

Conquests

LITTLE IS WRITTEN ABOUT CHINGGIS'S actual role in combat, but plenty of evidence shows his ability as a master of both strategy and grand strategy. This is yet another difference between him and any previous steppe leader, with the possible exception of Attila almost a millennium before. Chinggis not only had big dreams for his people; he saw the larger picture as well. His invasions were only undertaken with an eye to security. First, in the wake of the 1206 khuriltai and the army and social reorganization, he mopped up any remaining pockets of resistance on the steppes. Some leaders of defeated tribes were able to escape and even reestablish themselves elsewhere, but he knew where they were and would get to them in his own time.

Second, he began preparations to take on the major power on the continent, China. Luckily for him there were two rival dynasties, the Chin in the north and the Sung in the south, so he could assume the assistance of one against the other. In order to completely secure his base, however, he needed to neutralize a third, relatively minor power in western China, the state of Hsi-hsia. It was the home of an erstwhile steppe tribe, the Tanguts, who had settled into a sedentary lifestyle. They still maintained a credible army based on cavalry, but had also built walled cities on which to base their national defense. Chinggis needed to secure his right flank before invading China proper. Chinggis managed to overrun the countryside in two campaigns (1205–7 and 1209), but he could not capture the major walled cities as he had no siege weapons.[30] He did, however, sufficiently impress the ruling family with his abilities that they signed a treaty swearing vassalage, sealing it with a dynastic marriage between Chinggis and the king's daughter. Hsi-hsia promised to provide troops upon request any time Chinggis needed them.

By 1211 Chinggis was prepared to invade China. The Chin emperor (to whom Chinggis was technically a vassal since his days allied to Togoril, or Ong Khan) had recently died, creating in the capital city the typical disorder that comes with a change of leadership. Further, the ruling dynasty was made up of Jurchens, also former steppe peoples, not ethnic Chinese and therefore unpopular with the citizenry. All this worked in Chinggis's favor, even though he faced an army much larger than his own, perhaps 120,000 cavalry and 500,000 infantry (though it was scattered across the empire). Chinggis probably entered China with 65,000 men. He picked up more manpower with a defection by some of the border Onggud tribesmen and a revolt of the Khitans from the region of Manchuria. Chinggis's first goal was to control the frontier along the Great Wall. The second goal was to conquer southern Manchuria and its tribal population. Subedei, though subordinate to fellow commander Jebe's command during the first years of the China campaign, was involved in achieving both goals. It is said that Subedei made a name for himself as the first man to scale the walls of the city of Huan-chou, a strategic city on the frontier.[31]

Hard fighting followed, for the Chinese army possessed talent and training, but more defections weakened the Chin leadership until finally the Mongols laid siege to the capital at Chung-tu, modern Beijing. Although he had earlier refused to parlay, Chinggis did now, in 1214, since his troops were beginning to suffer from disease and the walled city still resisted him. A treaty was signed with another new emperor, but when he established a new capital further south, Chinggis took that as a sign the Chin were trying to regroup, so the war picked up again in 1214. This time Chung-tu was captured.

The primary lesson learned in this first war against China was that the Mongols needed siege equipment. Chinggis thus began to hire or draft Chinese (and later Persian) engineers to fill that need. As a leader, Chinggis had a firm grasp of reality, and valued innovation over tradition. He had no mania to preserve the old ways if new methods were necessary. From captured Uighers he adopted the practice of writing, in order to modernize his population and to facilitate administration. He embraced the concept of new weaponry when siege engines were necessary, and he incorporated nonsteppe peoples into his army and even his ruling council just as he had done with defeated tribesmen.

Chinggis left troops in Chin territory to keep an eye on things while he returned to Mongolia to suppress some uprisings. During this period he had made contact with Shah Muhammad II of Khwarezm, recent conqueror of an area encompassing territory from the Persian Gulf to modern Kazakhstan, north of the Caspian and Aral Seas. Chinggis had hoped to not only maintain a passive presence to the rear while he dealt with the Chin but also reopen the Silk Road for income for his nascent empire. After initially positive relations between the two leaders, the shah altered his attitude. Fearing that Mongol traders were actually on spy missions, he agreed to a subordinate's plan to slaughter an entire caravan. Chinggis, not surprisingly, demanded compensation as well as the head of the transgressing subordinate, the governor of the city of Utrar. The shah had killed or humiliated three Mongol ambassadors, which for Chinggis was tantamount to a declaration of war. He tolerated national insults no more than he did personal ones.

Before he could punish Shah Muhammed for his crimes, however, he had to secure his flanks. This involved suppressing two old enemies. Kuchlug of the Naimans had escaped his tribe's major defeat and fled to Kara Khitai, bordering Khwarezm to the northeast. There he married the king's daughter in 1208, and usurped the throne in 1210. He proceeded to oppress the mainly Muslim population. He was technically in league with the shah (who had helped him in his seizure of power) but there was more distrust than friendship. Chinggis could not mount an invasion of Khwarezm with Kara Khitai under hostile control on his left flank. There were also some reorganized Merkids just north of the Syr Darya (Jaxartes) River who could prove troublesome. Chinggis sent two of his Dogs, Jebe and Subedei, to handle the situation. Jebe was assigned to defeat Kuchlug while Subedei went with Chinggis's son Jochi to deal with the Merkids. Both were ultimately successful.

Like the Chin Empire, that of Khwarezm suffered internal leadership problems. Muhammad II was a minority ruler who inherited much of his empire from his conqueror father. Real power rested with the army, made up of primarily Turkish troops with no ties to the Persian, Afghan, and other peoples of the empire. Muhammad was at odds with his mother, an aristocrat with strong ties to the military leaders. She was a power not only behind the throne but often in opposition to it. The internal disorder benefitted Chinggis, who hoped the Khwarezm population would look

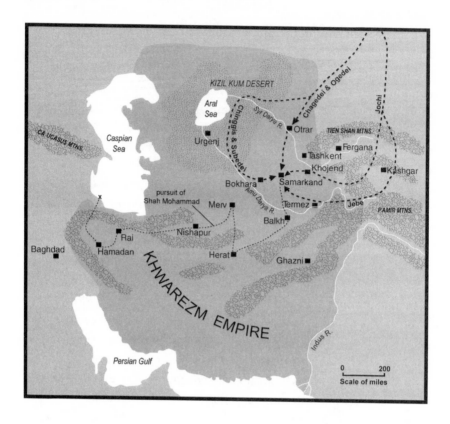

on him as a liberator rather than conqueror. This was supported by his well-known policy of allowing complete religious freedom. Thus, though the defenders of Khwarezm vastly outnumbered the Mongols, they lacked sufficient unity and motivation.

Muhammad dispersed his army across a broad front along the Amu Darya frontier in a cordon defense based on a number of walled cities. His son and chief commander, Jalal-al-Din, proposed a concentration of troops forward, along the Syr Darya, to meet the Mongols at the end of their march, when they would be tired. Given the Mongol plan, Jalal-al-Din (had he won his initial battle) might have been able to defeat the Mongol attacks one by one. It was not to be. No one else was willing to bet everything on a single battle in the open. Muhammad also had to disperse his troops to maintain order over a disaffected, heavily taxed population.

The invasion of Khwarezm was the textbook version of Outflanking Tactic B, the strategic flanking movement. Early in the year 1220 Chinggis deployed his main force of 30,000 (under two sons, Ogedei and

Chagedei) in the center to focus the Khwarezmian army's attention and give the impression that the cordon defense would work. Their job was to capture Otrar and punish the offending governor who provoked the war initially, then work southeastward toward the capital city of Samarkand. Meanwhile, Chinggis's son Jochi with three tumens would take his forces southward from Kara Khitai into the mountains, through the passes into the Fergana River valley, in order to threaten the eastern end of the Khwarezmian line. Jebe took a small force even farther southward before turning west down the Amu Darya toward Samarkand. Chinggis took the third part of the army (another 30,000) along with Subedei farther to the west, where it disappeared unnoticed and captured the Turkoman city of Zarnuk, for the sole purpose of contacting a man who knew a chain of water oases through the Kyzyl Kum desert.[32]

With Muhammad focused on three forces approaching his capital from the northwest, east, and southeast, he was shocked when Chinggis and Subedei emerged from the desert in April and appeared before the city of Bokhara, a hundred miles west of Samarkand. Not only was he threatened from yet another direction, but any hope of support from the west was now impossible. Muhammad gave a few more orders for troop deployment, then fled southward for his life. The rest of the campaign was a series of successful sieges of those cities that resisted and peaceful occupations of those that did not. In a matter of months, Chinggis virtually destroyed a kingdom, almost entirely by the use of strategic moves that left the defenders unable to respond. At every decisive point, surprise permitted him to assemble locally superior forces, though his overall strength was less than Mohammed's.[33] Just as importantly, Chinggis possessed what no other nomad army ever had: siege equipment. The ability either to fight in the open or successfully conduct sieges negated Muhammad's strategy. Jalal-al-Din tried to rally forces in Afghanistan and remained a threat for several years, but he died in Kurdistan in 1231, virtually alone.

Chinggis concentrated his center of gravity more rapidly than the Khwarezmians. The Mongols threw the effects of their superior mobility upon the most decisive points in the kingdom, and each operation in the campaign set up follow-on operations that helped the Mongols destroy Khwarezm's ability to fight.[34] By spreading out his army, necessary though it may have been, Muhammad allowed the Mongols to gain local superiority at each city they attacked. The fact that no city held out for more than a few weeks meant that even had the Khwarezmians desired to send reinforcements, they had no time to do so.

What is remarkable about the operation is the four-prong attack, with each prong moving in complete isolation from the others, knowing what to do in advance without having to maintain contact between the prongs.[35] Liddell Hart observes: "In these brilliantly conceived and harmoniously executed operations we see each of the principles of war—direction, mobility, security, concentration, and surprise—woven into a Nemesis-like web in which are trapped the doomed armies of the Shah."[36] Some sources say the invasion was planned by Subedei, others by Chinggis. Either way, it proved that Chinggis had developed both the tactical methods to win battles and the strategic vision to win wars. Subedei took what Chinggis had created and implemented it in operations where he was far away from any supervision, where his own vision and battlefield acumen would be demonstrated.

Subedei and Jebe were given the task of pursuing Muhammad, to kill him or bring him back to Chinggis. After a lengthy chase, Muhammad escaped to a small island near the south coast of the Caspian, where he died sometime between December 1220 and February 1221. Having traveled a great distance already, Subedei then suggested a remarkable feat, which was approved: an exploratory mission to continue on east and then northward around the Caspian Sea, through the Caucasus Mountains, and into the region of the Kipchak nomads. There they would link up with Chinggis's son Jochi, who would explore westward from Khwarezm.[37] Chinggis thus sent the two Dogs on what came to be called the Great Raid, a two-year reconnaissance around the Caspian Sea, over to the upper shores of the Black Sea, and back home to report.

Eastern European Warfare

CHINGGIS FELT SUFFICIENTLY COMFORTABLE with his Asian conquests to begin to think about expeditions westward, to Russia and eastern Europe. In the thirteenth century Russia was a collection of principalities with little or no mutual loyalties. Owing to their position on the frontier between Europe and Asia, their military exhibited characteristics of both cultures. As did the Europeans, they based leadership on aristocracy that fought as heavy cavalry. Byzantine influence remained dominant until the early thirteenth century, with the Russian cavalry equipped with straight sword, bow, mail cloak, segmented helmet, and large, round shield.[38] The aristocracy kept bodyguards (*druzhina*) also made up of cavalry, in units that could number as high as 5,000. The older veterans of the bodyguard were lancers, the younger troops were light cavalry archers. Units consisted of 100 and 1,000 men drawn from urban militia and a general levy called the *smerd*, something like the *fyrd* of England. The prince's armory or that of the city supplied arms and armor. Most principalities also had auxiliary horse archers made up of steppe tribes that had drifted or been driven westward.

Russian forces deployed normally in five sections: vanguard, center, and rear units flanked by cavalry. The smerd were often placed in the center, supported by foot archers shooting from behind shields. Their bows were made of wood and cedar and were about six feet tall. Heavy and light spears were both produced, the lighter ones probably used as javelins. Those with swords carried a straight, double-edged blade modeled on the western European pattern. The aristocrats also used maces, battle-axes, or war hammers. Body armor was *kolchuga* (chain mail), scale mail, or lamellar. The helmet included a half mask or full mask with eye slits and breathing holes.

In eastern Europe the Hungarian royal household, much like the Russians, was now conspicuously modeled on those of the country's western neighbors. The Hungarians, however, depended a bit more heavily on light cavalry made up from nomadic steppe warriors.[39] Steppe nomads had been moving into the region of Hungary ever since the fifth century, when it was settled by the remains of Attila's Huns. The Hungarians tried to emulate western European warfare, but could not always adapt it to the talents of their migrant populations; the elite of society trained in western modes of warfare may have formed a majority of heavy cavalry by the end of the twelfth century.[40] The light cavalry retained its steppe weaponry and wore little or no armor. The heavy cavalry would charge with lances made of ash about ten feet in length. There was not, however, much in the way of finesse in the European heavy cavalry; they relied on straightforward power and little else in the way of tactics.[41]

Infantry was playing an increasingly important role in western Europe, especially with the development of crossbows, but in eastern Europe they played only minor roles, with little contemporary descriptions of their tactics available. With the dependence on heavy cavalry, there was little impetus to train or even pay much attention to the peasant infantry. Thus, when combat occurred there was no coordination between the two arms.[42] Finally, because their armies were based on the feudal system, the Europeans had a major drawback in the fact that vassals were required for only a set number of days per year. This proved disastrous when fighting the Mongols, who campaigned year-round.[43]

The Great Raid and the Battle of the Kalka River

SUBEDEI AND JEBE MUST HAVE STARTED OUT the Great Raid with at least some siege equipment, because they captured a number of cities in late 1220 while awaiting Muhammad's death. Many cities failed to learn from the experiences of the cities farther east that surrender meant survival, resistance meant slaughter. As the Great Raid was a reconnaissance in force, there was no real attempt to conquer, but merely to gain what supplies were necessary by intimidation or pillage. Subedei and Jebe led two tumens northwestward into what is today Azerbaijan and Georgia, and after gaining some supplies from the governor of Tabriz, they spent the beginning of 1221 on the Moghan steppe where the Kura and Araxes Rivers empty into the Caspian. They passed the time in a mild January expanding their forces with local Kurdish volunteers.

In the spring they made their way up the Kura valley toward Tiflis (Tblisi). The Georgians had an army of some repute, supplemented with a large contingent of Kipchak cavalry. King George III (the Brilliant, or the Resplendent) led a force out to confront the Mongols as they entered Georgian land. Numbers vary wildly concerning the Georgian army, anywhere from 10,000 to 70,000 including 30,000 Kipchaks; regardless, they were no match for Chinggis's Top Dogs. Jebe's feigned retreat worked to perfection, and Subedei's ambush and Jebe's counterattack broke the Georgian army. A similar battle and defeat occurred a few months later, and then the Mongols were gone, pushing north for more information. They extorted supplies and mountain guides from the shah of Shirvan in Derbend, then crossed the Caucasus Mountains in the winter. Guides led the forces through a circuitous route while, on the far side of the mountains, a Kipchak force with multiple tribal allies awaited their emergence. Unable to withdraw or break through the 50,000-man force facing them,

Subedei split his enemy by bribing the Kipchaks to leave. He then slaughtered the remaining forces, after which he followed up the Kipchaks and defeated them, fetching back his bribe.

Now in the spring of 1222, the Mongols scouted southern Russia and turned west. Jebe took his tumen to explore up the Don River while Subedei took his along the north shore of the Black Sea to the Crimea. There he encountered some Venetians, people as expert in trade as the Mongols were in warfare. They made a deal: the Venetians would make detailed reports of economic strength and military movements in the countries that they visited and spread Mongol propaganda, while in return the Mongols would trade solely with the Venetians and destroy any rival trading posts.[44] Subedei made good on his agreement, pillaging and wiping out two Genoese trading posts in the Crimea as he departed to rejoin Jebe. The two rode west in late 1222, across the Dnieper to the Dniester on the far northwest corner of the Black Sea. Mongol scouts brought in prisoners for interrogation, with interpretation via Chinese scholars who specialized in learning languages. The Mongols also gathered information on the economic geography of the region, as well as its people's military abilities. When they were satisfied with their information and their loot, Subedei and Jebe headed north.[45]

The Kipchaks had scattered after their last encounter with the Mongols. Some fled north, others west. One chieftain, Khotian, was father-in-law to a Russian nobleman, Mstislav the Daring of Galicia. Khotian convinced him of the Mongol threat and managed to gain some cooperation from other nobles, all of whom brought their troops to the west bank of the Dnieper in the spring of 1223. As the Russians were gathering across the river on the western bank, the Mongol scouts reported that the Kipchaks (known to the Russians as the Polovets) were also gathering further north in order to join with the Russian forces. Subedei sent envoys to the Russians saying he had no cause to fight them, only the Kipchaks. Knowing absolutely nothing of the Mongols, the Russians killed the ambassadors.

Seeing an overwhelming number in opposition, and knowing that Jochi and a few more tumens were supposed to be advancing from the Caspian region, Subedei and Jebe decided it would be best to retreat toward their reinforcements. (They soon learned Jochi was not coming.) They left a minghan behind to keep an eye on the Russians congregating on the island of Khortitsa in the middle of the Dnieper. While the Russian forces approached as many as 80,000 men (again, historians vary in their guesses from 30, 000 to 90,000), with an unknown number of Kipchaks on the way, the army's major failing was a lack of leadership or, more correctly, too much leadership. As is the nature of nobles, it was difficult to decide who was in charge, Msistislav ("the Daring") of Galicia or Msistislav of Kiev. Thus, there was no coordination of strategy.[46]

Mstislav the Daring lived up to his name by leading an amphibious landing of 10,000 men on the eastern bank and engaging the Mongol rear guard, which they soon wiped out. With this initial success, the other Russian princes hurried to battle to avoid being left out of the glory and loot. The remainder of the Mongol force was in sight, so the chase was on. It lasted for nine days. With no command coordination, the various Russian units spread across the countryside, jockeying for position to engage the retreating Mongols. Even the Kipchaks who had caught up to the Russians, and who should have known better, believed

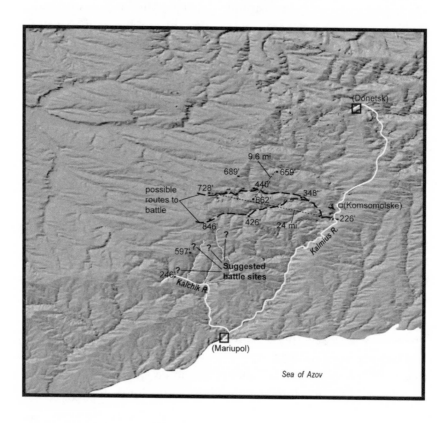

that Subedei and Jebe were in retreat. Mongol tactics were not a secret in the thirteenth century, especially to other nomads, but they frequently worked anyway.[47]

No one knows the route of withdrawal or the exact site of the battle that ensued. The land to the east of the Dnieper rises gradually for about a hundred miles, with small east-west valleys along the way. One of the main questions surrounds references to the rivers called the Kalmius and the Kalka, which may actually have been the same.[48] This river flows into the Sea of Azov at modern Mariupol. Approaching from the west, within twenty to thirty miles of the Kalmius the ground becomes much more hilly and broken. While none of the terrain is impassable (it's primarily farm and pastureland today), only a couple of valleys lead fairly directly to the Kalmius; they emerge into the river valley near modern Komomols-koye, about forty-five air miles upriver from its mouth at Mariupol. In his book on the Mongols, Leo de Hartog writes that the Kipchaks and Gali-cians crossed "the little Kalka River, which flows into the Sea of Azov."[49] The Kalmius flows into the Sea of Azov, but the modern Kalka River does not. Some historians suggest that the battle site is at the modern Kalka River, running north-south on the western side of the broken terrain mentioned above, which feeds into the Little Kalchik and then into the Kalchik. Others suggest not the Kalmius but the Kalchik as the Kalka River, but the terrain makes this questionable. The Kalchik runs mainly northwest-southeast, making it more of an avenue down which the Mongols would have withdrawn rather than a river near which to make a stand. Further, the right bank is much steeper than the left, so staging an ambush after a river crossing would be difficult. The Kalchik empties into the Kalmius within the city of Mariupol.

I favor the Kalmius site as the Kalka River of old. The river on the western side of the broken ground would provide something of an ambush spot for the Mongols, certainly; however, given the terrain approaching that site from the west the attackers could approach the spot along a relatively wide front. By placing the ambush on the Kalmius, the pursuers would be obliged to enter through one of two valleys, thus narrowing their front and being a more likely location for successive waves of Russians to ride up on each others' backs and create the confusion described in the accounts of the battle. After the Mongols had retreated for nine days, another few miles would not have made any difference in

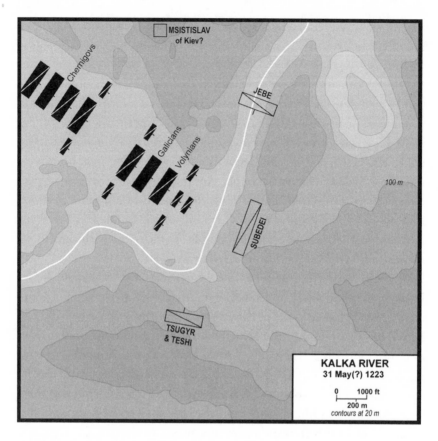

KALKA RIVER
31 May(?) 1223

0   1000 ft
200 m
contours at 20 m

the fatigue or readiness of the troops, and given the Mongol expertise in ambushes a narrower front makes sense.

The date of the action is disputed, but 31 May 1223 is generally accepted. Descriptions of the battle are very sketchy and in many places contradictory. The lead units seem to have been those of Mstislav of Galicia and his father-in-law's Kipchaks (also known as Cumans as well as Polovets). When the Galicians crossed the Kalka, they found the Mongols had faced about. It would have been easy for Mongol units to have deployed upstream and downstream. Some descriptions begin with the Mongols stopping before the river, then turning on the Russian-Kipchak force with light cavalry archers firing through smoke the Mongols had created with firepots. This divided the Kipchaks from the Russians, and the Mongol heavy cavalry drove a wedge between the two, forcing a Kipchak rout. The initial units had been closely followed by those from Volynia and Kursk, with Mstislav of Kiev bringing up the rear. They could not deploy with the Kipchaks fleeing through them, so the Mongols were soon sur-rounding the troops from Volynia and Kursk. The survivors fled all the way back to the Dnieper, stragglers being picked off the whole time. At the Dnieper, Mstislav of Kiev defended a fortified hilltop for three days until finally surrendering on a false promise of clemency.

In another description, the Kipchaks arrived first. As they were pri-marily light cavalry, they would have outdistanced their heavy-cavalry allies. The Russians came in close behind, however, followed by the infantry and the baggage train.[50] They were met by the Mongol heavy cavalry with their lances and swords, which drove the Kipchaks into a rapid retreat right into Mstislav's Galicians. If the Mongol heavy cavalry were the first into action, that would be an exception to their standard practice of softening up the enemy with arrow fire. The Russians' disor-ganization would have made it impossible for the pursuers to prepare for a concerted, hand-to-hand assault. The Kipchaks broke, followed by the now disordered Galicians, all of which continued to disrupt other units arriving on the scene. Only Mstislav of Kiev had the time and presence of mind to laager his wagons, which they turned in to a slow-moving fort to protect their retreat as the rest of the army made a mad dash westward.[51]

Another account also describes the action on the east side of the river. The Mongols had a rear guard maintaining contact with the pursuers, while Subedei divided the bulk of his army in three sections: himself in the center, Jebe to the right, and the left flank (including some 5,000 Brodniki tribesmen) commanded by Princes Tsugyr and Teshi. The Russian force advanced with the Kipchaks in front followed by Danill Romanovich and the army of Volynia. Mstislav of Galicia was next, forces from Chernigov and Kursk behind him, with the Kievans last in line.

The Kipchaks and Prince Danill's troops crossed the river and the cav-alrymen continued to ride, rather than form up for a concerted action. Mstislav's Galicians were just across the river when the Mongol heavy cavalry struck and broke the Kipchaks. The ensuing jumble of troops thus included Kipchaks, Volynians, and Galicians, all being forced back into the Chernigov cavalry, in the middle of the river. The Mongol wings joined in, striking Russian troops on both sides of the river. When Mstislav of Kiev came in sight of the melee, he ordered his men to circle the wagons on a nearby hilltop. Subedei ordered the princes of the left wing to surround and pressure the Kievans while he and Jebe pursued the forces in retreat.

Given the possible rivers, terrain, and traditional Mongol tactics, the Kalmius of today as the Kalka seems the best location. By taking their stand on the eastern side of the hill country, the Mongols would channel the pursuing Russians into a valley, albeit a wide one. Emerging from the valley at speed, there would be even less time and space for Russian redeployment. The Mongol rear guard, leading them through the valley, could easily become the vanguard upon emerging and joining the main force already deployed on the eastern side of the river. This would also give much more cover to the flanking units than they would have gotten at the river on the western side of the hills. This also means that the retreat would have had to go back up the valley before the various units fled straight for the Dnieper or scattered to their various homelands. Had the battle taken place on relatively open ground to the west as some suggest, the Mongol wings almost certainly would have spread out farther and not allowed any retreat, as occurred later at the Sajo River in Hungary. Fighting in narrower confines east of the hills would make the huge encirclement impossible, but Subedei probably would have assumed a large enough enemy casualty count at the river to make the pursuit of survivors fairly easy.

But what of Mstislav of Kiev? Many sources describe a slow retreat within a moving wagon laager. However, de Hartog gives a different description: "Watching from the western bank of the Kalka [he] could, or would, do nothing to help his namesake. After the prince of Galich's [Galicia's] defeat the prince of Kiev realized that a retreat would be fatal before an enemy who reacted so quickly. He therefore entrenched himself on a dominating hilltop, but before he could complete his defences Jebe and Subedei attacked."[52] The *Novgorod Chronicle* says that Mstislav "never moved at all from his position; for he had taken stand on a hill above the river Kalka, and the place was stony, and he set up a stockade of posts about him and fought with them from out of this stockade for three days."[53] He would be much more likely to find a stony prominence on the Kalmius side of the hills than on the western side.

The battle at the Kalka River was a masterful piece of maneuver on Subedei's part. Movement to contact (retrograde movement, in this case) for a meeting engagement is the best description of how this battle came to be. When the chosen ground was reached, Subedei engaged in a deliberate attack, defined as a fully synchronized operation that employs the effects of every available asset against the enemy. All the characteristics of the offense were employed, most especially concentration: massing effects without massing large formations, manipulating their own and the enemy's forces by some combination of dispersion, concentration, deception, and attack, or in this case, all of the above. Subedei controlled the tempo for nine days, keeping just enough Mongols in view of the Russian advance guard to maintain contact without bringing on a general engagement until the time and position was right. Finally, Subedei displayed audacity, necessary to negate the disadvantages of numerical inferiority.

Once the Kipchaks and Russians stopped their attack and made for the rear, the Mongol exploitation was immediate, never giving anyone except the rearmost (now the foremost in the retreat) units any time to make a stand or organize for combat. The Mongols undertook pursuit for the hundred miles back to the Dnieper, when Russian forces were either able to escape downriver or were killed in the chase. Meanwhile, the Mongols maintained the necessary force to keep pressure on the Kievan defensive position until it was obliged to surrender. If, indeed, the battle was fought west of the hill country, then the Mongols missed a golden opportunity to forgo the pursuit since the terrain was perfect for a nerge-style encirclement. The *Novgorod Chronicle* reports that after the battle, only one man in ten returned home. Since this is a phrase used multiple times in the work, it probably was just a euphemism for massive casualties; a nerge would have made sure no one returned home.

Aftermath

SUBEDEI AND JEBE ENGAGED IN RANDOM ACTS of destruction to reinforce the lesson of the Russian defeat on the local population, then moved homeward in response to orders to link up with Chinggis's son Jochi in the region above the Aral Sea. They met on the Volga and moved upriver to engage the Volga Bulgars, but instead were ambushed themselves by the Bulgars and obliged to retreat, the only defeat of the entire Great Raid. As the army approached the outer limits of the old homeland, Jebe contracted a fever and died. Jochi and Subedei joined Chinggis a few days later on the Irtysh River and, after telling the story of their experiences, they headed for home, leaving occupation forces in the captured territories. Upon returning, Subedei requested that Chinggis allow him to recruit an army of defeated steppe peoples to garrison outposts on the western frontier; Chinggis agreed. This may well be the first instance in Russia of the Mongol *tamma*, a structure that was both a nomadic garrison force and the nucleus of a regional tribal federation in conquered territories.[54]

In 1226, Chinggis began another campaign against the Tanguts of Hsi-Hsia. They had reneged on their promise to provide troops for the Khwarezm campaign and, as usual, Chinggis had no toleration for disloyalty. This time the nation was entirely subdued, not just turned to vassalage, but during the campaign Chinggis fell from his horse. Recovery was slow, but he continued to command troops in another war against the Chin Dynasty. A lifetime of activity came to an end in 1227, when Chinggis died around age sixty-five. His eldest son, Jochi, had died a few months earlier. Just before the Khwarezm campaign, Chinggis had named his number three son, Ogedei, to succeed him. Ogedei was not a great general but could mediate between his more aggressive brothers. Further, the naming and acceptance of the successor continued the existence and growth of the empire. Chinggis managed to set up an empire that long survived him, a virtually singular action in the annals of nomadic peoples. His incorporation of tribes into one population proved the key, and the traditions he established remained for generations.[55]

Invasion of Europe and the Battle of Mohi (Sajo River)

IN 1230, OGEDEI SENT THREE TUMENS to suppress the rejuvenated Jalal-al-Din in southern Khwarezm. In that same year the offensive was renewed against the Chin. When the Mongols met some unexpected early setbacks, Subedei was given command and ordered to capture the Chin capital at Kaifeng. During 1232 Ogedei and his brother Tolui both became extremely ill, probably through an excessive intake of alcohol. Subedei thus operated independently, negotiating an agreement with the Sung Dynasty in southern China to assist against the Chin. The allied force finally took Kaifeng and, in 1233, Subedei left a governor and went home. The Sung quickly swallowed up lands along their northern border, including Kaifeng, where they killed Subedei's governor. The Mongol frontiers were not completely secure.

Within a decade of Chinggis's death, Ogedei had run through much of the empire's wealth. In spite of all the pillage and loot gathered during Chinggis's reign, the cost of building a capital city at Karakorum, maintaining an ever-growing administration, and supplying Ogedei's alcohol needs had proven extremely expensive. Taxes and tribute were not enough; more conquest and pillage was necessary. At a khuriltai in 1235, various proposals were entertained. Subedei, now the senior general, convinced the sons and grandsons of Chinggis to think big. Subedei proposed to launch two major invasions in completely opposite directions, striking both eastern and western frontiers: China and eastern Europe. Chinggis himself would hardly have dreamed bigger.[56] Merchants, scouts, and spies had all confirmed that European kings, princes, and popes were still too busy fighting among themselves to coordinate any serious effort against the Mongol armies.

With Batu, a direct descendant of Chinggis, officially in command, the expedition left in the fall of 1235. Ogedei gave them a core of veterans and instructions to pick up more men on the frontier by whatever means necessary. The tamma (frontier garrisons) Subedei had organized on the frontier after the Great Raid certainly came into play at this point as a way to enlarge his army quickly. By the following spring Subedei and Batu led 50,000 Mongols, 20,000 conscripts, and several corps of Chinese and Persian engineers. Ten princes joined the expedition.[57] First, the various Russian principalities would need to be conquered, and then the invasion of eastern Europe could begin.

The opening offensive was launched in two prongs: Subedei and Batu led their forces to the city of Bulgar, at the junction of the Volga and Kama Rivers, while Princes Mangu and Budjek cleared out the steppes of the lower Volga, killing or capturing what eastern Kipchaks remained in the region. A handful fled farther west to offer their services to the Hungarian king, Bela, while the survivors were incorporated into the Mongol army or sold as slaves. The summer and fall of 1236 were spent training the new recruits in Mongol tactics. In December, with the army now numbering at least 120,000 and possibly as many as 200,000, the invasion continued, aided by the frozen rivers acting as highways for Mongol horses. One after another the Russian cities fell. In early 1238 the army divided into two prongs. The first, under one of Subedei's subordinates, fought and defeated Grand Duke Vladimir 120 miles north of

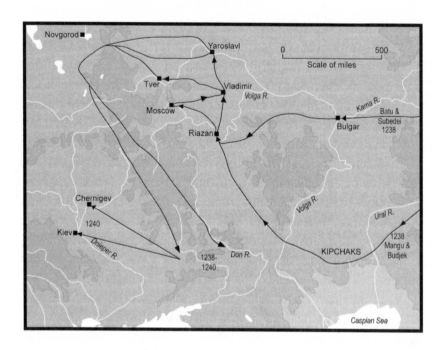

Moscow. The second prong, with Subedei and Batu at the head, drove on Novgorod.[58] Novgorod was saved by lucky timing: the spring thaws made travel virtually impossible, so the Mongols turned south.

From the summer of 1238 to the spring of 1240 the Mongols ceased their conquests and camped on the southern Russian steppes. In spite of their string of victories, they had suffered enough casualties that they needed some reinforcements and perhaps more time to fully integrate the captured Kipchaks. In early summer 1240, however, they were on the move again, capturing and destroying Pereiaslav and Chernigov before arriving at Russia's major city, Kiev, in November. The Mongols were so impressed with the city's beauty that they offered, as at so many other cities, peace for submission and tribute. As happened so often before, the Mongol emissaries were killed. The decision to do so came from Prince Danil, who had succeeded Mstislav the Brave of Galicia, and so should have known what the Mongol response would be.

Every other city the Mongols had taken on this campaign had boasted no better defenses than wooden walls, allowing siege engines and fire to make short work of them. Though Kiev had some stone walls, the attack focused on the weakest section, the Polish Gate, and this siege likewise lasted no more than a few days. With the northern Russian principalities and the southern steppe subdued, the Mongols headed west from Kiev for Europe.

Subedei divided the army into two expeditionary forces. His intelligence gathering had informed him of the potential forces opposed to him if the Europeans were allowed to mass. Subedei knew that King Bela of Hungary was related by blood or marriage to Polish dukes, a German duke, and the king of Bohemia. The territories abutted each other and could be expected to work together. Thus, with Hungary the primary target, the other three had to be kept busy while Subedei did his work.[59] Princes Baidar and Kaidu led two tumens (some sources say three) into Poland.[60] Their job was to create sufficient havoc with Polish armies that German and Bohemian forces would either march to assist the Poles or stay home to protect their own lands. All this was designed to protect the strategic right flank of the main Mongol thrust into Hungary.

Batu and most of the princes would force the Carpathian passes due east of the ultimate targets of Buda and Pest. Prince Kuyuk would swing farthest to cross the southernmost Carpathian passes through Transylvania, engaging what armies he could find in the south. Most authors place Subedei in the center with Batu, but a contemporary reference mentions a Mongol general in the south identified as Bogutai, which many seem to think was a variant on "Baghatur," Subedei's nickname, meaning brave or valiant. He probably led a column through the mountains on Batu's left flank then marched north to join the primary attack at the Hungarian capital cities. These moves were to be started in the dead of winter, when the snow would be the most packed and easiest for the Mongol ponies to traverse. It also would surprise the Hungarians, as European warfare was always undertaken in warmer weather. Thirty thousand garrison and line-of-communication troops had been left in Russia, so the European invasion force numbered between 100,000 and 120,000.

In Hungary, King Bela IV was planning as thorough a defense as he could. Unfortunately, he received little cooperation. Europe's two major armies, that of the Holy Roman emperor, Frederick Hohenstauffen, and that of the pope, were so busy preparing for war against each other they could not spare any time or resources for Bela. Things were little better within Hungary itself. Forty thousand Kipchak/Cuman warriors had appeared before Bela, led by King Khotian. Fleeing the Mongols, Khotian

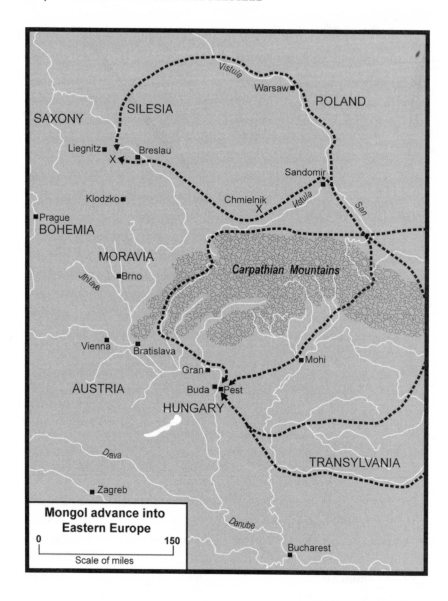

Mongol advance into
Eastern Europe

0   150

Scale of miles

offered his services to Hungary in hopes of saving himself and his troops. Bela jumped at the chance to expand his force with veterans of warfare against the Mongols, but to ease the hostility of the nobility he obliged the Cumans to accept Christianity; they readily agreed. Unfortunately, that did not set as well with the Hungarian nobles as Bela had hoped. They were in a long-standing power struggle with the king and were not happy to see his personal army expanded with foreigners. Besides, what if they were really a fifth column? Maybe they were actually in league with the Mongols? Suspicions ran high.

Further, many nobles and citizens thought the entire Mongol threat might be a giant hoax. Bela attempted to rouse the citizenry by sending envoys through the countryside carrying bloody swords; in eastern Europe the Mongols were coming to be known as Tartars, from the mythical Tartarus, or hell.[61] Unfortunately most people failed to heed the warning. The threat was obvious, however, to anyone who cared to look. Subedei had sent Bela a demand for immediate surrender, since the king had given safe haven to Mongol subjects, the Cumans. Further, many Mongol envoys had not returned, and killing them was always a mistake.

Even with these direct threats, Hungarian nobles acted like a modern Congress, arguing minutiae and personal privilege in the face of crisis. They demanded guarantees of Cuman loyalty, as well as payment in gold and in power for their assistance. The stalemate continued even after 10 March, when a messenger arrived with the news that the Mongols were attacking through the Carpathian passes. Bela pleaded, but the barons continued to resist. The Hungarian army stood by, awaiting orders.[62] Not until four days later, when more messengers reported the passes were now in Mongol hands, did anything happen in Buda or Pest—and it was not was Bela had hoped for. Bela promised to keep the Cuman leaders under house arrest, but after a patrol captured a Cuman fighting alongside the Mongols, the nobles thought they had that was sufficient "evidence" that the Cumans were playing both ends against the middle. Nobles and citizens attacked and killed King Khotian. The assassination had dire consequences. Prior to this the Cumans had regarded themselves as allies of the Hungarians and were willing to support them; now they turned against Hungary and fled the country, sacking towns and villages on their way out of the region.[63] Thus Bela lost not only a huge contingent of troops, but a force that knew the enemy. All he had now was a group of self-centered political generals.

In the north, Kaidu and Baidar succeeded in their mission. They attacked and captured the town of Sandomierz before the Poles even knew an invasion was coming. They defeated a Polish army outside Krakow and then moved on to Breslau. With growing urgency, Henry of Silesia gathered a 40,000-man army and occupied the town of Liegnitz. Wenceslas of Bohemia was marching to join him with a further 50,000.

Before he could do so, however, Baidar arrived with two tumen. He knew Wenceslas was only a day or two away, but Henry did not. Rather than be shut up inside the city indefinitely, Henry deployed his forces outside the city on 9 April. The standard Mongol feigned retreat did its work again, spreading out the overeager pursuers until they could not act in unison. Henry's army was destroyed; Wenceslas withdrew to protect Bohemia. His army occupied the passes into the country and successfully kept Mongol forays out. Unconcerned, Baidar rode south to join Batu, pillaging Moravia along the way. In this campaign a relatively small Mongol force had eliminated all possibility of intervention by Bela's allied armies many times its size, allowing it the time and opportunity to join Batu.[64]

In southern Hungary, Kuyuk was covering the far left flank as Baidar was handling the far right. His three tumens defeated Magyar forces at Hermanstadt and Weisenburg at the same time Baidar was defeating Henry at Liegnitz in Poland. Meanwhile, the central Mongol thrusts came together on the plain east of the Danube, gathering before Pest in late March and early April. They made no attempt to invest Pest or cross the Danube to engage Bela's growing army on the west side. Without knowing how many more troops Bela might yet raise, the Mongols packed up and left. Subedei proceeded to slowly withdraw his army eastward, just as he had prior to the battle at the Kalka River, keeping contact with the pursuing Hungarians as they marched farther and farther from their home base.[65]

In retrospect one wonders how the Russians and Europeans could be fooled so many times, but at least Bela had the foresight to keep his army together, rather than engage in a wild pursuit as had occurred so many times previously. Just past the village of Mohi, below the junctions of the Sajo and Hernad rivers, Batu and Subedei had their battlefield. They took their forces across the single stone bridge on the Sajo and disappeared into the woods beyond the river. When the Hungarians arrived and scouted the east bank, they found nothing but hoofprints. This seemed a good position to make camp, on the west side of the river facing the lone bridge. The size of Bela's army is disputed, anywhere from 50,000 to 100,000.

They set up camp on the west side of a bend in the Sajo and chained their supply wagons together in a giant laager perhaps half a kilometer across. On the surface, establishing a strong defensive position would make sense, but only if the Hungarians were armed for defense. Instead,

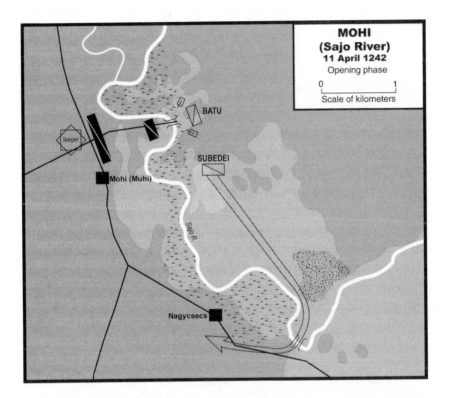

they were a heavy cavalry army, needing room to operate. Still, with no
sign of Mongols in the immediate neighborhood, it seemed to be the
right thing to do. Bela and his advisors made a basic mistake in their
plan for the outlay of the camp, however: they pitched their tents too
close to one another and in a haphazard manner. The ropes holding
down the tents slowed the movements of the men and their animals,
which were tied up next to them. The camp apparently had no streets,
and movement in it must have been difficult in daytime and nearly
impossible at night.[66]

Bela seized the bridge and placed 1,000 men on the east bank to hold
it. Today, the land within the bend of the river holds Lake Koromi; in
1241 marshes reportedly were along both sides of the river from the
Sajo-Hernad junction southward. The Hungarians apparently depended
on those marshes to cover their flanks. Though occupying the bridge
appeared to be favorable for the Hungarians, in fact, Subedei had laid a
masterful trap. As the bridge was the single point of crossing in the area,
by giving the bridge to the Hungarians it seemed as if the Mongols had

continued in their eastward movement. Bela could thus be sure of continuing the pursuit the following day.[67]

Assuming 100,000 men at the start of the European invasion, three tumens sent to Poland and three more through Transylvania in the south, this would mean a Mongol force at the Sajo River of 40,000. Assuming an upper estimate of 120,000 at the beginning and only two tumens sent to Poland, then the Mongols at Mohi would number 70,000. Batu established camp some five miles from the bridgehead. Whether through direct observation or the reports of scouts, he knew the Hungarian numbers and disposition. The plan was for him to assault the bridgehead and then the camp while Subedei led three tumens downriver. They would build a temporary bridge to cross well to the south, and then hit the Hungarian right flank and rear.

Batu launched his assault on the bridgehead just before dawn on 11 April 11 1241. Bela's brother Koloman commanded the covering force, and they put up a fierce resistance. Once pushed back across the bridge, they stood their ground against Mongol attempts to wedge themselves across the narrow stone structure. Success finally came with the Mongol introduction of seven trebuchets, which began to bombard the force on the west side of the river with explosives. The ammunition may have consisted of pots of burning naptha or perhaps pots of burning gunpowder. If the latter, it probably was used more to create a smoke-screen than do any real damage, but the explosions were certainly enough to scare European horses and dishearten European soldiers. With the Mongol bridgehead on the west bank, the trebuchets now increased their range and drove the Hungarians farther back toward their camp as the Mongols advanced behind the rolling barrage. This seems to mark the first time in European history that smoke delivered by indirect weapons fire, outside of a siege, was employed. This masked the movement of the assault troops, demoralized the Hungarians, and focused their attention to the front while Subedei was preparing his flank attack.[68]

If Batu planned all along to use his trebuchets in this fashion, then it is a terrific example of the Mongols' grasp of tactics. If he decided on the spot to use them, upon facing the unexpectedly stubborn resistance displayed by the knights, then the action shows the ability of the Mongols to adapt on the spot to whatever tactical problem faced them.[69]

Bela's forces rallied and charged the Mongols, who were able to keep up their traditional arrow storm but were limited in their ability to flank

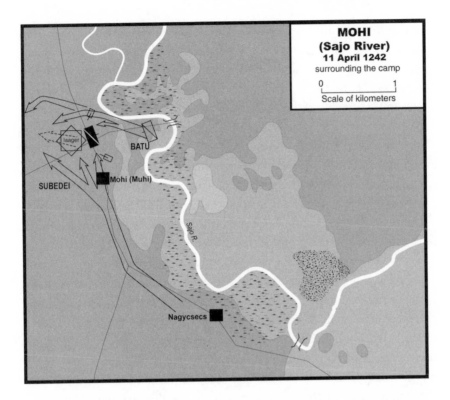

their enemy. Indeed, the repeated charges of heavy cavalry caused serious Mongol casualties, but Batu's forces endeavored to not only hold on but to stretch their line to the right. Batu started this battle with no more than four tumens under his direct command, and they now faced the full force of the Hungarian army of perhaps 100,000. This focused Hungarian attention just where it was supposed to be, for when Subedei's flanking force arrived it struck the Hungarian army in the rear. The Hungarians had little choice but to retreat into their laager, which now became the target of the trebuchets' explosives. Batu's force stretched to its right as Subedei's maintained pressure on the camp and stretched to its left. They did not, however, link up—they left a gap between their forces. Some sources mention a gorge open to the west, but modern terrain maps do not show it. Still, it was an opening and, while a contingent of Knights Templar threw another assault at the Mongols, many of those in the laager took the opportunity to make a run for it.

It was not, of course, a Mongol mistake. Foot soldiers and knights alike dropped their heavy armor and weaponry to make their best speed, but they could not outrun well-placed Mongol cavalry waiting for them. The result was slaughter in the open rather than slaughter in the camp, which occurred as well. Contemporary casualty reports put the Hungarian losses at 70,000. No numbers on Mongol casualties are available, but they were certainly severe. Nevertheless, within three days the Mongols were again at Pest, which now lay undefended. They destroyed the city, but did not immediately cross the Danube.

As in most of the Mongol battles, Subedei led a retrograde movement to contact. Once the Hungarians were encamped and deployed, Batu launched a deliberate attack against the bridgehead and, once across it, against the Hungarian army itself. His attack really was a feint, even though it was probably in greater force than Subedei's flank march, which was the hammer to Batu's anvil. Batu's attack was not a surprise in and of itself, but the use of trebuchets as battlefield artillery and the introduction of gunpowder were both major surprises to the Hungarians. The Mongol commanders failed to dictate the tempo as much as they desired, since Subedei's flank march took longer than expected owing to difficulty in bridging the river. The Mongols certainly succeeded in exploiting the victory, since both the Hungarians on defense and those on the run were destroyed. The pursuit started with the Mongols merely chasing fleeing Hungarian troops, but ended with the whole Mongol army appearing before Pest.

After about a year of pillaging across the countryside and reconnaissance missions as far as Vienna, the Mongol army left for home. That was certainly not its original intention, for Subedei's overall vision for the campaign was to reach the Atlantic in an operation that would take as many as eighteen years. Two primary reasons explain the Mongol leaders' decision to leave Europe, one political and the other practical. Ogedei had died, and it was necessary for Batu and the other princes to return home for a khuriltai to elect the next great khan. Also, the terrain was becoming increasingly difficult for a horse-bound society to live on. Gone were the massive steppe grasslands that were their home. They also would be facing more and more fortified towns and cities with fewer and fewer local troops to recruit as they advanced. Almost certainly they could have defeated European armies, but they just as certainly could not have adapted to Europe's landscape.[70]

Back in Karakorum, the khuriltai, after much debate, elected Kuyuk as the new great khan. Batu, who boycotted the meeting upon learning he would not be elected, stayed in Russia, the region he had inherited from his father, Jochi, and established what came to be called the Golden Horde. Subedei was assigned in 1244 to campaign against the Sung, but it was a short assignment. He was soon back on the steppes, where he died in 1248. For another four generations his descendants held positions of authority. His son Uriyangqadai was a major player in the defeat of the Sung Dynasty. Both father and son received posthumous honors, with Subedei being canonized as Chung-ting ("Loyal and Steadfast").[71]

Generalship

CHINGGIS AND SUBEDEI WERE SOMETHING of a two-headed general. Chinggis established the Mongol system and army, and oversaw its grand strategy and political actions at home, in the field, and in the conquered territories. Subedei learned at the master's feet and came to be his closest colleague, probably aiding Chinggis in details of invasion planning and execution, as best seen in the sweeping flank attack against Khwarezm that brought them to the gates of Bokhara. Subedei was certainly the originator of the reconnaissance in force that became known as the Great Raid, and Chinggis trusted him so implicitly that his only instructions were to return within three years. Both had a vision of what the Mongol nation could do and how far it could go, and both worked tirelessly to accomplish those great goals. All of the principles of war were mastered by these two.

At all levels, the generals established an *objective* at the outset and planned meticulously to achieve it. They realized what the enemy center of gravity was in each campaign. In the tribal battles, it was the enemy commander. In virtually every case Chinggis wanted the manpower another tribe could provide for the Mongol nation, and he could not trust former enemy leaders to remain loyal—although he did come to trust individual enemy soldiers, such as Jebe. In the campaign against Hsi Hsia, the center of gravity was the enemy capital, to force submission. In China, it was the emperor of the Chin and later of the Sung. In Khwarezm, it was Shah Mohammad and, when he was out of play, his son Jalal-al-Din, for they were the ones potentially capable of reorganizing resistance forces. In an analysis for the U.S. Army Command and General Staff College, Major Glenn Takemoto describes the Mongol objectives: "The Mongols sought to destroy the Clausewitzian trinity [government-army-population] at every level of war. At the strategic and operational levels, they sought the moral collapse of the people through terror, paralysis of the government through decapitation, and destruction of the army through piecemeal annihilation."[72]

Another consistent theme is that Chinggis or Subedei always took the *offensive*. In order to secure their frontiers, they always had to take war to a neighboring country. On the battleground, Chinggis was flexible to changing conditions. This is best shown in his adoption of Chinese and Persian engineers to assault walled cities, the bane of every other nomadic army. Additionally, every feigned retreat was designed to bring an enemy army to a particular predetermined location in order to counterattack and destroy it.

Centuries before Napoleon used the concept of "march divided, fight united," Chinggis had already developed it. His superior intelligence network allowed him to strategically divide in the face of the enemy but converge in *mass* on an objective at a given time. Four separate advances into Khwarezm massed at Samarkand, each of the forces having local superiority along its line of march. On the battlefield of Kalka, Subedei stretched out a stronger enemy force in such a way that enemy troops committed themselves to battle piecemeal, giving him local superiority over each successive enemy unit.

Any general who fights outnumbered has to master the principle of *economy of force*, and the superior intelligence the Mongols gathered made this possible, for they always knew where their enemy forces were positioned so they could be blocked, misled, or defeated by the minimum number necessary. This was best illustrated at Sajo River with the holding operation at the bridge while Subedei's force engaged in a flank march.

The most significant—and successful—component of Mongol strategy and tactics was *maneuver*. It all came from speed and discipline. The toughness of the Mongol soldier and his horses made rapid movement possible, both over long marches and in ambush. The training in maneuver and response to commands in the hunting nerge showed itself constantly on campaign. The goal of maneuver is to place the enemy in a disadvantageous position, and the feigned retreat brought army after army into that situation. The sixteen maneuvers outlined above, from harassment to encirclement, are timeless in their effects, but the instant response to commands made the Mongols unequaled in execution.

Another principle of war we see exercised, particularly by Chinggis, is *unity of command.* As he was the leader, in politics, planning, and execution, Chinggis's entire rise to power reflects his goal of achieving this unity. If there was a potential Mongol weakness, however, it was here. A royal personage had to be in titular command, as Batu was in the invasion of Russia and eastern Europe, but during his lifetime Chinggis made sure that a trusted general was the one who truly made the operational decisions. After Chinggis's death, however, with the division of empire among the sons, this became increasingly difficult to enforce. Subedei shared command with Batu at Mohi, but Subedei was the one who made the battlefield decisions. When Batu considered withdrawing from the field at Mohi in the wake of the severe casualties he had taken beating back the Hungarian assaults, Subedei made the final call: you and your princes can go, but I'm staying and fighting. Batu stayed.

Security was another key aspect of Mongol warfare, and one that Napoleon would redevelop in the nineteenth century. The Mongol intelligence network was superior to anything possessed by any other army or government, and it also was a channel for disinformation. Keeping the enemy guessing, whether it was on the battlefield or on campaign, was a hallmark of Mongol warfare. Advanced scouts alerted the Mongols to enemy positions, but also screened the movements of the main body with harassment. Baidar's invasion of Poland was nothing more than strategic security for Subedei's Hungarian invasion. The ability to have fast-moving messengers, or to send messages by flag or arrow, kept the Mongol army continually aware of enemy and allied positions.

Surprise is what the Mongol art of maneuver was all about. Whether it was Chinggis with the giant pincer movement into Khwarezm or Subedei's placement of flanking units on the Kalka River, the enemy never knew what to expect, and what they did expect was always wrong. The utilization of siege weapons surprised Shah Mohammad, who based his entire defense on holding cities. Using those same weapons tactically at the Sajo River was technically and psychologically devastating. The speed of the Mongol army's movement also created strategic and operational surprise.

One would think that dividing forces across hundreds of miles in order to come together at a particular spot at a particular time, and without modern communication equipment, would be nearly impossible.

However, the Mongol communication methods created an ability to coordinate movement across both countries and battlefields. With all sections of the army on the same page, complexity becomes *simplicity*. Further, the constant training of the troops enabled them to instantaneously execute all orders; extended descriptions of movements prior to battle were not necessary.

As any commander knows, victory creates its own high *morale*. For Chinggis, it meant more than that. The entire subjugation campaign to bring all the tribes into one nation meant bringing everyone into the same way of thinking. His creation of the yasa to break down tribal differences probably did as much to mold his army as any action Chinggis ever took. The development of unit loyalty, from the smallest to the largest formations, has always been key to maintaining morale. Unbiased discipline also contributed, as it always does, to chain-of-command loyalty. Promotion through excellence rather than birth or favoritism also was a motivating factor, as soldiers were rewarded for their hard work and commitment to their leader. Further, the reputation Chinggis's army established over time influenced enemy morale, especially in the cities that decided surrender under lenient terms was a better option than useless resistance and annihilation.

Exploitation is one area in which the Mongols could be accused of going too far. While the goal of battle is to destroy the enemy's will or ability to resist, for the Mongols the goal was destruction. During the steppe wars, Chinggis showed his determination by killing every member of the Tatar tribe taller than a wagon wheel's axle. City after city in his later campaigns was burned to the ground and the citizens slaughtered. There were, however, some exceptions. Nomadic enemy soldiers could and usually would be brought into the Mongol army and nation. Citizens of enemy cities, if valuable as craftsmen or engineers, were spared and sent to Mongolia. But as seen at the Kalka River and in the wake of the battle at the Sajo River, annihilation of the enemy army was the goal, and it came very close to being accomplished.

ALTHOUGH CHINGGIS ESTABLISHED a multigenerational empire, his dream of an all-encompassing and perhaps never-ending empire was no more possible for the Mongols than for any other population. He did accomplish more than any other nomadic leader, but in the final analysis what he sought was an impossible dream. Acquisition of loot has to have a purpose. Once it is acquired, it is either kept or traded for something else tangible. One cannot continually acquire goods and live in mobile tent communities. The Mongols, like so many other conquerors, were eventually absorbed by the conquered. Nevertheless, they did establish a military that was without equal in training, discipline, national identity, and an overall success that has never been equaled. The empire of Napoleon did not cover a third of that possessed by Chinggis Khan.

Subedei had an almost unbroken string of victories; only a defeat by the Bulgars on the way home from the Great Raid marred a stellar career. Like Chinggis, he knew his enemies and knew himself—Sun Tzu said that such knowledge would produce victory in a hundred battles. Subedei also lived on in modern times. In the mid-nineteenth century a Russian officer, Lt. Gen. Mikhail Ivanin, faced steppe cavalry tactics while fighting Uzbeks in Turkestan. His analysis of that style of warfare was published in 1846 as *The Art of War of the Mongols and the Central Asian People*, which became required reading in tsarist and then Soviet military academies. It became standard Soviet doctrine (known as "deep battle") in the 1930s thanks to Mikhail Tukhechevsky, Red Army chief of staff. As Subedei biographer Richard Gabriel writes, "By 1937 the Russians had—in a doctrinal and tactical sense—essentially reinvented the Mongol army with modern equipment. The Red Army was the largest and most mechanized army in the world, and its commanders were better trained in operational control of large units over great distances than those of any officer corps in the West. . . . [Tukhechevsky] had reconfigured the Russian armies in the image of the armies of Genghis Khan and Subotai."[73] Proof that some people do learn from history.

9

Jan Žižka (1360?-1424)

Leader of Hussite Forces during the Early Catholic Crusades

To most of his contemporaries he was, it seems, not so much an individual character as a great and frightful natural phenomenon: a terrific power, sent by God to save the Law of God and to punish the sinners; or, to his enemies, a great scourge of humanity, but even so: sent by God. That it was God indeed, who made him do what he did, was the firm conviction of Žižka himself.

—Frederick Heymann, *John Žižka and the Hussite Revolution*

THE YOUNG LIFE OF JAN ŽIŽKA is a matter of much speculation, without even heroic legend to attempt to fill the gaps. Born in the Bohemian town of Trocnow, he seems to have been from a family in the minor nobility. He thus had some social standing, although sources disagree as to his family's financial condition. Perhaps the most significant experience of his youth was the loss of sight in an eye, although how it came to be lost is also a matter of conjecture; it may have been from a childhood accident or from a teenaged fight. Some sources say Žižka was a nickname meaning one-eyed; his real name was John Trocnowski.[1]

In 1306 the royal line in Bohemia died out, and the crown was offered to the Germanic House of Luxemburg. In 1347, King Charles IV began something of a nationalist movement by establishing the University of Prague, a center of learning not controlled by the church and thus a rare forum for free thinking. Charles died in 1378 and was succeeded by Vaclav

IV as a dual monarch, both king of Bohemia and king of the Romans (i.e., Germans).[2] In 1380 a Žižka is listed as entering King Vaclav's service as a hunter. Vaclav loved to hunt, far more than ruling his domain, and as he was well known for not standing on formality, it is probable that he became quite friendly with young Jan. Jan's rapid advancement at court supports this supposition, as do the politico-military events surrounding Vaclav's reign.

The key players in the trouble brewing in Vaclav's kingdom were of the House of Luxemburg. Vaclav's younger brother Sigismund was king of Hungary. Vaclav also faced trouble with the Bohemian nobility, who chafed under any sort of rule; many of these nobles rallied around Henry of Rosenberg in 1395, creating the League of Lords, which allied with Sigismund and his cousin Margrave Jost of Brandenburg. King Vaclav had

the assistance, however, of the youngest Luxemburg brother, Duke John of Görlitz, as well as Jost's brother Prokop, margrave of Moravia. Large-scale fighting broke out in 1399 with the nobles on both sides backing bands of retainers and supporters that engaged in widespread pillage and guerrilla warfare. Sigismund convinced the Bohemian nobles to remove Vaclav as king of the Germans and replaced him with Rupert III (Sigismund later got himself elected to that position in 1411). The fighting continued into the early years of the fifteenth century, taking place throughout Bohemia and neighboring Moravia. The conflict was "fought out on three levels: the personal and political struggles between the two kings and the two margraves of the House of Luxemburg; the feuds of the barons, who supported one or the other side; and finally the guerilla warfare of the mercenary bands employed by the barons," according to Žižka's main biographer, Friederich Heymann.[3]

Žižka's name features regularly as an enemy in the records kept by the Rosenbergs, so it is certain he was fighting for one of these irregular bands in Vaclav's service. His unit was commanded by Matěj Vůdce and was under the control of the lords of Lichtenburg, another of the noble families. Žižka apparently did not hold a command position; indeed, he apparently drew little attention from his own leaders other than as, perhaps, a useful junior officer.[4] The fighting waned about 1406, when Vaclav's ally Prokop died; Vaclav also made peace with Henry of Rosenberg and Margrave Jost, while Sigismund was diverted by issues in Hungary. However, support for or against the king of Austria (also fighting his own brother) drew in some of the marauding bands, so some pillaging continued for several more years. During these times of troubles, Žižka had come to the attention of John Sokol, the most militarily talented of the Bohemian nobles, who had placed himself under Vaclav's banner. Sokol apparently had seen something in Žižka the previous commanders had not; in the guerrilla warfare Žižka had shown himself to be a natural leader.[5] In 1409 Žižka joined himself to Sokol, who had been hired by the king of Poland to fight the Teutonic Knights.

The Poles had recently allied themselves with Lithuania, which had long been targeted by the Teutonic Knights as a pagan nation. That changed in 1386 when Lithuanian prince Jagiello became king of Poland and converted his nation to Christianity. The Knights had come to dominate Prussia since their arrival at the beginning of the fourteenth century and, with no pagans to fight, expanded their holdings just because they could. They had the finest heavy cavalry in the region and no organized resistance to slow them down. However, with Poland and Lithuania united, an organized government now could place an army in the field that might present a real threat to the Knights. The Polish cavalry was made up of bold nobles on outstanding mounts, proving themselves a fit rival.[6] The Lithuanians were primarily light cavalry on the Asiatic model, having faced the Mongols for many decades. Unfortunately, the Polish-Lithuanian infantry was poorly armed and trained, no match for the Teutonic Knights in open battle except in terms of bravery.[7] Hence, the government needed to recruit soldiers from Bohemia, who at the time were considered to be superior to almost anyone in central and eastern Europe.[8]

During the Battle of Tannenberg between the Knights and the Polish royal forces in July 1410, Sokol was with the Polish king Władisław. Whether Žižka was with him is debated. However, Žižka got either first-hand experience of fighting heavy cavalry or exposure to high command procedures. He stayed with Sokol as the Polish army moved deeper into the Knights' lands, and was involved in the capture and subsequent defense of the fortress of Radzyń, staying there until the 1411 peace treaty went into effect. Unfortunately Sokol died during the siege, and Žižka lost both his patron and mentor in warfare.

By 1411 Žižka was in Prague, employed in Vaclav's household guard. (His official title, *portulanus regius*, or doorkeeper, was much the same position held by Subedei when he joined the Mongols.) Žižka seems to have gotten closer to King Vaclav as well as to his wife, Queen Sophia, whom he regularly escorted to church. It was on those Sunday trips that Žižka must have first heard the preaching of Jan Hus, a proctor at the University of Prague who was on his way to upsetting the religious life of east-central Europe. A follower of the English theologian John Wycliffe, Hus believed in the ultimate authority of scripture over the church hierarchy. His sermons, as well as his teachings at the university, horrified the Catholic nobility of Bohemia, who were predominantly of German heritage in keeping with the lineage of the House of Luxemburg. The two main criticisms Hus leveled at the church were its worldliness and its practice of "communion in one part," wherein the priest received both the wine and the bread, but the communicants received the bread only.

Hus argued that the practice violated the scriptures, and he called instead for "communion in both parts," or *sub utraque specie*: hence his followers came to be known as Utraquists. Hus's sermons must have affected Žižka. Heymann comments, "We know that at that time Hus had his most faithful and most determined adherents among the King's courtiers. . . . There is no doubt that Žižka later fought for what he believed to be Hus's tenets, though we may be much less certain whether Hus, had he lived, would have approved of Žižka's fierce ways." [9] It is true, however, that Hus was often described in the same words that would be used to depict Žižka: bold, fiery, powerful, and popular.[10]

The more popular Hus became, the more the German nobles pushed for church action. When the Czech ecclesiastical authorities condemned Wycliffe's works in 1408, Hus refused to recognize their action; the archbishop of Prague excommunicated him, as did Cardinal Collona, speaking for "anti-pope" Pope John XXIII. The city of Prague was laid under an interdict until Hus was removed from the city. Hus appealed the ruling to a general council in 1411 and received another excommunication in return. In 1412 Vaclav convinced him to leave Prague for a castle in the country, but this only gave Hus the opportunity to take his message to the peasants. In 1414, Hus was summoned before the Council of Constance to answer a charge of heresy. Hungary's King Sigismund, who hosted the council, granted Hus safe passage to and from Constance. When the council condemned Hus and his teachings, however, Sigismund reneged on his promise; Hus was burned at the stake in 1415. In his history of the Moravian Church, J. E. Hutton describes the execution: "At last the cruel fire died down, and the soldiers wrenched his remains from the post, hacked his skull in pieces, and ground his bones to powder. As they prodded about among the glowing embers to see how much of Hus was left, they found, to their surprise, that his heart was still unburned. One fixed it on the point of his spear, thrust it back into the fire, and watched it frizzle away; and finally, by the Marshal's orders, they gathered all the ashes together, and tossed them into the Rhine."[11]

The execution was a turning point for Bohemia. There is always a risk in killing popular religious leaders: if their followers don't dry up and blow away, they hunker down and get tough. That's what became of the new movement, the Hussites.[12] Sigismund was held responsible for not enforcing the safe conduct of Hus to Constance, and all Germans in Bohemia felt the citizens' hostility. A group of 452 nobles signed a document protesting the execution of Hus, and public opinion turned against the Catholic Church. In towns where the Hussites dominated, Catholic priests were expelled and monasteries attacked. In the country-side, pro-Hussite noblemen distributed parish offices to priests identified with Hus.[13] In response, the Council of Constance in 1417 declared a mass excommunication of all Hussites. Vaclav tried to enforce the ruling, offering cash rewards for information identifying Hussites and ordering their churches to be seized and destroyed. Prisons were soon filled while hundreds were burned at the stake, drowned, or died as slaves in the Kutná Hora silver mines.[14]

Persecution only hardened Hussite resolve, however. Although there was some success suppressing believers in Prague, the peasants organized themselves and began to fortify towns and hilltops. The old town of Nemějice, some fifty miles south of Prague, was renamed Mount Tabor, and became the soul of the Hussite movement and the headquarters for Jan Žižka.

The Hussite movement gained new leadership under the priest Jan Zelivský, more a firebrand than Hus himself. He and Žižka got the Hussite rebellion against the Catholic Church under way at the end of July 1419. On 6 July Vaclav had replaced the Hussite councilors of the New Town of Prague with hard-line Catholics, signaling a restoration of Catholic priests throughout the city's churches and a corresponding removal of the Hussite priests. On 30 July Zelivský held mass and served the communion in both kinds, then led a march through the streets that ended up at the New Town Hall, where they discovered a number of the Catholic councilors the king had appointed. They demanded the release of the Utraquists being held in prison. When the councilors refused, the mob broke in and threw thirteen of them from the windows into the street below, where those who survived the fall were killed.[15] (A similar defenestration in Prague two centuries later would set off the Thirty Years War.) This proved entirely too much for the increasingly vacillating Vaclav: he died of a stroke two weeks later.

Whether Žižka actually led the citizens in the defenestration is ques-tioned, but he was soon elected captain of the Hussite troops to serve in Prague; by late October he had seized Vysehrad Castle, which dom-inated the southern approach to the city. The situation across Bohemia was fluid, with no single Hussite faction in charge and Hussites making a wide spectrum of demands. There were relatively conservative groups that wanted limited reform, mainly the communion in both kinds. Others, epitomized by the force centering on Mount Tabor (the Taborites), were increasingly millenarian, calling for a war against the church in order to bring on Christ's second coming. Conservative and reform groups among the Catholics also vacillated. Queen Sophia, whom Sigismund had named regent, wanted to preserve the peace (and the government) in spite of her own Hussite leanings. She reinforced Hradčany Castle to defend the western half of Prague and waited for outside aid.

Warfare of the Time

BY THE LATE FOURTEENTH AND EARLY FIFTEENTH CENTURIES, the era of heavy cavalry in the form of the armored knight was declining. In France the English longbow was reestablishing the dominance of the infantry; the Swiss pikemen were doing the same with a reborn but more effective phalanx. Neither of these developments, however, had reached eastern Europe by the time of the Hussite wars, so the German aristocrats still dominated the invading armies. On the other hand, they were hardly the only military arm deployed in combat; infantry, especially crossbowmen, outnumbered the mounted knights.

The relative importance of the knights is the subject of much debate. Some scholars have argued that in spite of the increasing number of infantry from the lower classes, the aristocrats were still the dominant arm with their heavy cavalry. The charge of the heavy horse breaking through anything in its way was receding, but it could still play a decisive role in coordination with the other arms.[16] The early Middle Ages (up to about 1300) actually saw few wars and few battles outside the Crusades, so the knights suffered few casualties in European warfare, which may have given impetus to the concept of their bravery and overall success.

The knights had reached the apogee of body armor by the time of the Hussite wars. Chain mail continued to be used by soldiers in the fourteenth century, but as longbows and crossbows were able to break the rings and penetrate, new, more capable defensive wear was needed. Ultimately, this led to the development of plate armor, initiated in the thirteenth and early fourteenth centuries and lasting well into the sixteenth century.[17] Plate armor was developed first for the upper body and later for the limbs as well. The suits of armor for which knights are today best known were a trade-off between protection and weight. A standard suit of armor weighted fifty to sixty pounds. Thus, an unhorsed rider was at the mercy of swarming infantry, especially on muddy terrain. While astride his charger, however, armed with a strong straight sword and with a lance supported by a bracket fastened to the breastplate (an *arrêt de cuirasse*), the heavy cavalryman of the fifteenth century remained a formidable warrior when intelligently used.[18]

Siege warfare dominated the era, and infantry was a vital component. After the start of the fourteenth century, as battles became more frequent and casualties mounted, what had once been chivalric combat between Christian soldiers became class warfare. Perhaps the most convincing reason for the increased numbers of battles after 1300 is that infantry was beginning to dominate the battlefield. Although several battles during the Middle Ages had been fought using primarily infantry and in some instances these troops had been victorious, the myth of cavalry superiority prevailed.[19] Perhaps the fact that the defeated aristocrats were saved for ransom while defeated peasants were without financial worth finally motivated the peasants to see killing knights as retribution for being ignored. Certainly the increasing sense of freedom and self-worth felt by Hus's peasant followers could account for their disregard for the lifestyle, and the lives, of their "betters."

Infantry training came from an almost guild-like organization in the cities and towns. As military historian Dennis Showalter suggests, "If each task had its specific skill, taught and supported by specific guilds and craft brotherhoods, was it not correspondingly reasonable to divide up the labor of military service, and to provide specialists in this craft as in all the others? From a few experienced captains and armorers held on retainer, the permanent armed forces of Europe's cities and city-states tended to increase during the fourteenth century."[20] Infantry levies were expected to provide their own weapons and acquired some training either at fairs or under the direction of local commanders. As in all militia, training standards varied wildly and there was no training in cooperation with the cavalry. In Germanic states the basic unit of manpower was the *gleve*, numbering up to ten men with at least one horseman in the group. This varied, however: in Swabia a gleve denoted four horses; in Nuremberg, it meant two horses and a spearman; in Strasbourg, five horses; in Regensburg, one spearman, one archer and three horses. Further, there could be a variety of attendants, servants (who may or may not have fought), and archers.[21] Each city had a set number of *gleven* they were to provide when called upon. Ten gleven were commanded by a *hauptman* (captain), a hundred commanded by an *oberhauptman*.

Infantry tended to carry what weapons were handy: townspeople used clubs or spears, peasants employed farm implements. The only infantry technology was the bow and crossbow. Although crossbows were easy to use and required little training, there were still some professionals (like the Genoese) who were specialists and widely used as mercenaries. By the early 1400s the crossbow had evolved into a sophisticated weapon made of steel. Although it could launch a bolt at a high velocity, the increased power required increased technical measures to cock the bow, which lowered the rate of fire. The crossbow's penetrating power versus the knight's armor led to a constant game of tag through the medieval period, and a crossbowman had minimal time to launch a bolt and reload with a cavalry charge approaching at high speed. Only large units of crossbowmen behind some sort of protective screen could hope to break a charge once it was under way. Generally, crossbowmen tried to prevent cavalry's forming-up process with harassing fire, for they were lambs at the slaughter in an open field.[22]

It was these types of soldiers and weapons the Hussites faced: heavy cavalry to break an enemy's line followed by infantry to take advantage of the disorder. Thus, the best way to defend against such an assault was, as noted above, from behind some sort of protective screen. Žižka made defense the key to his battles, but kept his defense mobile by employing wagons that had been specially adapted to stop arrows or bolts and to provide a position for missile fire to cause disorder among the attackers. The concept of circling wagons to provide a quick defensive position had been used at least as early as the Roman experience in Gaul. A Gothic wagon fort was employed at the Battle of Adrianople in 378, and the practice was used regularly by the Byzantines. The Mongols likewise used the tactic, and brought the practice into Eurasia. It has been suggested that the Teutonic Knights at Tannenberg retreated into what came to be called a *wagenburg*, or wagon fort.[23] The formation was also called a tabor, from the Czech word for camp. Ernest Dupuy and Trevor Dupuy call it "one of the simplest and most effective tactical systems in history."[24]

Žižka's contribution was to use wagons as specially constructed war machines that could create a sophisticated defense; this became the main part of his tactics.[25] He started with common baggage wagons and modified them for maximum defense. First, he had a quick release harness developed to get the horses away from the wagon and the harness poles made removable to get the wagons end to end as close to each other as possible. The wagons were then chained together and any gaps between them covered with a removable shield called a pavise. An extra wall of boards was suspended from the side facing the enemy, with the bottom board covering the wheels and access underneath. This board had loopholes for crossbow fire. On the opposite side an opening, often with a ramp, facilitated reinforcement and resupply. Each wagon was ten feet long and held a crew of sixteen made up of crossbowmen and hand gunners as well as soldiers with threshing flails and polearms such as halberds. Completing the wagenburg were small cannon placed between the wagons.[26]

Even though the concept of a wagenburg was not new, Žižka perfected it by constantly training his drivers. On hand or flag signals they could very quickly deploy into circle, square, or triangle formation. Signal flags raised on the leading and trailing wagon of each file controlled the maneuvers. The wagon line moved ahead in four columns: two outer ones and two inner ones.[27] The wheels of the tabor were large and usually iron rimmed. The front pair projected out slightly from the body, allowing one front wheel to be locked into place with the rear wheel of another tabor and chained together.[28] The forming up and chaining together took one to two hours. Given more advance notice of the enemy approach, the Hussites would strengthen the position with ditches and throw the excavated dirt under the wagons for extra security against infiltration. The first time Žižka used the formation he had but seven wagons, but as his army grew he regularly deployed 180 wagons, which created a position some 2,500 yards in circumference.

While peasants provided the bulk of the manpower, Žižka did have some nobles in his army with cavalry expertise. They stayed within the wagenburg until the enemy charge had been broken; then the defenders would open a gap and the cavalry would engage in pursuit. The infantry were the backbone of the army, however. They were protected by whatever armor they could scavenge after the battles, so there were no standardized uniforms. Since most soldiers did their fighting behind wagon walls, helmets were the most necessary armor. The broad-brimmed iron "kettle hat" was the typical helmet of the Germanic lands and appeared in many slightly varied forms.[29] Weapons included standard swords and maces, supplemented with peasant farm tools: knives, hatchets, pitchforks, and scythes. The threshing flail, with spikes added, became the Hussite trademark weapon. In yet another change from normal warfare, peasant women also aided in building defenses and even engaged in combat. After one battle in 1420, Hungarians captured 156 armed Hussite women dressed as men. In another battle in 1422, Hussite women fought openly alongside the men, often with the same intensity and ferocious zeal as the men, for they were involved in a holy war. The last reference to Hussite women in battle was in 1428.[30]

Perhaps most important in the Hussite arsenal was the use of gunpowder weapons. While they certainly did not invent them or even improve on them, almost all use of such weapons to this time had been only in sieges. The handguns were basic in construction: an iron tube some sixteen inches long was fastened to the end of a short wooden pole, long enough to hold firmly under the arm but short enough for the gunner to reach the rear of the tube with a smoldering wick to light the touchhole. The weapon was somewhere between .50 and .70 caliber. It was virtually impossible to aim, so only had any effect when fired at a crowd. In German sources these are referred to as *Pfeifenbüchsen* or "pipe guns," a reference to the musical instrument rather than to a tobacco pipe. In Czech the expression is *pistala* or *pischtjala*, meaning a fife. This may be the origin of the word *pistol*.[31]

Some sources say slightly larger guns were mounted within the wagons, but the cramped conditions make this unlikely. The somewhat larger *tarasnice* (a small cannon) was mounted on a stand and placed behind the pavises between the wagons. Later, the even larger *houfnice* (from which comes the word *howitzer*) was mounted on wheels. Both handguns and tarasnice had been in general use since the 1380s, and it should be noted that Žižka didn't make any innovations in gunpowder weaponry. It was his tactical exploitation of the devices from mobile bases that mark his contribution to warfare.[32] As Charles Oman comments, "It was evident that these war-waggons, when once placed in order, would be impregnable to a cavalry charge: however vigorous the impetus of the mail-clad knight might be, it would not carry him through oaken planks and iron links."[33]

The Opponents

WHILE KING SIGISMUND OF HUNGARY was deciding how to proceed against the Hussites in Bohemia, fighting flared up again in Prague. At the beginning of November 1419, one of Sigismund's princes had attacked and slaughtered a band of Hussite pilgrims; that news spurred the Hussites into action. Žižka's forces stormed across the Charles Bridge into the western half of Prague. Days of fighting with royalist forces destroyed much of the area, but Queen Sophia finally negotiated a truce. The Hussite citizens of Prague were granted the right to communion in both kinds in return for the removal of the throng of countryside pilgrims and the return of Vysehrad Fort (in the south part of the city) to royal control. Žižka was disgusted with this Utraquist agreement to abandon such a significant point of defense for the city, so he took his Taborite followers out of Prague to prepare the defenses of Plzen, which covered the main road into Bohemia from the west. The temporary unity of the moderate and radical Hussites fell apart for the first time, but not the last.

Meanwhile, the Catholic royalists saw the outcome of the Prague fighting as a victory over the Hussites, especially Žižka's extreme Taborites. In the heavily Germanic city of Kutná Hora, site of the silver mines that provided much of Bohemia's wealth, Hussites were convicted of heresy and hanged in large numbers. Indeed, the numbers became so large that to save time the authorities began to throw prisoners into abandoned silver mines instead of hanging them. Such punishment inflamed not only religious hostility but ethnic hatred as well. One of the key demands of the Hussites had always been to hold their services in Czech rather than Latin, as well as to have the Bible translated into the vernacular. For the Bohemians, "Catholic" increasingly came to mean both German and upper class. Thus, the Hussite wars were class oriented as well as religious and nationalistic.[34]

At the same time, moderate nobles had sent representatives to Sigismund to negotiate: he would be welcomed as king of Bohemia if he would guarantee communion in both kinds, support the Hussites against the church's persecution, and fight against corruption in the church. Sigismund foolishly declined any compromise, assuming he could amass sufficient military power to crush any resistance. He had difficulty convincing the Germanic princes to provide enthusiastic support, however, so he convinced the recently enthroned Pope Martin V to authorize a crusade. Martin agreed on March 17, 1420, when his legate Ferdinand, bishop of Lucena, read from the pulpit the text of the bull *Omnium plasmatoris domini*. This proclaimed a crusade with the task of exterminating all "Wyclifites, Hussites, other heretics, and those favoring, accepting, and defending such heresies,"[35] and contained the usual addition that men fighting this war for the church would expiate all their sins. Sigismund thus rallied supporters from across the Holy Roman Empire to join his cause, and he gave the order for his soldiers to execute on the spot any Hussite who refused to recant.

The Hussites responded with calls for a holy war of their own, with heavenly rewards also guaranteed. Jan Zelivský preached that all those who had voted to burn Jan Hus were guilty of murder because it was done by hate and not for the cause of faith. In his work on the Hussite wars, Thomas Fudge writes, "By extension and implication, the crusade itself was nothing but militarism based on malice and was therefore murder on an unimaginable and unconscionable scale. . . . The counter-crusading anthem of the heretics *Ktoz jsú bozí bojovníci* [You who are the warriors of God] identified death at the hands of the wicked crusaders as martyrdom. 'You who are the warriors of God. . . . Christ will reward you for all that is lost. . . . Whoever gives their life for him . . . Shall gain life eternal.'"[36]

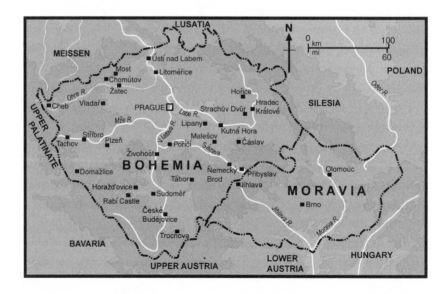

With Catholic nobles in Bohemia beginning to enforce both Sigismund's and the pope's commands, Žižka's arrival in Plzen was well timed. He had begun work with the priest of the city, Father Nicholas Koranda, to strengthen the defenses. Meanwhile, he decided to lay siege to the town of Nekměř just to the north. Royalist forces under Lord Bohuslav of Svamberg approached, and Žižka repulsed them with his hand gunners and crossbowmen firing from inside his seven wagons. This surprise response obliged Bohuslav to retreat, and Žižka led his men back to Plzen. The Battle of Nekměř marks the first application of the war wagons that was to be Žižka's hallmark.[37]

Battle of Sudoměř

ŽIŽKA LED THE DEFENSE OF PLZEN through March 1420. The citizens of the city, more moderate than Žižka or Father Koranda, finally convinced Žižka to negotiate with Bohuslav rather than face their fate if the city was taken by storm. Bohuslav agreed to let the Taborites leave under safe passage. The group of 400 men left on 23 March in twelve war wagons with a number of regular transport and baggage carts carrying women and children. Bohuslav, however, did not hold to his promise of safe passage. Messengers were sent out secretly from Plzen to inform the king's followers all over the country of the impending movement of the little caravan that would surely be at the mercy of any strong force sent against them. Two royalist groups responded.[38] Two columns met at Písek, about twenty miles west of Tabor. They numbered 2,000 mounted men, called the "Iron Lords" by the locals. One thousand were under the command of Henry of Hradec, the grand master of the Knights of St. John, based in Strakonice. The rest were led by Peter of Sternberg.

Žižka was traveling on relatively flat terrain, but in an area full of fish ponds. Seeing the mass of cavalry approaching from the north, he drove his wagons onto a dam between two ponds, both drained for the winter. Here he lined up his twelve wagons end to end and chained them together. His deployment obliged the royalists to attack on a very narrow front. The Hussite cannon caused more panic than actual damage among the horses; the raised position of the defenders and the length of their spears, halberds, and flails were equal to the assaults from the knights' lances. Henry's Knights of St. John failed to break through on their initial assault in late afternoon, so they dismounted to try their luck on foot. Casualties are described as heavy on both sides and three of the wagons were reported damaged, but the combination of guns, bows, and farm implements kept the attackers at bay.

Peter of Sternberg's force tried to flank the line of wagons by attacking through the empty but very muddy pond on the Hussite right flank. Their horses quickly mired themselves in the mud, forcing the knights forward on foot. Their armor also caused them to move slowly, and Žižka's peasants came out of reserve with their flails and pitchforks to deliver a beating to the bogged-down knights. The melee was still going on as darkness fell, and in the confusion the knights at times attacked each other. Žižka's annalist describes the early darkness and fog as a miracle sent to befuddle the knights; a Catholic chronicler claimed the Hussite women spread veils and scarves on the ground to trip the attacking horses and knights.[39]

Sources for the battle at Sudoměř lack a lot of detail, but two key results emerged. First, it was the beginning of Žižka's career as a tactical leader, with his successful use of war wagons as the main element in the defensive formations. Second, it made Žižka, at that point in his fifties, a Bohemian national hero.[40] Occurring as it did almost exactly as the pope

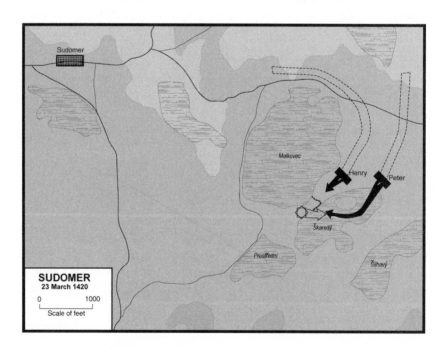

SUDOMER
23 March 1420

0   1000
Scale of feet

announced the crusade against them, the battle gave the Hussites a major morale boost.

As the forces approached each other, Žižka led his opposition to a meeting engagement on his own choice of ground, quickly chosen as it may have been. The rapidly deployed defensive wall of the war wagons gave him the element of surprise, as did the use of gunpowder weapons to panic the horses. On the defensive, Žižka used the terrain to max-imize the strength of his defense, with both flanks covered by the empty ponds creating a narrow front to funnel the enemy's charge. That gave the attackers fewer heavy cavalry at the point of attack. The position was aided by the wagon fort and use of firepower to break the normal power of a heavy cavalry charge. Both mounted and dismounted, the knights were at a disadvantage, primarily in their lack of missile weapons compared with the concentrated fire of the Hussite defenders. Owing to the nature of the defense and his lack of manpower, Žižka was unable to engage in an offensive defense until the royalist flanking movement. Here, he was able to employ his small reserve of unarmored manpower and woman-power to take advantage of the immobility of the armored attackers in the mud. There was no pursuit or exploitation, as exposing infantry even to a defeated cavalry force on open ground would have snatched defeat from the jaws of victory.

The next day the defeated royalists were gone, and Žižka moved on to Tabor. He arrived on 27 March to a tumultuous reception. Soon the citizens settled down to elect their leaders: Žižka was named one of four captains and took over the organization and training of the army, while Nicholas of Hus served as the political head of the community. Žižka thus took on a new role, the central focus of which was to improve the Hussite forces.

If Žižka had a dominating principle in his work of creating a new mil-itary organization, it was to disregard the traditions of centuries. He had to use to the best advantage whatever manpower and arms were available, which often meant relying on new technologies and innovations that had not been employed before.[41] Žižka had by this time decided to use his war wagons as the center of his military operations. As he had primarily peasants and a few city artisans upon which to draw for his troops, he played to their strengths. Artisans made the weaponry, including forging guns of various sizes. The peasants, who had handled wagons their entire lives, received directions in how to work together to quickly form up the wagenburg, unhitch the horses, chain the wagons together, and man them for battle. Coupled with the native talent of his men, Žižka also had their religious fervor on which to draw for motivation. Not only did Žižka create a perfect style of warfare for his followers, he also trained them to an extent unknown in medieval times. The force received on-the-job training as well when Žižka led an early-morning attack on the nearby town of Vozice. One of the enemy commanders at Sudoměř, Nicholas Divoký, occupied the town and its castle. The surprise of the attack forced the garrison into the castle, while Žižka's men grabbed anything of military value, including horses and prisoners (which were exchanged for thirty Taborites captured after Sudoměř). Thus did he form the basis of a cavalry force for counterattack in battle and scouting on the march.

On 16 May, word arrived of a royalist threat in Prague, and within two days Žižka and his army were in formation and on the move.[42] He led 9,000 men to Prague: 5,000 infantry, a few hundred cavalry, and the remainder war and supply wagons. The first day they covered fifty miles, at the end of which they drove a 400-man royalist cavalry force away from the town of Benesov. A three-pronged force of royalists totaling 13,000 men converged on the Hussite force near the village of Porci, just south of Prague. Žižka deployed his wagenburg atop a hill and beat back the attackers, inflicting about fifty casualties. That was enough for the Italian mercenary commander to call for a withdrawal. The Hussite force entered Prague on 21 May.

Žižka immediately began strengthening the moat on the south side of town facing Vysehrad Fort while simultaneously beginning a siege of Hradčany Castle. King Sigismund, basing himself in Kutná Hora, seemed paralyzed. He would do no more than feint against Prague, diverting Žižka just enough to slip supply wagons into Hradčany, but he refused to offer battle. Žižka finally gave up on the siege and turned to strengthening the city's defenses. Meanwhile, after losing a force in an abortive siege of Tabor and another at Hradec Krolové, Sigismund finally decided to head for Prague in mid-July 1420. Žižka realized that in order to keep from being besieged himself, he needed to keep open the one remaining road to the outside, which ran east over Vítkov Hill and overlooked the south bank of the Vltava. He ordered the hilltop fortified.

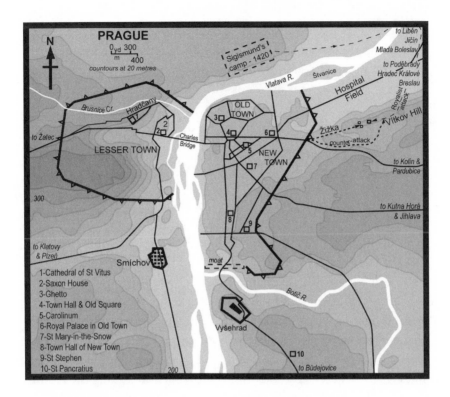

The Battle of the Vítkov

SIGISMUND'S ARMY OF 80,000 came from all across the empire, reportedly from thirty-three principalities and kingdoms from almost all of Europe except Scandinavia. It was more infantry (ca. 45,000) than cavalry (ca. 35,000 heavy and light), and most of the troops were mercenaries. They set up camp north of Prague on high ground overlooking the Vltava River and the Old Town. With Vyšehrad and the Lesser Town occupied by the royalists as well, the Hussites were surrounded on three sides.

The steep sides of Vítkov Hill had been cleared of cover. On the west end of the ridge stood an old watchtower. Žižka ordered the watchtower strengthened and a rampart-backed ditch constructed across the hundred-yard width of the hilltop, with a tower built on either end of the dirt embankment. The flanking positions could only hold about 30 troops each, but Žižka apparently assumed he could reinforce them before an assault could be launched. He was wrong.

Sigismund planned two attacks as diversions. On 14 July one came out of Hradčany and assaulted the Charles Bridge; the second came north out of the Višerhad against the south flank. When these were under way, he sent 7,000–8,000 cavalry across the Vltava far to the east where the river turns north. This allowed the cavalry to approach the hill on a shallower slope, then charge across the top of the ridge. Not until the cavalry had already crossed the river were they noticed, and Žižka rushed to put reinforcements in play. In the meantime, the handful of defenders behind their parapet had to hold on as best they could.

Luckily, the terrain favored the Hussites in the same way the dike had served them at Sudomer, narrowing the front the attackers could utilize. Thus, thousands of cavalry were reduced to dozens as they assaulted the defense across a mere hundred yards of frontage. The ditch did its duty of slowing down the charge, possibly even obliging some knights to dismount and fight on foot. The maneuverability of the unarmored peasants fighting with their flails from behind their parapet and shooting arrows from the towers also proved effective. Žižka led a small force toward the western end of the hill to give the beleaguered soldiers direct aid. He also sent a larger Taborite and Prague force along the road to climb the hill further to the east in order to strike the attackers' flank. Heymann describes his relief effort: "Finding the situation critical, he threw himself into the fight, trying to hold the remaining bulwark with his little troop at all costs and at the risk of his life. From this moment till the arrival of the larger Taborite force there was only a short interval, but this was the military and psychological crisis of the battle."[43]

With all attention focused on Žižka's struggle, the flank attack was a complete surprise. It was the typical deployment of the Taborite troops, with a priest in the lead carrying the host, followed by archers, with the rear brought up by peasants with their flails and spikes.[44] Unprepared for the assault, the knights broke and ran or rode away, possibly losing more men in the hasty retreat down the steep hillside than in the battle itself, some 300–500 men in total. A sally of Hussite reserves emerged from the Porcini Gate and pursued the retreating imperial troops across Hospital Field. The royalists made no further attack, but Žižka had the defenses strengthened nonetheless.

Žižka's preparation for the battle had included the strengthening of existing defenses and the construction of new ones, all before the emperor's forces were deployed. He failed to provide adequate security, however, for the imperial attack was on them quickly and without advanced notice, forcing an undermanned garrison to take up the defense. Luckily, the prepared positions were strong and the terrain favorable for the defense. From the initial stand, Žižka launched his counterattack. Although he could not control the tempo of the battle, he could concentrate sufficient reinforcements at the point of the enemy attack to both hold the position and hold the attackers' attention. With the battle raging along the western end of the ridge, no one had time to notice the outflanking force on the move. The fact that they were on the reverse slope, away from the royalist camp, aided in the surprise.[45] The surprise flank attack was successful enough to make up for the disparity in numbers, since the counterattack was made up of perhaps 3,000 troops. Any further attempt at exploitation would have been foolish, as they would have been chasing the retreating troops across the Vltava River and into the imperial camp.

The losses were minimal for Sigismund's army. Nevertheless, they were enough to cause discontent and the first desertions. To make matters worse, the summer heat combined with epidemics to decimate the royalist forces. As Sigismund continued to do nothing, rumors even began to spread through the camp that he was conspiring with the Hussites.[46] Seeing his army falling apart, Sigismund made a few political moves. He went to the Catholic-controlled Hradčany Castle and had himself crowned king of Bohemia in St. Vitus Cathedral. It was a less than satisfying occasion, as he had hoped for pomp and circumstance in the wake of a major victory. He then lifted the siege by moving his remaining forces (ca. 16,000) to Kutná Hora, site of the silver mines he needed to control even if he held nothing else. Practical as these moves were, their value was far overshadowed by the precipitate rise in Hussite morale at holding on to their half of Prague and obliging the retreat of a massive force. The Hussites scored another victory later in the year. But by the end of the year, Sigismund had mobilized a new army, which stood before Prague. Once more the Taborites came to assist and, in a victorious battle below the castle of Vyšehrad, Prague and the Hussite movement were saved on 1 November 1420.[47] Hradčany Castle and the western side of Prague fell to the Hussites a few months later.

Through the second half of 1420 Žižka had to engage in some intra-Hussite fighting. The poorest people of Bohemia not only embraced the teachings of Hus but carried them further into a millennial belief that a completely equal society would bring about Christ's second coming. The middle class and minor aristocracy opposed this for economic more than religious reasons, and Žižka depended on the city burghers (his own background) for the majority of his support. Thus, the poor who rallied around the most radical priests found themselves suppressed and ultimately defeated in battle. Some survivors left for more radical settlements, but the bulk of the poor, both rural and urban, realized that what progress they could make in advancing themselves in any socioeconomic way was by following Žižka. The fortress town of Tabor was still regarded as one of the more radical communities, but it was controlled by the middle class. By early 1421 Žižka had solidified his position as commander in chief of the Hussite forces, in and out of Tabor.

Early in 1421, Sigismund had withdrawn from Bohemia back to Germany, leaving the Hussites time and opportunity to deal with their own issues, and bringing an end to the first crusade. For the Hussites, the absence of any crusaders gave them the chance to spread their own influence. Many towns were attacked, with sieges lasting at times a few days and other times a few months. It was during one of these sieges that Žižka suffered a significant injury: during the siege of the town of Rabi, near the Hussite-held city of Tachov, Žižka led the first assault and was hit in the face by an arrow. This took out his second eye and almost killed him, but several weeks in Prague allowed him to recover his health, though he was now blind. It mattered little: Žižka fought some of his greatest battles and campaigns after he lost his second eye. Although he could have sustained himself on his reputation alone, his talents were undiminished.[48] His reputation did indeed precede him, however. In late July German forces from Meissen crossed the border to successfully relieve the Hussite siege of Most. The Hussite Prague army was reconstituted a month later with Žižka in command and marched back to face the leading elements of the second crusade. When news arrived that Žižka was leading the Hussite force toward them, even as he was still recovering from his wound, the German army turned and went home rather than face him.[49]

The second crusade consisted of larger forces than the first; estimates range from 120,000 to 200,000. The crusaders had orders to kill all Czechs but small children. The initial force marched east out of the Upper

Palatinate through Cheb on the way to Zatec, a Hussite stronghold. A second force came out of Meissen in three prongs, attacking a number of towns northwest of Prague before joining with the first army. Zatec was soon invested, but held off six major assaults. Collapsing morale from the crusaders' failures and Hussite sallies were compounded by word on 2 October that Žižka's army was on its way. Again, that was all the Germans needed to convince them to pack up and retreat. To make matters worse for them, a fire broke out in their tent city just before they were ready to leave. The defenders sallied out and inflicted serious damage on the already hurting crusader force, leaving them with a total of some 2,000 dead. Worse still, this defeat came even before Sigismund got his army moving, leaving the second crusade in a less than hopeful state.[50]

Kutná Hora and Německý Brod

A THIRD OFFENSIVE FROM THE SOUTH kept Žižka busy through the autumn of 1421. During that time Sigismund was finally getting his offensive under way. A Hungarian force of 60,000 (including 23,000 cavalry) marched into Moravia under the command of Philip Scolari, an Italian mercenary general better known by his nickname Pipo Spano; Sigismund joined him in late October at the town of Jihlava on the Moravian-Bohemian border. Instead of immediately marching for Kutná Hora to recover the mint and mines, Sigismund practiced his normal hesitation and waited for reinforcements. This gave Žižka's army of 12,000 time to reach the city first (on 9 December) and strengthen its defenses. The imperial army also took twenty days to march the fifty miles from Jihlava to Kutná Hora. Heymann describes the advance: "All the time [Sigismund's] Hungarians destroyed Czech villages, burned the men, mutilated the boys, raped the women and girls. The behavior of his troops was so atrocious that not one of the Czech chronicles which describes this invasion omits reference to it."[51] Sigismund and Scolari arrived at Kutná Hora on December 21.

As the imperial army of some 50,000 approached, Žižka deployed his wagon fort in front of the city walls, stretched over a sufficient length to cover both western roads into the city. Scolari, in military command of this operation, stretched his cavalry in a thin line to face the wagons and attacked repeatedly throughout the day. The Hussite cannon inflicted heavy casualties, but this action also kept the Hussite attention focused to the west. Scolari and Sigismund appreciated the leanings of the Germanic citizens of Kutná Hora and had secretly contacted their leaders. With the battle raging outside the walls, an imperial cavalry force had swung wide south and approached the gate on the Malesov road, which conspirators opened to them. The small garrison Žižka had left in the city was quickly overwhelmed and the Hussites were now surrounded.

Žižka found himself in the most dangerous position of his career, but his brilliant mind was not daunted. Sigismund had delayed entering the city until he could do so in triumph; he was still in his headquarters on the imperial left flank. Žižka decided to launch an ambitious surprise attack, assailing the enemy leader's headquarters at sunrise. Knowing the enemy once again provide invaluable, as Žižka knew that Sigismund never put himself in danger; he always commanded from the rear. Thus, the Hussites were sure he would not lead any resistance that was aimed directly at him, being too interested in getting himself out of the way.[52] Just before dawn on 22 December, Žižka formed his wagons into line and opened fire on Sigismund's headquarters. No one expected this gunfire to come out of the night and, as Žižka had planned, panic ensued in the imperial ranks. Although the column stopped now and then to reload

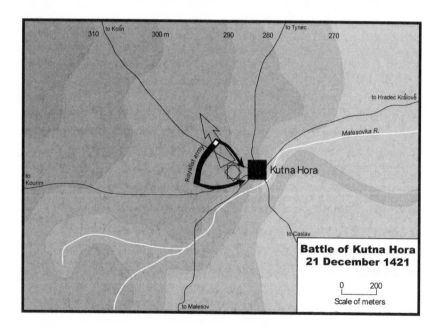

and shoot again, preventing a constant moving line of artillery fire, it was nevertheless enough to scatter the defenders and leave a hole in their lines through which the Hussites made their escape. Žižka's decision to attack at night had been a good one; a daylight gambit along these lines probably would not have been successful.[53]

As dawn broke the Hussite wagons were out of sight, and Žižka deployed them on a hill about a mile away and prepared for the pursuit, which never came. Once positive he would not be caught in the open, Žižka moved his men to Kolín, from whence he spent the next two weeks scouring the region for reinforcements. In the meantime, Sigismund (assuming his enemy was on the run and would not be a bother until spring, if at all) had settled himself into Kutná Hora. He could not quarter all his men in the town, so he dispersed them to villages around the region, paying particular attention to Cáslav, a Hussite stronghold just to the east, and to Nebovidy, about halfway to Kolín, to act as a covering force. Žižka took advantage of this dispersal on 6 January when he surprised the force at Nebovidy. Unfortunately, no sources give details of the next few battles, other than to say the Hussites attacked and the imperial troops broke. An anonymous late nineteenth-century description, probably taken from the George Sand biography of Žižka, says that Žižka "suddenly burst upon Sigismund's scattered troops like a thunderbolt. Hundreds of Hungarians were cut down at the first onslaught, and the panic spread with awful rapidity from village to village."[54] No one else provides any more detail.

What is important is that the crusaders fled toward Kutná Hora and created a panic there, especially in Sigismund's heart and mind. He fruitlessly begged the German town elders to defend the city from Žižka's army while he withdrew, then ordered the city burned rather than let it fall into Hussite hands. The citizens were hustled unprepared out of the town while a Hungarian cavalry contingent remained behind to light the fires. Their desire for loot, coupled with the speed of Žižka's pursuit, however, meant that few fires were actually set, and those were quickly extinguished. The pursuit continued, as did the panic. Sigismund decided to make a stand a few miles to the southwest at Habry. His advisors, particular Scolari, counseled against it: the troops were too demoralized. The advisors were right, though Sigismund didn't listen. When the Hussites did attack, the defenders once again turned tail. The rout was total, with the crusaders abandoning everything but personal arms in their haste.[55] Again, no details of assault or defense are available.

Sigismund fled for the Moravian border town of Jihlava. He crossed the Sázava River at Německý Brod, well ahead of his army, some of whom again tried to make a stand, but the hot Hussite pursuit forced a mad dash across the frozen river. It was not, however, totally frozen, and the breaking ice led to the drowning of a reported 548 knights. A hasty defense of the town was soon rendered useless by Hussite heavy artillery that made short work of the walls. An attempted negotiated surrender fell apart when a Hussite patrol found a particularly weak section of wall and broke through without orders, setting the fighting off once again.

In the wake of the Hussite victory and the ensuing pillage, and a similar lapse of control a year later, Žižka developed one of history's first sets of regulations of war, dictating the behavior of troops in and out of combat. Overall, the combat between 6–9 January 1422 cost the imperial forces at least 4,500 dead; there is no account of Hussite casualties, but they must have been very light.

The campaign beginning at Kutná Hora and ending at Německý Brod showed Žižka at his best on offense and defense. He had several days to prepare his wagenburg outside Kutná Hora, and it dealt heavy casualties to the imperial cavalry that attacked it. When he found himself betrayed by the townspeople and cut off, Žižka massed his combat power at a single weak point, the king's headquarters, and through firepower and psychological intimidation paralyzed his opponent and made good his own escape. Taking advantage of his opponent's assumption of victory, his innate proclivity not to fight, and the dispersed nature of his army, the offensive that began on 6 January combined all the elements of the offense: surprise, concentration, control of tempo, and audacity. His movement to contact led to a deliberate attack, followed by immediate exploitation and long-range pursuit. One has to be amazed at the ability of a blind general to command a breakout from encirclement, then follow it up with a cross-country pursuit of a broken enemy, and all in the dead of winter. This was not typical medieval warfare.[56]

In the grand strategic scheme of things, the campaign had major significance as well. It ended the second crusade and so disheartened Sigismund that he did not approach Bohemia himself for years. By keeping himself in Hungary and letting the German princes conduct the future crusades, he alleviated Bohemia's necessity to prepare for or fight a two-front war. Žižka's reputation, as well as that of his followers, remained one of the most important factors in the three crusades that followed over the next few years. One of the crusading armies barely got inside Bohemia when the sounds of Hussite soldiers singing one of Žižka's war songs frightened the invaders out of the country without a battle. Hans Delbruck notes, "Once the warlike character had gained the upper hand and had become completely dominant, the Hussites were preceded by a wave of fear so that the Germans dispersed before them whenever they simply heard their battle song from afar."[57]

Unfortunately for the Hussite cause, internal feuds caused more troubles than did invasions. Although the wagenburg tactic became standard for all Hussite forces, they used it against each other at times, as in the last of Žižka's great victories at Malesov against a rival religious faction. Žižka would ultimately die of the plague while preparing an invasion of Moravia in 1424, and his leadership position was ably taken up by Prokop the Great, who continued the long line of Hussite victories over German Catholic crusades. Finally, in 1434, a truce was signed that granted the Hussites some concessions. They remained outside the good graces of the church, which, however, did not reestablish its authority in Bohemia until two centuries later at the Battle of White Mountain at the start of the Thirty Years War.

Žižka's Generalship

JAN ŽIŽKA WAS CERTAINLY the most imaginative general of the late medieval–early Renaissance period. Although he was not the first to use gunpowder weapons, he was more forward-thinking than anyone of his time in how to employ them. His use of soldiers from the lower economic classes was also employed by England with the longbowmen of the Hundred Years War and by the Swiss pikemen, and as Charles Oman observes, contributed to "the overthrow of feudal cavalry—and to no small extent [to] that of feudalism itself."[58] The strengths of Žižka's leadership were his mastery of maneuver, surprise, simplicity, and morale.

The goal of *maneuver* is to place the enemy in a disadvantageous position. For Žižka, this meant obliging his heavy cavalry enemy to attack a position across terrain for which it was not suited. The first two battles covered, Sudoměř and Vitkov Hill, show this perfectly. The Bohemians were on narrow raised ground with steeply falling sides, forcing the attackers into a narrow front where their strength of numbers was negated. The Bohemians drew their enemy into an attack against a fortified position in order to employ superior firepower. The ability to force a disadvantageous position depended on knowing the nature of the enemy's mind-set as much as their tactics. Žižka knew the knights would not take a peasant force seriously, no matter what their position. Hence, he drew the imperial cavalry into attack after attack against fortified positions that horses could not penetrate and where infantry or dismounted knights had to fight hand-to-hand against soldiers with a height advantage in the wagons. The peasant defenders, using spears and flails, also had superior reach against foot soldiers armed with swords.

Žižka also employed maneuver in the offensive-defensive nature of his warfare. Although he did engage in siege work, that was a traditional practice of warfare albeit with the newly implemented heavy cannon. His wagenburg, however, could be used across most of the relatively level Bohemian terrain. Thus, he could take war to the enemy, but employ the strength of a defensive position against armies that did not employ the necessary weaponry. As long as Žižka carried the firearms and his enemy did not, all he had to do was make sure his wagenburg was deployed before the enemy struck. This, of course, is what made the wagenburg a relatively short-lived aspect of warfare, for armies would soon be employing their own firearms, and the wooden wagons could only absorb so much gunfire, unlike the archery fire they had dealt with in the early fifteenth century.

The first time any new tactic or weapon is introduced it produces *surprise*, and Žižka's wagon-borne firearms were no exception. This is what makes Žižka, like the other generals studied in this work, stand out: he saw the strengths and weaknesses of his own forces and the enemy's, and he adapted his strength to their weakness. His first two surprises therefore went hand in hand: the wagenburg and the peasant soldier. The shock of facing gunpowder arms in large numbers had to have amazed the knights at Sudoměř, no matter what actual damage was inflicted. This was the first time that guns had been used in massed defensive positions, and the effects were notable. The noise was terrifying in itself, and it combined with the gunpowder flashes and thick smoke to confuse enemy troops.[59] The horses apparently began to get over it after a time, for by the battle at

Kutná Hora the imperial cavalry attacked repeatedly throughout the day. Even if the actual damage inflicted by the handguns and small cannon was not great, it was supplemented by arrows and crossbow bolts.

The nature of the wagenburg would have been surprising enough when first encountered, but his quick shift from defense to breakout at Kutná Hora, as well as the fact that he attacked at night, again show Žižka's ability to think outside the box. He knew his enemy's general attitude toward the nature of combat and the personal attitude of Sigismund, and he played on them both to paralyze his enemy—even if he inflicted few casualties. In the battles that followed, his quick strikes and close pursuit were like nothing his enemies had encountered. This again was not normal medieval warfare, for the usual aftermath of battle was a peaceful withdrawal. The Hussites, however, did not act in accepted knightly fashion and the crusader knights don't seem to have adapted.[60] Heymann notes that while it was fairly common for medieval generals to pursue an enemy, "to follow up a victory by a continued pursuit over scores of miles, to press on after a beaten enemy so as to achieve his complete destruction—this was by no means usual or 'normal.' It was 'normal' only for Žižka who always acted according to the military needs of the situation as his unfettered mind saw them."[61]

Žižka's soldiers were a surprise to their enemies not necessarily because they were peasants, but because they were disciplined. Showalter observes, "Medieval armies lacked anything like a comprehensive command structure able to evoke general, conditioned responses. . . . At their best the civil militias of urban Europe were part-time fighting men. Their tactical skills were correspondingly limited."[62] Žižka benefited from his own military experience as a guerrilla fighter and also had the all-important motivating factor of religion to help keep his troops disciplined. Žižka did not really ask his soldiers to do anything out of the ordinary as far as their abilities were concerned, as driving wagons and handling tools were second nature. In this way Žižka brilliantly implemented the principle of *simplicity*. The gunpowder weapons were so basic that no real training was necessary to handle them. He also taught his army of farmers to fight as well as they could with the tools they knew best: scythes, iron-tipped grain flails, axes, rakes, picks, hoes—implements that turned out to be vicious at close quarters when wielded by people who were very strong, very motivated, and used to hard labor.[63]

Žižka's experience, coupled with a zeal that matched or exceeded their own, made him a leader his men could follow into any situation, and they could easily accomplish the assigned tasks within the wagons on the move or when deployed into the fortress. The Hussites' early victories sufficed to give them the confidence they needed to buy into the fixed way of doing things, and their do-or-die attitude of fighting for God against heretics and aristocrats tapped into their already existing attitudes and emotions. None of the disciplined movements or fanatical willingness to fight were things for which the invading crusaders were prepared. The most complex maneuver Žižka ever asked of his men was forming up in a straight line and following each other into Sigismund's headquarters, stopping periodically to shoot into the dark to keep the enemy disorganized. Other than that (and the necessary movements to create the wagenburg), all their actions were straightforward attack or defense. Only the two-pronged attack out of Prague up the Vitkov Hill showed anything like sophistication.

Žižka was also a skilled commander when it came to the principle of *morale*. Religion is an incredibly motivating cause, and Žižka used this to his advantage to keep the morale of his troops high. He showed himself to be more religious than the conservatives controlling Prague, but not as radical as the millenarian sects that emerged in the wake of Jan Hus's death. His belief was never in doubt, even when he made war against the radical factions, made up of the lowest rung of society. He maintained the loyalty of the rank-and-file Hussites and the respect of the conservatives, who looked for some sort of compromise with the church. But it was for social and economic advancement and freedom from outside rule, as well as religious freedom, that his people followed him. Žižka could therefore rely on the support of the country people and urban poor who brought their own weapons with them.[64]

While religion may have been the glue holding the army together, it was discipline that gave it shape. A disciplined force always has greater unit cohesion and therefore fights better than one lacking in those traits. Žižka set rigid standards: each man was assigned a place in ranks with a specific tactical mission. Straggling, disobedience, and disorderly conduct were severely punished. Promotion was based on ability rather than social status and the serf was considered the equal of the noble.[65] We have seen this same attitude in most of the generals discussed thus far: ability trumps birth. That was just as true concerning punishment, and equal justice maintained belief in the system.

And then, of course, there was the man himself. When he still had his sight, he fought alongside his troops. Sharing dangers and conditions always promotes loyalty to a leader. Then, when he completely lost his sight, he still commanded in the field for another three years. For a religious peasant army, that was surely a sign of God's grace. It also illustrates how Žižka's reputation became a demoralizing factor for his enemies. Žižka's regular victories gave him an air of invincibility on both sides of the battlefield, and the songs he wrote for his troops (a mixture of hymn and military instruction) were as frightening to his enemies as the Hussites' crude weapons.

Jan Žižka is unfortunately not a widely known figure outside central Europe, but no work on him or on the Hussites fails to describe him as a genius, the most talented general of his time. Although his wagenburg was effective for only a short period in military history, it shows what one imaginative leader can do with the materials at hand to exploit an innate but often unseen weakness in his enemy. Unseen, that is, except to a blind old man.

10

Oda Nobunaga (1534-1582)

Japanese Daimyo and Unifier

His skills at organization, his tactical flair and above all his visionary
use of military technology placed him in the front rank of generals.
His other outstanding characteristic was his great ruthlessness.

—Stephen Turnbull, *Samurai Commanders*

THE PROMINENT JAPANESE ODA CLAN moved from Echizen Province to Owari Province around the turn of the fifteenth century. Oda Ise Nyudo Josho was appointed deputy military governor of the province by Shiba Yoshishige, the de jure ruler of the province as military governor. Shiba, like most provincial military governors, lived in Kyoto rather than Owari and had little input into the day-to-day operations of the province; that was Oda's job. All was well until the outbreak of the Onin War (1467–77), a struggle between the military ruler of Japan, the shogun, and a number of the provincial leaders, the *daimyo* ("great name"). Japan had an emperor but the daimyo exercised local power with little if any attention paid to either emperor or shogun. Neither the shogun nor the emperor had enough power to restrict or control the feudal houses, which numbered some 260 by 1467. Thus, for all practical purposes, Japan by 1467 was in fact 260 separate countries. Each daimyo was independent and maintained personal armies.[1] Thus, even when the Onin War officially ended, inter-daimyo conflict continued in what was called the Sengoku (Warring States) Period. Only when Tokugawa Ieyasu established hegemony in the early 1600s did that era come to an end.

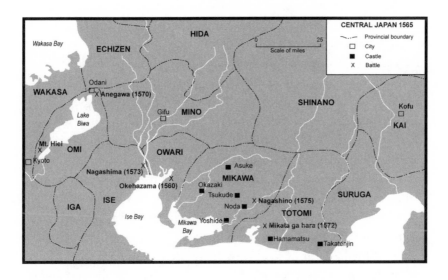

THE SHIBA CLAN FOUGHT among themselves during the Onin War, and the Oda took advantage of the rift to take over control of Owari Province. This, however, resulted in a split in the Oda clan. Two factions controlled half the province each: the Ise no Kami occupied the "upper" districts nearer the capital city of Kyoto, and the Yamato no Kami controlled four counties farther away in the "lower" districts. Through most of the first half of the 1500s the Ise no Kami branch was under the leadership of Oda Nobuhide, who seems to have held true power despite his subordinate position to Oda Michikatsu, the deputy military governor. In the 1540s Nobuhide organized attempts to expand his domains at the expense of neighboring provinces, a project in which he was only partially successful. In 1547 he lost a major battle to Saito Dosan, but the campaign had an interesting outcome. In 1549, Nobuhide married his second son and heir, Nobunaga, to one of Saito Dosan's daughters. This marriage cannot be seen as a sign of Nobuhide's deference, as it was Saito's daughter who moved to Owari Province. Rather, it seems to have been a formal acknowledgment by Saito Dosan of Oda Nobuhide's military strength.[2]

The second son mentioned above, Nobunaga, was born on 9 July 1534. Nothing is mentioned of his upbringing and youth other than that in his teen years he adopted a very eccentric behavior pattern that made many think he was mentally deficient. Whether this was youthful ego or a carefully designed facade is impossible to tell. Neither is it clear why he, as second son, would be heir. He did, however, inherit both a strong domain and influential in-laws when he took over leadership in April 1551 when his father died of disease. When constant prayers by local Buddhist priests did not bring about his father's recovery, Nobunaga took revenge. In the only full-length biography of Oda Nobunaga in English, Jeroen Lamers writes, "Nobunaga then had the bonzes [priests] thrown into a temple with the doors locked from the outside; he told the bonzes that, as they had lied to him about the health of his father, they had better pray to their idols with greater devotion for their own lives. After surrounding them on the outside, he shot some of them to death with harquebuses."[3] Some historians assume that this was a motive for Nobunaga's campaign to annihilate area monks later in his career.

Nobuhide had not been able to completely assimilate all of Owari, and the Ise no Kami faction was further split between Nobunaga and his brothers. It took four years for Nobunaga to begin his move to exercise preeminence. In 1555 he conspired with an uncle against a local official who was plotting against Nobunaga. This resulted in the acquisition of Kiyosu Castle and the end of the Yamato no Kami branch of the family. The following year he beat back attacks from two brothers; one, Nobuhiru, decided afterward to join Nobunaga, but the younger brother, Nobuyuki, remained hostile. In response, Nobunaga tricked Nobuyuki out of his castle in 1557 and had him murdered. It took two more years to capture the final resisting stronghold, but the successful siege of Iwakura, home of the original military governor, gave Nobunaga control of all of Owari Province.

Warfare of the Time

MEDIEVAL JAPANESE WARFARE prior to the Sengoku period meant samurai warfare. Although battles occurred with large numbers of conscript infantry, they carried no historical significance. In traditional samurai warfare, battles were large collections of individual combats. Warriors would announce themselves, pair off with opponents of similar rank, and fight with the high-quality swords for which the era is so famous. That formality began to disappear during the Mongol invasions of the 1100s, when a samurai who singled himself out before the steppe warriors immediately found himself pincushioned by arrows. The samurai thereafter became expert horse archers, with retainers and conscripts in support as infantry. The bow of the time (*yumi*) was some seven to nine feet tall, with the grip offset below center. It was a laminate of wood and bamboo. Like the Mongols, the Japanese designed their arrowheads in multiple shapes for differing functions and fired them from a finger-and-thumb release. The role of samurai as archer, however, was changing by the time of the Sengoku period, when firearms were introduced into Japan.

The samurai warrior wore rawhide or iron lamellar armor. Like the samurai sword, the iron plates would be manufactured with the iron being repeatedly beaten and folded over, to a final thickness of 2 mm. A complete suit of armor could weigh as much as thirty pounds. In the sixteenth century the breastplate became solid rather than layered, more like the European armor of the time. The samurai resembled the European knight, in fact, with the addition of the *sashimono*, an identifying device such as a flag, worn on the back. Samurais carried a *te-yari* (hand spear) or *mochi-yari* (held spear), which could vary in shaft length between 3.2 and 4 meters. Blade lengths varied enormously, from about 10 centimeters to 1.5 meters.[4] With or without armor, the samurai always wore one or two swords, even though by the Sengoku period the samurai was primarily a lancer, with the archery being taken over by lesser infantrymen. The yari spear gave its wielder an advantage, being a weapon as useful on foot as on horseback. The range of options for the samurai was thereby extended from their being elite archers to a role of greater versatility. The yari permitted the samurai to defend himself or take the fight to his enemy, in a way that the exclusive use of the bow had never allowed.[5] By the Sengoku period the samurai in battle was a swordsman almost as a last resort.

The bulk of the Japanese armies consisted of *ashigaru*, foot soldiers without sociopolitical rank. Traditionally these were peasant conscripts, which limited warfare to the off period between planting and harvest. They wore what was called a folding cuirass: folding armor consisting of dozens of small, card-sized plates of metal connected by metal rings. The cheapest armor had the plates sewn directly to a quilted lining.[6] The ashigaru may have worn sleeve armor, but almost certainly did not wear any leg armor. By the mid-1500s all armor was lacquered in the daimyo's personal color, usually with his crest painted on the ashigaru's cuirass. The greatest difference in appearance and protection came with the headgear. In place of the samurai's helmet and face mask, the ashigaru wore a simple iron jingasa, or war hat, which was usually shaped like a lamp shade, with a cloth neck guard hanging from the rear.[7]

As seasonal conscripts the ashigaru could use little more than farm tools or spears for weapons. By the Sengoku period, these peasant soldiers had become more valuable, both because damiyo preferred to limit casualties among their samurai and because missile weapons were more widely used. The bow and arrow take time and practice to master, so it became necessary to have full-time infantry to learn the weapons. When firearms were introduced, their shallow learning curve meant farmers could easily learn their use, but the need for more year-round campaigning again meant a reliable soldiery that the farmers could not provide. Nobunaga was the first commander who separated his soldiers from the agricultural laborers, and by doing so obtained a free hand to begin operations at any time of the year he chose.[8] This also gave them a greatly increased status and the ability to progress through the ranks. Toyotomi Hideyoshi, one of Nobunaga's primary generals (and his successor), advanced in this manner. The primary weapon for the ashigaru was the spear, used for both offense and defense. Nobunaga equipped his men with the longest possible spear at six and a half meters, more than three times the height of the man wielding it.[9] The spearmen formed the bulk of the front battle line, with archers and gunmen arrayed among them.

It is the firearms that make this period of Japanese military history significant. Accounts of the introduction of matchlock weapons to Japan are contradictory, although the generally accepted story is that Portuguese merchants shipwrecked on the island of Tanegashima sometime between 1542 and 1545 gave a demonstration of the weapon that so impressed the local daimyo that he ordered his metal workers to immediately begin copying it. Some historians question this version, pointing out that the "contemporary" account was actually written sixty years after the fact and that the possible introduction by the Mongols would significantly predate the Portuguese. Paul Varley notes that "there are other scattered accounts in the records of firearms—perhaps Chinese or Southeast Asian—in Japan before 1543, although none gives a clear idea of what these weapons may have looked like."[10]

The arquebus, or teppo, used in Japan was not as heavy as the original matchlocks of Europe, for it was not necessary to shoot from a rest. As leading Western expert on samurai warfare Stephen Turnbull describes the weapon, "The arquebus was a simple muzzle-loading musket fired by a lighted match that was dropped on to the pan when the trigger was pulled. It was already revolutionising European warfare, and similar models had helped bring about the victory of the Spanish general Gonzalo de Cordoba at Cerignola in 1503."[11] Although with a maximum range of 500 meters it outdistanced the bow, its maximum effective range against samurai armor was 50–100 meters or roughly twice that of the bow. Whatever the original source, Japanese ironworkers by the middle 1500s were making firearms in large numbers, as well as improving them. The danger of having a burning match three-quarters of an inch from the pan struck the Japanese as foolishly unsafe, so they made a modification by adding a pivoting pan cover that was kept shut, covering the priming powder, until the arquebusier was ready to fire. Flintlocks in Europe would later have the same pan cover.[12] Among other improvements were a larger bore to increase the bullet's effectiveness as well as standardizing the number of calibers so bullets could be mass produced. Japanese gun makers refined the comparatively crude Portuguese firing mechanism, developing a helical main spring and an adjustable trigger pull.[13]

By the time Oda Nobunaga came to power firearms had been in use long enough to make them a fairly normal part of the battlefield, even if not yet the dominant arm. Archers were never superseded by musket-firing infantry, but fought side by side with the gun companies; their rate of fire was much greater and their effective range was comparable. It is false to assume that the introduction of the firearm completely altered Japanese fighting methods; the arquebus was just one factor that contributed to a process that was already under way.[14] Nobunaga, however, was one of the first to appreciate the potential of the weapon, ordering 500 from the ironworks at Kunitomo in 1549. He heard about the power of the teppo, that supposedly nothing could stand against it, and he was very impressed. Nobunaga hired the best teppo marksman in Japan to be his teacher, and the troops learned to handle the weapon with fervor and a great amount of drill.[15]

On the other hand, Nobunaga did not immediately embrace firearms as a revolutionary weapon. According to Noel Perrin in his work on the history of firearms, Nobunaga is supposed to have told his followers, "Weapons of war have changed from age to age. In very ancient times, bows and arrows were the fashion, then swords and spears came into use, and recently guns have become all the rage. These weapons all have their advantages, but I intend to make the spear the weapon on which to rely in battle."[16] That attitude began to change over time, however, for by the 1570s he was depending on the firearms. Oda Nobunaga understood the importance of the new weapon quicker than any other daimyo, and he moved swiftly to gain control of all the gun-producing locations in central Japan. In the end he had five major and a number of minor arms foundries under his partial or full control and would develop a new fighting style based on the new weapon.[17]

The armies of Japan were organized along a standard format. In what could be seen as a Japanese version of the gleve system of the Holy Roman Empire, a daimyo like Oda Nobunaga could call on subservient nobles to provide manpower based on their income. Turnbull describes the system: The wealth of a landowner, or a fief holder, was expressed in *koku*, one koku being the amount of rice thought necessary to feed one man for one year. Feudal obligation required the supply of troops according to wealth. As a rule of thumb two mounted men and 20 foot per 1,000 koku would be supplied, although the proportion varied enormously from year to year and from daimyô to daimyô."[18] The army that resulted was a conglomeration of family, vassals, and ashigaru. "It could be computed, and was visibly identifiable, being made up from a hierarchy of units, each of whom had a vertically supportive role, and involved distinguishable weapon troops. . . . Each of these contingents was assigned its place on the battlefield, and fought independently under the overall command of one supreme general."[19] The commanding general, protected by his personal guard (*hatamoto*), would usually place himself on high ground in the central part of the battlefield in order to oversee the battle and send messengers to order unit movements. The messengers, or aides-de-camp, were called *tsukai-ban*. During a battle these elite mounted warriors, chosen from men who were already elite, would be in constant motion between the commander and the generals of the individual clan armies, taking messages and reporting back, surveying the situation, warning of new developments, and generally providing a battlefield communications system.[20]

The armies by the Sengoku period were primarily spear-carrying infantry. Analysis of paintings concerning battles of this period show that archers and gunners were arrayed on the front line amid spear units, acting primarily as skirmishers who did not engage in close combat. Nearly all the fighting was done by infantry armed with spears and swords, with spears by far the more prevalent.[21] Cavalry were outnumbered perhaps twenty to one, mainly seen as infantry unit commanders or tsukai-ban. Although Takeda Shingen's army, one of Nobunaga's main rivals, was well known for the discipline and aggressiveness of its cavalry, the decline of its importance was already well under way.

The Opponents

WITH HIS HOME PROVINCE and his own family finally under his control, Oda Nobunaga began to expand his horizons. Whether he intended from this early stage to actually try to unify Japan is debatable, but he knew that any sort of personal advancement had to have the blessing of the shogun in Kyoto. The position of shogun had long been contested by descendants of the Muromachi *bakufu* (ruling family), a contest that had been a major factor in bringing on the Onin War in 1467, but by 1477 they had become irrelevant, with the shogun rendered almost powerless.[22] Ashikaga Yoshiteru, shogun in the mid-1500s, had been unable to occupy his own palace owing to the fact that Miyoshi Nagayoshi, the daimyo of Omi Province (where Kyoto was located) had not allowed it. This was one of the overriding contradictions of Japan at the time: the shogun was virtually powerless though the supposed military leader under the auspices of the emperor, but at the same time, as a figurehead he commanded "A strange respect" from the daimyo.[23] Gaining the support of the shogun was therefore the way to gain friends and destroy enemies, something of a royal road. In spite of the lack of respect paid to the sovereign in those days, a blessing from the throne was essential to an aspiring leader.[24]

While Nobunaga needed the shogun, Ashikaga Yoshiteru likewise needed him. Yoshiteru wanted to play a more active role than he was able to, so he appointed Nobunaga as military governor, or *shugo*, in Owari Province.[25] The shogun had to walk a fine line between appointing an overly aggressive daimyo who would try to seize control and one he could control but who might be insufficiently powerful to protect him. For a daimyo to aim for dominance he had to be able to safeguard the shogun, which meant controlling Kyoto. Any attempt to do so, however, would provoke moves by the other daimyo either to stop such a move directly or to attack the home province of the first daimyo. During the first half of the sixteenth century, these daimyo were so busy fighting each other there was no real chance of national progress.[26]

Given the constant threat of aggressive neighbors, dependable allies were as vital as dependable troops. Often alliances were negotiated and sealed by marriages, as was indicated earlier by Nobunaga's marriage to the daughter of Saito Dosan. Later, Nobunaga would actively arrange alliances by this method, betrothing sons and daughters to allies as necessary. Other times these were voluntary, including the most important of Nobunaga's alliances, that with Tokugawa Ieyasu. Once a hostage to a rival daimyo to secure his father's cooperation in a campaign, Tokugawa, upon taking over his own clan, tied his fortunes to that of the Odas. It proved a mutually beneficial arrangement: Tokugawa proved to be a trusted and at times vitally important subordinate in battle, but he also used the military power that he accumulated to make himself shogun in the early 1600s.

Another factor in the Sengoku period was a religious movement established in the early 1200s that became a factor by the later fifteenth century, led by the monks of the Buddhist Jodo Shinshu or "True Pure Land" sect. They began to assert political power by uniting farmers, monks, and priests in armed bands known as *ikki*. Through acts of resistance and rebellion they came to challenge the rule of the daimyo in several provinces.[27] The most powerful Pure Land group was the Ikko-ikki, or Single-minded League, established by Rennyo. Although not interested in political power as such, the Ikko-ikki rejected control by outside authorities. Their claim on the souls of peasants and samurai meant potentially divided loyalties when the daimyo needed taxes and military service.

Nobunaga would be obliged to deal with the Ikko-ikki in the future, but his initial concern was with rival daimyo. He had the shogun's favor, but was he strong enough to be the protector, much less a national unifier?

The Battle of Okehazama

BY 1559, ODA NOBUNAGA had secured control over his home province of Owari, and he had a favorable visit with the shogun that same year. However, he was still a minor player and was soon targeted by a more powerful daimyo with designs on Kyoto and the shogun: Imagawa Yoshimoto of Suruga Province, some one hundred miles to the east of

Nobunaga. Although Imagawa had only on-again, off-again alliances with his eastern neighbors (primarily Takeda Singen of Kai), the other daimyo to his north and east were so involved in their own fighting that he thought it safe to make a move toward Kyoto in 1560. Over the previous two decades he had risen from the position of third son and monk-in-training to become ally (through marriage) to the powerful Takeda clan and master of not only his own province but also of Totomi and Mikawa. So with large land holdings and the powerful Takedas to cover his rear, Imagawa prepared to brush aside the upstart Oda Nobunaga and march on the shogun's domain.

Imagawa reached the border of Owari in mid-June, immediately launching attacks on Nobunaga's two forts along the coastal Tokaido road: Washizu and Marune. The attack against Marune was led by nineteen-year-old Tokugawa Ieyasu, daimyo of Mikawa Province and at this time a vassal to Imagawa. After capturing the castle, Tokugawa was given permission to stay behind and garrison the frontier fort at Otaka while the rest of the Imagawa army pressed forward.

When Oda, in his headquarters at Kiyusu, was informed of the invasion and attack on the two forts, he sent orders for the commanders to hold as long as possible. Two versions exist of the council meeting he held that evening. One is that he listened to recommendations from his senior advisors to stand fast and defend Kiyusu. The other version is that when news came of the loss of the two forts he brushed it off. In his book on samurai legends, Hiroaki Sato describes the scene: "His conversations that night contained nothing remotely related to military matters, as they consisted of social gossip. When he found it was very late, he gave his men leave to go home. His house administrators derided him among themselves, saying, 'Well, the adage, "When luck runs out, the mirror of one's wisdom clouds up, too," is certainly meant for this kind of behavior.'"[28] When news came the following morning, 22 June, of the advance of Imagawa's army, his response was much different. He had been up since dawn, and now supposedly he chanted a line from a Noh play: "Man's life is fifty years. In the Universe what is it but dream and illusion? Is there any who is born and does not die?" He then ate breakfast as he donned his armor.[29] He rode out of Kiyusu with only half a dozen retainers, but the rest of his officers gathered their men and caught up.

Oda's first stop was Zensho Temple, very near where Imagawa had established his camp at Dengaku-hazama, near the village of Okehazama. This was an area with which he had been familiar since childhood. Hazama means gorge or defile; thus Imagawa had picked a camp in a seemingly good defensive position, but without room to maneuver.[30] Oda set up his camp with banners flying within sight of Imagawa's position. Leaving a number of men to give the look of busy preparation, Oda led his men around the flank by way of Nakajima, overruling protests from his subordinates that the route went through rice paddies, which would force them to advance in single file. At this point his force numbered somewhere between 2,000 and 3,000. During Oda's maneuver a small force of 300 cavalry struck Imagawa's camp from Zensho and was easily driven off with a loss of 50 men. The unsuccessful assault further contributed to Imagawa's conviction that the Oda force could do him little harm. Imagawa saw this as a sign of divine protection, assuring him that nothing could withstand his power. He had songs sung in leisurely fashion as he continued to lay out his camp.[31] Local peasants and priests brought him and his men food and drink. Imagawa himself was enjoying a head-viewing ceremony, the objects of his appraisal sent to him by Tokugawa from the victory at Marune.

Oda at this point prepared to attack, again provoking protests from his officers. He silenced them by arguing that the Imagawa forces were tired after their march and battles and that they would be resting before continuing their march. Thus, they would be unready for an attack. (Unbeknownst to Nobunaga, the forces that had taken the castles were those of Tokugawa, who was far to the east; the army before him was rested and ready.) Oda told his men that speed was of the essence, instructing them to hit hard and fast, create panic, and not stop the pursuit for prisoners. As if to belie Imagawa's assumption of divine favor, a furious hailstorm struck just as Oda's men were positioning themselves for the attack. The storm abated at about 2 p.m. and Oda immediately ordered the charge. Nobunaga's orders had been to advance if the enemy retreated, but to fall back if the enemy rallied and attacked. There was no rally; Imagawa's first line of defense was immediately shattered.[32]

Nobunaga's men were on the enemy before they had even emerged from whatever shelter they had taken from the storm. This was no time for muskets, but hand-to-hand fighting with spears and swords. As the two armies began the engagement, Imagawa was still wrapped in his sense of security. Indeed, he thought the noise of the attack, at first, was merely a quarrel among his own men. He shouted to a passing soldier for silence, but the soldier proved to be one of Nobunaga's men, who killed him.[33] Nobunaga dismounted and fought alongside his men on foot. He hoped to fight Imagawa himself, but such was not to be. It mattered little, for the battle was over in minutes and the pursuit resulted in 2,500–3,000 enemy dead. Oda's casualties are not recorded but must have been negligible.

The battle at Okehazama was a meeting engagement dependent on surprise. It began with a feint and demonstration when Oda fixed Imagawa's attention by establishing his camp and launching a small cavalry attack from it. That, coupled with Imagawa's false sense of security, concentrated the enemy in their own camp located in a gorge. This was a poor decision on Imagawa's part, but he seems to have assumed that the steep hills on either side would offer protection, rather than bottle him up. Oda controlled the tempo of the battle, launching his attack rapidly in the wake of the hailstorm before the enemy could collect themselves. Carrying out an attack on an enemy force some ten times one's own size certainly indicates Oda's audacity. The pursuit was planned from the beginning and carried out to the utmost. The surprise, along with the death of their commander, immediately dispirited the Imagawa force, and they fled after putting up minimal resistance. Although the bulk of the force escaped death or capture, their complete dispersal was sufficient to make this an overwhelming victory.

Jeremy Black argues that the victory was more the seizure of an opportunity than a deliberate attack: "Nobunaga, who received good intelligence reports and was always aware of the enemy's position and actions, was feeling his way toward [Imagawa] Yoshimoto, brushing aside the Imagawa advance forces and presumably hoping to pressurize the main Imagawa army into withdrawing from Owari."[34] Oda did not maneuver them into the gorge nor could he have anticipated the storm, but the ability to read and react is one of the characteristics of the great battlefield general. Black's argument that this was not a strategically planned attack is valid, but from the sources it cannot be doubted that Oda marched out of Kiyusu looking for a battle, not merely to "pressure" Imagawa away.

The battle at Okehazama also had great political ramifications. The vassal Tokugawa Ieyasu had done nothing to aid or avenge Imagawa and carefully made no move to antagonize Oda. He would soon join his forces and the resources of his province of Mikawa to Oda's cause and prove to be not only an invaluable ally and battlefield subordinate, but an able heir to Oda Nobunaga's goal of unifying Japan. With Tokugawa on his side and the Imagawa clan in rapid decline, his eastern flank was secure; Oda could continue his drive to pacify territory to the north.

Although allied to the daimyo of Mino by marriage, Nobunaga's father-in-law Saito Dosan was murdered in 1566 by the daimyo's son. This motivated Nobunaga into action. With the able assistance of Toyotomi Hideyoshi, a foot soldier turned general who had risen through the ranks under Nobunaga's tutelage, Nobunaga built a castle-fort at Sunomata at a river junction on the Owari-Mino border. This dominated the plain of Mino and gave Oda a strong position from which to launch an assault that quickly carried his enemy's castle at Inabayama.

With Mino Province in his control in 1567, Oda established himself at Gifu (formerly Inabayama). Here he received word from the heir to the shogunate, Yoshiaki, who was exiled from the palace. The shogun praised his achievements and asked for aid in recovering territory his family had lost to rebellious vassals and in restoring the vacant throne. These two requests formed the authority for Nobunaga's further action. His motto, engraved on his seal, became "Rule the Empire by Force."[35] Rival daimyo in Ise and Omi tried to interfere, but by late 1568 Nobunaga had defeated their armies and, with Yoshiaki in hand, entered the capital city of Kyoto, where Yoshiaki was restored to his position on 28 December. Despite their initial alliance, the relations between the two deteriorated as time went by, with Nobunaga respecting the office of the shogun but not the person. He built a massive new palace for Yoshiaki while demanding he submit to terms that would reduce him to ceremonial status. Yohsiaki instead courted support from other daimyo while carefully not offending Nobunaga too greatly.

At the end of July 1570 Nobunaga and Tokugawa Ieyasu fought the daimyo of the provinces of Echizen and Omi, Asakura Yoshikage and Asai Nagamasa. Asai was Nobunaga's brother-in-law, but had long-standing ties to Asakura. The battle took place at Anegawa and was a traditional hand-to-hand battle, much of it fought in a shallow river. Although he outnumbered his opponents, Nobunaga needed Ieyasu to deliver a well-timed flank attack in order to save the day. Asakura and Asai were badly hurt but not eliminated as a threat.

The Ikko-ikki

WITH HIS FRONTIERS RELATIVELY SECURE, Oda Nobunaga prepared for a threat much closer to home: the Ikko-ikki. These religious communities comprised new-style warrior monks of the Shinshu sect. Turnbull explains, "The second term in the name, *ikki*, strictly means league. . . . The other word, *Ikko*, provides a clue to their religious affiliation. It means 'single-minded' or 'devoted,' and the *monto* (disciples or adherents of the Shinshu sect) were completely single-minded in their devotion and determination."[36] The Ikko-ikki grew out of the Onin War and out of the tradition of earlier warrior-monk sects. Whereas earlier sects had some trained fighters, they depended mainly on mercenaries; the Ikko-ikki recruited from the peasantry and depended on fanaticism. The Shinshu sect grew out of a breakaway movement from Pure Land Buddhism and was organized in the first half of the fourteenth century by Kakunyo, grandson of the Pure Land sect's founder, Shinran. He established the movement's headquarters at the temple holding his grandfather's ashes, Honganji.

The Shinshu sect turned away from traditional monasticism taught by other forms of Buddhism in order to preach that enlightenment came merely from uttering the name of Amida Buddha, for it grew from an inner urge placed there by Amida. This simpler form of enlightenment was attractive to the peasantry, who had neither the time nor spiritual drive to become monks. The Ikko-ikki communities were started by Rennyo, the eighth leader of the Honganji, at the end of the fifteenth century. Turnbull writes, "Their faith promising that paradise was the immediate reward for death in battle, the Ikko-ikki *monto* (believers) welcomed fighting; nothing daunted them. When the Ikko-ikki were about to go into battle, the sound of their massed *nembutsu* chanting chilled the blood of their enemies."[37] By Oda Nobunaga's time the Ikko-ikki were established in an area virtually equivalent in size to his own, and they were an opposing economic force as well as a military one. Further, when relations between Nobunaga and the shogun went sour, Yoshiaki began courting the Ikko-ikki as well as some of the daimyo. Clearly, the warrior monks and the new militant church, the Honganji, would have to be dealt with if Nobunaga was going to establish his dominion.[38]

The Ikko-ikki were based in temples throughout the region from Kyoto westward, but their three primary centers were at Enryakuji just to the north of Kyoto, Ishiyama Hongonji further to the south (the site of Osaka Castle today), and Nagashima some fifty miles east in the province of Ise, next to its border with Oda's Owari Province. All were built in easily defensible areas, Ishiyama Hongonji and Nagashima in marshy river deltas and Enryakuji atop Mt. Hiei overlooking the southwestern shore of Lake Biwa.

The Ikko-ikki traditionally fought with a halberd-type spear, the *naginata*, which sported a long, wide, curved blade. By the Sengoku period, however, they had not only adopted firearms but were engaged in manufacturing them as well, using the organized and cohesive nature of the Shinshu communities.[39] That same cohesiveness, coupled with discipline and motivation, allowed them to develop into masters of both offense and defense.

Oda Nobunaga began his struggles with the warrior monks in 1570. After his victory at Anegawa in midsummer, he launched an offensive into Shettsu Province, south of Kyoto, against the daimyo Miyoshi Yoshitsugu, leader of one of the clans threatening Kyoto. Miyoshi was able to draw on 3,000 arquebusiers from the nearby Ikko-ikki temple at Ishiyama Honganji, a reinforcement that obliged the Oda forces to withdraw. Turnbull asserts that "Nobunaga's army was stunned both by the ferocity of the surprise attack against it and also by the use of controlled volley firing from 3,000 arquebusiers."[40] This is the first mention of volley musket fire in history.

When Nobunaga marched to Mt. Hiei against a reconstituted army under Asai and Asakura in the winter of 1570–71, Ikko-ikki forces surrounded and forced the surrender of Ogie Castle, commanded by one of Nobunaga's younger brothers, who committed suicide in shame. That loss, coupled with the blame he placed on Buddhist priests for his father's death, must have renewed Nobunaga's personal hatred and coupled it with his political and military needs. Additionally, monks had again aided his enemies during the battle against Asai and Asakura, when 3,000 gunmen from the temple at Enryakuji struck the Oda flank.

Starting on 29 September 1571, Nobunaga moved to eradicate the league in a most brutal way. Starting with the town of Sakamoto at the foot of Mt. Hiei, Nobunaga's army of 30,000 moved toward Enryakuji at the summit in a scorched earth advance, destroying everything in its path. The Ikko-ikki could do little against Nobunaga's large and highly trained samurai army, which destroyed the temple at Enryakuji.[41] All the sources describe it as more slaughter than battle, with every structure burned and every person—man, woman, or child—killed in battle or taken captive and beheaded.[42] Nobunaga's reputation for cruelty grew primarily from this occasion, but the action was effective. Although the temple was later rebuilt, the army of monks based there was never revived.

Nobunaga next moved to focus on Nagashima. An earlier assault in May 1571 had been led by two of Nobunaga's subordinates. They tried to send their cavalry through the marshes but were bogged down in the mire, at which point they were slaughtered by Ikko-ikki gunners and archers. Most of the attacking force was killed. Nobunaga led the next assault in the summer of 1573, using his own arquebusiers to lay down a covering fire while another force struck the flank. Unfortunately for him, a sudden downpour doused the matches on his teppo. As soon as the rain stopped, the monks, who had covered their fuses during the storm, launched a counterattack. The volleys of fire decimated Nobunaga's force, with one bullet narrowly missing him.[43]

Oda Nobunaga finally defeated the Nagashima defenders in 1574 by allying himself with a force of pirate ships with cannon that destroyed the forts' watchtowers and stopped any reinforcement by sea. After capturing two outer forts, Oda was able to surround the fort and fortified monastery and starve the monks out. He refused to accept their surrender and burned 20,000 starving defenders as well as locals who had fled to Nagashima before the attack. His final victory over the Ikko-ikki came in 1580, when he was able to capture and destroy the Honganji temple in Osaka.

Little in the campaigns against the warrior monks shows original tactical brilliance, but by facing the monks' use of volley fire, Oda Nobunaga learned from it. Ironically, then, Nobunaga owed the Ikko-ikki armies a debt of gratitude, for it was they who taught him to be flexible in his fighting techniques and to adopt the volley fire as the most effective technique with the weapons.[44]

Battle of Nagashino

IF ANY DAIMYO POSED A SERIOUS CHALLENGE to Oda Nobunaga as a potential unifier, it was Takeda Shingen of Kai Province. An able general, he had conquered all or part of the provinces surrounding his own and certainly had his sights on Kyoto. To his southwest lay Mikawa, Tokugawa Ieyasu's province. With the fall of the Imagawa clan after the Battle of Okehazama, Takeda acquired the province of Suruga while he and Tokugawa divided the province of Totomi. In 1570, Tokugawa moved his headquarters to Hamamatsu in Totomi Province, which Takeda viewed as a provocative act. What ensued was a Takeda victory over a Tokugawa force (with some Oda allies) at the battle of Mikata ga hara in 1572. In a follow-up offensive the following year Takeda Shingen died; some sources say of disease, others of a wound inflicted by a sniper at the siege of Noda Castle in Mikawa.

Takeda Shingen was succeeded by his favorite son, Takeda Katsuyori. He was a talented soldier but alienated the twenty-four generals and advisors he inherited from his father. His rejection of their advice, coupled with the belief that he was born of an enchanted mother, made his followers less than enthusiastic. Nevertheless, they followed him into Mikawa Province in 1575 even though they argued against it—there was another threat from the north, that of the Takedas' long-time adversary Uesugi Kenshin. Without their right flank, securing an invasion of Mikawa was very dangerous, even if it was a continuation of the strategy his father, Shingen, had been pursuing. However, Katsuyori had a traitor inside Tokugawa's headquarters at the castle of Okazaki, who was to open the gates to him.

Entering Mikawa from the mountains to the north, Katsuyori was marching his men toward Okazaki when he learned that his plan had been discovered and the turncoat had been executed. This turn of events convinced him not to try for the stronghold but to turn southeastward toward Tsukude, a castle he had once controlled before its commander turned his allegiance to Tokugawa. However, he then bypassed Tsukude and marched to Noda Castle on the Toyokawa River, and marched downstream toward the coast to raid three of Tokugawa's castles in the region. Katsuyori attacked and burned two minor outposts of Yoshida Castle (Nirengi and Ushikubo), but failed to take the castle itself. He then pointed his army back upriver toward the final frontier castle, Nagashino. Turnbull observes, "Possession of Nagashino was an asset worth having. It had passed from Tokugawa to Takeda and back again, and covered one of the mountain passes to Shinano. . . Little Nagashino would be a good consolation prize with which to conclude his Mikawa campaign."[45]

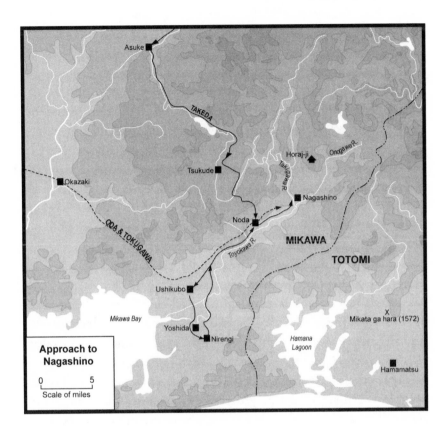

Approach to Nagashino

0   5
Scale of miles

On 14 June 1575 Takeda Katsuyori's troops placed themselves before Nagashino's western and northern faces, the only directions from which it was approachable. It was situated on a small cliff overlooking the junction of two rivers, the Onagawa and Takigawa, joining to form the southwestward-flowing Toyokawa. The fort was wooden, roughly 250 by 330 meters, surrounded by a stone wall and a dry moat. Outer defensive works covered the northern and western approaches. Okudaira Sadamasa commanded the 500-man garrison, who were armed with 200 arquebuses and a cannon.[46] Outnumbered thirty to one, the defenders mounted a gallant defense, repulsing each of Katsuyori's attacks. Katsuyori and his men tried to mine the castle walls, but the defenders foiled that attempt by countermining; samurai sent across the rivers on rafts likewise failed to make any headway, and Katsuyori's siege towers were shot to pieces. After a general assault on the castle was also beaten back, Katsuyori finally decided to starve the castle's defenders into submission.[47]

After four days of fighting, the fort's commander called for a volunteer to alert Oda Nobunaga to their plight. Torii Sune-emon stepped forward. He left in the night, swam past the Takeda guards, and made his way to Okazaki Castle, where Oda and Tokugawa were in residence. They had been alerted to the siege and were on the way with a force of 38,000, but Torii's message motivated them to move more quickly. Rather than travel with the army, Torii returned to Nagashino to report. Unfortunately, he was captured. Promising Takeda that he would approach the garrison and call out to them that they had been abandoned, he instead alerted them to the imminent relief. For this action he was crucified in front of the fort. Turnbull describes the result: "[T]he example of Torii Sune-emon is one of the classic stories of samurai heroism. Many in the Takeda army were moved by his example. . . . Whatever effect Torii-Sune'emon's bravery had on the enemy, its effect on the garrison was inspiring."[48]

As the Oda-Tokugawa force approached Nagashino, Oda decided against marching to the castle to relieve it but instead to deploy on the Shitaragahara Plain about three miles to the west behind the Rengogawa River. Oda was banking on young Takeda's impulsiveness; he was sure Katsuyori would abandon the siege to face him in battle. Arriving on the evening of 27 June, Oda deployed his men in a north-south line about a hundred yards west of the Rengogawa. The northern flank was covered by high ground (Mt. Gambo), while the southern flank was anchored on the Toyokawa River. The Renogogawa was neither wide nor deep, but the ground rose sharply on the western side. Using the naturally strong position, Nobunaga and his men made it stronger by building a palisade halfway between the river and their front lines. This fence, built in sections with openings every fifty yards, would provide cover for the gunners, break any cavalry charge, and provide paths for counterattacking infantry.[49] Behind the palisades he placed his arquebusiers, backed up by the remainder of the army.

The gunners are the primary source of controversy in this battle. Most secondary sources say this battle marks the introduction of musket volley fire, but as pointed out earlier, this had already been introduced by the Ikko-ikki. Almost all sources number Oda's gunners at 3,000. This is challenged, however, by Lamers, who points out: "The number of 3000 harquebusiers [sic] first appears in Oze Hoan's Shinchoki, but the far more reliable and earlier Shincho-Ko ki speaks of only 1000 harquebusiers.

Furthermore, many of the harquebusiers in action at Nagashino were not Nobunaga's own troops but had been temporarily dispatched by his captains. They joined Nobunaga only a few days before the battle, and it is questionable whether Nobunaga had much opportunity to train them in such a complicated action as rotating volley fire."[50]

The gunners deployed in groups of 30–50; given that the front was perhaps 1.25 miles, that means roughly one gunner per seven feet if they numbered 1,000 and did not fire in volleys. The deployment would be the same if they numbered 3,000 and fired in three ranks, as is often proposed. Turnbull supports the traditional view: "Behind the 2,000m palisade Nobunaga placed his remaining 3,000 matchlockmen. The gunners, arranged three ranks deep, were under the command of members of Nobunaga's horō-shū, his finest samurai. Their normal duties were to act as his personal bodyguard, and for Nobunaga to use them to command lower class missile troops shows the immense importance Nobunaga attached to the role of the ashigaru gunners."[51]

Takeda did indeed react as Oda had predicted, though his generals all advised against it. Leaving 3,000 men in the lines at Nagashino Castle, he led his remaining 12,000 through the night toward the enemy lines, moving in four groups of 3,000 through pouring rain. Takeda seems to have appreciated the weather, assuming it would make the matchlocks unusable. Again, Oda had learned that lesson from his first attack against Nagashima; this time his gunners were ordered to make sure their powder and fuses remained dry. Instead, the rain caused the low ground along the Rengogawa to become extremely muddy. The Takeda forces deployed

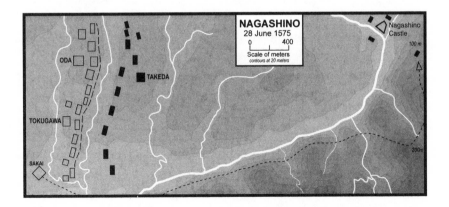

along a stream along the edge of a wood some 200–400 yards opposite the palisades. Once Takeda's forces left the wood line, there was no cover or concealment available except possibly the river's banks.[52] Takeda distributed his men in three commands, line abreast, parallel to Oda's army. Each command had roughly 1,000 cavalry with the remainder being infantry and support troops. The force under Takeda's direct command took position in the rear behind the central force.

As the Takeda army marched, Oda Nobunaga held a council of war. He secretly decided to send 3,000 men (including 500 arquebusiers) on a surprise attack against the Takeda force left behind at Nagashino. To launch a rear attack simultaneously, with the Takeda advance away from the security of their siege lines, would be a tremendous psychological advantage.[53] Their target was a force of 1,000 on Mt. Tobigasuyama, across the Omagawa River from the castle.

By 5 a.m. the Takeda forces were deployed on the edge of the woods. Takeda reasoned that the relatively short distance from the palisades would favor his cavalry, as they could cover it quickly and not take too many casualties from the gunners, who would be busy reloading by the time the horsemen struck. Further, his best unit, stationed on his far left, would sweep around the end of the fence and roll up the Oda flank.

At 6:00 the war drums began beating and the attack started. The charge from the woods to the river was unopposed, as Oda had ordered his teppo commanders to hold their fire until the enemy horse had come within fifty meters. However, on reaching the steep river banks the attack began to lose momentum, as the cavalry struggled. The Oda gunnery commanders exploited the fatal delay and ordered their men to begin laying down volley fire, each rank of gunners firing in rotation,[54] and the guns opened up. The range was such that an arquebus ball would penetrate the armor the samurai wore; it certainly would do damage to an unarmored horse. Thus, the first line of cavalry were hit while virtually standing still at the river bank. The survivors began to regain speed, but the terrain leading up to the palisades was uphill, and as the horsemen got closer to the line of gunners the damage was greater. Tunbull says that "modern experiments have shown that an experienced gunner could hit a man-sized target with five shots out of five at the shorter distance [30 meters], compared with one in five at 50m. The first volley was therefore fired at slow moving targets, while the second was delivered at a potentially greater accuracy but at a moving target. The third volley must have been fired at almost point blank range."[55] No one knows how many were killed in the initial charge. Some certainly survived, but any sort of unit cohesion was lost. Any horseman shooting a gap in the palisades would have found himself massively outnumbered and quickly dispatched. There was enough damage created in the cavalry units that the bulk of the survivors would have retreated.

Several more charges occurred throughout the morning. The battle devolved into hand-to-hand combat as the Oda forces charged out from the palisade. This continued until 1 p.m., when Nobunaga signaled his men to withdraw to the palisade. Temporarily disengaged, the Takeda forces began to retreat. Nobunaga ordered a pursuit, and despite the valiant attempts of Katsuyori's generals to fight a rearguard action, many Takeda samurai were run down and killed by the Oda cavalry.[56]

In addition to the question of the numbers of gunners, one source challenges the whole story of a full-scale cavalry charge. In his history of the samurai, Mitsuo Kure argues, "In the late Heian and Kamakura periods mounted samurai with bows indeed formed the main body of armies; but the introduction of new fighting techniques had changed the way in which mounted soldiers deployed, precisely to avoid the guns. At the time of Shitaragahara [Nagashino] the Japanese samurai dismounted to fight, supported by their retainers. . . . At the very least we may be confident that after the first wave of the Takeda assault had failed, they would know that the muddy ground was unsuited for cavalry charges."[57] Kure further asserts that the Takeda army was defeated primarily by the terrain, which not only slowed an assault by either cavalry or infantry, but had been enhanced defensively not just by the palisades but also by ditches and earthworks. He says that the second wave of the assault pulled down the palisades but immediately faced a ditch. "Attacks were made sporadically, probing forward piecemeal, perhaps using their own dead as fascines to bridge the ditch. . . . Neither Oda Nobunaga, Toyotomi Hideyoshi, Tokugawa Ieyasu or Takeda Katsuyori ever mentioned any particularly effective use of arquebuses, because the deployment of concentrated firepower was nothing new in Japanese tactics."[58] Lamers, however, whose definitive biography of Oda Nobunaga was the first to challenge both number of teppo and their use in volley firing, still supports the traditional view of cavalry's role in the battle: "Katsuyori gave away his advantage of speed by charging headlong into Nobunaga's line of defence, sacrificing his men to Nobunaga's superior firepower."[59]

Given the impetuosity Takeda displayed and the well-established reputation of his cavalry, it seems logical that the generally accepted version of the battle is correct. Firepower was a key factor, but the strength of the defense and the lay of the land were both overwhelming advantages for the defense. Even had the ground not been muddy, the river and the steeply rising western bank made a frontal assault virtual suicide against even 1,000 teppo. Casualty counts range from several thousand to 10,000 for Takeda Katsuyori and roughly 6,000 for the Oda-Tokugawa army. As a finishing touch, the diversionary raid against the covering force at the castle was also a huge success. The surprise attack quickly overwhelmed the isolated force on Mt. Tobigasu, and the garrison within Nagashino sallied to defeat the troops just outside the walls.

The Battle of Nagashino was the result of an approach march followed by a meeting engagement. Usually such a move results in an attack by the army on the move, but this time Oda's army took up the defensive, choosing terrific ground for provoking an attack by an impulsive commander. The river fronting the Oda lines provided the initial disruption of the attack, with the constructed defenses providing a second one. There were no spoiling attacks; Oda's orders were to stay behind the palisades until the attackers wore themselves out, after which the pursuit was launched. Having destroyed the bulk of the Takeda army, Oda and Tokugawa sent their men immediately out from their positions to pursue the retreating remnants, exploiting the effect of the defensive victory.

Nobunaga's Generalship

IN THE WAKE OF THE BATTLE OF NAGASHINO, Oda Nobunaga went on to conquer much of central Japan before he was ambushed by a traitorous subordinate, Akechi Mitsuhide, in 1582. Mitsuhide's men surrounded the temple at Honno-ji and fought their way into the courtyard, where one of them shot Nobunaga in the side with an arrow. Supposedly he pulled out the arrow, then took up his own bow and killed many of the attackers. He finally received a musket ball in his arm, which ended his resistance. It is said he turned and walked into a burning temple to end his own life.[60]

Modern judgments of Oda Nobunaga's character are not kind. Unlike many of the generals discussed thus far, he had few redeeming characteristics. One thinks of modern views of Alexander, best summed up in the title of one of his recent biographies, "killer of men." But as George Sansom notes in his history of Japan, Oda's methods "were utterly ruthless in a ruthless age."[61] A successful general, he was not an inspirational leader, though he received the loyalty of two talented men, Toyotomi Hideyoshi and Tokugawa Ieyasu, who would lead his armies and succeed him as unifiers of Japan.

Perhaps his primary military importance in Japan was his ability to innovate. He was among the first to recognize the potential of matchlocks, learning how to shoot and acquiring as many manufacturing centers as possible. Here he also encouraged the production of cannon. These had been used, as had the teppo, by pirates, but Nobunaga was the first to use them on a large scale on land, for both offense and defense. It is the arquebus, however, that is most important. Most accounts of the Battle of Nagashino credit Nobunaga with ordering firing according to rank, one group firing while the others reloaded. If indeed he fought in this manner, he was decades ahead of armies in Europe. As we will see in the next chapter, it was Gustavus Adolphus who introduced massed matchlock fire into European warfare during the Thirty Years War a half-century after Nagashino.[62] Oda Nobunaga promoted the manufacture of gunpowder as well, in order to be less dependent on foreign supply. He promoted the use of ashigaru as regular troops rather than militia, and by making them full-time soldiers gave them discipline and status that heretofore had only been in the hands of the samurai. He also began his own navy and experimented with the concept of ironclad ships.[63]

In the principles of war employed in this work, Nobunaga's strengths were objective, the offensive, security, and exploitation. From the beginning of his career, Oda Nobunaga set as his political *objective* the leadership of Japan: "Rule the Empire by Force." Strategically, he used his central location as a power base to which he would gradually gain land and men until he attracted the attention of the shogun and gained the necessary legitimacy to wage war on other enemies. In battle, the center of gravity for him was always the enemy army, whether in the open as at Okehazama and Nagashino, or in forts as at Mt. Hiei, Osaka, or Nagashima. Nobunaga benefited from the practice of the age of having daimyo lead their own armies, so "cutting off the head of the snake" was always a goal since surrender was not an option for such leaders. Subordinate commanders could become vassals, and he built his army in such a fashion, but rival daimyo (or religious leaders) ultimately would not survive defeat.

With the exception of taking up the tactical defensive at Shitaragahara, Oda favored the *offensive*. Although facing an invasion in his opening campaign, he refused to follow the advice of his older subordinates to defend his home castle. Instead, he took the initiative with a smaller force to ambush the Imagawa army at Okehazama. The speed of his reaction to the invasion, the analysis of the Imagawa position, and the fortuitous hailstorm amazed friend and foe alike. It was not, however, a tactic Nobunaga used often. He usually would not attack without a superior force and consistently did so after careful planning.

Although the battle at Nagashino is famous for Nobunaga's use of firearms for defense, he introduced the widespread use of both hand-held matchlocks and cannon primarily on the offensive. He defeated the warrior monks in their castles with gunpowder weapons, including seaborne cannon aboard the ships of mercenaries hired for the assaults on Nagashima. Nobunaga's early victories at Okehazama and Anegawa seem to have had no firearms employed, but the bulk of his campaigns after 1570 have them as an integral part of his army. His campaigns after Okehazama were strategic offensives, and he used this characteristic to his advantage tactically by choosing his battlegrounds when having meeting engagements. This is most apparent at Nagashino.

Nobunaga's attention to the principle of *security* is best seen in two well-recorded instances. When alerted to the Imagawa invasion of his province, he met with his advisors in Kiyosu Castle. As mentioned earlier, his conversations that night consisted of social gossip. Even though this was his first battle and he was but twenty-six years old, Nobunaga knew enough to keep his plans to himself. If any of his less-than-enthusiastic subordinates decided to transfer his loyalty to the stronger invader, he could have taken Imagawa some men but no information.

At Nagashino, Oda was again holding a council on the night before the battle. One of his younger officers, Sakai Tadatsugu, suggested a sneak attack on the small force besieging the castle. He spoke out of turn and was quickly reprimanded. Turnbull comments, "However, Nobunaga interviewed him in private later, and assured him that he supported the plan. His anger had merely been a camouflage to throw any spies off the scent."[64] Kure also comments on security precautions within the Oda forces that night, asserting that one of the reasons for Katsuyori launching the foolish attack was because Takeda's *ninja* scouts had all been killed by the Oda-Tokugawa troops before they could report the layout of the defensive position.[65]

Surely the principle of *exploitation* is the one at which Oda Nobunaga excelled. As noted above, the center of gravity was always the enemy army. Nowhere was this more true than in his battles against the warrior monks. In his battles against rival daimyo, his forces killed large numbers of defeated troops in pursuit, but with the monks it became a matter of massacres. Whether he held a grudge against the Buddhists for their broken promises to keep his father alive or he crushed them with a view to keeping the newly arrived European Christians happy so he could maintain a steady supply of gunpowder, he was intent on wiping them out. In his initial victory at Mt. Hiei, he left few survivors. Turnbull says, "Mount Hiei was virtually undefended except by its warrior monks. The attack had the prospect of being a pushover, but the ruthlessness with which it was pursued sent shock waves through Japan. . . . The next day Nobunaga sent his gunners out on a hunt for any who had escaped, and the final casualty list probably topped 20,000."[66] At Nagashima in 1574, Oda had another 20,000 monks and local inhabitants surrounded in a temple and fort compound. He refused to negotiate with them as they starved, and finally set fire to the complex and burned them all.

Following his victory at Nagashino, Nobunaga invaded the province of Echizen, north of Lake Biwa, the home of a large population of Ikko-ikki. As in the assault on Mt. Hiei, Nobunaga ordered a sweep through the province, killing anyone his soldiers encountered. They killed untold thousands; while his troops took countless men and women with them as slaves to their respective home provinces, they took no monks prisoner.[67] Only at his victory at Osaka Castle, the headquarters of the warrior monks, did Nobunaga show mercy. A long siege finally ended with an appeal for clemency by the emperor. Oda had arranged for the imperial letter to be sent in order to bring the battle to an end, but he honored the surrender agreement. He burned the buildings, but killed no more monks.

It is as an innovator that Oda Nobunaga stands out in Japanese military history. Like other commanders discussed in this work, he saw the technological wave of the future, and he rode that wave to both military and political victory. By creating larger standing armies of peasant warriors to supplement the traditional samurai, and by using that increased manpower to implement massed firepower, he was key to the decline of cavalry in Japan. A similar decline had been taking place in Europe for a century thanks to archers, pikes, and guns, but it came about much more rapidly in Japan because of the tactics Nobunaga implemented. Though remembered as ruthless and dispassionate, Nobunaga remains a critical figure in the formation of the Japanese military and the ultimate unification of Japan.

11

⚜

Gustavus Adolphus (1594–1632)

King of Sweden

While the world stands, our king, captaine, and master cannot be
enough praised.

—Robert Monro

GUSTAVUS ADOLPHUS'S GRANDFATHER, Gustavus I Vasa, is regarded
as the "Father of Sweden." He expelled Danish invaders from the country
and was named king in 1523. Gustavus continued to fight the Danes, as
well as the Russians, but on the domestic front he is most important for
introducing the Lutheran Church. He ruled until 1560, when he was
succeeded by his son Erik. Erik's eight-year reign, marked by increasing
insanity, came to an end when he was deposed by his half-brother John.
John was king of Sweden and Finland until his death in 1590; during his
reign he fought wars with Denmark and Russia. John's marriage to a Polish
princess made it possible to place his son Sigismund on the throne of the
Polish-Lithuanian Commonwealth in 1587. Upon John's death, Sigismund
assumed the kingship of Sweden and Finland as well. He ruled from the
Polish capital at Krakow with his uncle Charles as regent in Sweden. Sigismund, raised as a Catholic, had agreed not to interfere with Lutheranism
in his home country; Poland was a Catholic nation. Thus, it was Sigismund's support for the Counter-Reformation that motivated Charles to
seize control and have the Riksdag (the Swedish legislature) name him
king. A Swedish victory over the Poles at the Battle of Stångebro in 1598
led to Sigismund's official deposition the following year.[1]

Charles's son Gustavus thus came to be in line for the Swedish throne only after a tumultuous succession process. Charles ruled with the advice and consent of the Riksdag, and during his reign he consolidated Sweden's borders and its religion. He taught Gustavus the lessons of ruling well and appointed good tutors for his son's education. Gustavus's primary tutors were Johan Skytte ("one of contemporary Sweden's rather sparse intellectual luminaries")[2] and Johan Bure, an expert in runes and Swedish history and myth. Under the direction of these teachers Gustavus became fluent in five languages and did passably well in five others. His teachers saw a young man grow up with a great appetite for learning, excelling in languages, literature, and science. He became well known for debating nobles and, when his father allowed it, visiting ambassadors and aristocrats. He therefore developed a speaking style that amazed all who came in contact with him; he was regarded as a first-class orator as well as military leader.[3] Along with the "book learning," his father gave him lessons and experience in governing. Charles was often at odds with the Riksdag and could show a strong aggressive streak when opposed. Gustavus learned tenacity from his father, but also learned from observation that in dealing with government, words can sometimes be more effective than actions.

At fifteen Gustavus grew bored with intellectual pursuits and acted the feckless role of a teen-aged prince. He did, however, show a continual interest in military affairs. He had spent much time among military officers and had received a bit of tutelage from Jakob de la Gardie, who had been in the service of the great Dutch general Maurice of Nassau for some years; from Maurice would come Gustavus's reforms for the Swedish army. Turning sixteen in December 1610, Gustavus felt himself ready for action, and he asked his father for assignment to the east to fight against the Russians. He was denied, but did not have to wait long. In early 1611 the Riksdag declared him to be of age to fight, and the Danes (and their Norwegian subjects) were invading about the same time. The Danish army under King Christian IV captured the city of Kalmar on Sweden's southeastern coast and raided across the countryside, capturing some towns and destroying others. In April 1611, Gustavus was knighted and sent to collect troops to fight for the relief of Kalmar. He quickly recaptured the isle of Öeland, directly opposite Kalmar. He also was successful in the destruction of the town of Christianopol (modern Kristianstad) by outfitting his soldiers in his enemy's traditional clothing—his first use of deception as a combat technique.[4] Gustavus launched a surprise night attack and captured the town quickly; he then ordered the population to leave and burned it to the ground. A few other small actions met with success but in the fall of 1611 Charles, who had been in deteriorating health for some time, finally died. At only sixteen, Gustavus now found himself king and commander in chief.

With two fortress cities in Danish hands, Gustavus broke with contemporary strategic thinking and did not lay siege to either. Instead, he launched an attack into Danish-held territory to the west. It failed, but he launched another, hoping to draw the Danes out of the cities and into the open. They would not comply, however, but instead prepared a naval assault on Stockholm. When Gustavus learned of this, he force-marched his 1,200-man force 240 miles in a week to reach the capital before the attack. There, he put every available man in the city in uniform and awaited the assault. Seeing the large force arrayed against him and not knowing many were civilians, King Christian withdrew. Little more fighting was done and a peace was concluded in 1613. Gustavus negotiated the return of both fortresses, Kalmar and Älvsborg, though he had to buy back the latter. Denmark was out of the way, but Russia and Poland still presented problems.

Gustavus's cousin and rival, Sigismund of Poland, refused to discuss a peace treaty but did extend an existing truce for another five years.[5] Gustav used the time productively. His first move was to address his remaining rival, Russia. At that time Poland ruled much of northwestern Russia, and the Russian nobles were not happy with Sigismund. They offered the throne of Muscovy to Gustavus's younger brother, Charles Phillip. Gustavus hesitated, however, and the throne went instead to a Romanov. Gustavus apparently believed that trying to control such a vast area was more than Sweden could handle, or more trouble than it was worth. As Nils Ahnlund, one of Gustavus's primary biographers, notes, "He had not an atom of confidence in the Russians. He considered that he had a very good notion of their national character, and believed that when dealing with them, even under conditions of peace and friendship, it was essential always 'to keep the possibility in view of having to fight.' His policy was innocent of illusions."[6]

Sweden already held outposts on Russia's Baltic coast (notably Novgorod), and in 1614 Gustavus launched an invasion from there. The primary action was the siege of Pskov, which Gustavus wisely broke off as the winter approached. Little else happened, and a peace treaty was signed in 1617 that gave Sweden control of the entire Russian Baltic coast, and by extension control of all of Russia's overseas trade. In this brief campaign, Gustavus made two key military decisions. First, he displayed the importance of armies versus positions. He told his second in command, Jakob de la Gardie (his tutor on the Dutch tactics of Maurice), that Novogorod was not to be held to the last man if besieged. The city was valuable for trade, but not as important as an army of veterans. Second, he imposed the strictest discipline on his troops: there was to be absolutely no pillage and rapine. All supplies were bought and paid for from the locals, and any failure to follow those orders merited a death sentence. Such a reputation would serve Gustavus well in the future. With two enemies now at peace and a third under truce, the young king now began to implement the improvements to his army that would take him to his fame.

Warfare of the Time

SINCE THE MIDDLE OF THE SIXTEENTH CENTURY, the battlefield had been dominated by the pike. The millennium-long ascendancy of cavalry had begun its rapid decline in the face of long-range firepower in the form of English longbows and gunpowder weapons. While they stopped the charges of the heavy cavalry knights of the Middle Ages, the bowmen and gunners needed protection. Ultimately, the bow fell from widespread use in Europe owing to the difficulty in learning to handle the longbow effectively and the relatively short range and slow reloading of the crossbow. The gunpowder weapon that came to the fore was the arquebus. It also had limited range and a slow reloading time, but it was the easiest to teach recruits how to use. Over time the arquebus evolved into a heavier matchlock musket. Essentially a very large arquebus, a matchlock could weigh as much as twenty pounds. It had a bore of twenty millimeters and fired a two-ounce ball, twice the weight of an arquebus shot. One man could operate this gun by use of a separate, forked rest to support the barrel. Its portability, stopping power, and 400-yard range made it so useful that in spite of its inaccuracy musketeers gradually replaced half the arquebusiers in Spanish infantry units, and most European armies took up the musket.[7]

That is where the pike came in. Its length kept cavalry at bay while the gunners reloaded. The Swiss had first introduced the massed pike formation reminiscent of the ancient Greek phalanx, but it had been perfected by the Spanish in the form of the tercio. In open terrain, the square of pikemen provided the only place of safety where the infantry gunners might take refuge from the enemy's heavy cavalry. In turn, the musketeers' or arquebusiers' fire could support the pikemen's defense, and the enemy's heavy infantry or the attacking heavy cavalry would provide fine targets for arquebus balls.[8] The tercio numbered between 1,000 and 3,000 men, depending on the nature of the terrain. The outer ranks wore some armor and were equipped with pikes fourteen feet long. The next ranks inward were unarmored pikemen, and the center was made up of armored men wielding halberds with wooden shafts about six feet long and a metal spearhead with some sort of blade on one side and a hook or spike on the other. Primarily a defensive formation, the tercio also was used on the offense in battles similar to phalanx warfare, pikes against pikes. The tercio took infantry otherwise vulnerable to charges from cavalry and made them a sort of hedgehog, invulnerable and unstoppable. These slow-moving formations would crush anything in their way, unless it was another such massive square, in which case neither side would gain a decisive advantage. The tactics of the period provided no effective means of penetrating this type of defense.[9]

The muskets were the longer-range offense and defense. In order to maximize the firepower with slow-loading weapons, the Spanish developed the tactic of the countermarch. The gunners would line up in a file ten or twelve men deep. The man at the front of the file would fire his musket, then turn and march to the rear where he would begin the reloading process. The second man in line would follow suit, and so forth until the first gunner was once again at the head of the file, reloaded and ready to fire. The musket was slower to reload even than the arquebus and a musketeer could at best fire a shot every ninety seconds, but the range and hitting power (it was able to pierce plate armor at a hundred yards) made up for it.

When it came to cavalry, the day of the armored knight was gone, and for a time the cavalry reverted to scouting and foraging roles. They began to enjoy something of a resurgence with the development of the wheel-lock pistol, however. The pistol included a steel wheel attached to a spring that the gunner could wind with a wrench and then cock. Then, working on the same principle as a cigarette lighter, when the gunner released the spring, the turning wheel struck flint, sending sparks into the pan, igniting the powder, and thereby firing the gun.[10] Although more efficient than the matchlock, it was far more expensive and required a gunsmith to repair the mechanism, whereas a matchlock rarely broke down. For cavalry, however, a matchlock was impossible to use with any degree of effectiveness because it was a two-handed weapon. A wheel-lock could be cocked for later firing and discharged with one hand. A cavalryman would carry two pistols in holsters and a third in a boot and became a force to harass a tercio and potentially cause enough damage to create an opening for charging infantry.

German mercenary cavalrymen developed the tactics to maximize the effectiveness of the wheel-lock pistol. They wore armor for close-in protection, as well as a helmet. They then charged at a trot in a line of small, dense columns, each several ranks deep, and with intervals of about two horses' width between files. As they approached a tercio, the front-rank horsemen each emptied their three pistols and then swung away sharply to the rear—a tactic called the caracole.[11] Thus, the cavalry developed their own version of the countermarch. This took a lot of practice to do well and could be broken up by a countercharge.

This was the way European armies fought for several decades prior to the Thirty Years War. Since the 1560s the Spanish had kept their armies in the United Provinces of Holland, hoping to suppress Protestantism. In an intermittent Eighty Years War, the Dutch learned weapons and tactics from the Spanish, and began to alter them. The architects of this change were Maurice of Nassau and his cousins, William Louis and John. Maurice was not a spectacular general in the field, often too hesitant when haste was called for. Even so, he transformed a motley group of mercenaries and part-time militia into a professional fighting force that was enough to win him a lasting place in the evolution of modern war.[12] Although the Dutch operated with a core of native soldiers, they also depended on the mercenaries, who had been the soldiery of Europe for decades. Naval difficulties with the English hurt the income from the New World vital to Spain's economy and military goals, and irregular pay to their soldiers in northern Europe caused discontent and mutinies. A growing nationalism coupled with a growing navy gave the Dutch both motivation and money to maintain themselves as the war dragged on, and it was those two factors that gave Maurice what he needed to overhaul his army.

Maurice, son of William the Silent, was named at age twenty-one to be an admiral of the Dutch navy and commander of armies opposing the Spanish. The titles did not translate into power, as he was under the authority of a confederation of states that was extremely difficult to make effective. With too many heads of state jockeying for power, Maurice's noble status gave him influence but not control, so it is even more remarkable that he successfully remade an entire military system while a war was going on. The basis of his reforms came from study of the old Roman and Byzantine military texts, the Renaissance bringing about a fascination with all things from the classical world.

Maurice realized the major problem with the tercio: it was a big target. With artillery still too large to easily maneuver around a battlefield the tercio's size was a problem, but if employed properly the muskets could provide enough firepower to break a mass of pikemen. Maurice understood that to increase firepower, one would have to bring more guns to bear at once and increase the speed of reloading. Maurice reduced the size of the formations from 2,000 to about 600, made up of companies consisting of 130, and ranged them no more than 10 ranks deep, as opposed to the 25–30 ranks of the tercio. More units meant more guns along a greater front. A more rapid reloading procedure could keep the guns firing faster, and if two or three ranks fired at the same time before retiring to reload, a lot of lead would be flying. In his work on the military revolution of that age, Geoffrey Parker writes, "We can date the Dutch discovery of the 'volley' technique very precisely: it first appeared, in diagrammatic form, in a letter from William Louis to his cousin Maurice dated 8 December 1594, and the author asserted he had derived the idea from an assiduous study of the military methods of the ancient Romans."[13] (This is twenty years after Nagashino saw the use of volley fire.) Thinner lines not only created massed firepower but presented a smaller target for return fire.

To further increase firepower Maurice developed iron foundries in the United Provinces to cast cannon, for which he began the standardization of bore and shot, casting only three sizes: 12-, 24-, and 48-pounders, all large artillery pieces and difficult to maneuver. These guns were placed in front of the infantry, who were deployed in a checkerboard formation, as the ancient Romans had been, in order to advance and retreat through the gaps. Cavalry units were placed to protect the flanks. Maurice's reforms achieved two objectives. First, the battalions were more mobile and better suited to operating in the marshy terrain of the Netherlands. Second, they were much handier than the larger tercios both in offense and defense.[14]

To make these improvements work, it was necessary to have more than short-term enlistees. The population of the United Provinces was no more than a million people, most of whom were dedicated to farming or trade. Maurice would therefore be obliged to use mercenaries. The difference was that these men were hired for long service, not the seasonal fighting that was typical of the age. Once hired, the soldier now received something almost no mercenary ever had: a regular paycheck and regular supplies. In return for these, he had to undergo intense training, which developed both discipline and unit cohesion. Again, this was something not seen in western Europe since ancient Roman times. Smaller also units meant more units, which meant more officers and noncommissioned officers. These men were usually Dutch rather than foreign, as most of the mercenaries tended to be. Thus, the officer corps had loyalty to the state, and the soldiers developed loyalty to the unit. Pikemen, musketeers, and cavalry working together took constant practice, something no short-timer would have been interested in. The reintroduction of drill into the army was an essential part of Maurice's reforms and a basic contribution to the modern military system.[15]

The negative side of the lengthened front was that more men had to actually face the enemy and exercise courage, since there were no longer massed ranks within which a new recruit could be lodged until he had seen some action. This, again, is where the discipline created by the drill and the unit cohesion came into play. Just how effective such training would be was illustrated in the two battles the Dutch army actually fought under Maurice; they were both victories, but hardly overwhelming ones: Turnhout in 1597 and Neiuwpoort in 1600. These suggest that there were still improvements to be made in order to achieve notable victories, but they laid the foundation on which Gustavus built.[16]

Gustavus took what Maurice had created and adapted it for Sweden and for a more aggressive style of warfare. From a manpower standpoint, Gustavus used Swedes as officers and soldiers, thus creating a truly national army. Mercenaries were simply too independent to form a standing army. Michael Howard observes, "Armies were in a continual state of deliquescence, melting away from death, wounds, sickness, straggling, and desertion, their movements governed not by strategic calculation but by the search for unplundered territory. It was a period in which warfare seemed to escape from rational control; to cease indeed to be 'war' in the sense of politically-motivated use of force by generally recognized authorities, and to degenerate instead into universal, anarchic, and self-perpetuating violence."[17] Instead, Gustavus drew on the conscription system initiated by his grandfather and expanded by his father. One man in ten from a community was liable for military service, and the remainder of the citizens provided the necessary taxation and supplies to maintain them. This offered sufficient manpower to create a strong defense force for a population of a million and a half, but to go campaigning would require more. Thus, Gustavus was obliged to fill his ranks with mercenaries when away from home. They, however, would be forced to learn the Swedish way of war.

The soldiers were organized in squadrons of just over 400 men, almost equally pike and musket. They were deployed with the pikemen in the center and the musketeers equally divided on both flanks, all arrayed six deep. Attached to each squadron was a unit of 96 musketeers for reconnaissance or reserve. Three or four squadrons made up a brigade. The infantry were equipped with improved arms. The musket the Swedes used had, like the Dutch, been produced in a standardized caliber. Already the powder horn, used to carry and measure the gunpowder charge, had been replaced by the single cartridge. A premeasured amount of powder was stored in a wooden vial, with numerous vials carried on a bandoleer around the gunner's neck. Gustavus improved this further by introducing (or perhaps merely expanding the use of) the paper cartridge, with both powder and musket ball combined in one disposable package. The Swedes also abandoned the matchlock for a "snaplock" (an early flintlock). They were issued in great numbers during the 1620s, and not just to artillery and bodyguards as in other armies. One of the main reasons Gustavus introduced this was the difficulty in Sweden of finding material with which to make the match cord.[18]

The Swedes not only manufactured a lighter musket, but by removing the need for a rest, the number of movements necessary for reloading decreased and the rate of fire thereby increased. The two-rank volley instituted by the Dutch was also changed to three ranks. When the musketeers had their weapons loaded and had completed the shoulder-to-shoulder rearrangement into three ranks, the front rank knelt, the second rank stooped, and the rear rank stood, then all three ranks simultaneously fired.[19] Gustavus also altered the nature of the countermarch, whereby the musketeer marched to the rear of the line to reload and await his turn to fire again. After the front three ranks fired, they would stand fast to reload as the following three ranks stepped forward, hence creating almost a rolling barrage.[20]

The pike underwent a transformation in the Swedish army as well, shortened from sixteen feet to eleven. The metal point extended from a sheath long enough to keep the pike from being broken or hacked off in close combat. Although the pike remained the sole defense for the musketeers, Gustavus used it for more than keeping the enemy at bay. For him the pike was the battle-winning weapon, a leftover from tercio-style warfare. The goal of the musketeers was to break the enemy line in order for the pike-wielding infantry to finish the job.[21]

Shot, however, was not to be provided only by musketeers. Another of Gustavus's innovations was light artillery. Cannons had long been standard equipment, but were primarily used in siege warfare (very common at the time) with minimal but increasing use on the battlefield. Their size meant that once set in place, they were extremely difficult to move, hence of mixed effectiveness against moving targets. Prior to Gustavus, artillery was considered to be a technological specialty, usually operated by civilian engineers. The gunners often scorned the requirements of standard military discipline and were scorned by the regular army in return. Gustavus made them military professionals as well.[22]

Maurice had improved the artillery by standardizing bore and shot, but even his guns were large. Gustavus had his foundries cast cannon in 24-, 12-, and 3-pounder sizes. The smallest gun became mobile, drawn by one horse or (in case of need) three men. At 625 pounds, it could be hauled where needed and set up quickly, and it was easier to adjust and maintain fire on targets. Initially Gustavus used a copper-barreled gun wrapped in mastic-coated rope with a sheath of leather, but by the time of his German campaign metallurgy had so improved that the replacement 4-pounder was solid metal. Improvements in gunpowder helped immensely to standardize pressures in the tube, thus permitting reduction in thickness of the barrel. As with the musketeers, a prepackaged cartridge simplified loading and assured a high rate of fire for the guns. This weapon completely changed the role of artillery on the battlefield.[23] Gustavus also introduced grapeshot, firing up to twenty-four smaller balls at once in place of one large cannon ball. The Swedish army could thus produce more, and more concentrated, firepower than any army in Europe. Constant practice increased not only the professionalism but the accuracy of the gunners. With these changes, the Swedes had the finest artillery in Europe, and historians have argued that the modern role of artillery on the battlefield truly began with Gustavus.[24]

"For all that, it was Gustavus Adolphus's cavalry that became the true decisive weapon and that most fully bestowed offensive power upon his army."[25] So says Russell Weigley, but different authors have their views of which arm was really key to Swedish victories. The cavalry under Gustavus was primarily made up of Swedes, usually the nobility or the wealthy farmers. Gustavus did not employ them as scouts or in the caracole maneuver, the normal roles for horsemen of their day. He wanted to restore the days when cavalry used their weight and speed for shock power. Hence, although the cavalry were armed with the wheel-lock pistols, their primary weapon was the saber. Each cavalry unit had a musket unit attached, so they could approach the enemy at the same speed, and the musketeers could deliver a massed volley that would disorganize the enemy sufficiently to allow the cavalry to launch their charge. The musketeers would reload during the charge to assist with a second wave or cover a retreat, as necessary. Gustavus also attached 3-pounder guns to his cavalry for the same purpose. As mentioned earlier, the role of gunfire was to open a hole in the enemy formation, and the cavalry would use cold steel to finish the enemy off.[26]

The Opponents

FIREPOWER, CLOSE COMBAT, and cavalry charge all have their proponents as the key to Gustavus's improved military system. One thing is sure, however: the alterations came during and as a result of the campaign against Poland in 1621. With Denmark and Russia out of the way, and the Swedish army beginning to adapt its version of the Dutch system, the war against Sigismund was the proving ground for weapons and tactics. Details of the war itself are minimal, but the overwhelming shock of the lance-armed Polish cavalry convinced Gustavus to alter his own tactics. Also during this war, in 1623, Gustavus instituted his first artillery company, which by 1629 had expanded to six companies forming a regiment under the command of Lennart Torstensson. The Swedes conquered Livonia (in modern Estonia) fairly quickly and moved the war into Prussia. There, victories were a bit harder to come by, especially when Holy Roman Emperor Ferdinand (who was also Sigismund's brother-in-law) provided an army to assist in the Polish defense. In a battle at Sztum on 29 June 1629, the Swedes came off second-best in a somewhat inconclusive battle, at which Gustavus was almost captured. The battle did, however, bring about another truce between the two powers, as Sigismund was tired of fighting and Gustavus wanted to enter the war going on in Germany.[27] Hence, both sides were open to the offers of mediation from England and, more importantly, France. As Basil Liddell Hart writes, "Gustavus was wanted on a greater stage, and [French Cardinal] Richelieu's master mind pulled the strings to release him for the new part."[28] The Treaty of Altmark began yet another truce, this one to last for six years; this freed up Gustavus to go to war against the Holy Roman Empire, France's rival.

The Polish war had turned the Swedish army into a finely tuned machine made up of combat veterans. The soldiers and Gustavus had matured from the experience. Theodore Dodge comments, "Under Gustavus' careful eye, every branch of the service during these campaigns grew in efficiency. Equipment, arms, rationing, medical attendance, drill and discipline, field-maneuvres, camp and garrison duty, reached a high grade of perfection. . . . Not only had Gustavus learned to know his generals and men, but these had gauged their king."[29]

Gustavus's rationale for invading German territory is the topic of much debate. He quickly became to the German people the champion of the Protestant cause, even though their princes were slower to embrace his crusade. Although Gustavus certainly made war against the Catholic Holy Roman Empire and sought Protestant princes as allies, his motives certainly could have been political rather than religious. In a speech in 1629, Gustavus remarked:

> The Papists are on the Baltic. . . . [T]heir whole aim is to destroy Swedish commerce, and soon to plant a foot on the southern shore

of our Fatherland. Sweden is in danger from the power of the Haps-burg; that is all, but that is enough; that power must be met, swiftly and strongly. The times are bad; the danger is great. It is no time to ask whether the cost will not be far beyond what we can bear. The fight will be for parents, for wife and child, for house and home, for Fatherland and Faith.[30]

When he landed in the province of Pomerania, Gustavus issued a "press release" that was translated and distributed across Europe. It listed his reasons for invasion: diplomatic insults, imperial aid to Poland during the recent war there, imperial designs on the Baltic region, and oppression of the Germans by the emperor. There was no mention of military goals or of religious motivations. Gustavus's chancellor, Axel Oxenstierna, later averred the invasion was "not so much a matter of religion, but rather of saving the *status publicus*, wherein religion is also comprehended."[31]

Gustavus later began to posit the idea of a Protestant league of sorts, which some have suggested meant that he had imperial designs of his own. His major biographers, Ahnlund and Michael Roberts, agree that there was no divorcing politics from religion. It may have been some, any, or all of these motives. Or, to the cynic, none of them: some think he fought for fighting's sake.[32]

When Gustavus and his army of 13,000 arrived near Peenemünde on the Pomeranian coast in July 1630, he had but one ally, the port city of Stralsund. The city had been under siege by imperial forces the previous year, and Gustav had dispatched 5,000–6,000 men under the Scottish mercenary Alexander Leslie to stiffen the resistance. The imperial forces' goal had been to seize the city and take over the fleet in its harbor to create a naval force strong enough to dominate the Baltic, a project hatched between Sigismund and the Spanish (yet another reason for Gustavus to go to war). The reinforced garrison at Stralsund proved too difficult to overcome, so the attention shifted to another port, Wismar.

Although Gustavus had income from tolls from Prussian and other Baltic ports, he needed other sources of financial support as well as mil-itary assistance. In 1631 the French diplomat Cardinal Richelieu (angling to increase French power at the expense of the Holy Roman Empire) entered into an agreement to provide a monthly subsidy. He realized the danger of an overly strong Hapsburg empire and was willing to finance efforts to combat it; local princes under more direct threat were less willing. Only those whom Emperor Ferdinand had dispossessed from their lands came to Gustavus's aid, and that was little more than moral support.

As for his enemies, Gustavus faced primarily Count Johann Tserclaes Tilly, a professional soldier of great experience, who had started his military service in 1574 at age fifteen. Having seen Protestant forces destroy his home province of Brabant in the Spanish Netherlands, he had a passion for revenge. He served in the wars against the Turks and rose through the ranks. He was named an imperial field marshal in 1605; later that year he accepted the position as commander of the Bavarian military. When Bavaria created the Catholic League in 1609, he became commander of its forces. During the Thirty Years War (starting in 1618), he led armies in Bohemia and Denmark, winning an unbroken series of victories. By the time he came to face Gustavus, however, he was of advancing years and declining abilities. Tilly was an excellent commander and had a grasp of strategy at least as good as Gustavus's, but was wedded to the tercio style of fighting. He has at times been depicted as over-the-hill, but he was not without some of his old talents.[33] Often fighting alongside Count Albrecht von Wallenstein, Tilly became supreme commander when Wallenstein was removed from his position shortly after the Swedish forces arrived. Subordinate to both was Field Marshal Count Gottfried Pappenheim, commander of the imperial cavalry. Still comparatively young, he was almost a caricature of a fiery cavalry leader. He was at times brilliant, but too hotheaded to be consistent and often insubordinate. He despised Tilly, thinking him senile.[34] For almost a year the two sides played a game of position. Gustavus spent six months capturing as many cities along the coast as he could in order to maintain his lines of supply. He campaigned into the north German state of Mecklenburg and brought it under his control. The Swedish army was growing with the addition of local mercenaries, and Gustavus was determined to maintain supply depots to keep his army from engaging in pillage and thus alienating the population. By the end of 1630 he had established secure supply bases, but picked up few allies. The elector of Brandenburg refused to cooperate with Gustavus, and in February 1631 the elector of Saxony, John George, called a conference of Protestant leaders to his capital in Leipzig and proposed a defensive alliance to field a neutral force that

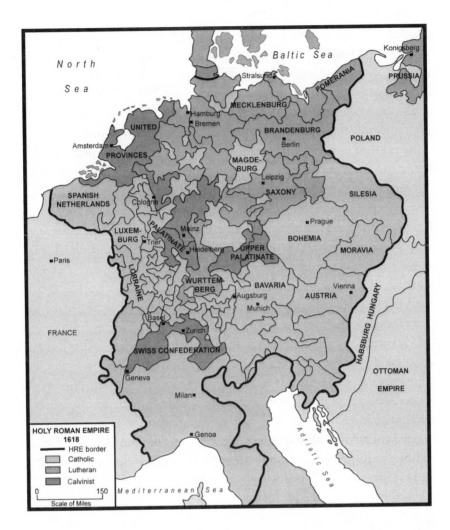

North Sea

Baltic Sea

Königsberg

Stralsund

PRUSSIA

POMERANIA

MECKLENBURG

Hamburg

Bremen

BRANDENBURG

POLAND

UNITED

Berlin

Amsterdam

PROVINCES

MAGDE-
BURG

Leipzig

SILESIA

SAXONY

Cologne

Prague

LUXEM-
BURG

Mainz

BOHEMIA

Trier

PALATINATE

Heidelberg

UPPER
PALATINATE

MORAVIA

Paris

LORRAINE

WÜRTTEM-
BERG

BAVARIA

Vienna

Augsburg

AUSTRIA

Munich

Basel

Zürich

HABSBURG HUNGARY

FRANCE

SWISS CONFEDERATION

OTTOMAN
EMPIRE

Geneva

Milan

Adriatic Sea

**HOLY ROMAN EMPIRE
1618**

——— HRE border

☐ Catholic

▨ Lutheran

■ Calvinist

0   150

Scale of Miles

Genoa

Mediterranean Sea

would support neither Sweden nor the empire. Such an attempt to avoid commitment was futile when the two opposing armies met to fight in Saxony, and John George had to make a choice.

Quick campaigns of misdirection kept Tilly off balance while Gustavus captured Frankfurt an der Oder, which gave him a strong strategic position as well as a riverine line of supply. In early May 1630 he finally convinced the elector of Brandenburg to ally with him, but had to reconvince the wavering elector in June by marching on Berlin and threatening it. Gustavus still met reluctance from John George. Meanwhile, Tilly's forces expanded a blockade of the city of Magdeburg into a full-scale siege. Gustavus had sent one of his generals, Dietrich von Falkenberg, to organize the city's defense, but the inhabitants were more worried about their own safety than the overall progress of a war that had dragged on for fourteen years. Hearing of the Brandenburg alliance and fearing a quick Swedish march to relieve the city, Tilly's forces on 20 May stormed the city and took it. The result was 25,000 of the 30,000 citizens killed in the siege, the pillaging, or the fire that burned most of the city to the ground. Tilly's army had been starving and looted the city, but the fire destroyed what long-term succor it might have provided. Still hungry, Tilly had no choice but to march on to unplundered Saxony if his men were to be reprovisioned. Russell Weigley comments, "Tilly was an experienced veteran soldier and a generally sound commander, [but] he had mismanaged the logistics of his 1631 counteroffensive. Misman-agement of logistics was not difficult, of course, after much of Germany had been the scene of marching and countermarching for many years and had repeatedly been picked bare of sustenance."[35]

Tilly sent word to John George to join him or be invaded. That threat, coupled with the outrage over the destruction of Magdeburg, finally convinced the Saxon elector on 11 September to join forces with Gustavus. It was not a ringing endorsement of the king of Sweden or the Protes-tant cause, and Gustavus would always have doubts about John George's dependability. After all, it was only Tilly's capture of John George's capital of Leipzig that pushed him to an alliance. They joined forces on the 15th, and two days later the armies were in battle.

Breitenfeld

BOTH ARMIES WERE SHORT OF SUPPLIES, but Tilly was expecting rein-forcements from the south. A conflict in Italy had just been brought to a close, and imperial forces were on their way to aid him. All he had to do was sit tight in Leipzig once he captured it, fatten up his men, and choose his own time for battle when the relief army arrived. Further, he believed that his veterans could easily handle the Swedes, even though they had made little progress against them in the past several months. In a council of war on the 15th, Pappenheim claimed the neither the Saxons nor the Swedes were anything to worry about.[36] Tilly's army numbered 21,400 infantry and 9,900 cavalry, with 26 artillery pieces.

Gustavus arrived in Düben, twenty miles north of Leipzig, to join with John George on the 15th, just as Leipzig was falling. He commanded 14,742 infantry and 8,064 cavalry plus 54 artillery pieces. John George brought 12,100 infantry, 5,225 cavalry, and 12 guns.[37] The primary difference between the two armies was not numbers but experience, since the Saxons were for the most part recently called up militia and had few veterans. The one bright spot in the Saxon army was Lieutenant General George von Arnim, formerly second in command to Wallenstein and a veteran of the imperial campaign against the Swedes in Poland. Unfortunately, he had just assumed the position of army commander the previous June, so he had too little time to whip the troops into shape. From Düben, the combined force marched south to engage the imperialists. Between the two armies ran a small river, the Loder. Although Pappenheim's cavalry did engage in some minor harassment, Tilly did not attack during the river crossing. Had he placed his troops there and awaited an attack, the outcome could have been radically different. According to Liddell Hart, "The formality of the time is well shown by the failure to fall on Gustavus during this crossing."[38] Hans Delbruck's explanation is more practical: "[Tilly] did not do so, probably in order to allow his artillery first to fire on the enemy while he was involved in his deployment."[39]

During Tilly's council of war on the 15th, he proposed staying inside Leipzig and forcing Gustavus to waste men assaulting it or waste time besieging it; after all, reinforcements were just a few days away and could put the Swedes between two fires. The older officers agreed, but the younger officers rallied around Pappenheim, whose nature despised anything but the offensive. Reluctantly, Tilly agreed to fight in the open, perhaps because of taunts that he was too old or afraid to meet Gustavus in battle.[40] It is possible that Tilly overruled the more numerous younger officers but gave Pappenheim permission to take 2,000 horsemen in order to reconnoiter the enemy approach.[41] This was not a wise move. Tilly had exercised wisdom in deciding to remain behind Leipzig's walls, but unfortunately for him, giving Pappenheim an inch was the same as giving him a mile. The young cavalry commander would launch a reconnaissance in force that would oblige Tilly to march to the rescue.[42] Loosing Pappenheim and expecting him to follow orders to merely scout the enemy was too much to ask. Who knows—Pappenheim may actually have thought he could defeat the Saxons and Swedes by himself.[43]

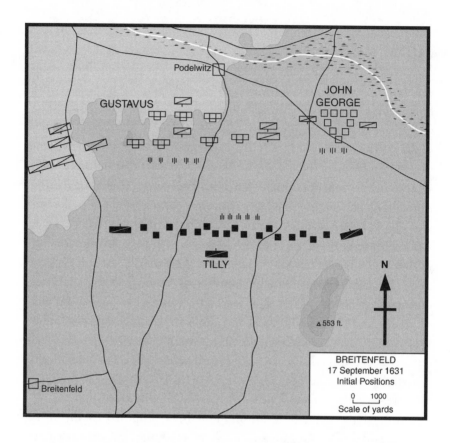

Pappenheim's sally was on the 16th, and Tilly soon began marching his men out of Leipzig. Tilly spent the balance of that day deploying his troops initially in a defensive position, a stance he had rarely taken.[44] Accounts vary, but Gustavus seems to have encamped north of the stream on the night of the 16th. He deployed in line of battle while still on the other side of the river, and his men slept in position. As mentioned, Gustavus's army crossed the Lober against minimal cavalry resistance, then marched forward to face the enemy. Gustavus commanded the center of the army, with Marshal Count Gustav Horn on the left and much of the cavalry on the right under Marshal George Baner. The Saxons under John George and Arnim were deployed on the left flank. The Saxons used the tercio formation but little is known of their exact deployment; possibly it was in a pyramid of units with the point toward the enemy and cavalry on the flanks. With both Saxons and Swedes posting cavalry on their wings, the center of the line thus became predominantly cavalry, but for the mixing of musketeer units as Gustavus had designed.

Tilly was atop a very low ridge and deployed his army with the infantry in the center and cavalry on the wings, the traditional format. Sources disagree on whether his infantry was deployed in twelve or seventeen tercios, but they were divided into imperial troops next to Catholic League troops, who had fought with Tilly the longest. He deployed them line-abreast rather than in the normal checkerboard fashion, probably in order to match the width of the Swedish line. Cavalry was assigned fairly equally to both flanks, Pappenheim commanding on the left and Furstenburg on the right.

The field is open and slightly rolling, so neither side really had a height advantage. Oddly, half the sources describe a mist on the morning of the 17th while the others describe it as dusty and windy. The Swedish army had received their exhortation from their king; the senior officers had been given a less stirring, more pragmatic talk on the need for discipline and flexibility. They decamped about 9:00 and reached the battlefield near noon. They faced imperial cannon fire as they deployed, but soon Torstensson's artillery was arranged along the front, and the Swedish forces' superior number of guns, as well as their ability to load and fire three times faster than the imperial gunners, gave them the advantage as the duel went on for more than two hours. Further, the tercios received terrible damage. The imperial formations were too big to miss, and the effect was disastrous. The forward ranks took the brunt of it, but any ball passing through a man in front still had 10 or 12 more behind him to hit, and for every pikeman who went down there fell an iron-tipped pike to trip fellow soldiers.[45]

Sometime between 2:00 p.m. and 2:30 the armies began to move. The cavalry charged first, although it is disputed if Pappenheim made the first move (a safe assumption) or Furstenburg. Furstenburg's assault on the Saxons bore fruit quickly. For mostly untrained militia, the two-hour cannonade had been frightening enough (with some 1,000 Saxons killed). Now they could see the enemy begin to move toward them and hear their battle cry "Jesu-Maria!" Croatian cavalry led the charge, red cloaks streaming and sabers flashing, screaming unintelligibly as they moved forward.[46] For the supposedly unwieldy tercios, Tilly had them moving in an oblique, a form of advance to be perfected a hundred years later by Frederick the Great. They initially marched not straight ahead but half right, then pivoted half left toward a Swedish flank opening ever wider as the Saxons began to run. It was vintage Tilly and worked as it often had in the past—at least against the Saxons.[47] The Saxon gunners in front broke first, and soon it was learned that John George was galloping away at top speed. The entire Saxon army fell apart and ran, some stopping only to loot the Swedish baggage. The Swedish left was completely broken, and Tilly sent his infantry to take advantage.

On the western side of the field, Pappenheim's cavalry rode up to the mixed cavalry-musketeer units. They fired their first volley from the caracole, whereupon the Swedes responded with massed musket fire and a cavalry sally. Pappenheim quickly withdrew and moved further to his left in an attempt to turn the flank. Gustavus sent in reserves as Baner pulled back to present a refused flank. Pappenheim's second caracole fared no better than did his first. Neither did the third, fourth, or even seventh attack. By 4 p.m. his men had taken a beating from the constantly reinforced Swedish line and massed muskets. Pappenheim withdrew from the field as Tilly was leading his infantry against the collapsed Swedish left flank.

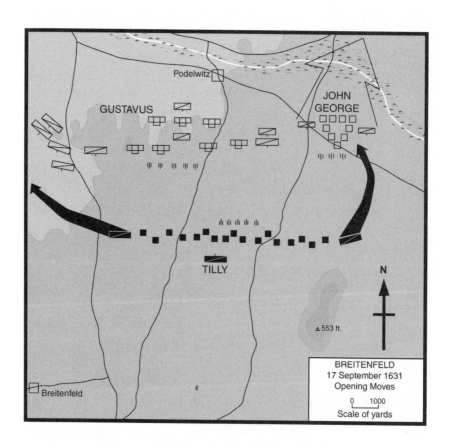

Tilly and Furstenburg were as shocked as Pappenheim had been when they found, instead of an exposed army, another refused flank, this one deployed by Horn. The slow-moving tercios were being easily outmaneuvered by the smaller Swedish units. Horn, however, did not stand and fight, but attacked the imperial forces as they were trying to recover from their charge against the Saxons and change face to meet the new threat. Soon, the imperial ranks were nothing but confusion; and then it got worse. With Pappenheim on the run, Baner's wing advanced and swung east to occupy the ground where Tilly's army had stood before their charge. That imperial charge had left all their artillery behind, and the Swedes quickly seized the guns and aimed them at the rear of the imperial army. Musket fire and attacks from the Swedish lines coupled with cannonballs tearing through their forces from behind: it was more than the imperialists could possibly stand. They too began to waver and run, and the Swedes were quick with the pursuit.

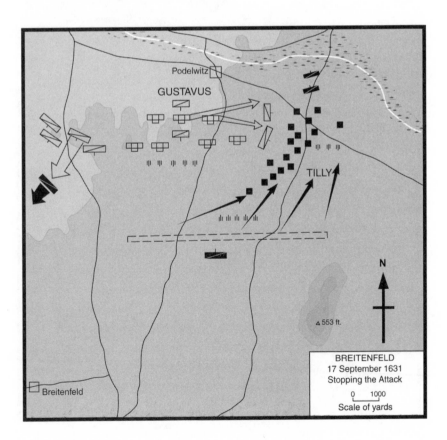

It was an overwhelming victory. Tilly, wounded in the battle, fled the field leaving behind 7,600 dead, 6,000 made prisoner on the field, and another 3,000 taken captive the following day in Leipzig, where a tercio and some stragglers had fled. Thousands more were cut down in the pursuit, died of their wounds, were murdered by the Saxon peasantry, or simply deserted. The imperial forces lost all 26 guns and 120 regimental flags. Pappenheim was also among the wounded.[48] Swedish losses were 2,100; the Saxons lost 3,000 on the field and while being pursued.

Gustavus led his men to Breitenfeld on an approach march leading to a meeting engagement. After more than two hours of an exchange of opening fire, he received the imperial attack. On defense his right flank disrupted Pappenheim's attack with much greater firepower than the attacking cavalry could deliver. This led to a separation of enemy forces when Pappenheim withdrew and Tilly attacked the Saxons. For the first time in centuries a force was made up of units able to quickly move about

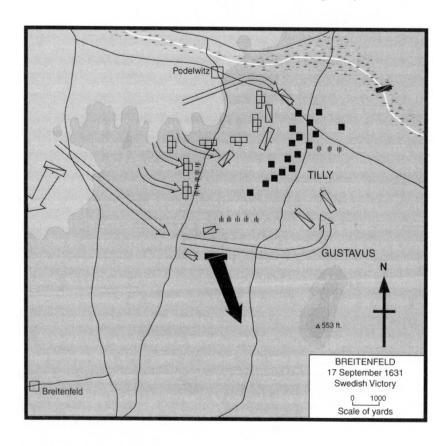

Podelwitz

TILLY

GUSTAVUS

N

△ 553 ft.

BREITENFELD
17 September 1631
Swedish Victory

0   1000
Scale of yards

Breitenfeld

the battlefield, and the Swedish reserves were committed in sufficient numbers to both strengthen the refused flank and to extend it so it could not be ridden around, as Pappenheim had intended. When Baner's men went over to the offensive, Gustavus could reconstitute his reserve and back up Horn's refused flank. Once on the offensive, his men exploited the situation by capturing the enemy guns and turning them on the enemy rear. With the imperial force caught in midmove out of its north-eastward attack against the Saxons trying to face about toward the new flank, Horn's attack was perfectly timed and executed. His men maintained sufficient offensive pressure to back the crumbling tercios against some neighboring woods, but spent so much time attacking their front that several thousand escaped. Pappenheim's reorganized cavalry arrived on the field to stop close pursuit of the imperial retreat to the west.

The victory was one of the maneuverability of the Swedish units versus the size and weight of the tercio. Conversely, it was a victory of the weight of Swedish firepower over the limits of that produced by the tercio. Gustavus won because his forces could deliver much more firepower than the enemy. The infantry in their extended formations used their superior muskets, and the superior Swedish light artillery moved forward with the infantry, delivering canister fire within yards of the enemy.[49] The day of the caracole was dead, that of the tercio was on its deathbed. The battle proved to be a dramatic endorsement of Gustavus's linear system and cavalry. The Swedish deployment in two lines to make a reserve enabled Gustavus to protect his flanks and differed in no serious respect from the use made of their second lines by Scipio and Caesar. Few military men in Europe missed the lesson to be learned here, as Gustavus himself was to see the following year when he faced Wallenstein at Lützen. The success of the Swedish army and tactics in the war may be gauged by the efforts of Sweden's opponents to copy them.[50]

Breitenfeld was also a victory for Gustavus's methods of training as well as his organization. The mutual trust gained between officers and men as well as king and men gave them the confidence to persevere when almost half the army broke and ran. When all is said and done, the elite military spirit of the Swedes won Breitenfeld. The Saxons buckled under the pressure, but not the Swedes.[51]

In the days following the battle Gustavus failed to maintain pressure on the defeated Tilly. Instead, he turned his attention more toward

Bohemia, where he dispatched John George's army. This failure to crush his opponent robbed him of the decisive victory Breitenfeld could have been, although it was a major morale boost for Protestants throughout Germany, and therefore brought Gustavus allies, reinforcements, supplies, and money. Some argue that Gustavus should have made immediately for Vienna. Tilly's broken force was the only one available to stop him, and seizure of the city could have forced Emperor Ferdinand to the peace table.[52] Liddell Hart, however, agrees with Gustavus's plan to maintain secure bases and gather allies: "The scheme was wise and far-sighted, took into calculation all the political and military elements of the situation, and was based on broad, sound judgment. For seventeen hundred years, no one had looked at war with so large an intelligence. . . . What he has taught us is method, not temerity."[53] Had Vienna been a national or even an imperial capital, its capture may have been decisive, but it was merely Emperor Ferdinand's home rather than a true seat of government. J. F. C. Fuller's analysis covers most of the strategic bases that may have led Gustavus to decide against going directly to Vienna. First, the roads were bad, winter was coming on, and Gustavus possessed no detailed maps. Additionally, without the Catholic army destroyed, a move to the south would expose his supply lines. Instead, by moving westward through Catholic territories to the Protestant Palatinate, he would tap into new sources of supply while denying them to the imperialists. And finally, occupation of the Palatinate would bar Spanish Hapsburg access from Italy to the Protestant United Provinces, against whom Spain had been warring for decades.[54]

With John George leading his army and a band of Bohemian exiles toward Prague, therefore, Gustavus pointed his army southwestward. Although Tilly did quickly recover from his wounds and gather together another army of 25,000 men, there were no major battles. At Wurzburg Tilly faced a badly outnumbered Swedish army but followed orders from his boss, Maximilian of Bavaria, to bring his troops back for home defense. Thus, Gustavus continued—slightly more cautiously—to move to Frankfurt-am-Main (captured 27 November) and thence to Mainz (taken on 22 December). Finally he settled into winter quarters, master of a wide swath of German territory running from the French frontier to the Baltic.

The campaign of 1632 started out with bad news for the Swedes. Tilly had been replaced as imperial commander (though he still commanded the Bavarian–Catholic League troops) with Wallenstein. Fabulously wealthy with massive holdings in Bohemia, Wallenstein was a master of raising and equipping armies. Unfortunately for Emperor Ferdinand, he was without scruples or loyalty to any cause but his own advancement. That is why Ferdinand had given in to pressure from Maximillian of Bavaria to sack him shortly after Gustavus's army had landed in 1630. To regain Wallenstein's services the emperor would have to pay dearly in lands and power, but he was desperate after the Swedish offensive had both crushed the imperial army at Breitenfeld and advanced easily through central Germany. Wallenstein agreed first only to a three-month commission to raise an army; accepting command would come later with more imperial concessions. The emperor was desperate, and Wallenstein took advantage of that the situation, demanding unconditional control over the army and whatever territory he conquered, as well as assurance that the emperor would issue no military commands without Wallenstein's approval.[55]

The second problem the Swedes faced in 1632 was manpower. Gustavus, Tilly, and Wallenstein were all raising armies, so mercenaries could pick and choose where they wanted to give their services. Thus, Gustavus had been unable to recruit the 200,000-man army he had hoped for, and he was forced to enter into a short-term truce with Maximilian of Bavaria in order to buy himself some time to expand his ranks. Unfortunately, Marshal Horn violated the truce by seizing Bamberg, a Bavarian possession. Tilly massed superior forces at Bamberg and forced Horn's retreat on 9 March. This hurt Gustavus's reputation and pushed him into action sooner than he had planned in order to reestablish his military credibility.

The Swedish army was also suffering from the loss of Saxon support. John George had shown his true colors once in possession of Prague by losing his nerve and opening negotiations with the emperor. Nothing came of it, but with Wallenstein returning to his home country with his new army, John George had to decide between the immediate threat of the imperial forces or the distant threat of Gustavus's wrath and his seemingly invincible army. When Wallenstein communicated to John George that he could return to Saxony unmolested, the elector abandoned Prague and went home. His army commander, Arnim, did nothing to stop him, and Gustavus's representative, Count Heinrich Thurn, had no sufficient force to do so either. This, coupled with Horn's mistake at Bamberg, undid Gustavus's original 1632 strategy. He had hoped to invade though Saxony into Bohemia or, barring that, move north to fight Pappenheim. He now decided to march into Bavaria and fight with Tilly's reconstituted army. Thus, he could defeat a weaker army before concentrating on the larger one.[56]

Gustavus retraced his path from Frankfurt-am-Main back to Würzburg and then on to Nuremburg, which welcomed him with open arms. Joining with scattered detachments summoned to the campaign, he marched southward to Donauwörth on the Danube, where he quickly ejected Tilly's garrison. Gustavus seized the high ground and placed Tortensson's artillery to bombard the city. The imperial force lost 800 dead in the cannonade and a further 500 prisoners as they abandoned the place.[57] Leaving 2,000 men behind to hold the town, Gustavus marched toward Tilly's army. Tilly had chosen a good defensive position near the town of Rain between the north-ward-flowing Lech and Ach Rivers, which empty into the Danube. The Lech was in flood, and Tilly had destroyed all the nearby bridges as well as any boats that could be used to either ferry troops across or build a pontoon bridge.

Tilly could hardly have had a stronger position. On the east side the river-banks were either woods or marsh. Most of his 22,000 men were in a fortified camp at the town of Rain some 800 yards from the river; a redoubt was built halfway between that camp and the Lech. This earthwork was fronted by spiked chevaux-de-frise barricades to the south and west and manned by two infantry battalions and a dozen guns, with heavier 12-pounders in the main camp. All the artillery had the riverbank easily in range. Tilly occupied Rain with a portion of his right wing and Augsburg to the south with a strong detachment. He then distributed the remainder of his army at the points between the two places where the river might be crossed. Small bodies of cavalry were placed at intervals to give warning as to enemy movements. The distance north to south was sixteen miles.[58] Certainly no one in his right mind would force a river crossing in the face of such opposition.

Gustavus's subordinates agreed with Tilly on that point, but Gustavus did not want to spend the time to go farther south looking for a bridge. He thought a delay would give Wallenstein time to join with Tilly and create an overwhelming force. (He was unaware that the new imperial commander had no intention of marching to Tilly's aid, although he did send a contingent of 5,000 men as reinforcement.) Gustavus knew that the bulk of Tilly's force would be new conscripts or militia, so he banked on their inexperience to allow him to force a crossing.

The point Gustavus chose was near the town of Oberndorf, where the Lech made a westward bend and an island was in the center of the river.

Gustav deployed his army along the river facing Tilly's redoubt outside
Rain. Instead of attacking, the Swedes dug in, creating three redoubts of
their own by the evening of 13 April. Once constructed, they could hold
24 heavy guns that could pound Tilly's entrenchments; the largest guns
would be able to reach the main camp farther to the rear. The 14th saw an
inconclusive artillery duel with little damage done to either side.

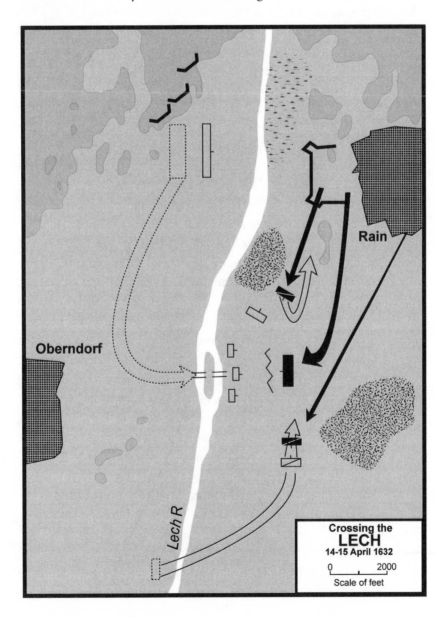

Rain

Oberndorf

Lech R

**Crossing the
LECH**
14-15 April 1632

0 _____ 2000
Scale of feet

All of this, however, was a feint. Gustavus had instructed his men to drag boats from the Danube and tear apart local houses for building material, and throughout the night of 14–15 April prefabricated pieces of bridgework were hauled out of Oberndorf to the riverbank opposite the island. An initial force of 334 Finns rowed across to the island and dug in on the east side. By 5:00 a.m. on 15 April the Swedes were ready. The bridge sections were in place, and the Swedes had also constructed supporting earthworks holding 18 guns and 2,000 musketeers. Tilly had been completely deceived.[59] At 8:00 a.m. men began swarming across the bridge until three brigades were on the island.

As this was happening, however, some of Tilly's patrols discovered the action and reported to him. He quickly brought reserves toward the crossing point. Again the Finns were the leading element across to the far side of the Lech, where they began to dig in under fire. Gustavus's artillery kept Tilly's men from advancing, but not from felling trees and building a defensive position. To assist the men finishing the bridge and crossing the Lech, Gustavus had stacks of wet hay, green wood, and gunpowder burned to create a thick smoke that blew across the river into the imperial faces.

Both sides reinforced their positions throughout the day. Tilly directed Count Johann von Aldringer to move round the swampy ground, charge with his cavalry those who had already crossed, and seize the bridgehead. Aldringer obeyed the order with alacrity. He turned the marsh and led his men with daring. But the Swedes had second-guessed him and had formed up to await his attack. The cavalry charge, though pressed with vigor, was turned back.[60] Aldringer was wounded in the head during the fighting, and Tilly stepped up his activities among the troops, exposing himself to fire to stiffen their morale. During the intense fighting that followed the imperial forces suffered serious losses, and Tilly, continuing to expose himself to enemy fire, was struck in the knee by a 3-pounder cannon ball.[61] With the two senior commanders wounded and removed from the field, command fell to Maximilian of Bavaria.

With the fighting so intense at the bridgehead, Gustavus ordered 2,000 cavalry to ride upstream, ford the river, and attack the imperial flank from the south. Imperial cavalry met this thrust but were driven back after some hard fighting. By 6:00 the setting sun brought the battle to an end. Maximilian, with little military training, decided to withdraw the imperial army during the ensuing darkness. He knew that if he abandoned his position he would be exposing his home province of Bavaria to Gustavus's occupation and potential destruction. Nevertheless, he decided saving the troops was too important, and made the call to abandon the field and Bavaria. It was a masterful retreat, so well conducted the Swedes did not know it was taking place. Not a man or gun was lost in the withdrawal.[62] However, imperial forces left behind almost 3,000 dead; Swedish casualties numbered around 2,000.

Gustavus's crossing of the Lech can stand as a model for such an operation. Whereas much of the battle at Breitenfeld was reaction on his part, the Lech showed his ability to read the terrain, use it to his advantage, and implement surprise. This was a deliberate attack that fully fills its definition: a synchronized operation that employs the effects of every available asset against the enemy defense. Gustavus set the tempo by deploying in full view of the enemy and then holding their attention while implementing his main concentration against a weakly held point. The bridging of the river and the landing on the imperial side was a total surprise, and a deliberate smoke screen probably had not been used in Europe since the Mongols invaded Hungary. His only failure was his inability to exploit or pursue his enemy, because of the skillful retreat of Maximilian's troops. He did, however, achieve his goal of opening a path into Bavaria, which he proceeded to pillage.

The successful passage of so well defended a position added to Gustavus's growing reputation. He could have crossed his army farther downstream and attacked from the south without having to fight it out on a bridgehead, but Gustavus himself was impressed with the earthworks the imperial army had constructed and could not believe anyone would abandon such a strong position. So a difficult battle awaited him no matter what the avenue of approach. In an analysis for the U.S. Army Command and General Staff College, Major Mark Connor writes, "Though one of his least famous actions, the passage of the Lech River is a shining example of his ability to recognize his army's condition, establish its goal, and concentrate decisive combat power—all the while protecting his soldiers."[63] The key was the misdirection Gustavus employed, which probably would have made Subedei smile.

GUSTAVUS NEXT HAD TO MEET the redoubtable Albrecht von Wallenstein, once again the commander of imperial forces. Born in 1583 to poor but noble parents, Wallenstein served in wars against the Turks and Hungarian rebels, coming to the notice of the Hapsburg monarchy. In 1609 he married a wealthy widow; she died in 1614, leaving him a very rich man. He married into more wealth in 1617 and financed a cavalry squadron that same year to fight against the Venetians. By the time the Thirty Years War broke out in his home country of Bohemia the following year, he was a powerful and influential man in the eastern Holy Roman Empire.

In the early years of the war Wallenstein fought for the imperial cause and rose in rank to become Duke of Friedland in 1625. He gained more land and income as the war progressed, becoming Duke of Mecklenburg after helping to defeat the Danes in 1628. His increased military and political standing proved threatening to many of the imperial nobility, since he had no loyalty to empire or church. Through the urging of many of the nobles, primarily Emperor Ferdinand's son Maximilian of Bavaria, Wallenstein was removed from his command in 1630, just after Gustavus had landed on the Baltic shore. Wallenstein went home, managed his estates, and bided his time, for he knew the time would come when Tilly would fail and the emperor would be in need.

At Rain, Wallenstein was in no mood to march to Tilly's aid, and his command position made him answerable to no one. Much more a strategist than a tactician, Wallenstein grasped that Gustavus continually kept his mind on his lines of communication back to Sweden. Liddell Hart comments: "Wallenstein, the first grand strategist, appear[s] to have grasped the principle of *unity of command*, appreciating that to counter Gustavus, the absolute chief of a military monarchy, equal power and freedom of action was essential."[64] Although the Swedes ran rampant through Bavaria, Wallenstein did nothing to stop them. After all, that was Maximilian's territory; after Maximilian had played a key role in having Wallenstein removed from command two years earlier, why should he care what happened to Bavaria? Wallenstein was busy expelling the Saxons from Bohemia, which not only secured his own base, but threatened Swedish supply lines and bases. Thus, he saved Vienna without having to defend it.

Wallenstein had raised an army of 40,000. Like Gustavus, he realized the value of regular pay and supply for the troops' morale, and his territory of Friedland provided plenty of both. In early summer he summoned

Maximilian to bring his Bavarian army to join him. The two joined forces at Eger and with 60,000 men moved toward Nuremberg. Gustavus had at first planned to march on Saxony to revitalize John George, but news of the huge imperial army gave him second thoughts. Instead he retreated into Nuremberg's friendly environs, but with only 20,000 men. Wallenstein approached the city in July 1632 but did not use his three-to-one manpower advantage for an assault. Instead, he established himself in a strong encampment on rugged ground around the castle of Alte Veste to the southwest. There he waited on hunger to do its work, although Gustavus had laid in two months worth of supplies. There were, Wallenstein calculated, insufficient supplies for men and horses, so Gustavus would have to fight or starve. Either way Wallenstein was in a good position, for he was able to maintain his own supply situation fairly well for a time.[65] In August Gustavus's chancellor Oxenstierna arrived with a further 30,000 men; Wallenstein did nothing to stop their juncture. He believed that more men in the city meant quicker starvation, even though he was finding it increasingly difficult to keep his 60,000 as regularly fed as he had hoped.

The Battle of Lützen

GUSTAVUS WAS FINALLY FORCED to challenge the imperial forces. In early September 1632 he launched an attack on Alte Veste, but the rough terrain made it difficult for his men to maneuver and bring their artillery to bear; after severe losses Gustavus withdrew back into Nuremberg. His reputation had taken a beating as much as his army had, and with poor food and morale his German soldiers began deserting and his allied leaders became disaffected. He finally abandoned the city after trying futilely to interest Wallenstein in a peace treaty. He headed for Austria, hoping to consolidate his hold on the Danube and prepare for the following year's campaign.

Maximilian urged a pursuit, but Wallenstein was looking at a bigger picture. With his joint armies he intended to race for Saxony; thus either he would come upon John George and Arnim alone and force them to make terms, or he would draw Gustavus off from Austria. But Maximilian had had enough of Wallenstein, and he took the rest of his army home to reoccupy and hopefully rebuild Bavaria.[66] With his army reduced by one-third by Maximilian's retreat, and then reduced further by starvation and desertion (after all, there was no victory in which to gather loot), Wallenstein himself was seeing his army dwindle to about 30,000 — roughly the same as Gustavus's if John George joined him. Learning that the Swedes were heading once again for the Danube, Wallenstein followed his plan to march on Saxony in early October. So each planned to raid, make a foray into the each other's base, and, he hoped, put his adversary on the defensive.[67]

Gustavus once again showed his abilities, even after the recent setback at Alte Veste. Learning of Wallenstein's move, Gustavus reversed course and followed him speedily, force marching his men some 400 miles in seventeen days to catch the imperial troops before they could meet the Saxons. In early November Wallenstein captured Leipzig, joining forces with Heinrich Holk and Pappenheim (who had been campaigning in the north). Gustavus met his ally Bernhard, Duke of Saxe-Weimar, with reinforcements at Erfurt, some 50 miles southwest of Leipzig; together they had just under 20,000 men. They rested there for five days before slowly moving toward Leipzig. On 8 November they captured the village of Naumburg and began erecting earthworks; they were now 20 miles from Leipzig.

Wallenstein, who had intended to march on Torgau to seize the bridge there and isolate the Saxon army, now turned back to meet the Swedes. Outside Weissenfels, on 12 November, his army deployed as Gustavus rode nearby with a cavalry reconnaissance. Gustavus withdrew to Naumburg to strengthen his defenses while sending a message to Duke George of Lüneburg to bring his 2,000 cavalry from Torgau to join him. Seeing the Swedish defenses, Wallenstein withdrew toward Leipzig. What happened next is open to some debate. William Guthrie's 2002 detailed account of the battle follows the traditional viewpoint: "[Wallenstein's] next decision is difficult to understand; in fact it was one of the most bizarre of the war. On November 14, Gustav heard, to his mingled joy and disbelief, that the Imperial army had broken up into corps and gone into winter quarters. . . . Wallenstein, it would seem, assumed that the camp at Naumburg was the Swedish winter quarters, that the king was suspending operations for the year."[68] The imperial commander spread his men out in various directions to spend the next few months pillaging the Saxon countryside to stay alive and at the same time needle John George. He was sure that if the Swedes moved, he could rally his army soon enough to fight. Guthrie notes that Wallenstein was suffering from gout and also was in a deteriorating mental state; he believed that the Swedes were suspending operations "because he wanted to believe it."

Others argue that Gustavus's entrenchment was merely a feint meant to confuse Wallenstein, and that the imperial decision to divide the army and live off the land until battle loomed was a surprise. Wallenstein, however, was not going into winter quarters.[69] He could not dislodge Gustavus from his strong position, and he could not feed his army on local supplies. Further, Pappenheim had been successful in controlling northern Saxony, and wanted to return to there and resume his independent command. Wallenstein agreed, on the condition that he capture Halle (some twenty miles to the northwest of Leipzig) on the way. Pappenheim departed with 5,000 men, about 2,000 of whom were cavalry. Wallenstein was in command of 15,000–18,000, and Count Matthias Gallas was marching from Bohemia with a further 6,000–7,000 to establish himself at Grimma, some 20 miles southeast of Leipzig. So with a respectable force on hand and two other forces within a day's march, he seemingly felt secure.

The problem was that Gustavus was also only a day's march away and a surprise attack would leave Wallenstein without assistance. What happened next is one of the "what-ifs" of this campaign, and perhaps the war; the whole history of the next two days, from the Swedish point of view, was a string of accidents and cruel strokes of fate.[70] Wallenstein positioned a small force at Weissenfels, halfway between Lützen (his headquarters) and Naumburg. Early on 15 November he sent a few hundred Croat cavalry under Count Rodolfo di Colloredo to fetch them and bring them back to the main body. Just as they were joining up, however, Gustavus's army approached in battle formation. The small imperial force retreated to a marshy stream called the Rippach and threw together a hasty defense on the eastern side. The Swedish advance guard could not estimate the enemy numbers in the trees on the far bank, and so awaited the remainder of the 18,000 men to arrive. Colloredo, usually considered a mediocrity, sized up the situation at a glance and acted correctly. He sent warning to Wallenstein while deploying his meager forces along the stream. For two hours, they held up the Swedish advance. By the time Gustavus was able to break through and reach Wallenstein's headquarters at Lützen, it was already dark, and battle was impossible until the next day.[71] If the small imperial force had indeed been withdrawing, an hour's delay on Gustavus's part would have made his approach unopposed. Likewise, a more aggressive Swedish advance guard could have broken the small force and Wallenstein would have been caught unawares, his army forced to flee or fight unprepared. As it was, the small force of cavalry under Colloredo managed to prevent the imperial army from suffering a potentially devastating assault.

Gustavus's men were marching in battle order, so they encamped on the eastern outskirts of Lützen. His deployment looked the same as it did at Breitenfeld, minus the Saxons. After sending a horseman to Pappenheim to get his force back from Halle on the double, Wallenstein spent the night deploying his men and digging defenses. He formed his infantry in the center in three lines with five regiments in front, two in the second line, and one in reserve. The 1,000-man infantry brigades deployed in the center were, in effect, battalions; Wallenstein had clearly realized the maneuverability of smaller formations and had abandoned the tercio.[72] Cavalry units were on the flanks: Colloredo's Croats on the imperial right, Field Marshal Heinrich Holk on the left.[73] The artillery Wallesntein placed both in front of his infantry and on his right near some windmills on the edge of town. Between the two armies ran the road to Leipzig, in this stretch a causeway with ditches on either side. Wallenstein wisely placed musketeers on his side of the road in order to be protected as they lay down fire on the advancing Swedes.

By dawn both sides were in position, and both were waiting on cavalry to arrive. Gustavus learned, however, that Duke George was not coming from Torgau, being ordered by Arnim to stay in place and protect Saxony. On the other side of the field Wallenstein waited anxiously for Pappenheim. In spite of the bad news that he would receive no more cavalry, Gustavus was in a good mood and ready to fight, having a slight edge, 19,000 men to Wallenstein's 16,770, but he knew that every passing minute worked against them: the enemy had 10,000 reinforcements en route, while Gustavus had none.[74]

Indeed, more than minutes were passing. The day broke on 16 September with fog and mist, sufficient to hide both armies. Gustavus's plan was to hold the imperial center and right wing while swinging his personally led cavalry against the imperial left. He had a 1,000-man advantage in numbers on that side, but as it turned out he needed more. When the fog finally lifted at 11:00 he quickly sent his men forward as the imperial artillery opened up. The first problem for the Swedes came almost immediately. The hidden musketeers in the ditches surprised the attacking cavalry, which could not easily jump the ditches, and paths across them were at irregular spots. In seconds, the Swedish cavalry was milling about while imperial musketeers fired into the disordered masses.[75] The infantry following up were able to clear the ditches, but the impetus was lost. The advance continued, however, and made slow but steady headway against the imperial left wing. At the same time, on the western flank, Wallenstein ordered the town of Lützen to be burned, and the smoke blew directly into the attacking Swedes, creating visibility just as limited as it had been under the morning fog.

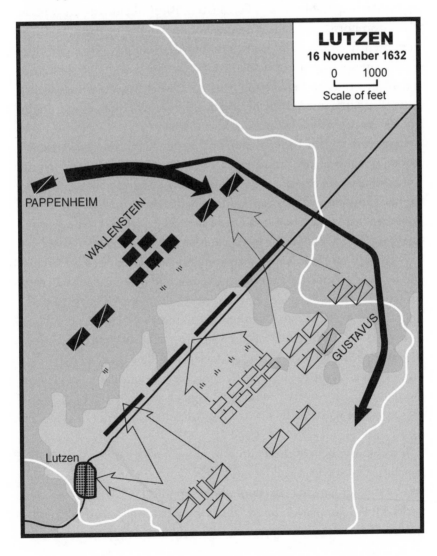

LUTZEN
16 November 1632
0   1000
Scale of feet

PAPPENHEIM

WALLENSTEIN

GUSTAVUS

Lutzen

Duke Bernhard of Saxe-Weimar commanded the Swedish left and was the most affected by the smoke. His moved his wing forward under musket fire from the walled garden around Lützen and from the artillery to his front at a windmill. Soon, however, the smoke hid his movements and he was able to cross the road, drive away the musketeers in the ditch, and break the cavalry screen. That was the end of his luck, however; when cavalry reserves attacked him and the gunfire from the walls resumed, he had to withdraw back across the road.

Seeing Gustavus's advance coming on his left, Wallenstein ordered reserves to help hold the line. Fortunately, Pappenheim arrived at noon with 2,300 horses and took command of the crumbling flank. His men were tired from the all-night march, but the young commander's legendary energy would not be denied. He would lead the imperial left-center into the gap made by Gustavus's cavalry attack, while cavalry units would hit Gustavus's flank and move around his rear, rolling up the Swedish line. That was the plan, at least.

Unfortunately for Pappenheim, by the time his assault was launched around 1:00, his enemy had advanced to the road. The Swedes had improvised a defensive line utilizing the musketeers and regimental guns, and Pappenheim's advancing troops were immediately hit with a wave of firepower against which they stood little chance. Pappenheim himself was one of the first to fall, struck by two musket balls and a cannon shot.[76]

Even without their leader, Pappenheim's men continued the attack. Croat cavalry struck the far right squadrons and drove them back, then rushed past them to swing wide and strike the Swedish baggage park. Imperial general Ottavio Piccolomini, taking over from Pappenheim, slowly pushed the Swedes back across the road. Displaying his unparalleled battlefield presence once again, Gustavus rallied the remnants of his original attack, sent for reserves to reinforce his right flank, and fell on Piccolomini. The imperial commander quickly turned to face Gustavus's charge, allowing the badly mauled Swedish infantry to dig in along the road.

It was somewhere in this confusion, about 1:00, that the unthinkable happened: Gustavus was shot and killed. Word spread quickly on both sides. It did not have the effect one might suppose, however. Piccolomini, under Holk's command, had withdrawn according to orders to rally around Wallenstein, who apparently did not know of Pappenheim's fate.

This left the imperial center-left virtually leaderless. On the Swedish side some, realizing that their leader had fallen, fled, but Gustavus's chaplain began singing hymns and rallied the troops. He would not confirm the death and stopped the potential flight as Gustavus's second in command, Bernard Saxe-Weimar, quickly reorganized the units along the road. The Swedish second line was under the command of Field Marshal Dodo von Knyphausen, a steady veteran. He kept the reserves under strict control, assuring them that the king was only wounded. He fed units to Bernhard on the left for a second assault on the windmills, which was also beaten back in hard fighting. Knyphausen sent units to the road to reinforce or replace those that had taken the brunt of the fighting.

At about 3:00 the battle fell into a lull. Both sides had lost key commanders and thousands of men; both were in roughly the same positions they had started; and both were bringing up reserves. On the Swedish side, Bernhard Saxe-Weimer assumed command. He had received confirmation of the king's death, but rather than allow chaos to erupt, he used the information to his advantage. He rallied his men to avenge their fallen monarch.

Since the Swedish right and imperial left flank units were both trying to recover and hold their ground with minimal forces, Bernhard decided to launch one more assault against Lützen and the windmill batteries. At about 3:30 he began the attack; Wallenstein threw in all the reserves he could. The battle went back and forth for an hour and a half, until finally Bernhard's men stood around the windmills and Wallenstein could send no more men forward. The continual smoke coupled with the setting sun brought the battle to an end. It had been a long and costly fight; casualty numbers vary widely, but seem to average some 5,000 to 6,000 dead on each side.

GUSTAVUS BEGAN HIS MOVEMENT to contact at dawn on 15 November. The delay at the Rippach slowed his approach, and could well have cost him the battle. As it was, the battle at Lützen did not allow for him to engage in anything but a deliberate attack. Though his plan was sound, Gustavus was forced to execute his scheme in a blinding fog against an inadequately reconnoitered position, in addition to smoke from the fire ordered by Wallenstein. All of this limited the command and control he might have exercised.[77] Tactically, the battle was a draw, but since

Wallenstein withdrew his army to Leipzig and then to Bohemia, the Swedes could claim the strategic victory. There was no exploitation or pursuit. Had Wallenstein employed Pappenheim's infantry, which arrived on the scene just after dark, he might have been able to eke out a victory for the empire. However, he was ill with gout and fearful of the arrival of John George's force, whose numbers he exaggerated.[78]

Gustavus's Generalship

IT MUST BE SAID that of all the generals covered in this work, Gustavus's actual on-the-field leadership more often than not shows less talent than the others. His spirit matches any of them, however, and the developments he introduced were absolutely central to seventeenth-century European warfare. Without a doubt his real strength is in perfecting the organization and tactics begun by Maurice, as well as improving the weaponry of the time. As with Scipio's adaptation of the Carthaginian sword and tactics, Gustavus introduced the flexible unit of combined arms and the light artillery. His cavalry tactics were not, of course, new, but a reintroduction of its traditional striking power. In his massive work on military history, Archer Jones observes, "Gustavus's modification of cavalry doctrine, with its stress on shock in combat with other cavalry, became standard. . . . The most enduring legacy of Gustavus's changes was moving the infantry one more step in its evolution as the major force on the battlefield."[79]

On a larger stage, Gustavus also reintroduced the long-service national army with its concomitant discipline and esprit de corps that had always characterized the Roman army on which he based it. While some have argued that Gustavus's developments constituted a complete military revolution, his reign certainly at least marked a turning point from medieval and Renaissance warfare into the modern age. David Chandler writes, "The King of Sweden made the most significant contribution to the development of the art of war in the seventeenth century. . . . Gustavus created the first truly modern army; one that was destined to be widely copied in France, the United Provinces and England."[80]

When it comes to analyzing the military principles Gustavus employed, many commentators praise his adherence to the principle of *security*. Other than the crossing of the Lech, however, Gustavus's attention to security seems woefully missing. This work will focus instead on his adherence to the principles of mass, economy of force, and morale.

At all three of the battles discussed, Gustavus saw the enemy weakness and put his *mass* at that point: the exposed flank and rear of Tilly's tercios once they had moved into their attack, the river crossing at the Lech, and Wallenstein's left flank at Lützen. At Lützen, Gustavus strengthened his own cavalry flank in order to overwhelm the enemy. Had he been able to launch his attack at daybreak, as he intended, Pappenheim's cavalry would not have arrived to stop him and the battle could well have been over quickly; even the imperial musketeers in the ditch caused only a relatively short delay. At Breitenfeld, he swung his army's center and right flank across the field to hammer Tilly against Horn's anvil. At the Lech, his placement of the bulk of his artillery on the crossing zone kept Tilly from launching a successful counterattack, although his inability to get a large number of men across the river in a hurry negated the surprise effect of the move. At Alte Vesta Gustavus's forces were too small at first to be effective, but he did wait for the arrival of reinforcements before assaulting the position. However, a massed force here probably would not have availed him anyway, given the rough terrain and strength of the imperial defenses. Had the pressure of a lack of supplies not impelled his decision there, he probably would not have tried the battle.

In all of the battles he fought, Gustavus was sure to maintain an adequate reserve; at Lützen it was almost half his army. Since his plan there was to hold the center while sweeping the flank, his deployment of forces was the correct decision. Only when the flank attack was driven back and his own center was threatened did the commitment to the front line prove too small. On the other hand, the ability to virtually replace the entire front line with fresh (though less veteran) units certainly saved the day for the Swedes. At Breitenfeld, his defense of his right flank against Pappenheim's attack was masterful. By having Baner refuse the flank and sending in support from the reserve in increments, Gustavus kept the line from either breaking or being surrounded. Once Pappenheim was chased from the field and Horn was being pressed on the left by the victorious tercios, the remainder of his reserve (as well as those recalled from the right) could hold that line until the rest of the army made its move on Tilly's flank and rear. At the Lech, he had sufficient forces deployed downstream, across from the imperial defenses, to convince Tilly a river crossing there was a real possibility. Thus, a smaller force was able to bridge the river and establish the foothold. Just enough cavalry sent to cross the river to the south and hit the imperial flank helped roll up the enemy line, while a secondary cavalry crossing, though it failed to engage, forced enemy attention to the north of the bridgehead.

Maintaining and harnessing his troops' *morale* was Gustavus's overwhelming strength. Everything he did, from building the army to leading it, was intended to keep his men focused. His conscripted regiments were formed from neighborhood drafts, giving a regional bond to each unit. The training and discipline, even the orders to dig (which was beneath the dignity of most mercenaries), all served to bond the soldiers into strong unit cohesion. During the siege of Riga, when Gustavus made his soldiers dig trenches and traverses to approach close to the walls, he got down in the dirt with his men. As a result, the morale of his army was superb. He took such pains with planning of transport and supply that he was the first commander in modern Europe successfully to fight winter campaigns.[81] Regular pay and supply also kept the troops happy. It was the dedication to supply that convinced Gustavus to move slowly early in his campaign in order to establish supply bases and a secure line of communications. As the war progressed and the proportion of Swedish soldiers in the ranks diminished to as low as 10 percent, he motivated the army by maintaining, as best he could, the supply and pay.

Most of all, the troops respected and followed Gustavus not only because of his victories (which always brought in recruits) but because of the fact that he was a soldier's soldier. He partied with the aristocrats, but he also lived in the field, ate soldiers' rations, and did not fear combat. Not for nothing was he called the "Lion of the North." His reconnaissances were personal and exposed, and he was in the thick of the fighting in a way not seen since Belisarius; indeed, that was his ultimate downfall.

IF GUSTAVUS DID NOT EQUAL some of the other generals studied here in battlefield brilliance, his ability to adapt his army to new weaponry and tactics, and adapt those weapons and methods into effective and long-lasting modes of warfare, puts him in these ranks. Dodge comments, "For many centuries war had been conducted without that art and purpose which Alexander, Hannibal, and Caesar so markedly exhibited. But in the operations of the Swedish king we again find the hand of the master.

We recognize the same method which has excited our admiration in the annals of the noted campaigns of antiquity, and from now on we shall see generals who intelligently carry forward what Gustavus Adolphus rescued from the oblivion of the Middle Ages."[82] Or as a more modern observer notes, "His administrative, tactical, and operational practices were widely imitated and more than any other general of his age, he mastered the various elements that comprise leadership in combat. He was a great captain of men, imposing his will and determination on the army, which he infused with the sense that there was nothing it could not do."[83]

12

John Churchill, Duke of Marlborough (1650–1722)

English General

> Kirke has fire, Lanier thought, Mackay skill and Colchester bravery, but there is something inexpressible in the Earl of Marlborough. All their virtues seem to be united in his single person. I have lost my wonted skill in physiognomy if any subject of your Majesty can ever attain such a height of military glory as that to which this combination of sublime perfections must raise him.
>
> —Prince of Vaudemont to King William III

JOHN CHURCHILL'S LIFE is a prime illustration of the phrase, "It's not only what you know, but who you know." He could not be included in this work if not for his military talent, but he would probably never have been able to demonstrate that talent but for the proper connections. John's father, Sir Winston Churchill, backed the losing royalist cause in the English Civil War. This cost him his estate and obliged him to move in with his Parliament-supporting mother-in-law. He enjoyed some revival of fortune when the 1660 Restoration brought Charles II to the monarchy, and Winston was knighted and served in Parliament. Still without serious income, Winston's connection with the king gained court positions for his first two children, Arabella and John. Arabella was named maid of honor to the first wife of James, Duke of York, heir to the throne. Not long thereafter she became James's mistress. John was appointed a page at age sixteen and quickly learned the smooth manners

314

necessary to advance in society. Prince James noticed his interest in things military and procured John a position in England's small military establishment in the King's Guards. John's advancement on the social ladder depended entirely on connection rather than merit, but given the time and circumstances it was not uncommon for someone in John's position to act thus.[1]

A number of opportunities for service and combat followed over the next few years. In 1768 Churchill volunteered to serve in Tangier, a North African outpost included in the dowry of King Charles's wife. Here soldiers and marines fought Moors on land and sea, gaining the type of hard-fought experience that later soldiers would find on the Northwest Frontier of India.[2] He followed this by serving aboard ships in the Mediterranean fleet fighting the pirates of Algiers. In 1672 England went once again to war with the United Provinces (Holland) as an ally of France. In this conflict he served on the Duke of York's flagship and distinguished himself in combat, so much so that Prince James named him an officer in the Marine Company over men with greater time in service. This also gained him a position in James's court. A career in the navy at this point seemed to be in the offing, but he was soon fighting on land.

James had an illegitimate nephew, the Duke of Monmouth, who led a force of British soldiers to assist the French army fighting the Dutch. His unit was posted under the command of the premier French general of the time, Marshal Vicomte Turenne. Again Churchill was in the thick of the fighting. Turenne, a master general, had little respect for the British troops' value and had no qualms about using them in combat, where they suffered high casualty rates.[3] Churchill was involved in three assaults against the Dutch fortress at Maastricht, the final one breaking through and producing victory. For this success, Churchill was not only praised by Turenne for his bravery but was also congratulated by French king Louis XIV, who had observed the battle. In February 1674 the Dutch signed a peace agreement, but not all British troops went home. Churchill remained in service as commander of an English regiment in French service. He thus saw more action, fighting in three battles in the second half of 1674.[4] These actions were under the direction of Turenne, allowing Churchill even more exposure to the master's touch. In the winter campaign across the Vosges Mountains he learned firsthand the value of forced marches and careful organization.[5]

He returned to England with glory and further recognition in James's court. He also began courting a lady-in-waiting, Sarah Jennings, a fifteen-year-old maid of honor to James's second wife.[6] They were a perfect match, in spite of the ten-year age difference. They married two years later. When James's daughter Anne married Prince George of Denmark in 1683, personal and political connections blossomed. Churchill escorted George from Denmark to England for the wedding, and Sarah moved to join Anne's household, where soon the two became fast friends.

These connections became more important as Prince James, Duke of York, became King James II in February 1685. In early summer the Duke of Monmouth invaded England in order to press his own claim to the throne. Churchill was quick to respond, and put his experiences in both Tangier and France to good use. In the biography of his forebear, Charles Spencer writes, "As soon as he heard that Monmouth had landed at Lyme . . . Churchill set out to head off the threat. With him went only a small column of foot and an inconsequential body of horse. However, Churchill's march echoed the approach of his mentor, Marshal Turenne, by relying on speed and decisiveness to surprise the enemy. He appreciated that the key to defeating Monmouth was to harry him. The renegade duke could not be allowed to settle."[7] By keeping Monmouth on the move, Churchill prevented him from gathering either supplies or supporters. Some West Country militia rallied to him, but constant harassment by Churchill's professionals wore them down physically and psychologically. At the Battle of Sedgemoor on 5 July 1685 the royal troops easily defeated the last of the rebel force.

Unfortunately, James began pushing a strong Catholic agenda in spite of the conditions laid out during the Restoration. The Churchills, both Protestant, had to walk a fine line as King James drew John increasingly into his inner circle. Churchill tried to warn the king against antagonizing Parliament, but to little avail. A covert group of Protestant military officers began to gather around Churchill. Always able to smooth over any opposition or confrontation, he found his powers of diplomacy stretched to the limit.

Everything came to a head in 1688 when James had a son. This indicated the potential for a long-term Catholic dynasty in a Protestant country, and James's appointments of Catholics to important positions in government and the military motivated many in Parliament to look somewhere else for a replacement king. As negotiations began with Stadtholder William of Orange, married to James's sister Mary (a Protestant), Churchill continued to try to moderate James's religious activity, but without success. Forced into a choice, John picked his faith over his monarch and pledged loyalty to William when he came to the throne in the Glorious Revolution of 1688, the bloodless coup that confirmed the Protestant faith as dominant in England.

His choice was not well rewarded. William was suspicious of Churchill and realized the potential problems that could arise from his close relationship with Anne, who also had a claim to the throne. Churchill did what he could to assure the new monarch of his loyalty, even convincing Anne to cede any claim to the throne while William or Mary lived. Still, William remained suspicious, even though he did grant Churchill the title of Earl of Marlborough. With the Dutch in the middle of yet another war with France and William in need of all the troops he could get, an English force was detailed to Holland. William allowed Marlborough to maintain his rank as lieutenant general. As the English army was undergoing reorganization and Catholics were under investigation, many men had left the army to join James in Ireland; still, 8,000 were detailed to Flanders with Marlborough in command.[8] Marlborough did his job well, organizing and training the soldiers and performing admirably in combat.

The next few years were difficult for everyone. William had to suppress a Catholic campaign in Ireland, where Marlborough led a lightning campaign against Cork and Kinsale, which eased the burden on William's primary campaign elsewhere. Marlborough landed near Cork with some 4,000 troops on 22 September 1690, linking up with cavalry from William's army under the Duke of Würtemberg, who gave Marlborough his first taste of handling awkward allied generals as he would be obliged to do as long as he worked with the Dutch.[9] He also was appointed to a Council of Nine to advise Mary on governing while William was in Ireland. Still, for the most part William preferred Dutch advisors (and soldiers), which did not sit well with many in England. A few, including Churchill, occasionally wrote to James II, who had gone into exile in France. In 1692, an argument between Queen Mary and her niece Princess Anne led William to dismiss Marlborough from his military and court positions. He even spent six months in the Tower of London accused of treason, until the charges were proven to have been the result of forged documents. Not until Mary died in 1695 did he recover his position and begin, finally, to receive some of William's grudging appreciation.

During Marlborough's time off the scene, William continued the Nine Years War in Flanders against Louis XIV's France. William was not a brilliant commander and the war was slow, owing to the fact that it consisted primarily of sieges of the seemingly countless fortresses along the frontier. Had Marlborough been in the king's favor, he would have been obliged to accompany William on these campaigns and (as a subordinate commander) engage in a style of warfare alien to his nature. That certainly would not have endeared him to his king. He would only have chafed under such orders or violated them. In reality, his being out of the picture was better for him in the long run.[10]

Several years after his return to service, war was brewing once again in Europe. Charles II of Spain was dying, and there were two potential claimants to the throne: Philip of Anjou (grandson to both Charles and Louis XIV) and the Habsburg archduke Charles of Austria, whose father was Holy Roman emperor Leopold (brother to Charles II of Spain). Given that the last war between the French and Anglo-Dutch forces (the war of the League of Augsburg, ended in 1697 by the Treaty of Ryswick) had been a great strain on French resources, Louis was not looking to get involved in another conflict any time soon. William, who hated Louis and feared his ambition, approached the powers in play to develop a solution. This they did, without Spain's input. The Partition Treaty of 1698 named an infant prince of Wittelsbach as a compromise monarch, with both France and the Holy Roman Empire receiving substantial territorial compensation for not pushing their own claims. After the baby prince died, a second treaty the following March gave Emperor Leopold's son the throne in return for France receiving Naples, Milan, and Sicily. Unfortunately, Leopold wanted it all. "Leopold intransigently insisted that his son was the sole rightful heir, while Louis, dreading a war, proved reasonable beyond all expectations," writes John Wolf.[11] Louis agreed to the second treaty, but the Austrians did not.

Nobody in Spain, however, wanted the Spanish Empire divided, nor did they believe that landlocked Austria should control Spain's overseas colonies. With papal support, the Spanish aristocracy convinced the dying Charles to keep the empire together and will it to his grandson Philip of Anjou. When Charles finally died in November 1700 and his last will and testament was read, Louis had no real choice other than to support his grandson's claim. Emperor Leopold readied for war, but England and Holland still pursued compromise. Then, Louis provoked both of them. In the name of Spain he sent French troops to occupy the fortresses of the Spanish Netherlands, modern Belgium. He then ordered all Dutch and English shipping banned from Spanish ports. Finally, after William died in early 1702, Louis recognized James II's Catholic son over Protestant Anne as the rightful monarch. Challenges to Dutch security and income, and to England's income and religion, were enough to convince the Dutch and the English to ally with Leopold and the Holy Roman Empire.

Warfare of the Time

THE THIRTY YEARS WAR had created across Europe immense fatigue, as well as immense fear. Reports on the devastation of the Germanic states vary, but a huge percentage of the population died and the physical and economic recovery took decades. Attempts were made to alleviate similar future suffering at the hands of marauding mercenaries by the widespread adoption of "rules of war" codified by Hugo Grotius. The Treaty of Westphalia that ended the war in 1648 had some of its foundations built on these rules. The primary goal was to stop making civilians victims of warfare, and the rise of professional armies that individuals such as Gustavus Adolphus implemented went a long way toward achieving that goal. The nation that set the pattern for increasing professionalism was not Sweden (whose star waned after Gustavus fell) but France.

France's suffering in the war had been more financial than otherwise, since the war was not fought on its soil. Still, the superior performance of professionals had been proven and, after a bit of its own civil war, the government began taking serious measures to upgrade the military. This began at roughly the same time a new monarch came to the throne, Louis XIV. He had the assistance of two able administrators who completely reworked the nature of France's military structure. In 1668 Michel le Tellier was appointed to the post of secretary of state for military affairs; he was aided and ultimately succeeded in this position by his son, Francois Michel Tellier, better known as the Marquis de Louvois, who orchestrated the transformation of the army into a truly royal force, and became the first great civilian minister of war in any country.[12] One of his major accomplishments (though not completely fulfilled) was to address the corruption among army officers. It was not uncommon to list more manpower in one's unit than actually existed, in order to be provided with more money and supplies. Limited inspection visits made this easy, even though it could prove dangerous in wartime when one expected to field an army of a certain size when such numbers did not exist. Further, having responsible soldiers (rather than the traditional prison recruits) became a priority. Advancement became possible through merit and not just birth or purchase of a commission.

Up-to-strength units received the best possible training and supplies. In order to accomplish the second item, the ministry developed a system of supply magazines. Regular food on campaign meant no need to pillage, which both maintained positive civil relations and gave soldiers fewer opportunities to leave camp, something that usually resulted in unmilitary activities and behavior. What Gustavus had tried to implement, regular food and pay, became established and successful policy under the French regime, which did much to expand the army significantly as well as increase the number of talented officers through the merit system.[13] Other countries had to follow suit or be completely at France's mercy.

The infantry made up about one-fourth of the French army. Foot soldiers were organized by the turn of the century into battalions of thirteen companies of 40–50 men each, armed with matchlocks or flintlocks. The transition from the older, heavier, less dependable weapon had not completely taken place by 1700. Indeed, in the French army it almost did not take place at all. For some reason King Louis XIV disliked flintlocks, even for a time ordering they be abandoned, but luckily for him cooler heads convinced him otherwise.[14] The flintlock offered an increased rate of fire, two to three shots per minute as opposed to two shots in three minutes with the matchlock. Without the need to worry about a long, burning fuse, soldiers needed less space to reload, so they could be lined up in tighter formations, increasing the firepower. There was another area in which the French had not advanced, and that was their rejection of the paper cartridge, carrying both powder and ball.[15] Most other European armies had adopted the paper cartridge used by Gustavus. The French continued to deploy their men in five or six ranks, better for resisting attacks but not designed to put as much lead in the air as fewer ranks would have allowed.

Two new things appeared among the French infantry under Louis XIV at the end of the seventeenth century. One was the socket bayonet invented by the fortification-engineering genius Sebastian Vauban, which led to the death of the pike. Earlier attempts at using bayonets resulted in the plug type, which was stuck in the barrel and therefore prevented the weapon from firing. A ring bayonet merely slipped over the barrel and easily fell off. Vauban's device slipped over a lug that held the bayonet in place once it was rotated. With the bayonet's ability to provide the sharp points that charging horses did not want to encounter, the pikeman was removed from the field by 1700. Thus, everyone on the line now had a musket, increasing firepower even more. The second was the introduction of the grenadiers, who along with their standard weaponry of flintlock, bayonet, sword, and hatchet carried 12–15 grenades. These were hollow iron shells filled with gunpowder, which had first appeared in the Middle Ages. In 1667 four men from each infantry company were trained in throwing grenades and termed "grenadiers"; four years later one company of grenadiers was assigned to each battalion. Physically large and strong, they became an elite soldiery designated for difficult assignments.[16]

French cavalry was divided into three classes. Louis XIV's time witnessed the introduction of *cavalerie légère* or light cavalry, which used to be the heavy cavalry. It was renamed because the new cavalrymen did not wear heavy armor as previously. In 1690 came the introduction of modern light cavalry, the hussars.[17] The third class was the dragoons, or mounted infantry. Each carried a musket, pistol, saber, and shovel. The shovel meant that he could entrench himself just like regular infantry, but with his horse he could also be used in long-distance service such as transport escort.[18] Regular cavalry were equipped with a sword with a three-foot straight blade, two flintlock pistols carried in saddle holsters, and a shorter musket called a carbine. Just as the grenadiers became elite infantry, Louis's army introduced elite cavalrymen in the form of *carabiniers* who were given rifled carbines. In October 1690 they were formed into their own company. In late 1693 these companies were grouped into a new unit called Royal Carabiniers, 100 companies strong—a sort of elite reserve cavalry division.[19]

In spite of the return of power tactics with the cavalry of Gustavus Adolphus's Swedes, the French retained many of the older practices. The French cavalry was not used for shock, as Gustavus had used his, but as mobile musketeers.[20] Just as in the older cavalry, they attacked in the car-acole, using pistols or carbines. The main difference was that the horsemen now fired in volleys of three ranks, expanding their firepower somewhat.[21] The French tended to mass their cavalry on the wings with the infantry arrayed in the center. Nothing special is indicated in the early seventeenth-century sources about French artillery, an interesting omission, since artillery became one of the French specialties by the middle of the eighteenth century.

The English and Dutch armies were organized along virtually parallel lines, which is probably not surprising given their common head of state. They were not, however, anywhere near as large as that fielded by Louis. Neither England nor the Dutch Republic could call up military force on a whim, since both had elected governments that held the purse strings. The Dutch army was far larger than that of England, since the Dutch had been fighting for generations, first against Spain and more recently against France. King James had attempted to increase and profession-alize the English army, but his thinly concealed religious motives kept Parliament from allowing much of anything beyond a national defense force. When William came to the throne in 1688 the total enlistment was roughly 35,000–40,000 men, of which some 11,000 were based in the Netherlands. It had a number of veterans from the wars against the Dutch in the 1670s and more recently in the suppression of rebellion in Ireland. In order to assist his home country he expanded the English army to as many as 60,000, though many of them fought in Ireland. After the War of the League of Augsburg ended in 1697, the army was reduced to a mere 7,000.

English infantry, like the French, had thirteen companies to a battalion, twelve of foot and one of grenadiers, each company numbering 60 men at full strength. They also carried the flintlock, which had a maximum range of about 250 yards though only a 50–60 yard effective range. They too used the socket bayonet and thus had relegated the pike to a ceremonial weapon for officers and noncommissioned officers (NCOs). Unlike the French, they deployed in an extended line only three ranks deep, all of which fired. The major difference in tactics was that the battalion was arranged into platoons. When the battalion was deployed (with half the grenadier company on either flank) it was divided into eighteen equal sections, or "platoons." As the enemy came into range, instead of firing by ranks, six of the platoons spaced through the battalion fired their muskets and then began reloading. The second set of six platoons would then fire and begin the reloading process, followed by the third firing of platoons.[22] Having one-third of the battalion firing at a time meant a round of gunfire would normally take about thirty seconds, at which time the first platoon was ready to begin the process again; thus, an almost constant fire was maintained. This allowed the NCOs to keep their platoon under control, and one-third of the force was always loaded and ready for unexpected developments. In most battles, however, this was more theory than reality. Once combat started the excitement began to outweigh the discipline, and the platoon fire broke down into individuals shooting their muskets as soon as reloaded rather than waiting for the command.[23] Although Marlborough did not institute this practice—it had grown out of Gustavus's army—he insisted on year-round drills and practices with live ammunition, both in season and out, and thus helped create the most devastating infantry in Europe. Usually no more than a few minutes of this kind of firing was sufficient to break the morale or formation of most opponents. The following bayonet charge then tended to be decisive. This constant practice and maintenance of unit cohesion was one of Marlborough's keys to victory.[24]

His cavalry tactics, like those of the Dutch, also grew out of Gustavus's philosophy. The English cavalry were divided into horse and dragoon units, light cavalry not coming into play until later. The horse soldiers were organized into troops of 40–60 troopers (three troops to a squadron) and armed with straight sword, pistol, and sometimes carbine. As the Swedes had done, Marlborough rejected the caracole tactic; instead he trained his Anglo-Dutch cavalry in the true cavalry charge with cold steel, but delivered at a fast trot with his squadrons knee-to-knee in two ranks. The momentum of the charge was sustained by the reserve squadrons. He had so little faith in the firepower of cavalry (and so much in the shock value) that his troopers were allowed no more than three pistol balls each.[25] Marlborough tended to keep a fairly large cavalry reserve and use them for the breakthrough assault and pursuit.

Like the French dragoons, the English were mounted infantry with a variety of roles. Described in the field manuals of the day as "mounted musketeers," they were to assist wherever needed. Like the French they were used both on the battlefield and for detached duty as well as some engineer duty, clearing obstacles and such.[26] At the beginning of the War of the Spanish Succession, the English had fifteen regiments of horse and nine of dragoons. The Austrian imperial army also employed hussars, light horsemen for reconnaissance and harassment.

While the English artillery was little different from that of any other nation of the time, Marlborough gave it special attention. The siege guns were still too large to be hauled around with the army on campaign, so the largest guns on the battlefield would be 6- or 9-pounders. Marlborough spent time situating his cannons and developed the tactic of moving them forward after the opening volleys of an engagement. He also added smaller guns, 1.5-pounders and 3-pounders, to increase battalion firepower.[27] The 3-pounder could fire solid cannon balls to a range of about 450 yards and grapeshot to about 300 yards, though it was usually reserved for close-in fighting. Getting the increased firepower onto the field, and siting the guns himself at times, meant that Marlborough could readily assist his infantry and cavalry operations. He had an average of 100 guns at each of his four great victories, Blenheim, Ramillies, Oudenarde, and Malplaquet. This meant usually 1.34 guns per thousand men.[28]

While Marlborough was commander of Dutch forces only when they were serving alongside the English forces, he also had Austrian troops. Austria had come out of the Thirty Years War politically strong, and the emperor had maintained a standing army after the Treaty of Westphalia in 1648. Austria had been busy, however, with regular offensives against the Ottoman Empire as well as acquiring, then trying to hold on to, Hungary. This meant that the imperial army was spread thin, having to operate in the Balkans and Italy as well as trying to stymie Louis's aspirations toward empire. Thus, it was a veteran army but one stretched to the limit by enemies and the time committed to various wars. The cavalry became the best arm of the Austrian army. It was that army that introduced the modern light cavalry, the hussars, which were of Magyar origin and used for skirmishing and reconnaissance.[29] Luckily for the Austrians, and for Marlborough, they had the services of a general who was virtually Marlborough's equal, and some think his tactical superior: Prince Eugene of Savoy.

Although the Savoy territory was under French authority and Eugene's mother had been mistress to Louis XIV, he had been rejected from French military service. A slim boy, described by Spencer as "effeminate," he just did not look like a soldier, and Louis quite brusquely told him so. Instead, Eugene offered his services as an eighteen-year-old with no experience to the Austrian government and from his first combat showed remarkable bravery. He also developed into as good a strategist and tactician as was active in the era. He and Marlborough became fast friends and fought together at Blenheim and Oudenarde.

The Austrians suffered a serious disadvantage in matters like supply, equipment, and above all numbers. While not particularly innovative, however, the army had marvelous commanders and an emperor who trusted them.[30] During the War of the League of Augsburg, Eugene fought the French in Italy and handled them severely. Finally realizing his mistake in dismissing the young Eugene, King Louis is said to have offered him a marshal's position, the principality of Champagne, and a huge pension, all of which Eugene rejected. From 1697 to 1699 he fought the Turks and defeated them decisively at Zenta in September 1697.[31]

As for French generals, the great ones by this time had passed on. Marshal Count Turenne was the class of his era and certainly Marlborough was glad to have served under his command and picked up some lessons. His immediate predecessor (and rival during the French civil wars) was Louis de Bourbon, the Prince de Condé, also known as "The Great Condé." Both had risen to high command near the end of the Thirty Years War and had also fought in the various conflicts with the Dutch. The master of siege warfare, both offensive and defensive, was Sebastian Vauban, but he was far more an engineer and master of siegecraft than a combat commander. Still, Louis's army was not without some talent, although his generals tend to be overshadowed by Marlborough and Eugene. Some, like the dukes of Tallard, Villeroi, and Bourgogne were political appointees with little to recommend them, but some, the duc de Villars and duc de Vendôme in particular, had real talent.[32]

The Opponents

IN SPITE OF THE GROWING HOSTILITY, peace negotiations began in May 1701, but with little serious hope of a positive outcome. A large proportion of Englishmen thought that a land war was unnecessarily costly and that the navy should be depended on to protect English commercial interests.[33] (One can easily see parallels to some twentieth-century

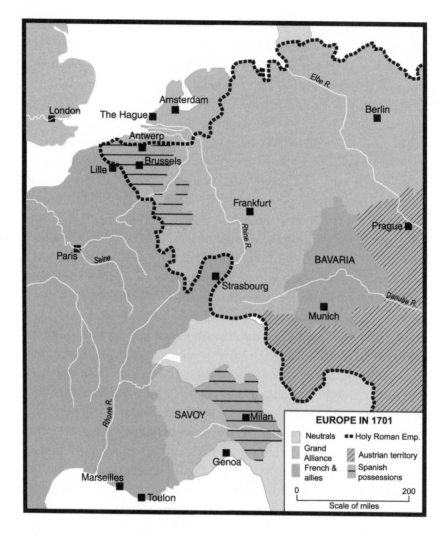

arguments about air power.) On 7 September, England, the United Provinces of the Netherlands, and the Austrian Empire signed the treaty of the Grand Alliance of the Hague: Holland promised to contribute 100,000 soldiers, the English 40,000, and the empire 82,000. Over time, several Germanic states also joined. Marlborough had signed the treaty for England; after finding William's favor again after Queen Mary's death, Marlborough had favorably impressed the king with his command in Ireland; William appreciated talent when he saw it. Luckily for England and Holland, William was able to put aside personal feelings in order to resist France.[34] On that, both men were in agreement.

Fighting alongside Louis were Spain and a number of Italian states (Savoy, Piedmont, Mantua, and Milan). Most importantly, Louis signed an alliance with Elector Maximilian II Emanuel of Bavaria, whose young son had been recently in the running for Spain's throne. Max, as he was known, was upset with the Austrians for not paying him for his support against the Turks and because Louis promised him the viceroyalty of the Spanish Netherlands, as long as he could keep the alliance forces at bay. He started in his new role by forcing Dutch garrisons from some of their frontier fortresses.[35] A hero of the wars against the Turks and intimate with the strengths and weaknesses of the Austrian military, Max assumed the war would be short and France would win. If he could defeat the Austrian forces, he could have a throne in Vienna if not a son on the throne in Madrid.

Even before war was declared in May 1702, fighting had been taking place in Italy, where Austria and Spain had long struggled against each other. The Austrians committed a 30,000-man army under Prince Eugene. He fooled the Franco-Spanish generals by marching his force through less commonly used mountain passes to surprise and defeat them at Carpi in July 1701. He then took a strong defensive position and beat back a force of 100,000, inflicting 2,000–3,000 casualties with a loss of just over 100. The defeated armies went into winter quarters, Eugene laid siege to Mantua, and some Italian nobles began changing sides.

In 1702 the Dutch forces opened the fighting in April. Skirmishes along the frontier between the Spanish Netherlands (modern Belgium) and the United Provinces (modern Holland) remained limited. Along both sides were large numbers of fortresses, the slow taking or retaking of which had dominated the last war. This dependence on fortresses for defense effectively limited thoughts of offense. It was this clash of philosophies that was to dominate the relations between the Dutch government and generals on the one hand and Marlborough and Eugene on the other. At the end of June 1702 the Dutch government (without a strong candidate for commander in chief) had ordered its generals to follow Marlborough when in joint operations.

The offensive-minded Englishman struggled with the defensive-minded Dutch, both the government and the generals. After almost constant warfare for more than twenty years, the Dutch were not anxious to lose manpower in big battles. Also, they doubted Marlborough's abilities. After all, who was he but some political appointee who had never had large-unit command experience? Thus, although he technically commanded in joint operations, getting the operations approved by the Dutch government proved close to impossible. Siege warfare was what they knew, and that was what they intended to practice.[36] When Marlborough commanded a joint operation into the Spanish Netherlands and threatened the lines of communication of the primary force along the French front under Marshal Louis François, duc de Boufflers, his subordinate Dutch generals could not convince themselves to follow orders to attack, even though the French force was exposed in the open on three occasions. He failed to inflict a major defeat on a French army, but he did accomplish what the Dutch wanted: Boufflers's retreat led to the capture of a number of fortresses. Frustrated on the battlefield, he was rewarded off it by receiving a new title, Duke (rather than Earl) of Marlborough.

The following year proved indecisive as well. It got off to a good start with the Dutch capture of Bonn, but during the summer French forces under Villars linked up with those of Max of Bavaria. With more than 70,000 troops on hand, Villars argued for an advance on Vienna. Max, however, wanted to link up with French forces in Italy before a Vienna campaign. King Louis sided with Max, who led 16,000 men in a disastrous campaign. In the Brenner Pass between Austria and Italy, the peasants harassed the Bavarians unmercifully, driving them back and costing Max half his force. Meanwhile, Louis of Baden aided the allied cause by capturing Augsburg, but was forced out of the city late in the year. Both sides did gain strategic victories: Savoy changed sides and joined the Grand Alliance, blocking French access to the Alps and Italy, but a rebellion in Hungary against the policies of Emperor Leopold diverted troops from the Grand Alliance to a new eastern front. Inconclusive sieges on the western front accomplished little for either side; Marlborough was unable to force French forces in the Netherlands into an open battle.

The 1704 campaign marked the first serious victories for the Alliance and for Marlborough's view that the enemy army was the center of gravity. With the large Franco-Bavarian force still in a position to threaten Vienna, Marlborough devised a plan for saving the city by defeating the enemy in the open, rather than in a siege. He was aided in this campaign by the fact that King Louis had removed Villars as the French commander working with Max. Villars was not one to suffer fools gladly, and he viewed Max as such when the elector would not cooperate in any move toward Vienna. After a loud confrontation, both men appealed to Louis, Villars offering to give up his command, and denouncing his ally and his supporters as "swindlers, traitors, and falsehearted fools." Max responded that he would not work with someone so rudely outspoken. Louis accepted Villars's resignation and replaced him with the incompetent duc de Marsin.[37]

The Blenheim Campaign and Battle

MARLBOROUGH'S ORIGINAL INTENT for the 1704 campaign was to march up the Rhine, turn right, and advance up the Moselle, threatening Villeroi's position north and west of the Meuse River and, he hoped, drawing French forces away from Max and the Vienna offensive. Urgent appeals from the emperor for more direct action swayed him, though they certainly did not sit well with the Dutch. After conferring with Queen Anne and advisors in London, Marlborough decided to bypass the Moselle and march to the Danube in order to alleviate the threat to Vienna and hopefully fight a decisive battle. In order to make this a successful campaign, secrecy was vital. Marlborough therefore made open plans to fight along the Moselle, telling no more than a few close associates of his true intent. He had a difficult time convincing the Dutch Estates-General to allow him to campaign as far as the Moselle; had he revealed to them his real goal they never would have cooperated. He conceded to their demand that 60,000 men under Field Marshal Hendrik Overkirk stay on the northern frontier to guard against a French advance. The rest he prepared for campaign, also planning on picking up German reinforcements along the way and joining Prince Eugene at the Danube. He ordered that regularly placed supply depots be established along his route in order to maintain constant supply: this would keep the local population happy by their profiting from the passing army without being harassed by it.

On 19 May Marlborough led 21,000 men out of the town of Bedburg, marching southeast along the left bank of the Rhine. He led the way with cavalry, while his brother, Charles Churchill (a newly appointed general), led the infantry and artillery. The supply depots were three to four days march apart, and Marlborough planned to never have his cavalry and infantry more than two days apart. Sure enough, the northernmost

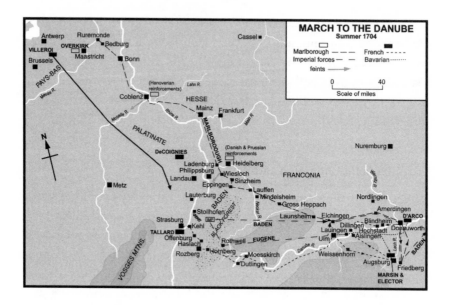

French army under Tallard began to shadow Marlborough at a distance, ignoring the Dutch frontier. Marlborough's first stop was Bonn, a logical base for an advance up the Moselle. There he received unfortunate news that a body of French reinforcements had evaded Louis of Baden's covering force on the upper Rhine and had attached themselves to Marsin and Max, bringing their numbers to 70,000.

Forty miles further up the river, the Moselle empties into the Rhine at Coblenz. When Marlborough and his cavalry arrived they did not turn to proceed up the Moselle, but crossed a pontoon bridge onto the far bank and rode directly east to Mainz. When the rest of the army arrived and followed suit, the French realized the Moselle offensive was a ruse. Villeroi passed the shadowing on to Tallard, who also paralleled the English force, staying on the western side of the Rhine. Not until several days up the Rhine did the allied soldiers themselves begin to grasp their ultimate destination. A British officer commented, "It was so much a secret, that General Churchill (the Duke's brother) knew nothing of the matter till this time; and Villeroi's constant attendance on our marches, shewed that the court of France was as much in the dark as we were."[38]

By the end of June Marlborough's army, supplemented by German units along the line of march, joined with those of Louis of Baden and Prince Eugene. The march to the Danube was a magnificent example of military deception, and also of a major feat of logistics. The French plans toward Vienna were thwarted and the allies took the initiative.[39] Indeed, the French marshals took counsel of their fears and turned to King Louis for direction, all bemoaning their respective fates. Marsin's letter warned that Elector Maximilian might take his family and treasure and flee for Hungary. Louis in response divided the army in France into three segments. Tallard would cross the Rhine from Strasburg into the southern Black Forest and lead 35,000 men to join with Marsin. Villeroi would hold the defensive lines at Stollhofen to the west of the Black Forest, where he would keep Eugene pinned down, the French hoped, and then be prepared to support Tallard if necessary. A third force under Marshal Robert de Coignies would guard the west bank of the Rhine between Philippsburg and Mainz.

While Eugene remained for a time in the Black Forest, Margrave Louis of Baden marched his men to meet Marlborough's army at Launsheim on 22 June, making the combined force some 80,000 men. Louis had a significant numerical advantage at this time, so Marlborough wanted to draw the Franco-Bavarian forces out into the open. Many of his heavy guns had not arrived, so an attack on the primary Bavarian camp at Ulm was ruled out. The combined force marched down the left bank of the Danube, past Lauingen, and on 2 July appeared outside the Schellenberg fortress at Donauwörth. This proved a major surprise to the fortress commander, Jean Baptist, the Comte d'Arco, who with his 11,000 men was working to upgrade the defenses.[40] It was late in the day and the margrave's political position outranked Marlborough's military one, though it had been decided that they could exercise command on alternate days. Margrave Louis was not a stellar general, being dedicated to siege warfare and so slow some imperial leaders suspected his loyalty. Indeed, he had fought alongside Elector Max against the Turks and they were related by marriage. Marlborough had to convince Margrave Louis to take advantage of the unprepared garrison. They had neither the time nor the artillery to besiege the city, and the longer the delay in attacking the more time d'Arco would have to strengthen the walls. Unfortunately, the troops had been marching since dawn down muddy roads. A quick assault would of necessity be somewhat piecemeal, but D'Arco would not expect it and Marlborough had great faith in the abilities of his troops.[41]

Marlborough chose the direct route for the attack, up a steep hillside. He sent 6,000 men in three lines in the first wave, supported by eight battalions directly behind and another eight echeloned to the right. He also had 35 squadrons of cavalry, which he formed close behind and to the right of his main force.[42] At about 6:15 p.m. the lead force of 6,000 grenadiers and volunteers charged at the strongest point of the defense, just uphill from the unrepaired Fort Augustine. English cannon fire was very accurate, and the English were soon fighting hand-to-hand on the parapets. A French defender wrote an account of the battle: "The English infantry led this attack with greatest intrepidity, right up to our parapet, but there they were opposed with courage at least equal to their own. Rage, fury, and desperation were manifested by both sides, with the more obstinacy as the assailants and assailed were perhaps the bravest soldiers in the world."[43] After two failed assaults in an hour's fighting, the English fell back to a dip in the ground where they were protected from enemy fire.

All of this, however, was diversion, designed to draw as many reserves as possible to the right flank of the defense. As the assault ended, a new one began on the defenders' left, where the fortifications were not in good repair. Here, Baden somewhat surprisingly led a mixed Anglo-imperial force into the now lightly held section of the defense. They quickly broke through and swarmed onto the defenders' flank and rear, while Marlborough rallied his men for a third assault. Pressed from both sides, the defenders broke and ran for the river, where a pontoon bridge broke under their weight. The pursuing cavalry showed no mercy.

The assault cost the allied army 1,500 killed and 4,500 wounded, most of them British. So many casualties in so short a space of time was rare, and the news was not well received in London. The defenders, however, suffered much more heavily. D'Arco commanded some 14,000 men, roughly 11,000 infantry and 3,000 cavalry. A British witness recorded, "The loss of the enemy was computed to be about 7,000 killed, 2,000 drowned, and 3,000 taken, with everything they had."[44] The Bavarian elector had been marching to the town's relief but arrived too late; he instead moved south to the stronghold of Augsburg. He ordered Donauwörth to be destroyed and the garrison to join him, but the French commander fled without carrying out his orders and the allies captured the town intact. They now held a secure crossing over the Danube, had captured a large amount of supplies, and seized the initiative. With Donauwörth in allied hands, the

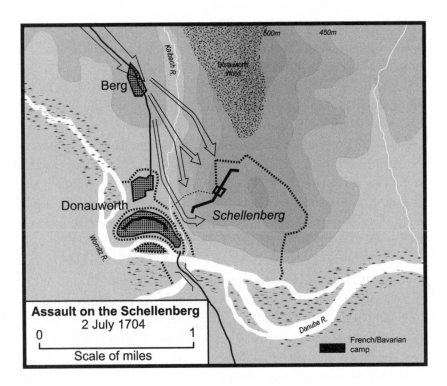

Assault on the Schellenberg
2 July 1704
0   1
Scale of miles

French/Bavarian camp

road to Vienna was blocked and the Bavarian towns and rich countryside were wide open.[45]

In spite of this costly success, the overall situation remained bleak for Marlborough and his allies. Max and Marsin refused to come out of Augsburg, mainly because they had received word that Tallard was marching to their aid. Eugene, however, was between the two French forces and delayed Tallard's advance, as did the 8,000 supply wagons he had to navigate through the Black Forest. Perhaps one-third of the French force became stragglers.[46] By late July both forces joined their respective sides. As Tallard marched, Marlborough grew desperate to draw the enemy out of Augsburg. Military historian Russell Weigley comments that he therefore "embarked on one of the less admirable ventures of his career. He turned his army loose to plunder and devastate Bavaria, with the idea that the cries of his subjects might cause the Elector to either make peace or, at least, to disperse his army for the protection of the countryside."[47] This action partially achieved the desired effect. Maximilian did spread out some of his troops, and even considered negotiating, but Tallard's arrival on 5 August ended that hope. On the other hand, the juncture of the armies brought about the real potential for a pitched battle, which had been Marlborough's ultimate goal.

Once the Franco-Bavarian army was collected, Tallard marched it along the north bank of the Danube, hoping to cut Marlborough's lines of communication. Marlborough sent Baden with 15,000 men to besiege Ingolstadt. Many sources claim this move was designed to remove the cautious general from the planning for a decisive battle. In reality, the idea to capture Ingolstadt was Baden's own. Nonetheless, Marlborough and Eugene do not seem to have been sad to see him off. Although these two had only known each other for less than two months, they were as closely attuned as Chinggis and Subedai. Marlborough sent for his forces to rally at Rain (site of Gustavus's victory over Tilly), while Eugene held his force on the north bank at Hochstadt for forward observation.

With the arrival of Tallard's forces, Tallard superseded Marsin, but he could not give orders to Elector Maximilian. That proved to be a key factor in the upcoming events. When Marlborough had sent his men to loot the Bavarian countryside, Max had sent out forces to garrison key towns for protection. They were still deployed across the area, leaving the three generals in command of a force that was primarily French though technically commanded by the Bavarian. The question before them was: what would the allies do? The three were fairly sure that their vast numbers were sufficient to oblige the allies to abandon the Danube region, probably retreating into Franconia. Thus, all that was necessary was to keep together and allow that to happen. In order to avenge the recent pillaging, Max was eager to set out in search of the allied force. "However, Tallard was less hasty, preferring to await the arrival of the recalled Bavarian detachments," writes Charles Spencer. "When the Elector persisted, Tallard replied icily: 'If I were not so convinced of Your Highness's integrity, I should imagine that you wished to gamble with the King's forces without having any of your own, to see that no risk would happen.'"[48] They decided to move forward to the town of Hochstadt, from where they could deploy in a strong defensive position.

That movement obliged Eugene to withdraw slightly and call for Marlborough to bring up his forces, now numbering 38,000 after detaching 15,000 with Margrave Louis to besiege Ingolstadt. Marlborough brought his men across the Danube at Donauwörth and marched four miles along the north bank to join Eugene at Münster. On 11 August their forces were combined, and the enemy was deploying just to the west between the villages of Hochstadt and Blindheim, along a stream called the Nebel. A personal reconnaissance gave Marlborough and Eugene a good view of the ground and the layout of the enemy forces. Tallard had chosen his bivouac site more for defense than for a battle. After all, he was used to siege warfare and not rapid action. This was all Marlborough needed to implement a great surprise.[49] This complacency was compounded by intelligence gathered by the French from allied prisoners that Louis was leaving Ingolstadt to join Marlborough and Eugene, at which point they would all retreat northward. Marlborough, however, had sent those prisoners to be captured and give this disinformation.

The allied army was on the march by 3:00 p.m. on 13 August. The plain around the Nebel is a large semicircle of wooded hills overlooking the Danube. However, the approach from the east is through narrow passages, and the allied army could not arrive all at once. Luckily for the allies, a morning mist covered their arrival, and by the time it began to lift Marlborough's forces were already lined up along the Nebel. The French, meanwhile, were not in their normal deployment of infantry in the center

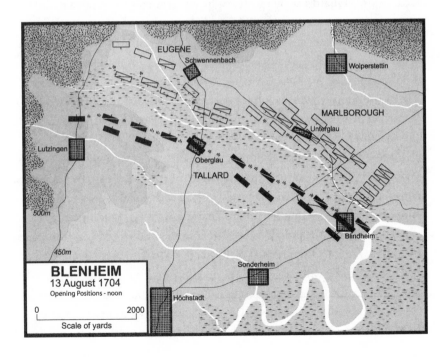

and cavalry on the wings. The force that had arrived with Tallard was arrayed northwest-southeast between the villages of Oberglau and Blindheim. The elector and Marsin were to the left in an almost east-west line from Oberglau to Lutzingen. The Nebel flowed across their front, but was only about ten feet wide, not very deep, with marshy ground along both sides. Almost their entire front was cavalry, with infantry units arrayed in a second line. Blindheim and Oberglau were both occupied by infantry and were the right and center anchors of the line. The force numbered between 56,000 and 60,000 with 90–100 guns.

The allied Anglo-Imperial force had between 52,000 and 56,000 men and only 60 guns. The numerical difference between the forces meant little to Marlborough, who had great faith in his men and their training.[50] He fronted his line with infantry, cavalry in a second line, and infantry in a third, massing around the village of Unterglau. He put his strongest effort on his left against the village of Blindheim. When Eugene's forces arrived they passed behind Marlborough's to deploy opposite the elector and Marsin. Eugene deployed infantry along the Nebel near Oberglau and put most of his cavalry on the far right flank. The plan was for Eugene's troops to hold the French left wing in place while Marlborough took care of Tallard's army on the right wing. A front line of cavalry was unusual, but apparently Tallard depended on the mud along the Nebel to significantly hamper any allied advance. With the allies deployed, Tallard decided not to alter his forces. He apparently was going to wait for Marlborough to bring his men across the river, then force them back into it.[51] While the British were trying to recover their lines after the crossing, Tallard expected his artillery and enfilading fire from Blindheim and Oberglau to pin them down.

Marlborough saw that Blindheim and Oberglau were the keys. Both were strongly defended, and those became the focal points for his attacks. One of Marlborough's major biographers, David Chandler, writes, "Marlborough did not disappoint Tallard in selecting this apparent death-trap for his main assault, but the Duke's eagle eye had not failed to notice several weaknesses in the French position. If the garrisons of Blenheim and Oberglau could be effectively contained within their positions, Tallard's center would be dangerously exposed. . . . It would be difficult for the French commander to ensure full co-operation between his two flanks."[52] Thus, Blindheim became the target of the initial assault. The village of

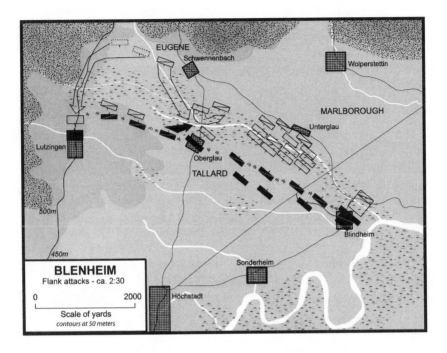

EUGENE
Schwennenbach
Wolperstettin
MARLBOROUGH
Unterglau
Lutzingen
Oberglau
TALLARD
500m
Blindheim
450m
Sonderheim
BLENHEIM
Flank attacks - ca. 2:30
0   2000
Höchstadt
Scale of yards
contours at 50 meters

some 300 houses was defended by the best French infantry available, in sixteen battalions with another eleven arrayed behind the village. Twelve squadrons of dismounted dragoons held the ground between Blindheim and the Danube.

The battle started, as was customary, with an exchange of artillery fire. Marlborough's men had to withstand some four hours of this while Eugene's men moved into position. Also, the engineers were trying to position pontoons to aid in crossing the Nebel, for the stone bridges across the stream were easily within musket range of Blindheim and Oberglau. Marlborough had his men lie down most of the time in order to try to avoid some of the artillery fire. Just past noon he received word from Eugene that the right flank units were in position and he was ready for battle. At about 12:30 the attack began with Lord Cutts leading twenty battalions of infantry and fifteen squadrons of cavalry against Blindheim. These were the cream of the British forces, and they took a terrible beating. They retreated and attacked again. Their bravery frightened Lieutenant General Philippe, the Marquis de Clérambault, commanding the defense, so he called up the reserves and had the dragoons leave their flanking position and come into the village as well. He also brought in infantry

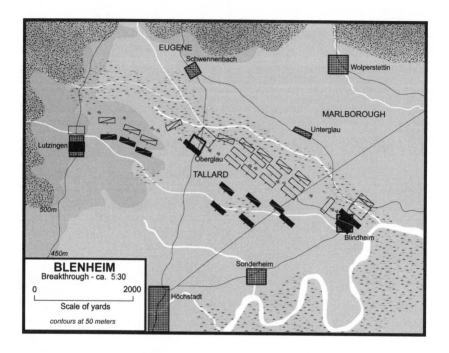

reserves from the center of Tallard's line, weakening that sector. Tallard was at the time on the far side of the battlefield conferring with Marsin and Maximilian. Blindheim now held twenty-seven battalions; troops were packed so tightly into the village they could barely move, but they made easy targets for English muskets. A mere nine battalions, primarily recruits, remained to support the French cavalry in Tallard's lines.

With the struggle going back and forth, French cavalry tried to assist in throwing back the assaults. This is where Marlborough's philosophy of aggressive cavalry tactics paid off. Tallard had just returned from the left wing when he saw eight squadrons of his elite cavalry being driven back by five squadrons of British cavalry. Even though a relatively minor action, it still shook Tallard's morale.[53]

With Blindheim sucking in French resources, Marlborough ordered units on his right to attack Oberglau while units in the center began to cross the Nebel and form up on the far side. Tallard was once again out of the picture, now looking into the situation at Blindheim as the advances took place. At Oberglau, however, the French were doing just fine without him. Ten battalions under the prince of Holstein-Beck assaulted the well-defended position and were not only repulsed but pursued by the defenders, primarily the Irish "Wild Geese," who served with the French after William drove them from Ireland. As they came out of their defenses cavalry units joined in, and it looked as though Marlborough's right flank might collapse. The infantry held the French cavalry at bay long enough for the retreating British cavalry to reform and recover the field. For assistance, Marlborough sent an urgent request to Eugene for more cavalry support. Hard-pressed himself, Eugene sent some squadrons anyway while he kept up his attack with infantry. Meanwhile, Marlborough brought up some artillery to aid in the assault, gathered together cavalry and the re-formed infantry under Holstein-Beck, and personally led the charge against the village.[54]

On the allied right wing Eugene had his hands full. Marsin and Maximilian had decided to defend the Nebel rather than let the enemy across, and they were doing a good job of it. Imperial cavalry had tried to sweep the far right flank and had captured some guns near Lutzingen, but a Bavarian counterattack regained the lost ground and guns. A second cavalry charge fared no better, nor did a third. After Eugene dispatched cavalry aid to Oberglau, he was immediately back into the thick of the fight. The three failed charges had begun to dishearten some of the troops and there was a feeling of panic, but after he shot two men for running, the others took heart. Declaring, "I wish to fight among brave men and not cowards," Eugene joined units of Prussian and Danish mercenaries.[55]

The allied regrouping after the initial repulse at Oberglau kept up pressure on the village and brought in a few more French reserves, further weakening the French center. Now was the time for Marlborough to strike. Weigley describes the scene: "Choosing with superb military instinct—the hallmark of the warrior, reaching beyond the intellectual qualities of the educated professional soldier—the moment when the fight was most fluid and ready to be resolved by a fresh effort by either side, Marlborough ordered a general assault and threw in his massed cavalry."[56] His reserves had crossed the Nebel and deployed on the French side, two lines of cavalry in front with two lines of infantry in support. Artillery was also hauled across the pontoons and brought to bear. Marlborough now deployed 80 fresh squadrons against the 50–60 tired French squadrons, plus 23 battalions of British and German infantry against the remaining 9 French battalions. The lessons taught by Gustavus came to life again, as infantry and cavalry worked together. The British cavalry charged,

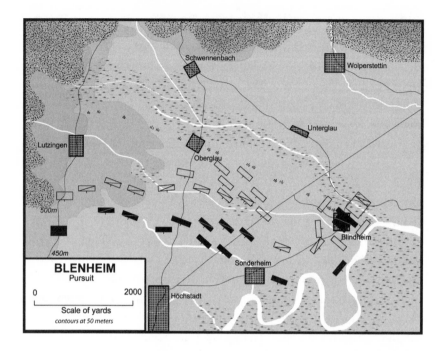

then withdrew between gaps in the infantry battalions, which blasted the pursuing French cavalry, which were then chased by the re-formed British horsemen. That, in addition to the newly placed artillery, broke the French center and the rout was on. The massed advance was more than the French cavalry could take, with even the elite Maison du Roi in headlong flight.[57]

Once Tallard began to fall back, allied infantry split to surround both Blindheim and Oberglau, as well as strike Marsin's rear. Pressed by Eugene in front (who was by now making good progress on the far flank near Lutzingen) and the victorious allies on their right, Marsin and Maximilian had no choice but to join in the retreat. They withdrew in better order, trying to make for Hochstadt. The 27 battalions in Blindheim surrendered about 9:00 that evening, their commander having fled on horse and drowned in the Danube. With the surrender of some 10,000 troops, the psychological effect was tremendous across western Europe, for the concept of French invincibility had been proven false.[58]

In a time when casualties were usually numbered in the hundreds or a few thousand, the Battle of Blenheim (as the German village came to be known in its anglicized form) was horrific: more than 4,500 allied soldiers killed and almost 8,000 wounded. Of the British soldiers engaged, one in four was killed or wounded, and some 40 percent of the British officers were casualties. The number, of course, was much higher on the losing side. Spencer recounts, "Marlborough intercepted reports sent from Duttlingen to the French court by survivors. These conceded that 40,000 of Louis's and the Elector's men had been killed, wounded, or captured at Blenheim. . . . Perhaps most revealing is the statistic calculated by Marlborough's biographer, Archdeacon Coxe: of the 4,500 Franco-Bavarian officers who fought at Blenheim, only 250 were not killed, wounded or captured."[59]

The allied approach march began at roughly 3:00 a.m. but, owing to rougher terrain on the northern flank of the march, Eugene's deployment delayed what could have been a surprise attack. Having surveyed the battlefield site the day before, Marlborough already had in mind the deployment of all three arms for best coordination in a deliberate attack. His primary tactic was feint and demonstration, successfully tying down large numbers of enemy troops while at the same time creating a weak spot for his main assault. The breakthrough allowed for only temporary pursuit as it was late in the day; therefore, there was no real attempt at immediate exploitation, although operations over the next few months took advantage of the victory. The most important military effect was the virtual destruction of the Franco-Bavarian force. Strategically, it allowed for capture and securing of all major strong points along the Danube and Rhine as well as potentially laying France open to invasion. Politically, it saved Vienna and the empire from collapse and took Bavaria out of the war. J. F. C. Fuller remarks on the importance of the battle: "Had Marlborough been defeated, the Elector of Bavaria would have replaced the House of Habsburg on the Imperial throne; Munich would have ousted Vienna; and the Empire itself would have become a satrapy of France. . . . For England, Blenheim was the greatest battle won on foreign soil since Agincourt. It broke the prestige of the French armies and plunged them into disgrace and ridicule."[60]

All accounts of the battle praise Marlborough, but many are quick to point out he did not accomplish the victory alone. Dodge notes the centrality of Eugene's presence on the battlefield: "Had Eugene not contained nearly half the enemy, Marlborough would scarcely have been able to break the centre. . . . [W]e must cheerfully allow him full half the credit for this great and decisive victory."[61] A more recent biographer notes that Eugene's holding operations had been as crucial to the whole battle as had his preparation for action in the days leading up to it. Marlborough and Eugene highly praised each other.[62] Eugene not only fought superbly, but he faced the superior opposition, outnumbered by some 10,000 men on his wing of the battle. This was a tribute to his talent and courage, that he could keep a much larger force occupied, detach men to help Marlborough in his time of need, and still be advancing when the French troops began to break.[63]

The Battle of Ramillies

UNFORTUNATELY, THE SUCCESS AT BLENHEIM did not translate into larger dividends. Although the allies did occupy Trier in November 1704 and had a strong position for an offensive up the Moselle, neither that avenue nor an assault against Strasbourg would open a road to Paris, the surest way to bring King Louis to the peace table on terms favorable to the allies. Any advance west from the Rhine faced the need for sieges of major cities; any advance through Flanders meant besieging an even larger number of fortresses. To further trouble the allies, King Louis managed to refit his army quickly. Thus, 1705 negated the initiative gained in 1704. Some successes were still achieved: Marlborough managed to break through the seemingly impregnable lines of the Brabant, a string of defenses stretching from Antwerp to Namur. This gained a few fortresses but there were no major battles to inflict serious harm on the French. One flagrant missed opportunity on the Ijssche River led to the resignation of a major Dutch general and a promise from the Dutch that they would, indeed, take his orders on the battlefield rather than continually argue as they had been doing. The positive effect of this offensive was not only breaching the lines of Brabant but destroying a section of the defensive front about twenty miles wide.

At the beginning of 1706 it seemed that the focus of the war was going to shift to Italy, where Eugene was fighting. The Dutch government told Marlborough he could go if he did not take any Dutch troops with him, but a defeat of his ally Louis of Baden convinced them that he needed to stay and conduct a campaign in Flanders. At the opening of the fighting season in early spring, Marlborough was at Maastricht, preparing for what

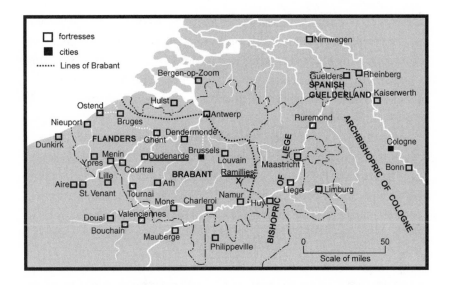

he expected would be another year of maneuver without much fighting. He was wrong.[64] King Louis, buoyed by the early success, became a bit more aggressive in northern France. He ordered Villeroi, stationed in Flanders with 60,000 men, not to avoid battle. Louis's more talented general, Villars, was stationed on the upper Rhine with 40,000 men. Marlborough did not expect Villeroi to go on to the offensive right at the start of the campaign season, without even waiting for Villars to bring reinforcements. Recent successes by the French had made Blenheim a distant memory, and a general underestimation of Marlborough's capabilities proliferated.[65] After he had pierced the lines of the Brabant the previous year, Villeroi assumed Marlborough would try a movement toward Namur. This was perhaps the only thing he got right that month, for although he was confident that he could handle the British, historians have described him as "inept" and "the worst of the French chiefs."[66]

Marlborough led his forces out of Maastricht on 22 May, lacking many of the promised reinforcements from some of the German states. He marched his army through the destroyed section of the Brabant lines with the intent, as Villeroi assumed, of threatening Namur. The allied forces moved westward through Merdorp as Villeroi led 74 battalions and 128 squadrons (60,000 men) southward from Louvain. Marlborough could barely believe scouting reports that the French were on the move toward him. He called up his Danish mercenaries at the double quick, bringing his forces up to 74 battalions and 122 squadrons (62,000 men). Both commanders were surprised by their proximity to each other. As Chandler comments, "The tactical intelligence of both sides thus left something to be desired; the 'fog of war' was very evident. Yet both sides knew the site for the forthcoming battle well enough, for it was a location of some strategic importance."[67]

About dawn on a very foggy 23 May, 600 dragoons stumbled into a French foraging party and exchanged a few shots. Word immediately went back to Marlborough, who arrived with his staff before the town of Ramillies about 10:00, when he observed Villeroi's army marching north to south across a gently rolling plain. The battlefield and the French deployment were reminiscent of Blenheim, except the northern

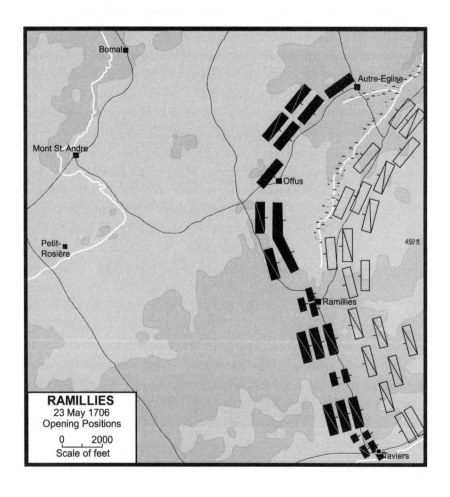

RAMILLIES
23 May 1706
Opening Positions
0   2000
Scale of feet

flank curved toward rather than away from the oncoming allies. On the left (northern) flank was the town of Autre-Église with the Petit Gheet stream flowing south. It was swollen from rains over the previous few days and in some places was 200 yards across (though shallow) with marshy terrain on both sides. Next was the smaller town of Offus, then Ramillies, then on the far right flank was the town of Taviers, sitting on the Mehaigne River. Most sources have the town anchoring the French right, but contemporary sources imply the French troops were actually behind a tributary of the Mehaigne just to the west of the village. As Tallard had at Blenheim, Villeroi believed himself to be in a strong defensive position. His infantry occupied the villages and were in a solid line from Ramillies to Autre-Église, with cavalry deployed behind them. In the southern part, between Taviers and Ramillies, the ground was open, gently rolling farmland that offered excellent fields of view. Though still somewhat muddy, it was good cavalry country.[68] Indeed, the majority of the French right wing was cavalry, 82 squadrons including the elite Maison du Roi.

Marlborough had some major advantages as his army came up. First, Villeroi, by using the villages as anchors, had his men arrayed in a convex line. This would make it much more difficult for units from either flank to reposition themselves if needed. Conversely, Marlborough's line would be concave, bringing his flanks closer together and thus having much shorter interior lines. Second, the British right wing, deployed along the Petit Gheet, was backed by a hill. Marlborough would use the reverse slope to move men without the French being able to observe. Third, the Anglo-Dutch army had the advantage of superior artillery in this battle. The proportions were the opposite of Blenheim: 90–100 guns for Marlborough to only 60 for the French. The allied deployment placed the bulk of the British infantry and cavalry on the right wing with the Dutch infantry and cavalry and Danish cavalry covering the left, opposite the massed French cavalry.

The allies went into action first, about 1:00 p.m. Dutch infantry quickly occupied Taviers on the south flank, causing the French to move fourteen squadrons of dragoons and a number of Bavarian infantry battalions to hold the line. They failed. Just as the dragoons dismounted Danish cavalry units arrived and drove them from the scene, with the infantry soon in retreat with them. This removed some of the infantry units stationed on the French right wing.

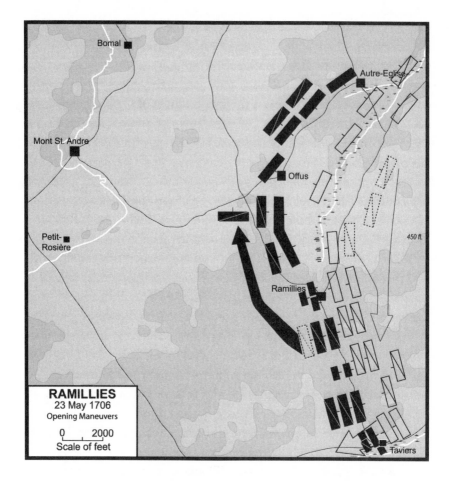

As this was happening, Marlborough ordered his British infantry under General George Orkney forward toward the Petit Gheet. Given the width of the stream, this was probably a feint, but contemporary records are not clear. They did go forward with pontoons to throw bridges across the stream. Whether it was a feint or real attack did not matter, for it had the desired result of drawing Villeroi's attention. Whether Marlborough knew it or not, Villeroi had been given orders from King Louis for this engagement, not only to engage but how to do so, with the king telling him, "Pay particular attention to that part of the line which will endure the first shock of the English troops." Given a command by the king meant that no matter what actually happened during the ebb and flow of the battle, the orders must be obeyed.[69] (Changing rules of engagement ordered periodically from the Pentagon in the Vietnam

War come to mind.) When the redcoats started approaching the stream, Villeroi followed his monarch's instructions and brought both infantry and cavalry units from south of Ramillies to reinforce his left wing.

At the same time, twelve allied battalions assaulted Ramillies, four from the front and eight from the south, with the intent of neutralizing the French artillery situated to support the cavalry in case of attack. They got off to a good start, but the Maison du Roi cavalry counterattacked. A back-and-forth battle ensued as Overkirk's Dutch cavalry came into play. Given the sheer intensity of the attacks against Offus and Autre-Église, and the massing of the Dutch and German brigades against Ramillies, Villeroi was happy to follow his monarch's decree, pulling more reserves from the French right flank.[70] With infantry support (which the French cavalry now lacked) the allies to the south were able to hold off the French and allow the Dutch to re-form. Still, they had lost ground, and the infantry assaulting Ramillies was now exposed. Stationed on higher ground behind the lines, Marlborough saw the potential for disaster and made two decisions. First, he recalled Orkney's assault across the Petit Gheet. Second, he followed that withdrawal with an order to the British cavalry to withdraw behind the hill mentioned earlier.

If the British attack across the Petit Gheet had been a feint, Marlborough must have intentionally not mentioned that to the commander, General Orkney. The attack had actually been succeeding, with infantry across the stream and assaulting both Autre-Église and Offus. With the former almost in his possession, Orkney was not happy with the recall order. Ultimately, it took the arrival of General William Cadogan, Marlborough's second in command, to convince him to disengage. The battalions grudgingly withdrew, but easily handled some French formations that tried to follow.[71] As the British units re-formed on the east side of the stream they lined up on the hillside, threatening a second assault. Though the retreat was not a popular order with the troops who had been so close to capturing the two villages, it was the wise one, for they could not have known that the massed reserves were lined up just beyond the villages, waiting for them to emerge.[72] Colonel Robert Parker, a participant in the battle, described it thus: "But the front line halted on the summit of the hill in full view of them, and there stood, ready to march down and attack them. As soon as our rear line had retired out of sight of the enemy, they immediately faced left, and both horse and foot, with a good many

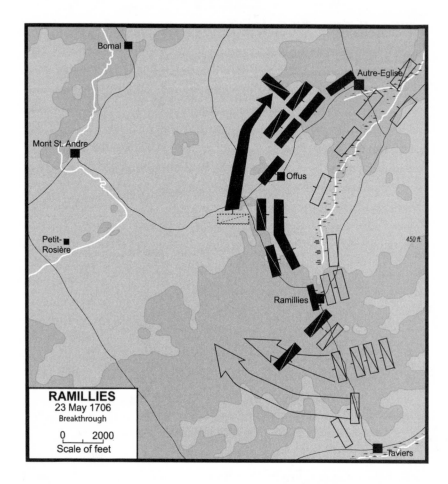

RAMILLIES
23 May 1706
Breakthrough

0   2000
Scale of feet

squadrons, that slunk out of the front line, marched down to the plain, as fast as they could; by this time the greater part of our horse of the left wing had arrived there also."[73]

As this shift of units from the allied right to their left was taking place, Marlborough was massing his infantry reserve in the center to follow up on the Ramillies assault. He led the attack himself, having one horse shot out from under him and seeing an aide killed by a cannon ball as he ceded his horse to his commander. Chandler observes, "Some commentators assert that Marlborough was wrong to expose himself so rashly.... But the Duke was a skillful assessor of a difficult situation, and was probably aware that his personal intervention would play an important part in rallying the horse." This assessment was correct; time was won for the arrival of the transferring squadrons, and the allies gained an advantage in numbers.[74]

It was now approaching 6:00 and time for the killing blow. Across the open plain south of Ramillies came masses of allied cavalry. Immediately following came the Danish cavalry from the far southern flank where they had earlier driven the Bavarians from the Taviers area. At the battle's height, 25,000 cavalry from both armies were engaged and the struggle lasted two hours. Although the Maison du Roi acquitted themselves admirably, they could not withstand the superior numbers on front and flank. Neither did they have the infantry support necessary to repel the cavalry, as the allied side possessed. The French began to withdraw to the northwest. Villeroi saw what was happening too late; with his entire right wing in flight, the allied cavalry could now fall on his flank. As the French right wing collapsed, Marlborough swung his southern units into

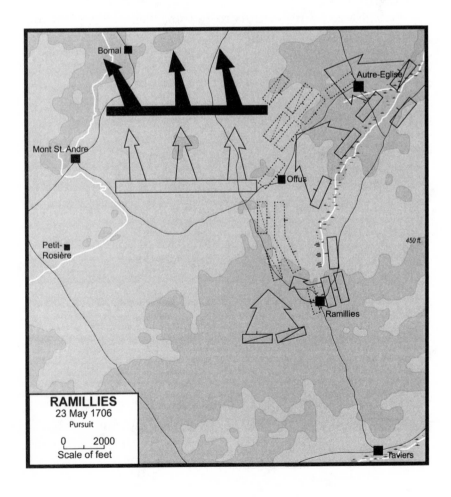

a line perpendicular to the French and began advancing north into their now exposed flank. That, coupled with the intense pressure coming onto Ramillies, was more than they could stand.[75]

Ramillies soon fell and the assault on the remainder of the French line began. Unable to turn and face the onslaught, unable to move forward toward the marshy stream, Villeroi tried to react, ordering his unused cavalry to turn and face the new threat. As Corelli Barnett vividly describes, "But as the spark of fear leaped from man to man all fifty squadrons rode in panic through the fleeing French infantry. . . . The fugitives took to the fields and woods like wild creatures, and all that evening and night the English cavalry . . . hunted them down with remorseless pleasure."[76] Unlike the aftermath of Blenheim, there was still enough daylight and fresh horses to completely exploit the retreat, which became a rout.

In fact, it was a British victory to outshine Blenheim. Of Villeroi's original 60,000 men, he withdrew into the defenses at Louvain with but 15,000; all the rest were killed, wounded, captured, or missing. Allied losses were just over 1,000 dead and some 2,500 wounded. The French lost all their artillery and supplies. They soon lost even more, as the allies swept the French from the Spanish Netherlands. In less than a month, Louvain, Brussels, Gavre, and Bruges fell, while a dozen other major fortresses capitulated without resistance, so demoralized were their garrisons. Ramillies thus proved to be a perfect illustration of exploiting a victory both tactically and strategically.[77] Within six weeks almost all of the Spanish Netherlands was in allied hands. Almost every fortress the French had occupied before the war in order to assist the Spanish garrisons was retaken, many without a fight.

The Battle of Ramillies was a classic meeting engagement, since both armies had stumbled into each other at the site. In Marlborough's movement to contact he had certainly hoped for an open battle, but he had expected it later and in a different location. In spite of the relative haste of the deployment, Marlborough was familiar with the ground and quickly grasped the weaknesses in the French deployment. As at Blenheim he started with a demonstration on both flanks, though the assault on the southern flank at Taviers proved successful and became the initial move that began to roll up the French right wing. On the French left, the demonstration also proved initially successful, although it was not intended as a breakthrough but to draw in reserves. Chandler comments,

"Marlborough's skill for sizing up a position, his skill at controlling the form and detail of a major conflict, had been once again amply demonstrated."[78] Once the French cavalry retreat began, the exploitation was immediate; both the cavalry on the plain and the infantry at Ramillies pushed the exposed flank. The immediate exploitation was followed by both a tactical pursuit that broke the French force and a strategic pursuit that pushed French forces almost completely out of the Spanish Netherlands.

The Battle of Oudenarde

SOON AFTER RAMILLIES came more good news. In Italy, Eugene had captured the city of Milan after the French commander there, the duc de Vendôme, was recalled to assist the crumbling situation in France. This effectively took France out of the picture in Italy; the French still occupied some cities but had no field army in-country. With two major losses, one would think that Louis XIV would be in a good mood to negotiate, but military success bred allied political failure. Once again the Dutch let Marlborough down, happy to have accomplished what they had in 1706. Marlborough was ready to go for the French throat, but was overruled by political complacency.[79] The new emperor in Vienna, Leopold I, spent too much of his time focused on the Hungarian revolution and establishing Austrian power in Italy, which (according to the original alliance agreement) should have been ceded to Spain. The Dutch government, now in charge of the lower Netherlands, quickly lost its initial goodwill by imposing heavy taxes on the Catholic residents. The Dutch also were not happy to learn that Britain was planning on keeping Gibraltar as well as Port Mahon on Minorca. So with all the new infighting among the allies, the French had a year's respite to regroup. In 1707 they fielded a strong army on the Netherlands frontier, staged a destructive raid into German territory, and gained power and prestige in Spain. Further, Eugene led an attack on Toulon, but it was poorly organized and failed to seize the French Mediterranean port city.

In 1708 both sides were ready to get back into the game. Vendôme was ready to take his large force of 110,000 back into the Spanish Netherlands and recover some lost fortresses. Marlborough was stationed in Holland, Eugene was on the Moselle, and the elector of Hanover (the future

George I of England) was on the upper Rhine. Eugene and Marlborough decided to join forces and look for a battle. Coupling Eugene's 45,000 imperial troops with 90,000 British and Dutch troops would overwhelm any enemy in the neighborhood.

Vendôme was a good general, but he was saddled with the Louis, duc de Bourgnogne (Duke of Burgundy), Louis XIV's grandson and no great military mind. Burgundy did, however, have rank and the willingness to exercise it. In late May 1708 the French crossed the frontier, moving in the direction of Brussels. Marlborough moved to block their path, and the French started marching farther east toward Louvain. Again Marlborough headed them off. At this time he got bad news: Eugene was having trouble getting everything prepared and was arguing with the elector. Thus, in order to arrive at all, he had to leave manpower behind. Not until 29 June did he start his march, and with only 15,000 men. The French commander, the duc de Berwick, was three days behind him in pursuit with 27,000. Eugene and Marlborough had to join forces and strike against Vendôme's army before Berwick could either catch up to Eugene or alter his march to join Vendôme.

Luckily for Marlborough, arguments between Vendôme and Burgundy took up the remainder of the month of June and into July; the marshal wanted to march east to besiege Huy while the duke wanted to march northwest to Ghent to take advantage of the growing disaffection with Dutch rule. Finally word came from Versailles to follow the duke's plan. Unfortunately, focused as Marlborough was on his own plans and preparations, he ignored intelligence reports of French intentions. On 4 July a French cavalry force left Vendôme's army to "forage." At the same time, a separate force marched quickly from Menin northward to Bruges. By employing speed and deception, small forces broke into Bruges and Ghent, taking them both without a fight. The rest of Vendôme's army was quickly away from Marlborough and into Ghent before he could react. Winston Churchill commented on his ancestor's plight: "At a stroke, the French had made themselves masters of the middle Scheldt [River] and the canals leading to the coast. . . . This *coup* returned much of Spanish Flanders into French hands, and constituted a serious blow to Marlborough's prestige and thus to the morale of the Allied army."[80] With these two key cities in hand, the French began laying siege to Oudenarde on the Scheldt River; control of that river would isolate Flanders to the west.

The usually well-balanced Marlborough fell into a depression approaching despair. He probably was also suffering from a severe fever. The arrival in camp of both Eugene and the British second in command Cadogan broke the spell, restoring his morale as well as that of the army.[81] The brothers-in-arms were quickly planning moves. In their camp at Asch, intelligence reports arrived alerting them to another French move. After seizing Ghent, the French had taken up a forward position some seventeen miles to the southeast at Alost. The Anglo-Dutch camp at Asch was eight miles due east of Alost. The scouting report said the French were marching south, probably to the town of Lessines, to cover the approach to Oudenarde. Marlborough and Eugene had to get there first. They sent Cadogan ahead with an advance team of cavalry and infantry; he got there at 4:00 a.m. on 10 July, well before the French. The rest of Marlborough's army was there by 11:00, having marched thirty miles in thirty-six hours. When the French army on the march learned of this rapid movement, they had no choice but to alter their route. Chandler observes, "The French (Burgundy not desiring to force a battle at this stage—to Vendôme's disgust) forthwith swung away northward towards Gavre, intent on placing the Scheldt between the Allies and themselves, and called off the blockade of Oudenarde as the Allies began to pour over the Dender [River at Lessines]."[82] The French failed to fight the Anglo-Dutch force piecemeal as it arrived at Lessines; perhaps they could do it at Oudenarde.

The French established themselves at Gavre, eight miles downstream (north) of Oudenarde, while at 1:00 a.m. on 11 May Marlborough sent Cadogan and 10,000 men straight for Oudenarde. They carried bridging equipment and encountered no enemy scouts along the way. By 10:30 they had reached the river and begun work, constructing pontoon bridges and strengthening the stone bridges in the town. Although the French could see the activity from a distance, they apparently believed it was foragers or the British garrison, rather than the advance force of Marlborough's army. They continued to move at a leisurely pace southward from Gavre to begin their deployment on high ground near Huyshe. Meanwhile, Marlborough had been alerted to the relative movements of the two forces, and the bulk of his troops were in a mad dash to assist. Early in the afternoon the advance guard completed the first bridges and British and Dutch infantry along with Hanoverian dragoons began to take up

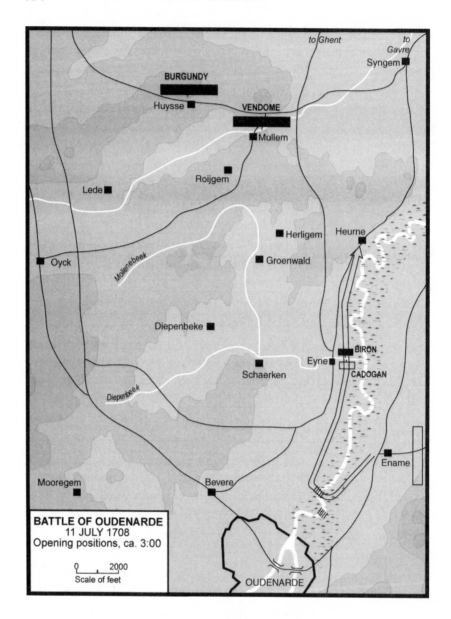

BATTLE OF OUDENARDE
11 JULY 1708
Opening positions, ca. 3:00

0   2000
Scale of feet

positions. Past the river lay open farmland, rising upward, cut by three streams: the Norken, Diepenbeek, and Mollenebeek.[83]

The commander of the French advance guard finally came close enough to the bridges to confront reality: not only were they built and guarded, but in the distance he could plainly see the bulk of Marlborough's army approaching. He alerted Vendôme, who quickly ordered several Swiss mercenary battalions of the advance guard forward to seize the bridges; he would send forward cavalry support and bring up the rest of the army. Unfortunately for the French, senior officers again took counsel of their fears. The ground along the Scheldt on which the cavalry would have to ride was thought to be too marshy to cross, although nobody seems to have actually gone forward to inspect it. The support column thus halted on the command of Vendôme's chief of staff. When Vendôme himself arrived, he demanded to know why the troops were not advancing. Vendôme decided not to override his chief of staff's decision, so unhappily countermanded his earlier order. He then rode off to find Burgundy to see about formulating another battle plan.[84]

The Swiss battalions did not receive the withdrawal order. Marlborough and Eugene arrived on the scene about noon and ordered Cadogan to drive the Swiss out of their position at Eyne. This was accomplished quickly, and the British line extended as far as Heurne. The next arriving British units went past Eyne to the northwest and occupied Groenwald. With an allied line forming, Vendôme met with Burgundy and recommended withdrawal. Had the initial attack been made with deliberation, it would have been the French establishing a line, and one much closer to the Scheldt. Now, the initiative was lost. The inconsistency of the dual command showed itself again. The royal pulled rank on the general, ordering an attack. Vendôme unhappily returned to his wing of the army and began sending units forward with intent of outflanking the allies to the west. Burgundy, however, did not get involved. He brought his wing forward from the Huysse heights past the Narken to the higher ground around Roijgem. Here he was informed that the ground to the front, along the Mollenebeke, was also too marshy for cavalry to operate. This too was untrue, but Burgundy also believed the terrain report, and he, with his half of the army, spent the rest of the battle as observers.

The battle developed in parallel, with allied units deploying between Herlingem and Schaerken along the east bank of the Mollenebeek, while arriving French units marched onto the field and deployed opposite them. Just as Vendôme thought he was getting units around the allied flank, new units would cross the pontoon bridges and take up position to the left of the defending units, turning westward along the southern bank of the Diepenbeek. Through the late afternoon, one French unit would reach

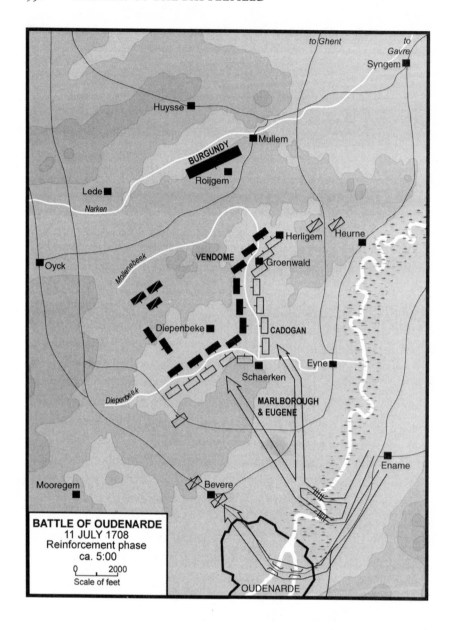

BATTLE OF OUDENARDE
11 JULY 1708
Reinforcement phase
ca. 5:00
0   2000
Scale of feet

the far flank just as an allied unit would arrive to oppose it. Vendôme was in the thick of the fighting, "in the front line, pike in hand, as if he could beat a way to victory by his own physical efforts."[85] Burgundy watched from behind. At one point Vendôme sent a messenger to Burgundy, ordering (or suggesting) he bring the stationary troops down on top of the allied flank at Herlingem. Again, "marshy terrain" kept this from happening, and the messenger returning the negative response to Vendôme was killed on the way.

The final units of the allied army were finally arriving. Owing to the collapse of one of the pontoon bridges, these Dutch and Hanoverian soldiers had to march through Oudenarde (earlier the cavalry had been ordered to take the southern route to facilitate the infantry crossing the pontoons). With the reserves arriving on the field, Marlborough sent Eugene to take command on the right while he oversaw the left. Meanwhile, Vendôme was redoubling his efforts to break through, finally capturing Groenwald and Hermlingen. Marlborough sent fresh Hanoverian troops into the far western lines, withdrawing the committed troops back through them (but leaving their colors behind to give the impression they were still there). The relieving troops pressed the French across the stream, while the newly relieved troops marched behind the lines to aid Eugene. Marlborough illustrated his mastery of the battlefield in employing this tactic and having it succeed.[86] With the reinforcements Eugene retook both villages.

With the entire line stabilized, Marlborough now had the opportunity to deliver his killing blow. He ordered the Dutch troops under Overkirk to march northwest from Bevere onto the high ground called the Boster Couter, from which they could fall on the French right flank. At about 7:00 p.m. the flank attack began, with eight battalions under General Week passing the headwater of the Diepenbeek and turning east. About a half hour later twelve squadrons and sixteen battalions were in position past Oyck and received the order to charge. They accomplished a total surprise, and the French right flank began to fall apart as it approached 9:00. They tried to put up a fight but could not handle frontal and flank pressure in what was beginning to look like a single envelopment that would close a ring around the French. Before it could close the allied troops withdrew to the north, as did their commanders.[87]

Chandler writes, "Casualty figures are, as usual, hard to establish with any accuracy. The Allied figures are generally agreed to have been about 825 killed and 2,150 wounded, but the French claim they lost only about as many ... and a mere 1,800 prisoners (including 300 officers). Some Allied sources put the French loss as high as 6,000 killed and wounded besides 9,000 prisoners and a further 5,000 deserters."[88] Although nightfall

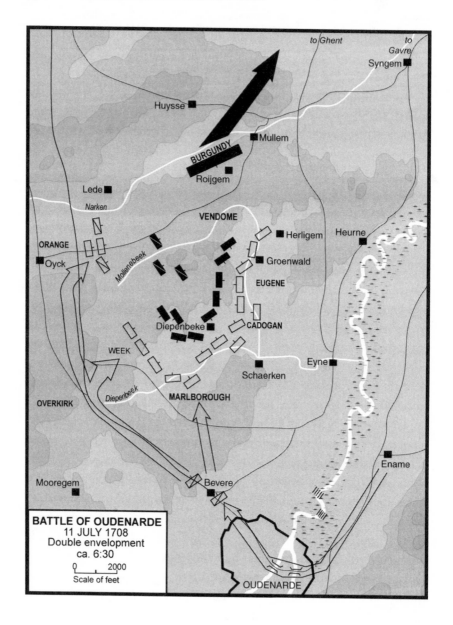

BATTLE OF OUDENARDE
11 JULY 1708
Double envelopment
ca. 6:30

0   2000
Scale of feet

prohibited immediate pursuit, the darkness did have one beneficial effect on the allied prisoner count. Eugene ordered French Huguenot troops in the allied army to call out in their native language and to beat the drums, sounding the French order for retreat; French troops marched to the sounds of those drums and became captives.

Although both armies knew the other's general location and their intent to march to Oudenarde, the battle became a textbook example of a meeting engagement. Neither army had the time to choose good ground or to make well-thought-out decisions. Vendôme correctly ordered a hasty attack by his advance guard on the allied advance guard and bridgehead; unfortunately for him Cadogan's attack overwhelmed what became an exposed Swiss infantry unit. The immediate pursuit gained a forward position at Heurne and Groenwald, the latter becoming the initial point of contact as well as the focal point of the most intense fighting throughout the afternoon. After hours of hasty attack and defense, Marlborough was finally able to implement a deliberate attack with his flanking movement. Immediate exploitation was curtailed by darkness, while the pursuit ordered the next morning ran into a well-organized rear guard that drove them off and allowed the remains of the French army to retreat into Ghent.

Marlborough's Generalship

THE REMAINDER OF THE CAMPAIGN SEASON of 1708 proved successful for the allies. They recaptured the fortresses lost at the beginning of May and successfully besieged the most important French fortress city of Lille. Unfortunately, this did not bring about an end to the war any more than had the spectacular successes of 1706. The following year the armies were at it again, with Marlborough winning another victory, though an extremely costly one, at Malplaquet, south of Mons, on 11 September. He also had some success in penetrating the line of fortresses known as the Ne Plus Ultra, but it was not enough to either force a peace or maintain his own military and political position. Growing fatigue over the war in Parliament and the English public worked against his goal of a military-political success. The relationship between Queen Anne and Sarah Churchill, Lady Marlborough, soured as well. The friendship between the two that had taken Marlborough to power eventually led to his demise when Sarah grew too domineering for the queen to handle any longer. "When the Whigs were driven from office in 1711, Marlborough was dismissed from his command," notes Spencer. "He was accused of having prolonged the war to his own advantage."[89] The Marlboroughs fell from grace in 1708, and many of the next years were spent on the continent, where they were more appreciated. The crowning of George I in 1714, however, brought Marlborough back into high military command, for the new monarch had fought under Marlborough in the Netherlands and admired his skill as a general and leader.

Most English historians regard Marlborough and Wellington as the two greatest generals of their history, with the two exchanging first and second place depending on the author. I will discuss Wellington later in this book. Marlborough's strengths as a general include mastery of the principles of objective, offensive, mass, unity of command, and morale.

By holding political and military positions simultaneously, Marlborough had a terrific grasp of what needed to be done militarily in order to achieve political *objectives*. Unlike most of the Dutch leaders, he saw the enemy army as the center of gravity. Thus, all his battles were fought with the intent of destroying armies. His ultimate failure lay in the fact that there were too many enemy armies, and the defeat and virtual destruction of one—as certainly happened at Blenheim and Ramillies—did not cripple the whole French military system. One of Louis XIV's advantages lay in the fact that he could keep up the war by personal choice, which none of the allied leaders could do (with the exception of the emperors in Austria). Thus, while Marlborough could maneuver an enemy into a battle that was locally decisive, victory tended to have only a regional effect. Chandler writes, "From first to last he was the proponent of the major battle as the sole means to break an enemy's military power and thus his will to resist. In this he was following the advice given by Turenne to Condé in the preceding generation: 'Make few sieges and fight plenty of battles; when you are master of the countryside the villages will give us the towns.'"[90]

On the battlefield, Marlborough was always quick to read the terrain and locate the enemy's weakness. Even at Oudenarde, where time was of the essence and he could not personally reconnoiter, his trusted aides knew his mind and discovered the unoccupied high ground to the west from which to launch the decisive attack. Possibly no general since Alexander was as good at finding or creating weak points in enemy lines. Eventually, however, the tactic of threatening a strong point and drawing in reserves, used at the three battles discussed in this chapter, became too predictable. At Malplaquet in 1709, French marshal Villars did not rise to the bait as his predecessors had. The result was not an overwhelming victory for the allies but a slugfest that forced the enemy from the field, though in good order and with fewer casualties than the allies.

Marlborough was also master of the *offensive*. Since he was always looking for a battle, he often wrong-footed his opponents by rapid marches to the battle site. This was best illustrated at Oudenarde, when his men marched twice as fast as the French to occupy Lessines—an advance that a Dutch general described not as a march but as a run. The allies then threw pontoon bridges across the Scheldt while the French were leisurely moving into the area from Gavre. When Vendôme received news of this rapid movement, he reportedly responded with disbelief: "If they are there, then the Devil must have carried them. Such marching is impossible."[91] Marlborough's advance to the Schellenberg caught the defenders unprepared, and the allied appearance at dawn at Blenheim was a shock to the French.

While Marlborough's army for most of the afternoon stood on the tactical defensive at Oudenarde, he was the aggressor at all his battles. At Blenheim and Ramillies, the French generals thought themselves to be in strong defensive positions, so they gladly let him take the initiative. At Oudenarde, the opening fight between the two advance guards virtually determined which side would hold the initiative, and Cadogan gained that for the allies (with some help from faulty terrain reading by French officers). In all three battles, the offense was always controlled, intended to hold the enemy and focus his attention away from the decisive point. In this Marlborough was fortunate to have less-than-able opposing generals at all three battles, although Vendôme certainly would have been a worthy opponent had he not been overruled by the inexperienced Duke of Burgundy. Once battle was joined there was no letup, no time to allow the enemy commander to assess his situation and make any moves other than in reaction.

In all his battles, the factor Marlborough was most intent on employing was *mass*. He made sure that he had functioning combined arms, with cavalry, infantry, and artillery all trained to work together—a lesson learned from Gustavus. He was able to employ dragoons as extra infantry, a service Gustavus did not develop, and mobile artillery supported all attacks. All of Marlborough's battles, as illustrated in the discussion above, were designed to isolate enemy forces into as small an area as possible, such as the wall at the Schellenberg; Blindheim and Oberglau in 1704; Ramillies and Autre-Église in 1706; and Hermlingen, Groenwald, and Schaerken in 1708. All these moves drew in enemy reserves and weakened sections of their line. Then, more combined arms in his own reserve would be massed against that weak point: the unrepaired walls at Schellenberg overrun by the elector of Baden's attack, the marshy center of the lines at Blenheim, the open plain between Ramillies and Taviers, and the west flank at Oudenarde. Although quick assaults won all these actions, the combination of cavalry and infantry in mutual support was instrumental in stopping counterattacks and giving the horsemen time to regroup and maintain cohesion while the enemy horse became tired and disorganized.

In the area of *unity of command*, one sees perhaps the most remarkable aspect of Marlborough's character. Although he was an extremely able diplomat, his relationship with Prince Eugene of Savoy had nothing of the negative aspects of political diplomacy. There was no false modesty nor playing to one's strengths or weaknesses, as we see in his actions with members of government. Here was one of those rare times in history when two men meet and have an instant connection, seeing each other's value and recognizing how one might work off of the other's strengths. Although Eugene was certainly a brilliant leader in his own right, he must have seen in Marlborough not only a man senior to himself in age and in numbers under his command, but also an equal in talent and vision on the battlefield. That Marlborough acted as commander in chief when they worked together is not only a tribute to his talent but to a remarkable humility on Eugene's part. The two had little in common as far as personal bearing or habits were concerned, but it was only battlefield ability and trust that mattered. Count de Biron, who had led the French advanced guard at Oudenarde and was captured afterward, noted the relationship between the two and their subordinates, commenting on "a deep respect on the part of all the general officers for these two chiefs."[92]

Ultimately, Marlborough was *the* commander of the British army. He had loyal subordinates such as Cadogan and his own brother, Charles Churchill, on whom he depended greatly, but whether in planning or in execution Marlborough made the calls. He was able to enhance this ability to command by employing extremely effective aides-de-camp who made sure nothing happened on the battlefield that he was not immediately aware of. According to Chandler, "The Duke also took more than usual care in choosing his aides. . . . They served as Marlborough's eyes—a truly vital function on days of battle for any one man to keep full control over every sector. Marlborough's much noticed knack of appearing at points of the greatest crisis and danger were frequently due to information brought back by his aides."[93] Thus, he was always able to respond to enemy movements and could be on hand to rally his men when they were hard pressed or to launch the final attack when the time came. As battlefields grew larger along with the armies, such intelligence gathering became more and more vital. Jeremy Black comments, "Marlborough's battles were fought on a more extended front than those of the 1690s, let alone the 1650s, and thus placed a premium on mobility, planning and the ability of commanders to respond rapidly to developments over a wide front and to integrate and influence what might otherwise have been in practice a number of separate conflicts. Marlborough was particularly good at this and anticipated Napoleon's skilful and determined generalship in this respect."[94]

Such was the trust from his subordinates that they responded when needed, as did a hard-pressed Eugene by dispatching a cavalry unit to aid in beating back a French thrust at Oberglau during the battle at Blenheim. Cadogan's withdrawal from Autre-Église was not done willingly, but in the end he trusted Marlborough to see the big picture even when localized success seemed assured.

The trust exhibited by his immediate subordinates was reflected as well by the rank and file, a tribute to Marlborough's mastery of the principle of *morale*. Although Marlborough was one of the first modern commanders to run up high casualty counts, his men loved him anyway. Primarily this was because he paid particular attention to logistics. The French had in Louis XIV's time begun to implement the arsenal system of storing all manner of supplies for an entire army. Marlborough did one better by having consistent supplies on campaign. In the rapid march to the Danube in 1704, he showed this to its greatest benefit. The marches started at 3:00 a.m. but were always completed before noon brought the heat of the day. Every third or fourth day the column would stop to gather another few days' worth of rations, so they were never without food and did not have to forage. New shoes for the entire army awaited them during their stop in the Heidelberg-Frankfurt area. This had an amazing effect not just on morale but on character. Black observes that Marlborough "secured the affection of his soldiers by his good nature, care for their provisions and vigilance not to expose them to unnecessary dangers, and gained [that] of his officers by his affability. . . . The poor soldiers who were (too many of them) the refuse and dregs of the nation, became tractable, civil, orderly, and clean, and had an air and spirit above the vulgar."[95]

Marlborough also differed from almost all the generals of his time by not traveling in style. He ate at junior officers' mess and oftentimes slept on the ground. He also walked the battlefield and endangered himself, and few things are as important to a common soldier as seeing such action. By sharing fully in the experiences and dangers facing his troops, Marlborough motivated the soldiers to do their best. Black again observes, "The trust he engendered enabled him to make calls on their endurance that few others would dare contemplate. . . . Marlborough's characteristics as both man and soldier provided him with the *charisma* that caused him to never forfeit the confidence, loyalty or affection of his rank and file. . . . Above all, as Wellington noted, 'He was remarkable for his clear, cool, steady understanding.'"[96] He was one of the first to maintain a medical corps on campaign. The care of the sick and wounded tended to be very basic, but soldiering was always a rough pastime. Regiments had surgeons and surgeon's mates, and Marlborough had the army camp followers deputed to act as nurses after major battles. Starting in 1705 a commissioner for sick and sounded was an established post at Marlborough's headquarters.[97] Again, attention to the common soldier's welfare paid overwhelming returns in the field.

One rarely sees this type of devotion from the troops. Alexander and Caesar received it, as would Napoleon and Lee in the future. It contrasts with Wellington's virtual disdain for his soldiers and their lack of devotion in return. Marlborough's soldiers, however, affectionately referred to him as "Corporal John," and their devotion to him was based on more than basic material concern. Philip Haythornthwaite notes, "As one of his officers, Robert Parker, remarked, it was impossible to appreciate the joy with which a glimpse of Marlborough was greeted unless one was actually part of the army, every man of which realized that no lives would be risked unless he was confident of success."[98]

IN COMPARING MARLBOROUGH AND NAPOLEON, J. F. C. Fuller writes, "The one was the forerunner of the other, as well as heir of Gustavus Adolphus; for by breaking down the formalities of late seventeenth-century warfare and returning to the ways of the great Swede, Marlborough opened the road for Frederick and Napoleon. Marlborough broke away from this type of [siege] warfare and returned to the offensive strategy of Gustavus and the attack tactics of Conde and Cromwell. He did so because he was imaginative enough to see into the military changes of his day and appreciate their meaning."[99] Marlborough, perhaps even more so than Gustavus, was the first modern general in that he had not only a national army with which to fight but national armies to fight against, making his task more difficult than that which Gustavus faced. He had the same disappointments as the Swedish king as well, in that he could never make his battlefield triumphs translate into long-term political gains. As Russell Weigley observes, "Marlborough, ably seconded by Prince Eugene of Savoy, restored decisiveness to the battlefield. At Blenheim and Oudenarde he well-nigh attained the goal that over the centuries has been a will-o'-the-wisp pursued by all resolute commanders, the practical destruction of the enemy army that confronted him on the field. . . . Nevertheless, a brilliant generalship's restoration of decisiveness to battle proved insufficient to restore decisiveness to war."[100] Frederick and Napoleon would restore, and be the last gasp of, the warrior kings who controlled battle, war, and peace.

13

Frederick II (the Great) (1712–1786)

King of Prussia

That was the tremendous respect which the king gained in the eyes
of the opposing commanders. Why did they so seldom take advantage of the favorable opportunities that he offered them frequently
enough? They did not dare. They believed him capable of everything.

—Hans Delbruck

THE TERRITORY OF BRANDENBURG, around the city of Berlin, was
the birthplace of what would become the mighty Prussian state and,
eventually, modern Germany. In 1415, the Holy Roman emperor Sigismund defaulted on a loan to Frederick Hohenzollern. Collateral for the
loan was the electorate of Brandenburg. In the wake of the defeat of the
Teutonic Knights at the Battle of Tannenberg in 1410, the order fell into
decline, and in 1466 the Knights named a Hohenzollern as their new
grand master. In 1525, the grand master converted to Protestantism and
privatized the Knights' land for himself and his heirs. Two lines of the
Hohenzollern family agreed to merge the territories in the event of one
line having no heir; such an event occurred in 1618, and Brandenburg-
Prussia came into official being.

Late in the Thirty Years War Frederick William, also known as the
Great Elector, became leader of the province. He suppressed local governments and built up an army of 30,000 men with which he sought
to curry favor with the Holy Roman emperor. Building on Dutch and
then French military models, the Brandenburg-Prussian army became

respected, if not dominating. His son Frederick became elector in 1688 and remained subservient to the empire. Under his leadership the army grew to 40,000 and during the War of the Spanish Succession, Prussian officers learned warfare from the master commanders Marlborough and Eugene. In return, they gained international respect as well as power and prestige. Bavaria, by backing the losing side in the war, was on a downward slide while Brandenburg-Prussia became the preeminent German state. In 1701 Frederick took the title king of Prussia, as Brandenburg was still under imperial authority. Upon his death in 1713 his son became King Frederick William I.

King Frederick William continued transforming the army into a force as dominant as its state. Prussia became a military state; 83,000 men served out of a population of 2.25 million (although many of the recruits were foreigners). By the time of his death in 1740, Frederick William's territory was tenth largest in Europe, his population thirteenth largest, but his army stood at fourth largest. To accomplish that feat took more than military manpower; it needed the efforts of the entire population. For Frederick William, this meant bringing the entire population into a semimilitary lifestyle. Everyone from noble to peasant acted like soldiers, and the economic and social life of Prussia revolved around the army. Discipline for the entire population was the order of the day.[1]

Aided by Prince Leopold of Anhalt-Dessau (a veteran of service under Marlborough), the army became a model of discipline and precision. Leopold developed the cadenced step and introduced the iron ramrod, while Frederick William introduced the plain dark blue uniform, which broke from the tradition of more decorated and fashion-conscious uniforms. Christopher Duffy points out that "[t]he new style accorded well with the movement of Pietism which was abroad among the Lutheran people and nobility, and which stressed the virtues of service, honesty and industry."[2] Frederick William created not only a large army but the best-drilled and most disciplined one in Europe. Nothing to him was as important. "He transformed the royal parks of Berlin and Potsdam into parade grounds," Duffy notes. "In his creative work for the Prussian army Frederick William's achievement far surpassed the activity of his more famous son, Frederick the Great. Stout, bad-tempered Frederick William was the man who regularised the recruiting of the army at home and abroad, who cemented the peculiar bond between the King of Prussia and his officer corps."[3]

Personally, Frederick William was a hard taskmaster with his family as well as with his troops. He preferred the company of rowdy friends (known as the "Tobacco College"[4]), though he spent sufficient time with his wife to father fourteen children. His disdain was saved particularly for Crown Prince Frederick, born in 1712. The young man was his mother's son: quiet, studious, artistic, and (worst of all in his father's eyes) Francophile. His father harassed him at every possible turn, in public and private. Pushed to the breaking point, Frederick at age eighteen made the foolish mistake of running away to France with a close friend, Lieutenant Hans von Katte. As a result Frederick was imprisoned for fifteen months while von Katte was beheaded.

All of this harsh treatment was not without its long-term positive effects. Early on Frederick learned to still his temper and tongue, and he developed a cold and calculating nature, which he used against his father. He could stand expressionless before his father's tirades, knowing that such passivity angered the older man even more. "The less Frederick William was able to hide his emotion from others, the more the crown prince learned to do so," writes Gerhard Ritter. "If we ask what character traits first became recognizable in the behavior of the adolescent boy, we discover above all an amazingly stubborn self-assurance, ambition which could not be deflected by any humiliation, the power to mask his feelings from others, and . . . great cunning in getting his way."[5] The intellectualism he developed under his mother's tutelage served him well after his release from prison. Frederick acted as though he had learned the lesson his father had intended, and he became an untiring student of military history and the nuts and bolts of operating Prussia's army. He also seemed to cooperate in the political marriage his father arranged for him in 1733. Although there was a wedding, one can hardly say there was a marriage; Frederick barely acknowledged his wife, Princess Elizabeth Christine of Brunswick, and they never had children.

Frederick received a colonelcy upon his release from prison and devoted his public life from that point forward to his army and his nation. In 1734 he saw his first combat. He served with a Prussian contingent fighting under the command of Eugene of Savoy in a campaign against France. Philip Haythornthwaite writes, "Eugene affirmed that Frederick showed all the intelligence, courage, and skill to become the greatest soldier of his time, and this recommendation so impressed Frederick

William that he appointed Frederick as Major-General. . . . By the closing months of the life of Frederick William, Frederick had so rehabilitated his reputation that the King accepted him as a worthy successor."[6]

After his death, Frederick William's *Political Testament* showed him to be a much deeper intellect than he portrayed. He had seemed a caricature to much of Europe, rejecting the trappings of monarchy for the company of soldiers; even odder was his apparent fascination with overly tall soldiers. He formed a grenadier regiment of 3,000 men all more than six feet tall and had some tall cavalry troopers as well, though they were rarely good horsemen. The surest way to curry favor with him was to send him some tall men for the regiment.[7] The *Testament* disclosed, however, that much if not all of this public image was a false front: Duffy quotes the *Testament*: "Only under the guise of these spectacular eccentricities was I allowed to gather a large treasury and assemble a powerful army. Now this money and these troops lie at the disposal of my successor, who requires no such mask," he wrote in *Political Testament*.[8] If indeed Frederick William's public persona was a fraud to ensure the successful future of his country, as the opening of his *Political Testament* indicates, he ranks as a great actor and brilliant political mind. It is his son who takes on the sobriquet "the Great," however. With his calculating personality and his military inheritance of three generations dedicated to building an army, Frederick on becoming king in 1740 was poised to earn his nickname.

Warfare of the Time

ON THE SURFACE, armies and warfare of the mid-eighteenth century differed little from half a century earlier when Marlborough dominated European battlefields. Indeed, outside Prussia such was the case. Inside the country, however, the future of warfare was being created. The Prussian kings had been as dedicated to making a national army as Gustavus Adolphus had been in Sweden. Although as king and commander Gustavus had earned the loyalty of the Swedish army, in Prussia the state became the object of loyalty, more so than the monarch. Much of that devotion results from the national focus on military production mentioned earlier. The soldiers were recruited by geographic region (the cantonment system) and quartered in private homes in their neighborhood when not in fighting season. This created a bond between civilian and soldier. Barracks became a more common sight in Berlin as Frederick's reign progressed, but in the early days the practice of local garrisoning meant "the troops could be kept together under close supervision, and assembled quickly and quietly in the event of mobilisation."[9] The "close supervision" would be exercised by the local noble, whose military service was not optional.

"Although a new man made a passable soldier inside twelve months, it took six years to mould a really steady, reliable infantryman," notes John Childs.[10] Underlying all the Prussian military before and after Frederick was discipline, such as had not been seen since Sparta. In 1747 Frederick wrote, "The discipline and the organization of Prussian troops demand more care and more application from those who command them than is demanded from a general in any other service. If our discipline aids the most audacious enterprises, the composition of our troops requires attentions and precautions that sometimes are troublesome."[11] Although the use of the cantonment system aided somewhat in maintaining unit cohesion, the large-scale use of foreign troops led to an almost constant problem with desertion. This was addressed in many ways: "night marches were avoided, and men detailed to forage or bathe had to be accompanied by officers so that they could not run away. Even pursuits of the enemy were strictly controlled 'lest in the confusion our own men escape.'"[12] Everything was done, especially when on campaign, to make sure officers always had eyes on their men. Haythornthwaite describes how: "measures taken to enforce this discipline were draconian: physical beatings by NCOs, branding, running the gauntlet (under which the prisoner could die) and execution—barbaric treatment resulting from Frederick's belief that a soldier must fear his superiors more than the enemy."[13] Minor punishments were left to officers' discretion, primarily beatings with sticks or fists. Worse offenses could be punished in a variety of ways, including "chaining to bedsteads, the *Eselsreiten* (riding a sharp-backed wooden horse), and the painful process of *Krummschliessen* by which alternate arms and legs were bound tightly together by leather straps. Incorrigible thieves were branded deep on the hand . . . while men involved in desertion plots sometimes had their noses or ears cut off in addition to the other punishments that came their way."[14]

As mentioned previously, the key individual in developing the theories of Prussian military doctrine was Leopold I, nicknamed "the Old Dessauer." After his service with Eugene in the War of the Spanish

Succession, Leopold became field marshal and chief of staff. While the kings employed the army and even trained with it, Leopold was the potter who molded the clay. Under his command, "the officers discovered that they were expected to make military duties their first concern in life, even in peacetime, which was something of a novelty in contemporary Europe." And it was not only the officers who were influenced by him: "The Old Dessauer was an expert in the formation of crown princes, and for the instruction of Frederick he compiled a *Clear and Detailed Description*, which was based on the orders of the day which were issued in the campaigns against the Swedes between 1715 and 1720."[15]

Thanks to Leopold, the Prussian infantry had also become virtually the only force in Europe employing the cadenced march, in which every soldier started off on his left foot then marched in step to an accompanying drumbeat. Using this cadenced march resulted in tighter formations that were able to maneuver much more quickly. This allowed the units to advance farther before having to stop and dress the lines, and also created more compact columns to employ a greater mass of firepower.[16] Before this time all armies marched in route step, with no coordination at all. This meant that units gradually became more spread out while on the march, making it more difficult to form up and prepare for maneuver. The Prussian army stayed in step, so stayed in ranks. Deployment was therefore far more rapid and organized. Childs points out that "[o]nce the cadenced step had been universally adopted much of the hassle and uncertainty of taking troops from column into line disappeared, as the intervals between ranks, battalions and files could be maintained precisely on the approach march and translated direct into the correct spacing in the battle line by a simple wheel to the left or right. Frederick the Great drilled his infantry to the point where they could swing out of column of march into line of battle within a few minutes and advance straight into the attack."[17] Other European armies might take as much as two hours to perform the same action. Frederick wrote that "promptness contributes a great deal to success in marches and even more in battles. That is why our army is drilled in such a fashion that it acts faster than others. From drill comes these maneuvers which enable us to form in the twinkling of an eye."[18]

Upon assuming the throne in 1740 Frederick began expanding his army, primarily the infantry, with the intent of doubling its size from its

existing one of 80,000. (That goal was not reached until the outbreak of
the Seven Years' War in 1756.) Between 1740 and 1743 fifteen infantry
regiments (at 1,700 men each) were added, as well as twelve regiments
designed primarily for garrison duty in Prussia's forts. The Prussian
infantry consisted of grenadiers, two companies per regiment, chosen for
their reliability and aggressiveness. They needed both traits, as these units
often took the greatest casualties. The rest of the infantry, fusiliers, were
the standard troops, using muskets of less-than-stellar quality. Based on
the Liege-manufactured musket of Frederick William's day, Frederick's
proved to be "a clumsier and more eccentric version of the typical military flintlock of the day. . . . [T]he Prussian musket remained one of the
worst in Europe. Firing was a decidedly uncomfortable experience, for
the trigger was set too far forward in the guard, the comb of the butt
rose so high as to make aiming almost impossible, and . . . the long barrel,
the bayonet and the cylindrical ramrod combined to make the weapon
muzzle-heavy by three pounds."[19] Still, it was a rugged weapon firing a
.75 caliber ball. Since discipline demanded reloading and firing at speed,
aiming was ignored; however, the shots were famous for falling far short
of their target owing to the weapon's imbalance.

In the Seven Years' War Frederick filled his ranks with militia and "free
battalions," or mercenaries. During the War of the Austrian Succession,
he developed a small light infantry organization, used more as scouts and
guides than skirmishers; they developed into that more typical role in the
Seven Years' War and afterward.

For the most part Frederick's army fought in the standard linear tactics
of the day, with two lines roughly 200 yards apart, each made up of
three ranks of musketeers (although he often used only two ranks when
his manpower was short). Firing was done by platoons, the formation
Leopold had learned in Marlborough's service. The Prussians held two
distinct advantages: a far more rapid deployment on the battlefield,
and an increased rate of fire that resulted from the constant training
and discipline. In training, the Prussian soldier could fire five shots per
minute, almost twice that of his enemy; in combat, however, both rate
of fire and regularity in volley fire diminished, as was true in all armies.
Still, the Prussians always threw more lead than their opponents could.
Had they had better muskets, the damage would have been that much
greater. Childs notes another disadvantage: "The intention to break the

opponent's morale rather than his bones produced another limitation upon accurate musketry. The advantage went automatically to the side which loosed off more volleys in a given space of time, and this led Frederick the Great to put more emphasis upon speed of fire and rapid reloading than upon accuracy."[20] Still, battles of the time were not long exchanges of musket volleys, but more dependent (especially in the Prussian army) on the bayonet charge. Starting in 1741 Frederick ordered the bayonets to be permanently affixed when soldiers were on duty. He wrote in 1747, "It is not fire but bearing which defeats the enemy. And because the decision is gained more quickly by always marching against the enemy than by amusing yourself firing, the sooner a battle is decided, the fewer men are lost in it."[21] In retrospect, he should have focused more on improving his firepower. In biographer Christopher Duffy's opinion, "For the best part of the first two decades of his reign Frederick was deluded into thinking that the awe-inspiring sight of advancing troops was a more effective weapon than the bullet. This miscalculation must be regarded as his greatest error in his capacity as military technician."[22] By the time of the Seven Years' War, Frederick had become more appreciative of the benefits of firepower.

Frederick's most famous contribution to contemporary warfare was the oblique attack. This was a wise adaptation given that he was usually outnumbered in battle. "There can be no doubt that Frederick, who once wrote that he had read just about everything that had ever been written on military history, already had in mind the thought of the oblique battle order when he went into his first war," writes Hans Delbruck.[23] The concept goes back to Epaminondas of Thebes and his use of the refused flank at the Battle of Leuctra. In later times, the concept was discussed by the first Duke of Prussia (1500s), Raimondo Montecuccoli (1600s), then the French soldier and theorist the Chevalier Folard, Jacques François de Chastenet of France, and the Austrian Ludwig Khevenhüller in the 1700s. Therefore what Frederick did was to update and fine-tune a theory that had been discussed for a long time.[24] It began its evolution in peacetime experiments in 1747, but hints of it might be seen as early as the Battle of Chotusitz in 1742. The maneuver started with the concept of holding back one wing of the army as the rest partially wheeled into the enemy flank. According to Bevin Alexander, "A commander should strengthen one wing of his army and employ it to attack the enemy flank, while holding back another, smaller wing to threaten the enemy's main force and keep it from changing position. Since the enemy army would already be deployed, it could not switch troops fast enough to the threatened flank before Frederick's columns struck. Frederick said an army of 30,000 could beat an army of 100,000 using this method."[25]

Over the years it evolved into an attack in echelon, with the refused units coming into the attack successively against the enemy flank. Such an advance limited the enemy's ability to redeploy and attack the Prussian flank, as it was refused. So unlike Epaminondas attacking with only one unit and holding the others back, Frederick would have the entire line advance, with fresh units coming into action along the line. This style of advance had two main advantages. Each unit could more easily maneuver itself over broken ground if it was not worried about maintaining an extended line. It also fooled the enemy, as Brent Nosworthy notes: "Looking at the Prussian infantry from a distance, the enemy was unable to discern the formation being employed, and, in fact, thought that the Prussian infantry was advancing in total chaos. The enemy was able to see that the infantry line was fragmented; but was not able to perceive any ordered relationship between each division of line."[26] Frederick used this movement to fulfill his primary battlefield goal, to put maximum force at the enemy's weakest point. Thus, even an army outnumbered overall could attain localized superiority. Frederick believed unwaveringly in the strength of the oblique attack, insisting that other armies ought to be employing it: "All weak armies attacking stronger ones should use the oblique order, and it is the best that can be employed in outpost engagements; for in setting yourself to defeat a wing and in taking a whole army in the flank, the battle is settled at the start. Cast your eyes on this plan."[27] In what could be equally advantageous, the oblique order could cover a withdrawal if the attack didn't go well, as happened at Prague in 1757. R. R. Palmer describes how the maneuver accomplished either purpose: "Frederick's purpose in favoring this type of battle was, in case of success, to gain a quick victory by rolling up the enemy's line, and, in case of failure, to minimize losses, since the refused wing maneuvered to cover the withdrawal of the wing engaged. Frederick's superior mobility and coordination gave a special effectiveness to these flanking movements."[28]

Although he inherited the best possible infantry, at the outset Frederick's cavalry was the shame of his army. Haythornthwaite describes the cavalry as "[p]roficient only at ceremonial drill on foot, [and] Frederick claimed that they could not manage their horses and were commanded by officers totally ignorant of what was required of them in action. The cuirassiers he described as 'giants on elephants,' who could neither manoeuvre nor fight, and who fell off their horses even on parade; they were so bad, he claimed, that 'it isn't worth the devil's while' to use them."[29] This became dangerously clear to Frederick at his first battle as king, at Mollwitz in 1741. His cavalry fled from the Austrian cavalry, which would have won the battle had they not been turned back by the stalwart Prussian infantry. Frederick's improvements in this arm, therefore, were both quick and effective. Frederick recruited cavalrymen not from the society as a whole (as with his infantry) nor from the landed gentry and nobility (as with his officers). Instead, he looked to the better-off peasants who had sons who were used to being in the saddle and (initially, at least) could provide their own mounts. The foreign-born recruits came from the same condition. This provided the Prussian military with young men who already were familiar with what a horse could do, and they proved more loyal, as Hawthornthwaite notes: "The cavalry contained the smallest proportion of desertion-prone impressed peasants and unreliable mercenaries; indeed, Frederick's *Instructions* indicate that the presence of cavalry picquets were a principal discouragement to desertion, so the cavalry had to be reliable."[30] Although they were trained to operate in as disciplined a manner as were the infantry, they did not undergo the same harsh discipline. The new cavalry arm was first organized and led by Frederick Wilhelm von Seydlitz, "probably the most gifted leader of men in eighteenth-century Prussia. . . . Seydlitz believed that it was not enough for an officer simply to order a man to do something: he must be in a position to show him how it ought to be done, and to do it in an exemplary style."[31]

Frederick removed the giants from the cavalry, although he knew that size and power were necessary to his plan of reintroducing shock to cavalry tactics. The cuirassiers were the heavy cavalry, named for the heavy iron breastplate, or cuirass, that they wore. These were the descendants of the knights of medieval times, armed with a straight sword, two pistols, and a carbine. The dragoons had been developed in the Thirty Years War in order to provide mounted infantry; by Frederick William's time they were full-fledged cavalry but lacked the armor. They carried a longer carbine with a bayonet and a straight sword. The hussars, or light cavalry, originated in Hungary and were used primarily for patrol work, raiding, and flank security. The hussar concept was slower to catch on in Prussia. "For a long time the Prussian hussars could be written off as just another of Frederick William's bad military jokes—more gaudy, perhaps, than the Giant Grenadiers, though not nearly as expensive," Duffy writes. "The king himself admitted that 'a German lad does not make such a good hussar as an Hungarian or a Pole.'"[32] That view changed by the time Frederick was king, for many a German lad found the most attractive aspect of the hussar's role was his almost unique opportunity for plunder. It was the hussars who also had the role of pursuit in the wake of victory. That freedom of action out of sight of the high command, however, was one of the main fears of a king worried about desertions. The hussars had a more colorful uniform, somewhat Turkish in its aspect, as inherited from the Austrian light cavalry (Hungarians and Croats) who had inherited theirs in wars against the Ottoman Empire. They too carried a carbine but their sword was curved, again as a nod toward their Middle Eastern roots.

Although the new cavalrymen usually arrived with a modicum of horsemanship, much more had to be taught. Two years was the minimum training, during which "each man was instructed in the skills of riding and horsemanship until he was complete master of both himself and his mount in all situations. Only after the completion of this basic initiation was he taught how to fire his pistols and carbine from horseback and to fight from the saddle with the sabre."[33] The cavalry were trained to operate as efficiently and in as orderly a fashion as were the infantry. Frederick's most basic advances came in the area of training, where systematic methods were employed to instruct the trooper in a variety of required drills, exercises, and maneuvers. He was also responsible for the introduction of revolutionary new cavalry tactics: the charge at the gallop, the charge in echelon, the charge in column, and maneuvering while moving, as well as the use of light cavalry in close-order fighting on the battlefield.[34] Although each style of cavalry had its assigned role, they all trained to do each other's jobs. All three types of Prussian horsemen received the same basic instruction so that their functions were quickly and easily interchangeable, so a cuirassier could when needed be a scout or a hussar could charge into battle. This flexibility was unique to the Prussians.[35]

Although the horsemen carried firearms, Frederick disallowed their use in almost all circumstances, and certainly during the charge. As time went by, Frederick became more wedded to the concept of speed equaling power, so the cavalry in their charge started their gallop at greater and greater ranges. According to Nosworthy, "In 1748, Frederick demanded that they charge 700 yards (trot: 300; gallop: 400). In 1750 this was increased to a total of 1200 yards (trot: 300; gallop: 400; and full speed: 500). This was increased to an incredible 1800 yards in 1755, with the last 600 yards at full speed."[36] All of this had to be done in formations almost as tight as those practiced by the infantry. Seydlitz, although somewhat lighter handed in disciplinary measures, still drove his men in daily practice and in peacetime army maneuvers. "The cavalryman's equipment was made as light as possible to enhance speed and increase the fury of the charge," writes Trevor Dupuy. "Close order and alignment were achieved by constant drill, and Prussian cavalry could move with the same precision and perfection as the infantry. Eight to ten thousand mounted men could charge for hundreds of yards in perfect order, then after a melee re-form for movement almost immediately."[37] Enemy infantry squares with bayonets (if they could be formed quickly) offered some defense, but they could maintain a line only against trotting horsemen. The galloping attack en muraille (as a wall) was key in most of Frederick's victories.

Frederick was much more interested in the cavalry than he was in artillery, despite the rising prominence of the latter; however, he also brought the concept of speed to his artillery.[38] Even though smaller and lighter cannon had been on the battlefield for some time, the Prussians made them even more mobile. Ernest Dupuy and Trevor Dupuy point out how "Frederick carried one step farther the artillery tactical developments of Gustavus Adolphus. He created the concept of the horse artillery (as opposed to conventional horse-drawn artillery) in which every cannoneer and ammunition handler was mounted, so that the light guns could keep up with the fast-moving, hard-riding Prussian cavalry."[39] The Prussian artillery arm, as in all the European armies, was manned by civilian contractors, engineers who were looked down upon by all other arms. In the days of Frederick William, General Christian von Linger oversaw the artillery and reduced the guns to four sizes: 3-, 6-, 12-, and 24-pounders (determined by the weight of the cannon ball). The two smaller guns were assigned to the front lines with the infantry while the larger two were deployed farther to the rear and massed to focus on a particular section of the enemy army. The gun barrels alone weighed in at 988 and 1,800 pounds respectively, so rapid movement was not possible. The smaller guns, however, were moved about rapidly by three-horse and four-horse teams.

Improvements during Frederick's reign came thanks to Lieutenant Colonel Ernst von Holzmann. He developed the caisson, a box carrying ammunition and powder added to the limber supporting the cannon's trail. This allowed the gun and crew much more independence, able to operate further away from the battalion or regimental ammunition supply. Holzmann also introduced a better method for adjusting the gun's elevation. The Austrians had developed a wedge placed under the rear of the cannon to be slid in and out to control elevation and depression. Holzmann added a screw mechanism to the wedge so it could be more finely adjusted. Most of the time all the guns fired solid round balls, which did damage to solid targets but also to individuals as the shot bounced through infantry lines "like a bowling ball gone berserk,"[40] taking lives and removing body parts. For short-range work, however, Holzmann crafted the idea of employing canister rounds, cylinders of sheet metal or wood that enclosed scores of shot about the size of walnuts. The lightly built cylinder disintegrated as it left the muzzle, and the shot sprayed over a wide arc.[41] Grapeshot was a variation on the canister, with larger shot. Frederick also came to appreciate the value of the howitzer, "a stubby, heavy-calibre chambered piece, specially designed to throw explosive shells without cracking the brittle cast iron of their casing."[42] The howitzer was traditionally a siege gun designed to lob cannonballs in a high arc over walls; Frederick began using the weapon on the battlefield to strike at hidden targets in dead ground behind the enemy. Most of these improvements, however, did not go into effect until the latter part of the Seven Years' War.

The Opponents

ALTHOUGH THROUGHOUT HIS REIGN he shifted alliances when he deemed it necessary, Frederick's primary opponent was Austria. Whereas his forebears had subordinated themselves to the emperor in Vienna, Frederick realized that to strengthen the security of his territory he needed extra land to fill in the gaps between his holdings. The most necessary land was

Silesia, the pathway from Bohemia into Brandenburg. Although Brandenburg and Prussia were politically a single entity, in 1740 they were not joined
physically; West Prussia (under Polish control) lay between them. Thus,
Frederick's overall goal was both defense and unification. With the death of
Charles I in Vienna just a few months after Frederick came to power in 1740,
the confused situation in Austria invited Frederick to begin his project. As
Charles's successor was his daughter, Maria Theresa, it was an open question
how many European powers would recognize her as a legitimate ruler. Over
the previous several years all the major powers had signed the Pragmatic
Sanction agreeing to recognize a female successor, but just how many would
come to the aid of potentially weak twenty-three-year-old queen? Frederick
had demanded cession of the Duchy of Silesia as his price for honoring the
agreement. The law there did not allow a female ruler, and he claimed a
relation to the last duke of Silesia. Frederick seized the opportunity.

He was correct in assuming Austria was fragmented and unprepared for
war. "He was wrong, however, in his assessment of the energy, strength and
wisdom of the new Austrian ruler, by far the most distinguished monarch
the Habsburgs ever produced, and in the fervent support she was to receive,"
Albert Seaton asserts.[43] The first assistance for Maria Theresa came from
Hungary, a nation recently at odds with Austria but befriended by Maria
Theresa's father, Charles. A standing Hungarian force protecting the southern
frontier from Turks provided 39,000 infantry and 6,000 cavalry. Coupled
with the existing Habsburg army, which had recent experience against the
Turks, the Austrian resistance proved stronger than Frederick had anticipated. However, the Austrian infantry's method of fighting was no different
than that of any other country: linear warfare. The cavalry trotted forward
in a line, then at twenty paces fired their pistols and spurred their horses.
Neither had the discipline or speed of the Prussians. The Austrians' edge was
in their light troops with superior scouting and harassment abilities, but on
the battlefield they used muskets and bayonets like all other European armies.

At first Frederick's December 1740 invasion met little resistance, with
the Prussian army occupying just about every city in Silesia before the
Austrians could react. Frederick hoped that a fait accompli, followed by
his reassurance of support for Maria Theresa's claim to the remainder of
Habsburg lands, would be sufficient to keep her from reacting. But, Ritter
asserts, "[h]e did not know that this woman possessed more courage and
a greater sense of honor than all the men at her court. That she had been

robbed of Silesia without so much as a warning made it impossible for her to acquiesce. She would rather risk extreme peril than accept such an insult. In her person, Habsburg's ancient imperial pride rose up against the faithless vassal."[44] It only got worse for Frederick, as the other countries he expected to move in and grab parts of the empire, such as France and some of the Germanic states, failed to do so. The diversions he expected never materialized, and Maria Theresa was able to focus her military efforts on him rather than on her western frontiers.

In the spring of 1741, an Austrian army under Field Marshal Wilhelm Count Neipperg marched out of Bohemia with the intention of severing Frederick's army from its supply bases in Berlin. In desperation, Frederick marched north to avoid being cut off, but ran into the Austrian army at Mollwitz on 10 April.

Frederick had wanted to avoid such a situation. Earlier reports of Austrian forces in Bohemia motivated him to pull his forces back and together. On 29 March, however, he was convinced otherwise by his senior advisor Kurt Christoph Count von Schwerin, who believed that the better idea would be to keep the troops dispersed in order to maximize foraging. When Frederick concentrated his forces and began moving he had a numeric and qualitative edge: 21,600 Prussians to 19,000 Austrians, of whom 10,000 were infantry and most of those recruits. An infantry battle should certainly go Frederick's way, but as he was deploying his forces early in the afternoon of 10 April his right wing was struck by an overpowering cavalry attack that not only sent the Prussian horse flying but threatened to crumple the entire army. Frederick himself was in imminent danger of being captured. "No one expected anything like it," Ritter notes. "How long had it been since a Prussian ruler had personally fought in battle? The fate of Gustavus Adolphus and Charles XII may have flashed before the eyes of the Prussian generals, and the natural excitement of their young commander-in-chief probably interfered with their tactical dispositions."[45] Frederick took his senior commander's advice and fled, with Austrian hussars hot on his heels. The remainder of the Austrian cavalry, however, re-formed and prepared to charge the Prussian lines. The years of discipline paid off; neither cavalry nor infantry could make headway against the immovable Prussian lines. The Austrians withdrew at dark, losing the battle but winning the campaign, for Frederick halted his invasion.

The young king wasted no time identifying mistakes and addressing them. He observed the strength of the infantry and the poor quality of the "damnably awful" cavalry. His own mistakes? He allowed the army to remained scattered when he should have concentrated it; he allowed himself to have his lines of supply cut; and he spent too much time deploying before the battle. Deciding to keep his army in camp at Mollwitz, Frederick immediately began making improvements. He depended on Leopold of Anhalt-Dessau and his sons to keep up the infantry training while he turned to the cavalry. He began to look to a hussar officer, Lieutenant Colonel Hans Joachim von Ziethen, whose "skill in light cavalry tactics was such that his hussars led the way for the total regeneration of the Prussian cavalry."[46]

As Frederick worked on his army through the quiet summer of 1741, Bavaria, Saxony, and Savoy went to war against Austria. This obliged Maria Theresa secretly to promise to leave the Prussians in Silesia in return for a cease-fire, but she reneged on her promise within two months. In the spring of 1742 Prince Charles of Lorraine led an Austrian army against the Prussians. At the Battle of Chotusitz in mid-May, the Prussian cavalry initially gave a good account of themselves but were scattered by a counterattack while trying to re-form. On the Prussian left Prince Leopold held the village of Chotusitz in bitter fighting before he was finally forced back. During his withdrawal, Frederick, on Leopold's right, brought his men out of a hollow where they had lain unobserved and launched them at the now-exposed Austrian flank. At this surprise, the Austrians broke and fled.

This defeat led to the Treaty of Breslau in mid-June (ratified in late July) whereby Maria Theresa ceded Silesia in return for an end to hostilities. Apparently, neither she nor Frederick really believed this would end the fighting for that province. However, as Theodore Dodge observed, "Frederick had learned good lessons. He had gained self-poise, and a knowledge of the hardships of war, the meannesses of courts, and the fact that he could trust no one but himself and his devoted legions. He was disenchanted. War was no longer glory, but a stern, cold, fact."[47]

With some breathing space from his Austrian opponents, Frederick watched political events and worked on his army. For two years he built his treasury back up and expanded his forces to 140,000 men. He also introduced a new innovation: peacetime field maneuvers.[48] In the meantime, Bavaria—a Prussian ally—had been losing continually to Austrian forces, and the pro-Austrian alliance grew larger when England joined the Dutch and several Germanic states to fight the French. In the summer of 1743 Frederick renewed Prussia's alliance with France, which, under the leadership of Louis XV, was eager for some more glory. Hoping for a Franco-Prussian offensive into Austria, possibly even threatening Vienna, Frederick broke the Peace of Breslau and led his armies into Bohemia in August 1744.

The Prussians quickly captured Prague and continued south, but unfortunately for Frederick the French did not keep the Austrians busy. With sufficient allies to keep an eye on the less-than-aggressive French, the Austrians moved their army eastward to deal with Frederick. Everything went against him all at once: bad weather, breakdown of supply, harassment by the enemy's light troops, epidemic. His generals thought he was going too far too fast, but they could not influence him. He finally took his army back to Silesia late in 1744 in bad shape, with at least 17,000 desertions along the way. "Totally demoralized, the proud army finally returned to Silesia," Ritter observes. "Every weakness of troops trained to unquestioning obedience but incapable of independent action had been laid bare."[49] Indeed, the confidence the First Silesian War had given him took a major blow as well, and Frederick was learning to balance his own views with considered advice. He could not depend on subordinates alone, as he had at Mollwitz, but he could not ignore them as he had done on this campaign.

With Frederick's army severely weakened and the ego of its leader bruised, Maria Theresa saw her opportunity to punish Prussia and regain Silesia, and in 1745 sent her army out of Bohemia under the command of Charles of Lorraine. He had overseen the recovery of Bohemia, but he had had the expert advice of the veteran field marshal Count Otto Ferdinand von Traun, who was now in command of forces facing France. Still, Maria Theresa thought him just the right man for the job. Reed Browning asserts, "What was needed in Silesia was not cunning or brilliance, but rather the conventional skills of a seasoned commander. These Prince Charles could muster—and he [as her brother-in-law] could bring too all the prestige that attaches to relationship to royalty."[50]

The Battle of Hohenfriedberg

CHARLES HAD A GOOD PLAN. With 55,000 Austrian and 20,000 Saxon troops at his disposal, he would put the bulk of his troops in Bohemia into a drive on the Silesian capital of Breslau, a secondary force would feint from Moravia to draw off some Prussian troops, and a screen of light troops would harass the Prussian supply lines. Charles also had spies alerting him on Prussian plans and movements. He confidently looked forward to finding a demoralized enemy whom he could sweep from the field.

The Prussian intelligence service, which was always one of Frederick's primary weaknesses, outdid themselves this time, however. One of Charles's spies was actually a double agent and Frederick took full advantage of him. Not only did Frederick know the Moravian force was a diversion, but he also used the spy to pass on the disinformation that he planned to withdraw toward Breslau, just as Charles already assumed. Frederick led Charles to believe that the Prussians would behave as they had done in 1744, retreat to the north to avoid being cut off from their supply base at Breslau. To strengthen this idea, he evacuated part of southeastern Silesia. In reality, Frederick intended to go on the offensive with 70,000 men as soon as the Austrians could be lured down to the plains of Silesia.[51]

When Austrian forces crossed the mountains from Bohemia into Silesia at the beginning of June 1745, they met no resistance. That Frederick would not contest the passes further confirmed the Austrian notion that the Prussians would not fight anytime soon. Thus, when the army debouched onto a plain facing east toward the Striegauer River and the town of Striegau[52] (their goal for the following day), they made no particular effort to secure their perimeter. After all, the Prussians were miles away and the Austrian troops were tired from their strenuous climb. The 19,000 Saxons encamped on high ground near Pilgrimshain, and the lines stretched roughly south-southwest to Günthersdorf, with the 40,000 Austrians deployed down to Thomaswaldau, then southeast to Halbendorf.

Frederick had observed the Austrian positions firsthand. He endeavored to do this before all his battles in order to exercise what he termed coup d'oeil. "The coup d'oeil of a general is the talent which great men have of conceiving in a moment all the advantages of the terrain and the use that they can make of it with their army," Frederick wrote. "The coup d'oeil is required of the general when the enemy is found in position and must be attacked. Whoever has the best coup d'oeil will perceive at first glance the weak spot of the enemy and attack him there."[53] In this case, Frederick decided to hit the Saxons on the high ground first, then drive south into the Austrians. The 59,000-man Prussian army began a night march in complete quiet. The normally active Austrian Croat light cavalry were not on patrol. The Austrians were blissfully ignorant of the approach, Frederick's double agent having assured Charles that the Prussians were not within striking distance. The Prussian forces reached the Striegau at midnight, caught their breath for a couple of hours, and then moved across the stream and onto the plain. Duffy describes the Prussian plan: "The columns were to pass the Striegauer-Wasser in the region of Striegau, Gräben and Teichau and make northwards in the general direction of Pilgrimshain until they had covered enough ground to be able to form a line of battle. The Prussians were then to advance to the west, with the right leading in a staggered echelon of brigades."[54] The cavalry was primarily deployed on the right and it was their mission to hit the Saxons at dawn to start the battle. The infantry for the most part faced the Austrians, intending to launch their attack as the Saxon wing crumbled.

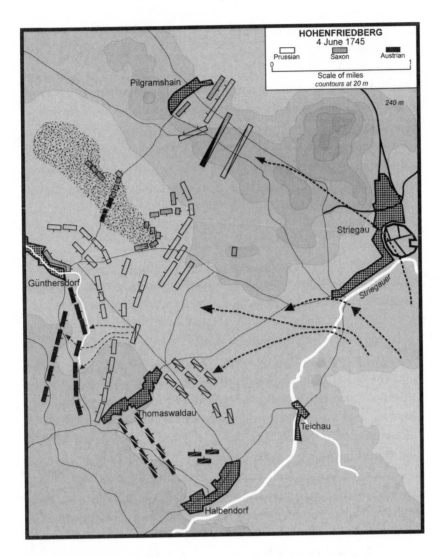

First contact came at 4:00 a.m. when leading elements of the Prussian cavalry stumbled into some Saxon grenadiers on the Breite Berg, a hill between Striegau and Pilgrimshain. The Saxons quickly fled, leaving the Prussians with good ground for artillery. Rather than allow the retreating grenadiers to rouse the defense, the Prussian cavalry pressed the attack. The Prussian cuirassiers found themselves facing stiff resistance and called for support from the dragoons and hussars, who were glad to assist, "and within a few minutes dragoons, hussars, cuirassiers and enemy mounted grenadiers were engaged in a deadly hand-to-hand combat, swirling about like a swarm of bees."[55] After two charges the Saxon cavalry broke, but they had bought some time for the infantry to form up. Meanwhile, Prince Leopold Max was bringing twenty-one Prussian infantry battalions directly from the line of march into attack formation. Under Frederick's philosophy that cold steel was more important than firepower, the Prussians advanced with shouldered muskets, through intense musket and artillery fire, until they saw the whites of the Austrians' eyes. The Prussian attack did not break the Saxon infantry immediately. Not until 7:00 a.m. did they abandon the field.[56] Frederick supposedly told his men to show the Saxons no quarter, "an order thoroughly congenial to troops now possessed by what one of them called a 'demonic bloodlust.'"[57]

The Saxons received no assistance from the Austrians, slowly emerging from their tents. Prince Charles had heard the firing and assumed it was the Saxon assault on Striegau. Not until retreating Saxons approached his headquarters did he learn differently. Charles ordered his cavalry on his far right flank into the battle, but they were engaged immediately by Prussian cavalry so could not aid the Saxons. The cavalry battle on the southern end of the battlefield swayed back and forth. A dozen Prussian cuirassier squadrons found themselves cut off from the rest of the army when a bridge across the river collapsed, but quick action by Ziethen's hussars finding and crossing a ford saved the day. The Prussians finally gained the upper hand and the Austrian cavalry broke. "By 7:00 a.m. the Prussian situation was truly enviable," Browning notes; "they had shattered the allied cavalry on both wings and had put the Saxon infantry to flight. Only the Austrian infantry still contested the field, stripped of its ally and exposed as never before in the war."[58]

The Austrian infantry bravely stood in their lines and exchanged volleys with the Prussians. As the Prussians advanced, a gap appeared in the middle of their infantry. Following along behind the infantry all morning was a Prussian cavalry unit, the Bayreuth dragoon regiment. Seeing the widening gap and fearful that a counterattack might exploit it, they exploited it themselves. Over a fairly short distance they broke into a trot and then quickly into a gallop through their own lines and into unsupported Austrian infantry. A quick volley was all the Austrians could loose before the horsemen were in their midst. Dennis Showalter describes the result: "In less than half an hour the Bayreuth Dragoons took no fewer than sixty-seven colors—a far greater tribute to the force of their charge than the five guns that could not be withdrawn, or the 2,500 prisoners who compared their maximum foot speed to the pace of a running horse and sensibly threw down their arms."[59]

That, for all intents and purposes, marked the end of the battle as the rest of the Austrians either fled or surrendered. The battle was over by 9:00 and no serious pursuit was launched, for the Prussian infantry had no more strength and the cavalry could not be quickly re-formed. The casualty count uncharacteristically favored the Prussians, who lost some 900 dead and 3,800 wounded; the Austro-Saxon dead numbered more than 3,000 and the wounded some 10,700.

The success at Hohenfriedberg came about as a result of Frederick's approach march followed by a deliberate attack. There was little exploitation or immediate pursuit, owing to his ongoing fear of desertion; indeed, so ingrained was the order against breaking their lines that the Prussian troops cleared the field of enemy forces without a man engaging in a single act of looting. Frederick fulfilled all the characteristics of the offense in this battle. He gained surprise through both disinformation and the secretive night march. He hoped to implement the oblique order in this battle, with stronger forces on his left facing the Austrians while the cavalry and fewer infantry struck the Saxons on the left flank with the intent of a "swinging gate" movement onto the Austrian position. He was in control of the tempo of battle, even though the enemy infantry put up stout defenses. Had he used his firepower on the advance this probably would have been even more to his advantage. Although the two armies had roughly equal numbers, Frederick showed his audacity by acting completely against the expectations of his foes; by not pausing at any point but quickly reacting to changes on the field, he gave the defenders no opportunity to do anything but defend.

Hohenfriedberg was Frederick's most impressive victory thus far.[60] Frederick here showed that he was rapidly transforming himself into a great general. He had learned from his mistakes in previous battles and began showing the characteristics for which he would be best known. The oblique order may or may not have been attempted here; if he intended to use it the deployment in the dark surely hampered it. Further, with the quick movement of infantry marching toward the fighting being redirected toward the Austrians, as other units were deploying in the southern area, implementing the oblique certainly would have been a challenge on the parade ground, much less on the battlefield.

In the wake of the battle the Austrian survivors quickly re-formed and conducted a safe withdrawal back across the mountains, with the Prussians close behind. For the next three months Frederick's goal was to feed off Bohemian crops for his troops and fodder for his horses. This would lessen the demands on his logistics as well as deny those same supplies to the Austrians should they try to reenter Silesia. Frederick's army skirted the western side of the mountains up to the Elbe, with the Austrian force following slowly along behind. Hohenfriedberg had not disheartened the Austrians; indeed, Maria Theresa's husband, Prince Francis, was elected Holy Roman emperor. Frederick, as elector of Brandenburg, voted against him, but promised his support in return for (not surprisingly) full claim to Silesia. Maria Theresa was still not ready to agree, so her armies tried one last time to defeat Frederick and drive the Prussians away. Charles stole a march on Frederick in September 1745 and placed himself once again athwart the Prussian lines of communication.

At first glance, what became the Battle of Soor (Sohr) was Hohenfriedberg in reverse. The Austrians staged a night march through heavily wooded terrain, emerging before dawn and seizing high ground overlooking the Prussian camp. Frederick was overconfident of the enemy's lack of resolve and laid his camp out without paying attention to security. In particular, he neglected to occupy or even place guards on the high ground to the Prussians' right, which was the route of his line of march back to Silesia.[61] The Austrians, outnumbering Frederick's 22,000 by two-to-one, were poised to strike a killing blow but held their hand. Charles would not attack into the early morning fog and mist, and that gave Frederick's quickly reacting troops time to deploy. Frederick threw a cavalry attack around the far right flank of the hill atop which the mass of the Austrian force was located. The Austrian cavalry stood still, firing at long range, when Frederick's cavalry emerged from a narrow valley and attacked uphill against a force twice their size. They succeeded in seizing the hilltop as Prussian infantry attacked from the opposite side. The rest of the army advanced all along the line, and the Austrians soon were retreating back into the woods. The Prussian discipline and drill of so many days and months in camp proved the deciding factor as the Austrians failed to take advantage of their opportunities. "From this day on dated [Frederick's] European reputation as a military leader, and the belief in his invincibility," remarks Ritter.[62]

A few other minor battles took place through November into December, with Frederick's hussars doing good work in harassing the Austrians and seizing supplies. As the year came to a close, Maria Theresa had had enough for the time being. On 25 December she signed the Treaty of Dresden, in which she accepted Frederick's recognition of Francis as Holy Roman Emperor in return for ceding Silesia. Frederick went back to training and drilling his army.[63]

Fighting between Austria and France continued for some time after Prussia left the war, but Frederick was intent on getting his army back up to strength and preparing for whatever future conflicts might arise. He had no illusions about the permanency of Austria's cession of Silesia. He also saw the rising hostile power of Russia as a threat he would sooner or later have to face and recognized that the Prussian army would have to adapt in order to do so successfully. In the decade after Silesia's acquisition Frederick wrote his directives on warfare, known today as *The Instruction of Frederick the Great for His Generals*, finished in 1747. It was revised in 1748 under the title of *General Principles of War*. A confidential set of instructions and meditations on war, one copy was sent in 1748 to Frederick's successor with a request that it should be shown to no one. In January 1753, an edition of fifty copies was printed and sent to a list of his most trusted officers. Frederick ordered each recipient on his oath not to take it with him in the field, and should the officer die arrangements should be made to have the book returned whole and unharmed.[64] In the book, Frederick advocated principles he saw as necessary for successfully conducting a campaign. The book's first chapter addressed the Prussian army's main problem, keeping soldiers from deserting. There followed chapters on planning for a campaign, reading enemy intentions, conducting the campaign, and conducting a battle, including his oblique order. Duffy summarizes some of the elements covered: "In the final articles, Frederick dealt interestingly with the element of chance in warfare, the evils of councils of war, and the cost of a winter campaign, returning in Article XXIX to his new battle tactics, a system 'founded on the speed of every movement and the necessity of being on the attack.'"[65]

In his personal life, Frederick became famous for his work ethic, rising at 4:00 a.m. to work on matters of state. After a modest lunch he would study and work on his musical skills until evening, finish up more paper-work after supper and retire at 10:00. He built his army up to 150,000 men and maintained the vaunted Prussian training and discipline. The number of cannons doubled, and the cavalry expanded almost as much. He also instituted war-gaming maneuvers in the field to observe and perfect his oblique attack. "In a comprehensive test of overall readiness, Frederick assembled the Army once a year for maneuvers," write A. S. Britt and colleagues. "The generals, as well as the troops, demonstrated their profi-ciency. Marches, tactics, logistics, and new equipment were subjected to the King's scrutiny. Every detail went through his exacting inspection."[66] Two of his generals on their own initiative began experimenting with all-arms divisions. Duke Ferdinand of Brunswick developed a concept of marching in four separated all-arms columns; although it was never perfected in Prussia, it would enjoy major success when redeveloped by Napoleon.[67] Frederick also refilled his treasury. All these exercises proved necessary when, by 1756, his enemies had massed against him.

Meanwhile, spurred by the embarrassment of losing Silesia, Maria Theresa began improving her military, introducing drill and discipline in the style of the Prussian army and upgrading artillery. General Leopold von Daun oversaw a commission to implement Prussian-style tactics and write new regulations, as well as implement summer maneuvers as Fred-erick had done. Her army expanded to 200,000, but the improvements were just beginning when the next war arrived. In spite of their numbers, plus that of the allied armies that would soon join in, Austria wisely adopted an overall defensive strategy that would play on its major strength over the Prussians: their light troops. As Daniel Marston recounts, "These troops, also referred to as *Croates* and *Pandours* by contemporaries, were made up of soldiers from the Balkan frontier regions. . . . The Austrians used this military corps as light troops, employing them to reconnoiter, forage, and skirmish. They were deployed on the flanks of the army as it marched, and would report on the movements and dispositions of the Prussians before battle. During battle, they would attack the flanks of the Prussian lines, trying to get them to fire and break ranks."[68]

As was often the case in European history, peace was merely a tem-porary break in the action between wars. Grudges from the War of the Austrian Succession still festered, but new alliances were necessary to gain revenge or protect possessions. The only constant was the Anglo-French hostility, primarily played out in North America with sideshows in India and the Caribbean. Maria Therese wanted to regain Silesia and, if possible, reduce Prussia to the minor state it traditionally had been. Frederick's goal was to hold on to the gains from the last war and, if possible, conquer Saxony. The Russians were afraid of Prussian desires along the Polish frontier, which they were interested in conquering.[69] To achieve their goals, or to watch each other's backs, Austria allied itself with Russia. Fearful of this powerful new alliance, Frederick concluded an alliance of his own with Britain, whose primary Continental concern was the German state of Hanover, home of the new English royal family since George I's accession in 1714. This Treaty of Westminster, completed in January 1756, so outraged the French that after their ten-year alliance agreement with Prussia lapsed in 1757, they formally joined the Austro-Russian alliance, along with Sweden and Saxony. Haythornthwaite points out that "[i]t was an alliance in which all except France had designs on Prussian territory, designs which if successful would have reduced Prussia once again to a minor principality."[70] As Russell Weigley observes, other powers in Europe ganged up on Prussia as they would Germany almost two centuries later, fighting against a state aiming at military dominance.[71]

With Austria and Russia both focused on him, Frederick decided on a preemptive strike against Saxony. In late August 1756 he marched 63,000 men (less than half his army) into Saxon territory. The Saxon army numbered a mere 18,000, and it quickly withdrew into a strong defensive position at Pirna. Frederick's goal had been to make quick work of Saxony, then use the Elbe River valley to advance into Bohemia. He had no time for a siege if he was to strike Bohemia while Austrian forces were still dispersed, so he left a covering force at Pirna and marched south. The Austrians responded by sending a relief force under Irish immigrant Maximilian Browne, who encountered the Prussians at the Eger River.

After a week of skirmishing, Frederick staged a flank march on the Austrian camp at Lobositz. He launched a cavalry assault in the early morning fog and saw it repulsed, as was a second. Improved Austrian artillery took its toll against both cavalry and infantry when Frederick committed them, but finally superior Prussian discipline broke the Austrian line. The Austrian troops withdrew in good order under artillery covering fire. Both sides started with roughly 30,000 men and ended the day with roughly 3,000 casualties. The Austrians demonstrated their improved training, but Frederick held the field. The besieged Saxons in Pirna soon surrendered, and Frederick achieved his first goal as the fighting season of 1756 came to an end: Saxony was his. He relieved all the Saxon officers but forced the remaining soldiers into the Prussian army. This proved an unwise move since he did not scatter them throughout his own units but left them in their existing Saxon contingents. These units deserted wholesale whenever the opportunity arose.

Frederick got off to a strong start the following year. In the spring of 1757 the Prussian army streamed into Bohemia in four columns, converging against the Austrian army just to the east of Prague. Although in a strong position, the Austrians left a gap in their center as they attempted to reinforce against the Prussian cavalry pressing their right flank. Frederick took advantage of the opportunity and won a solid victory. Duffy summarizes the state of affairs afterward: "Thus Frederick had taken on an Austrian force of approximately equal size and had driven it from its prepared position in the face of almost every conceivable obstacle and accident. . . . At the same time the Prussians had plenty of food for thought. They had lost over 14,000 men (actually more than the Austrians) and among that number were included Field-Marshal v. Schwerin and what Frederick called 'the pillars of the Prussian infantry.'"[72] The victory was not long celebrated. The remains of the Austrian army withdrew into Prague, forcing Frederick to lay siege; only a month later, a relief army under Leopold von Daun arrived and dealt Frederick a serious defeat at Kolin in mid-June, forcing the Prussian army back into Silesia. Six weeks later a French army overcame a force of Germans protecting Hanover, and by early September they controlled the province. This gave France an open road into Saxony. To make matters worse, at the end of August a Russian invasion through Poland into East Prussia gained a quick victory over Frederick's holding force there. Luckily for Frederick the Russians pulled back into Poland for the winter, but he still had serious French and Austrian threats to deal with.

The Battle of Rossbach

FREDERICK WAS LUCKY that Austrian marshal von Daun was overly cautious and did not seize the momentum after the battle at Kolin to press the Prussians completely out of Bohemia. Temporarily saved in the east by the Russian withdrawal and aided in the south by Daun's lack of vigor, Frederick decided to strike westward against the encroaching French, who, having taking Hanover, now threatened Saxony. The French army was initially under the command of General Charles de Rohan, Prince of Soubise. It was reinforced by a coalition army of German imperial states loyal to Maria Theresa under the nominal command of Field Marshal Prince Joseph Friedrich von Sachsen-Hildburghausen. The command was nominal because it was a coalition: 231 states contributed troops, and Hildburghausen soon learned that the term "chain of command" meant little when so many generals and princes were in the army with their own ideas of how things should be done.[73] The command structure was further weakened by the soldiers they commanded. The quality of the French soldier had deteriorated badly in the decade since the War of the Austrian Succession, and French officers were often dandies who had no concept of discipline. A French officer captured after Rossbach described his army as "a traveling whorehouse." Hildburghausen's so-called *Reichsarmee* thus lacked any coordination. Showalter points out that though in previous wars "Imperial troops had performed well as part of larger entities once they learned their trade, [i]n 1757, . . . they were being sent against the best fighting army in Europe with less than six months' experience in working together, with supply and administrative services even weaker and more disorganized than those of France."[74]

Thus, attacking through Saxony certainly seemed the wisest choice. Leaving General A. W. Bevern with 36,000 men to protect Silesia from an Austrian offensive out of Bohemia, Frederick led 10,000 men to Dresden. There he combined his force with 12,000 men under Maurice (Moritz) of Dessau. Together they marched westward past Leipzig to Erfurt in far western Saxony, arriving on 13 September. Soubise, not yet joined by Hildburghausen, abandoned the town and relocated southwestward to Gotha. For the next four weeks the two armies crossed and recrossed the same ground, reacting to each others' moves. Not until mid-October was there a major move, when 3,400 Austrian Pandours launched a surprise attack on Berlin. Not knowing how large the force was, Frederick took 14,000 men to relieve the city as the rest of his force pulled back east of the Saale. That convinced the Franco-German commanders to advance. They were bluffed out of their offensive by Frederick's new commander of cavalry, thirty-six-year-old Friedrich Wilhelm von Seydlitz. Seydlitz used his cavalry so aggressively at Gotha that Soubise was convinced the entire Prussian army was at hand. Fredrick was quickly back in Saxony with his main force by

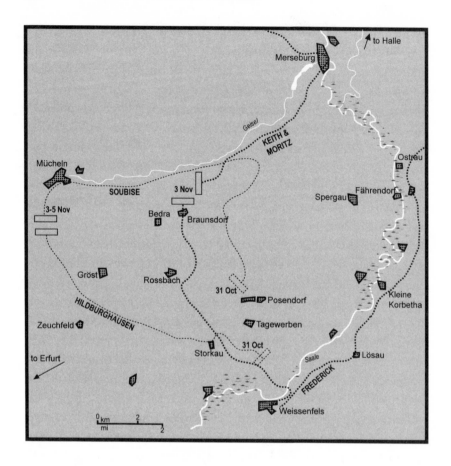

the 28th after he learned that the attack on Berlin had been no more than a raid. Hildburghausen, however, had advanced again east across the Saale River, and Frederick hoped to catch the imperial forces on the move. He broke his force into three prongs to cross the river at Merseburg, Halle, and Weissenfels. Unfortunately, when he reached the town of Wiessenfels the imperial troops retreated and burned the bridge behind them. Hildburghausen withdrew toward Erfurt. Soubise had considered opposing Prussian crossings at the two other towns after burning the bridges there as well, but pulled back to Müchelin, where he was joined by Hildburghausen. Together they numbered some 42,000 troops (though Friedrich estimated them at 60,000).[75] The initial French deployment was on the Schatau Heights in an east-west line, but Hildburghausen convinced Soubise to swing ninety degrees and face east with a north-south line.

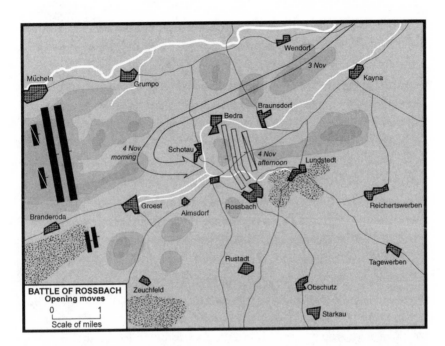

BATTLE OF ROSSBACH
Opening moves
0   1
Scale of miles

Frederick's three prongs converged on the town of Braunsdorf early in the evening of 3 November. He had roughly 22,000 men, whom he deployed along a line anchored on the north by the village of Bedra and on the south by Rossbach. Forces probing the French position early had withdrawn in the face of intense artillery fire, so Frederick decided to await developments rather than charge uphill against superior numbers. Fortunately for Frederick, Soubise thought that the repulse had cowed the Prussian king. Finally, Soubise got up the courage to launch an attack, which his staff and Hildburghausen had been pressing. The two allied commanders decided to abandon their high ground and swing east by the Prussian left flank. Soubise wanted to hit the flank but Hildburghausen preferred a sweep behind the Prussians to threaten their lines of communication. This would force them to retreat back across the Saale or meet on open ground.

Why would the allies not stay in their virtually impregnable position? Primarily it was a matter of supply. Recent French reinforcements had arrived with no food of their own, straining the resources of an army that had been living off the land. Had the Prussians not arrived, Hildburghausen had been planning on withdrawing farther west to a supply base at Unstrut. The allied force had to move or starve. It was November and by that time of year most armies were already in winter quarters.

Further disagreements between the two commanders used up most of the morning of 5 November, and it was approaching noon by the time camp broke and the allies deployed for the march in three columns of infantry. Frederick assumed that their desperate supply situation was forcing them to move toward their base, and ordered his men to stand firm and wait. He posted a lookout to keep an eye on them while he sat down to eat. Seydlitz, however, thought the allies were maneuvering for an attack, so he ordered his cavalry to prepare for action. He was proven correct when the lookout informed Frederick that the French had turned east with the cavalry moving ahead as the infantry in three lines dragged along, losing their marching order as they made the eastward turn. The king was quick to act when he realized his position. At 2:15 p.m. the Prussian camp disappeared, in a matter of a few minutes, as the army faced about. Frederick ordered Seydlitz to lead the 4,000 cavalry eastward behind the cover of Janus Hill and position himself at its far end. The artillery, which had begun to prepare when the cavalry did, were quick to move as well. They were sent to the top of Janus Hill where they commanded an unobstructed field of fire as the enemy marched by. The infantry deployed between Rossbach and the hill, hidden behind some woods.

The quick Prussian movement had not gone unobserved by French lookouts on a rise overlooking the village of Almdorf, about a mile west of Rossbach. Hildburghausen and Soubise jumped to the conclusion that their movement had accomplished its goal of forcing Frederick into a retreat. Not wanting to let him get across the Saale, the cavalry picked up their pace to get ahead of the "retreat."

Within an hour of the Prussian move eighteen artillery pieces were atop Janus Hill. Showalter describes the initial action: "At 3:15 the process of [allied] disillusion began when the Prussian heavy guns opened fire. They did some damage, but not enough to halt the allied advance. Instead, the allied horsemen quickened their forward pace, accepting some disorganization as a fair price for getting out of the artillery's killing zone."[76] The gunfire was the signal for Seydlitz to attack. While the allied cavalry hurried forward in line of march, Seydlitz came around the corner of Janus Hill with his cavalry spread out in attack formation. Frederick's main biographer, Thomas Carlyle, observes: "'Got the flank of them, sure enough!'— and without waiting signal or further orders, every instant being precious, rapidly forms himself; and plunges down on these poor people. 'Compact as a wall, and with an incredible velocity,' says one of them."[77] Although outnumbered by the allies 57 squadrons to 38, the Prussian cavalry's initiative carried the day. The Austrian units in the lead slowed the charge only momentarily. Soubise joined the fray with another 16 squadrons of French cavalry to try to halt the retreat. However, it made little difference as Seydlitz committed the 18 squadrons of his second line. These units crashed into the allies in an attack around both flanks. Within half an hour the allied cavalry were being forced back and ultimately off the field of action.[78] Seydlitz, wounded, led a hot pursuit as the allied cavalry fled at top speed.

Meanwhile, the lagging allied infantry advanced toward the Prussian artillery's kill zone. As Seydlitz had mounted his charge the Prussian infantry had emerged from the woods. The Prussians had had time to deploy in oblique order with the mass of troops on the left flank to swing around the head of the French column.[79] The units in echelon marched across the allied front, but then deployed in an unusual manner, which Showalter describes: "Instead of the familiar two straight lines of battalions, Frederick used his second line to extend the left flank of the first, forming an obtuse angle. This was done at a certain risk, since the final Prussian formation provided no significant reserves to plug gaps or cope with surprise tactical threats."[80]

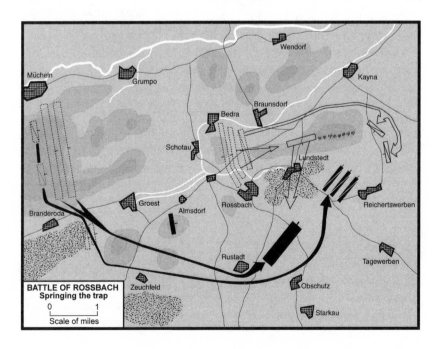

BATTLE OF ROSSBACH
Springing the trap
0   1
Scale of miles

Indeed, there was a potential tactical threat from the French, who were experimenting with the concept of attacking in column, foreshadowing the tactics of the French Revolutionary and Napoleonic armies. Two things kept the French from success: the typical Prussian fire discipline and the surprising reemergence of Seydlitz. In too many battles throughout history pursuing cavalry have taken themselves out of a battle in the thrill of the chase. Seydlitz broke with that unfortunate tradition and rallied his horsemen once the allied cavalry were safely out of the way. The returning cavalry struck as the Prussian infantry was delivering its normal devastating fire. Joined with the artillery barrage from on high and the sight of their cavalry broken and in flight, the allied infantry could stand no more demoralization. Carlyle comments: "French and Imperials throw weapons to the ground, run south from battle. Only two Swiss regiments retire in order. The Prussians pursue to Obschütz, taking numerous prisoners and most of the baggage. Darkness alone saves the enemy, who are in frantic flight south to Freiberg and beyond. The Prussians continue the pursuit, but it is dark and the men are tired. Frederick halts the infantry just east of Obschütz."[81]

Allied casualties were 3,000 killed and wounded, with 3,000 to 5,000 taken prisoner. The Prussians lost around 550, mostly among the cavalry since no more than seven Prussian battalions had actually been able to fire their guns before the allies broke. Carlyle ranks the battle high in military history: "Seldom, almost never, not even at Crecy or Poictiers, was any Army better beaten. And truly, we must say, seldom did any better deserve it, so far as the Chief Parties went."[82]

Since both armies were on the offensive; the allies used an approach march to stop what they assumed was a Prussian withdrawal, while the Prussians launched an attack that could be described both as hasty ("minimal preparations to destroy the enemy") and as a spoiling attack (to disrupt an expected enemy attack, striking while the enemy is most vulnerable). Frederick benefited from the allies' shortcomings: disagreement between commanders, lack of reconnaissance, disorganization on the march, and failure to coordinate infantry and cavalry. This should not, however, take away from his brilliance in grasping the value of the terrain while creating a plan and deploying his troops virtually on the fly. He exercised all the characteristics of the offense: surprise from all three arms; concentrating his cavalry to scatter superior numbers while his infantry did the same; dictating the tempo, though the battle was so short there was no real opportunity to alter it; and audacity, by attacking an army twice his size and not deploying in standard fashion but inventing his single-line infantry deployment on the spot. Seydlitz was the key to both the beginning and ending of the victory, arriving just in time to throw into headlong flight an army that was wavering from concentrated artillery and infantry fire. Like the Prussians, most of the allied army saw no action since only the lead elements engaged. Seydlitz successfully exploited the break but Frederick stopped any serious pursuit, as was his general practice. "Rossbach was an odd encounter. The standard patterns did not hold true. It was a contest between an agile army with brains and a clumsy army without any."[83]

Although virtual destruction could have resulted from a hard pursuit, Frederick needed his army whole. One threat was negated, but the Austrians were still active, and he needed to shift both his focus and his troops as quickly as possible. "Rossbach was at least as much an Imperial as a French defeat," Weigley notes, "but the lost battle proved to abate considerably such enthusiasm as the French had been able to generate for their unaccustomed alliance with the Habsburgs. Frederick had by no means swum out from his sea of troubles, but he could comfort himself that the shore might be in sight."[84] First, however, he had to swim to the opposite shore to salvage the situation in Silesia.

The Battle of Leuthen

WHILE FREDERICK WAS CAMPAIGNING against the allies, the Austrians under von Daun had finally begun to show the energy they failed to display after Kolin. The 38,000 men Frederick left under Bevern to defend Silesia were miserably failing in their task. "The Duke of Bevern, left to hold in Frederick's absence, had been outfought and outgeneralled at every turn," Showalter asserts. "Bevern was out of his depth in independent command against heavy odds. The Austrians took full advantage of superior numbers to hold him in check while overrunning Silesia's fortresses."[85] Still, it was not as successful for the Austrians as it might have been. Von Daun was joined in command by Charles of Lorraine, Maria Theresa's brother-in-law. He was even less aggressive than his co-commander (Simon Millar recounts how "Kaunitz, the great Austrian Chancellor at this time, expressed the frustrations of the court when he remarked that the only way to get the campaign moving again would be to recall Prince Charles"[86]). Had Frederick been in their place, Silesia and most if not all of Prussia would have been subdued by early November. Thus, the slow and steady Austrians overwhelmed Bevern but not the enemy country. By 13 November the town of Schweidnitz had surrendered; a week later the Austrians approached Breslau, where Bevern stood with 28,000. After a brief fight on the 23rd Bevern was in retreat across the Oder, leaving behind a garrison of just ten battalions of disaffected Silesians. They surrendered the city quickly. For a late-season campaign it was enough for the Austrians to be satisfied with their progress and sanguine about the next year's possibilities.

In Saxony, Frederick had spent ten days gathering men and supplies while allowing his men to recuperate. By mid-November, though, he was on the move toward Silesia. He left behind a small holding force and sent 6,000 men on a diversionary raid into Bohemia; that had the effect of drawing off some Austrian forces that might have stood in his way. Frederick took some 13,000 men on a march that covered 180 miles in fifteen days. He sent cavalry general H. J. von Ziethen to gather up the remains of Bevern's force and meet him on the march; Bevern had been captured after the rout at Breslau, perhaps purposely in order to avoid facing Frederick. On 2 December Ziethen met Frederick at Parchwitz with 25,000 men, a remarkable feat given the fleeing army's total disorganization after Breslau. With a combined 38,000 men Frederick was determined to do or die. He did not chastise the defeated soldiers, but welcomed them with food and

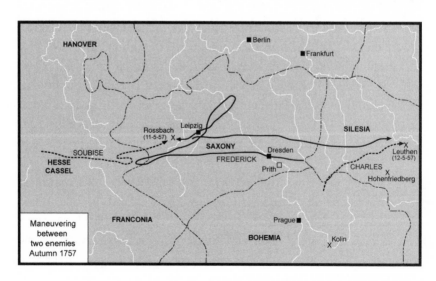

Maneuvering between two enemies Autumn 1757

drink and stories of the massive victory at Rossbach. Frederick himself walked through the camp and engaged the soldiers in man-to-man banter. "Orderlies carried casks of wine and baskets of bread and meat, and by the campfires he ate and drank with his soldiers, listened to their tales, heard their complaints," recounts Robert Asprey. "It was drunken talk in part, certainly coarse talk, often humorous, decidedly human. He was a soldier among soldiers."[87] The old Prussian pride began to reemerge. Frederick gathered his generals around him and gave an impressive pep talk, made all the more so by its calm presentation. The exhausted Frederick all but whispered to his commanders that this was an all-or-nothing proposition, win or die. Three to one odds against us. The future of Prussia at stake. Bravery would be rewarded, cowardice punished. I'll look after your families if you die. Showalter likens the speech to theater or modern locker-room inspiration: "Like all great performances, Frederick's blended sincerity and artifice in a way impossible for anyone to separate. . . . His 'Parchwitz speech' became the eighteenth century equivalent of an important contemporary sporting event: even people who were not there could remember every detail of what they saw or heard."[88]

After giving the officers and men a day to ponder his words and actions, he began moving the troops on 4 December. The Austrians had learned of his approach and were shocked at the speed of his movement. They then proceeded to make a terrible mistake: they marched out of Breslau and the prepared defenses they had overcome a few weeks earlier in order to meet Frederick in the open. Still, with the confidence they had gained after defeating Frederick at Kolin, Daun and Charles apparently thought an open battle would, indeed, decide the fate of Prussia in their favor. While not known for their aggressiveness, they were both veterans with victories under their belt and command of an experienced army with initiative. Plus, they outnumbered Frederick almost two to one: Frederick's roughly 38,000 against their own 66,000 (though some sources place their numbers as high as 80,000). They also had 210 guns to his 170 and deployed on ground of their own choosing. Unfortunately, it was the wrong choice. The position they selected, stretching north-south either side of the town of Leuthen, was well known to the Prussians from their annual maneuvers. They may as well have contacted Frederick and asked him where he would like to fight.

Early on the morning of 4 December the Prussians were advancing on the town of Neumarkt when the townspeople told them of a contingent of Croats in the town, laying out a new camp and baking bread for the advancing Austrian army. Frederick sent cavalry behind the town, then into it, scattering the enemy and capturing an army's worth of fresh bread, along with killing or capturing two-thirds of the 1,000 Croats. Basing himself at Neumarkt for the remainder of the day, Frederick learned of the Austrian deployment. He decided on a quick strike before they could dig in.

The Austrian position stretched over almost five miles, the right flank anchored to the north by the village of Nippern, then Frobelwitz almost two miles to the south, and Leuthen a mile further, and the left flank by Sagschütz. The deployment was typical: infantry flanked on both ends by cavalry, with the artillery arrayed front and center. A mixed infantry-cavalry force was held in reserve behind Leuthen. The right flank was covered by the Zettel-Busch, the only serious patch of woods on the entire battlefield. The left flank did not reach to the marshy area of the Schweidnitzer-Wasser, which could have prevented a sweep around that end. On the other hand, the Austrians did have time to throw up some quick defensive obstacles on the southern end of their lines. Daun and Charles intentionally lengthened the line in order to hamper Frederick's ability to use his oblique order attack. Or so they thought.

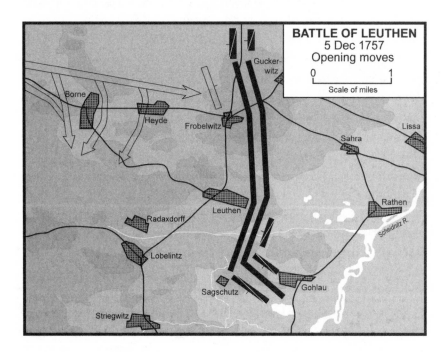

At 4:00 a.m. the Prussians arose and within two hours were marching eastward in four columns, infantry to the inside and cavalry on the outside. Frederick rode with an advance guard consisting of his few light infantry and all his hussars. At dawn they approached the village of Borne, held by an advanced force of hussars and Pandours, the same units that had performed well against the Prussians at Kolin. Not this day. The Austrians were unprepared for the size and speed of the attacking force charging out of the darkness. A few hussar regiments managed to escape, but eleven officers and 600 troopers were taken prisoner. They were paraded past the advancing infantry to buck up morale. The fleeing hussars alerted the Austrians of the Prussian arrival, and Daun and Charles ordered their men out of bivouac and a thousand yards forward into position. Frederick rode through Borne to the small village of Gross-Heidau then on to the Schönberg, where the battlefield panorama spread before him. The oblique attack, which he had designed and implemented with mixed success since Hohenfriedburg, would be perfectly executed on this day.

He kept his advance guard cavalry in a position plainly visible to his enemy. He was determined to convince the Austrians that he would indeed try his oblique attack, but on their northern flank. With his cavalry, and the appearance and disappearance of various infantry units, the enemy took his bait. Commanding the Austrian right was an Italian, General J. Lucchese, who called for reinforcements as soon as the feint was made. A second call for aid convinced Daun that the attack probably was going to strike that end of the line, so he sent the eight battalions in reserve north. Daun himself decided to look over the threatened section; while he was gone Prince Charles sent General J. B. Serbelloni's cavalry reserve from the south to reinforce Lucchese. All of this played perfectly into Frederick's hand, for as his feint was demonstrating in the north, the bulk of his army took a right turn at Borne. They converged their four columns into two and marched south in the dead (unobservable) ground behind a series of low hills that ran parallel to the Austrian lines. It was Rossbach again, but this time the enemy was not on the march while the Prussians positioned themselves to strike. Even when an occasional Prussian unit appeared through a gap in the hills, the Austrians dismissed them as deserters, or perhaps a retreating army protected by what could be a covering force to the

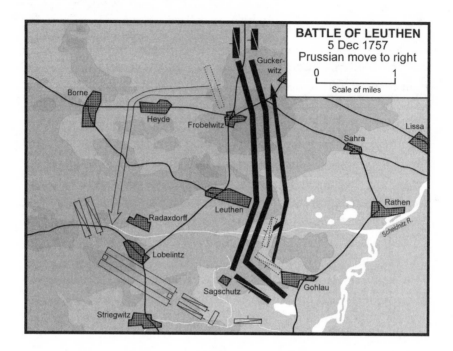

north. After all, Frederick was well known for attacking only when he had a numerical advantage.

By early afternoon the Austrian right was strengthened, and the Prussians began to emerge opposite their left flank. The lead infantry units were six battalions led by Prince Karl von Bevern (not to be confused with the Duke of Brunswick-Bevern captured after the Breslau battle) supported by Ziethen's fifty-three cavalry squadrons and some 12-pounders placed atop the Glanzberg overlooking the village of Sagschütz. The Austrian commander on the southern flank, General Franz Nadasti, quickly grasped what was about to happen and sent an urgent call for reinforcements, which was initially ignored. Frederick had ridden south to direct the battle and rode along the line, making sure the proper intervals for the oblique attack were maintained between the battalions, which finally numbered twenty in the front line and eleven in the second line.

At 1:00 the cannons fired, the fifes and drums began playing, and the attack started. "Starting from the right, the assault began, each battalion standing still until its right-hand neighbor had covered 50 paces," Britt and colleagues write. "In this manner, an oblique advance commenced at the moment when the advance guard rammed into the strong point at Sagschütz. . . . Ten battalions under Maurice [to whom Frederick had given command of the infantry] overpowered the Württembergers while a battery of 12-pounders enfiladed the Austrian forward line and poured a world of devastation on frightened men."[89] The troops stationed around Sagschütz were Württembergers and Bavarians, not the highest-quality troops in the Austrian force. They soon began to buckle, but Nadasti counterattacked with his cavalry. That slowed the advance somewhat, but Ziethen's horsemen soon gained the upper hand, routing the Austrian cavalry and capturing fifteen guns. With the Austrian line breaking Frederick sent his artillery into the gap and onto the Judenberg and then the Kirchberg, from where it raked the retreating troops and the second line.

Charles and Daun, who had stationed themselves on the northern wing with the reinforcements, were slow to grasp the reality of the situation. "In earlier battles the Austrians had been understandably reluctant to abandon strong positions, natural or artificial, to risk a tactical counterattack against the formidable Prussians," Showalter asserts. "Here nothing stopped them but high-level inertia reinforced by misapplied experience."[90] They finally realized what was happening and tried to salvage the situation by establishing a new line, perpendicular to the first, at Leuthen. Troops to the north were ordered to wheel left and face the Prussians, while the retreating troops were rallying to extend the line eastward from the town. Although the Austrians were able to reposition themselves, the battalions were not able to fully deploy and in some places were massed thirty deep instead of the standard three ranks. This made them an easy target for the rapidly advancing Prussian artillery; guns placed on the Butterberg could not miss.

While the battle for the town of Leuthen began about 3:30, Lucchese and Serbelloni saw an opportunity to get into the battle by riding around Frederick's army's new right flank and striking the left end of the Prussians in their parallel line. It was a good idea, but fate was still favoring Frederick. On the low hills that had screened the infantry movement stood forty cavalry squadrons under General Georg Wilhelm von Driesen. As the Austrian cavalry was deploying from column to line for their assault, Driesen's cavalry struck. There was a mad melee for a time, but as more

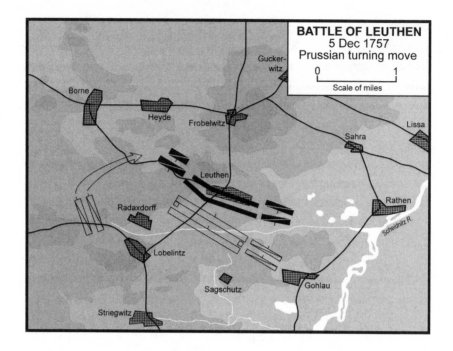

Prussian squadrons hit the Austrians confusion became chaos, which Fletcher Pratt describes: "He was charged front, flank, and rear, all at once. It was like Seydlitz's charge at Rossbach; Lucchesi himself was killed and his men scattered as though by some kind of human explosion."[91] The Austrian horsemen began retreating—right into their own infantry, who were being pushed out of Leuthen. That signaled the beginning of the end as "whole battalions of the enemy threw down their muskets and fled. Such troops as sought to make a stand were swept away in the stream of fugitives."[92]

For once Frederick engaged in pursuit, personally leading whatever cavalry units he could rally around him. Joined by Ziethen he rode down the road toward Breslau, wanting to keep just enough pressure on the retreating Austrians that they could not re-form and establish a defense at the Schweidnitzer-Wasser (the Weistritz River). There were a few skirmishes but by nightfall the Austrians were in full flight. Frederick settled himself into the castle at Lissa as his infantry, singing the hymn "Nun danket alle Gott" ("Now Thank We All Our God"), joined in the pursuit.

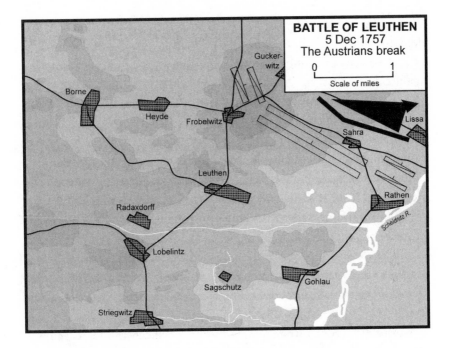

It was as complete a victory as Rossbach, but not as cheaply won. The Prussians' casualties numbered more than 1,000 officers and more than 5,000 men, or some 20 percent of their force. The Austrians were hurt much more: 3,000 officers and men killed, another 6,000–7,000 wounded, 12,000 more men taken prisoner on the battlefield, for a total loss to the Austrians of one-third of their army. It only got worse as the Prussians took another 10,000 prisoners during the pursuit.[93] It then got worse still, for although the Austrian commanders returned home, they left 17,000 men as a garrison in Breslau, which fell to the Prussians on 20 December. The retreating 37,000 were harried out of Silesia into Bohemia through terrible winter weather.

Leuthen became over time one of the classic battles studied by historians and military men worldwide. Britt and colleagues explain why: "The battle is in itself a complete lesson in tactics—deception, maneuver, inspiration, and resolve—gathered together into a volume on generalship, without one chapter missing. It was also a solid exclamation point to a year that had plumbed the depths of the Soldier-King."[94] Frederick's movement to contact was an approach march that led to a deliberate attack, including all arms. There was no surprise that there was going to be a battle; both sides were prepared. The surprise came from the feint and demonstration early in the day followed by the flanking march leading to his best use of the oblique attack. The concentration of his main force against the flank of the enemy gave him massive local superiority against an overall larger enemy force. By maintaining pressure, particularly with the constant advance of his artillery into successive points of high ground, he dictated the tempo throughout. While his attack was audacious, it was not a simple plan, especially concerning the deployment of his infantry battalions for the oblique attack. Having the time to do so depended on freezing the bulk of the enemy forces in their positions, which he accomplished by the feint, which shifted the Austrian reserves and the attention of their commanders.

Frederick's contemporaries thought that Leuthen was his finest victory, and most historians agree. The oblique attack, which had been in development for years, showed itself to perfection. The victory at Leuthen was against a larger, well-disciplined army, unlike the troops he had defeated at Rossbach.[95] From a strategic standpoint, Rossbach and Leuthen saved Prussia. Frederick spent the winter rebuilding his force; he then tried to strike Austria through Moravia rather than Bohemia. A mixture of inconclusive victories and losses followed until all Europe, exhausted, gave up the fighting in 1763.

However, Frederick's best days were behind him. He led the army again in 1772 when Prussia, along with Russia and Austria, divided Poland among themselves. In 1778–89 Frederick started another war with Austria over the Bavarian Succession, but little fighting occurred, and Catherine of Russia helped negotiate a settlement. Frederick had not kept up the extreme training regimen of the past, and the troops became slack, ultimately living off their reputation rather than their ability. That remained the case even after Frederick's death, but that attitude came to a rude end in 1806 at the hands of Napoleon.

Frederick's Generalship

BY TAKING A SMALL COUNTRY and transforming it into a major player in European politics, Frederick had emulated Gustavus. However, the many improvements Gustavus implemented became standard practice in European armies; other than the development of horse artillery later in the Seven Years' War, such was not the case with Frederick's legacy. Although military leaders from across the Continent came to Prussia, all they seemed to take away were the trappings of military power, rather than the practice of it. "In Europe generally military men sought to express their admiration for things Prussian by imitating every conceivable external of Frederick's army, rather as a savage might adorn himself with the feathers of an eagle in an attempt to endow himself with the creature's qualities," Duffy argues.[96] Few men anywhere at any time would so dedicate themselves to the management of details in the depth and breadth of the military.

I find that Frederick's strengths were best shown in the principles of the offensive, mass, surprise, simplicity, and morale. In his 1747 instructions to his generals, prepared after the War of the Austrian Succession, Frederick writes: "I have often said that for Prussians I would choose only unassailable positions or else I would not occupy them at all, for we have too many advantages in attacking to deprive ourselves of them gratuitously."[97] In other words, since perfect defensive positions were few and far between, the nature of the Prussian military argued against going on the defensive. Indeed, everything about the training of the Prussian military was about the best way to attack the enemy. Even in the battles where he was attacked, as at Soor, Frederick launched his forces onto the *offensive* as quickly as the enemy had been stalled. "Like the Romans," Dodge writes, "he laid down one rule: Never wait for your opponent's attack. If you are on the defensive, let this be still of an offensive character in both campaigns and battles."[98] His instruction to the infantry to close with the bayonet rather than "amusing" themselves by firing their muskets was intended to close the gap between the two forces as quickly as possible. His instructions to his cavalry were to get their horses to the gallop as quickly as possible in order to close more quickly as well as to build momentum. Even at his first battle, Mollwitz, whence he had to flee for his life, his army began the battle on the attack even though it finished it victoriously on the defense. As David Chandler asserts, "He taught the importance of offensive action. 'War is only decided by battles,' he declared, in marked contrast to earlier generals."[99]

At Hohenfriedberg Frederick marched through the night to catch the Austrians and Saxons unawares at daybreak. At Rossbach the French thought they were on the offensive, but it was Frederick's charging cavalry and rapidly deploying infantry that won the day. At Leuthen the Austrians were deployed, awaiting him with superior numbers, and he launched the classic example of the oblique attack. Ten years before the battle he had written that troops in entrenchments were at the disadvantage: "It is because whoever is enclosed in them is restricted to one ground and whoever attacks can maneuver freely; he who attacks is bolder then the one who defends himself."[100] Find the weak point and throw the weight of your force there—it was a lesson Napoleon learned well.

The main failing of Frederick's use of the offensive, however, was his lack of willingness in almost all cases to engage in pursuit.

Related to the proper use of *mass* on the battlefield is *maneuver* (getting the mass of your troops to the right place at the right time) and *economy of force* (use the minimum number of troops necessary for diversions and holding actions). Since in none of the three battles discussed did Frederick choose the battlefield (other than partially so at Rossbach), then maneuver ("places the enemy in a position of disadvantage," as the U.S. Army Field Manual phrases the principle) can't fully be exploited. One could argue, however, that by their placement on these three battlefields, Frederick's enemies virtually placed themselves at a disadvantage. Neither does economy of force always apply, as secondary objectives were not held by minimum forces other than at Leuthen. So in following up on the principle of the offensive discussed above, selection of the target on the battlefield becomes the most important aspect of Frederick's victories.

Indeed, the objective of his ongoing project to perfect the oblique attack is a lesson in where to employ the mass of one's force: at the point where the enemy is at the greatest numerical disadvantage. The goal of the oblique was to mass Prussian forces on a flank, where only the endmost enemy units were able to engage the attacking force. Hohenfriedberg was a battle of roughly equal forces, but Frederick's goal from the instant he knew the Austro-Saxon deployment was to strike both flanks. The Prussians achieved surprise as well as local superiority in numbers on both the enemy flanks there, the flanking units being cavalry. Hence the attacking Prussians were not only able to strike a smaller frontage of troops but they were also able to avoid the bulk of the Austrian artillery fire. At Rossbach, his cavalry force overall was smaller than the allied horse troops, but by striking them while still in march formation, the Prussians in the wider attack formation overwhelmed the allied frontage. When the infantry came into action the story was the same: the Prussian infantry deployed in line across the path of the allied force and was able to bring concentrated fire on their much narrower front lines. In both cases, defeat and retreat of the frontline troops led to disorganization and rout of the troops to the rear.

At Leuthen the Prussians were able to strike the enemy flank twice. The infantry to the south easily began to roll up the Austrian left flank with vastly superior forces at the point of attack, bringing about "perhaps the greatest day in the history of the Prussian army."[101] When the Austrians redeployed and their cavalry tried to implement their own flanking attack, they found themselves the victims instead of the instigators, thanks to Driesen's cavalry force, which had trailed the main body of the Prussian army and was opportunely located to crush the Austrian counterattack. Frederick could not take credit for Driesen's attack, but the concept had been pounded into his subordinates for years so the counter-counterattack is, in retrospect, really not too surprising. As Archer Jones points out, "In his other offensive battles he had less success that at Leuthen, but in every one he attempted to assail the enemy from an unexpected direction where he could anticipate finding the foe weaker than in front."[102]

When it comes to the principle of *surprise*, given the relatively minor attention Frederick gave to scouting and intelligence gathering, it would seem likely he would be surprised much more often than his opponents. At the strategic level this is true, but on the battlefield he was usually able to catch the enemy off balance. As Bevin Alexander writes, "The *real* challenge is to deliver a blow *without* being first thwarted or deflected by the enemy, who may recognize the decisive point as quickly as the attacker. A commander's principal problem, therefore, is disguising his intention so as to keep his opponent from subverting his effort by some decisive action of his own."[103] In his initial battle at Mollwitz Frederick made the mistake of deploying too slowly and forfeiting the element of surprise, but the discipline and determination of his infantry was sufficiently unexpected to enable them to defeat the Austrians. At Chotusitz his flank attack in the middle of the battle, with a force hidden in dead ground, shocked the Austrians and forced their withdrawal. At Hohenfriedberg his intelligence was perhaps the best it ever was, especially with his placement of a double agent with the ear of the Austrian commander. Here Frederick caught the Austro-Saxon force completely unprepared for any Prussian force in its area. His attack at dawn was certainly one of the primary factors in the Prussian victory.

Rossbach, however, was one of the greatest examples of battlefield surprise anywhere, anytime. His enemy was convinced the Prussians were in full retreat. The troops in Soubise's headlong dash never expected the cavalry wall they ran into. The use of the terrain to screen Prussian movements was rarely more masterful, and the sudden appearance of the infantry deployed across their front was nearly as much a factor in the rout of the allied infantry as was the concentrated Prussian musket fire. A French officer said it all: "Never did Army behave worse; the first cannon-salvo decided our rout and our shame."[104] Finally, the use of the terrain as well as the diversionary feint completely fooled Daun and Prince Charles at Leuthen. The ability to oblige the enemy to commit his reserves early to the wrong part of the battlefield is a dream all generals share and few realize. Dodge notes how "Frederick held Hannibal up as a pattern. 'Always,' said the king, 'lead the enemy to believe you will do the very reverse of what you intend to do.'"[105]

Unfortunately for Frederick and Prussia, Leuthen was the last time he was able to implement his oblique attack. By that point the Austrians were learning his tactics and deploying to avoid it, primarily by refusing their flanks and denying him the exposed flank he needed. Over time he adapted to the changes with greater firepower rather than the elan on which he had long trusted.

Possibly the most excellent talent Frederick possessed was his coup d'oeil, his ability to instantly read the terrain and the enemy's positions. For him, like the blind Jan Žižka, the best battle map was in his head. In his *Instructions* he mentions the need to use this talent both on the march and when the enemy is deployed; this foreshadowed Rossbach and Leuthen: "The *coup d'oeil* is of great importance . . . when you encounter the enemy on your march and are obliged to choose ground on which to fight instantly. . . . The judgment that is exercised about the capacity of the enemy at the commencement of a battle is also called *coup d'oeil*."[106]

This capacity to absorb all the key elements of terrain and enemy positions meant that Frederick could develop a plan almost instantly. Although the training for and execution of the oblique attack was complicated and required precision, Frederick's battle plans were never complex. "His was no hard and fast system," Dodge asserts. "He did what was most apt. His battle plans were conceived instantly on the ground. What was intricate to others was simple to him and to the Prussian army."[107] Although he scouted the enemy position in advance at Hohenfriedberg, he decided on and implemented the deployments at both Rossbach and Leuthen in a matter of minutes.

Frederick was also masterful in his ability to maintain troop *morale*. On the surface, someone not familiar with military training might think that the Spartan discipline imposed on the Prussian soldier would break his spirit rather than motivate it. After all, it was Frederick who famously opined that the soldiers needed to fear their officers more than they did the enemy. Of course the opposite occurs: ability to overcome difficulty creates pride and self-confidence. All elite soldiers know this. This is why the Prussian army was the creme de la creme of eighteenth-century armies. To this end, Frederick did not create the famous Prussian discipline, but he perfected what he had inherited from his father and grandfather.

As we have seen with other generals, to be effective one needs to show his men he is willing to share their burdens and their dangers. A less disciplined army may have rejected Frederick's leadership in the wake of his debut at Mollwitz, but they followed their orders, and at Chotusitz and Hohenfriedberg they learned that their soldier-king was a man of determination. As Samuel Lewis notes, "Although his army was disciplined, experienced, and confident, he nevertheless clearly expressed what was required of every officer and man, both in camp and on the battlefield. He cared for and protected his force even though he was of royal blood."[108] Frederick was never one to put on airs; he was famous for his unkempt uniform. He kept his men better fed and supplied than most generals of the time, either carrying food with the army in his own lands or living off the land in enemy territory.

He also knew that his role was, at times, to be the actor. Historians debate whether his actions prior to Leuthen were the results of personal exhaustion or well-implemented psychology. He walked softly, he did not berate defeated soldiers (although some of their generals were punished), he provided extra food and drink. He walked among the men and engaged them with unwonted familiarity, even though there are stories of blunt talk from some of his troops. He was even called "Old Fritz" to his face by men in the ranks. But he knew the value of his presence. It may not have been worth 40,000 men, as Wellington was supposed to have said about Napoleon, but since the days of ancient Greece men have respected the leader who stands among them. Frederick wrote to his nephew, "You cannot, under any pretext whatever, dispense with your presence at the head of your troops, because two thirds of your soldiers could not be inspired by any other influence except your presence."[109] He did not lead from the front like Alexander or Belisarius, but he put himself in harm's way on many occasions. It paid off. Biographer David Fraser remarks that Frederick had "the divine spark of leadership, the gift of communicating energy and inspiring confidence in tired, frightened, dispirited men. . . . Frederick, the Prussian soldiers knew, was always where the fight was the hottest, was watching every shift, every twitch of the battle with the eye of a master, was asking no more of any man that he would hazard himself. . . . Frederick thought fast, decided fast, spoke and wrote fast. All bore witness to his extraordinary calm in moments of crisis."[110]

FOR THE REMAINDER OF THE SEVEN YEARS' WAR Frederick's defeats outnumbered his victories, and some of his losses were severe. However, he and his army managed to survive the setbacks and come out of the war with both territory and reputation intact. His contributions to warfare and his smashing victories were sufficient to earn him the "Great" sobriquet. "No one else accomplished what he was able to do with linear tactics," Dupuy asserts. "[H]e achieved the utmost possible within the limits set by technology and by the political and social conditions of Prussia in the eighteenth century."[111] The greatest contemporary tribute to Frederick was the mass of foreign soldiers who went to Prussia to learn from the master who, as noted above, mainly grasped the trappings of power instead of the reasons behind it. Ritter asserts that "[a]fter the Seven Years War he occupied the same position among the generals of Europe that once had been Prince Eugene's: Frederick was the universally admired, studied, and emulated preceptor of modern war."[112]

Frederick, however, declined in his advancing years as the army became a shell of its former self. "The brotherhood of endurance faded in peacetime, as discipline became an end in itself instead of a means of making war," Showalter writes. "The fellowship of arms eroded as the King's capriciousness broke careers without hope of redress. By the mid-1770s the army was focused on Frederick not as king, not as commander in chief, but as totem."[113]

The great tragedy of his accomplishments was that they were so good the Prussians would not change as time passed. In his glory days Frederick could see what was necessary and adapt, as he did with his cavalry and artillery, but his successors did not. Instead, they gloried in the mystique, which was ultimately shattered by Napoleon in 1806 at the battles of Jena and Auerstadt. His spirit, however, continued to motivate generations. The cavalry tactics used by Napoleon and others came from Prussian roots; the obsession with massed firepower dominated German military thinking through World War II; Moltke depended greatly on maneuver and mobility in his victory in the Franco-Prussian War a century after Frederick's time.[114] In these imitators and many others, Frederick's success as a commander is continually reestablished.

14

Napoleon Bonaparte (1769–1821)

French Emperor

He knows all; he understands everything; he can achieve anything.

—Abbé Emmanuel-Joseph Siéyès

ONLY ONE OTHER TIME IN THIS WORK have two contemporaries been discussed: Hannibal and Scipio. Hannibal was the elder and long in the field before Scipio arrived, a much younger man. Scipio learned from Hannibal and adapted Carthaginian weaponry and methodology into a new style of Roman warfare. Such is not the case with Napoleon and his contemporary, Wellington. The two were of almost identical age and, while there are a number of striking similarities in the lives of the two men, it cannot be said that either adopted the other's techniques. As in the earlier pairing, we also see the two generals moving in opposite directions, with Scipio and Wellington peaking at their abilities as Hannibal and Napoleon were past their best days.

Napoléone Buonaparte was born on 1 August 1769 into the minor nobility, son of Carlo and Letizia Buonaparte, on the island of Corsica. The island had long been ruled by Genoa and had only recently (1761) managed to expel the Genoese rulers. It was not exactly independent, however, as Genoa proceeded to sell Corsica to Louis XV, who invaded and established a French administration in 1768. The Corsicans were not terribly pleased with this new overlord and resisted the French presence; however, they failed to gain their sovereignty. Carlo Buonaparte decided to go along with the new order and befriended the French governor, the Marquis de Marbeuf. This connection opened the way for young Napoléone to attend military school in northeast France at Brienne, in the Champagne region some fifteen miles north of Reims. He was a student there from 1779 to 1784, when he was transferred to the Ecole Militaire in Paris; in 1785, at the age of sixteen, he entered into military service with an artillery regiment in the Rhône River valley. In the summer of 1788 he entered artillery school at Auxonne, just outside Dijon in eastern France.

This proved perhaps the most important move in Napoléone's life up to that point, for the school was run by Baron Jean-Pierre du Teil, who along with his brother was probably the premiere artillery expert in the world. Du Teil took a fancy to the young man, seeing signs of a sharp intelligence.[1] Like many of the generals studied in this work, Napoléone became a voracious reader, primarily of history and military works but also of mathematics. Du Teil also gave the young man special exercises to hone his skills. Napoléone became a master at reading terrain and effectively employing cannons. No general in this work appreciated big guns like he did. He grasped an unrivaled knowledge of ballistics and also developed his talents as an architect and draftsman. He learned from du Teil's brother Jean the importance of massing artillery at key instants in battle.[2]

A year into Napoléone's artillery training, the French Revolution broke out in July 1789. Since his father had died in 1785 and had been a minor noble, Napoléone was not a target of any backlash against aristocrats. Not until 1791 did the Royal Artillery School come under political fire, with du Teil forced to emigrate along with many of the high-born officer candidates. Napoléone, however, embraced the revolutionary cause as the Royal Army was collapsing. He took leave from his regiment in October and went home to Corsica, where he became lieutenant colonel of the Ajaccio Volunteers, part of the National Guard established by the revolutionary government. He achieved this rank by election, which meant lying, cheating, stealing, and stabbing in the back, described by one biographer as "a contest violent and corrupt even by eighteenth-century small-town Corsican standards."[3] The election was confirmed after he made a trip to Paris in August 1792, and Napoléone spent the following several months suppressing Corsican independence movements. Such actions and attitudes resulted in threats by local patriots that were sufficient to convince him and his family to abandon the island for France; he never returned to his homeland. From that point forward, his name was Napoleon Bonaparte and he was French to the core.

Facing some royalist movements around the country, the Revolutionary Committee decided in January 1793 to execute King Louis XVI along with his family, friends, and supporters. This would make enthroning a new monarch much more difficult. The resulting Reign of Terror hardened some of the counterrevolutionary groups. On the south coast, the city of Toulon declared itself in favor of a return to royal rule, expelled revolutionaries, and invited the British and Spanish to occupy and defend the city. In early August the revolutionary army arrived to begin a siege, but it faced extremely stout defensive works as well as English warships; the early part of the siege proved less than successful. On his way to Nice in mid-September to deliver some gunpowder, Napoleon stopped at Toulon to pay his respects to a fellow former Corsican and, owing to the wounding of the artillery officer in charge, found himself assuming that position. He also found himself in the middle of mass chaos. The army commander at Toulon, General Jean-François Carteaux, had no talent. Napoleon had some connections with the political officers on hand who were reporting back to Paris, and with their support he assumed not only command of the four cannons and two mortars available, but also began organizing every aspect of the force that had any connection to artillery. He imported sacks of earth from Marseilles in order to build ramparts. He created an arsenal at the nearby village of Ollioules and had blacksmiths and carpenters working to repair muskets, cast musket balls and cannon balls, and build the necessary transport vehicles. He imported skilled workers from Marseilles to create case shot for his cannons and shells for his mortars. He reorganized the artillery company, obtained more gunpowder, and scrounged more cannons from the surrounding region. He soon had a complement of almost a hundred artillery pieces.[4]

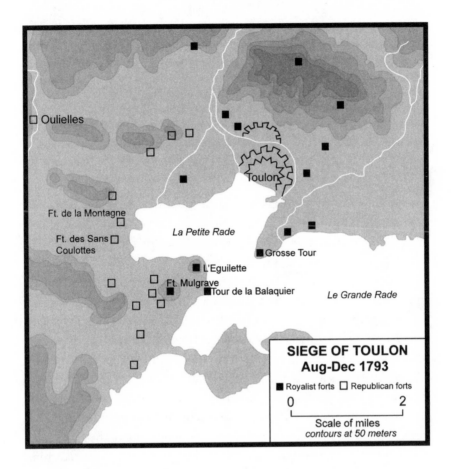

□ Oulielles

Ft. de la Montagne

Ft. des Sans
Coulottes

La Petite Rade

Grosse Tour

L'Eguilette

Ft. Mulgrave

Tour de la Balaquier

Le Grande Rade

Toulon

SIEGE OF TOULON
Aug-Dec 1793

■ Royalist forts □ Republican forts

0   2

Scale of miles
contours at 50 meters

The challenge for the besiegers was not just the city's fortifications but the English fleet in the harbor, which had grown immensely by capturing dozens of French ships based there and had greatly expanded the defenders' firepower. Here Napoleon first showed his coup d'oeil. He grasped that the key to taking the city was not in overcoming its walls and gun positions; instead, the center of gravity was the allied fleet. Remove that and the city could not survive; leave it in place and supplies could be brought indefinitely. His first batteries, Forts de la Montagne and des Sans Culottes, were constructed to bombard the western end of the inner harbor (La Petite Rade), and although their initial cannonade produced little in the way of damage, it did convince the British commander in Toulon, Admiral Lord Alexander Hood, to pull his ships closer to the

Toulon docks. The western end of the harbor was too shallow to bring in his warships for counterbattery fire.

David Chandler, the premier Napoleonic military historian, writes, "The young officer soon made his presence firmly (and unpopularly) felt at every council of war meeting. From the first he appreciated that the key to the defences of Toulon lay in capturing Fort l'Eguilette. Sited on a high promontory overlooking the narrow passage between the greater and lesser anchorages, the latter could be rendered untenable for Hood's fleet if cannon shot was fired against it from the fort."[5] The first attempt against the post was too weak and failed; the British responded quickly to strengthen their hold on the area. At the end of September they landed more than 500 British and Spanish troops. The British engineers quickly built a large and imposing position known as Fort Mulgrave—nicknamed "le petit Gibraltar" by the French—on the heights overlooking the point, and manned it with twenty heavy cannon and four mortars.[6] This stymied the French effort for a time, while allied reinforcements arrived by ship from Naples and Sardinia, bringing the defense forces up to almost 9,000 against the 15,000 French besiegers, who held significantly less favorable ground. Still, the superior numbers allowed the French to regularly harass the outlying allied posts, keeping them on edge and short of supplies. The French, meanwhile, had little problem delivering sufficient provisions from Marseilles. There were political moves among the force commanders but Napoleon spent his time building up new batteries, earning the respect of all. Through October both sides received reinforcements, with the Spanish holding the majority among the defenders in both men and ships.

In mid-November a professional soldier took charge of the siege: General Jacques Dugommier. Along with him came Baron du Teil, Napoleon's old mentor from artillery school. He gave the young artillerist both freedom and approval for his emplacements. Although du Teil was greatly senior in rank and experience, he generally deferred to Napoleon's decisions since they generally mirrored his own. Between 14 and 30 November, Napoleon built eight more batteries. By month's end, his thirteen batteries with a total of thirty-seven cannon and twenty-six mortars presented a considerable threat to both Fort Mulgrave and the western side of the harbor.[7] The increased firepower kept allied ships even further at bay, leaving Fort Mulgrave dangerously isolated.

On 30 November the allies launched an attack out of Fort Malbous-
quet (on the north shore of the inner harbor) against the batteries just to
the north. Early allied success, however, turned to failure when overpur-
suit led to disorganization, which counterattacking French forces were
able to exploit. At the end of the day many French guns were disabled,
though neither side gained or lost any significant position. However,
the allies had suffered a significant number of casualties, including the
mission commander, General Charles O'Hara, who was wounded and
captured. Napoleon was among the leaders of the counterattack. This, and
his constant exposure to fire during the construction of his batteries, did
much to endear him to his men.

The successful counterattack was followed almost immediately by a
council of war to discuss what would be the key battle of the siege. Napoleon was involved in the planning—although he was certainly not its
primary architect, as later memoirs would claim. The council resulted in
attacks on three points around Toulon, to keep the allies from knowing
where the main effort would be focused. This eventually came at Fort
Mulgrave, which, after two weeks of constant pounding from Napoleon's
guns, fell to French assault after fierce fighting. With that stronghold out
of the way, Napoleon led the final assault to seize the position at Fort
l'Eguilette. Napoleon urged on his troops until his horse was shot out
from under him; he then led on foot, receiving an enemy bayonet at the
fort's parapet and suffering a bad thigh wound. The assault was so quick
that the allies did not have the time to spike their cannons before the
Frenchmen seized them.[8]

By the following day Napoleon had ten cannons in position and began
firing on the British ships. Admiral Lord Hood saw the handwriting on
the wall and ordered not just the harbor but the city to be abandoned.
The ships, crowded with wounded as well as royalist civilians, sailed
away in the night. At 9:00 a.m. on 19 December Toulon became the
property of the French Republic. Napoleon, according to British officer
William Sidney-Smith, rounded up anyone who appeared to be a col-
laborator, massed them in the city square, and mowed them down with
artillery. By Napoleon's own account, however, trials were held and a few
hundred executed. In his book on the siege of Toulon, Bernard Ireland
writes, "The anger of the Committee of Public Safety at what it viewed
as the prolonged betrayal of Toulon could be assuaged only through

terrible vengeance. Its original intention was to raze the town totally but, as this made no practical sense, penalty was exacted from its unfortunate remaining inhabitants."[9] Napoleon, owing to the severity of his leg wound, probably had nothing to do with the ensuing deaths of as many as 6,000 civilians.

Although detractors link him to the slaughter, French contemporaries saw Napoleon as one of the major heroes of the battle. Chandler observes, "Although technically he was never more than artillery adviser to a succession of commanders in chief, Major Buonaparte was generally recognized as being the mastermind behind the success. . . . [He] had hit upon the secret of success by appreciating the military problem correctly. . . . And so at last Napoleon Buonaparte had emerged onto the scene of European History."[10]

Warfare of the Time

IN THE WAKE OF THE SEVEN YEARS' WAR, the French government became determined to overcome its military's extremely poor showing.[11] Embarrassing defeats like Rossbach motivated the French high command to improve the nation's army. Napoleon actually developed almost no new methods of fighting; he inherited a newly developed system from three main theorists and reformers of the prerevolutionary era, Guibert, Bourcet, and Gribeauval. Their work, undertaken during the last decades of the monarchy, would lay the basis for Napoleon's success.[12]

Jacques Antoine Hypolite, Comte de Guibert, who wrote his *General Essay on Tactics* (*Essai général de Tactique*) in 1772, was a critic of the entire European political system and the means of warfare it employed. What, he asked, were the results of the wars of the late seventeenth and eighteenth centuries? Nations with shattered economies that could neither afford war in the first place nor succeed in their stated goals at its conclusion. What was needed, according to Guibert, was something of a throwback to the days of the wars of religion, when masses of manpower fought for ideals. The new ideal, however, would not be Catholicism or Protestantism, but national pride and glory. Mobilize the nation, create a national army, and follow a charismatic and visionary leader: this was a virtual blueprint for Napoleon's career. Although he never foresaw nor advocated anything like the French Revolution, Guibert did desire a national will. Military historian Russell Weigley writes, "The Age of Enlightenment and Reason had already brought forward the idea that all institutions of government ought to be in harmony with the spirit and desires of the people. From this idea, Guibert drew the concept of a citizen's army. If the armies of France could embody the vigor of the French nation at large, then indeed France could resume its former glorious place in the European military constellation."[13]

In Guibert's conception, the army itself would be handled differently than before. Speed was of the essence, and therefore large baggage trains were anathema. So, too, was the concept of the army moving as a single mass. The army instead would be divided into divisions or corps and move along parallel routes toward a single objective, at which place they would reunite for battle. Each division, moving along its own route, would carry minimal supplies and acquire most of its provision from the countryside. This idea would result in a much more mobile style of warfare than had been seen previously in Europe. Breaking armies into divisions promoted maneuverability and speed of both march and deployment for battle. This, too, became a hallmark of Napoleonic warfare.[14] Once the divisions came together for battle, their individuality remained a positive aspect, as marching by division allowed variations in the terrain to be exploited more easily.[15] When the French army adopted a new training manual in 1791, it was based heavily on Guibert's theories.

Pierre de Bourcet published *Principles of Mountain Warfare* (*Principes de la guerre des montagnes*) in 1771, after working on it for seven years. He had served as chief of staff for a number of senior generals, and his expertise was well known. He was appointed to direct the newly established French staff college in the wake of the Seven Years' War, and his text was available at first only to his students. It was later published by France's War Department, but with limited distribution to officers, and not outside the army. Thus, Napoleon was first exposed to Bourcet's *Principles* during his training at Auxonne. Bourcet's ideas reflected those of Guibert, arguing the need for speed as well as deception. Thus, his army divisions were larger (corps sized) and moved over a greater front, making it difficult for an enemy to anticipate which was the main column and what would be its target.[16] Bourcet was more strategically minded, however, while Guibert's theories were more at the operational or grand tactical level. Bourcet saw army divisions marching directly into battle from a number of directions, rather than marching to a battlefield and forming up opposite the enemy in parallel lines. This called for excellent communication between the divisions. For Napoleon, moving his army across a massively wide front became a trademark.

Napoleon's training and specialty was with artillery, an arm that was also undergoing a major transformation in the prerevolutionary era. By the time of the Seven Years' War, other countries had begun manufacturing smaller cannon for more mobility on the battlefield, while the French were still focused on artillery as siege weapons. Bitter experience in battles against Prussian and English armies brought them to the realization they needed to adapt their theories. In 1763, Jean Baptiste Vacquette de Gribeauval was assigned to oversee the modernization of French artillery. He had worked with the head of the Austrian artillery forces during the Seven Years' War, during which the Austrians had developed the finest artillery arm in Europe. Using the Austrian guns as models, Gribeauval redesigned the French pieces to be more maneuverable than before. Instead of fifteen horses, his 12-pounder cannon could be moved by six horses or fifteen men. Also like Frederick's guns, the new French artillery could be transported across obstacles easily and moved as quickly as infantry.[17] Gribeauval was also responsible for two technical innovations: the elevating screw to more accurately adjust for range, and a graduated rear sight. These, as well as the adoption of Dutch casting methods, made the French guns highly accurate.

Napoleon inherited from the du Teil brothers the opinion that artillery fire on the battlefield should be just like that in a siege: massed fire at a single point to break down the defense. The increased use of smaller guns on the battlefield, however, brought about the view that placement on high ground was not the best position for maximum damage. Artillery usually fired cast iron balls, which were most effective when fired at a level trajectory about chest high. Whether flying through the air or bouncing along the ground, they caused serious wounds and death. Higher trajectories meant less bouncing, hence less damage. Therefore, gunners preferred flat, open, hard ground.[18] As that was just the type of ground that facilitated linear warfare and cavalry charges, the use of artillery naturally became more widespread and deadly. Napoleon increased the number of guns to four per one thousand men, each gun having at hand 300–350 rounds.

Along with these developments came a debate over how best to actually engage the enemy. Since the time of Gustavus Adolphus armies had been deploying in linear formations in order to maximize the firepower of inaccurate arquebuses and muskets. To be effective, this demanded disciplined troops who would stand and take casualties while delivering their fire. The question that Napoleon and contemporary generals faced was whether a citizen army could be sufficiently trained to handle that pressure, as had the professional armies that had dominated the battlefield for more than a hundred years. If not, how could these citizen soldiers best be employed? One answer was the use of infantry as if it were pre-gunpowder cavalry, for shock attacks. The soldiers were deployed not in line but in column and sent forward in a rapid bayonet charge. Harking back to the concept of othismos in ancient Greece, the depth of the column and the momentum generated by the pressure of the rear ranks upon men in front could create sufficient shock effect sufficient to puncture and break the enemy's line.[19] This recalls the Athenians at Marathon; speed could diminish the effect of firepower given the slow reloading time necessary for the musket. Other advantages of this column formation were the ability to better cross rough terrain, the concentration of officers and noncommissioned officers giving an example of leadership, the smaller target that would be presented to the enemy line formation, and the fact that the unit could more easily form into a defensive square should cavalry attack. The battalion column was one or two companies wide, making it a front of 50–80 men, and a depth of 9–12 men. This would make it 30–60 yards wide and 12–15 yards deep. It was therefore still wider than it was deep, but significantly narrower on its front than the shallow line it would be attacking.[20]

On the other hand, the column could not produce much firepower, and if the soldiers in the defending line were well trained they could maintain a fairly steady rate of fire by ranks, somewhat negating the slow reloading. The compromise, and the formation favored by Napoleon, was a combination of line and column, known as *l'ordre mixte*. This would usually be a battalion in line flanked by two battalion columns. Chandler observes that l'ordre mixte was "ideally adapted for the exploitation of success, the assumption of the defensive or an abrupt change of front; in other words it could perform almost any role with a minimum of delay."[21] The size of the formation could vary up to a divisional line with brigade flanking columns. If columns alone advanced onto the field, they would do so in order to gain position as quickly as possible before deploying into line to begin the actual exchange of fire. It was during that shift that the French troops were most vulnerable; Chandler notes that the French columns "habitually attempted to carry out these instructions, but often delayed the final evolution until it was too late."[22]

Another addition to the military repertoire was the large-scale introduction of light infantry as skirmishers. Skirmishers had been used during the War of the Austrian Succession and the Seven Years' War, introduced by the Austrians, who learned the practice in their wars against the Ottomans. The French began using them during the War of the First Coalition (1792–95) in order to soften up the enemy line before the main attack. Military historian Trevor Dupuy in his *Evolution of Weapons and Warfare* notes that "by 1793 all battalions were acting as light infantry, dissolving into skirmisher swarms as soon as action was joined. These fighting methods, sometimes called 'horde tactics,' were in turn superseded after 1795 by a tendency to return to properly controlled assault columns, preceded by skirmishers whose functions were reconnaissance and disruption of the enemy by individual aimed fire."[23] Significantly, this French skirmishing system was not performed by special light troops but by regular soldiers. Thus, during the Wars of Revolution the swarm, or horde, could disrupt the normal linear tactics. They later became more specialized, often marksmen; in the Prussian forces they were called *Jägers*, hunters. As such, they were used to counter the enemy's skirmishers and to pick off officers, thus diminishing command and control functions.[24] These soldiers in the French army were called *tirailleurs;* later Napoleon introduced the *voltigeurs*, who were to go into battle with the cavalry. Usually one company per battalion was designated as skirmishers, though at times entire battalions might be deployed as such. French skirmishers gained a solid reputation for the effectiveness of their harassing fire.

In spite of the adoption of the 1791 manual, during the Wars of Revolution the mode of warfare depended on the man in command, though the government attempted to dictate a constant offense, usually with the bayonet. This sounded good to politicians in Paris but was of little practical use on the battlefield. Once the national conscription, or *levée en masse*, was introduced in late summer 1793, manpower became a French advantage. The French column attack became stereotypical, but wasn't quite as bayonet-oriented as believed. Early in the Wars of the Revolution the French system became more flexible, shifting between line and column, using skirmishers and artillery as the situation called for.[25] This system brought two battalions of recruits together with one of veteran regulars. The regulars deployed and fought in line flanked by the new men. The battalion in the center used the veterans' discipline to maintain sufficient fire while the recruits were thrown at the weak points created in the enemy lines. Napoleon developed this ordre mixte all the way to divisional level.[26] Coupled with the increased production of arms, the French ordre mixte produced both firepower and shock.

All that was missing was cavalry. The French fielded the arm, of course, but the troopers were few in number and lacking in effectiveness, as many of the former cavalry officers were nobles who had not fared well in the Revolution. Napoleon expanded the role of light cavalry, depending on them for both reconnaissance and as a screen for his widely separated divisions. The screen effectively provided early warning of enemy movements and also denied the enemy the ability to know just where the French army was located. Light cavalry also proved extremely effective in the pursuit. On the other hand, Napoleon also revived the true heavy cavalry. Dupuy writes that Napoleon's cavalry, "provided with horse artillery and used in great but articulate masses and in surprise operations against hostile cavalry and infantry," was very effective, particularly as it was often used against enemy troops who were already shaken by massive artillery fire or by infantry attack. "During the early Napoleonic Wars, under outstanding leaders, and by its impetuous charges, French cavalry was generally superior to the best cavalry in other European nations."[27]

Other than the more mobile horse artillery, virtually none of the weaponry of the Napoleonic era differed to any great extent from that of Frederick's day. The standard French infantry weapon was a .69 caliber smoothbore musket introduced in 1777. Though Napoleon had enhanced light infantry, the regular blend of fusilier and grenadier remained fairly standard. The main advancement was the development, thanks to Guibert and Bourcet, of the independently acting division made up of all arms, which made for speed and ease of supply. In his classic work on strategy, Peter Paret observes that living off the land was facilitated by Napoleon's warfare style of combined arms in the corps organization. He notes that "the extended army covered much ground . . . but also, and primarily, enabled its component parts to move more rapidly, gave them greater flexibility, and multiplied the commander in chief's operational choices."[28] The separated corps could move and converge into a variety of formations: echelon, wedge, or *en potence* with one flank reinforced. Napoleon also introduced what became known as the *batallion carré:* He moved his army in four corps in a rough diamond shape along separate lines of march, roughly a day's march apart. "Each self-contained, all-arm corps was capable of engaging or holding off several times its own number for several hours, during which time the neighboring formations could move up to its support or to outflank the enemy," Chandler explains. "This dispersal was carefully controlled, and the appearance of disunity was stronger than the reality."[29]

The batallion carré worked both for intentional and surprise contact with the enemy. All the corps marched toward a predetermined site where the enemy army would be located; Napoleon cared little for other targets, such as cities or fortresses. The enemy army was the center of gravity, the key to breaking an enemy's will and forcing his surrender. If, however, along the line of march the advanced cavalry screen stumbled into an unexpected force, the corps nearest at hand would engage. The two closest corps would come up on either side, looking for which enemy flank was weakest. The farthest corps would come up and act as a reserve. Either way, the goal on the battlefield was the *manoeuvre sur les derrières*, the flanking move that would either result in positioning the corps for an attack on the enemy rear or oblige the enemy to redeploy to protect his flank or line of communications, which would create an exploitable weakness somewhere else along the line. Once the weak spot was discovered, the reserve would be thrown in to break the line and begin the pursuit. In Chandler's view, "In this way Napoleon fused battle with maneuver, and thus made possibly his greatest contribution to the art of war."[30]

The Opponents

THE AUSTRIANS, WHO FOUGHT AGAINST NAPOLEON more than any other power, went into the Napoleonic Wars with the traditional linear tactics of the century, apparently unaware of (or unconcerned with) developments in France. The Austrian generals favored defense over offense, firepower to break the enemy charge rather than to break the enemy line. They had increased the professionalism of their forces in the wake of their experiences against Frederick, improving their performance as the Seven Years' War progressed after their defeat at Leuthen in late 1757.[31]

The Austrians began to change their tune, however, when the French revolutionaries won victories against them and other European armies with their attacks in column. Although they attempted to adopt the French tactics for themselves, the Austrians were far less successful with these maneuvers. The revolutionaries won their early battles as much by numbers and the willingness to accept high casualties, both of which came from the spirit of the times in France. Such nationalism could not be matched in the Austro-Hungarian Empire, composed as it was of Germans, Czechs, Flemings, Walloons, Croats, Serbs, Poles, and a number of smaller ethnic populations. Without nationalistic fervor to draw on, the Austrian army had to rely on traditional tactics until a sufficiently peaceful period should occur when reforms might be considered. As it happened, that was not until 1804–5. When the Austrians met Napoleon in northern Italy, they were facing an army whose revolutionary elan had cooled somewhat, but which had a commander for whom they were unprepared.

The French first ventured into the Italian Peninsula in 1792 in an effort to secure their southeastern frontier from a hostile but weak House of Savoy. They were quickly victorious but made no further immediate forays into the neighboring states, most of which were owned or dominated by Austria. When the Wars of the Revolution began in earnest, the French government was more worried about its eastern frontier. After initial French successes against coalition invaders into France in 1793–94, the southeast became the object of the French army's first offensive moves.

Napoleon, who had been in and out of prison in direct relation to changes in the revolutionary leadership, had finally proved himself worthy to the new Directory under Paul Barras by suppressing a Paris revolt against Barras's government in July 1794. This later earned him appointment to command of the French Army in Italy. The Austrians allied with Piedmont had kept French armies at bay until 1796, when the Directory decided to make war against Austria with a main effort through the Rhineland and a diversionary offensive into Italy. The plan was to have the Army of the Alps under Count F. E. Kellerman pin down the Piedmontese army while Napoleon marched along the coast road in a flanking move. Napoleon took command of a starving army led by veterans who despised him for his political appointment. The two commanders in the region, Andre Massena and P.F.C. Augereau, each thought he should be in command rather than this boy general. Napoleon's charm and acumen, however, won them over on their first meeting.[32] He convinced his new subordinates that the divided Austrians could be beaten separately; he convinced his troops that victory would lead to full bellies and full pockets. Indeed, it has been supposed one of the reasons for the 1796 offensives was to enhance the French treasury by living off enemy territory and pillaging the enemy's wealth.

Although the French were outnumbered by the Austrians (47,000 to 37,000), the enemy were in two separated columns. Napoleon here first introduced one of his signature strategies, that of the central position. Using the divisional concept from Guibert, he posted a minimal force to the east to hold back one Austrian army while he took the bulk of his forces against the western enemy in mid-April. This resulted in the defeat of Austrian general Michael Colli's army of 25,000 on the 22nd, after which Piedmont agreed to sign an armistice. Napoleon then force marched his men to his eastern detachment and obliged the other Austrian army to retreat. Now with the numerical advantage (and a victory under his belt), he pressed the Austrians hard. In early May he introduced his manoeuvre sur les derrières for the first time.[33] He left a holding force in front of Austrian general J. P. Beaulieu while he led the bulk of his army up the Po River to Piacenza, where he crossed in order to cut the Austrian lines of communication back to their base in Mantua. Again the Austrians retreated without fighting, although they lost their rear guard to Napoleon's advancing troops at Lodi on 10 May; the French were in Milan five days later. The Austrians by the end of the month were back in Trent and Mantua.

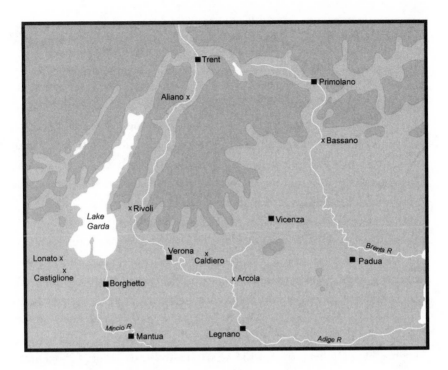

Napoleon soon laid siege to Mantua, a task that would occupy him off and on for almost a year. For the remainder of 1796 Napoleon marched his men across northern Italy in constant attempts to either beat back Austrian thrusts toward Mantua or trying himself to force his way through the Alps. He won victories over a variety of Austrian generals. At Castiglione in early August and Bassano in early September he defeated General Dagobert Wurmser, who did manage to reinforce Mantua though he was captured in its fall in February 1797. From November 1796 through the spring of 1797 Napoleon's main opponent was Field Marshal Josef Alvintzi (or Alvinczy), a decorated veteran of the Seven Years' War, War of the Bavarian Succession, and the invasion attempts to restore the French monarchy.

The Battle of Rivoli

IN JANUARY 1797 THE AUSTRIANS sent Alvintzi to try once again to lift the Mantua siege. The Austrian plan was to approach along three lines of advance to face Napoleon's forces spread in a broad line to cover all possible attacks. The first army of 9,000 marched from Padua toward Augereau's forces near Legnano; the second of 6,000 marched from Vicenza toward Messena's forces at Verona; the third, 28,000 men under Alvintzi, left Trent down the valley of the Adige River toward B.C. Joubert's force at La Corona. Napoleon also had a force to the west under Brigadier General Louis Rey (4,500 men), to the south Brigadier General Jean Lannes (6,800 men) maintained a watch on the Papal States, and Major General Philibert Sourier with 8,500 men maintained the siege at Mantua. The first two Austrian attacks began on 12 January, pressing hard on both Augereau and Massena. When Napoleon learned, however, that Alvintzi had pushed Joubert back to the plain at Rivoli, he decided that he would concentrate the main effort there. He ordered Augereau to cover the eastern flank while he sent Massena north to reinforce Joubert, followed by the cavalry reserve. Rey was also ordered to join. Napoleon rode with his chief of staff, Louis Berthier, to join his army, confident he could win no matter the odds.[34]

Joubert, outnumbered almost three to one, fought a delaying action southward to the village of Rivoli. He arrived there before dawn on 13 January and deployed just to the north of Rivoli along the Trombalore Heights. Flowing from the northeast, the Tasso Brook fronts the heights and swings south, then southwest, west and south of Rivoli. Two miles to the north of the village looms Monte Baldo, snow covered at that time of year. The Adige runs southward through a deep valley to the east, from which Osteria Gorge connects the valley to the plain between town and heights. The Austrians spent the 13th setting up three camps among the Monte Baldo foothills and one to the west at Lumini. Two columns also were approaching down either side of the Adige. Joubert spent the day waiting for orders from Napoleon, which never came. At midnight he decided he could not possibly hold the position and began preparing his troops for withdrawal. Less than two hours later, however, Napoleon arrived himself and stopped him. Quickly looking over the Austrian deployment, Napoleon decided he had plenty of time to place his own arriving forces before Alvintzi would begin his attack. Chandler observes, "It was clear the village of San Marco was one key to the position; its possession by the French would divide the Austrian assault in two, and Bonaparte at once ordered its reoccupation. The battle was obviously going to be a race against time; everything depended on the speed of the reinforcements' arrival to counteract the progressive commitment of the scattered Austrian detachments."[35]

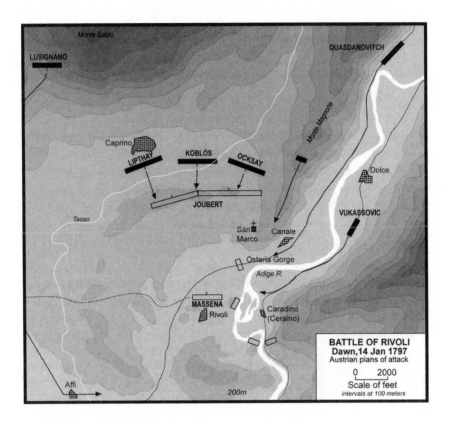

Joubert's men redeployed along the Trombalore Heights, with units occupying the chapel at San Marco (anchoring the right flank) and the Osteria Gorge. They managed to occupy the chapel just before Austrian troops arrived with the same mission. A quick attack in the dark drove the Austrians back along the Monte Magnone ridge. At 6:00 a.m. Massena's division arrived with other detachments, having marched more than twenty miles along ice-covered roads during the night. This gave Napoleon 23,000 men and 40 guns against 28,000 Austrians with 90 guns.[36] As Massena's men arrived one brigade was posted to the west to hold back the Austrian force that would march from Lumini, while the remainder went into reserve in Rivoli. Napoleon decided that in order to buy himself some time he would have to launch a spoiling attack to disrupt Alvintzi's plans. Accordingly, Joubert attacked with his entire force at dawn, but they were forced back. The Austrian right flank, under General Anton Lipthay, broke the attackers before them and moved to outflank the

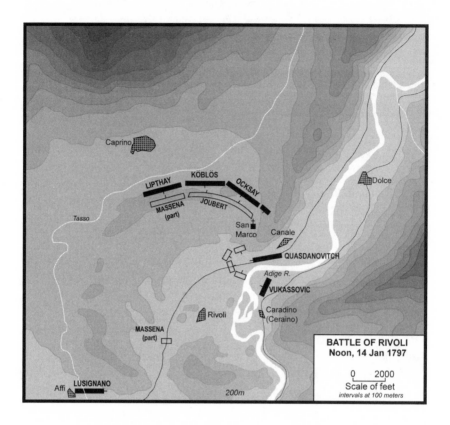

French, but Napoleon led half of Massena's reserve forward just in time to stabilize the line back on the heights.

With the battle now fully engaged along the center, the Austrian forces along the Adige arrived and positioned themselves opposite Osteria Gorge. Philipp von Vukassovic, on the east side of the river, deployed his artillery and began firing on the French holding the gorge. General Quasdanovitch meanwhile positioned his 7,000 men for the assault. He succeeded in pushing the French out of the gorge and sent troops to seize the San Marco chapel, now unoccupied, as its defenders had left to push back the Austrians coming down Monte Magnone. Joubert, his hands already full trying to maintain his position along the heights, had to rush three battalions to the chapel; they arrived just in time to beat the Austrians to it.

By late morning things were looking grim for Napoleon and the French. The Austrian force from Lumini under General Franz Joseph Lusignan had driven back Massena's holding force and was now threatening to place the French in a pincer. Quasdanovitch's forces were massing for an assault up the gorge. Using the last of his reserve from Rivoli to counter Lusignan to the south, Napoleon then thinned Joubert's line facing a waning Austrian attack in order to place more manpower and artillery above the gorge. When Quasdanovitch's men charged up the gorge and onto flat ground, they were met by 15 French cannons pouring grape-shot into the close-packed ranks. This was followed by a counterattack of 500 infantry and cavalry. When the leading unit panicked and ran, the gorge became choked with confused, defeated men.[37] With his right flank now secure, Napoleon sent the remainder of Joubert's and Massena's men on the heights into a general advance against tired Austrian troops who had neither artillery nor cavalry to support them. To complete the turnaround, Lusignan's flanking force was not only stopped by the last of the reserve but was itself struck in the rear by Rey's force, which was just arriving on the scene. Lusignan withdrew up the slopes of Monte Pipolo, where he soon surrendered.

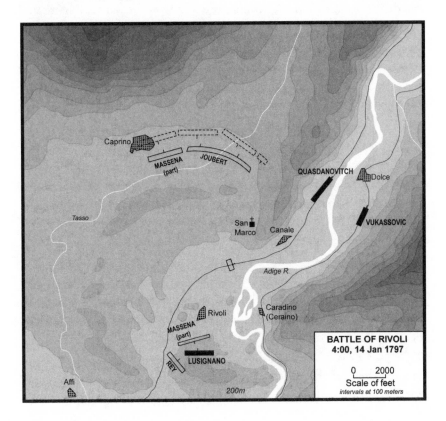

Napoleon was preparing a full pursuit when word came from Augereau in the south that the Austrian columns under Major General Johann Provera that had launched the earlier diversionary attacks were now pushing across the lower Adige toward Mantua. Napoleon was obliged to limit the pursuit to Joubert and Rey while he took Massena's men back to assist Augereau. Even without a massive pursuit effort after Rivoli, the Austrian army collapsed into rout, with half the army either casualties on the battlefield or deserting on the retreat.

The Battle of Rivoli saw Napoleon start with a spoiling attack, after which he spent most of his time on defense, a rarity for him. He had no chance to deliberately surprise his enemy to start the battle, but his rapid movement of troops on the battlefield allowed him to gain limited surprise at Osteria Gorge; further, Rey's timely arrival was something Lusignan could not have anticipated. The key to the victory was Napoleon's ability to concentrate forces in the right place at the right time, giving enough localized victories to demoralize the Austrians before the deliberate attack from Trombalore that won the battle. Pursuit and exploitation occurred, but not to the point of destroying the enemy army, which was always Napoleon's goal.

Rivoli proved to be the final turning point in the French campaign in Italy. Some historians have argued that it ranks among the best of Napoleon's battles and was key to turning the tide against Austria. Not only did it take out almost half of Alvintzi's army, it secured Napoleon's reputation.[38] Provera's force was unable to relieve Mantua, being caught between Augereau and Massena, and was forced to surrender. The garrison in Mantua, after a last attempt to break out, was obliged to give up the city owing to starvation. Napoleon controlled northern Italy and quickly used the breathing space to launch an attack on the Papal States, which resulted in a peace treaty and a large monetary payment that kept the war going. Austria created another army under its best general, Archduke Charles, but Napoleon's moves through the Alps toward Austria (though more bluff than actual threat), along with another push from the French at the Rhine, convinced the Austrians to agree to an armistice that became the Peace of Campo Formio in October 1797.

Napoleon rode his newfound fame to greater political power, convincing the French government to let him try an expedition to Egypt to threaten Britain's ties to India. The expedition proved a disaster, but

Napoleon demonstrated that his propaganda skills equaled or surpassed his military abilities: he arrived in Paris before news of his failure and just in time to take advantage of political turmoil. He not only landed on his feet, but staged a coup in early November 1799, whereupon he took the title of first consul in a new government.

Napoleon then reestablished his military credentials with another victorious campaign over the Austrians in northern Italy, ending with a treaty in February 1801. A treaty with Britain the following year ended the War of the Second Coalition, and he was rewarded with a new constitution, which named him first consul for life. This led to a Senate proclamation naming him emperor of France, followed by his self-coronation in December 1804.

Yet even with this remarkable ascension to power, Napoleon was not satisfied. He decided that in order to achieve his highest ambitions he would have to eliminate Britain, so he began gathering forces at Bolougne in 1805 for a cross-channel invasion.

It was in the first few years of the nineteenth century that Napoleon had time to mold the army into his own model described earlier. Between 1801 and 1805 fighting was irregular, although only the year in the wake of the Treaty of Amiens (March 1802) was there official peace. The army organized and trained at Bolougne came to be called Le Grande Armée, and it came into being as Napoleon was beginning the recreation of empire. At Bolougne the men trained in large-unit exercises and were officially organized into the corps formations. All the lessons of Guibert and Bourcet were coming to fruition.[39]

Politically, 1805 saw alliances coming together. France and Spain signed a treaty in January; England's William Pitt the Younger and Russia's Czar Alexander did so in April. England knew Austrian forces were vital to defeating Napoleon, but two unsuccessful wars had Austria wary of trying for a third. However, Napoleon's 1804 execution of a Bourbon prince involved in an insurrection plot against him raised monarchical ire. The French ruler's growing ambition scared Austria as well. His proclamation of empire had rattled them, and his ensuing consolidation of northern Italy was a direct threat. Austria had been building up its armies for several years. When Napoleon crowned himself the king of Northern Italy in March 1805, this proved to be too much. Austria joined with Britain and Russia to create the Third Coalition in August 1805.[40]

The Austrian minister of war, Field Marshal Archduke Charles (Emperor Francis's brother), had begun the process of reforming the army in 1801, but with irregular results. The light infantry units raised in 1798 for the War of the Second Coalition had recently been disbanded for the old Prussian reason that they could not be controlled. The frontiersmen the Austrians had been using for the purpose, the *grenzers*, were being forced into a regular army discipline that stifled their irregular warfare skills. Additionally, the vast number of ethnic minorities in the polyglot Austrian Empire required that the army be widely dispersed in order to maintain the government's authority and spread the cost of maintenance. Unfortunately, that dispersion meant that mobilization would be slow.[41] England, as usual, provided money rather than manpower, which removed the economic objection to war. Political infighting at the court in Vienna also brought the war party into influence over Emperor Francis; throw in Russian manpower to support the offensives and the next war was under way in late summer.

The Russian army that contributed to the coalition effort was of mixed effectiveness. In the 1790s it had been undergoing erratic reforms under the equally erratic Czar Paul, whose assassination in 1801 brought Alexander to the throne. Although a Russian army had performed well under one of the premier generals of Russian history, Alexander Suvarov, in Italy in 1799, it was for the most part an untested force. As has always been the case with Russia, its vast distances obliged a widely scattered army, which meant training standards were haphazard and coordinated peacetime maneuvers virtually impossible. Nevertheless, the soldiers were solid and at times inspired, when well led.[42] The officers were drawn from the upper classes, as was normal at the time, but some foreigners served as well. At the regimental level, the gentry often started as noncommissioned officers and then moved up, but they were so poorly educated that many were illiterate. They were usually loyal and stubborn, but were not self-motivated.[43] The upper classes also provided officers by purchase or appointment, but although they attended cadet schools they had no training for the staff positions to which they were appointed. The cavalry forces of the Russian army were adequate, but not up to the standard of either Austria or France. There were vast numbers of Cossack light cavalry, but they were relatively effective only in raiding and harassment; additionally, forces stationed to protect the frontiers with the Ottoman

Empire and Sweden limited the numbers that could be committed to a central European war.

Archduke Charles was replaced as Austrian minister of war by General Karl Mack von Lieberich, a member of the war party, who promptly told the emperor the Austrian army was ready for action. Archduke Charles retorted that this was nonsense, but the court swayed the emperor to commit to action against France. Mack proposed an offensive while Napoleon's army was still stationed on the English Channel. Unfortunately for the Austrian army, he also tried to introduce some immediate reforms, though they could not possibly be implemented in the weeks before combat was joined.

Charles took command of some 100,000 men along the Adige in northern Italy, along with his brother John who commanded smaller forces holding the passes through the Tyrol. Mack's force (originally under the command of Archduke Ferdinand), numbering roughly another 75,000, was to march up the Danube toward the French frontier, where they were to be joined by a 55,000-man Russian force under Marshal Mikhail Kutuzov at the city of Ulm. This would be the main thrust of the allied offensive, with Strasbourg as its initial target. In Prussia, a northern army under Russian general Levin Bennigson with some 45,000 men was trying to encourage the reluctant Prussians to join in. Mack predicted it would take Napoleon sixty-nine days to move his army from the Channel to the frontier, five days longer than it would take Kutuzov to join him. Had the French army been as slow as the Austrians and Russians, he may well have been correct.

It was in this transition from the English Channel to the frontier that the training and reorganization of the French army began to be illustrated. Napoleon, correctly predicting Ulm (in southern Bavaria) as the Austrian destination, knew he was closer to the city than were the Russians. All he had to do was move faster than the Russians and defeat Mack alone at Ulm; once that was accomplished, he could move toward Vienna to take care of Kutuzov. Everything depended on speed, and that was Napoleon's watchword.[44] The strategy of marching separately and fighting united meant that 200,000 men in seven corps had to move along parallel routes at similarly high speeds—an ambitious advance that would test Napoleon's newly implemented tactics and training.

Meanwhile, Marshal Massena in Italy would keep Archduke Charles busy. As Ulm was on something of a traditional invasion route, Napoleon obliged Mack's assumptions by sending his cavalry to the Black Forest, the traditional eastbound invasion course. While they held Mack's attention, Napoleon and his army crossed the Rhine between 27 September and 3 October. Mack's force (minus small garrisons scattered through Bavaria) held Ulm and awaited Russian reinforcement. He was therefore shocked when he learned that the troops to his east were French, not those of his allies. Before it was too late, Archduke Ferdinand managed to escape the city with some cavalry. As the French corps arrived in line, each one moved further east and then south, encircling Mack who tried desperately to break out. Every probe met French troops. Hopelessly outnumbered and outmaneuvered, Mack was obliged to surrender his 24,000 men and 80 pieces of artillery on 20 October.[45]

Napoleon's victory at Ulm was one of the most brilliant and complete of all time, one that would have made Sun Tzu take notice. As Weigley observes, "Napoleon did not worship battle. He made battle serve him; he did not seek battle for its own sake. . . . Napoleon could be a strategist of finesse as well as a strategist of overpoweringly forceful blows."[46] Although not without casualties, the victory was more one of maneuver than combat, though a number of small battles took place as each arriving corps placed itself farther and farther around Mack's position until he was surrounded. Between the skirmishes, the encirclement, and the pursuit the Austrians suffered some 60,000 casualties to no more than 2,000 Frenchmen.[47] This victory was quickly followed up by the capture of Munich a few days later and the news from northern Italy that Massena had inflicted a defeat on Archduke Charles, immobilizing his forces for a time. This news was dampened somewhat, of course, by that of the French navy's virtual destruction at the Battle of Trafalgar.

Actually, the defeat at Trafalgar was the beginning of a series of incidents that had the emperor screaming at his subordinates. The Russian army under Kutuzov began withdrawing eastward immediately upon hearing the news from Ulm. Napoleon sent his marshals in pursuit, but by doing so lost the ever-important close communication needed to make his style of warfare effective. First, assuming Kutuzov would stand before Vienna, Napoleon sent Joachim Murat and Jean Lannes dashing for the city. When Kutuzov instead retreated northeast in order to link up with other Russian forces, Murat and Lannes let him go in favor of being the first to the Austrian capital. They managed to bluff their way into capturing a key bridge across the Danube, but they failed to remember Napoleon's dictum that the center of gravity was the enemy army, not a physical location. Vienna meant nothing to Napoleon except as a source of supply. Other marshals also moved too slowly in the pursuit; the one force that kept contact, E.A.C.J. Mortier's 8th Corps, was alone and out of touch with the others and fell victim to an ambush by Kutuzov. All this incompetence was made worse by the fact that the army was exhausted to the point of collapse by the marching and fighting. Supplies had not been provided along the way, and the resultant looting of the local population did nothing to make for a welcoming populace. Further, one of the corps had passed through the Prussian province of Anspach, potentially provoking Frederick William III into succumbing to Russian and Austrian pleas to join the coalition. Sensing the potential for disaster, Napoleon began establishing supply dumps to assist his advance or, if necessary, a withdrawal.[48]

The Battle of Austerlitz

KUTUZOV'S RETREAT TOOK THE RUSSIANS closer to their reinforcements while stretching Napoleon's lines of communication almost to the breaking point. On 19 November Kutuzov, having passed through the Moravian frontier city of Brunn (Brno), reached Olmutz and met the Russian 2nd Army and Czar Alexander. The Imperial Guard arrived soon thereafter, as did Austrian emperor Francis with some 35,000 to add to the Russians, bringing their total up to 89,000. Things now seemed to be going the allies' way: they outnumbered the forces Napoleon could gather into the area; the Prussians were seriously considering joining in and launching an offensive over the Rhine; and Archduke Charles and his brother John had broken away from Massena and were marching out of Italy with another 80,000 men. With both Czar Alexander and Emperor Francis on hand, however, political ends began to weigh more heavily than military realities. Although Kutuzov was technically in command, real orders now came from the czar, "whose military experience qualified him to drill a battalion on the parade ground."[49] Kutuzov's recommendation, along with that of Emperor Francis, was to keep withdrawing and so pull Napoleon even farther from his supplies and reserves. Delay would only strengthen the allied armies with new reinforcements while obliging the French to pursue them over territory empty of supply. A little patience, a Prussian alliance, and the arrival of Archdukes Charles and John, and a half million men could be brought to bear.

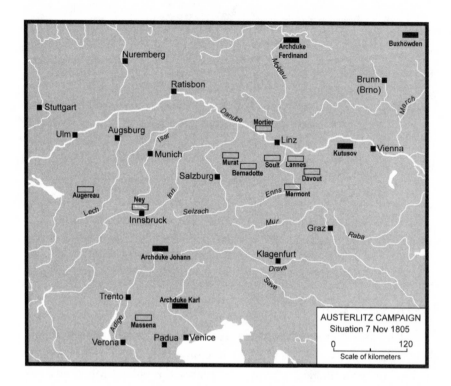

AUSTERLITZ CAMPAIGN
Situation 7 Nov 1805

0   120
Scale of kilometers

In the final days of November 1805 Napoleon showed his mastery in understanding the minds of his opponents. He had long tried to ally himself with Alexander, and so must have known the czar's personality and weaknesses well. Aware that Olmutz could not supply the increasing number of troops there, Napoleon knew that the allies would have to move soon. First, he played into the czar's correct assumptions that the French were hopelessly overextended. Supplies captured at Ulm, Vienna, and towns along the way were proving insufficient to maintain the army for much longer. This and the approaching winter weather affected the French troops' morale as they continued to march deeper into enemy territory. Straggling became a major problem and those in the ranks began to despair.[50] When Emperor Francis offered an armistice on the 27th, Napoleon quickly sent an envoy with his response, but primarily to gauge the temper of the enemy commanders and spread the story of dissension within the French ranks. All this enticed Alexander to push his luck. In his biography of Napoleon, Frank McLynn writes, "Pursuing his career as a great actor, the Emperor agreed to an interview with the

Russian emissary Count Dolgourouki (29 November) in which he feigned confusion, uncertainty and an ill-disguised fear. So brilliantly was he toying with the enemy and so confident of his own mastery that he had actually chosen his battleground on 21 November."[51] That battleground was in front of the town of Austerlitz, some dozen miles east of Brunn.

Napoleon's second move was to take some of his 53,000 men from Brunn to occupy Austerlitz temporarily, and then withdraw them as if in a hurry. This would not only give the allies the town but the high ground just outside it to the west, the Pratzen Heights. Abandoning high ground to occupy a position just below it seemed the height of military stupidity, just what the eager Czar Alexander would assume. At the same time, Napoleon strengthened a hilltop just to the north of the Heights and deployed the remainder of his army behind a small stream, the Goldbach, running north-south parallel to the Heights. This would plainly illustrate his inferior numbers and further bait the allies. What his enemies didn't realize, however, was that he had couriers riding for Vienna to order L.N. Davout to bring his corps at top speed; others rode to Bohemia with the same orders for Jean-Baptiste Bernadotte and his corps. Bernadotte's men arrived on the afternoon of 1 December; Davout's men marched sixty miles in seventy hours to arrive early in the morning of 2 December, the day of battle. French strength reached 73,000 men.

In spite of his best planning, however, Napoleon was surprised that the Austro-Russian army moved as quickly as it did. Thus, some of the rapid withdrawal was not stage-managed. As the allied army came onto the battlefield from Olmutz to the northwest, they saw a steep hill alongside the road to Brunn rising some 100 feet over the surrounding area. This the French called the Santon, after a similar hill from their Egyptian campaign. Napoleon directed Marshal Lannes to construct strong defenses and site artillery here. It was key to Napoleon's plan, and also gave the allies the impression that he was planning a defensive battle on this northern end of the Pratzen plateau. As the allies debouched onto the plain to look down on the Goldbach, they saw a handful of small settlements along the stream and some frozen ponds off to the south. Thus, the terrain features narrowed the front on which the allies would have to operate.

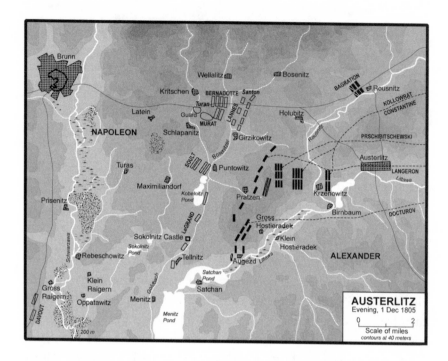

The allies' plan was to give the impression of attacking the northern position while sending roughly half their force to the south with the intention of both cutting off the lines of communication from Vienna and rolling up the French army in a wide, sweeping flanking movement. Indeed, Napoleon had deployed only minimal forces at the southern end of his line in order to convince the allies of the wisdom of their plan. Marshal Lannes was on the left, to cover the road to Brunn and deliver a supporting attack against Prince Peter Bagration. Davout was on the right, reinforced by one division from Marshal Nicholas Jean Soult's corps, to confront the Russian main effort. Soult, located in the center, was to launch the main attack north of Pratzen, supported by Bernadotte, while Murat and the Guard were in reserve, prepared to exploit success either on the left or in the center.[52]

At about 1:00 a.m. on December 2, the commanders of the various allied columns were briefed on the plan of attack by its designer, Austrian chief of staff Franz von Weyrother. The meeting proved almost useless. Weyrother had the confidence of Czar Alexander, but almost no one else. Russian officers paid him little attention as they had no respect for the Austrian army in general. Austrian officers supported the plan without questioning any of its strengths or weaknesses, as they were a minority in the overall force and needed solidarity in the face of Russian contempt. They might have done better to evaluate it, however; Weyrother's plan was based entirely on Napoleon's apparent weakness, and it had no contingency for any French countermoves. It was overly complicated, calling for multiple moves in the darkness across too narrow a front for proper deployment. The only officer to recognize this, grasping the big picture and wiser methods, was Kutuzov, but he was out of favor and ignored. The allies suffered from the twin concepts of fear and honor: once they decided on battle, they were deceived into accepting it on the worst possible terms by their own pride.[53] To further harm the attack, the orders in German had to be translated into Russian for distribution to the seven columns involved and were not delivered to everyone before the operation was scheduled to begin.

On the French side the divisions were placed and ready. Napoleon had dinner with his marshals on a hill called the Turlan just to the west of the Santon position. Gunfire far to the south alerted him to the earliest allied movements, about midnight. He rode out for inspection, found the probes farther south than he had anticipated, at Tellnitz, and alerted both Soult and Davout as to the likely new allied axis of advance. C. J. Legrand's force of 6,000 would take the initial brunt of the massive allied assault; how long his troops could use the rough ground, woods, streams, and villages to slow the enemy advance would determine the success of Napoleon's plan. Strong points existed at Tellnitz and Sokolnitz, but overall the southern section of the French line was the better part of two miles wide. Legrand was lucky to have obstacles along his front that aided in the defense: a vineyard on a reverse slope, a ditch, garden walls, and houses. Moreover, the narrow space between the Goldbach Stream and the Satchan Pond offered limited frontage to the attackers.[54] Nevertheless, even if Davout's men arrived in time to assist, the defenders would still number less than 13,000 against perhaps four times that many attacking them.

At 7:00 the first allied units began their advance. The Goldbach valley was shrouded in fog, completely hiding the French deployment. The first contact took place at Tellnitz an hour later, and French light infantry quickly bloodied the Russians. A back-and-forth battle for the village ensued, with both sides holding it in turn as each received reinforcement. By 9:30 the Russians finally took the village for good and proceeded to cross the Goldbach. The support columns were slow to arrive, and the commanders had been ordered to advance together, forcing them to wait. The allied attack on

Sokolnitz followed much the same pattern, though it started an hour later owing to the Austrian cavalry repositioning themselves from the southern to the northern end of the Heights by riding across the front of the infantry columns. Still, Davout's men arriving on the field aided in the defense of both positions until forced back by overwhelming numbers. Thus, as the morning progressed, the Russians made fairly steady progress but the French remained well organized in their fighting withdrawal.[55]

Although the low ground was still shrouded in fog, the Pratzen Heights were early open to view from Napoleon's command post on the Zuran, a hill southeast of Kritschen. As the sun came up and burned away the last of the mists along the Heights, Napoleon could see the masses of enemy troops pouring forward.[56] Turning to Marshal Soult, Napoleon asked how quickly his men could climb to Pratzen. When he was told it would take twenty minutes, Napoleon announced that they would wait another quarter of an hour. According to McLynn, "Napoleon's military genius was never more evident. By intuition he knew the exact equilibrium point at which the Pratzen would be sufficiently clear of allied troops to make Soult's task easy, but not yet so denuded that reinforcements from the heights were likely to overwhelm the hard-pressed French right."[57]

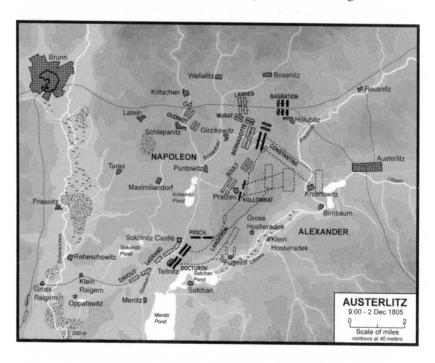

AUSTERLITZ
9:00 - 2 Dec 1805
0   2
Scale of miles
contours at 40 meters

The northernmost allied column to be committed to the southern attack was the last to move, as it had the shortest distance to march. It was made up mostly of weakened Russian battalions that had marched all the way to the Inn River to join Mack at Ulm before turning around and marching all the way back to Olmutz, and then back yet again to Austerlitz. The rest of the column was made up of a mixture of Austrian regulars and reservists with little training and no experience. They had just begun their march toward Sokolnitz when Soult's 17,000 men emerged from the mist and caught them full in their extended flank. Such an attack would test even the best-trained soldiers, so it is a testament to the Russian and Austrian troops that they managed to hold the village of Pratzen for three hours before finally being forced to abandon the battlefield.[58]

Kutuzov was with the two emperors when the French emerged out of the fog. Alexander immediately lost all the bravado with which he had been commanding up to this point, while his old general reacted quickly by calling up the Russian Imperial Guard from its reserve position. The first counterattack came at 10:30; it was beaten back. The second, led by the Guard cavalry, broke through the French position, but Napoleon had his own Guards handy and they recovered the situation. To the north,

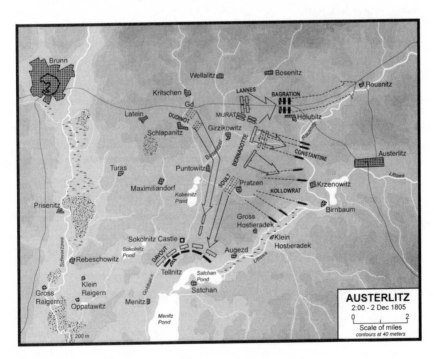

Murat led the bulk of the French cavalry onto the field and engaged Bagration's cavalry force, some 10,000 horsemen in a massive melee. Lannes's infantry kept up the pressure, and Bagration began to withdraw eastward up the same road he had advanced down that morning. Between Lannes to the north and Soult to the south marched Bernadotte's corps as the allied army was split in two. Bernadotte's men pressed forward, while Soult's men were directed to the south to strike the allied left wing from the rear, hammering them onto Davout and Legrand's anvil. By midafternoon French artillery was pounding the enemy down the heights. The only possible route for their escape was across the frozen Satchen Pond. Hundreds fled across it, only to be drowned as French cannon fire broke the ice. From that point the retreat became a rout.[59]

By 5:00 on the afternoon of 2 December it was all over. Bagration alone in the allied army had managed to withdraw in good order. The Austrians managed to regroup east of Austerlitz and withdraw into Hungary, escaping the French pursuit, which mistakenly went up the road toward Olmutz. The Russians lost some 11,000 killed and wounded, the Austrians another 4,000. The allied total for prisoners was a further 12,000. The French losses were no more than 2,000 killed and almost 7,000 wounded, with just under 600 taken prisoner.

The following day, Emperor Francis sent a representative to Napoleon asking for an armistice and a meeting; the conference led to the Peace of Pressburg, signed just after Christmas. Alexander led the remains of his army through Poland back to Russia. McLynn records a message he sent to the French force following along behind him: "Tell your master that I am going away. Tell him that he performed miracles yesterday; that the battle has increased my admiration for him; that he is a man predestined by Heaven; that it will require a hundred years for my army to equal his."[60]

Masterful as Napoleon was on the offensive, Austerlitz showed him to be a master when he had to stand his ground. He prepared his defense during the days he had while waiting for the allies to appear. Indeed, had the allies sped their advance, they could have caught him without reinforcement and probably gained a victory. Napoleon's use of terrain was the key to the entire battle: the low ground effectively hid his troops on the morning of the attack; the natural and man-made characteristics of the villages along the Goldbach made his right wing successful; the fortification of the Santon anchored his north flank and made it virtually impenetrable. His security was excellent, keeping his numbers and dispositions secret from his enemy, except for what he wanted them to see; at the same time, his envoys supposedly discussing peace were in fact gaining accurate views of allied numbers and plans. The stout defense of the southern Goldbach completely disrupted the enemy plans and negated their superior numbers. This, plus Lannes's defense of the Olmotz-Brunn road, focused the allied forces on the flanks and opened their center for the French counterstroke. Napoleon's ability to virtually direct the enemy forces into his own plans allowed him to mass his key striking force and keep it hidden until the last moment, at which point it concentrated on the weakest section of the allied position. His flexibility was shown by his placement of forces: had the allied attack in the south succeeded, Soult's force as well as the Imperial Guard could have pivoted to face the threat. Not needing the reinforcement, Napoleon was able to pick the perfect time for Soult's advance as well as when to commit elements of the Guard to counter Kutuzov's commitment of the allied reserves.

Chandler sums up the offensive-defensive nature of the victory: "A last lesson that Austerlitz teaches us is that the counterattack or tactical offensive is the true key to defense. Strategically Napoleon was undoubtedly on the defensive, but this did not dissuade him from reassuming the tactical initiative all along the battleline (once the trap was sprung), thus snatching overwhelming victory from the jaws of apparent defeat."[61]

PEACE WAS SHORT-LIVED. Although the Prussians wavered about joining the Austro-Russian coalition, they received news of Austerlitz before they acted. The impressive French showing cooled their ardor temporarily, but Napoleon's occupation of much of Germany upset the Prussian royal family, especially Queen Louisa, who had a particular hatred of Napoleon. The French emperor also proceeded to dismantle the Holy Roman Empire and replace it with the Confederation of the Rhine, under his protection and encompassing most Germanic states, including Hanover. Napoleon had offered Hanover to Prussia in exchange for the small provinces of Cleves, Berg, and Neufchatel; additionally, Bavaria would trade Ansbach for part of Bayreuth. All these territorial changes would serve two purposes for France: they would consolidate Napoleon's holdings in central Europe and alienate Great Britain from a potential ally.[62]

Indeed, Prussia took control of Hanover but the queen and the war party in Prussia continued to exert pressure on King Frederick William to ally with Russia and go to war. When the Russians reported that Napoleon was offering to return Hanover to Britain, in August the Prussian king rallied his nerve and sent an ultimatum to Napoleon, demanding he withdraw all his forces from German territory. Napoleon's reply came in the form of an invasion.[63] Long before any Russian troops could conceivably arrive to assist, French troops were into Saxony and aimed at Berlin. The Prussian army found itself stumbling into two battles, at Jena and Auerstadt in mid-October, which resulted in two stunning defeats at the hands of Napoleon (at Jena) and Davout (at Auerstadt). On the 24th Napoleon was in Berlin and his cavalry officers were sharpening their swords on the steps of the French Embassy.

Frederick William, however, managed to retreat with some troops to the east, where he joined with advancing Russian forces in Poland. Napoleon led his army to Warsaw and spread the gospel of nationalism, which the Poles were not terribly excited to hear. Napoleon nevertheless gathered together some locally raised troops and supplies, and chased the Russo-Prussian force through Poland in the dead of winter. The two armies finally clashed at Eylau on 7 February 1807 and fought one of the era's bloodiest battles. Aided by a strong defensive position and bitter winter weather, the Russians fought the French to a standstill. Had their commander not lost his nerve and withdrawn in the night, he might have been able to claim a victory over the hard-pressed French.[64]

If Ulm, Austerlitz, and Jena and Auerstadt were the pinnacle of Napoleon's military accomplishments, Eylau marked the beginning of his long slide toward ultimate defeat. Bloodied by the Russians and accomplishing no more than a draw, Napoleon showed himself to be beatable. Although his opponents took note, no country immediately moved to follow up on what may have been a shift of momentum. Instead, the traditional Continental powers stayed passive, and Napoleon redeemed his reputation with a major victory over the Russians at Friedland four months after Eylau. With the Russians chastened and a peace treaty with them in hand, Napoleon turned his attention to Italy and then to Spain, where his attempt to invade Portugal and deny the British a base of operations was provoking a Spanish popular revolt. Napoleon spent much of 1808 in Spain trying to restore order for the new king, his brother Joseph. A resurgent Austria, however, sent him back to France in early 1809 to suppress yet another challenge to his rule.

Napoleon's break-up of the Holy Roman Empire cost Emperor Francis II not only his title (he became Francis I, emperor of Austria-Hungary) but also territory—neither of which made for a passive rival. In the wake of these embarrassments, Archduke Charles rose to favor once again in Vienna and was given the job of reforming the army. Although he reached his position of field marshal because of his birth, he was indeed a talented commander with a number of victories against French forces in the Low Countries and Italy. He had spoken against the war in 1805, a position that was proven justified and resulted in renewed confidence in his judgment in 1806. Dedicated as Charles was to reform, however, he was still not the visionary that Napoleon was. He reorganized the army on the combined arms *corps d'armee* system, and was able to expand it to 279,000 men, primarily by instituting an expanded Landwehr (national guard) for garrison and replacements, as they could not be brought up to traditional training standards without the long-service commitment. The corps system did not speed the army's marches, however, as Charles kept the same supply system in place, in order to not alienate the population through which they passed. He also attempted to simplify the field manuals and make military service somewhat more attractive by shortening enlistments and reducing the abusive discipline. Difficult as it was to make a multinational force loyal to a single entity, Charles focused on creating regimental elan in order to maintain morale and discipline.[65]

Unfortunately, the revised manual was in some ways more complicated, and the multinational nature of the Austro-Hungarian army made any sort of motivation short of intense discipline limited in its effectiveness. The light infantry and light cavalry talents of some of the ethnic minorities, such as the Croatian Pandours of the Silesian and Seven Years' Wars, were still viewed as untrustworthy by the bulk of the Austrian officer corps. The primary change for the infantry was experimenting with the use of the third line as skirmishers, but it was not widely employed. For the cavalry the main problem was a dearth of mounts. Charles had learned from the French, particularly in the nature of artillery deployment, which he reorganized into an independent arm as in the French army. Artillery had traditionally been an Austrian strong point, and he determined to make it so again.[66]

As the Austrians were improving, the French army was deteriorating. Although forces garrisoned Italy and Germany in relatively strong numbers, the bulk of the army's focus was the campaign in the Iberian Peninsula. Wide commitments coupled with increasing casualties meant Napoleon had to strain for manpower, which he found by calling up draftees earlier than scheduled and by relying on allied forces. Napoleon's preparations gave him 170,000 troops in southern Germany, with 50,000 of the German troops from the Confederation of the Rhine. However, almost half of his growing army were recent conscripts.[67] In order to give the recruits more confidence, since long-term training was now impractical, artillery firepower was increased. Napoleon also began to depend more on mass than maneuver: although he would never abandon the concept of speed in the attack, he became less subtle in his views, aiming for mass at the weak point early in the battle, eschewing his traditional maneuvering. This gave the new troops more confidence but limited flexibility.[68]

The commander in Germany was Chief of Staff Marshal Louis-Alexandre Berthier, a man much better at administration than command. Napoleon was relying not only on client states for men and materiel but also on Czar Alexander to assist him if the Austrians got out of hand. After the Battle of Freidland in 1807 the Russians had signed the Peace of Tilsit, which officially made them allies of France. Alexander, however, had let the Austrians know that he would not intervene, regardless of his promises to Napoleon. One of the primary questions was whether the confederation troops would rally to their new master who had freed them from Austria, or fight him in order to gain independence from any outsider. Archduke Charles was hoping for the latter.

The Battle of Wagram

THE NEWLY REORGANIZED AUSTRIAN ARMY consisted of eleven corps. One was detailed to Poland to suppress any action by the pro-French regime there. Two were sent to Italy to keep busy Napoleon's stepson, Eugene, and Franco-Italian forces poised to march through Dalmatia. The remaining eight corps were to invade Bavaria in order to provoke a war of liberation. The original plan called for six corps to march from Bohemia into Bavaria while the remaining two corps marched parallel, south of the

Danube. Napoleon soon revised his own plan, however, to send the bulk of his army up the Danube on the south bank in order to better screen any possible French move toward Vienna.

The invasion started on 9 April 1809, rather sooner than Napoleon thought the Austrians could take the field. He was still in Paris when the semaphore system alerted him to the attack. Sending messages ahead to Berthier, Napoleon was not far behind. Berthier was overwhelmed and clearly anxious to have his emperor take charge when he arrived on the 17th at Donauwörth. Napoleon immediately began moving his corps where needed to stop the Austrians and then begin pushing them back. Most of the French thrust was south of the Danube, finally pushing Charles to Ratisbon (Regensburg). The Austrian rear guard held the French at bay long enough for Charles to evacuate most of his troops to the north bank of the Danube and destroy the bridges behind him. Although Napoleon later claimed to be proud of winning his next five engagements between Ratisbon and the Iser River, they were not conclusive; Charles managed to escape with the bulk of his forces intact.[69] He withdrew into Bohemia, leaving the path to Vienna virtually unobstructed. Napoleon chased a force under General Johan Hiller to the city and entered on 10 May, but the Austrians had abandoned the city (except for the citadel) and retreated across the Danube, again destroying the bridges behind them.

Napoleon's army was now reduced to 82,000, while the Austrians across the river had 115,000. Napoleon refused to wait for more men to arrive. He had been slowed somewhat in his advance by spring rains, which now were flooding the Danube—something for which he was unprepared, having fought his previous campaigns here later in the year. While he considered what materials were necessary to cross the river, Hiller joined with Archduke Charles, who had arrived from Bohemia. Napoleon hoped to cross the river quickly and prevent the enemy from joining forces, but the destroyed bridges kept him from doing so. At this point, the flooded Danube was as much as 2,000 yards wide, so gaining sufficient material to build new bridges took four days.[70] Just to the east of Vienna the Danube is filled with a multitude of islands, the largest of which is Lobau. Marshal Davout's corps managed to build pontoon bridges to a few small islands from the south bank of the Danube over to Lobau, from which a fairly narrow strait from the north bank of the island led to a landing between the villages of Aspern (to the west) and Essling about two miles to the east.

Across this single bridge Napoleon pushed 30,000 men on 21 May, followed by another 25,000 the following day. The Austrians had them cornered with 100,000 men. Napoleon's orders to his men were uncharacteristically vague: cross the river and engage the enemy. Seizure and fortification of the two villages were vital to securing a bridgehead, but he gave no such directives. Dodge notes, "At other battles—Austerlitz, Jena, Friedland—he had been more careful. Or had he, as many contemporaries allege, been spoiled by success so far as to believe that he could not fail in any undertaking, that no enemy could stand against him, whether he took proper precautions or not?"[71] The two marshals in combat were Lannes at Essling and Massena at Aspern; though they were outnumbered almost two to one and outgunned three to two, the French at times seemed on the verge of victory in a battle that raged back and forth for two days with both villages changing hands multiple times.

Ultimately, Austrian stubbornness and the flooded Danube made the difference. Not only did rising waters weaken and at times break the pontoon bridge, but the Austrians sent massive logs and ultimately a burning, floating flour mill that broke the bridge for good just as reinforcements were preparing to cross and a major French assault on the Austrian center showed signs of possible success. Fatigued and low on ammunition, the French could not prevail, and Napoleon ordered a withdrawal to Lobau Island at dusk on the 22nd. Casualties on both sides numbered more than 20,000 (including Marshal Lannes, dead of wounds), but the Austrians claimed a victory by bloodying Napoleon's nose.

Napoleon withdrew into seclusion in Schönbrunn Palace for a day and a half, before emerging with renewed vigor. He needed a victory to erase the possible effects of Aspern-Essling, just as Friedland had negated the setback at Eylau. One thing certainly favored him in the wake of the battle: he still owned Vienna and Lobau Island. He could thus maintain his army as more men arrived through the month of June, and he could establish a strong base on the island and prepare multiple bridges for a return match. He also learned that the Austrian expeditions to Italy and Poland had both met with failure, and he could draw on Eugene's forces to cover his right flank. Viceroy Eugene's force had defeated Archduke John at Raab (to the southeast, halfway to Budapest) in mid-June, slowing an already slow Austrian reinforcement. Napoleon also benefited from

Charles's inactivity, as the archduke's primary goal was to use his success and his improved strategic position to enter negotiations on favorable terms. Unfortunately, that was unacceptable to his brother and the war faction in the government, and their rejection of his plans seems to have taken a heavy psychological toll. Charles withdrew into himself for several weeks, in spite of the fact that he commanded a force currently larger and more strongly positioned than the French.[72] After all these years too many Austrians still seemed to be underestimating Napoleon.

By the end of June 1809, Charles had less than 150,000 troops, which included the untrained militia recruits, as Emperor Francis kept insisting that Charles detach men to aid the failing Polish expedition. Additionally, Austrian cavalry and artillery units were lacking sufficient horses. The Austrians did just about everything they could to waste their success in May. Napoleon, on the other hand, had been reinforced to almost 190,000 men, and he had been busy occupying a number of other islands near Lobau. From here he began both openly and secretly to build bridges in order to keep the Austrians guessing as to where a crossing might take place. Weigley writes, "In fact, he decided that there was not much chance to engender further mystification or to achieve any real measure of surprise in crossing his big army, so on the night of 3–4 July he began pulling additional troops into Lobau. On the stormy night of July 5 Massena's IV Corps floated another pontoon bridge and began filing out of Lobau, not directly into the old Aspern bridgehead, where Charles expected the French, but farther east."[73]

Although Charles had a corps stretched from Aspern–Essling–Gross Enzersdorf dug in facing the river, the bulk of the army was drawn up in a strong defensive position well away from the Danube. Charles deployed on the Russbach Plateau to the northeast of Aspern and Essling. The plateau's rectangular situation presented a front parallel to the Danube; along its northwestern and southwestern edges ran a stream called the Russbach. The banks of the stream were both steep and tree lined, presenting a natural obstacle to any assault. Further, the approach to the stream from the west consisted of some 100 yards of boggy ground. On the opposite western bank was a cliff, 30–60 feet in height, known as the Wagram; on its western corner stood the village of Deutsch-Wagram. The ground further west rose gently toward the major height on the battle-field, the Bisamberg, which anchored the Austrian right.[74] Three corps were on the escarpment overlooking the stream and the large Marchfeld plain. Two more corps were behind and to the west of the Bisamberg, and a cavalry corps stretched out over the three miles between the two. Nothing was there to stop any French river crossing away from Aspern.

The crossing began after dark on the night of 4-5 July and proceeded without a hitch. The feint near Aspern, coupled with the thunderstorm that struck late in the afternoon, made for a completely unopposed operation. The French engineers had outdone themselves in preparation, not only constructing numerous bridges for quick deployment but also driving piles into the Danube riverbed to stop any floating bridge busters like the ones that had ruined the operation in May. Three corps under Massena, Oudinot, and Davout were deploying for battle by dawn on the 5th. In his work on Napoleon's decline, Alistair Horne describes the operation: "To have moved the best part of 100,000 men in the dark, across two sets of pontoon bridges . . . in close proximity to a supposedly vigilant enemy, all with virtually no loss of life, was a feat that would have been difficult to rival even in the Second World War, with all its modern mechanization and communications. It showed Napoleon, his commanders and above all General Bertrand and his Corps of Engineers at their very best."[75]

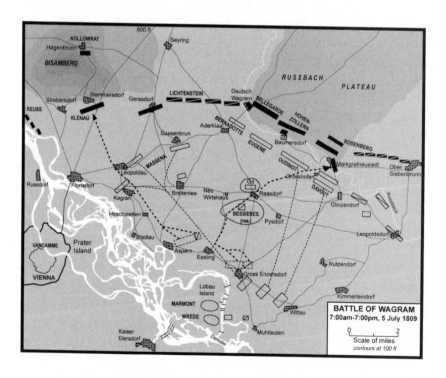

The men crossed due east from Lobau to the road running south-east from Gross Enzersdorf, the anchor of the Austrian forward position's left flank. With these three corps deployed by noon and more troops crossing behind them, Napoleon set the attack into motion. Massena struck the Gross Enzersdorf and immediately began pushing the Austrians toward the Bisamberg. Oudinot and Davout made for the Russbach to face the far left of the main Austrian line; Eugene and Bernadotte followed them and deployed to their left, four French corps facing three Austrian corps across the Russbach. J. B. Bessiers established a reserve in the center near Raasdorf. By late afternoon on the 5th little fighting had taken place and the French had deployed far forward. Massena's corps stretched more than two miles from the Danube to Sussenbrun, facing Marshals Johann von Klenau and John Charles Kollowrat in front of the Bisamberg. Charles assumed that the deployment phase was sufficient for the day's activities, but Napoleon was never one to waste daylight. At 7:00 he ordered his men forward in a probing attack, as he could not determine the strength of the Austrians on the Wagram heights. He sent his four corps forward toward the Russbach along the Deutsch Wagram–Markgrafneusiedl line.[76] Although the French made some initial gains, the attack was too uncoordinated. Further, allied Italian and Saxon troops, both dressed in white uniforms, exchanged fire while mistaking each other for Austrians. At dark both sides settled in, but the French could count their rapid advance across the Marchfeld to be a major success.

Napoleon's next move was to start one of his traditional attacks sur les derrières. With Eugene and Bernadotte holding the Austrians around the village of Deutsche Wagram, Oudinot would press forward while Davout would swing around the Austrian left at Markgrafneusiedl, gain the plateau, and begin rolling up the Austrians' flank. Once they began to break, then Jacques MacDonald would lead elements of Eugene's Army of Italy to the village of Wagram to break the Austrian center. Not knowing just where Archduke John's 13,000-man force might be, Napoleon positioned light cavalry forces to the east to serve as both an advance warning and a bar to John's troops should they appear. In order to cover MacDonald's flank, Massena was ordered to send a division to the rear to cover the Aspern River crossing while moving the rest of his force to the right, concentrating between Aderklaa and Sussenbrunn. Napoleon's object was not to separate the two wings of the army in front of him, but to drive between Charles's army and John's.

After weeks of inactivity, Charles wasted no time preparing a counter to the French advance. He assured his brother the emperor, stationed on the Bisamberg, that all was going according to plan. Little did Napoleon know that his repositioning of forces was playing directly into the Austrian plan. Knowing that the weakest point of his line was the center, held only by reserve cavalry, Charles wanted to bring his forces together with an advance along his entire line. He had to attack first, join his forces in the center, and force the French back into a tight fishhook formation in which they would be unable to maneuver.[77] From the Bisamberg, Klenau was to advance straight ahead parallel to the Danube with the goal of securing the bridges and threatening the French left flank and rear. Kollowrat would parallel him with an attack on Süssenbrunn while Prince John Lichtenstein would lead the grenadiers and cavalry in an attack on Aderklaa, the pivot point of the French position. Austrian artillery on the plateau would pound the French center while Charles led H.J.J. Bellegarde's corps forward on Aderklaa from the northeast. Karl Rosenberg would strike Davout's flank, aiming for a double envelopment. Clemens Hohenzollern would remain on the high ground in reserve.

Charles had a good plan but for two problems. First, he expected his brother John to arrive in the nick of time to finish off the French with an attack on their right rear; John, however, was too far away to be of any assistance, though neither Charles nor Napoleon knew his position. Second, the Austrian army stretched over an eleven-mile front, making communication and coordination difficult, especially in the dark or in the midst of the smoke-enshrouded battlefield after the sun came up. Napoleon therefore had the advantage of manpower and interior lines.

As dawn was about to break at 4:00, Rosenberg began the second day's fighting. He advanced on Davout out of Markgrafneusiedl and caught the French by surprise. Upon hearing the gunfire, Napoleon assumed Archduke John had arrived. He gathered the Guard and marched to Davout's support, only to find the talented marshal had stopped the Austrian attack and begun his advance as originally ordered. Relieved to learn that the situation was in hand, he was then alerted to the Austrian advance in the center. Here all could have collapsed: Bernadotte had abandoned

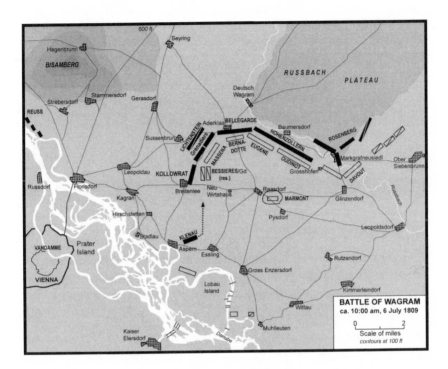

Aderklaa without orders in order to facilitate the link between Massena on his left and Eugene on his right. He also removed his men from the artillery fire coming from the heights. Napoleon ordered Bernadotte and Massena to retake the village at all costs. They did, but Charles led a counterattack that drove Bernadotte's Saxons into a panic. Bernadotte, who the evening before had loudly criticized Napoleon's battle plan, found himself relieved of his command in the middle of the battle.

By 9:00 Aderklaa was back in French hands, but just then Napoleon learned that the Austrians had begun their advance along the Danube. The Austrian 3rd and 6th Corps had at last advanced from the Bisamberg, though they were four hours late. Still, Massena was busy with the Aderklaa and would be hard pressed to respond.[78] The Austrian columns easily pushed through to Aspern and drove back the division covering the bridge before coming under fire from French artillery on Lobau. Klenau then faced his army left and marched north toward Breitenlee. Kolowrat's force was just then approaching Süssenbrun. Napoleon turned his attention to the latest threat, aided by a less than rapid Austrian seizure of the opportunity to strike from the rear. Luckily for Napoleon, Eugene had seen the threat posed by the Aderklaa fighting and had begun to turn his men in that direction, ordering Marshal MacDonald to face his corps and artillery to the west rather than the north. With that sector being strengthened, Napoleon pulled Massena's force out of the line to face to the south and recover the river crossings. As Chandler says, "This was a daring expedient, but the crisis called for desperate measures, and Napoleon had every confidence in the skill of perhaps his ablest subordinate."[79]

To cover Massena's withdrawal, Napoleon ordered his reserve Guard cavalry to stop the oncoming Austrians. They failed, but bought enough time for the Guard artillery to bring up 60 guns (soon reinforced to more than 100) and place the Austrian advance under fire. That slowed the Austrian troops down sufficiently to shift MacDonald's corps even farther around to the west from Aderklaa and create a strong flank position with 30,000 men. MacDonald wheeled left and met the Austrian advance at Sussenbrunn; some of Eugene's men and the Guard came to assist. It was just enough to counter a tiring Austrian advance, which ground to a halt. By late morning the Austrians had failed in their plan, and Napoleon was ready to take charge.[80]

The time had come to shift from defense back to offense. On the far French right, Davout, who had spent the morning waiting for ammunition resupply after the Austrian dawn assault, finally managed to capture Markgrafneusiedl and force Rosenberg back onto the plateau. Rosenberg had called on Hohenzollern for reinforcements, but pressure from Oudinot and Eugene had frozen him in position. The Austrians were fully committed, but no longer advancing. Massena had retaken Aspern and Essling, so the southern flank was secure. Napoleon ordered MacDonald to push 8,000 men at the Austrians around Süssenbrunn with Gerasdorf as his target; Oudinot and Eugene were to push west and northwest to force back Hohenzollern and Bellegarde, while Davout was ordered to implement his original orders and sweep around the Austrian left onto the plateau.

MacDonald's attack was designed to both break the Austrian line, if possible, and keep Charles from shifting any men to aid Rosenberg. Macdonald led l'ordre mixte with eight battalions in line and nine battalions in column on either flank. The attack succeeded at first but took a heavy beating from Austrian artillery, which inflicted some 5,000 casualties; the Austrians then rallied and counterattacked.[81] As MacDonald's battle was being fought, Oudinot's force aided Davout driving onto the plateau. Eugene's force moved obliquely on Deutsch Wagram and captured it, turning to the left to aid MacDonald. At this point, Charles saw that the day was lost and ordered his men to withdraw, which they did in remarkable order. By evening they had consolidated themselves and remained a cohesive force, obliged to leave the field but not really beaten.

The opening of the battle saw Napoleon surprise the Austrians with the location of the river crossing, but not with the timing of it. Since Charles did not choose to deploy in a forward defense, the French were allowed to concentrate on the north bank of the Danube with virtually no serious resistance. There was no real tempo to control, as the bulk of the day was spent in deployment rather than fighting. The hasty evening attack across the Russbach was a surprise but lacked sufficient preparation; the entire operation was almost a reconnaissance in force to determine the location and strength of the Austrian army.

The second day found Napoleon beaten to the punch, with the Austrians gaining the initial surprise on Davout's corps and then following it with another on the French left flank. Charles, unfortunately, had too great a battlefield and too-distant generals to dictate the necessary tempo, which Napoleon regained about noon. He then rearranged his forces to meet the Austrian assault and launched the counterattacks necessary to win the day. The orderly Austrian withdrawal coupled with the exhaustion of the French army resulted in no exploitation or pursuit for a few days.

Charles is to be congratulated for his ambitious offensive in the wake of his weeks of inactivity. His army acquitted themselves well, and he was in the thick of the fighting and slightly wounded during the day. Charles was wise to disengage while his army was still intact. The withdrawal from the field was done in an orderly fashion, a difficult move at the best of times.[82] The Austrians had stood toe-to-toe with the French and given as good as they got. Had the subordinates been more aggressive or Archduke John arrived prior to late afternoon, the battle could easily have been an Austrian victory. Losses were horrendous on both sides: more than 6,800 French killed, almost 27,000 wounded, and another 7,000 taken prisoner; 40 generals were among the casualties. The Austrians lost some 6,500 killed, plus more than 18,000 wounded and almost as many missing or captured.

For Napoleon, it was the apex of a successful career from which ensued his long descent toward Waterloo. He showed at the start of the campaign that the French corps d'armee system was as good as ever as he constantly outmaneuvered the Austrians all the way to Vienna. Aspern-Essling, however showed that he was either far too confident of his soldiers' abilities or he was too vain of his own abilities to care about his men. His traditional preparation was not there, and his army paid the price. As Chandler comments, "There is scant defense for his hasty and ill-considered decision to make an unprepared crossing of the Danube in mid-May."[83] Once he reverted to his old ways, the July crossing of the Danube and the deployment to the Marchfeld was error free. What followed, however, was no Austerlitz, and Charles, whatever his faults, was no Czar Alexander. Still, Napoleon showed that he could master even potential ruin. "Many commentators place Wagram among his greatest battles in terms of tactical skill," Chandler notes, "and there is no doubt that the way in which he retrieved one critical situation after another, refusing to show perturbation at even the most perilous moments, show Napoleon, the soldier, at his best."[84]

After Wagram, however, victories were fewer and much further between. This is due to both the declining numbers of veterans as the battles became more costly and the increasing quality of the opponents as they adapted to Napoleon's style of warfare. Although the French army that fought at Wagram and later did not have the quality of the one that fought the Austrians in 1805, it still could not be taken for granted. In his work on the Napoleonic wars, Rothenberg comments that "the fighting qualities of his troops were high, if only because less experienced troops often fought more aggressively than veterans who had acquired survival skills. The combat performance of Davout's and Massena's corps was equal to anything in the past, indeed all corps fought well. Italians and Bavarians matched French performance at Wagram, and the Saxons did very well on the first day and [were] routed on the second because of Bernadotte's poor leadership."[85]

Napoleon's Generalship

MOST NAPOLEONIC COMMENTATORS argue that the French emperor was no developer of tactics or systems like Frederick; rather, he became a master of the system he inherited from French military theorists immediately before the Revolution. Rothenberg asserts that he "was not a great innovator but imposed his genius and personal leadership on the huge, largely conscript armies he inherited from the Revolution. He perfected their offensive, mobile and ruthless way of war."[86] Chandler also comments on Napoleon's interweaving of strategy and grand tactics, saying, "Napoleon fused marching, fighting and pursuit into a single remorseless process, affording his enemy no time to draw breath."[87]

It was that march-into-battle concept that Napoleon developed, perfecting what is today called the operational level of warfare. His tactical skill is not to be ignored, however. While he did not lead from the front, he was meticulous in setting his units on the battlefield in order to best coordinate the three arms.[88] It is the grand tactical area of warfare, of course, with which this work concerns itself. Napoleon was exceeded only by Chinggis Khan and Subedei in his mastery of the principles of war; Napoleon's thoughts on warfare, however, are much more readily available than those of the Mongol leaders. At the same time, Napoleon himself scorned "rules of warfare." He had the necessary coup d'oeil to deploy his men correctly, hold back a reserve, let the enemy attack, and then exploit mistakes.[89] None of his battles were identical, and his use of the various principles of war was fluid and ever changing. He particularly shined in the areas of objective, offensive, mass, economy of force, unity of command, surprise, and morale.

In 1797, Napoleon said, "I see only one thing, namely the enemy's main body. I try to crush it, confident that secondary matters will then settle themselves."[90] In almost all warfare up to the late eighteenth century, the object of warfare, or center of gravity, was a location: usually the enemy capital city, which the enemy would do anything to defend. In contrast, Napoleon ignored cities as goals, but used them to manipulate his enemy's movements. By threatening a capital, like Vienna in 1805 or Berlin in 1806, he knew he could draw the enemy army to its defense. In his article "How Good Was Napoleon?" Jonathan Riley says, "For Napoleon, the centre of gravity at the operational level was almost invariably the enemy's army, and the decisive act in achieving his strategic objectives was its destruction in battle by the fastest means available. By this means he would break the enemy's will to resist so that all else—the conquest of territory in particular—would follow."[91] As the enemy army was his *objective*, it would present itself somewhere between where he crossed the frontier and the target location. There, on the path to the city, he would find and attempt to destroy it. A collection of buildings cannot defend a country, Napoleon asserted; only an army can. Destroy the army, and the country has no choice but to surrender.

On the battlefield, the objective was connected to that same concept. Threaten the line of communications back to the capital, or wherever the primary source of supply lay, and the enemy would move the bulk of its force to protect that line. By doing so, the enemy forces would weaken themselves somewhere else on the field, providing Napoleon with the perfect point at which to strike. This concept was illustrated in his first major battle at Toulon, where his strategy was to threaten the navy, the royalist source of supply. With that threat accomplished, the battle was over. At Wagram, the source of supply was not the point to threaten, since Vienna was already occupied; instead, Napoleon chose to cut the possible line of assistance to the east from where Archduke John was advancing. Like Alexander, he always looked to create a weakness in the enemy line and pounce when it was exposed.

Napoleon was also master of the *offensive*. As he wrote, "Making war offensively; it is the sole means to become a great captain and to fathom the secrets of the art."[92] Riley argues that Napoleon "rarely fought a defensive battle, even when he was strategically and operationally on the defensive. There are arguably only three occasions when he did so: Leipzig in 1813, and La Rothière and Arcis in 1814. Even then, he only did so as a last resort."[93] Offensive action operated on both the strategic and tactical levels. As mentioned above, Napoleon usually let his enemy attack first, which means a tactical defensive stance, a position he put himself in at Rivoli and Austerlitz. However, any such defensive situation was intended to be temporary, held only until the enemy weak point appeared. To look at Napoleon's campaigns from Italy forward, only in the wake of the capture of Moscow in 1812 was he forced on to the defensive. Multiple coalitions were formed and declared war on France, but only at the end of his career was any fighting done on French soil; he always took his army against the enemy in their own countries.

Napoleon went to great lengths to make sure he went into battle with numerical superiority, but the most important aspect of his battles was, as his primary contemporary analyst Henri Jomini explains, to find the enemy's decisive point and strike it with as much force as possible. "When you have resolved to fight a battle, collect your whole force. Dispense with nothing. A single battalion sometimes decides the day."[94] At Rivoli Napoleon was outnumbered in total, but never at any particular point. This was his true battlefield genius: to move his units in the midst of battle to the location where he would have the localized advantage. He did the same thing strategically, always trying to get his army between two opposing forces in the "central position." This way he could divide his army, using a small holding force against one opponent while massing the rest of his troops against the other. At Ulm his overall numerical superiority allowed him to surrounded Mack's Austrian army, while at Austerlitz the bulk of his army struck the weakened Austro-Russian center. His shifting of units on the second day at Wagram saved his army by enabling it to never be outnumbered at any point. Napoleon reflected on the principle of *mass* in his writings: "The art of war consists, with an inferior army, of always having more forces than your enemy at the point where you attack, or at the point which is attacked; but this art cannot be learned either from books or from practice. It is a feeling of command which properly constitutes the genius for war."[95]

This principle, however, was one of the factors in his ultimate undoing. The great losses of men at Eylau, Aspern-Essling, and Wagram were indicators that Napoleon was becoming less subtle in his battles. Instead of always creating an opportunity by obliging the enemy to weaken some part of his own line via maneuver, he began to rely increasingly on firepower followed by manpower; this was especially true after Wagram, when he increased the guns committed to the Guard and reintroduced the concept of distributing guns among the infantry. In his work *How Great Generals Win*, Bevin Alexander writes, "As Emperor Napoleon, however, he possessed such enormous armies and so much confidence in his military ability that he no longer depended upon speed and surprise but relied upon sheer mass or offensive power to win his victories. . . . Napoleon purchased victories at the cost of great losses of manpower—on both sides. With virtually a blank check on the resources of his empire, Napoleon lost his resolve to win by guile and deception."[96] As we will see in the next chapter, his inability to even find the enemy army's decisive point at Waterloo, coupled with his inability to force the British army to weaken itself anywhere along its line, proved more than Napoleon could overcome.

Intent as he was on superior numbers, Napoleon never wasted manpower. His grasp of *economy of force* is best illustrated by the fact that he always maintained a sizable reserve, which indeed became a larger and larger percentage of his force as time went by and he grew his Old, Middle, and Young Guards. He benefited from having marshals who knew his views and could, in most cases, hold positions against superior enemy forces while the mass (usually including the reserve) was committed to the decisive point. At Rivoli he thinned his front lines facing the bulk of the Austrian assault in order to join with his reserve and beat back Quasdanovitch's attack on the French right flank, and then sent those forces back to the center to launch the winning counterattack. Massena's corps was stretched to the limit at Rivoli and again at Wagram, but he always did what Napoleon needed in order to stabilize the situation and bring about victory. Davout's corps arrived in the nick of time to hold the French right flank, then beat back Rosenberg's surprise attack and still turned the tide of battle with the flank maneuver that had been his original mission.

When Napoleon implemented the corps d'armee system, the concept was that if an individual corps stumbled into an enemy force, it could launch a spoiling attack or stand its ground, as necessary, until reinforcements could arrive. Napoleon always depended on minimal forces to exert maximum effect while the main force and reserve finished the battle. Rarely did those corps commanders disappoint him.

Napoleon's maxim 64 asserts: "Nothing is so important in war as an undivided command: for this reason, when war is carried on against a single power, there should be only one army, acting upon one base, and conducted by one chief."[97] In volume 31 of his correspondence, entitled *Notes on the Art of War*, he muses explicitly on the principle of *unity of command*: "Unity of command is of the first necessity in war. You must keep the army united, concentrate as many of your troops as possible on the battlefield, and take advantage of every opportunity, for fortune is a woman: if you miss her today, do not expect to find her tomorrow."[98] In some ways this is a reflection of Napoleon's personality, for it is virtually impossible to imagine him sharing anything. Perhaps the trial of being forced to serve under a succession of incompetents at Toulon reinforced his high opinion of himself, but once he secured his first independent command in Italy, he was the sole determinant of what the army would do.

Napoleon benefited from the fact that unity of command was a principle not often followed by his opponents, perhaps best indicated at

Austerlitz where two emperors commanded the Austro-Russian coalition. This made for a muddled chain of command as well as the problems of communicating orders in two languages. Likewise, arguments between commanders, primarily Mack and Archduke Charles, weakened the Austrian effort in 1805, resulting in the disaster at Ulm. In contrast, Napoleon, as commander in chief and head of government, had only himself at the head of the chain of command.[99] The implementation of the corps d'armee system would seem on the surface to fly in the face of the concept of unity of command, as virtually self-contained small armies operated outside of Napoleon's direct command. In reality, although he gathered about him subordinates he could trust to fight independently for a short time, he only allowed them to do so until he could arrive with the rest of the army and take over. In this system, however, we also see some of the problems that led to eventual decline. Napoleon needed good corps commanders to act semi-independently and follow orders, but they could not be so talented as to challenge his reputation. Thus, he kept some men who were brave and loyal, like Marshals Murat and Michel Ney, though he himself admitted they could not be trusted alone or with large commands.

Napoleon also began to suffer as his ambitions built an empire: he could not be everywhere at once, and someone had to be placed in independent command in Italy or Spain when he was fighting the Austrians, Prussians, or Russians. Here, trust overrode talent and his placement of his brother in political and military control of Spain ended up losing France the Iberian Peninsula. He fared better in Italy with stepson Eugene de Beauharnais as viceroy, but Napoleon had to make sure that talented marshals were there to assist Eugene, and he dispatched regular letters to give him advice. On the other hand, Eugene never had to deal with the popular revolt or the British army that Joseph Bonaparte faced in Spain.

All that being said, on the battlefield Napoleon was the master no matter where the fighting took place. And one cannot argue that any of his subordinates, talented as they may be, had acquired his level of reading and reacting. "It depends on him alone to conquer difficulties by his own superior talents and resolution," said Napoleon.[100]

At the strategic level, the repeated use of the principle of *surprise* was certainly the result of Napoleon's obsession with speed, a reputation he developed from his earliest days of command in Italy. His soldiers' complaint that the emperor employed their legs more so than their guns is indicative of this penchant. Before battle, Napoleon's appearance in the enemy's proximity was almost always days, if not weeks, prior to his expected arrival. His corps d'armee wide-front movement covered by a cavalry screen ensured no enemy could keep tabs on his movements and prepare for him.[101] This alone was the reason for the surrounding and capture of Mack's army at Ulm.

Shortly after Ulm, at Austerlitz, one of the greatest surprises in all military history occurred when Napoleon so skillfully used the terrain, the enemy commanders' expectations, and the timely arrival of Davout on the Austro-Russian flank. Although surprised himself on the second day at Wagram by the Austrian offensive, he had pulled off the greater surprise the previous day by his deployment across the Danube even though the Austrians knew the French army was on the island of Lobau and was building up its forces there. The weeks in preparation were unprecedented, but the rapid deployment of three corps across bridges and into the field accomplished complete tactical surprise.[102]

Probably no aspect of Napoleon's leadership gains more comment, however, than his ability to motivate his men and maintain *morale*. Riley writes, "And there is no doubt that his personal presence was a huge force multiplier: where the dreaded cries of '*Vive l'Empereur!*' arose, French troops took heart, and their enemies despaired."[103] His enemies knew that; Wellington said that Napoleon's presence on the battlefield was worth 40,000 men. He knew how to motivate; Martin van Creveld describes what underlay that ability: "A good understanding of the native qualities of the French soldier: a knack for resounding phrases; an encyclopedic memory for faces, often assisted by careful but well-concealed homework; and a talent for stage management—all these are indispensable for understanding why so many followed him for so long."[104] Indeed, if one could but master Napoleon's ability to inspire, one could accomplish much in any field.[105]

Napoleon had the one characteristic necessary for loyalty: the ability to win consistently. Troops are always more impressed with winners, especially if there is an aspect of personal gain as well, and Napoleon was not one to limit his soldiers' looting. Soldiers also respond to the general who exposes himself to the same dangers they face, and Napoleon had the reputation of having risen through the ranks and leading from the front at

Toulon. Although he rarely put himself in the front lines in later times, he was always close enough to be exposed to danger. Had he not been, given the battlefields of the day, he could not have made the quick adjustments necessary for victory. Although he slept in Schönbrunn Palace in Vienna, he was also seen sleeping on the ground just before the crossing of the Danube in July 1809. Napoleon may not have been the "soldier's soldier" that Hannibal or Caesar was, but he was no stranger to his troops in any of his campaigns.

Unfortunately, all that had an element of show. He was often extremely callous toward his men. His maxim number 15 states: "The first consideration with a general who offers battle should be the glory and honour of his arms. The safety and preservation of his men is only the second."[106] He is widely reported to have privately commented that a million men's lives were nothing to him and would flippantly comment on what soldiers would do "for a scrap of ribbon." As for rewards, he could be very generous with promotion and cash; he even adopted the children of his dead soldiers after Austerlitz, promising that the boys would be brought up at the imperial palace, the girls in the palace at Ste. Germaine. He may have been more than a little cynical, but his men loved him for his promises and actions.[107]

Although Napoleon tended to dismiss the idea of prebattle speeches (though there were many after the battles), he did what he could to keep the army from succumbing to the rumors that are rife in all military camps in all times. He distributed usually heavily spun press releases to maintain civilian morale as well. Thus, he became known for making propaganda a regular arm of the military. He realized the importance of morale and made sure the soldiers were often updated with orders of the day or speeches. Propaganda for him became almost as important as infantry, cavalry, and artillery.[108]

BRILLIANT AS HE COULD BE ON THE BATTLEFIELD—and Ulm and Austerlitz are masterpieces that can stand side by side with any victories in history—Napoleon was a victim of himself more than his enemies. Of all the generals studied in this work, he most represents the heights and depths of leadership. Only Alexander was so negatively affected, in the end, by vanity. Theodore Dodge has perhaps the best summation: "Napoleon's strategy shows a magnificence in conception, a boldness in execution, and a completeness and homogeneity not shown by any other leader. The other captains can only stand beside him because they built so that he might add; they invented so that he might improve. But while Napoleon reached a height beyond the others, they did not show the decrease of genius which he showed." He opines that Frederick did more with less and was "steadfast in victory and defeat alike." For their accomplishments politically, he calls Caesar the "most useful man of antiquity; Napoleon comes near to being the most useful man of modern times."[109] But they cannot stand, in quality of character, to the other great captains.

15

Arthur Wellesley, First Duke of Wellington (1769–1852)

British Field Marshal

We would rather see his long nose in the fight than a reinforcement
of ten thousand men any day.

—Captain John Kincaid, 95th Regiment

OF ALL THE MEN discussed in this work, probably none was less likely
to become a great captain than Arthur Wesley. Even Marlborough and
Caesar, though sons of lesser nobility raised in no serious military environment, had at least some connection to a soldier in the family of one
sort or another. Apparently none of any note had been in the Wesley heritage since the days of Richard I's invasion of Ireland in 1369, when a forebear named Colley settled into what became known as the Anglo-Irish
Ascendency. Arthur's grandfather, Richard Colley, inherited the estate
of a distant relative named Wesley in 1728. Colley changed his name
to Wesley and, when granted an Irish peerage, took the title of Baron
Mornington, the name of his new estate.[1] The second Baron Mornington, Arthur's father, was later named Viscount Wellesley; upon his
death his eldest son, Richard, altered the spelling of his surname Wesley
to Wellesley. Arthur, however, kept the original spelling for some time.

Arthur's father was a music professor at Trinity College in Dublin,
just a few blocks away from Arthur's 1769 birthplace. As the third son
of fairly minor nobility he had little to no future within the family, as

primogeniture ruled that as first son Richard inherited title, lands, and wealth (or debt, as the case may be). Arthur therefore had to depend on his eldest brother's good graces; as it turned out, his brother treated him well and had the favor returned. Growing up, however, he depended on the will of his mother, who had scant faith in his future. His father had abandoned Dublin for London when Arthur was seven. Arthur went to school in Chelsea until his father's death in 1781, when his mother sent him off to school at Eton. The three years he spent there were unremarkable, though one author asserts that one can see the beginnings of his character emerging: "a belief in himself and his capabilities that his ten subsequent years of doing very little indeed entirely failed to dent."[2]

If Arthur's character was developing, one could not see it in his schooling, for his grades were mediocre and he could not grasp Latin or Greek. A year in Brighton with a private tutor followed, and in 1785 he moved with his mother to Brussels. There he spent a year learning French, but apparently little else. His mother removed herself back to London the following year, leaving him at a military-finishing school in France. It was Arthur's year here that began to reveal some changes. In his new school he learned fencing, horsemanship, and the theory of fortifications, but the primary focus was to instill the virtues of honor and nobility. It was not a difficult course but he emerged from it a much more well-rounded young man, fluent in French.[3] He began to show some interest in potentially following a soldier's career, the path of other younger, less accomplished sons of aristocrats.[4] His brother Richard accommodated him by arranging to purchase a commission for him as ensign in the 73rd Highlanders. This was something of a hollow position, as the regiment was at the time stationed in India and Arthur did not travel to join it. He bought another commission in the 76th Regiment of Foot; when they sailed for India in January 1788 he moved to the 41st and stayed in England. These unit changes meant nothing to his consistent position, an aide to the viceroy in Ireland, which he held for six years. Over the next five years he held positions in three more regiments (two of them cavalry), finally buying a majority, then a lieutenant colonelcy, in the 33rd Regiment of Foot.[5]

This last position was second in command of an infantry unit, yet Arthur had as yet no military experience other than wearing the uniforms. However, with the French Revolution in full swing and the first coalition of European countries marshaled against the government that had executed King Louis XVI, Arthur began to feel the need to see some action. He had also recently been unlucky in love, which added to his dissatisfaction. The one talent he had exhibited to this point in life, playing the violin, was ruthlessly expunged: he burned the instrument and began studying war. In his dual biography of Wellington and Napoleon, Andrew Roberts observes, "If Wellington was to become a professional soldier, rather than an uninspired amateur, he needed to foreswear gambling and hard drinking—which he also did soon afterward—and take his commission in the 33rd Foot seriously."[6] His first attempt to get a combat assignment came to naught, but in late June 1794 his regiment landed at Ostend to defend the Dutch from French aggression. An Anglo-Dutch force had recently been defeated and blamed the Austrians for a lack of support. Arthur soon found himself in command of a brigade consisting of his regiment, the 41st, some dragoons, and artillery, all of which relocated to Antwerp. The fact that he was appointed to brigade command despite never having seen combat was expected since he was the senior officer. However, command of such a large detachment did show that his superiors saw some potential in him.[7] Very soon his unit found themselves, with the rest of the army, being pushed back. Here, in mid-September 1794, Arthur saw his first combat at Boxtel in the Netherlands and gave a good account of himself, overseeing his unit's repulse of a French assault.[8] It was a promising start, but without any follow-up. The army went into winter quarters and suffered through the bad weather and worse supply situation. Forced to retreat even further into Hanover, the whole army was removed in the spring of 1795. Young Arthur Wellesley learned first hand the need for solid bases and lines of supply. "I learnt what one ought not to do, and that is always something," he observed many years later.[9] That in itself showed that the young man was quickly maturing.

Warfare of the Time

THE BRITISH ARMY HAD CHANGED LITTLE from the time of Frederick the Great. Indeed, the official drill *Regulations* had been adopted in 1764, in the wake of the Seven Years' War. Those rules, however, reflected more the British experience in North America's French and Indian War than it did warfare on the continent. Thus, there was somewhat more of an emphasis on light infantry and skirmishing tactics than was seen in most

European armies. The 1778 edition of the *Regulations*, introduced in the midst of the American Revolution, was almost completely ignored. To confuse matters further, the rules were not enforced army-wide: some regiments stuck with the old rules, some tried to implement the new ones, some freelanced their own maneuvers, and some ignored both books.[10] Much depended on the particular regiment's experience. Had they been stationed consistently in England or Ireland, they followed "the book." Had they been stationed overseas and seen some fighting in America or India, they adapted the rules to the realities of combat they had experienced.

Two things altered this situation in the army in which Wellesley was ensconced. The first was Colonel Henry Dundas's publication of *Principles of Military Movements* in 1788. Dundas served on the Irish staff, from whence no one expected anything of excellence. Over the next three years, however, all the Irish regiments learned his way of soldiering. It proved so impressive that a condensed version was adopted as the *Regulations* of 1792.[11] The second thing that changed Wellesley's situation for the better was the appointment of the Duke of York to the position of commander in chief in 1795. Although his expedition to assist the Dutch, as mentioned above, was a failure, he was serious about creating a first-class army. The whole army embraced the Dundas maneuvers, and this revolutionized the British army. Before, every battalion had its own way of operating; now, an order to a brigade was quickly obeyed through the ranks.[12] That Dundas had the ability to express himself clearly and simply was one of the major strengths of the new drill manual. The virtue was that it provided battalion-level tactics with a standard set of moves that could be adapted to any tactical situation.[13] The Duke of York also did much to improve the lives of the soldiers, issuing greatcoats, regularizing the supply system, expanding hospital services, and developing programs for taking care of soldiers' families. He also oversaw a major barrack-building program to ease the burden on the civilian population, who had often been obliged to quarter soldiers. This also aided in developing unit cohesion, limited the opportunities for desertion, and made the drill regular and consistent.

The infantry organization was altered, based not only on the new rule book but also on the lessons learned in the American Revolution. The type of warfare fought in America (small unit actions and skirmishing) could not be translated directly into Europe, where the armies were many times larger, but the concept of light infantry was incorporated and taken more seriously. At paper strength, each regiment consisted of ten 100-man companies, with one company being designated as grenadiers and a second as light infantry. Frederick had distrusted the light infantry since he could not exercise control over them; their need for independent thought and action ran counter to his Prussian discipline. British discipline was almost as harsh but, like the Prussians', it was necessary for the linear warfare practice of firing by ranks. In the new order, three ranks were dictated: front rank kneeling, second rank standing against their backs, third rank touching the backs of the second rankers to their front. In reality this appeared only on parade, as the front rank almost never actually existed in combat. As did Frederick's army, the British fought almost exclusively in two ranks, both standing. Even though Dundas's manual called for platoon firing (or file firing), in use since Gusatavus's time, it was dropped in favor of massed volleys. British officers had learned in America (rather than from Frederick's theories) that the huge explosion of fire at close range followed by the bayonet charge resulted in fewer casualties for the attacking force.

As had been the case since the introduction of firearms to warfare, the standard firearm of Wellesley's day was a notoriously inaccurate weapon. The troops carried what was widely known as the Brown Bess, a smooth-bore flintlock musket in service for many years. The Indian Army carried a similar weapon with a 39-inch barrel as opposed to the Brown Bess's 43 inches. Over time the shorter-barreled weapon became the standard and was used in Wellesley's forces in Spain and at Waterloo. "Don't fire until you see the whites of their eyes" was the standard procedure for determining when an aimed shot might reasonably be expected to hit a specific target. After 100 yards the accuracy rate was no better than 50 percent, and firing at targets 300 yards distant (though the gun's range was greater than that) was a waste of powder. Further, the black powder used at the time created such billowing smoke that actually sighting the enemy line, much less an individual soldier, became difficult if not impossible after a volley or two. A 14-inch socket bayonet completed the weapon; it was not often used, but the British soldier showed real expertise when it was. Primarily it was effective when the infantry formed into squares to resist cavalry attacks. The bayonet then did what it was originally designed to do: act as a pike.

Dundas described eighteen basic maneuvers for battalions that could be easily demonstrated on the parade ground and implemented for deploying on the battlefield. He also included ten pages on light infantry tactics (other manuals spoke to them), but admitted that the heavy infantry was his main topic. Although it was the army commander who arranged the regiments at the outset of battle, the battalion commander gave the orders once the units deployed and the battle began. The regular orders Dundas had categorized were supplemented by bugle calls, which also became standardized in this time period. Drumbeats also indicated movements in addition to merely keeping pace on the march. Though there were great differences between drill fields and battlefields, the ease of maneuver learned at drill provided confidence and flexibility when needed in battle, thereby creating effective troops and units. Wellesley's success in Portugal and Spain owed much to the introduction of the Dundas rules.[14]

The light infantry was one of the companies on the wings of the battalion. The members were to operate in pairs (one loading while the other fired) in front of the rest of the battalion and were supposed to be marksmen. Once deployed in the open, they would harass enemy formations and generally create havoc. Like a cloud of mosquitoes, they were difficult to get away from or kill.[15] They fired at individual targets, acting at times as snipers aiming at high-value targets. When deployed with the rest of the battalion, however, they volley-fired like everyone else. The light infantry soldiers at the time were equipped with rifled muskets, although the technology to make them widely available was still more than fifty years in the future. The worries Frederick had expressed about desertion by the Prussian forces did not apply in the British army. One can imagine that desertion in a war zone would be minimal since all fighting was outside Britain: where would one go if home was not available? There was also the aspect of being something of an elite. Good soldiers provide their own discipline through unit pride, comradeship, and support from their fellows.

The cavalry in general was usually overlooked in favor of the actions of the infantry. In the early 1790s the British cavalry arm numbered less than 15,000 men, about 17 percent of the army total. By 1795, with war against Napoleon definitely decided upon, the number of horsemen went up, but their percentage of the overall force remained the same or declined. From

1807 to 1815 the total number was between 26,000 and 29,000.[16] In India, few British cavalry units served; instead the Indian forces depended more on locally recruited manpower. Going into the Napoleonic era the basic horsemanship training was not standardized but developed at the regimental level, as were tactics. Each regiment numbered just over 500 men divided into three squadrons of two troops each; the troops numbered 70 privates plus officers and noncommissioned officers (NCOs). Although there were basic similarities in required uniforms and equipment, the cavalry regiments showed a variety of uniform styles dependent on the taste or wealth of their commander, who was responsible for acquiring the clothing from private contractors. Regiments were officially designated as heavy cavalry or light, but in practice there was little difference. Unlike the dragoons, cuirassiers, and hussars of Frederick's army (and Napoleon's), British cavalry was used for scouting, skirmishing, or assault as needed.

The basic weapon of all British cavalry was the saber. Debates raged over the relative merits of straight-thrusting swords and curved slashing blades. Not until 1796 were two styles officially mandated. The regiments designated as heavy cavalry received a straight sword without a sharpened tip, but with both edges of its 35-inch blade sharpened for some 12 inches back from the tip. Thus, it was not a thrusting sword as its straight blade would imply; not until 1815 and later was the point sufficiently sharp to use as a stabbing weapon. The light cavalry received a slightly curved 31-inch blade designed for the slashing cut. Its effectiveness was described in a number of accounts, one of which describes cuts to the Frenchmen's heads: "the appearance presented by these mangled wretches was hideous. . . . as far as appearances can be said to operate in rendering men timid, or the reverse, the wounded among the French were far more revolting than the wounded among ourselves."[17] The cavalry carried firearms, but they were of irregular and generally poor performance. Attempts at standardization failed, and the sword remained the cavalryman's primary weapon. Lances were not used in the British army to any great extent, although Wellesley employed irregular cavalry in India that did carry them. In the Indian cavalry forces each horseman had a carbine and two pistols, all flintlocks.

Tactics were straightforward: deploy in two long ranks and charge. Walk to 250 yards from the enemy, then trot to 80 yards, then break into a gallop to contact. Usually this was performed well enough. The problem came after initial success. Since the first use of horsemen in combat, maintaining order in the pursuit had always been far more the exception than the rule. Wellesley regularly cursed his cavalry for overpursuing, losing cohesion, and being ripped apart by counterattacking French horsemen. The primary uses of light cavalry, scouting and screening, were not extensively taught in British service, although they were part and parcel of warfare in India. In spite of its lack of training, however, the British cavalry proved itself able when it counted: the scouting patrols made sure that British forces were never surprised by French troops in the Portuguese or Spanish campaigns.

As for artillery, it was a matter of the gunners rather than the guns in most cases. British cannons were not greatly different from those of other European powers.[18] Guns were organized into brigades of between six and twelve cannons (the term *battery* came into use later). As seen in previous chapters, the guns varied in size and were designated by the weight of the shell they shot. Horse artillery were normally 3-pounders, field artillery was more a variety of 6-, 8-, 9-, and 12-pounders. Anything heavier was siege artillery (or artillery of the park) and not normally deployed unless walled cities needed reduction. All the field artillery fired solid round shot as well as canister (or case) shot in which a can of musket balls was fired to give a shotgun effect. This latter was only used at close range, and the majority of the ammunition carried by all armies was round shot. Horse artillery was normally used for covering advances or retreats, rather than as the quick-moving direct-support guns that Frederick had designed in the Seven Years' War.

Most gunners were still more engineers than anything else, looked down upon by "real" soldiers. Horse artillerists, however, were not only more widely accepted but actually came to be regarded as elites. Both, however, rose by seniority rather than merit or purchase since commissions were not for sale in the Royal Artillery. Still, there were generals of artillery, and one Corsican artillerist in French service actually became the emperor of France. In India the nature of the gunners was much the same, but horse artillery was more widely used. All members of the Indian service were recruited locally from both the Indian and European populations and were under the direct control of the East India Company. Artillery proved to be a multifunctional tool for both offense and defense, attempting to destroy both enemy defenses and the enemy guns damaging one's own army.

All three branches of the service were of a high quality in India: just like the infantry and cavalry in Britain, the gunners in India were well trained and very professional in combat.[19] This is interesting given that it was to an extent a private (or at best semigovernmental) army raised and operated by the East India Company with somewhat limited input from the military authorities in London. Indeed, it was only in the late 1700s that the English began to seriously pursue a policy of hegemony in India rather than trade.

The Opponents

AFTER HIS EXPERIENCE IN HOLLAND, Wesley spent the next several months of 1795 in garrison duty in Dublin. He lobbied for an active posting, or at least a higher political position than aide-de-camp to the governor-general of Ireland, but nothing came of it. The 33rd Regiment was ordered to join a force sailing for the West Indies, but an extended period of severe weather led to its cancellation. This was the third time Wesley had potentially been posted to the West Indies, where he certainly would have served in obscurity if not died of the multiple maladies that ravaged European armies in the area. Finally, in mid-1796 his regiment sailed for India; it arrived in February 1797. This would prove to be the first major step on Wesley's road to greatness. He finally achieved full colonel in May 1796, and he began to look on India as his path to prominence. He took along a well-chosen library to immerse himself in the ways of Indian warfare.[20] For a year Arthur was on his own, without the assistance his brother Richard had given him throughout his career. In April 1798 the relationship was reestablished when Richard was appointed governor-general of India. It was at this point that the family name was officially altered from Wesley to Wellesley.

The British Indian Army was made up of three types of units. The first were on loan from the English government, the so-called king's troops. Then there were units consisting of primarily English soldiers, which had been raised by the company. Finally, there were units recruited locally, made up of Indian troops and NCOs (sepoys) but with English officers. The artillerists were all English, some recruited locally and some in England, but most of them had trained at the gunnery school at Woolwich in England. The officers of the king's soldiers were considered to be superior in rank based on length of service instead of assigned rank. This occasionally made for some testy relationships on campaign. The Englishmen in Indian service thought themselves better soldiers but envied their counterparts' ability to purchase commissions, which was not the practice in the company's army.

The Indian subcontinent in the late eighteenth century consisted of a variety of principalities technically under the leadership of the rapidly declining Mohgul Dynasty but in reality very independent. India had been a center of Anglo-French rivalry since before the Seven Years' War, and most local armies had European officers in command or advisory positions. This does not mean that the locals knew nothing of warfare outside their traditional environment and fought well only because of the outside training, however. Indian warfare was sophisticated before the Europeans arrived, and since the Portuguese first entered the Indian scene in the late fifteenth century and early sixteenth, the Indian military had been adapting itself to foreign weaponry. Military leaders were quick to study European methods of warfare, as well as learn from the Persians. Indeed, Indian metalsmiths quickly developed improved versions of European weapons. Portuguese officials writing to their home government commented on the fact that artillery produced in India was generally superior to that produced contemporaneously in Europe. The local smiths had thousands of years of collective experience and excelled in the production of steel, brass, and bronze.[21] Muskets had already been in use for generations, and the Indians were masters of irregular cavalry warfare.

Every principality maintained armed forces, but the most warlike of the Indian ethnopolitical groups were the Marathas. In the early sixteenth century, Marathas served as mercenaries in armies of Muslim kings of the Deccan region of central India. The great Maratha leader Shivaji between 1664 and 1680 created the powerful Maratha Confederation.[22] The confederation became much looser after Shivaji's death, but the Marathas honed their skills in the mercenary trade. Like all mercenaries, they had to be good to stay employed so they were quick to adopt anything that would enhance their abilities, whether weapons or tactics. For example, they developed artillery-based fire superiority before the Europeans did and introduced it as an antipersonnel weapon instead of one used primarily against defensive positions.[23] As the Marathas had defended their lands with chains of forts, they were used to employing artillery on the defensive as well.

From the European point of view, however, the Marathas were primarily a light and irregular cavalry force. Indeed, that was traditionally the case. For more than a century and a half prior to Wellesley's arrival the Marathas had been used what were called bargi-giri, predatory light horse tactics, mainly against Mughal army supply lines.[24] The Maratha and other Indian armies also employed *pendharis* (guerrillas), who were used as harassing forces on enemy supply lines and were paid with whatever loot they could acquire. Thus, the British came mistakenly to believe that the Marathas were little more than brigands. When necessary, however, the Maratha cavalry could form up and charge in line like any European force.

It was the infantry that the British most overlooked. Comments by multiple observers prior to the Second Maratha War dismiss the Maratha infantry with barely a second thought. They learned differently when the war began. Although Shivaji was a master of guerrilla warfare, he used infantry to hold a chain of forts to protect and define Maratha territory in western India. He also developed combined operations with infantry and cavalry. This technique became more solid under the leadership of Peshwa Baji Rao I, who used his infantry to better employ his outstanding artillery force.[25] Still, in the time between Shivaji in the mid-1600s to Baji Rao in the late 1700s, the emphasis in Maratha armies had become predominantly placed on cavalry, with infantry just beginning to come back into favor as the British military presence and ambitions grew. Peshwa Baji Rao I made use of both column and line, with linear tactics predominating. At the Battle of Babhoi in 1731 the Marathas showed their talent for artillery coverage of their infantry advance. As this was an intertribal battle it went unnoticed by the Europeans in India at the time, hence they had not learned these lessons when they met the Marathas later.[26] Perhaps the major Maratha defeat at the hands of the Afghans at Panipat in 1760 convinced the Marathas to upgrade their infantry.

There are two people generally nominated as responsible for this resurgence of infantry in India. One was Hyder Ali, sultan of Mysore, in south central India. He still depended mainly on cavalry but employed both infantry and artillery with skill. He fought two wars against the British and held them at bay, but his son Tipu (or Tipoo) could not do so. Farther north in the Maratha Confederacy, Mahadji Scindhia brought in European aid by hiring the Frenchman Benoit de Boigne. De Boigne's battalions quickly proved their worth to Sindhia and by 1789 had established him as the supreme warlord of northern India, including Delhi. De Boigne's 2,000-man force bore the brunt of most of the fighting and showed training along the British lines rather than in use of the French tactics being introduced at the time.[27] De Boigne's leadership, rather than his organization and tactics, may have been the deciding factor in his success according to Randolf Cooper in his work on the Anglo-Maratha wars: "In the past many authors have portrayed de Boigne's impact on Mahadji's forces as nothing less than a military revolution in the 'transformation' of the 'Maratha army' with the introduction of 'European discipline and drill.' But those descriptions were essentially derived from nineteenth-century British military myths offered up as an explanation to answer the nagging question of how the Marathas—a supposed nation of 'freebooters'—could pose such a credible military challenge to what was a historically contemporary superpower."[28] Whatever the truth of the matter, what remains is that the Maratha infantry at the turn of the nineteenth century was underestimated by British officers. They viewed it, moreover, as a mistake to strengthen their own infantry. This weakened their greatest strength, mobility, while it strengthened an arm in which their Anglo-Indian enemy was dominant.

The British political authorities had slowly expanded their influence deeper into India by what were termed subsidiary alliances. If a local prince would agree to become subsidiary to the company, ceding his authority over foreign policy, the company would provide military protection with its army. The subsidiary prince would provide maintenance for these forces and extra troops in case of war. With this practice the company slowly reached into the Indian body politic from its original bases at Calcutta, Madras, and Bombay. Weaker princes like the nawab of Oudh saw this policy as a way to keep themselves safe from enemies. Other princes saw the agreements as a way to supplement their own forces in conflicts with neighbors. This put company forces into a variety of temporary alliances with princes that alternately favored or opposed their subsidiaries. It was this system that ultimately led to wars against Mysore and the Marathas.

The Maratha Confederacy by the 1790s was a political entity in name only. The titular head of the confederacy was the peshwa, originally the prime minister but now with little command authority. He was headquartered in the city of Poona, southwest of Bombay. The other Maratha states were led by Scindhia of Gwalior, Holkar of Indore, the gaikwor of Baroda, and the raja of Berar, all of whom had originally been generals who were awarded lands for their service. Gwalior and Indore were involved in a family feud, Berar was isolated from the capital to the far eastern part of the confederacy, and Baroda (just north of Bombay to the west) always maintained a friendly relationship with the British.[29] Scindhia (in the northern part) was the strongest of the princes and had the latest Mughal emperor in his debt for helping him maintain the throne in 1791. Before he could use this authority to exercise serious influence in the confederacy, Scindhia died in 1794 and was succeeded by Daulat Rao Scindhia, a teenager. Still, the confederate states cooperated one last time in a war against the nizam of Hyderabad, crushing him in 1795. Immediately afterward, the princes fell out among themselves in a dispute over the successor to the peshwa, whose estates were south of Bombay.

This was the situation into which the Wellesleys arrived in India. The initial problem they faced was the reintroduction of French influence into India, thanks to negotiations between Napoleonic agents and Tipu, sultan of Mysore, who, while keeping up a seemingly friendly correspondence with the British, was at the same time secretly negotiating with Napoleonic agents from Mauritius. French officers trained his army.[30] Richard Wellesley consulted Arthur for plans to deal with Tipu. He confirmed the analysis already given by the commander in chief in India, General Sir John Shore: it would take time to gather a siege train and wait out the monsoon season. Arthur soon showed himself to be quite an expert on India and its military situation, sending extremely detailed memoranda to Shore as well as his brother the governor-general.[31]

In 1799 the company forces, allied with the nizam of Hyderabad, invaded Mysore—due south near the bottom of the subcontinent—with the intent of defeating Tipu and solidifying British authority. Colonel Arthur Wellesley served under the command of General Sir George Harris. Wellesley did not perform well in a night skirmish against a prepared position, but his troops cleared the obstacle the following day. After driving off a French-led force along the way, they laid siege to the capital city of Seringapatam from early April until 4 May. Wellesley commanded the third-line reserves as the other two forces assaulted a hole in the walls battered by a month's cannonade. The city was taken and Tipu was killed.

Arthur received command of the city, which he held for a year and a half, proving himself quite acceptable to the inhabitants.[32] During this time he also commanded an expedition against a guerrilla force of as many as 50,000 under Dundia Wagh, operating in the northern area of Mysore, and in this case distinguished himself. After a long campaign destroying the guerrilla bases, the British finally surprised Dundia Wagh with 5,000 cavalry in the open. Wellesley commanded about 1,600 British and local cavalry. Without hesitation Wellesley deployed his men in line and led the attack from the front, saber in hand.[33] The British conducted this operation with the assistance of a number of surrounding powers, including the Marathas, as Dundia Wagh was an outlaw who threatened everyone. Thus, Wellesley got the opportunity to see his future enemy in action.

The next three years consisted primarily of administrative duties for Wellesley, but he was promoted to major general in April 1802. War with the Marathas was brewing. The members of the confederacy began to fight among themselves. As noted earlier, the position of the peshwa had diminished over the years, but it still held some cachet. Peshwa Baji Rao II, who was hardly a model of decorum or honesty, had managed to alienate the two major Maratha powers, Scindia and Holkar. In the fall of 1802 Holkar defeated the peshwa's forces outside his capital at Poona. Holkar seized the city but failed to rouse any support. Needing a powerful ally, Baji Rao reluctantly signed the Treaty of Bassein on 31 December 1802, making himself a subject of the East India Company. This overt cooperation and cession of territory to the British was more than the other Marathas could stand. However, now that the treaty was in place, Governor-General Wellesley could put troops in the field to protect Rao. If the Marathas went to war, so much the better: with the political bonds of the confederacy weakened, Richard Wellesley thought the time was ripe to expand the company's influence.

The Battle of Assaye

RICHARD PUT ARTHUR in command of company forces in the south central part of India known as the Deccan. General Arthur Lake commanded forces in the north that were to protect Oudh and capture Delhi in order to "protect" the Moghul emperor (and further the

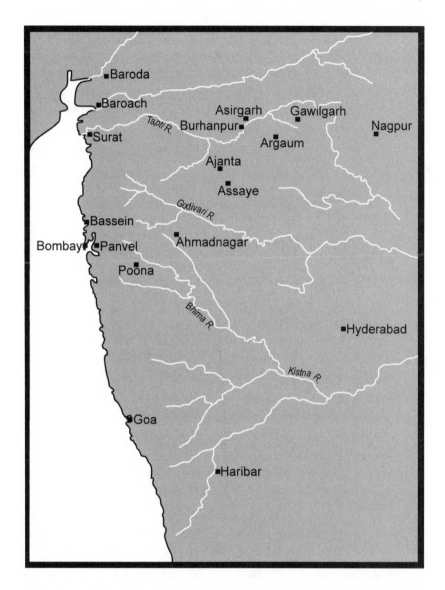

company's influence at the same time). Richard gave Arthur wide-ranging authority, to determine if the Marathas were going to war and to act without consultation in response. This was a move both politically savvy and practically minded. Richard could trust his brother to be both; if he made a political mistake, however, Richard could exercise deniability. Should circumstances arise under which Arthur was attacked, he would not have to wait weeks to get a message to Calcutta asking permission to respond.[34] The plan of action was to settle the situation peacefully if the other Maratha states would follow the lead of their peshwa into a subsidiary alliance, raising the question of whether the peshwa had signed the treaty for his own lands or as prime minister of the entire confederacy. If the other states would not follow along, then war was deemed inevitable. The other states did not follow.

Arthur had occupied Poona and restored Baji Rao II to his position, and used the city as his base of operations. He had some 11,000 men; a further 4,000 were to the northwest in Gwaikar, and another 9,500 were based in Hyderabad to the east. Wellesley gathered what supplies he could from the Poona area, but Holkar had burned much of the region when he withdrew to his homeland.

Given his campaign against Dundia Wagh, Wellesley felt himself sufficiently knowledgeable to handle the Maratha army. He launched his offensive in August 1803 against the hill fort of Ahmadnagar. This fell within two days, to the great amazement of a Maratha chieftain, who remarked: "These English are a strange people. They came here in the morning, surveyed the wall, walked over it, killed the garrison and returned for breakfast."[35] Ahmadnagar provided Wellesley with a forward base of supply. His plan was to carry his own supplies by bullock train, yet move quickly enough with pontoons to create bridges and maintain pressure on the Marathas so they could not stay in one place long enough to gather supplies. Surprisingly, Wellesley's army could march twenty-three miles in a day. The first major obstacle was the Godavari River, but an advance force had constructed a large number of wicker and leather boats, and the army was completely across in three days (by 25 August). Wellesley's eastern force under Colonel James Stevenson had advanced from Hyderabad and positioned itself at Jafarabad at the junction of the Kaitna and Purna Rivers.

By 29 August 29 Wellesely's force had reached Aurangabad, where he met with Lieutenant Colonel John Collins, who had just left the position of British representative to Daulat Rao Scindia's court. Collins had often seen the Maratha infantry in action; Wellesley had not. Collins tried to warn the much younger Wellesley what to expect: "The Colonel tried to persuade Arthur that Sindia's army was different and the conventional threat that it posed was very real. A single one of Sindia's five brigades, when accompanied by its artillery park, packed enough firepower to maul Wellesley's Army of the Deccan.... 'I tell you. General, as to their cavalry

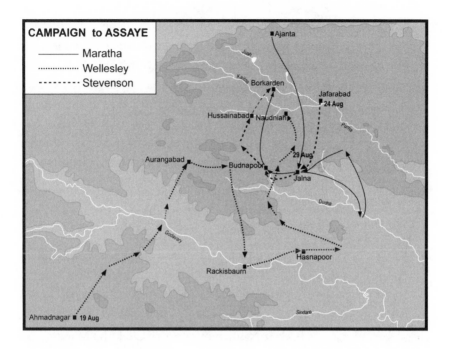

[meaning the enemy's], you may ride over them wherever you meet them; but their infantry and guns will astonish you.'"[36] Wellington and his staff dismissed the old man as out of touch, but were later to be haunted by his wisdom. Collins reported that Scindia's last response to peace negotiations was evasive, which did not change the situation—the offensive would go on. Instead, intelligence reached them that Scindia was planning a quick thrust between Wellesley and Stevenson toward Hyderabad, which could be a feint or could be an attempt to cut the British supply lines.

For the next week the two British and one Maratha force crisscrossed the countryside, jockeying for position. Scindia was not able to break free of Wellesley's pursuit and so decided on battle. He sent for 17 battalions of his elite infantry, expertly trained and equipped and commanded by European officers.[37] Wellesley decided that he needed to gather his forces for what looked like a set-piece battle. Stevenson met him at Hasnapur on 8 September, having launched a number of cavalry raids of his own against Scindia's camps and supply columns. Word soon arrived that Scindia was withdrawing north to meet his infantry in the hills around Borkarden; he also met with the Raghuji Bhonsle, raja of Berar, who brought a large army.

On 21 September, Wellesley met with Stevenson again at Budnapoor and developed his plan to bring the Marathas to battle in the open. He sent Stevenson on a wide left hook to come down on Scindia from the northwest while Wellesley would take his force east, then north to Naulniah near the Purna River. This would put Scindia between them. Both forces began their marches early on 22 September. By midday on the 23rd Wellesley's force reached Naulniah, about six miles from the river. At that point Wellesley received information that the Marathas had proceeded out of Bokarden and were encamped along the Kaitna River. He rode forward to inspect the ground and found the report to be true. The Kaitna had steep banks at that point and a direct assault was impossible. Wellesley immediately decided to see if he could quickly deploy across the Kaitna downriver and perhaps strike the Maratha flank before they could reposition themselves.

Wellesley knew he was outnumbered and outgunned, but decided to press forward, although he deployed only part of his force. He had left his baggage under guard back at Nauliah in hopes to catch the Marathas on the move, as the initial reports said they were. When he found them not marching but ready for battle, and realized they knew his force was there, he decided retreat was not an option. Seeing their great superiority in cavalry, Wellesley believed that a withdrawal now would further distance him from Stevenson and give the Marathas the central position to try to defeat them in detail. He decided to seize the opportunity.[38] He also knew that if he didn't press forward, he would lose the element of surprise. Even though the Marathas were aware of his presence, he did not think they would be ready for a quick attack. Additionally, Wellesley recognized that any attempt to withdraw would have a negative morale factor.[39]

Wellesley took his force downstream to a ford, crossing with his English battalions and his sepoys but leaving the allied cavalry of Mysore and Peshwa on the south bank to protect his forces from any potential Maratha cavalry attack on that side. As soon as the British began fording the three-foot-deep stream they came under long-range Maratha artillery fire. It was random since the gunners could not see the British force but effective nonetheless, with one of Wellesley's aides being decapitated by a cannonball. Wellesley had seven infantry battalions numbering 3,170 men, four regiments of cavalry numbering 1,200, and a relative handful of artillery, 22 guns with none larger than a 6-pounder.

This seemed ridiculously small compared to the Maratha army arrayed across the field. Daulat Rao Scindia had been joined by three *campoos* (brigades) of infantry, each numbering eight battalions. These were referred to as regular troops, trained by Europeans and usually officered by them as well. Berar brought another force of 6,000 infantry. The Maratha right flank was manned by the regular troops trained by a Belgian, Sumroo, here commanded by Jean Saleur. The center was under the command of the Hanoverian Anthony Pohlmann, who had taken over from the retired de Boigne, the creator of Scindia's regular infantry. To the left, next to Assaye, was the least-talented campoo, commanded by the Dutchman John James duPont. At least 100 cannons deployed across the Maratha front. The regulars numbered about 15,000 soldiers under European officers. Apart from the regular battalions, Scindia and the state of Bhosle had other units numbering between 10,000 and 20,000 infantry and 30,000 armed horsemen, who may or may not have been trained soldiers.[40] Although Wellesley hoped that the Marathas would not be able to maneuver in time, the Marathas surprised him with their quick and disciplined response. They established a front of about a mile with both flanks anchored by the Kaitna River on their right, the Jua River and the town of Assaye on their left. Behind the infantry and artillery the massed cavalry were formed.[41] A second line of infantry deployed perpendicular to the first, from Assaye westward along the Juah River.

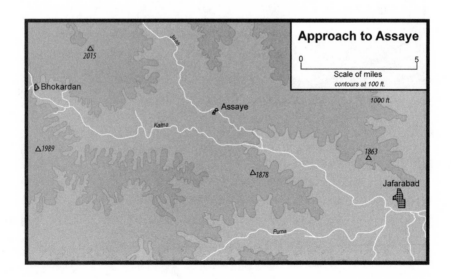

There is some discussion as to the nature of the European leadership in the Maratha forces. At the outbreak of the war British officers serving in the Maratha armies were offered bounties by the British to desert, and many did so. Instead of making better offers to maintain the officers, the commander of the regulars, Pierre Perron, decided to fire all British and Anglo-Indian officers. This immediately cut the skill level of the regular Maratha infantry forces by a significant amount, and also provided the company army with a number of men intimately familiar with the Maratha army.[42] Thus, the midlevel officer corps at Assaye may well have been less than top-notch. Recent Indian military historian Pradeep Barua describes this situation, asserting that early in the battle when one of the regular brigades deployed to meet the British, "it did so awkwardly by moving in a line formation, rather than marching in column and then deploying to fight in line. The inability to execute such a simple maneuver would seem to indicate that the veteran brigade, which had conducted far more complicated maneuvers under intense fire, was indeed devoid of most of its command element."[43]

Wellesley's initial idea was to move against Assaye to strike the Maratha infantry's flank and rear, but the enemy's rapid repositioning made that idea virtually suicidal. Instead, he decided to strike the far right Maratha

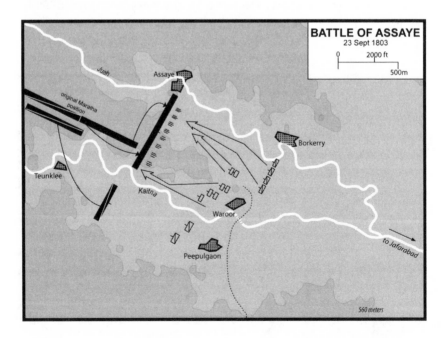

flank and drive it back, hoping to have the whole Maratha infantry line swing away to the northwest. Thus, the firepower located in Assaye could never come into play. He rode out to each battalion with orders. The 78th Highlanders on his far left would lead the attack along the Kaitna, with the other units following along in echelons to one flank in a manner reminiscent of Frederick's oblique order.[44] The 74th Highlanders held the right wing with units of the Madras Native Infantry in between. The cavalry, stationed to his right, would cover the flank against any Maratha counterattack. The light infantry companies of each battalion moved forward as skirmishers as the units deployed from column into line.

As Wellesley's men were deploying they came under intense artillery fire, which they could do little to counter as their smaller 6-pounders could not match the 9- and 12-pounders the Marathas employed. The Maratha artillery wrought immense havoc, destroying the British artillery at long range. As the infantry advanced, they too were badly hurt by round shot as well as chain shot.[45]

The British advance thus started badly. Although Wellesley had given orders personally to each unit, the skirmishers did not turn toward the enemy but kept marching toward Assaye; the 74th followed them rather than abandon them to their fate. This took them away from the rest of the infantry. They quickly suffered horrendous casualties from artillery fire and began falling back. Maratha cavalry around Assaye followed them, along with Pohlmann's closest infantry units. As the 74th withdrew some 150 yards, they stopped and formed squares, which successfully kept the enemy attacks at bay.[46]

Meanwhile, Wellesley had stationed himself with the 78th on the far left and was leading the remainder of the infantry toward the battalion on the far left of the Maratha line. Pohlmann's regular infantry was fronted by some 60 cannon only 700 yards away. The assault was textbook. At 60 yards the Scots of the 78th stopped, fired a volley, reloaded, and advanced with fixed bayonets. When they reached the guns they fired again, and the fighting became hand-to-hand. Some gunners defended their guns to the last, a few fled, some fell to the ground feigning death. The Scots moved on, fired a volley at the infantry, reloaded, and fired a second. At this point some of the European officers mounted their horses and fled, and British cavalry came on the scene and charged the breaking infantry lines. The massed fire and advancing cavalry caused the Maratha center to break, opening a 900-yard gap, and the Marathas abandoned some 40 guns.[47] Some of the sepoys broke ranks to give chase but the 78th re-formed to face a cavalry counterattack. Twenty thousand Maratha light cavalry began riding toward the Scots, but a solid line and a solid volley convinced them not to press the attack.

As the 78th and the Madras infantry battalions were breaking the Maratha right wing, Wellesley heard the sounds of the Assaye guns and quickly learned of the bad position in which the 74th found themselves. He ordered the 19th Light Dragoons and the 4th and 5th Native Cavalry to ride to the rescue. The cavalry were outstanding. They drove back the units milling about the British squares, then pushed the fleeing Marathas into units south of Assaye. They struck Pohlmann's northern sector as Wellesley was breaking the southern part of the line.[48] The cavalry almost overpursued their enemy, but the commander rallied them before they got too close to Assaye and launched all the remaining cavalry at the collapsing Maratha infantry.

The Maratha infantry retreated in fairly good order to the second line established along the south bank of the Juah. Wellesley's infantry and cavalry now had a full head of steam and were preparing to attack, but the Marathas had one last trick up their sleeve. Once the British and Madras infantry broke through, some of the "dead" Maratha gunners came back to life, turned their guns around, and fired into the backs of their enemies. Wellesley personally faced about with a cavalry and an infantry unit and rode down the revived gunners and captured the artillery. With most of the artillery now gone, the Maratha infantry fled. In spite of their large numbers, their cavalry did little in the battle.[49] As the Maratha infantry were backed up against the Juah, the 19th Light Dragoons crossed the river just downstream from Assaye and attacked some of the retreating units. They inflicted severe damage until the British commander was killed, which caused the attack to stop.

The three-hour battle tapered off as the sun set. The bulk of the Maratha force crossed the Juah and retreated in good order, leaving behind all their artillery, numbering between 90 and 102 guns. The gunners who played dead were made to quit playing the part. Given the fact that Wellesley's force had been on the move since daybreak and had suffered more than one-fourth of their force as casualties, there was no immediate pursuit. (Wellesley did, however, lead a force the following morning at dawn that pursued the retreating Marathas and captured an encampment of them.) The casualty count was 198 British and 258 Indian officers and men killed, 442 British and 695 Indians wounded; this was 27 percent of his force. The Maratha losses were some 1,200 killed and perhaps four times that number wounded.

The battle at Assaye was a meeting engagement resulting from Wellesley's quick march to the scene upon receiving intelligence of the Maratha whereabouts. His analysis of the ground and the best method of launching a hasty attack was as worthy a coup d'oeil as any Frederick could have accomplished. He was unable to surprise the Marathas in spite of his rapid deployment, but he controlled the tempo by keeping up constant pressure all along the Maratha lines. Only the opening Maratha cannonade kept him from making all the movement decisions. Assaulting an army many times the size of his own, with virtually no artillery support, was the virtual definition of audacity. After quickly locating the weakest point in the enemy line, Wellesley's force was intended to be wholly concentrated on the enemy right flank; only the actions of the skirmishers and the 74th Regiment kept this concentration from being complete. The fatigue and heavy casualties among his army kept Wellesley from engaging in any rapid exploitation, but a delayed pursuit did succeed in catching and destroying a part of the retreating enemy. Philip Mason, in his book on the Indian army, comments, "Assaye has always been described as a general's battle, and so it was; to fight at all was the General's sole decision and the operation was designed entirely by himself. Few indeed have been the commanders who would have ventured on so daring a plan or carried it through with such courage, resolution and dash. But it was also, in another sense, a soldier's battle, illustrating in the highest degree the confidence men feel in a general who knows what he is about."[50]

Wellesley's war against the Marathas continued for the remainder of 1803; he followed up Assaye with two lopsided victories at Argaun in late November and the siege of Gawilgarh in mid-December. In the north, General Lake was scoring victories of his own, so Maratha morale was broken by the end of 1803, and the war came to an end. Wellesley enjoyed the fruits of victory. Having already been appointed major general, as noted, he was now also made a Knight of the Bath and received rewards that ultimately totaled £42,000. Company power was extended well into India; Wellesley's presence there, however, came to an end in March 1805, and he reached England in September. His time in India had transformed both his leadership and tactical abilities on the field, and he returned a man well versed in the art of battle. From colonel to major general, he commanded units from battalion to corps size, learning important lessons in morale, supply, and operations with foreign troops. All of this would serve him in good stead when he served in Portugal and Spain.[51]

An analysis for the U.S. Army War College states six basic lessons that Wellesley learned in India: the value of logistics; attention to detail in training and supply; how to handle large bodies of men, both in and out of combat; the value of surprise in the midst of battle, especially against larger forces; physical and mental stamina for the person in command; and that the French were beatable.

Back home he left the army for a time, marrying his sweetheart from his early, poor Irish days, though the result was hardly a storybook marriage. He served in Parliament for a time and spent time back in Ireland as Irish secretary. He finally longed to return to overseas service, but in those days the Royal Navy was doing most of the fighting. His success in India was personally satisfying, but not particularly impressive to the high command. After all, it was "just" India and he was "just a sepoy general." Wellesley managed to secure a minor command in an expedition to Denmark, where his unit was involved in the capture of Copenhagen. He served on a surrender commission and came home to England with a bit more attention focused his way.

In 1808 Napoleon declared war against Britain's ally, Portugal, after dominating the Spanish government for some time and finally appointing his brother Joseph as the new king. Britain responded by sending an expedition to indirectly aid its ally, by appointing Wellesley to lead an attack on Spanish South American colonies. Once again he managed to avoid this sidetracking of his career when the operation was cancelled. Instead of sailing for Buenos Aires, he and 9,000 men went to Portugal; a further 5,000 sent from Gibraltar were to join them. Before they arrived in Lisbon, an invading French force attacked a small town nearby and slaughtered the population. This led to a mass popular rising by the Portuguese people. Much the same thing was taking place in Spain. In March 1808, a force of 100,000 French troops marched into Spain, forcing King Charles IV and his heir, Ferdinand, to abandon the throne. The people rebelled and rallied around Ferdinand, and the French were brutal in suppressing the movement.[52]

In March 1808, Wellesley's 14,000 men landed at Mondego Bay, roughly a hundred miles north of Lisbon, and quickly began their march to liberate the Portuguese capital. A skirmish at Roliça drove a small French force back. At this point, Wellesley was superseded in command with the arrival of Sir Harry Burrard, who halted the advance until more reinforcements could arrive under the command of General Sir John Moore. Wellesley was thus standing on the defensive when a 13,000-man French force came out of Lisbon toward him. Seeing them coming, Wellesley deployed his men along a ridge at Vimeiro and dealt the French a severe defeat at little cost to his own troops. Burrard arrived and prohibited a pursuit, even though it almost certainly would have captured Lisbon. Wellesley was not happy.[53] He had his first victory in Europe, albeit an incomplete one. It was not to be his last. To add insult to Wellesley's injury, Burrard's superior, Sir Hew Dalrymple, took overall command. Dalrymple had not seen action in fourteen years, was near retirement age, and was no more aggressive than Burrard. Wellesley found himself in the role of a lion commanded by lambs.

The Peninsular Opponents

BY 1808 THE FRENCH ARMY under Napoleon dominated almost all of Europe. This resulted from a combination of Napoleon's leadership and the nationalist spirit of the troops. In the immediate wake of the execution of Louis XVI in 1793, most European powers banded together to suppress the French Revolution and restore the monarchy. The revolutionary government had purged most of the officer corps, so the armies that took the field were enthusiastic rabble who won because of strategic speed, swarming tactics, and remarkable bravery against lethargic European armies. Once whipped into shape by Napoleon, they not only defended France but spread across western Europe, defeating Austrians, Prussians, Russians, and anybody else who chose to fight. Throughout this time Spain was an ally, but a hesitant one. Napoleon's removal of the legitimate monarchs and the placement of Joseph on the throne therefore was designed to strengthen the southwestern flank. Although Joseph proved a good king and gained some local support, the initial action motivated extreme Spanish resistance, and French troops had to be sent in to support the new king. When Portugal refused to join in a Continental boycott against Britain, Napoleon sent troops there as well.

The French army in Spain resembled French troops elsewhere. The swarming tactics mentioned earlier were somewhat formalized into skirmishers and light infantry, which Napoleon strengthened with horse artillery. In the regular infantry, the company numbered 140 men, and six companies made up a battalion. Three or four battalions made a regiment, two or three regiments made a brigade, two or three brigades made a division, and a collection of divisions made a corps. The cavalry was patterned on that used by Frederick's Prussians: light cavalry for patrol and pursuit, heavy cavalry for shock attack, and dragoons in between for either or both roles. Revolutionary French armies had little cavalry, but Napoleon remedied that shortcoming and his cavalry units were first-rate—as good as any in Europe. He also expanded the number of cannons per unit in order to maximize firepower on both offense and defense.

The revolutionary forces had won success by attacking in columns rather than the standard linear tactics; this gave them power at a single point for breaking through enemy lines. The usual tactic was to send a large force of skirmishers and light infantry well in front of the main columns, and these would harass the enemy sufficiently to create enough disorganization for the columns to be effective. Unfortunately, if the enemy was not sufficiently disorganized and the breakthrough did not occur, the column formation limited firepower and created confusion to the rear. To prevent this, forces in column marched onto the battlefield behind the light infantry screen and then rapidly deployed into line just before the assault. Wellesley countered this move by using the terrain to his advantage whenever possible, and his favorite tactic was to deploy his men on the reverse slope of a hill, concealing the number and arrangement of his troops from the enemy. Light infantry skirmished in front as the enemy advanced. Thus the advancing French were usually unable to deploy from column to line until at the crest of the hill, at which point the British would already be deployed and have their massed musket fire ready.[54] This became Wellesley's signature move in Portugal and Spain.

Wellesley's primary problem throughout his peninsular campaign was manpower. He had the only significant force of British soldiers and therefore could not afford either defeats or even costly victories. He was aided by forces supplied from both Spain and Portugal, though the quality of the troops, and their motivation, varied widely. The French brutality proved a great morale factor for both Spanish and Portuguese, but they never completely trusted British motives.[55] These troops were, however, vitally necessary to both the British army and their own countries if the French were to be both defeated and removed. The Spanish did serious damage to the French armies with guerrilla warfare, reportedly killing an average of 100 French soldiers per day. Since, however, it was Portugal that was Britain's ally and the base for all operations, it was there that troops had first to be raised. At the beginning of the war the Portuguese army had been almost useless. To try to whip them into shape Wellesley requested the appointment of William Beresford, to which the authorities in London agreed. Michael Glover, in his book on the Peninsular Campaign, describes him thus: "Although a field commander of only moderate ability, he was an organizer of genius. He had need to be. As one of his British staff wrote, 'The Portuguese soldier is naturally indolent. He falls with the greatest facility into slouching and slovenly habits, unless he is constantly roused and forced to exert himself.'"[56]

Beresford not only trained the Portuguese but also commanded them in battle. He did both jobs well. Beresford was named marshal of the Portuguese army in 1809 and brought with him a number of British officers to serve at all levels of the army. The result was remarkable, and the Portuguese came to be considered almost the equal of British soldiers, described by Wellesley as "the fighting-cocks of the army."[57] Meanwhile, it was not until 1812 that the rebel Spanish government granted Wellesley command of its armies. Wellesley took them into his forces only on the condition that he was in total command and his orders would not be overridden, no promotions or demotions would be made without his recommendation, and the Spanish government would do its best to keep its troops paid and equipped.

Wellesley also commanded two German units, the King's German Legion and the Brunswick Oels. Both brought with them their own organizations, staffs, cavalry, and artillery. Their infantry were well trained, and their light infantry battalions had companies of expert riflemen that were employed very successfully for skirmishing and sniping.

The main difference in the British army of the Peninsular Campaign was the influence of General Sir John Moore with the support of the commander in chief, the Duke of York. Moore was a forward-thinking soldier intent on developing soldiers through good training and trust rather than the lash and iron discipline. In this he succeeded quite well.

Moore acted on the Dundas rule book and believed in the trained, alert soldier with self-motivation. Officers should earn the respect of their men and be models of self-discipline. Add to these concepts extensive drill and training, and remarkable results ensued.[58] Since all soldiers in the British army were recruits, they were more motivated than those who would have been conscripted or pressed into service, and Moore believed it was vital to use that sense of volunteerism. By 1808 desertion was almost nonexistent, and the British army was the best for its size in Europe. Further, the continued development of loyalty to the regiment kept the necessary esprit de corps that all effective armies must have. Wellesley himself did not necessarily look with such attitudes on his soldiers, but his ability to win was enough to develop loyalty from his troops.

The Battle of Vittoria

WELLESLEY'S FIRST VICTORY of the Peninsular Campaign, the previously mentioned battle at Vimeiro, could not have had worse consequences. His two superior officers, Dalrymple and Burrard, responded to a French offer to negotiate, which resulted in the Convention of Cintra, under which the French army in Portugal, faced with a British army and surrounded by angry Portuguese, should be evacuated back to France. Further, it should be evacuated in British ships and allowed to take all its arms and loot. Dalrymple and Burrard agreed.[59] The news of this outrageous agreement was met in London with a recall of the two commanders and Wellesley to face a court of inquiry. All the charges were ultimately dismissed and swept under the carpet. The testimony did reveal, however, that Wellesley had performed well in the field and been overruled by his superiors at the negotiating table. Parliament voted to thank Wellesley for the victory at Vimeiro, Dalrymple was dismissed as governor of Gibraltar, and Burrard was retired to duty in England. As was often the case with military scandals, it had been smoothed over so as not to ruffle feathers. Wellesley retired to Dublin with what seemed to be a bleak outlook for his career.[60]

Sir John Moore took over the war in the peninsula with some success until Napoleon himself arrived for a season and drove the British army out of Spain after the Battle of Corunna, during which Moore was killed. Napoleon went back to war against the Austrians, and Wellesley was summoned to take sole command in Portugal to save the British effort. He returned to Portugal in April 1809 and made his presence felt almost immediately. Within three weeks of his arrival he had defeated Napoleon's Marshal Soult at Oporto and begun planning future campaigns. At the end of July he defeated Napoleon's brother Joseph at Talavera, for which he was given the title Viscount Wellington. In spite of this initial rapid offensive, he knew that he did not have the numbers as yet to challenge the French to one decisive battle. He thus realized that an Iberian campaign would be a long one and instituted what came to be called his "cautious system." This took advantage of the mountainous Portuguese terrain to establish garrisons from which to launch harassing raids. In the meantime, he trusted Beresford to whip the Portuguese army into shape.[61]

Wellington spent the next four years fighting French troops across Spain and Portugal, on the offensive when he could and on the defensive when he must. He accomplished his mission to defeat the French forces while at the same time husbanding his own, which obliged retreating at times when superior numbers made discretion the better part of valor. By the spring of 1813, however, he had finally secured Portugal sufficiently to invade Spain once again, swearing at the outset of the campaign that he was saying good-bye to Portugal forever.

On orders from Napoleon, Joseph had moved the capital from Madrid northwestward to Villadolid, near the junction of the Duoro and the Pisuerga Rivers. Joseph's position was deteriorating in the wake of news in February 1813 of his brother's disastrous invasion of Russia. Napoleon needed 15,000 veterans from Spain back in France in order to have some foundation for rebuilding his army. The forces departed under the command of Marshal Soult (with whom Joseph did not get along), and the new commander assigned to Joseph was an old friend, Marshal Jean-Baptiste Jourdan, who, as Glover describes him, "could not be called an outstanding soldier but [was] honest and obedient, both rare qualities among the marshals in Spain, and [whose] theoretical appreciations of the situation were often more realistic than those of many more renowned figures."[62]

Joseph and Jourdan were looking at a terrible situation. Although Wellington had been pushed out of Spain back into Portugal the previous autumn, the Spanish guerrillas were creating havoc across the country, and large numbers of French troops had to be employed just to maintain

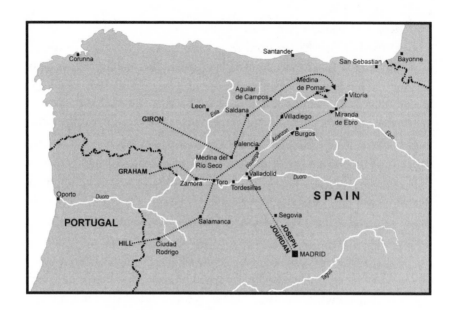

something resembling secure lines of communication from central Spain back into France. The French Army of the North, 20,000 men, struggled to control the region between the Ebro River, the Pyrenees, and the Bay of Biscay. During the early months of 1813 the 17,000-man French Army of Portugal marched north to assist. The Army of the South, made up of 35,000 men, was deployed in a curving line from Madrid to the Duoro River at Toro, and the Army of the Center supported it in the area of Segovia and Villadolid. The French had decided to try to hold what they could; virtually the entire peninsula south of the Tagus River had been abandoned to the guerrillas.

Joseph and Jourdan suspected that Wellington would try to repeat his strategy of 1812 and drive toward Madrid by way of Salamanca, and Wellington went to great lengths to convince the French leaders they were correct. In the spring he trained his new Spanish troops virtually within sight of Ciudad Rodrigo, where a relatively brief but successful siege had occurred in January 1812. Lieutenant General Sir Rowland Hill commanded some 30,000 men in this area, and he started the offensive on 22 May. Six cavalry brigades rode ahead as a wide screen, followed by the Light Division. Behind this there was only an undersized corps consisting of one British, one Portuguese, and two Spanish divisions.[63] Joseph's main force, stationed along the Duoro between Toro and Tordesillas, was strengthened to 50,000 and prepared for the attack. Ciudad Rodrigo and Salamanca fell with virtually no fighting. Then . . . nothing.

While Joseph and Jourdan pondered Wellington's next move, it struck them by surprise from the northwest toward the French right flank at Toro. This was the main force of some 42,000 under Lieutenant General Sir Thomas Graham. These troops had gone through the supposedly impenetrable tracks through the mountain range of northern Portugal and then driven across the Esla River to Zamora before the French were aware of any enemy forces in the area. Joseph and Jourdan had no choice but to withdraw their army to Villadolid to avoid being outflanked.

Wellington, who had been conspicuous during the display before Ciudad Rodrigo, had secretly moved himself over to Graham's force, and he took control of both forces at Toro, then marched northeast parallel to the Pisuerga River. In an advance that Napoleon himself might have envied, Wellington kept a heavy cavalry screen along the river to hide his army's movements behind it. This force moved so quickly that by the time Joseph retreated to Villadolid his army was on the verge of being flanked; he withdrew further to Burgos and found himself in the same situation. Wellington's maneuvers kept the French on the run, with little happening other than an occasional cavalry or artillery duel. On 13 June the French blew up the castle at Burgos and withdrew further northeast toward France.[64] The British and their allies had yet to fight much more than a skirmish, but they had the French army on the ropes.

Unfortunately for Wellington, however, the French got to move across much easier ground than did he. An analysis of the coming battle describes the country as "mountainous and criss-crossed by gorges and good defensive positions. Indeed the area north of Burgos is unlike any other part of Spain, with wooded plateaux fringed with sheer drops and ravines. . . . It was also terrain through which the French thought it impossible to bring guns and wagons."[65] The allied force moved so quickly even through this terrain, however, that the French were never able to take advantage of its defensive strengths. The British crossed the Ebro unopposed and moved east toward Vittoria, where Joseph and Jourdan had decided to make a stand behind the Zadorra River.

The French deployed in a potentially good position. The Zadorra flowed west through Vittoria then turned south to join the Ebro. Parallel between the Ebro and the Zadorra were the Heights of Puebla. All around the city of Vittoria were multiple villages with thirty to forty houses each, all of which could be fortified. The Zadorra River ran along the northern and western approaches to the town while hills covered northern and southern flanks. Jourdan correctly saw that an attack could only come from the west, so he directed the establishment of three successive lines deployed northward from the Heights of Puebla on the southern flank.[66] If Wellington attacked as presumed, Joseph was well positioned with 57,000 men, including 9,000 cavalry and 104 guns. His hand would be considerably stronger when the Army of the North under Lieutenant General Baron Bertrand Clausel arrived with a further 15,000–30,000 men; he was due on the scene no later than 21 June. The position deteriorated, however, when intelligence came in reporting some British movement to the north, although this was not taken too seriously at first. In spite of the fact that they had been victims of Wellington moving across supposedly impassable terrain, Jourdan and Joseph still believed the hills north and northwest of Vittoria were too difficult for troops to pass. When they learned of troops movements to the north, they first thought the British might be flanking them and heading for Bilbao. Just to be on the safe side, Jourdan withdrew his third line of defense from the western plateau and placed it along the Zamorra River running east-west above

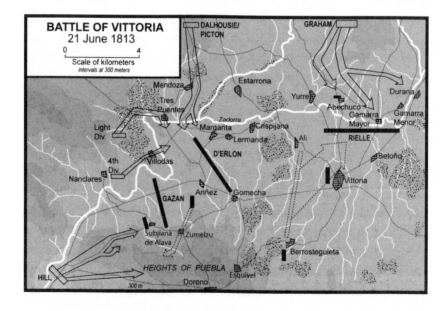

BATTLE OF VITTORIA
21 June 1813
0   4
Scale of kilometers
intervals at 300 meters

Vittoria.[67] Unfortunately, this left a five-mile gap between the troops under Rielle near Vittoria and those of Honoré Gazan and Jean-Baptiste d'Erlon to the west.

Wellington, outnumbering the French by about 15,000 men, also had the advantage that Joseph and Jourdan were not sure just where he was. Thus, he was able to divide his forces into four parts and strike from the southwest, west, northwest, and north. The initial force of 30,000 men under Hill was to proceed up the Zadorra through the pass at Puebla and move along the slopes of the Heights of Puebla to strike Gazan's line on its left flank. Once they were engaged, Wellington would push forward the 4th Division—3,000 infantry and 4,500 cavalry—from the west across the Zadorra from Nanclares against Gazan's right, while the Light Division would cross upriver at Tres Puentes. The Earl of Dalhousie, with Lieutenant General Sir Thomas Picton as second in command, led just over 14,000 men across the Monte Arato to cross the river to the east of Tres Puentes. Finally, Graham and a mixed force of British, Portuguese, and Spanish troops would swing farther east and try to cut off the road from Vittoria northeast toward Bilbao and Bayonne. All these forces were aided by the fact that the French had not destroyed a single one of the ten bridges across the Zadorra.

Early in the morning of 21 June Wellington looked across the Zadorra from high ground overlooking Nanclares. He saw Joseph and Jourdan, completely unaware of the impending threat, inspecting their lines. Hill, after clearing away some skirmishers along the east bank of the Zadorra, began his attack on the French far left flank about 8:00. This caught Joseph's attention, but he did not send any reinforcements as Wellington had hoped. Dalhousie's attack was slow in starting, his force having crossed some very rough terrain. Picton's division was in front and ready to go, but Dalhousie's division was still coming up. Wellington decided to launch his attack from Nanclares to keep the French focused to the west, when a Spanish informant alerted him to the unguarded bridge at Tres Puentes. The Light Infantry Division was quickly dispatched and established an unopposed bridgehead across the river with a hussar regiment right behind it. Seeing the taking of the Tres Puentes bridge and tired of waiting for Dalhousie to arrive, Picton led his division across the river on his own initiative, leaving his superior to go into action when he arrived on the scene.

Graham's force, with a twelve-mile march to reach its jumping-off point, was in position by 10:00. His instructions were to interdict the road northeast out of Vittoria toward France and, if the opposition was not too great, to flank Rielle's lines along the Zadorra.[68] He appeared on the heights overlooking Vittoria, and Jourdan completely misinterpreted his arrival. Jourdan was convinced this was a feint to draw off reserves from the "real" attack in the west. Rielle, commanding the force facing Graham, knew better and withdrew most of his picket forces back from the north side of the river, leaving only a brigade to defend the village of Abechuco. Rielle would thus be left to his own devices as Jourdan decided to draw off more troops from the center to combat Hill's attack along the heights.

On the front lines, Gazan was thinning his line to move manpower to contest the heights. This so weakened his center that the village of Subjiana de Alava fell to Hill without a fight. Joseph and Jourdan were in the center of the French army. Gazan, seeing the British 4th and Light Divisions poised to cross the river, surmised Wellington's plan, but Jourdan would have none of it, convinced that everything but Hill's assault was a diversion. Jourdan shifted units from d'Erlon's force to the heights as well, while ordering Gazan's right wing units to recapture Subjiana. Thus, when Wellington sent his two divisions across the river at Tres Puentes and Villodas, they were approaching d'Erlon's right flank and were positioned to strike Gazan's right rear. D'Erlon could not respond, having sent units to the south to aid on the heights; plus, Picton's division had crossed the river at noon and was now on d'Erlon's flank.

Graham, finally seeing Picton's troops going into action, began his own advance. The French unit left at Abechuco put up little resistance, but his Anglo-Portuguese troops could not cross the river against Rielle's stiff resistance and superior cannonade. A Portuguese division moved east to try its hand at Gamarra Mayor but met the same heavy fire. A Spanish brigade under General Francisco Longa swung even further east to attack Durana, held by a Spanish brigade in Joseph's service. Again, French artillery kept the attackers at bay until late in the day, when Longa's men finally forced their way across the bridge and secured the road. Had Graham not held back some reserves he might have sent men downstream to Yurre and turned Rielle's left.

As Picton and Dalhousie drove east along the river against stout resistance, the Light and 4th Divisions continued to press forward. Wellington wrote in a dispatch after the battle, "The troops advanced in echelons of regiments in two, and occasionally three lines; and the Portuguese troops in the 3rd and 4th divisions, under the command of Brigadier General Power and Colonel Stubbs, led the march with steadiness and gallantry never surpassed on any occasion."[69] The French fought impressively as well. They tried to form a new line of defense based on Lermande and Gomecha, but they were too hard-pressed on both their front and their left flank, as Hill began a steady advance along the Heights.[70] Jourdan finally realized he had been mistaken in his analysis of Wellington's intent. At 1:00 he ordered Gazan to withdraw to a line just in front of Vittoria. Although his men were engaged, Gazan followed orders, beginning a phased withdrawal, pulling back one brigade through another, but the pressure was too much to allow a stand.[71] Not until 6:00 that afternoon was the last line of defense reached, roughly a mile from Vittoria. With all his army across the river and the French in retreat, Wellington finally brought up his artillery and began constant harassing fire. Within an hour of the general advance the French army was broken and in full rout. Escape to the northeast was cut off by Graham's forces, so the only route to run was the road east to Pamplona, which was little better than a cart path.

The French lost some 6,000 killed and wounded, with 2,000 taken as prisoners, but the high command managed to escape. The French army was not just routed, but lost almost all its equipment, including virtually all of its 150 cannons. The pursuit could have been long and deadly but for the amazing loot available to the British troops, who could not resist. (They had not been paid in months.) As a result, the allied pursuit was haphazard. Although some of Wellington's infantry chased their opponents for several miles, the cavalry seems to have been conspicuous by its absence.[72] Joseph's army had a large number of noncombatants retreating with him to France, and they left behind "stores as well as baggage, wagons, three thousand carriages, chests full of money, eagles, standards, horses, mules, pet monkeys and parrots."[73] The loot included the payroll for the French army, 5 million francs, plus Spanish and French gold coins and at least 500 French prostitutes. The Spanish royal art collection was captured as well, much of which went to England, where it remains. Wellington offered to return it to the Spanish monarch when Joseph was dethroned, but Ferdinand awarded it to him as a gift from a grateful nation.[74]

Although Wellington lost some 5,000 men killed and wounded, the battle at Vittoria could hardly have been a more complete strategic victory. Glover describes the international response: "The victory at

Vittoria irrevocably broke the French kingdom in Spain. . . . On hearing of the victory the Russian army sang a *Te Deum*, the only occasion on which this was done for the victory of a foreign army. In Germany, Beethoven composed a 'Battle Symphony' [*Wellington's Victory*, op. 91] to commemorate the occasion."[75] Austria, pondering a Napoleonic offer of truce, decided against it and rejoined the coalition against him.

From a tactical point of view, Vittoria had its high points and lows. There was insufficient coordination between columns, and on the battlefield there was often confusion among the attacking regiments, which caused some opportunities to be missed. On the positive side, the British troops proved their prowess was not limited to a single division or regiment. Picton's advance on his own initiative was key to the early breakthrough, and the final cannonade proved sufficiently powerful to turn defeat into rout. Additionally, the terrain had much to do with whatever difficulties were encountered.[76]

Wellington, by dividing his forces and timing their respective actions, engaged in a deliberate attack with all of his army; he held back nothing in reserve but his artillery, which came forward as the tide turned. Although Joseph and Jourdan deployed around Vittoria in order to fight, Wellington's appearance was a surprise. By convincing Jourdan that Hill's attack was the main thrust, he managed to concentrate the French forces in the wrong area of the battlefield while his virtually equal columns were able to strike in multiple locations. Since the French spent the day playing defense, Wellington controlled the tempo of the action from beginning to end; only on the Heights of Puebla were there setbacks, and they did not matter to the outcome of the battle. Wellington's plan was not particularly audacious, even though he did divide his forces and have them operate across an area several miles across with little to no communication between units other than visual orientation. The pursuit and exploitation were minimal, owing to roads clogged with noncombatants, nighttime rains, and the inability of his troops to keep from looting.

Wellington gathered together what manpower he could find the following morning in order to begin the pursuit. He was not particularly successful; he would later claim that he had lost more men to plunder than to battle. Still, the French under Joseph were in no mood to do anything other than escape back to France. From Paris, Napoleon sent Marshal Soult to the border to try and salvage something of the debacle. Soult managed to mount strong defenses of San Sebastian and Pamplona, but they finally fell to storm on 31 August and 30 October respectively. By 9 November Wellington had crossed the Pyrenees into France, leaving his Spanish soldiers behind to avoid any vengeance against French civilians. Soult continued trying to halt the advance, but with more room to maneuver Wellington continually outflanked him. A four-day battle at St. Pierre in early December was the last major combat. The British occupied Bordeaux on 12 March 1814, and Soult had no choice but to position himself behind the defenses of Toulouse. Wellington stormed the city and captured it on 10 April, ignorant of the fact that in the wake of the Battle of Leipzig Napoleon had abdicated his throne four days earlier. Wellington received the news with unaccustomed levity, spinning on his heels, snapping his fingers, and crying "Hurrah!" His five years of unremitting hard work had finally paid their dividend. On 11 May 1814 he was accorded the highest honor his country could bestow, the Dukedom of Wellington, following his recently awarded Order of the Garter.[77] He had, after Vittoria, also been promoted to field marshal.

Wellington spent the next year being toasted and celebrated wherever he went, even among the foreign ministers of Europe gathered at the Congress of Vienna. All was not over, however, for in late February 1815 Napoleon escaped from his Elba exile and marched on Paris. Every force sent by the new king, Louis XVIII, to stop him turned coat and joined the returning emperor. Luckily the other European powers could react quickly in the political realm, as they were gathered in Vienna. Unfortunately, a quick military reaction was another matter. Russian troops had a long march to rejoin the coalition forces and Austria had to reassemble her army. The two powers in a position to react quickly were Britain and Prussia. Wellington took command of the British and Dutch armies in Brussels while Field Marshal Gebhard von Blücher marched his Prussians west to join them.

The Opponents

THE ONE THING WELLINGTON MOST WANTED, and could not get, was time. He knew that if Napoleon could be kept passive in France, then overwhelming numbers would soon arrive to crush the returning emperor. Wellington had studied Napoleon's 1814 operations and been deeply impressed. He knew that it would be best to have overwhelming strength as at Leipzig, and hoped he could wait for Prince Karl Schwarzenberg's 210,000 Austrians, Johann von Frimont's 75,000 Austrians, and Mikhail Barclay de Tolly's 150,000 Russians.[78] Napoleon, of course, was not foolish enough to allow that to happen, so Wellington had to do the best with what he had.

On 28 March 1815 the British government had named him commander in chief of all British land forces. The army he commanded at Waterloo, however, was not even half British. The British had sent expeditions to the United States to try to successfully finish off the War of 1812, but had made no serious progress and had lost 2,000 veterans at New Orleans. Wellington's troops in Belgium were primarily recruits, well trained, of course, but unseasoned.[79] In June 1815 Wellington commanded just shy of 26,000 British troops.

The remainder of his force was made up of troops from northern Europe. He had the King's German Legion, which had served with him in the peninsula; its soldiers numbered 3,000 infantry and 3,000 cavalry. Hanover, their home province, had since the Congress of Vienna been recognized as a kingdom and was supplying a further 15,000 men, though mainly militia. The largest contingent of 29,500 men came from the United Netherlands, but the Dutch government demanded they remain an independent command under the 22-year-old Prince of Orange. Although he had spent some time with Wellington in the peninsula, the prince was in no way an experienced commander. Wellington must certainly have thought of the same Dutch political constraints placed on Marlborough's use of Dutch soldiers. The Dutch troops were also, for the most part, new recruits and were officered by former French servicemen. They had received basic training, but their raw state argued against counting on them too heavily.[80] The Duke of Brunswick provided 6,700 men in return for a British subsidy, and a further 7,300 came from the twin duchies of Nassau. Wellington's position was clearly less than ideal; although he had numbers, his troops lacked experience and efficiency. Additionally, most of the army spoke German or Dutch, which he could not. The units from Hanover, Brunswick, Nassau, and the Netherlands, although under his orders, had their own chains of command, supply systems, and training methods. This was not the force one would want with which to face Napoleon.[81]

The allied Prussian army was in rather better condition, though with its own problems. The Prussian army had been living on Frederick the Great's reputation for decades, until Napoleon crushed it in the twin battles of Jena and Auerstadt in 1806. Prussia was forced into an alliance with France, and its troops served under Napoleon in a number of campaigns, including the invasion of Russia. However, there had been an underground movement to rebuild and reform the army. After Napoleon's 1812 disaster, Prussia broke free and began putting its new army together along Napoleonic lines combined with traditional Prussian militarism. Thus, the army that marched into Belgium in 1815 had a number of veterans but also a number of new soldiers learning a new way of fighting. Luckily, the officer corps was composed of veterans, but the commander was not without his drawbacks. Gebhard von Blücher was in his early seventies, and something of a wild man. He commanded forces in the 1813 and 1814 campaigns against the French, whom he hated with a passion. Not only was he criticized for being too old, he was also known to favor wine, women, and gambling. He was nevertheless a feared commander; in his book on Blücher's army, Brigadier Peter Young observes, "He alone had the will-power, the drive, the optimism, the sheer guts to carry his raw army forwards. His quickness of decision, his presence of mind under fire, more than made up for his contempt for planning and cartography. With a Chief of Staff like [August von] Gneisenau to work out the details it was a positive advantage to the Prussians that Blücher did not concern himself with the minutiae of military administration."[82] He brought 117,000 infantry, 12,000 cavalry, and 296 guns.

Given the multiple weaknesses of the allied forces, Napoleon seemed to have a distinct advantage going into battle in the summer of 1815. His triumphant return from Elba to Paris brought the entire standing army of King Louis into his service, numbering some 180,000. A further 50,000 men, mainly officers, whom Louis had placed on extended leave to avoid paying, also returned. The last contingent of draftees, from 1814, brought in almost 100,000 more. Many more volunteered, perhaps wishing to trade life under the king for a return to the glory days of the emperor.

In spite of the impressive numbers, however, the French had to be spread thin to protect the frontiers. The large force also required a vast amount of resources to train and equip. Two hundred National Guard battalions were mobilized for manning fortresses; twenty battalions of veterans were assigned to train them. Civil officials were recalled to military posts and old regiments resurrected.[83] By early June the number reached over half a million, with a projected number of 800,000 by October. Plenty of weaponry remained from the previous two decades of war, and Napoleon was quick to get the armaments factories back into production. The main problem was not manpower but horses, the losses of which in the previous two decades had been proportionately larger than those of the soldiers. Thus, cavalry would be in somewhat short supply.[84]

Where Wellington was strong in experienced, dependable British subordinates, Napoleon had problems. Impressive as his total numbers may have been, his high-ranking officers proved to have been lower quality than they had once been.[85] His longtime chief of staff, Berthier, did not return to service and died from a fall (perhaps suicide) on 1 June. Marshals Soult and Ney had served Napoleon long and well, but had abandoned him after his expulsion to Elba. Napoleon forgave them and placed them second and third in command of his field army, but they were barely on speaking terms with each other. Soult took himself too seriously and could not be bothered with giving precise orders when battle came. Ney was given command in the field, but the years had worn on him and he may have been suffering from battle fatigue. He has been described as almost demented at times during the upcoming battle.[86] Other marshals had died. Murat, an outstanding cavalry commander, was both Napoleon's brother-in-law and king of Naples, but had infuriated Napoleon by rising up against the Austrians during his return to power. Murat was beaten, and the loss kept Naples from aiding Napoleon's return by securing France's southern front and diverting Austrian attention. Napoleon's anger overrode his judgment, and he refused to forgive Murat. Davout, another capable general, was made minister of war and left behind to maintain order in Paris.

The entire situation is reminiscent of one of Napoleon's aphorisms: Better an army of rabbits led by a lion than an army of lions led by a rabbit. Napoleon was not the lion he used to be. Many defeats since 1809 had robbed him of his mystique, and neither Wellington nor Blücher feared him. Some of the charisma was there, but it was not enough to cover some apparent weaknesses. One of his staff officers, Colonel Pétiet, had already noticed that the emperor was unable to spend as much time in the saddle as he used to: "His corpulence, his dull, pallid complexion, and his stiff gait made him seem quite different from the General Bonaparte I had known at the beginning of my career."[87] Given that in 1815 both Napoleon and Wellington were forty-six years old, their respective stars were on opposite paths.

The Battle of Waterloo

NAPOLEON, SUMMONING WHAT WAS LEFT of his leonine nature, made the first move. A quick victory was necessary, if there was to be any hope of awing the other nations into negotiations. With garrisons stationed in his frontier forts, Napoleon took the offensive. He surprised the allies by gathering and moving 89,000 infantry, 22,000 cavalry, and 366 cannons from various places around France on 6 June and having them ready to cross the Sambre River into Belgium nine days later. The old Napoleon seemed to be alive and well.[88]

That he would make the first move was not a surprise, but his target proved to be. Wellington assumed that his opponent would want to seize, or at least threaten, the Channel ports, which were vital for the British army's supply. Thus, he posted his army southwest of his headquarters in Brussels, placing them at Menin, Tournai, Ath, and Mons. Napoleon was famous for two maneuvers, and Wellington predicted the wrong one: the manoeuvre sur les derrières. Using this strategy, Napoleon would hold an enemy's attention to its front while moving the bulk of his force to its rear, threatening its lines of communication. However, finding himself outnumbered and facing superior enemy forces, Napoleon turned instead to the strategy of the central position. As David Chandler describes this strategy, "The traditional central position would then enable the French army to pin or mask each Allied army and destroy them one by one. Each wing would engage the attention of the enemy in its vicinity while the Emperor maneuvered the reserve and any other disengaged troops to fall on each force in turn."[89]

Thus, Napoleon aimed his army at Charleroi, splitting the 45-mile gap between Wellington in Brussels and Blücher in Namur. Blücher learned of Napoleon's intentions from a deserter, General Louis-Auguste-Victor Bourmont, on 14 July, and ordered his divided forces to come together for battle. He was working on the assumption that Wellington would move to his aid, as had been agreed between the two allies on 3 May. Chandler comments, "Although the Prussian concentration was going ahead as previously planned, it was nevertheless placing Blücher's army in increasing peril—for in warfare few movements are more dangerous than a forward concentration of troops in close proximity to a powerful and advancing enemy."[90] The first report of gunfire came from south of Charleroi at 4:30 on 15 June, with a message to headquarters arriving in Namur arriving at 9:00. Blücher had already begun concentrating his troops for an advance while alerting Wellington to the situation.

Just when Wellington received this communication is a matter of some debate.[91] Most sources record that it arrived at British headquarters at 3:00 on the 15th, making Wellington's reaction seem to have been very leisurely. He gave greater credence to reports of French demonstrations toward Lille and Dunkirk. Chandler notes that this interpretation of events "has indubitably harmed Wellington's reputation as a strategist. The Allies were fortunate to survive so blatant an error; normally only a single mistake was sufficient to deliver an enemy into Napoleon's hand, and by 3:00 p.m. on the 15th the Allied generals had already made two critical blunders."[92] Wellington did not really grasp the gravity of the situation until the night of the 15th, when word of fighting at Charleroi disturbed his dancing at a ball in Brussels. Realizing that Napoleon had "humbugged" him, he ordered his troops to prepare for a move to the southeast to assist the Prussians. Wellington met with his generals and ordered the army to Quatre Bras. The orders were quickly disseminated and the units began to march. He continued to dine and dance until 2:00, supposedly to convey a sense of calm to the crowd.

Wellington managed to get his army on the road early on 16 June, and reached the town of Quatre Bras, held by the young Prince of Orange, at 10:00. He then rode off to confer with the Prussians, who were about to be attacked at Ligny. Napoleon had to this point employed his plans perfectly. He sent his left wing northeast from Charleroi toward Quatre Bras under Ney, with orders to drive away the enemy along the Brussels road.[93] The right wing, under recently promoted marshal Emmanuel Grouchy, was to march northeast to defeat or drive Blücher back. The reserve under d'Erlon, who had fought at Vittoria, remained in Charleroi to assist whichever attack needed it most. With the orders given, Napoleon was on the move at dawn on the 16th with Brussels as his goal.

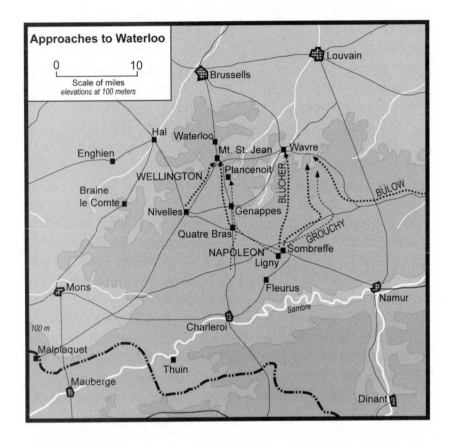

A victory over Wellington and capture of a capital city would do much to frighten other monarchs.[94]

Unfortunately for Napoleon, everything that had been going so right began to go wrong. Ney did not capture Quatre Bras as ordered. Grouchy ran into the Prussians farther forward than expected. Napoleon rode to investigate and decided on the spot to fight the Prussians first. He ordered the troops to deploy near the village of Ligny and sent word to Ney to bring his forces east and strike the Prussian flank. It took time for all of the French troops to march forward and into their deployments; meanwhile, Blücher's forces were also coming up in force. By the time Napoleon had sufficient men to launch his attack, the Prussians outnumbered him. Napoleon also ordered d'Erlon to bring up the reserves. The fighting went on throughout the afternoon of the 16th, and the French artillery seemed to have the best of it. As night was falling, however, rain began falling as well and the reserves had not arrived. Instead, they had been seen by the commander of the French rear guard and identified as enemy troops. Left with few options, Napoleon finally committed his Guard and managed to drive the Prussians from the field. The Prussians took a serious beating from the French artillery. Starting the day with 84,000 men and 224 guns on a front of seven miles, Blücher ended the day with a loss of 21 cannons and 25,000 killed, wounded, and captured. A further 9,000 fled eastward toward Liege.[95]

D'Erlon had not arrived in time because he had received conflicting orders, to join both Napoleon and Ney. He had first marched his men toward Quatre Bras, but found Ney unwilling to launch a major assault at what he wrongly assumed were superior numbers. He then marched his men to Ligny, arriving too late to take part in the battle. Had d'Erlon's force been committed at Quatre Bras the British would almost certainly have been badly beaten. The same can be said if they had been used against the Prussians. As it turned out, the lack of a reserve resulted in two indecisive battles instead of one overwhelming French victory. Still, Napoleon thought that the Prussians were sufficiently beaten to be shadowed by a relatively small force under Grouchy. The first intelligence reports had the Prussians withdrawing toward their base at Namur. He would take the rest of the army to reinforce Ney and defeat Wellington.

There were communication problems between allied forces as well. Blücher had taken a fall from his horse late in the battle and was out of action for several hours. His chief of staff, Gneisenau, assumed command in the meantime. Although the deserters and the wounded were retreating toward Namur to the northeast, Gneisenau took the bulk of the Prussian army north to Wavre. Neither the extent of the Prussian defeat at Ligny nor their destination were relayed to Wellington, however. Not until the following morning did a British patrol find Ligny in French hands. Wellington thus had little choice but to leave a rear guard in Quatre Bras while he gathered the remainder of his forces at Mont St. Jean, just south of the village of Waterloo on the road to Brussels. As the British began this move, they were aided by two strokes of luck. First, Napoleon's recurring illness struck him, and he was slow to issue orders, not sending the French out until noon on 17 June. That bought time for Wellington, as did torrential rains that fell that afternoon and evening as he settled in at Mont St. Jean.[96]

Adding to his good fortune, Wellington also heard from the Prussians, who informed him that they had reached Wavre at dark on the 17th and were within range of the proposed battlefield. Alistair Horne describes how "[o]ld Blücher, too, aided by liberal doses of his favorite medicine, garlic and gin, had recovered and was under way.... He dictated a letter to the British Field-Marshal assuring him that, 'ill as I am, [I will] put myself at the head of my troops and attack the right flank of the enemy immediately Napoleon makes any move against the Duke.'"[97] After stormy weather through the afternoon of the 17th and well into the night, the morning of the 18th saw Wellington and Napoleon facing each on two parallel ridges divided by waterlogged ground.

The area in which the battle took place is relatively small, some 5,000 yards wide and 1,500 yards across. The rains had turned the fields into a sticky mud, making life miserable for the soldiers, most of whom had camped in the open. As a result, the ground was not conducive to maneuvers and rapid marches, but instead favored the defense.[98] There are debates about how far in advance Wellington surveyed the ground. He may have seen it as early as his school days in Brussels. It is widely reported he pointed to the village on the map just before he left the ball in the early hours of the 16th. It is more likely, however, to have been a position almost forced on him by circumstance. Once he knew that the French were at Ligny and Quatre Bras, the road from the latter location to Brussels became the axis of movement. Given the nature of his grand tactics, to employ the reverse slope of a hill, the ground before Mont St. Jean was the only location Wellington could have profitably chosen. With armies facing each other on two ridges, somebody had to be on the defense, and the attacker was going to be at a disadvantage.[99]

Whether carefully chosen or the product of circumstance, the valley was perfect for Wellington's style of battle, which had become apparent in his days in the peninsula.[100] He deployed his font lines east-west along the crest of a ridge just north of the village of La Haye Sainte. These men were not as exposed as it may seem, however; the center of the battlefield was the north-south road to Brussels, and to Wellington's left for about a half to two-thirds of a mile, the Ohain road was not sunken but was bracketed by high, thick hedges that formed an obstacle to cavalry. To the duke's right of the crossroads, where the ground rises sharply, the road was sunken for about 400 yards, passing between embankments five to seven

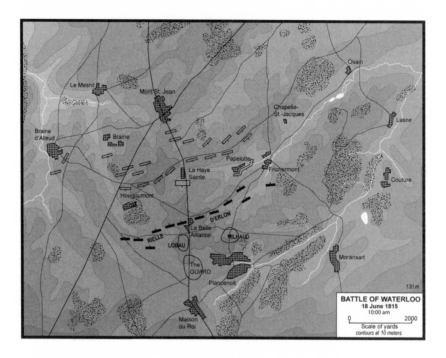

feet high before emerging level with the ground and descending gradually to Braine-d'Alleud.[101]

The remainder of Wellington's force was in dead ground on the north side of the ridge. Instead of sending out skirmishers, he placed units in three farmsteads: Hougoumont to the west, La Haye Sainte in the center, and Papelotte to the east. Papelotte was held by the Saxe-Weimar units that had seen the most difficult fighting at Quatre Bras and would be the first units to receive aid from the Prussians when they arrived. La Haye Sainte was held by the 2nd Light Battalion of the King's German Legion (500 men) supported by the British 95th Rifles in a sandpit just to the north. Hougoumont was garrisoned by the light companies of the Scots Guards and Coldstream Guards plus some 700 Hanoverians and men of the 2nd Nassau Regiment. The bulk of the British artillery and almost all the cavalry were on or behind the ridge. To the far western flank were 7,000 men of the Dutch-Belgian army at Braine-l'Alleud to cover a flanking attack to that side. Altogether there were some 30,000 men along the front and in the forward positions with another 22,000 in reserve. Still fearing a Napoleonic move to cut his lines of supply, Wellington unnecessarily placed another 17,000 men some ten miles farther west, well out of the battle zone.

Napoleon deployed his 1st Corps with 16,000 infantry, 1,500 cavalry, and 46 guns to his right under d'Erlon, who had spent the 15th marching between the two battles; thus, his men were the freshest. To his left, the 2nd Corps of 13,000 infantry, 1,300 cavalry, and 36 guns, all under Rielle, were positioned opposite Hougoumont. The remainder of his 72,000 men he held in the center, behind the mass of his artillery. His plan was to attack Hougoumont and draw Wellington's reserves there, then break through what would be the resulting weakened center after a massive cannonade. There would have been nothing wrong with this plan, had Napoleon had all day to implement it. Unfortunately for him, the rain had made the ground so muddy the cavalry could not operate effectively; more importantly, neither could the artillery. The cannons could not maneuver until the ground dried out and the mud would greatly nullify the effect of the cannonballs to tear through formations. He had little choice but to delay the attack until almost midday. He was ignorant of the fact that the Prussians were marching and that their shadow, Grouchy's 32,000 men, was not going to hinder them in any way.

So while waiting for the ground to harden somewhat, Napoleon inspected the troops. This was intended to raise the morale of his men and dishearten the enemy as well. Since so many British troops could not see the display, its effect on them was questionable; they could, however, hear the cries of "Vive l'Empereur!" as he rode along the lines. Wellington, who watched from his position, commented that Napoleon would soon learn what a "sepoy general" could do. He had no plan other to defend his chosen ground and react to Napoleon's moves. He had given a short-tempered response to the cavalry commander, the Earl of Uxbridge, the evening before: "Bonaparte has not given me any idea of his projects, and as my plans depend on his, how can you expect me to tell you what mine are?"[102]

Napoleon apparently wanted to press forward first with his 1st Corps on the right, to advance in oblique order with the leftmost unit in the lead. The order, however, seems to have been misinterpreted to mean that the left of the French line, 2nd Corps, would lead the attack. The attack began just before noon as Rielle's corps began to advance on the orchards around Hougomont farm. The Nassau and Guards light infantry held them at bay for some time, but were finally pressed back into the farmhouse complex. There the French made little headway against the extremely stout defense. With more of the Guards sent in after about an hour's fighting, the British force at this point ultimately numbered some 3,500; they drew into them some 7,000 French in what proved to be a battle within the larger battle. Rielle sent in more and more men, the "diversionary" attack taking on a life of its own. Wellington did not shift manpower to either flank as Napoleon had hoped.

At about noon the main batteries in the center of the French line opened up. This had been the key to breaking the Prussians at Ligny as it had been key to breaking the Austrians at Wagram. The French gunners, however, had little at which to aim if their intent was to break the British line. They lobbed shells over the ridge crest with no idea what effect they were having. To the veteran infantry in front, it appeared to be firing merely for intimidation, but to the units in the rear it was doing serious damage. British counterbattery fire from the sunken road on the ridge line did some serious damage as well, but Napoleon's 250-plus cannons outnumbered those of the British by 100. "With mounting uneasiness," Allessandro Barbero recounts, "the officers of the Allied infantry watched artillery caissons struck by enemy cannon-balls blow up before their eyes; . . . *Les belles filles de l'Empereur*, 'the Emperor's beautiful daughters'—as the French gunners affectionately called their 12-pounders—were doing their job well."[103] They needed to perform well, for off in the eastern distance trouble was approaching for the French army.

The French first spotted the oncoming force at about 1:30; Napoleon could not determine if the advancing troops were Blücher's or Grouchy's. He had sent word for Grouchy to march to the sounds of the guns (which he had indeed heard when they opened up at noon). Had the message arrived in time? Had Grouchy actually driven the Prussians away? In reality, it would have been a physical impossibility for Grouchy's men to be approaching the battle so soon, as they had actually begun the day marching to the northeast away from Waterloo. Whatever columns were approaching, they would enter the battlefield around Papelotte in about three hours.[104] Assuming the worst, Napoleon shifted his 6th Corps to the right flank to deal with the Prussians.

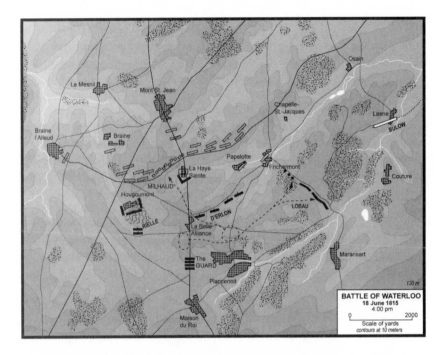

BATTLE OF WATERLOO
18 June 1815
4:00 pm
0   2000
Scale of yards
contours at 10 meters

With an increasing sense of urgency, d'Erlon's men began their advance at about 1:30. They made good progress at first, driving back the defenders at Papelotte, isolating the defenders within La Haye Sainte, and forcing the 95th to retreat from the sandpit. All seemed to be going well as a Dutch-Belgian brigade broke and ran, disrupting the advance of some of Picton's division. Had some cavalry been available this could have been key to a French victory. But there were none available, and British artillery fire and a counterattack by the 92nd Regiment broke the French charge. As d'Erlon's men began to retreat, the British cavalry came over the hill and rode many of the French soldiers down. Unfortunately, as so often happened throughout military history, the British horsemen did not know when to quit and found themselves in the midst of the French lines with no support. A French cavalry countercharge decimated the British cavalry, particularly the Scots Greys. The British cavalry took 50 percent casualties, 2,500 horsemen, failing to achieve what could have been a great success.[105] Despite these losses, the British cavalry did prevent the French from trying the British left wing again that day.

Wellington filled in his losses from d'Erlon's attack with men from his reserves, but more French attacks, primarily cavalry, were thrown across the field. With neither failure nor retreat an option and with valuable time passing, Napoleon ordered Ney to seize the La Haye Sainte farmhouse, at any cost. At 3:45 Ney led the charge, taking his men across the field, up the opposite hill, and into the British forces on the reverse slope. There the British formed fourteen squares, each of about 1,000 men, able to stand with muskets and bayonets against multiple cavalry charges. The largest assault, 12,000 horsemen, beat themselves against the squares and were obliged to retreat.[106] As the French cavalry were forced back across the Mont St. Jean ridge and to their own lines, the leading elements of the Prussian army were arriving along three parallel roads.

Depending on his right wing to hold the Prussians at bay, Napoleon ordered yet another massed cavalry charge at the British center. Its bravery and its defeat were repetitions of the previous attack. By 5:00 the remnants of the French cavalry were streaming back across the field, although the defenders of La Haye Sainte had finally run out of ammunition and been forced to abandon their position. Prussian troops were also pushing the French back and were threatening the village of Plancenoit. As the Prussians took and lost and retook the village, Napoleon shifted some of his reserves to assist. These were the Guard units, his elites, and a mere two battalions managed to beat back fourteen battalions of Prussians. The French line was temporarily stabilized.[107]

Napoleon had one last card to play. Certainly two major assaults on the British line had weakened them, he reasoned. Indeed, with the loss of La Haye Sainte the allied center was temporarily broken. Wellington deployed forward the last of his reserves and shifted his 7,000 from Braine-Alleud to the ridge overlooking Hougoumont. Unit commanders sent word to him for replacements or reinforcements, but no more existed. The British drew their flank forces to present as strong a line as possible along the ridge. Wellington himself led a unit of inexperienced Brunswickers, backed by two small units of cavalry.[108] It was 7:00 and Wellington had nothing left to commit. He prayed for Blücher or darkness.

Napoleon had had no more reserves when Ney called for them after taking La Haye Sainte, as they had been committed to his right against the Prussians at Plancenoit. With things somewhat stable there and with Wellington reeling in front, Napoleon could only do one thing to save the day for himself: commit the Imperial Guard.[109] The Guard had

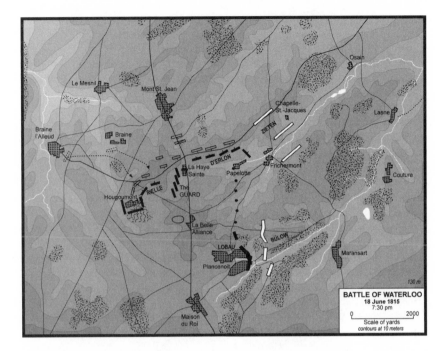

BATTLE OF WATERLOO
18 June 1815
7:30 pm
0   2000
Scale of yards
contours at 10 meters

just returned from Plancenoit when he ordered them forward. As they
marched toward the British lines, word spread of the Prussian arrival.
To stop these rumors, Napoleon ordered the word to be spread that the
newcomers were the men of Grouchy's column. This temporarily shifted
enthusiasm. He gathered together eleven battalions of the Old, Middle,
and Young Guard; five battalions, or 4,000 men, of the Middle Guard
took the lead. The Guard battalions marched in column formation, which
made for a lack of forward firepower as they approached the British line.
Further, they were unsupported by artillery or cavalry. All they had going
for them was their knowledge that they were the best Napoleon's army
had to offer.[110]

The charge got off to a good start, since the forward center of the
battlefield was now in French hands. Wellington had his men lie down
just below the crest of the ridge on the reverse side. They had done this
often during the day, and it greatly limited damage from the indirect
artillery fire. On the right side of the advancing French troops were two
battalions of grenadiers. They captured some artillery batteries, then
crossed the crest to face elements of Halkett's brigade, the 30th and 73rd
Foot. They almost drove the British troops back but for the arrival of

David Chassé's men with artillery, who began firing grapeshot into the French troops. To the French left were three battalions of chasseurs, which ran into the 1st and 2nd Battalions of the Foot Guards (later known as the Grenadier Guards). Now was the time to turn the tide. Wellington called out to the Foot Guards' commander, General Sir Peregrine Maitland, to engage with his infantry. They stood and fired at the French from a range of twenty yards, killing some 300 Frenchmen. The French Imperial Guardsmen kept advancing, but three more volleys broke their charge.[111]

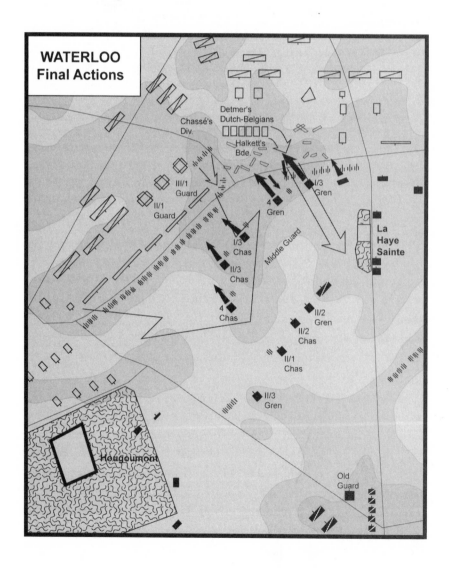

The attackers wavered, tried to return fire, and then fled into the battalions of the Old Guard, which were to be the second wave. Napoleon saw the assault faltering, followed by hordes of allied infantry and cavalry coming over the hill. With the Guard falling back, Wellington sensed the time was ripe for a counterattack. He waved his hat and the 40,000 men on the ridgeline burst forward.[112] Napoleon ordered the remaining Guard units into squares; they put up a minimal resistance before fleeing themselves. The Young Guard held out a while longer in Plancenoit, covering the retreat of the remnants of the French army. The French left some 32,000 casualties behind, as well as virtually all of their artillery.

Wellington won by fulfilling most of the tenets of a defensive battle. He had a day's head start in arriving at the battlefield, ground with which he was familiar, and personally placed his units. No defensive works could be constructed in the time he had, but the existing strong points of Hougoumont, La Haye Sainte, and Papelotte served him well. Security was his strength, as it had been in all his defensive battles: placing the majority of his troops on the reverse slope deceived his enemy as to his numbers, and played on the fears of Napoleon's subordinates who had faced Wellington in the peninsula and were aware of his tactics. Wellington was not one to use spoiling attacks on this day, but his ability to recover his guns on the ridgeline every time the French drove the gunners away allowed him to maintain fire on successive French attacks. Fortunately for him, Napoleon's army was sufficiently disjointed in their attacks that Wellington did not have to disrupt them with offensive actions. The forward strong points accomplished that goal. Wellington's deployment in dead ground not only deceived the enemy but allowed him to move reserves unseen. Thus, he was able to maintain his front line after each French assault. His final reserves, brought up from Braine l'Alleud, were perfectly placed to enfilade the attacking Guard units at the end of the battle and begin the pursuit immediately.

Wellington did not operate against Napoleon's flanks—that was Blücher's job. Although not under Wellington's direction (so the British commander cannot be credited with this flexibility), the Prussian flank attacks from midafternoon onward not only diverted French reserves but maintained enough pressure to keep the French from throwing sufficient reserves at Wellington late in the day. Wellington's greatest illustration of flexibility was in the nature of his defensive moves. He had no earthworks but used the existing strong points perfectly. His infantry squares did what they needed to do: break the French cavalry and quickly re-form into lines for the final assault.[113] Wellington used all military aspects of the terrain masterfully. The ridge provided both concealment from French observation and cover from the long-range artillery fire. The strength of the farm complexes proved sufficient that none could be taken until it was too late in the battle to make a difference.[114] Wellington covered the avenues of approach as well as his own lines to the flank and rear. His personal position was wherever he was needed; he rode all along the line throughout the battle, giving immediate directives in reaction to French moves. By occupying the road along the ridgeline, both sunken and covered by hedges, he kept all the ground in front of him in a covered field of fire.

Wellington and Blücher met immediately after the battle at La Belle Alliance. Which man was most responsible for the victory? Most give credit to Wellington, although some favor Blücher since without his flank attack the French would almost certainly have won the day. As Gordon Corrigan comments, "Arguments as to whether or not the Prussians, rather than Wellington, won the battle are irrelevant: had Wellington not relied upon Blücher to come and join him, he would not have fought the battle at all. As it was, the two commanders trusted and respected each other and the result was to the credit of both."[115] The Prussian cavalry were given the task of pursuit, but the exhausted horsemen went no more than a few miles to the Dyle River, where they stopped to rest. By the next morning the French army was out of touch. Napoleon hoped to regroup, but at each planned rallying point he found nothing but refugees or dead soldiers. He finally hustled to Paris to see if he could salvage a propaganda victory. Neither he, Wellington, nor Blücher ever saw battle again.

Wellington's Generalship

REVIEWS OF THE BATTLE at Waterloo almost always look at the multitude of mistakes made, primarily on Napoleon's part. While it is true he made more than was his wont, it still took a commander able to take advantage of those mistakes in order to emerge victorious. In considering the principles of war that Wellington best implemented, the clear choices are mass, maneuver, unity of command, and morale. Although he showed the elements of offensive in a number of battles and used surprise to his advantage at Vittoria, enough of his battles were fought on the defensive that these principles cannot be selected.

In the three battles discussed here, Wellington was outnumbered twice. Leading up to the battle at Assaye, he tried to implement a pincer movement with Stevenson's force. Should he have divided his forces and hoped for coordinated attacks across miles of unfamiliar terrain without communication between the two columns? On the surface of it, no. But neither would it have been wise to wait for Stevenson's arrival rather than attacking the Marathas on his own. In his book on the Anglo-Maratha Wars, Brigadier K. G. Pitre expresses the opinion that it "would have been logistically and strategically impossible to conduct this campaign with a single force. If Wellesley had combined both armies, the combination would have been not only hopelessly clumsy and slow, but totally incapable of guarding the Peshwa and the Nizam's territory. It could not have secured Ahmednagar and Jama. Moreover, both corps could not have advanced through the same defile on the same day."[116] Neither could he have withdrawn after making contact with the Marathas, for their cavalry would have harassed his column unmercifully. Once on the battlefield, however, his concentration of force was handled admirably. He used the *mass* of his troops at the Maratha right, breaking their line and forcing a withdrawal. Any other maneuver would almost certainly have ended in his destruction.

At Vittoria, although his forces were on separate lines of approach, they converged on the bulk of the French army along the Zadorra River line. The mass, three-fourths of his army, struck the front and both flanks of the primary French line, forcing a retreat. The fourth column was sufficient to accomplish its task of securing the road to Bilbao and, had it been more aggressively employed, could have been the anvil for the main attack's hammer.

At Waterloo, the use of mass only occurred at the end of the day. Wellington had no single decisive point to hold, and thus his numbers were dispersed across the battlefield. Only when the French had thrown in the Imperial Guard, and failed, did he get to use the mass of his force, which at that point was almost every man still upright. After being subject to attacks at almost all points, his entire line became the mass of his offensive as he went over from defense to offense.

Wellington also demonstrated the principle of *maneuver* from the earliest days in India. The battle at Assaye showed his ability to read terrain and respond almost immediately. Surprised to find the Marathas in a strong defensive position rather than in open formation as he had been led to believe, he saw the ability to shift his arriving troops around to the right to strike the Maratha flank. Again surprised by the speed of the Maratha change of front, he adapted his plan on the spot to deploy his forces more strongly to his left to strike the decisive blow while maintaining pressure on other parts of the enemy line. Corrigan asserts, "Assaye surely gives the lie to any suggestion that he was always cautious or lacked the speed of reaction to fight an encounter battle. Immediately upon realising that the Mahratta army were as close as they were, he had galloped straight to where he could see for himself, then in minutes had decided that the best option was to attack at once, had made his plan, issued his orders and had got the army under way."[117]

Vittoria was almost a textbook example of moving a force along separate lines. The entire 1813 Peninsular Campaign up to the battle at Vittoria showed Wellington's ability to continually threaten an enemy flank to force his retreat. His fast-moving army, operating in very rough terrain, kept the French army completely at bay until the French forces held their ground around Vittoria, where he was almost able to pull off a complete battle of encirclement.[118] Once the French decided to make a stand, his forces came together to oblige their retreat from the battlefield. Given the difficulties of communication over the miles separating the four columns, to assign routes and responsibilities to three men (while he commanded the fourth column) and have them come together, if not perfectly, then certainly in a sufficiently timely manner to accomplish his goal was a remarkable feat. The southernmost column operated virtually independently on the Heights of Puebla while Wellington was able to shift the line of attack immediately upon hearing of the uncovered bridge near Tres Puentes. The arrival of Picton and Dalrymple was almost fortuitously late, since Wellington's earlier attack with the Light Division meant the French northern flank was more exposed than it would have been had the two attacks been simultaneous.

At Waterloo, all of Wellington's maneuvering prior to the battle was in response to the surprise line of attack Napoleon chose and Ney's attack at Quatre Bras. After Quatre Bras, however, he was able to withdraw his men along lines he ordered to a battlefield of his choosing. Once the battle commenced, all of his maneuvering was again in reaction to attacks; the real maneuvering was his shifting of reserves from point to point as the battle progressed. It was the arrival of the flank attack by the Prussians that provided the bulk of the allied maneuver that day, but it was a move Wellington expected, even if he did not command it.

Wellington employed the principle of *unity of command* increasingly as his career progressed. This was due mainly to the very irregular quality of his subordinate commanders. In India he had few subordinates to worry about; as he and most of his officers were young, they learned together and were more likely to think alike. He learned some tactics from the Marathas and had no trouble implementing them without others who disagreed with his views. As Corrigan points out, "It was Wellesley and Wellesley alone who, without teaching, training or instructional manuals to help him, devised the tactics and organisation which won the war."[119] At Assaye, Wellington's personal reconnaissance gave him the opportunity to take in the situation and immediately move to action. Pitre notes, "His first infantry attack . . . unhinged the Maratha right flank. . . . An unexpected situation developed, when the 'dead' gunners turned their guns and started firing at the cavalry. Wellesley restored the position by employing his remaining infantry units who restored his rear area. . . . Wellesley ordered Maxwell's second charge, but in the time thus gained, he realigned his infantry for the second attack."[120] His constant movement around the battlefield was what saved the day after the skirmishers advanced in the wrong direction. He was on the spot to see the developing problem and order in the cavalry to save the exposed soldiers, and in doing so drive some Maratha cavalry back into their own lines.

In Portugal Wellington often complained about the low caliber of officer sent to him from England. In 1811, he wrote to the Horse Guards concerning some of his commanders: "I have received the letter announcing the appointment of Sir William Erskine, General Lumley and General Hay to this Army. The first I understand to be a madman. I believe you agree that the second is not very wise. The third may be useful."[121] Even had they been of better or even consistent quality, it probably would have made little difference; Wellington had little use for seconds in command: "It has a great and high-sounding title, without duties or responsibility of any description . . . excepting in giving opinions for which he is in no manner responsible."[122]

Almost all accounts of Wellington's command style reflect his disdain for those under him, and he not only rejected the concept of an immediate subordinate but also was not terribly fond of the idea of a staff along modern or even Napoleonic lines. He was not inclined to consult with subordinates on anything but technical matters, and he was not happy with the independent views of others.[123] He was, however, dependent on subordinates who would follow orders, since he was often in the thick of the battle on a large field and could not, as at Assaye, be everywhere. After the battle at Vittoria, he court-martialed a battery commander for moving his guns on the directive of another senior officer. At the same time, had Graham not followed his orders to the letter and cut the road to Bayonne, he might have been able to seize Vittoria instead and destroy the French army.

At Waterloo Wellington made sure each unit was properly placed and had a clear understanding of its orders; he then rode back and forth across the lines to move men and materiel as needed. Orders were sent off by aides-de-camp, but Wellington was completely hands-on during the battle, not only repositioning reserves but at times taking personal command of units whose officers were killed or wounded. In his analysis of Wellington as a commander, Michael Glover writes, "Three times he personally led up the wavering Brunswick battalions and the third time they stayed in line and did their duty. A rifleman of the Ninety-fifth recalled how during the French cavalry charges 'while we were in square the second time, the Duke of Wellington and his staff came up to us in all the fire, and saw we had lost all our commanding officers; he, himself, gave the word of command.'"[124] By taking control to such an extent, Wellington would have left his forces in dire straits had he been incapacitated or killed, which does not argue in his favor. Further, any failures would be laid only at his feet.

Wellington also employed the principle of *morale* to great effect, despite the fact that he is often criticized for displaying an uncaring attitude toward his soldiers. He certainly was not one to ride along the lines and whip up enthusiasm by his presence, as Napoleon or Alexander did. He famously called his troops "the scum of the earth," although he followed it up (less famously) with the line "but you can hardly conceive of such a set brought together, and it is really wonderful that we should have made them the fine fellows they are."[125] Many things transformed the drunks of the city slums into a trusted soldiery: the Dundas and Moore reforms implemented in the boot camps of England, the increasing development of the concept of loyalty to the regiment, and the willingness to follow a winner. Wellington may not have earned the adulation of the troops, but he earned their respect. For all his denigrating comments, Wellington respected his troops as well; as he said to his confidante Lady Salisbury, "I could have done *anything* with that army, it was in such splendid order."[126]

Wellington's aloof personality proved more an advantage than a drawback, for his apparent calmness under fire was essential to the men's morale. Russell Weigley comments that "[t]he calmness of the Iron Duke during the climactic phase of the battle [Waterloo] was also invaluable in shaping the outcome, holding the Anglo-Dutch army to its stubborn resistance against the desperate onslaughts of the French."[127] This characteristic, shown at his final battle, was also there in his younger days at Assaye: as a volunteer in the 78th commented, he was "in the thick of the action the whole time. . . . I never saw a man so cool and collected as he was."[128] Wellington rode back and forth along the Mont St. Jean ridge throughout the battle of Waterloo, fully exposed to enemy fire as subordinates were shot down on either side; nothing could have been done at that battle to more motivate the men following him. He may not have been in the middle of the fight like Alexander or Belisarius or Gustavus, but Wellington risked death nonetheless. John Keegan writes, "That he had been spared was unquestionably one of the most remarkable outcomes of the battle, for he had been exposed to danger from its beginning to its end. Of his personal staff of sixty-three, no less than twenty had been killed or wounded. . . . Moreover, he himself had consistently been within cannon range of the enemy and frequently within musket range—say a hundred yards. That he had been mobile only made his exposure more extreme, for he always moved *towards* not *away* from fire."[129]

Although his campaigns in Iberia were a mixed bag of advance and retreat, Wellington finished his career the victor in every theater in which he fought. He had strategic and tactical genius. As Chandler notes, "His generalship was a blend of calculated example, of 'heroic generalship' at many a critical moment and place on the battlefield, and of cool realistic appraisal of strategic realities and military capabilities. That remains as clear today as it has ever done before."[130] Chandler attributes four major strengths to him: he never feared the French way of fighting, he grasped his role in the overall grand strategy of wherever he fought, he was a master of logistics, and he developed great skill in minor tactics, especially in his signature use of the reverse slope on the defensive. Although Wellington had risen through the ranks through purchase, he had been wise enough to learn lessons at each level of command so he knew what was necessary in any situation. Philip Haythornthwaite notes that "he owed much of his success to the attention he always paid to the inferior parts of tactics as a regimental officer. It was his firm belief that before a commander can group divisions and move an army he must understand the mechanism and power of the individual soldier, then that of a company, a battalion, a brigade and so on."[131]

Perhaps the one word that best describes Wellington as commander is flexibility, or the ability to use what was at hand to accomplish his goals, no matter how it may have looked. His comparison between his own methods and those of his French opponents in the peninsula best illustrates his way of war: "They planned their campaigns just as you might make a splendid piece of harness. It looks well; and answers very well; until it gets broken; and then you are done for. Now I made my campaigns of ropes. If anything went wrong, I tied a knot; and went on."[132]

16

Conclusion

A Coup d'Oeil at the Great Commanders

Definitions, axioms, pet theories, and checklists abound, but leadership, like sex, is a doing thing.

—Henry G. Gole, "Leadership in Literature"

OUR SUBJECT IS *Menschenführung*, one of those clumsy-precise German words, which means "leading human beings." As historian and retired air force general Montgomery Meigs observes, "There seems to be no real conclusive body of thought on what makes a good general. So as a start point, study of the leadership attributes of generals, past and present, should be useful. Historians and commentators alike usually cite character as the essential ingredient of enlightened senior leadership, especially of military leaders."[1] Meigs goes on to propose four qualities of character for great commanders: intellect, energy, selflessness, and humanity. While these are without question essential, we might add decisiveness and speed on the battlefield, as well as the ability to both maximize one's own strengths while minimizing those of the enemy. Almost all the generals discussed in this work were at the cusp of a change in warfare and were often responsible for bringing about that change. But let's examine Meigs's more traditional list of attributes.

MEIGS SAYS THAT INTELLECT is the basis of competence, intuition, and will. Few of the generals considered here were products of institutions of higher learning (Meigs himself went to West Point); they all learned their craft through experience. Some, especially the most recent subjects, commented on their appreciation of history. Han Xin had the writings of Sun Tzu to which to turn for advice, while Belisarius had the writings of Vegetius.[2] The others learned what they knew from actual combat, as well as from whatever commanders they may have served under or against. Alexander learned from his father, Hannibal from his, Scipio from Hannibal, Žižka from his experience against the Teutonic Knights, Marlborough from Turenne, and so forth.

I would argue that what Meigs means by intellect should include another abstraction—"vision." This quality might include not only a willingness to use new weaponry (Scipio, Oda Nobunaga, Jan Žižka, Gustavus Adolphus) or even tactical innovations (Epaminondas, Frederick), but the oft-mentioned coup d'oeil—the ability to sum up the terrain, the opposition, and the correct offensive moves in a matter of moments. Can such a quality be learned? Perhaps—if one were to study the masters and look at the maps of their battlefields, or walk the battlefields and see what the generals saw, or look at any terrain and decide as quickly as possible where the lay of the land would help or hinder an offense or a defense. Acquiring this quality would probably require regularly war-gaming, a late development in learning to command.

The heart of the coup d'oeil is the ability quickly to determine an enemy's center of gravity, which means, in the strategic sense, choosing the enemy army as opposed to being locked on a fixed objective. In the tactical sense, it often means knowing how to find and eliminate the enemy commander. That certainly was Alexander's consistent goal, and Epaminondas's when Cleombrotus was killed at Leuctra. As I discuss below, knowing an enemy's weakness is often the center of gravity.

One also has to include imagination under intellect, meaning not only introducing new tactics but employing methods that almost exceed the conception of adversaries. The citizens of Tyre, for example, were certain that their island city and its walls were impervious to attack—until Alexander built a mole more than half a mile long from the shore, and developed weapons and siege engines to operate from ships against those walls. Long Ju, likewise, could not imagine that Han Xin would build a dam to entice him across the Wei River, only to have much of his army drowned and the rest isolated.

Second, we must consider energy, which is best displayed in the commander's involvement with the troops, during peacetime but more particularly during war. Before the battle, the generals covered in this book were in motion with their armies if not marching in the ranks, and whenever possible were scouting the battlefield before the fighting started. Jan Žižka was planning deployments even when he was blind. Whether they arrived in wagons or on horseback or by footslogging, they were in the field and in view. To accomplish what he did, Subedei needed to keep up with his troops' rapid movements. Leadership means not merely leading but being seen leading. Sitting in headquarters is not an option. To make his point, Meigs quotes General Matthew Ridgeway, who guided UN forces in Korea after Douglas MacArthur was relieved of his command: "A basic element in troop leadership is the responsibility of the commander to be where the crisis of action is going to happen."[3]

Energy is of course vital if one is going to actively be involved in the fighting, as Alexander was in all of his battles. Caesar certainly illustrated it at Alesia. And Belisarius seemed to be everywhere during the siege of Rome—coordinating troops, civilians, and construction when he wasn't firing arrows at Ostrogoth riders from the walls or leading cavalry operations. Even when not in actual combat, the general needs to be in a position to act and react. Wellington was always described as being where the action was hottest. One regular observation of Napoleon's declining days involved the lack of energy he demonstrated in comparison with early in his career. His physical ailments kept him from the Waterloo battlefield at its most important juncture.

Meigs's third quality, selflessness, is best illustrated when commanders place themselves in harm's way to achieve victory. As we've seen, most of the commanders in this book spent time in the field with their troops and sometimes suffered their privations, but without exception all of them were on or near the battlefield when the action started. From Epaminondas to Marlborough they were often engaging in combat themselves—as we've seen with Alexander, Hannibal, Caesar, and Belisarius in particular. Meigs observes that Marlborough was not "worrying about his own skin when he placed himself in danger at Ramillies and Oudenarde."[4]

Those who held themselves back from swinging a sword or firing a musket (Oda, Frederick, Napoleon, Wellington) were on the field, watching and directing the action and within arrow or gun range. In the political arena, some of these men were willing to act from behind the scenes, but the battlefield is a different kind of arena. A commander must truly be willing to sacrifice himself, as J. F. C. Fuller once wrote: "Death is the bandmaster of War, and unless all, from general to drummer boy, follow the beat of his baton, harmony must eventually give way to discord."[5]

The last of Meigs's qualities of greatness is humanity. As he expresses this quality, "The difference between winning and not winning lies often in the faith of the unit in their leader and in their ability together to persevere through that last final push that breaks the enemy's will. To engender that faith, generals must have a human touch and a feel for the troops."[6] Meigs's "human touch" may not be what most people would call humanity—concern about the lives and conditions of others. Yet it is how the soldiers under one's command would define it. Alexander and Napoleon were renowned for identifying individual soldiers by name and praising their performances. Napoleon in particular offered quick rewards for exemplary service. His comment on what men would do for a scrap of ribbon reveals a certain cynicism; on the other hand, he knew that that scrap of ribbon translated into status and often rank and monetary advancement. Oda exhibited little concern for the welfare of his individual soldiers, but by instituting the widespread use of ashigaru he offered a way for peasants to rise in status through military service.

Hannibal could not appeal to his veterans' sense of national pride— many were mercenaries and far from home—so he appealed to their personal pride by setting the example. The humanity these generals showed is what motivates all good soldiers: it binds individuals together and creates cohesion; it is the basis of brotherhood. Hannibal was a soldier's soldier; what man under him could do less? Žižka didn't let blindness keep him from the battlefield, and his men served him with greater devotion because of it.

Further, Žižka had a religious motivation that was unique among the commanders in this book. Religion played a remarkably small role in their fighting lives, it seems. Alexander may have viewed himself as divine, but was hardly intent on spreading Greek religion. Belisarius was a champion of Justinian, who was as well known for his religious reforms in the Byzantine Empire as for his foreign policy, but neither seems to have used "God and country" in motivating the troops. Gustavus, as a champion of the Protestant cause in the Thirty Years War, was probably the only other commander here whose faith in God inspired him in battle. Indeed just before his final cavalry charge he commented, "The Lord God is my armor."

Those are Meigs's elements. Other military thinkers have outlined other qualities, most of them connected in some way. U.S. Air Force colonel John Boyd believes that decisiveness is key to military victory and devised the so-called OODA loop: "observe," "orient," "decide," and "act."[7] This has to be done again and again as the battle develops and done faster than the enemy can. This also incorporates some of the aspects of "vision" discussed above—the coup d'oeil during which the commander chooses a deployment or method of attack, particularly one his opponent least expects. Decisiveness shows itself in battle by the commander's knowing when and where to strike. At Austerlitz, Napoleon not only set up the battlefield deployment but knew precisely where the enemy weak point would appear and when to launch his striking force.

The generals discussed here were quick to issue the necessary orders, knowing their men could and would implement them. Alexander could throw himself into the battle assured that his subordinates would do their jobs. Hannibal at Cannae could face an army far superior in numbers because he knew his men and because he had developed a bold plan. Han Xin could do the same at Jingxing. Though he did not have a close relationship with his relatively new troops, he could anticipate their abilities. At both Ramillies and Oudenarde, Marlborough demonstrated the ability to plan and deploy—almost on the run—even as his enemy was deploying simultaneously. None of these commanders ever exhibited hesitation. Even on defense, they knew when to seize the opportunity to counterattack.

Related to decisiveness is of course speed, a quality perhaps best demonstrated at the operational level. Whichever general can get his men to a battlefield before the enemy expects them has a distinct advantage. Sometimes this means the general gets to choose his battleground and create an ambush, like Hannibal at Lake Trasimene. Belisarius reached Rome so quickly the Ostrogoths had to abandon the city, setting up the year-long siege. Subedei paced his withdrawal in order to set up the ambush at the Kalkha River. Žižka had enough time to read the ground and deploy at Sudomer before the imperial forces attacked. At Hohenfriedberg and

Leuthen, Frederick got to the field before his enemy was fully deployed and created a surprise attack. So did Marlborough at the Schellenberg and Subedei at the Sajo River. The result is often a smaller casualty count for both sides, as was not the case at Lutzen, Blenheim, and Waterloo.

Speed in battle can be just as important. Epaminondas's deep phalanx running across the plain at Leuctra caught the Spartans in midmaneuver. Alexander began the battle at the Issus late in the day, before the Persians could read and react. Oda surprised Imagawa's army at Okehazama by rushing into his camp in the immediate wake of a hailstorm. Žižka broke out of his encirclement at Kutna Hora by striking in the dead of night against an unprepared Sigismund. Frederick's rapid redeployment at Rossbach caught the French cavalry and infantry completely unawares. Napoleon's rapid redeployment of troops at Rivoli beat back one uncoordinated Austrian attack after another until he could launch his counteroffensive.

In the end every great commander recognizes relative strengths and weaknesses—whether in a coup d'oeil, or over time. This applies to new tactics or weaponry, which can play a part in overturning an enemy's strength. For example, the deep phalanx at Leuctra broke the "invincible" Spartan force. The Persian chariots proved useless against the sarissas and discipline of Alexander's formations. Pompey's large cavalry force had no better luck against Caesar's smaller mixed cavalry and light infantry using their pila as stabbing spears instead of javelins. Oda's matchlocks broke the Takeda cavalry, just as the Hussite hand cannons helped to defeat the imperial knights—their armor became a liability once they were unhorsed. Žižka also negated the superior numbers of his enemies by deploying his forces in such a way that the enemy was obliged to fight on a narrow front. Gustavus's lighter artillery tore apart the imperial tercios, as did his quicker-firing musketeers. Napoleon's army was famous for its artillery; Wellington negated its effectiveness by employing the reverse slope at many of his battles in Spain, and most notably at Waterloo.

Connected to assessing strengths and weaknesses is using them to outmaneuver or outthink an opponent. Alexander played on—indeed relied upon—the Persians' sense of security in their positions at all of his battles with them. At Ilipa, Scipio negated the usually devastating effect of the Carthaginian elephants by means of a complex maneuver that placed cavalry and light infantry nearest them, so the elephants' size and strength were negated by swarms of arrows and javelins from the more mobile Roman forces. Frederick's classic outflanking move at Leuthen made moot the entire Austrian army position.

Conversely, the weakness of using Hussite peasants for soldiers became a strength when they proved far more mobile—able to use their wagons and farm implements for military purposes—and far more motivated than their opponents. The use of smaller forces to divert larger ones is probably the most effective way of benefiting from weakness. Han Xin's smaller force backed up against the Wu River at Jingxing focused the enemy attention away from the cavalry thrust to the rear. The Mongol tactic of the feigned retreat was always to give the impression of weakness or defeat.

Perhaps even more important than the coup d'oeil is the ability to foresee an opposing commander's moves. Sun Tzu wrote, "Know yourself and know your enemy and in a hundred battles you will not be defeated." This is the most consistently illustrated characteristic of the generals in this study.

It helps of course when an opponent is predictable or overconfident, as were the Roman generals Hannibal faced—Tiberius Longus at the Trebia River and Flaminius at Lake Trasimene; much the same Roman attitude resulted in the slaughter at Cannae. Belisarius took advantage of the overzealous Persian cavalry at Dara to strike both their attacking forces in flank or rear. Žižka knew that once the armored knights deployed they would not shy away from attacking his peasant wagenburgs, and thus defeated them multiple times. Subedei's opponents never caught on to the feigned retreat. Oda knew Takeda would throw his cavalry at him at Nagashino. Marlborough knew at Blenheim and Ramillies that the enemy would use villages as strong points, so he held them there and broke through weakly held portions of their lines elsewhere. At Rossbach Frederick took advantage of a command divided between two generals who were both sure of their abilities. And perhaps no commanders in any battle in history were as manipulated as the Russian and Austrian emperors at Austerlitz (though Mack at Ulm is in the running for the honor). Finally, Wellington's conversation with Picton just before Waterloo was a telling illustration of taking advantage of enemy habits: "Well, here they come in the same old way." "Yes, and we shall beat them in the same old way."

CAN THE STUDY OF THESE GREAT CAPTAINS confer any advantages today at the tactical and grand tactical levels of combat? Without question. At heart, whatever the abstraction that might have applied to their thinking, the actions taken by these great commanders of the past involve terrain and the deployments and are mainly boots-on-the-ground concepts. New technology does not make irrelevant history's lessons. As George Patton wrote to his son: "To be a successful soldier you must know history. Read it objectively. . . . What you must know is how man reacts. Weapons change, but the men who use them change not at all."[8]

GLOSSARY

Terms are synthesized from the U.S. Army Field Manual 100-5, *Operations*, pp. 7-01–7-09.

Characteristics of the Offense

1. *Surprise*—Commanders achieve surprise by striking the enemy at a time or place or in a manner for which it is not physically or mentally ready. Knowing the enemy commander's intent and denying his ability to conduct thorough and timely intelligence is crucial.

2. *Concentration*—The ability to mass effects without massing large formations is essential for achieving and exploiting success. Attacking commanders manipulate their own and the enemy's concentration of forces by some combination of dispersion, concentration, deception, and attack.

3. *Tempo*—The rate of speed of military actions; controlling or altering that rate is essential for maintaining the initiative.

4. *Audacity*—A key component of any successful offensive action. A simple plan, boldly executed, requires audacious leaders to negate the disadvantages of numerical inferiority.

Tactical Offense Forms

1. *Movement to Contact*—An offensive operation conducted to develop the situation and to establish or regain contact. It may also include preliminary diversionary actions and preparatory firing.

   - *Approach march*—used when a commander is relatively certain of the enemy's location and is a considerable distance from the enemy.
   - *Search and attack*—conducted by smaller, light maneuver units to destroy enemy forces, protect the force, deny area to the enemy, or collect information.
   - *Reconnaissance in force*—a limited-objective operation by a considerable force to obtain information and to locate and test enemy dispositions, strengths, and reactions.
   - *Meeting engagement*—the desired result of a movement to contact.

2. *Attack*—The purpose of an attack is to defeat, destroy, or neutralize the enemy. The same fundamentals apply to each type of attack. The differences lie in the amount of planning, coordination, and preparation before execution.

   - *Hasty attack*—the most likely result of a meeting engagement. The forces at hand are used with minimal preparation to destroy enemy forces before they can concentrate or establish a defense.
   - *Deliberate attack*—fully synchronized operations that employ the effects of every available asset against the enemy defense.
   - *Spoiling attack*—mounted from a defensive position to disrupt an expected enemy attack. One strikes while the enemy is most vulnerable: during his preparations for attack.
   - *Counterattack*

- *Raid*
- *Feint and demonstration*—A feint is designed to divert enemy attention from the main effort; it is a shallow, limited-objective attack. A demonstration is a show of force in an area where a decision is not sought; no attack is made.

3. *Exploitation*—The attacker extends the destruction of the defending enemy force by maintaining offensive pressure.

4. *Pursuit*—An offensive operation against a retreating enemy force, following a successful attack when the enemy cannot form an organized defense; its object is the destruction of the opposing force.

NOTES

Introduction

1. "Greatest Military Leaders" at George Patton Historical Society Library, http://pattonhq.com/militaryworks/leaderslist.html, 28 Oct. 2012.
2. Basil Liddell Hart, *Scipio Africanus: Greater than Napoleon* (Cambridge, MA: DaCapo Press, 1994 [1926]), p. xi.
3. Daniel L. Byman and Kenneth Pollack, "Let Us Now Praise Great Men," *International Security* 25 (4), Spring 2001, p. 107.
4. Kimberly Kagan, *The Eye of Command* (Ann Arbor: University of Michigan Press, 2006), p. 200.
5. David Chandler, *Marlborough as Military Commander* (Staplehurst, Kent: Spellmount, 2003 [1973]), pp. 318–19.

Chapter 1. Epaminondas

1. Nepos, *Vitae*, 2.1.
2. Ibid., 3.1–3.
3. Lynn, *Battle: A History of Combat and Culture.*
4. Spence, *The Cavalry of Classical Greece*, p. 151.
5. Xenophon, *Hellenica*, 6.4.11, in *Xenophon in Seven Volumes.*
6. Pritchett, *The Greek State at War*, vol. 1, pp. 134–43.
7. Luginbill, *Othismos*, p. 56.
8. Goldsworthy, "The *Othismos*, Myths and Heresies"; for another overview of the controversy, see Stylianou, *Historical Commentary on Diodorus Siculus*, appendix "The Nature of Hoplite Fighting," pp. 552–55.

9. Starr, *Ancient World*, pp. 211–12.
10. Diodorus, *Library*, 15.52.3–4.
11. Sextus, *Stratagems*, 1.12.5.
12. Diodorus, *Library*, 15.53. 4; 15.54.1.
13. Frontinus, *Stratagems*, 1.11.6.
14. Hamilton, *Agesilaus*, p. 187.
15. Polyaenus, *Stratagems*, 2.3.15.
16. Diodorus, *Library*, 15.55.2.
17. Xenophon, *Hellenica*, 6.4.13.
18. Devine, "Embolon: A Study in Tactical Terminology," pp. 201–17.
19. Buckler, "Epameinondas and the 'Embolon,'" pp. 134–43.
20. Goldsworthy, "*Othismos*," p. 8.
21. Xenophon, *Hellenica*, 6.4.13–14.
22. Ibid., 6.4.15.
23. Ibid., 7.5.24.
24. Nepos, *Vitae*, 9.4
25. Cawkwell, "Epaminondas and Thebes," p. 261.
26. Delbruck, *Warfare in Antiquity*, p. 166.
27. Hanson, "Epameinondas."
28. Lendon, *Soldiers and Ghosts*, p. 107.
29. Hanson, *Soul of Battle*, p. 46.
30. Goldsworthy, "*Othismos*," pp. 24–25, citing V. H. Davis.
31. Hanson, "Epameinondas," pp. 199, 206.
32. Lendon, *Soldiers and Ghosts*, p. 122.
33. Liddell Hart, *Strategy*, p. 34.

Chapter 2. Alexander

1. Plutarch, "Alexander."
2. Hamilton, "Alexander's Early Life," p. 119. This work provides a good overview of Alexander's upbringing, with references to the best known works of its time, which was the mid-1960s.
3. Hammond, "What May Philip Have Learnt as a Hostage in Thebes?"
4. Griffith, "Philip as a General and the Macedonian Army," p. 58.
5. Borza, "What Philip Wrought," pp. 107–8.
6. Delbruck, *Warfare in Antiquity*, p. 179.
7. Jones, *The Art of War in the Western World*, p. 22.
8. Different views of this issue are covered in Markle, "The Macedonian Sarissa, Spear, and Related Armor," pp. 329–30.
9. Jones, *Art of War*, p. 22; Heckel and Jones, *Macedonian Warrior*, pp. 13–18.
10. Worley, *Hippeis*, p. 155.
11. Barker, *Armies of the Macedonian and Punic Wars*, p. 88.
12. Tarn, *Hellenistic Military*, p. 65.
13. Hamilton, *Alexander the Great*, pp. 68–69.
14. Hammond, *The Genius of Alexander the Great*, p. 89.

15. Green, *Alexander of Macedon*, pp. 228–29.

16. Kutta, "Warfare in the Age of the Peloponnesian Wars and Alexander the Great," p. 16.

17. British Museum, BM 71537.

18. Diodorus Siculus, *Library*, 17.5.3–6.3.

19. On Darius's background, rise to power, and reign, see Badian, "Darius III"; also, for an overview of the state of the Persian Empire upon Alexander's invasion, see Briant, *Histoire de l'empire perse*.

20. For a more complete look at Alexander's campaigns to suppress rebellions after Philip's death, see Arrian, *The Anabasis of Alexander*, and Hammond, "Alexander's Campaign in Illyria."

21. For an overview of the ancient and modern (as of 1974) sources and an analysis of the Granicus battleground, see Nikolitsis, *The Battle of the Granicus*. For a deeper look into the battle and its relevance to the overall Persian campaign, see Devine, "Demythologizing the Battle of the Granicus."

22. For a look at Alexander's route of march and the establishment of supply bases, see Engels, *Alexander the Great and the Logistics of the Macedonian Army*, ch. 2.

23. Keegan, *The Mask of Command*, p. 26.

24. Arrian, *The Anabasis of Alexander*, 2.6–14.

25. Green, *Alexander of Macedon*, p. 228.

26. Warry, *Warfare in the Classical World*, p. 80.

27. Delbruck, *Warfare in Antiquity*, p. 192.

28. Hammond, *The Genius of Alexander*, p. 89.

29. Delbruck, *Warfare in Antiquity*, p. 195.

30. Keegan, *The Mask of Command*, p. 83.

31. Curtius, *History of Alexander*, 4.2.4–5.

32. Keegan, *The Mask of Command*, p. 82.

33. Ravilious, "Alexander the Great Conquered City via Sunken Sandbar."

34. Kern, *Ancient Siege Warfare*, pp. 213–15.

35. Curtius, *History of Alexander*, 4.4.14, 16.

36. Hamilton, *Alexander the Great*, p. 165.

37. Lendon, *Soldiers and Ghosts*, p. 119.

38. Curtius, *History of Alexander*, 10.5.26–29. http://luna.cas.usf.edu/~murray/classes/aa/source08.htm,

39. Borza, "The Conquest of Persia," p. 141.

40. Montagu, *Greek and Roman Warfare*, p. 30.

Chapter 3. Han Xin

1. Sima, "Biography of the Marquis of Huai-yin," p. 180. Westernized spelling of the Chinese language has changed over the years. At the time of this publication (1947), the Wade-Giles method dominated. Since the late 1960s, the Pinyin form has been the accepted method of spelling. Hence,

Han Xin becomes Han Hsin in Wade-Giles. Any quoted spelling in the Wade-Giles method will not be altered unless the change is markedly different.

2. Sima, "Biography," p. 182.
3. Sima, *Records of the Grand Historian*, pp. 164–65.
4. Information on weaponry and organization from C.J Peers, *Soldiers of the Dragon*, pp. 33–46; Richard Nable collection; "Ancient Bronze Weapons"; and "Weaponry of the Bronze Age."
5. Sima, "Biography," p. 185.
6. Sima, *Historical Records*, p. 122.
7. Paludan, *Chronicle*, p. 29.
8. Haichen, *Wiles of War*, p. 74.
9. Ah Xiang, "Han Dynasty," asserts 500,000 to 600,000; Hardy, *Worlds of Bronze and Bamboo*, p. 105, gives 560,000.
10. Haichen, *Wiles of War*, p. 75.
11. Sima, *Historical Records*, pp. 128–29.
12. Sawyer and Sawyer, *One Hundred Unorthodox Strategies*, p. 169; the translator John de Francis in Sima, "Biography," p. 189, n.42, discusses this in more detail, suggesting: "More probable than the use of airtight pontoons or wooden tubs was the use of log rafts or the flat-bottomed scows which are used today as ferries on the Yellow River."
13. Sima, *Records of the Grand Historian*, p. 168.
14. Ibid., p. 169.
15. Sima, "Biography," p. 192.
16. Haichen, *Wiles of War*, p. 140.
17. The Wei River discussed in this section is in modern Shandong Province and is not the same Wei River mentioned earlier that flows eastward past Chang'an to intersect the Yellow River.
18. Sima, *Records of the Grand Historian*, p. 71.
19. Sima, *Historical Records*, p. 133.
20. Sawyer and Sawyer, *One Hundred Unorthodox Strategies*, p. 172.
21. Ibid., pp. 172–73.
22. Sima, *Records of the Grand Historian*, p. 179.
23. Ibid., p. 74.
24. Sima, *Historical Records*, p. 136.
25. Ibid., pp. 136–39; the last hours of Xiang Yu's life have been dramatized in the opera and film *Farewell My Concubine*.
26. Sawyer and Sawyer, *Seven Military Classics*, p. 172.
27. Ibid.
28. Sima, *Records of the Grand Historian*, p. 169.

Chapter 4. Hannibal
1. Polybius, *Rise of the Roman Empire*, 3.11.
2. Livy, *Hannibal's War*, 21.10

3. Ibid., 21.3–4.
4. Goldsworthy, *Punic Wars*, pp. 157–58.
5. Hyland, *Equus*, p. 174.
6. Polybius, *Rise of the Roman Empire*, 3.114.
7. Warry, *Warfare in the Classical World*, p. III.
8. Sabin, "Face of Roman Battle," p. 10.
9. Connolly, "Roman Army in the Age of Polybius, p. 162.
10. The nature of fighting in a manipular formation, and the multiple views of how it may have been done, are discussed in Sabin's "The Face of Roman Battle," in *The Journal of Roman Studies*, vol. 90; also see Lendon, *Soldiers and Ghosts*, pp. 172–92, for a more psychological view of the Roman armies.
11. Prevas, *Hannibal Crosses the Alps*, p. 180.
12. Polybius, *Rise of the Roman Empire*, 3.68.
13. Ibid., 3.70.
14. Livy, *Hannibal's War*, 21.55.
15. Appian, *Foreign Wars*, 2.7.
16. Prevas, *Hannibal Crosses the Alps*, p. 191.
17. Polybius, *Rise of the Roman Empire*, 3.75.
18. Dodge, *Great Captains*, p. 43.
19. Mommsen, *The History of Rome*, book 3, ch. 5, http://ancienthistory.about.com/library/bl/bl_text_mommsen_3_5_5.htm.
20. Livy, *Hannibal's War*, 22.3.
21. Polybius, *Rise of the Roman Empire*, 3.80.
22. Livy, *Hannibal's War*, 22.3.
23. Polybius, *Rise of the Roman Empire*, 3.82.
24. Livy, *Hannibal's War*, 22.4.
25. Polybius, *Rise of the Roman Empire*, 3.84.
26. Livy, *Hannibal's War*, 22.6.
27. Ibid., 22.4.
28. Polybius, *Rise of the Roman Empire*, 3.112.
29. Appian, *Foreign Wars*, 4.20.
30. Lazenby, *Hannibal's War*, p. 79.
31. Goldsworthy, *Punic Wars*, p. 205.
32. Connolly, "Roman Army in the Age of Polybius," pp. 148, 162.
33. Lazenby, *Hannibal's War*, p. 82.
34. Polybius, *Rise of the Roman Empire*, 3.115.
35. Goldsworthy, *Punic Wars*, pp. 209–10.
36. Alexander, *How Wars Are Won*, p. 275.
37. Meikeljohn, "Roman Strategy and Tactics from 509 to 202 BC," pp. 12–13.
38. Delbruck, *Warfare in Antiquity*, p. 319.
39. Livy, *Hannibal's War*, 22.50.
40. Goldsworthy, *Punic Wars*, p. 213

41. Von Schlieffen, *Cannae*, p. 3.
42. Alexander, *How Wars Are Won*, p. 274.
43. Goldsworthy, *Punic Wars*, p. 157.
44. Dodge, *Great Captains*, p. 64.
45. Ibid., pp. 63–64.

Chapter 5. Publius Cornelius Scipio Africanus

1. Polybius, *Histories*, 10.3.
2. Livy, *Hannibal's War*, 26.19.
3. Polybius, *Histories*, 10.2.
4. Haywood, *Studies on Scipio Africanus*, pp. 25–26.
5. Liddell Hart, *Scipio Africanus: Greater than Napoleon*, p. 17.
6. Appian, *The Foreign Wars*, 23.88.
7. Lazenby, *Hannibal's War*, p. 136.
8. Ibid.
9. Haywood, *Studies on Scipio Africanus*, pp. 48, 51–52.
10. Scullard, *Scipio Africanus: Soldier and Politician*, p. 65.
11. Zhmodikov, "Heavy Infantrymen in Battle," p. 70.
12. Garba, *Republican Rome*, p. 11.
13. Wise, *Armies of the Carthaginian Wars* (London: Osprey, 1982), pp. 7–9.
14. Trevino, *Rome's Enemies*, p. 39. He gives good detail on the forging and the quality of the falcata (pp. 38–40).
15. Bagnall, *The Punic Wars*, p. 207.
16. Ibid., p. 208.
17. Livy, *Hannibal's War*, 26.45.
18. Polybius, *Rise of the Roman Empire*, 10.11.
19. Bagnall, *The Punic Wars*, p. 209.
20. Bradford, *Hannibal*, p. 161.
21. Goldsworthy, *Roman Warfare*, p. 108.
22. Polybius, *Rise of the Roman Empire*, 10.39. Scipio would have been the wise decision as he would have regained Spain for Carthage.
23. Meiklejohn, "Roman Strategy and Tactics," pp. 14–15.
24. Bagnall, *The Punic Wars*, p. 211.
25. Scullard, *Soldier and Politician*, pp. 74–75.
26. Ibid., p. 73.
27. Polybius, *Histories*, 11.20.
28. Livy, *Hannibal's War*, 28.12 n., p. 684.
29. Polybius, *Histories*, 11.20.
30. Liddell Hart, *Greater than Napoleon*, p. 51.
31. Livy, *Hannibal's War*, 28.14.
32. Polybius, *Histories*, 11.24.
33. Ibid., 11.24.
34. Livy, *Hannibal's War*, 28.16.
35. Montagu, *Greek and Roman Warfare*, p. 178.

36. U.S. Army Field Manual, 100–105, 7–2.
37. Liddell Hart, *Greater than Napoleon*, p. 63.
38. Livy, *Hannibal's War*, 28.14.
39. Lazenby, *Hannibal's War*, p. 149.
40. Goldsworthy, *Punic Wars*, p. 283.
41. Liddell Hart, *Greater than Napoleon*, p. 94.
42. Livy, *Hannibal's War*, 28.12.
43. Ibid., 28.14, n., p. 684.
44. Bagnall, *Punic Wars*, p. 214.
45. Goldsworthy, *Punic Wars*, pp. 323–24.
46. Bagnall, *Punic Wars*, p. 215.
47. Liddell Hart, *Greater than Napoleon*, p. 43.
48. Polybius, *Histories*, 11.20.
49. Meiklejohn, "Roman Strategy and Tactics," p. 19.
50. Polybius, *Histories*, 11.23.

Chapter 6. Gaius Julius Caesar

1. Plutarch, *Caesar*, in *Parallel Lives*, 1.2.
2. Ibid., 3.2.
3. Cary and Scullard, *History of Rome*, p. 243.
4. Greenough et al., *Caesar's Gallic War*, p. xvii.
5. Ibid., p. xviii.
6. Ibid.
7. Keppie, "Later Republic," p. 172.
8. Warry, *Warfare in the Classical World*, p. 153.
9. Carey et al., *Warfare in the Ancient World*, p. 107.
10. Keppie, "Later Republic," p. 172.
11. Ibid., p. 173.
12. Warry, *Warfare in the Classical World*, pp. 169, 170.
13. Goldsworthy, *Roman Warfare*, pp. 108–9.
14. Dando-Collins, *Caesar's Legion*, p. 23.
15. Ibid., p. 16.
16. Gilliver, in Gilliver et al., *Rome at War*, p. 36.
17. Rankin, *Celts and the Classical World*, p. 115.
18. Ibid., p. 115.
19. Herm, *The Celts*, p. 165.
20. Gilliver, *Caesar's Gallic Wars*, p. 89.
21. Herm, *The Celts*, p. 173.
22. Cary and Scullard, *History of Rome*, p. 261.
23. Gilliver, in Gilliver et al., *Rome at War*, p. 52.
24. Warry, *Warfare in the Classical World*, p. 163.
25. Jimenez, *Caesar against Rome*, p. 54.
26. Herm, *The Celts*, p. 188, 189.
27. Cary and Scullard, *History of Rome*, p. 263.

28. Lendon, *Soldiers and Ghosts*, p. 215.
29. Caesar, *Gallic War*, in Greenough et al., *Caesar's Gallic War*, 7.47–52.
30. Lendon, *Soldiers and Ghosts*, pp. 221–22.
31. Cary and Scullard, *History of Rome*, p. 263.
32. The exact location of Alesia is the subject of much debate, although Alise-Ste. Reine is the most likely given the discoveries of archaeologists there since the reign of Napoleon III. A summation of the debate over locations appears in Bianchini, *Vercingétorix et Alésia*.
33. Maier, "Oppida," p. 418.
34. Cary and Scullard, *History of Rome*, p. 263; Gilliver, in Gilliver et al., *Rome at War*, p. 70; Delbrück, *Warfare in Antiquity*, p. 498; Warry, *Warfare in the Classical World*, p. 167.
35. Delbrück, *Warfare in Antiquity*, p. 499; Gabriel, *Great Armies of Antiquity*, p. 90; Plutarch, *Parallel Lives*, 27.2.
36. Delbrück, *Warfare in Antiquity*, p. 499; Dando-Collins, *Caesar's Legion*, p. 58; Keppie, *Making of the Roman Army*, p. 92; Warry, *Warfare in the Classical World*, p. 170.
37. Warry, *Warfare in the Classical World*, p. 168. Warry writes that a pace equaled 5 Roman feet, a foot being one-third inch shorter than a modern English foot. Thus, 400 paces would measure 1,942 English feet, or 592 meters.
38. Anglim et al., *Fighting Techniques of the Ancient World*, p. 205.
39. Cassis Dio, *Roman History*, 40.40.2.
40. Caesar, *Gallic War*, in Greenough et al., *Caesar's Gallic War*, 7.76.
41. Delbrück, *Warfare in Antiquity*, pp. 499–500.
42. Caesar, *Gallic War*, in *Caesar's Commentaries*, 7.80.
43. Ibid., 7.84.
44. Ibid., 7.86.
45. Dodge, *Caesar*, p. 303.
46. Caesar, *Gallic War*, in *Caesar's Commentaries*, 7.87, 88.
47. Ibid., 7.88.
48. Dodge, *Great Captains*, p. 83.
49. Grant, *Twelve Caesars*, p. 33.
50. Cary and Scullard, *History of Rome*, p. 269.
51. Nofi, "Pompey the Great."
52. Liddell Hart, *Strategy*, p. 54.
53. Dodge, *Great Captains*, p. 90; for more information on the Spanish campaign, see Goldsworthy in Gilliver et al., *Rome at War*, pp. 128–32; Jimenez, *Caesar against Rome*, pp. 81–98; Jones, *Art of War*, pp. 75–80; and Delbrück, *Warfare in Antiquity*, pp. 515–27.
54. Goldsworthy in Gilliver et al., *Rome at War*, p. 135.
55. Liddell Hart, *Strategy*, p. 55.
56. Ibid., p. 56.
57. Dodge, *Great Captains*, p. 91.
58. Fuller, *Military History*, p. 191.

59. Appian, *Roman History*, 12.62.

60. Jimenez, *Caesar against Rome*, p. 148.

61. Plutarch, *Caesar*, 40.2.

62. Meier, *Caesar*, p. 395.

63. For a more complete discussion of the battle site, see Morgan, "Palaepharsalus—The Battle and the Town."

64. Caesar, *Commentaries*, 3.85.

65. Gwatkin, "Some Reflections on the Battle of Pharsalus," p. 109.

66. Goldsworthy, in Gilliver et al., *Rome at War*, p. 142; Meier, *Caesar*, p. 397; Boose and Gabriel, *Great Battles of Antiquity*, p. 389; Cary and Scullard, *History of Rome*, pp. 273, 622; and Warry, *Warfare in the Classical World*, p. 171.

67. Caesar, *Commentaries*, 3.86.

68. See McCartney, "On Aiming Weapons at the Face"; Wagener, "Aiming Weapons at the Face: A Sign of Valor."

69. Plutarch, *Pompey*, 64.1, and *Caesar*, 45.3–4, in *Parallel Lives*.

70. Plutarch, *Pompey*, 72.1.

71. Appian, *Roman History*, 12.82.

72. Reid, "Caesar's Counterinsurgency in Gaul," p. 43.

73. Grant, *Twelve Caesars*, p. 32.

74. Dodge, *Great Captains*, pp. 99, 103.

75. Goldsworthy, "Reassessing," p. 88.

76. Dodge, *Great Captains*, p. 92.

77. Goldsworthy, "Reassessing," p. 94.

78. Dodge, *Great Captains*, p. 96.

79. Ibid., p. 105.

80. Fuller, *Military History*, p. 199.

81. Goldsworthy, "Reassessing," pp. 92–93, 94–95.

Chapter 7. Belisarius

1. Stanhope, *Life of Belisarius*, p. 1.

2. Procopius, *Vandal Wars*, in *History of the Wars*, 13.II.21, p. 107.

3. Stanhope, pp. 1–2.

4. Gibbon, p. 1301.

5. Evans, p. 115.

6. Procopius, *Persian Wars*, I.XII.

7. Barker, *Justinian and the Later Roman Empire*, p. 114.

8. Nicolle, *Medieval Warfare Source Book*, vol. 1, p. 14.

9. Delbrück, *Barbarian Invasions*, p. 347.

10. Jones, *Art of War in the Western World*, p. 96.

11. Ibid.

12. Nicolle, *Medieval Warfare Source Book*, vol. 2, p. 13.

13. Oman, *Art of War in the Middle Ages*, pp. 12–13.

14. Greatrex, *Rome and Persia*, p. 39.

15. Gabriel, *Great Battles*, p. 278.

16. Greatrex, *Rome and Persia*, p. 38.

17. Bacon, *Critical Appraisal of Byzantine Military Strategy*, p. 31n.

18. Haldon, *Warfare, State and Society in the Byzantine World*, p. 193.

19. Gabriel, *Great Battles*, p. 280.

20. Nicolle, *Medieval Warfare Source Book*, vol. 2, p. 29.

21. Greatrex, *Rome and Persia*, p. 58.

22. Wilcox, *Rome's Enemies*, p. 9, 33.

23. Farrokh, *Shadows in the Desert*, p. 233.

24. Nicolle, *Medieval Warfare Source Book*, vol. 2. p. 21.

25. Procopius, *Persian Wars*, 1.14.25–26, p. 121.

26. Farrokh, *Shadows in the Desert*, p. 224.

27. Wilcox, *Rome's Enemies*, p. 33.

28. Nicolle, *Medieval Warfare Source Book*, vol. 2, p. 30.

29. Stanhope, *Life of Belisarius*, p. 14.

30. Greatrex and Lieu, *Roman Eastern Frontier*, p. 85.

31. Procopius, *Persian Wars*, 1.13.7, p. 104.

32. Zachariah, *Syriac Chronicle*, 9.2, pp. 223–24.

33. Malalas, *Chronicle*, 18.44, pp. 263–64.

34. Stanhope, *Life of Belisarius*, p. 16.

35. Procopius, *Persian Wars*, 1.13.13–14, p. 105.

36. Almost all sources cite Peroz as holding the rank of *mirranes*, or generalissimo as described by Mahon. Goldsworthy, however, says he was "of the Mihran house, an aristocratic family which produced so many Persian commanders that the Romans had come to believe that 'Mihran' was an actual rank" (*Name of Rome*, p. 411).

37. Procopius, *Persian Wars*, 1.13.18, p.107.

38. Differing sources on their battle maps identify the Immortals as either infantry (as in ancient Persia) or as cavalry. The "Immortal" concept of one stepping forward to replace a killed or wounded comrade seems to favor infantry, but they charged with Peroz's cavalry units on the Sassanian left. "The elite corps of the cavalry was called 'the Immortals,' evidently numbering—like their Achaemenid namesakes—10,000 men," writes Shahbazi, "History of Iran," citing A. Christensen, *L'Iran sons les Sassanides* (Copenhague: Levin & Munksgaard, 1936).

39. Procopius, *Persian Wars*, 1.14.4, p. 115.

40. Ibid., 1.14.33, p. 123.

41. Goldsworthy, *Name of Rome*, p. 413.

42. Procopius, *Persian Wars*, 1.14.37, p.125.

43. Greatrex, *Rome and Persia*, p. 181.

44. Procopius, *Persian Wars*, 1.14.39, p. 125.

45. Ibid., 1.14.50–51, p. 127.

46. Stanhope, *Life of Belisarius*, p. 20.

47. Procopius, *Persian Wars*, 1.18.24, p. 167.

48. Malalas, *Chronicle*, 18.464, p. 271; see also Cameron, *Procopius*, pp. 146–47.

49. Zachariah, *Syriac Chronicle*, 9.4, p. 226.

50. Barker, *Justinian and the Later Roman Empire*, p. 146.

51. Wolfram, *History of the Goths*, pp. 302–3.

52. Ibid., p. 303.

53. Burns, *History of the Ostrogoths*, p. 200.

54. Ibid.

55. Wolfram, *History of the Goths*, p. 303.

56. Gibbon, *Decline and Fall*, p. 1328.

57. Barker, *Justinian and the Later Roman Empire*, p. 153.

58. Stanhope, *Life of Belisarius*, p. 91.

59. Bury, *History of the Later Roman Empire* (p. 181n.), suggests that the number of 150,000 may have meant the entire Gothic population in Italy, which had been some 100,000 when they invaded half a century earlier. Given that the circumference of the walls was 12 miles, or just over 21,000 yards, 150,000 troops would have seemed sufficient to lay siege to more than half the city.

60. Dupuy and Dupuy, *Encyclopedia*, p. 187.

61. Procopius, *Gothic Wars*, in *History of the Wars*, 5.19.11, pp. 187–89.

62. Ibid., 5.20.16–18.

63. Ibid., 5.23.23, p. 225.

64. Gibbon, *Decline and Fall*, p. 1337.

65. Procopius, *Gothic Wars*, 5.24.13–17.

66. Ibid., 5.27.9–11, p. 255.

67. Ibid., 6.4.5, p. 319.

68. Barker, *Justinian and the Later Roman Empire*, p. 154.

69. Liddell Hart, *Strategy*, p. 66.

70. Ibid., p. 72.

71. Clausewitz, *On War*, p. 370.

72. Brogna, *Generalship of Belisarius*, p. 95.

Chapter 8. Chinggis Khan/Subedei

1. The spellings of names and places from Mongolia and China to the Middle East and eastern Europe are many and varied. There seems to be no authoritative spelling, so I have chosen what seem to be either the most common or used by the most authoritative sources. Thus, spelling will vary in quotes and will not be altered unless the spelling is unrecognizable. This will happen most often in place and tribal names.

2. Urgunge Onon's translation phrases it this way: "Chinggis Qahan was born with his destiny ordained by Heaven above. He was descended from Börte Chino, whose name means 'greyish white wolf,' and Qo'ai-maral, the wolf's spouse, whose name means beautiful doe, who crossed the lake and settled at the source of the Onon." Onon's primary claim to accuracy

is his own heritage, that of a Dawr Mongol, hence someone with much more of a native knowledge of the language. "The Dawrs were isolated from the main body of the Mongols for more than one thousand years, starting in the sixth century, when nomadic Turkic tribes penetrated present-day Mongolia. Scholars of Inner Mongolia confirmed in 1955 that the Dawrs speak an independent dialect of the Mongolian language, untouched by Orkhon Turkish and akin to the language of the History." Onon, *Secret History of the Mongols*, pp. 37, 29.

3. Kahn, *Secret History of the Mongols: The Origins of Chingis Khan*, p. 14.
4. The *Secret History* overlooks some events at this point. Temuchin was known to be thirteen when he rejoined his family although only nine when betrothed to Borte. What happened in the intervening years is unknown, although given the later close ties between him and his father-in-law, he may well have stayed the entire time with that tribe. Ratchnevsky asserts that the "custom of leaving a son with the future parents-in-law was widespread among the early Turkic-Mongol nomads" (*Genghis Khan: His Life and Legacy*, p. 21). Weatherford proposes that Yesugei intentionally moved Temuchin to a remote location to avoid a rivalry with a slightly older son by a previous wife (*Ghengis Khan and the Making of the Modern World*, p. 18).
5. Hildinger, *Warriors of the Steppe*, p. 110.
6. Allsen, "Rise of the Mongolian Empire," p. 334.
7. Onon, *Secret History of the Mongols*, p. 8.
8. Ratchnevsky, *Life and Legacy*, p. 31.
9. Man, *Genghis Khan: Life, Death, and Resurrection*, p. 89.
10. Ibid., p. 90.
11. Allsen, "Rise of the Mongolian Empire," p. 337.
12. Spuler, *Mongol Period*, p. 4.
13. Buell, "Subotei Ba'atur," p. 14, suggests that Jelme was Subedei's uncle.
14. Kahn, *Origins of Chingis Khan*, p. 51. The bulk of Subedei's biography in this section relies on Gabriel, *Genghis Khan's Greatest General*.
15. Kahn, *Origins of Chingis Khan*, p. 50.
16. Gabriel, *Subotai the Valiant*, p. 7.
17. Kahn, *Origins of Chingis Khan*, p. 111.
18. Ibid., p. 118.
19. Morgan, *The Mongols*, p. 84.
20. Ratchevsky, *Life and Legacy*, pp. 92–93.
21. Spuler, *Mongol Period*, p. 4.
22. Sinor, "Inner Asian Warriors," p. 137.
23. Alexander, *How Great Generals Win*, p. 71.
24. Gibbon, *Decline and Fall*, vol. 1, p. 797.
25. Kennedy, *Mongols, Huns and Vikings at War*, p. 122.
26. Weatherford, *Making of the Modern World*, p. 95.
27. Alexander, *How Wars Are Won*, p. 110.

28. McCreight, *Mongol Warrior Epic*, p. 71.
29. For a full description of all sixteen tactics, see Onon, *Secret History of the Mongols*, pp. 281–87.
30. Hildinger, *Warriors of the Steppe*, pp. 121–22.
31. Buell, "Subotei Ba'atur," p. 17.
32. Alexander, *How Great Generals Win*, p. 82.
33. Ibid., pp. 83–84.
34. Pittard, *Thirteenth Century Mongol Warfare*, p. 20.
35. Hildinger, *Warriors of the Steppe*, p. 127.
36. Liddell Hart, *Great Captains Unveiled*, p. 17.
37. Buell, "Subotei Ba'atur," p. 19.
38. Nicolle, *Medieval Warfare Source Book*, vol. 2, p. 105.
39. Nicolle, *Medieval Warfare Source Book*, vol. 1, p. 123.
40. Ibid., p. 128.
41. Marshall, *Storm from the East*, p. 91.
42. Legg, *Barbarians of Asia*, p. 290.
43. Miranda, "Khan: The Rise of the Mongol Empire," p. 17.
44. Chambers, *Devil's Horsemen*, pp. 24–25.
45. Man, *Life, Death, and Resurrection*, p. 187.
46. De Hartog, *Genghis Khan: Conqueror of the World*, pp. 120–21.
47. Trombetta and Ippolito, "Emergence of Sea Power."
48. Chambers, *Devil's Horsemen*, p. 28.
49. De Hartog, *Conqueror of the World*, p. 121.
50. Man, *Life, Death, and Resurrection*, pp. 189–90.
51. Ibid., p. 190.
52. De Hartog, *Conqueror of the World*, p. 122.
53. *Novgorod Chronicle*, p. 66.
54. Buell, "Subotei Ba'atur," pp. 19–20.
55. Legg, *Barbarians of Asia*, p. 283.
56. Ibid., p. 287.
57. Marshall, *Storm from the East*, p. 57.
58. Man, *Life, Death, and Resurrection*, p. 167.
59. Prawdin, *Mongol Empire*, p. 255.
60. Exactly which prince led which attack is difficult to tell from the multiple works on the campaign. Kadan Baidar is referenced as being in both the Polish campaign and leading a southern prong through Carpathians. Kaidu is usually identified as leading the Polish campaign, but in some sources his name is mentioned nowhere. As with the variation on names and places, the selection of commanders in this campaign will be somewhat arbitrary.
61. Jackson, *Mongols and the West*.
62. Chambers, *Devil's Horsemen*, p. 92.
63. Lukinich, *History of Hungary*, p. 70.
64. Alexander, *How Great Generals Win*, p. 89.

65. Man, *Life, Death, and Resurrection*, p. 271.
66. Kosztolnyik, *Hungary in the 13th Century*, pp. 155–56.
67. McCreight, *Mongol Warrior Epic*, pp. 128–29.
68. Ibid., p. 133.
69. Ibid.
70. Kennedy, *Mongols, Huns and Vikings at War*, p. 161.
71. Buell, "Subotei Ba'atur," p. 25.
72. Takemoto, *Back Azimuth Check*, pp. 22–23.
73. Gabriel, "Right Hand of Khan," p. 49.

Chapter 9. Jan Žižka

1. Wylie, *History of Protestantism*, book 3, ch. 13. Various translations provide a number of spellings: Žižka, Ziska, Zisca, Siska, etc. I will use the modern Czech spellings for all people and locations unless they are spelled otherwise in a quote.
2. Vaclav is the Czech spelling, but he is better known in the West as Wenceslaus; he also is called Wenzel in some sources.
3. Heymann, *John Žižka*, p. 25.
4. Ibid., p. 27.
5. Ibid., p. 29.
6. Jorgenson, "Tannenberg, 1410," p. 169.
7. Ibid.
8. Heymann, *John Žižka*, p. 30.
9. Ibid., p. 34.
10. Hutton, *History of the Moravian Church*, p. 31.
11. Ibid., p. 53.
12. Pribichevich, *World without End*, p. 86.
13. Cornej, "Hussite Art of Warfare," p. 67.
14. McGuire, "Jan Žižka and the Hussite Wars," p. 9.
15. Lambert, *Medieval Heresy*, p. 312.
16. Ayton, "Arms, Armour, and Horses," pp. 186–87.
17. Ibid., p. 110.
18. Ibid., p. 207.
19. Bennett et al., *Fighting Techniques of the Medieval World*, p. 123.
20. Showalter, "Caste, Skill, and Training," p. 412.
21. Gravett, *German Medieval Armies*, p. 7.
22. Hall, *Weapons and Warfare*, p. 18.
23. Holmes, *Oxford Companion*, p. 961.
24. Dupuy and Dupuy, *Encyclopedia of Military History*, p. 406.
25. Turnbull, *Hussite Wars*, p. 24.
26. Bloom, "The Hussites," p. 41.
27. Turnbull, *Hussite Wars*, p. 38.
28. Haywood, "Hussite Battle Tactics."
29. Turnbull, *Hussite Wars*, p. 21.

30. Klassen and Paces, "Women in Hussite Wars," p. 218.
31. Turnbull, *Hussite Wars*, p. 35.
32. Bloom, "The Hussites," p. 42.
33. Oman, *Art of War in the Middle Ages*, pp.125–26.
34. Nolan, *Age of Wars of Religion*, p. 429.
35. Hazard, *History of the Crusades*, pp. 593–94.
36. Fudge, "'More Glory than Blood,'" pp. 119, 120.
37. McGuire, "Jan Žižka and the Hussite Wars," p. 10.
38. Heymann, *John Žižka*, p. 92.
39. McGuire, "Jan Žižka and the Hussite Wars," p. 10; Turnbull, *Hussite Wars*, p. 33; "The Very Pretty Chronicle," reproduced in Heymann, *John Žižka*, p. 110.
40. McGuire, "Jan Žižka and the Hussite Wars," p. 10.
41. Heymann, *John Žižka*, p. 97.
42. McGuire, "Jan Žižka and the Hussite Wars," p. 11.
43. Heymann, *John Žižka*, p. 139.
44. Ibid.
45. Dickie, "Vitkov, 1420," p. 195.
46. Hazard, *History of the Crusades*, p. 597.
47. Macek, *Hussite Movement in Bohemia*, p. 43.
48. "John Žižka," p. 346.
49. McGuire, "Jan Žižka and the Hussite Wars," p. 21.
50. Ibid., p. 22.
51. Heymann, *John Žižka*, p. 291
52. Ibid., pp. 294–95.
53. Bloom, "The Hussites," p. 41.
54. "John Žižka," p. 352.
55. Fudge, *Magnificent Ride*, p. 104.
56. McGuire, "Jan Žižka and the Hussite Wars," p. 25.
57. Delbruck, *Medieval Warfare*, p. 494.
58. Oman, *Art of War in the Middle Ages*, p. 152.
59. Gravett, *German Medieval Armies*, p. 16.
60. Nicholson, *Medieval Warfare*, pp. 37–38.
61. Heymann, *John Žižka*, p. 305.
62. Showalter, "Caste, Skill, and Training," p. 411.
63. Wilkinson, "Žižka's Zeal," p. 36.
64. Macek, *Hussite Movement in Bohemia*, p. 48.
65. McGuire, "Jan Žižka and the Hussite Wars," p. 31.

Chapter 10. Oda Nobunaga

1. Hooker, "Warring States."
2. Lamers, *Japonius Tyrannus*, p. 23.
3. Luis Frois, quoted in ibid., p. 24.
4. Turnbull, *Samurai Warfare*, p. 56.

5. Ibid.
6. Bryant, *Samurai 1550–1600*, p. 31.
7. Turnbull, *Warfare*, p. 58.
8. Kure, *Samurai: An Illustrated History*, p. 73.
9. Bryant, *Samurai 1550–1600*, pp. 24 (chart), 50; Varley says the spear length in Nobubaga's army was 18 feet ("Oda Nobunaga," p. 109).
10. Varley, "Oda Nobunaga," p. 106.
11. Turnbull, *Samurai, World of the Warrior*, p. 97.
12. Bryant, *Samurai 1550–1600*, p. 50.
13. Perrin, *Giving up the Gun*, p. 17.
14. Kure, *An Illustrated History*, p. 75.
15. From "The Record of the Kunitomo Teppoki," quoted in Lidin, *Tanegashima*, pp. 134–35.
16. Perrin, *Giving up the Gun*, p. 14.
17. Lidin, *Tanegashima*, p. 146.
18. Turnbull, *Nagashino*, p. 15.
19. Turnbull, *Warfare*, p. 65.
20. Ibid, p. 67.
21. Varley, "Oda Nobunaga," p. 113.
22. Turnbull, *Samurai and the Sacred*, p. 77.
23. Ibid., p. 77.
24. Sansom, *History of Japan*, p. 273.
25. Lamers, *Japonius Tyrannus*, p. 42.
26. Sansom, *History of Japan*, p. 275.
27. Sharpe, *Samurai Battles*, pp. 112–113.
28. Sato, *Legends of the Samuraii*, p. 234.
29. Sadler, *Maker of Modern Japan*, p. 54.
30. Sansom, *History of Japan*, pp. 276–77.
31. Sato, *Legends of the Samuraii*, p. 235.
32. Kure, *An Illustrated History*, p. 145.
33. Sadler, *Maker of Modern Japan*, p. 55.
34. Black, *War in the Early Modern World*, p. 68.
35. Sansom, *History of Japan*, p. 278.
36. Turnbull, *Warrior Monks*, p. 15.
37. Turnbull, *Sacred*, pp. 77–78.
38. Sansom, *History of Japan*, p. 284.
39. Turnbull, *Japanese Warrior Monks*, p. 57.
40. Ibid., p. 58.
41. Sharpe, *Battles*, pp. 144–45.
42. Sansom, *History of Japan*, p. 284.
43. Sharpe, *Battles*, p. 145.
44. Turnbull, *Nagashino*, p. 13.
45. Ibid., p. 31.
46. Ibid., p. 33.

47. Hilbert, "Samurai Slaughtered," p. 67.
48. Turnbull, *Nagashino*, pp. 45–47.
49. Ledbetter, "The Battle of Nagashino."
50. Lamers, *Japonius Tyrannus*, p. 112.
51. Turnbull, *Nagashino*, pp. 60–61.
52. Ledbetter, "The Battle of Nagashino."
53. Turnbull, *Nagashino*, p. 57.
54. Sharpe, *Battles*, p. 150.
55. Ibid., p. 68.
56. Ledbetter, "The Battle of Nagashino."
57. Kure, *An Illustrated History*, p. 79. It should be noted that while Kure is not a historian by training, his resources are all Japanese works.
58. Ibid., p. 81.
59. Lamers, *Japonius Tyrannus*, p. 112.
60. Hilbert, "Samurai Slaughtered," p. 68.
61. Sansom, *History of Japan*, p. 310.
62. Turnbull, *Book of the Samurai*, pp. 95–96; Parker, *Military Revolution*, p. 140.
63. Turnbull, *Book of the Samuri*, pp. 309–10.
64. Turnbull, *Nagashino*, p. 57.
65. Kure, *An Illustrated History*, p. 81.
66. Turnbull, *Japanese Warrior Monks*, pp. 19–20.
67. Turnbull, *Sacred*, p. 84.

Chapter 11. Gustavus Adolphus

1. Ahnlund, *Gustavus Adolphus the Great*, pp. 4–16.
2. Ibid., p. 32.
3. Redmond, "Gustavus Adolphus, Father of Combined Arms Warfare," p. 2.
4. Ibid., p. 3. It should be noted that this story is not agreed upon by historians; some dismiss the detail of using disguise.
5. Dodge, *Great Captains*, p. 114.
6. Ahnlund, *Gustavus Adolphus the Great*, pp. 228–29.
7. Jones, *Art of War*, p. 195.
8. Ibid., p. 191.
9. Bobbit, *Shield of Achilles*, p. 99.
10. Jones, *Art of War*, p. 195.
11. Dupuy, *Evolution of Weapons and Warfare*, p. 116.
12. Rothenberg, "Maurice of Nassau," p. 37.
13. Parker, *Military Revolution*, p. 19.
14. Childs, "Maurice of Nassau," p. 22.
15. Rothenberg, "Maurice of Nassau," p. 43.
16. Parker, *Military Revolution*, p. 23.
17. Howard, *War in European History*, p. 37.

18. Brzezinski, *Army of Gustavus Adolphus*, vol. 1, p. 19.
19. Jones, *Art of War*, p. 223.
20. Haythornthwaite, *Invincible Generals*, p. 19.
21. M. Roberts, *Gustavus Adolphus*, p. 105.
22. Dupuy, *Evolution of Weapons and Warfare*, p. 135.
23. Ibid., p. 136.
24. Haythornthwaite, *Invincible Generals*, p. 22.
25. Weigley, *Age of Battles*, p. 16.
26. Baumgartner, *From Spear to Flintlock*, p. 253.
27. Haythornthwaite, *Invincible Generals*, p. 31.
28. Liddell Hart, *Great Captains Unveiled*, p. 86.
29. Dodge, *Great Captains*, p. 117.
30. Quoted in Rabb, *Thirty Years War*, p. 87.
31. Quoted in Parker, *Thirty Years War*, p. 122.
32. Maland, *Europe at War*, pp. 126–27.
33. Guthrie, *Battles*, p. 20.
34. Ibid.
35. Weigley, *Age of Battles*, p. 19.
36. Guthrie, *Battles*, p. 23.
37. Guthrie, *Battles*, pp. 20–23. This is the most detailed accounting of the two forces. Other authors give a wide range of numbers. Goodenough (*Tactical Genius*): 40,000 allied, 33,000 imperial; Alexander ("Swedish King"): 41,000 allied, 35,000 imperial; Childs (*Warfare*): 41,000 allied, 31,000 imperial; Fuller (*Military History*): 47,000 allied, 40,000 imperial; Haythornthwaite (*Invincible Generals*): 42,000 allied, 36,000–40,000 imperial; Parker (*Thirty Years War*): 41,000 allied, 31,400 imperial; Delbruck (*Dawn of Modern Warfare*): 39,000 allied and 75 guns, 36,000 imperial and 26 guns.
38. Liddel Hart, *Great Captains Unveiled*, p. 130.
39. Delbruck, *Dawn of Modern Warfare*, p. 204.
40. Haythornthwaite, *Invincible Generals*, p. 37.
41. Guthrie, *Battles*, p. 23.
42. Maland, *Europe at War*, pp. 130–31.
43. Wedgewood, *Thirty Years War*, p. 287.
44. Guthrie, *Battles*, p. 24.
45. Hollway, "Triumph of Flexible Firepower," p. 43.
46. Wedgewood, *Thirty Years War*, p. 289.
47. Showalter, "Gustavus' Greatest Victory," p. 48
48. Guthrie, *Battles*, p. 33.
49. Alexander, *How Wars are Won*, p. 171.
50. Goodenough, *Tactical Genius*, p. 75.
51. Bonney, *Thirty Years War*, p. 47.
52. Ibid.
53. Liddell Hart, *Great Captains Unveiled*, p. 126.

54. Fuller, *Military History*, p. 65.

55. Haythornthwaite, *Invincible Generals*, p. 41–42.

56. Guthrie, *Battles*, p. 165.

57. Ibid., pp. 165–66.

58. Malleson, *Battlefields of Germany*, p. 57.

59. Guthrie, *Battles*, p. 168.

60. Malleson, *Battlefields of Germany*, p. 59.

61. Connor, "Gustavus Adolphus and the Crossing of the Lech."

62. Guthrie, *Battles*, p. 169.

63. Connor, "Gustavus Adolphus and the Crossing of the Lech."

64. Liddell Hart, *Great Captains Unveiled*, p. 190.

65. Wedgewood, *Thirty Years War*, p. 311.

66. Ibid., pp. 313–14.

67. Jones, *Art of War*, p. 240.

68. Guthrie, *Battles*, p. 196.

69. Brzezinsky, *Lutzen*, pp. 31–32.

70. M. Roberts, *Gustavus Adolphus*, p. 177.

71. Guthrie, *Battles*, p. 197.

72. Brzezinsky, *Lutzen*, p. 42.

73. Guthrie and Brzezinsky differ radically on which units were placed in which positions and where the commanders were assigned; e.g., Holk on the imperial right flank and Colloredo in the center. The text follows Guthrie.

74. Guthrie, *Battles*, p. 205.

75. Ibid., p. 208.

76. Ibid., p. 210.

77. Ibid., p. 217.

78. Livesey, *Great Commanders*, p. 59.

79. Jones, *Art of War*, p. 241.

80. Chandler, *Atlas of Military Strategy*, p. 27.

81. Brodie and Brodie, *From Crossbow to H-Bomb*, p. 77.

82. Dodge, *Great Captains*, p. 133.

83. Rothenberg, "Maurice of Nassau," p. 55.

Chapter 12. John Churchill, Duke of Marlborough

1. Spencer, *Battle for Europe*, p. 44.

2. J. Jones, *Marlborough*, p. 14.

3. Ibid., *Marlborough*, p. 16.

4. Folkers, "Marlborough."

5. J. Jones, *Marlborough*, p. 17.

6. Hussey, *Marlborough, Hero of Blenheim*, p. 23.

7. Spencer, *Battle for Europe*, p. 52.

8. J. Jones, *Marlborough*, p. 42.

9. Ibid., p. 44.

10. Hussey, *Hero of Blenheim*, p. 40.

11. Wolf, *Emergence of the Great Powers*, p. 60.
12. Weigley, *Age of Battles*, p. 47.
13. Ibid., p. 52.
14. Ibid., p 74.
15. Chartrand, *Louis XIV's Army*, p. 21.
16. Childs, *Warfare in the Seventeenth Century*, p. 156.
17. Chartrand, *Louis XIV's Army*, p. 24.
18. Folkers, "Dragoon Regiments," in *Spanish Succession*.
19. Chartrand, *Louis XIV's Army*, pp. 34–35.
20. Chandler, *Military Commander*, p. 91.
21. Weigley, *Age of Battles*, p. 94.
22. Chandler, *Marlborough as Military Commander*, p. 92.
23. Wilson, "Warfare in the Old Regime," p. 91.
24. Ibid., p. 93.
25. Barthorp, *Marlborough's Army*, p. 10.
26. Ibid., p. 11.
27. Chandler, *Military Commander*, p. 93.
28. Barthrop, *Marlborough's Army*, p. 16.
29. Treasure, *Making of Modern Europe*, pp. 218–19.
30. Folkers, "Austrian Army," in *Spanish Succession*.
31. "Eugene," p. 156.
32. Chartrand, *Louis XIV's Army*, p. 12.
33. Kennedy, *Grand Strategies*, p. 15.
34. J. Jones, *Marlborough*, p. 57.
35. Folkers, "1701," in *Spanish Succession*.
36. J. Jones, *Marlborough*, pp. 62–63; see also Ostwald, "'Decisive' Battle," p. 699.
37. Morris, "Villars," p. 69.
38. Col. Robert Parker, quoted in Chandler, *Military Campaigns*, p. 31.
39. Standford et al., "Schellenberg," p. 36.
40. Chandler, *Military Commander*, p. 136.
41. Britt et al., *Dawn of Modern Warfare*, p. 79.
42. Churchill, *Marlborough, His Life and Times*, p. 382.
43. Duc de la Colonie, quoted in Standford et al., "Schellenberg," p. 39.
44. Parker, quoted in Chandler, *Military Memoirs of Marlborough's Campaigns*, p. 33.
45. Tincey, *Blenheim*, p. 36.
46. Chandler, *Atlas*, pp. 44–45.
47. Weigley, *Age of Battles*, p. 84.
48. Spencer, *Battle for Europe*, p. 223.
49. Britt et al., *Dawn of Modern Warfare*, p. 82.
50. Spencer, *Battle for Europe*, p. 224.
51. Derek McKay, *Prince Eugene of Savoy*, p. 86.
52. Chandler, "Blenheim," p. 32.

53. Chandler, *Military Commander*, p. 146.
54. Hussey, *Hero of Blenheim*, pp. 145–146.
55. McKay, *Prince Eugene*, p. 86.
56. Weigley, *Age of Battles*, p. 86.
57. Fuller, *Military History*, p. 152.
58. J. Jones, *Marlborough*, p. 96.
59. Spencer, *Battle for Europe*, pp. 296–97.
60. Fuller, *Military History*, pp. 153–54.
61. Dodge, *Gustavus Adolphus*, pp. 732–33.
62. McKay, *Prince Eugene*, p. 87.
63. Folkers, "Battle of Blenheim/Hochstadt," in *Spanish Succession*.
64. Britt et al., *Dawn of Modern Warfare*, p. 88.
65. J. Jones, *Marlborough*, p. 119.
66. A. Jones, *Art of War*, p. 278; Morris, "Villars," p. 69.
67. Chandler, *Military Commander*, p. 172.
68. Falkner, *Great and Glorious Days*, p. 100.
69. Britt et al., *Dawn of Modern Warfare*, pp. 88–89.
70. Falkner, *Great and Glorious Days*, p. 109.
71. Chandler, *Military Commander*, p. 176.
72. Falkner, *Great and Glorious Days*, p. 112.
73. Parker, quoted in Chandler, *Military Memoirs*, p. 60.
74. Chandler, *Military Commander*, p. 177.
75. Wolf, *Emergence of the Great Powers*, p. 74.
76. Barnett, *First Churchill*, p. 169.
77. "Ramillies (Offus)," pp. 372–73.
78. Chandler, *Military Commander*, p. 178.
79. Britt et al., *Dawn of Modern Warfare*, p. 92.
80. Chandler, *Military Commander*, p. 212.
81. Barnett, *First Churchill*, p. 204.
82. Chandler, *Military Commander*, p. 214.
83. Falkner, *Great and Glorious Days*, pp. 138–40.
84. Ibid., p. 142.
85. Barnett, *First Churchill*, p. 210.
86. Chandler, *Military Commander*, p. 220.
87. Livesey, *Great Commanders*, pp. 78–79.
88. Chandler, *Military Commander*, pp. 221–22.
89. Spencer, *Battle for Europe*, p. 330.
90. Chandler, *Military Commander*, p. 63.
91. Falkner, *Great and Glorious Days*, p. 142.
92. Barnett, *First Churchill*, p. 212.
93. Chandler, *Military Commander*, p. 71.
94. Black, *Britain's Military Power*, p. 56.
95. Ibid., p. 76.
96. Ibid., p. 329.

97. Falkner, *Great and Glorious Days*, p. 217.
98. Haythornthwaite, *Invincible Generals*, p. 94.
99. Fuller, *Military History*, p. 129.
100. Weigley, *Age of Battles*, pp. 102–3.

Chapter 13. Frederick II (the Great)

1. Britt et al., *Dawn of Modern Warfare*, p. 100.
2. Duffy, *Frederick the Great: A Military Life*, p. 3.
3. Duffy, *Army of Frederick*, p. 15.
4. Ritter, *Frederick the Great*, p. 24. Known in other sources as the "Tobacco Parliament."
5. Ibid., p. 25.
6. Haythornthwaite, *Invincible Generals*, pp. 104–5.
7. Baumgartner, *From Spear to Flintlock*, p. 308.
8. Bleckwenn, quoted in Duffy, *Military Life*, p. 4.
9. Duffy, *Army of Frederick*, p. 58.
10. Childs, *Armies and Warfare*, p. 108.
11. Frederick, quoted in Phillips, *Roots of Strategy*, p. 311.
12. Laffin, *Links of Leadership*, p. 142.
13. Haythornthwaite, *Frederick the Great's Army*, vol. 2, p. 5.
14. Duffy, *Army of Frederick*, p. 63.
15. Duffy, *Military Life*, p. 13.
16. Nosworthy, *Anatomy of Victory*, pp. 187–88.
17. Childs, *Armies and Warfare*, p. 125.
18. Frederick, quoted in Phillips, *Roots of Strategy*, pp. 394–95.
19. Duffy, *Army of Frederick*, pp. 80–81.
20. Childs, *Armies and Warfare*, p. 123.
21. Frederick, quoted in Phillips, *Roots of Strategy*, p. 396.
22. Duffy, *Army of Frederick.*, p. 90.
23. Delbruck, *Dawn of Modern Warfare*, p. 276.
24. Duffy, *Army of Frederick*, pp. 153–54.
25. Alexander, p. 240.
26. Nosworthy, *Anatomy of Victory*, p. 193.
27. Frederick, quoted in Phillips, *Roots of Strategy*, p. 380.
28. Palmer, "Frederick the Great," p. 101.
29. Haythornthwaite, *Frederick the Great's Army*, vol. 1, p. 3.
30. Ibid., p. 4.
31. Duffy, *Army of Frederick*, p. 93.
32. Duffy, *Army of Frederick*, pp. 98–99.
33. Childs, *Armies and Warfare*, p. 105.
34. Nosworthy, *Anatomy of Victory*, p. 164.
35. Childs, *Armies and Warfare*, p. 106.
36. Nosworthy, *Anatomy of Victory*, p. 170.
37. Dupuy, *Evolution of Weapons*, p. 151.

38. Duffy, *Military Life*, p. 321.
39. Dupuy and Dupuy, *Encyclopedia of Military History*, p. 611.
40. Alphin, *West Point History*.
41. Duffy, *Army of Frederick*, p. 115.
42. Ibid., p. 114.
43. Seaton, *Frederick the Great's Army*, p. 11.
44. Ritter, *Frederick the Great*, p. 82.
45. Ibid., pp. 83–84.
46. Haythornthwaite, *Invincible Generals*, p. 111.
47. Dodge, *Great Captains*, p. 146.
48. Ritter, *Frederick the Great*, p. 89.
49. Ibid., 89–90.
50. Browning, *War of the Austrian Succession*, pp. 213–14.
51. Seaton, *Frederick the Great's Army*, p. 19.
52. Today, in modern Poland, the town is Strzegom and the river the Strzegomka. Hohenfriedberg is now Dobromierz, Pilgrimshain is Zolkiewka, Gunthersdorf is Godzieszow, Thomaswaldau is Tomkowice, and Halbendorf is Granica.
53. Frederick, quoted in Phillips, *Roots of Strategy*, p. 341.
54. Duffy, *Military Life*, p. 60.
55. Ibid., pp. 60–61.
56. Showalter, *Wars of Frederick*, p. 80.
57. Browning, *Austrian Succession*, p. 216.
58. Ibid.
59. Showalter, *Wars of Frederick*, p. 81.
60. Weigley, *Age of Battles*, p. 175.
61. Showalter, *Wars of Frederick*, p. 84.
62. Ritter, *Frederick the Great*, p. 91.
63. Weigley, *Age of Battles*, p. 176.
64. Phillips, *Roots of Strategy*, pp. 309–10.
65. Duffy, *Military Life*, p. 78.
66. Britt et al., *Dawn of Modern Warfare*, p. 111.
67. Telp, *Evolution of the Operational Art*, p. 18.
68. Marston, *Seven Years War*, p. 24.
69. Ibid., pp. 13–14.
70. Haythornthwaite, *Invincible Generals*, p. 126.
71. Weigley, *Age of Battles*, p. 178.
72. Duffy, *Army*, p. 171.
73. Duffy, *Military Life*, p. 135.
74. Showalter, *Wars of Frederick*, p. 185.
75. Most writers use this number. Dupuy and Dupuy in their *Encyclopedia* give the figure 64,000, as does Baumgartner (*From Spear to Flintlock*); Alexander (*How Wars Are Won*) gives 60,000; Britt et al. (*Dawn of Modern Warfare*) numbers the force at 54,000, with the imperial troops in the majority; Weigley (*Age of Battles*) proposes 50,000.

76. Showalter, *Wars of Frederick*, p. 188.
77. Carlyle, *History of Frederick*, vol. 6, p. 256.
78. Millar, *Rossbach and Leuthen*, p. 29.
79. Weigley, *Age of Battles*, p. 184.
80. Showalter, *Wars of Frederick*, p. 189.
81. Carlyle, quoted in Asprey, *Frederick the Great*, p. 472.
82. Carlyle, *History of Frederick*, vol. 6, p. 259.
83. Britt et al., *Modern Warfare*, p.121.
84. Weigley, *Age of Battles*, p. 185.
85. Showalter, *Wars of Frederick*, p. 192.
86. Millar, *Rossbach and Leuthen*, pp. 41, 43.
87. Asprey, *Frederick the Great*, p. 475.
88. Showalter, *Wars of Frederick*, p. 195.
89. Britt et al., *Dawn of Modern Warfare*, pp. 123–24.
90. Showalter, *Wars of Frederick*, p. 198.
91. Pratt, *Battles That Changed History*, p. 221.
92. Duffy, *Military Life*, p. 152.
93. Millar, *Rossbach and Leuthen*, p. 88.
94. Britt et al., *Dawn of Modern Warfare*, p. 124.
95. Duffy, *Army of Frederick*, p. 179.
96. Ibid., p. 209.
97. Frederick, quoted in Phillips, *Roots of Strategy*, p. 385.
98. Dodge, *Great Captains*, pp. 168–69.
99. Chandler, *Art of War*, pp. 135, 142.
100. Frederick, quoted in Phillips, *Roots of Strategy*, p. 378.
101. Atkinson, "Infantry."
102. Jones, *Art of War*, p. 308.
103. Alexander, *How Wars Are Won*, p. 234.
104. Carlyle, *History of Frederick*, vol. 6, pp. 259–60.
105. Dodge, *Great Captains*, p. 172.
106. Frederick, quoted in Phillips, *Roots of Strategy*, p. 342.
107. Dodge, *Great Captains*, pp. 171–72.
108. Lewis, "Frederick the Great and the Battle of Leuthen."
109. Treitschke, *Confessions of Frederick*, p. 91.
110. Fraser, *Frederick the Great: King of Prussia*, p. 625.
111. Dupuy, *Evolution of Weapons*, p. 148.
112. Ritter, *Frederick the Great*, p. 148.
113. Showalter, quoted in Kolenda, *Leadership*, p. 139.
114. Laffin, *Links of Leadership*, p. 156.

Chapter 14. Napoleon Bonaparte

1. Neillands, *Wellington and Napoleon*, p. 12.
2. McLynn, *Napoleon: A Biography*, p. 36.
3. Roberts, *Napoleon and Wellington*, p. 10.

 4. Dwyer, p. 37.
 5. Chandler, "Right Man in the Right Place," p. 38.
 6. Chandler, *Campaigns*, p. 23.
 7. Forczyk, *Toulon 1793*, p. 57.
 8. Paschall, "Napoleon's First Triumph," p. 14.
 9. Ireland, *Fall of Toulon*, p. 288.
10. Chandler, *Campaigns*, p. 28.
11. Ross, "Napoleon and Maneuver Warfare," p. 3.
12. Liaropolous, "Revolutions in Warfare," p. 373.
13. Weigley, *Age of Battles*, p. 265.
14. Wasson, "Innovator or Imitator," p. 19.
15. Weigley, *Age of Battles*, p. 264.
16. Wasson, "Innovator or Imitator," p. 7.
17. McConachy, "Roots of Artillery Doctrine," p. 620.
18. Burbeck, "Napoleonic Artillery."
19. Weigley, *Age of Battles*, p. 268.
20. Muir, *Tactics*, p. 71.
21. Chandler, *Campaigns*, p. 346.
22. Ibid., p. 350.
23. Dupuy, *Evolution of Weapons*, pp. 156–57.
24. Muir, *Tactics*, p. 62.
25. Rothenberg, *Napoleonic Wars*, p. 27.
26. Haythornthwaite, *Napoleon's Line Infantry*, p. 3.
27. Dupuy, *Evolution of Weapons*, p. 159.
28. Paret, "Napoleon and the Revolution in War," p. 125.
29. Chandler, *Campaigns*, p. 154.
30. Ibid.
31. Seaton, *Austro-Hungarian Army*, p. 37.
32. McLynn, *Biography*, p. 109.
33. Chandler, *Atlas*, p. 90.
34. Britt, *Wars of Napoleon*, p. 14.
35. Chandler, *Campaigns*, p. 116.
36. Rothenberg, *Napoleonic Wars*, p. 46.
37. Shosenberg, "Battle of Austerlitz," pp. 39–40.
38. Dwyer, *Napoleon: Path to Power*, p. 271.
39. Esdaile, *French Wars*, p. 33.
40. Fisher, *Napoleonic Wars*, p. 13.
41. Ibid., p. 19.
42. Goetz, *1805: Austerlitz*, p. 38.
43. Rothenberg, *Napoleonic Wars*, p. 88.
44. Horne, *How Far from Austerlitz?* p. 79.
45. Harvey, *War of Wars*, p. 483.
46. Weigley, *Age of Battles*, pp. 381–82.
47. Horne, *How Far from Austerlitz?* p. 119.

48. Ibid., p. 121.
49. Glover, *Napoleonic Wars*, p. 110.
50. Ibid., p. 111.
51. McLynn, *Biography*, p. 342.
52. Britt, *Wars of Napoleon*, p. 53.
53. Kagan, *End of the Old Order*, p. 580.
54. Goetz, *1805: Austerlitz*, p. 123.
55. Weigley, *Age of Battles*, p. 388.
56. Horne, *How Far from Austerlitz?* pp. 154–55.
57. McLynn, *Biography*, p. 344.
58. Kagan, *End of the Old Order*, p. 595.
59. Shosenberg, "Austerlitz," p. 33.
60. McLynn, *Biography*, p. 345.
61. Chandler, *Campaigns*, p. 438.
62. Fisher, *Napoleonic Wars*, p. 42.
63. Seaton, *Austro-Hungarian Army*, p. 20.
64. Esdaille, *French Wars*, p. 41.
65. Haythornthwaite, *Austrian Army*, vol. 1, p. 8.
66. Seaton, *Austro-Hungarian Army*, p. 25.
67. Weigley, *Age of Battles*, p. 421.
68. Harvey, *War of Wars*, p. 662.
69. Horne, *How Far from Austerlitz?* pp. 263–64.
70. Weigley, *Age of Battles*, p. 425.
71. Dodge, *Napoleon*, pp. 258–59.
72. Rothenberg, *Last Victory*, pp. 130–31.
73. Weigley, *Age of Battles*, pp. 429–30.
74. Castle, *Aspern and Wagram*, p. 57.
75. Horne, *How Far from Austerlitz?* p. 273.
76. Castle, *Aspern and Wagram*, p. 61.
77. Rothenberg, *Last Victory*, pp. 173–74.
78. Chandler, *Campaigns*, p. 724.
79. Ibid., p. 725.
80. Dodge, *Napoleon*, pp. 312–13.
81. Connelly, *Wars of the French Revolution*, p. 163.
82. Riley, *Napoleon as General*, p. 98.
83. Chandler, *Campaigns*, p. 733.
84. Ibid., p. 732.
85. Rothenberg, *Napoleonic Wars*, p. 130.
86. Ibid., p. 34.
87. Chandler, *On the Napoleonic Wars*, p. 244.
88. Riley, *Napoleon as General*, p. 85.
89. Connelly, *Wars of the French Revolution*, p. 219.
90. Chandler, *Campaigns*, p. 141.
91. Riley, "How Good Was Napoleon?"

92. Napoleon, quoted in Chandler, *Campaigns*, p. 145.

93. Riley, *Napoleon as General*, p. 85.

94. Jomini, quote in Chandler, *Military Maxims*, p. 64.

95. Napoleon, quoted in Luvaas, *Napoleon on the Art of War*, p. 133.

96. Alexander, *Great Generals*, p. 122.

97. Chandler, *Maxims*, p. 76.

98. Luvaas, *Art of War*, p. 64.

99. Muir, *Tactics*, p. 151.

100. Napoleon, quoted in Chandler, *Maxims*, no. 61, p. 77.

101. Wood, "Forgotten Sword," p. 81.

102. Riley, *Napoleon as General*, pp. 119, 120.

103. Ibid., p. 85

104. Van Creveld, *Command in War*, p. 64.

105. Robert B. Holtman, quoted in Obstfeld and Obstfeld, *Napoleon Bonaparte*, p. 127.

106. Napoleon, quoted in Chandler, *Maxims*, p. 126.

107. Elting, *Swords*, p. 596.

108. Holtman, quoted in Obstfeld and Obstfeld, *Napoleon Bonaparte*, p. 125

109. Dodge, *Great Captains*, pp. 216, 219.

Chapter 15. Arthur Wellesley, First Duke of Wellington

1. Corrigan, *Wellington: A Military Life*, p. 2.

2. A. Roberts, *Napoleon and Wellington*, p. 6.

3. Corrigan, *Military Life*, p. 6.

4. Neillands, *Wellington and Napoleon: Clash of Arms*, p. 33.

5. Ibid., p. 34.

6. A. Roberts, *Napoleon and Wellington*, p. 8.

7. Corrigan, *Military Life*, p. 30.

8. Neillands, *Clash of Arms*, p. 34.

9. Boot, *War Made New*, p. 92.

10. Reid, *British Redcoat*, p. 20.

11. Ibid., p. 21.

12. Glover, *Military Commander*, p. 30.

13. Reid, *British Redcoat*, pp. 22–23.

14. Muir, *Tactics*, p. 75.

15. Ibid., p. 52.

16. Haythornthwaite, *British Cavalryman*, p. 3.

17. Ibid., p. 26.

18. Henry, *British Napoleonic Artillery*, p. 3.

19. Ibid., p. 26.

20. Kohli, *Iron Duke of Wellington*, p. 33.

21. Cooper, *Anglo-Maratha Campaigns*, p. 19.

22. Barua, "Military Developments," p. 604.

23. Cooper, *Anglo-Maratha Campaigns*, p. 59.

24. Ibid., p. 21.
25. Ibid., pp. 59–60.
26. Millar, *Assaye*, p. 21.
27. Barua, "Military Developments," p. 607.
28. Cooper, *Anglo-Maratha Campaigns*, p. 60.
29. P. E. Roberts, *History of British India*, p. 239.
30. Glover, *Military Commander*, p. 37.
31. Severn, *Architects of Empire*, p. 79.
32. Glover, *Military Commander*, p. 38.
33. Neillands, *Clash of Arms*, p. 36.
34. Cooper, *Anglo-Maratha Campaigns*, p. 78.
35. Chieftain, quoted in Neillands, *Clash of Arms*, p. 37.
36. Cooper, *Anglo-Maratha Campaigns*, p. 81.
37. Corrigan, *Military Life*, p. 73.
38. Mason, *Matter of Honour*, p. 256.
39. Severn, *Architects of Empire*, p. 178.
40. Pitre, *Second Anglo-Maratha War*, p. 64.
41. Kohli, *Iron Duke of Wellington*, p. 270.
42. Barua, *State at War*, p. 100.
43. Barua, "Military Developments," pp. 608–9.
44. Griffith, "Wellington—Commander," pp. 27–28.
45. Millar, *Assaye*, p. 61.
46. Ibid., p. 69.
47. Pitre, *Second Anglo-Maratha War*, p. 71.
48. Kohli, *Iron Duke of Wellington*, p. 273.
49. Bennell, *Making of Wellesley*, pp. 81–82.
50. Mason, *Matter of Honour*, p. 161.
51. Neillands, *Clash of Arms*, pp. 37–38.
52. Haythornthwaite, *Invincible Generals*, p. 203.
53. Ibid., p. 204.
54. Haythornthwaite, *British Napoleonic Infantry Tactics*, p. 43.
55. Harvey, *War of Wars*, pp. 696–97.
56. Glover, *Peninsular Victories*, p. 6.
57. Haythornthwaite, *Invincible Generals*, p. 211.
58. Neillands, *Clash of Arms*, p. 43.
59. Ibid., p. 61.
60. Harvey, *War of Wars*, p. 618.
61. Hendrick, "Campaign of Ropes," pp. 28–29.
62. Glover, *Peninsular Victories*, p. 96.
63. Ibid., p. 100.
64. Corrigan, *Military Life*, p. 242.
65. Hendrick, "Campaign of Ropes," p. 23.
66. Corrigan, *Military Life*, p. 246.
67. Esdaile, *Peninsular War*, p. 445.

68. Hendrick, "Campaign of Ropes," p. 39.
69. Gurwood, *Dispatches*, pp. 450–51.
70. Esdaile, *Peninsular War*, p. 448.
71. Neillands, *Clash of Arms*, p. 173.
72. Gates, *Spanish Ulcer*, p. 390.
73. Hibbert, *Wellington: A Personal History*, p. 134.
74. Chandler, "Wellington," p. 80.
75. Glover, *Peninsular Victories*, p. 124.
76. Weller, *Wellington in the Peninsula*, p. 265.
77. Haythornthwaite, *Invincible Generals*, pp. 224–25.
78. A. Roberts, *Napoleon and Wellington*, p. 144.
79. Nofi, *Waterloo Campaign*, p. 36.
80. Glover, *Wellington as Military Commander*, p. 191.
81. Hamilton-Williams, *Waterloo: New Perspectives*, p. 73.
82. Young, *Blücher's Army*, p. 11.
83. Chandler, *Campaigns*, pp. 1014–15.
84. Nofi, *Waterloo Campaign*, pp. 35–36.
85. Horne, *How Far from Austerlitz?* p. 365.
86. Ibid., p. 366.
87. Pétiet, quoted in Barbero, *The Battle*, p. 45.
88. A. Roberts, *Napoleon and Wellington*, p. 149.
89. Chandler, *Campaigns*, p. 1018.
90. Ibid., p. 1027.
91. See the debate on this in *War in History* between Peter Hofschröer and John Hussey, various issues starting in vol. 5, no. 2, 1998, and onward through 1999 (e.g., Hofschröer, "Did the Duke," and Hussey, "Toward a Better Chronology").
92. Chandler, *Campaigns*, p. 1028.
93. Hamilton-Williams, *New Perspectives*, p. 161.
94. Neillands, *Clash of Arms*, p. 236.
95. A. Roberts, *Napoleon and Wellington*, pp. 154–55.
96. Neillands, *Clash of Arms*, p. 240.
97. Horne, *How Far from Austerlitz?* p. 372.
98. Nofi, *Waterloo Campaign*, 179.
99. Howarth, "Waterloo: Wellington's Eye," p. 94.
100. Glover, *Military Commander*, p. 199.
101. Hamilton-Williams, *New Perspectives*, p. 266.
102. A. Roberts, *Napoleon and Wellington*, p. 172.
103. Barbero, *The Battle*, p. 103.
104. Ibid., p. 105.
105. Nofi, *Waterloo Campaign*, pp. 210, 211.
106. Alexander, *How Wars Are Won*, p. 139.
107. Wootten, *Waterloo 1815*, p. 68.
108. Ibid., p. 74.

109. Nofi, *Waterloo Campaign*, pp. 233–234.
110. Coote, *Napoleon and the Hundred Days*, p. 241.
111. Corrigan, *Military Life*, p. 326.
112. Chandler, *Campaigns*, p. 1089.
113. Weller, *Wellington at Waterloo*, pp. 166–67.
114. Esdaile, *Napoleon's Wars*, p. 557.
115. Corrigan, *Military Life*, p. 329.
116. Pitre, *Second Anglo-Maratha War*, pp. 75–76.
117. Corrigan, *Military Life*, p. 77.
118. Esdaile, *Peninsular War*, p. 454.
119. Corrigan, *Military Life*, p. 85.
120. Pitre, *Second Anglo-Maratha War*, p. 76.
121. Wellington, quoted in Neillands, *Clash of Arms*, p. 41.
122. Wellington, quoted in Corrigan, *Military Life*, p. 238.
123. Reid, *Wellington's Army in the Peninsula*, p. 19.
124. Glover, *Wellington as Military Commander*, p. 204.
125. Haythornethwaite, *Wellington, the Iron Duke*, p. 52.
126. Chandler, *Napoleonic Wars*, p. 163.
127. Weigley, *Age of Battles*, p. 534.
128. Hibbert, *Personal History*, p. 43.
129. Keegan, "Under Fire," p. 124.
130. Chandler, *On the Napoleonic Wars*, p. 165.
131. Haythornethwaite, *Wellington, the Iron Duke*, p. 15.
132. Longford, *Wellington: The Years of the Sword*, p. 442, quoted in Hendrick, "Campaign of Ropes," p. 2.

Chapter 16. Conclusion

1. Meigs, "Generalship," p. 4.
2. Publius Flavius Vegetius Renatus, author of *De re militari*, written in the late fourth century AD.
3. Meigs, "Generalship," p. 10.
4. Ibid., p. 11.
5. Fuller, *Generalship*, p. 28.
6. Meigs, "Generalship," p. 13.
7. Coram, *Boyd*, p. 334.
8. Patton, quoted in Carroll, "Sidelined Patton," p. 12.

SOURCES

Chapter 1

Anglim, Simon, Phyllis G. Jestice, Rob S. Rice, Scott M. Rusch, and John Serratt. *Fighting Techniques of the Ancient World.* New York: St. Martin's Press, 2002.

Buckler, John. "Epameinondas and the 'Embolon.'" *Phoenix* 39, no. 2 (Summer 1985).

Carey, Brian Todd, et al. *Warfare in the Ancient World.* Barnsley, UK: Pen and Sword Books, 2005.

Cartledge, Paul. "Hoplites and Heroes: Sparta's Contribution of the Technique of Ancient Warfare," *Journal of Hellenic Studies* 97 (1977).

Cawkwell, George. "Epaminondas and Thebes." *Classical Quarterly*, new series, 22, no. 2 (November 1972).

———. "Orthodoxy and Hoplites." *Classical Quarterly*, new series, 39, no. 2 (1989).

———. *Philip of Macedon.* London: Faber & Faber, 1978.

Davis, William Stearns. *Readings in Ancient History: Illustrative Extracts from the Sources.* 2 vols. Boston: Allyn and Bacon, 1912–13.

Delbrück, Hans. *Warfare in Antiquity*, trans. Walter J. Renfroe Jr. Lincoln: University of Nebraska Press, 1990 [1975].

Devine, A. M. "Embolon: A Study in Tactical Terminology." *Phoenix* 37, no. 3 (Autumn 1983).

Diodorus Siculus. *Library*, trans. C. H. Oldfather. 12 vols. Cambridge, MA: Harvard University Press, 1989.

Goldsworthy, A. K. "The *Othismos*, Myths and Heresies: The Nature of Hoplite Battle." *War in History* 4, no. 1 (1997).

Hamilton, Charles D. *Agesilaus and the Failure of Spartan Hegemony*. Ithaca, NY: Cornell University Press, 1991.

Hammond, N. G. L. *A History of Greece to 322 BC*. Oxford: Oxford University Press, 1967.

Hanson, Victor Davis. "Epameinondas, the Battle of Leuktra (371 BC) and the 'Revolution' in Greek Battle Tactics." *Classical Antiquity* 7, no. 2 (1998): 190–207.

———, ed. *Hoplites: The Classical Greek Battle Experience*. London: Routledge, 1993.

———. *The Soul of Battle*. New York: Free Press, 1999.

———. *The Western Way of War: Infantry Battle in Classical Greece*. Berkeley: University of California Press, 2000.

Hooker, J. T. *The Ancient Spartans*. London: J. M. Dent & Sons, 1980.

Lendon, J. F. *Soldiers and Ghosts*. New Haven, CT: Yale University Press, 2005.

Liddell Hart, B. H. *Strategy*. 2nd ed. New York: Praeger, 1967.

Luginbill, Robert. "Othismos: The Importance of the Mass-Shove in Hoplite Warfare." *Phoenix* 48, no. 1 (Spring 1994).

Lynn, John. *Battle: A History of Combat and Culture*. New York: Perseus Books, 2003.

Nepos, Cornelius. *Vitae*, "Life of Epaminondas," trans. John Selby Watson. London: Bell, 1902.

Pausanias. *Descriptions of Greece*, trans. W. H. S. Jones. 4 vols. Cambridge, MA: Harvard University Press, 1918.

Polyaenus. *Stratagems of War*, trans. Peter Krenz. Chicago: Ares, 1994.

Pritchett, W. Kendrick. *The Greek State at War*. 5 vols. Berkeley: University of California Press, 1971–91.

Sextus Julius Frontinus. *Strategems*, trans. Charles Bennett. New York: G. P. Putnam, 1925.

Spence, I. G. *The Cavalry of Classical Greece*. Oxford: Clarendon Press, 1993.

Starr, Chester. *A History of the Ancient World*. New York: Oxford University Press, 1965.

Stylianou, P. J. *A Historical Commentary on Diodorus Siculus, Book 15*. Oxford: Oxford University Press, 1998.

Warry, John. *Warfare in the Classical World*. Norman: University of Oklahoma Press, 1995.

Xenophon. *Xenophon in Seven Volumes*, 1 and 2. Cambridge, MA: Harvard University Press; London: William Heinemann, vol. 1: 1985; vol. 2: 1986.

Chapter 2

Alexander, Bevin. *How Wars Are Won*. New York: Crown, 2002.

Arrian. *The Anabasis of Alexander*, book 2, trans. E. J. Chinnock. London: George Bell and Sons, 1893.

Badian, E. "Darius III." *Harvard Studies in Classical Philology* 100 (2000).

Barker, Philip. *Armies of the Macedonian and Punic Wars: Organisation, Tactics, Dress and Weapons*. Cambridge: Wargames Research Group, 1971.

Borza, Eugene N. "The Conquest of Persia." In *The Impact of Alexander the Great*. Insdale, IL: Dryden, 1974.

———. "What Philip Wrought." *Military History Quarterly* 5, no. 4 (Summer 1993).

Bosworth, A. B. *Conquest and Empire*. New York: Cambridge University Press, 1988.

Briant, Pierre. *Histoire de l'empire perse: De Cyrus à Alexandre*. Paris: Fayard, 1996.

"Civil Engineering at Ancient Tyre," *Proceedings of the National Academy of the Sciences* 104, no. 22 (May 2007).

Carey, Brian Todd, Joshua Allfree, and John Cairns. *Warfare in the Ancient World*. Barnsley, S. Yorkshire: Pen & Sword, 2005.

Curtius Rufus, Quintus. *The History of Alexander*, trans. John Yardley. London: Penguin, 1984.

Davis, Paul K. *Besieged*. Santa Barbara: ABC-CLIO, 2001.

Delbrück, Hans. *Warfare in Antiquity*, trans. Walter J. Renfroe Jr. Lincoln: University of Nebraska Press, 1990 [1975].

Devine, Albert. "Alexander the Great." In Gen. Sir John Hackett, *Warfare in the Ancient World*. London: Sidgwick & Jackson, 1989.

———. "Demythologizing the Battle of the Granicus River." *Phoenix* 40, no. 3 (1986).

Diodorus Siculus. *Library*, trans. C. H. Oldfather. 12 vols. Cambridge, MA: Harvard University Press, 1989.

Engels, Donald. *Alexander the Great and the Logistics of the Macedonian Army*. Berkeley: University of California Press, 1978.

Fuller, J. F. C. *The Generalship of Alexander*. Westport, CT: Greenwood Press, 1988 [1960].

Green, Peter. *Alexander of Macedon*. Berkeley: University of California Press, 1991 [1974].

Griffith, G. T. "Philip as a General and the Macedonian Army." In Miltiades B. Hatzopoulos and Louisa D. Loukopoulos, eds., *Philip of Macedon*. Athens: Ekdotike Athenon, 1980.

Hamilton, J. R. *Alexander the Great*. Pittsburgh: University of Pittsburgh Press, 1973.

———. "Alexander's Early Life." *Greece and Rome* 12, no. 2 (October 1965).

Hammond, N. G. L. "Alexander's Campaign in Illyria." *Journal of Hellenic Studies* 94 (1974).

———. *The Genius of Alexander the Great*. London: Duckworth, 1997.

———. "What May Philip Have Learnt as a Hostage at Thebes?" *Greek, Roman and Byzantine Studies* 38 (1997).

Heckel, Waldemar, and J. C. Yardley. *Alexander the Great: Historical Texts in Translation*. Malden, MA: Blackwell, 2004.

Heckel, Waldemar, Ryan Jones, and Christa Hook. *Macedonian Warrior*. Oxford: Osprey, 2006.

Jones, Archer. *The Art of War in the Western World*. Champaign: University of Illinois Press, 1987.

Keegan, John. *The Mask of Command.* New York: Penguin, 1987.

Kern, Paul Bentley. *Ancient Siege Warfare.* Bloomington: University of Indiana Press, 1999.

Kolenda, Christopher, ed. *Leadership: The Warrior's Art.* Carlisle, PA: Army War College Foundation Press, 2001.

Kutta, Timothy. "Warfare in the Age of the Peloponnesian Wars and Alexander the Great." *Strategy and Tactics* 214 (January–February 2003).

Lendon, J. E. *Soldiers and Ghosts.* New Haven, CT: Yale University Press, 2005.

Markle, Minor M. III. "The Macedonian Sarissa, Spear, and Related Armor." *American Journal of Archaeology* 81, no. 3 (Summer 1977).

Montagu, John Drogo. *Greek and Roman Warfare: Battles, Tactics, and Trickery.* London: Greenhill, 2006.

Nikolitsis, Nikos. *The Battle of the Granicus.* Stockholm: Svenska Institutet I Athen, 1974.

Plutarch. *Lives,* "Alexander," trans. Bernadotte Perrin. Cambridge, MA: Harvard University Press, 1919.

Ravilious, Kate. "Alexander Conquered City via Sunken Sandbar." National Geographic News, 15 May 2007, http://news.nationalgeographic.com/news/2007/05/070515-alexander-great_2.html. Accessed 3 March 2006.

Tarn, W. W. *Hellenistic Military and Naval Developments.* Cambridge: Cambridge University Press, 1930.

Warry, John. *Alexander, 334–323 BC.* Oxford: Osprey, 1991.

———. *Warfare in the Classical World.* Norman: University of Oklahoma Press, 1999 [1980].

Worley, Leslie J. *Hippeis: The Cavalry of Ancient Greece.* Boulder: Westview Press, 1994.

Chapter 3

Ah Xiang. "Han Dynasty" *RepublicanChina.org.* 1998–2006. www.republicanchina.org/han.html. Accessed 16 August 2007.

"Ancient Bronze Weapons." *The Exhibition of Ancient Chinese Weapons at the Yin Cheng Gong Fa Association, North American Headquarters.* www.geocities.com/ycgf/museum.htm. Accessed 31 August 2007.

Hardy, Grant. *Worlds of Bronze and Bamboo: Sima Qian's Conquest of History.* New York: Columbia University Press, 1999.

Hardy, Grant, and Anne Behnke Kinney. *The Establishment of the Han Empire and Imperial China.* Westport, CT: Greenwood, 2005.

Lewis, Mark Edward. *The Early Chinese Empires: Qin and Han.* Cambridge, MA: Belknap Press, 2007.

Kaplan, Edward. *Gods and Demigods from Yao to Mao: A History of Chinese Statecraft.* Version 1.3, History 370, Winter 1997, Bellingham, WA. www.wwu.edu/~kaplan/H370/ap19.pdf. Accessed 4 September 2007.

Paludan, Ann. *Chronicle of the Chinese Emperors.* London: Thames and Hudson, 1998.

Peers, C. J. *Soldiers of the Dragon*. Oxford: Osprey, 2006.

Richard Nable Collection at the Young Museum of Cultural Arts. www.youngmuseum. com/the_richard_nable_collection.htm. Accessed 28 August 2007.

Sawyer, Ralph D., and Mei-chun Sawyer, trans. *One Hundred Unorthodox Strategies*. Boulder, CO: Westview, 1996.

———. *The Seven Military Classics of Ancient China*. Boulder, CO: Westview, 1993.

———. *The Tao of Deception: Unorthodox Warfare in Historic and Modern China*. New York: Basic Books, 2007.

Sima Qian. "Biography of the Marquis of Huai-yin," trans. John de Francis. *Harvard Journal of Asiatic Studies* 10, no. 2 (September 1947).

———. *Historical Records*, trans. Raymond Dawson. New York: Oxford University Press, 1994.

———. *Records of the Grand Historian*, trans. Burton Watson. 2 vols. New York: Columbia University Press, 1993.

Sun Haichen, trans. and ed. *The Wiles of War: 36 Military Strategies from Ancient China*. Beijing: Foreign Languages Press, 1991.

Sun Tzu. *Sun Tzu on the Art of War*, trans. Lionel Giles. Harrisburg, PA: Military Service, 1944.

Sun Tzu II (Sun Pin). *The Lost Art of War*, trans. Thomas Cleary. New York: Harper Collins, 1996.

"Weaponry of the Bronze Age." Hubei Provincial Museum, *Travel China Guide*. www.travelchinaguide.com/intro/focus/weaponry-bronze.htm. Accessed 1 September 2007.

Chapter 4

Alexander, Bevin. *How Great Generals Win*. New York: Norton, 1993.

———. *How Wars Are Won*. New York: Crown, 2002.

Appian. *The Foreign Wars*, trans. Horace White. New York: Macmillan, 1899.

———. *Roman History*, trans. Horace White. Cambridge, MA: Harvard University Press, 1972 [1912].

Brunt, P. A. *Italian Manpower, 225 BC–14 AD*. London: Oxford University Press, 1971.

Connolly, Peter. "Roman Army in the Age of Polybius." In Hackett, *Warfare in the Ancient World*.

Daly, Gregory. *Cannae: The Experience of Battle in the Second Punic War*. London: Routledge, 2002.

de Beer, Gavin. *Hannibal: Challenging Rome's Supremacy*. New York: Viking, 1969.

Delbrück, Hans. *Warfare in Antiquity*, trans. Walter J. Renfroe. Lincoln: University of Nebraska Press, 1990 [1975].

Dodge, Theodore A. *The Great Captains*. Totowa, NJ: Barnes & Noble, 1995 [1899].

Foulkes, Martin. "Livy's Characterizations of Individuals and Races in Book 21." 2006. www.dur.ac.uk/Classics/histos/1999/foulkes.html. Accessed 8 November 2007.

Goldsworthy, Adrian. *The Punic Wars*. London: Cassel, 2000.

———. *Roman Warfare*. London: Cassel, 1999.

Hackett, Sir John, ed. *Warfare in the Ancient World*. New York: Facts on File, 1989.

Hoyos, Dexter. *Hannibal's Dynasty*. London: Routledge, 2003.

Hyland, Ann. *Equus: The Horse in the Roman World*. London: B. T. Batsford, 1990.

Keppie, J. L. F. *The Making of the Roman Army*. Totowa, NJ: Barnes & Noble, 1984.

Lamb, Harold. *Hannibal*. New York: Bantam, 1963 [1958].

Lazenby, J. F. *Hannibal's War*. Warminster: Aris & Phillips, 1978.

Lendon, J. E. *Soldiers and Ghosts*. New Haven, CT: Yale University Press, 2005.

Livy. *Hannibal's War: Books 21–30*, trans. J. C. Yardley. Oxford: Oxford University Press, 2006.

Meiklejohn, K. W. "Roman Strategy and Tactics from 509 to 202 BC," part 2. *Greece and Rome* 8, no. 22 (October 1938).

Mills, Clifford W. *Hannibal*. New York: Chelsea House, 2008.

Mommsen, Theodore. *The History of Rome*, book 3, trans. William Purdie Dickson. 2006. http://ancienthistory.about.com/od/romehistorians/a/mommsencontents.htm. Accessed 3 November 2007.

Montagu, John Drogo. *Greek and Roman Warfare: Battles, Tactics, and Trickery*. London: Greenhill, 2006.

O'Connell, Robert L. "Carthage's Road to War." *Military History Quarterly* 13, no. 4 (Summer 2001).

Polybius. *The Rise of the Roman Empire*, trans. Ian Scott-Kilvert. London: Penguin, 1979.

Prevas, John. *Hannibal Crosses the Alps*. Cambridge, MA: DaCapo, 2004 [1998].

Sabin, Philip. "The Face of Roman Battle." *Journal of Roman Studies* 90 (2000).

Soren, David, Aicha ben Abed ben Khader, and Hedi Slim. *Carthage*. New York: Simon & Schuster, 1990.

von Schlieffen, General Field Marshall Count Alfred. *Cannae*. Leavenworth, KS: Command and General Staff School Press, 1931.

Warry, John. *Warfare in the Classical World*. Norman: University of Oklahoma Press, 1995.[1980]

Chapter 5

Appian. *The Foreign Wars*, trans. Horace White. New York: Macmillan, 1899.

Bagnall, Nigel. *The Punic Wars*. New York: St. Martins, 1990.

Bradford, Ernle. *Hannibal*. New York: McGraw-Hill, 1981.

Connolly, Peter. "The Roman Army in the Age of Polybius." In General Sir John Hackett, *Warfare in the Ancient World*. New York: Facts on File, 1989.

Dodge, Theodore A. *The Great Captains*. New York: Barnes & Noble, 1995 [1889].

Garba, Emilio. *Republican Rome: the Army and the Allies*, trans. P. J. Cuft. Berkeley: University of California Press, 1976 [1973].

Gabriel, Richard. *Great Captains of Antiquity*. Westport, CT: Greenwood, 2001.

Goldsworthy, Adrian. *The Punic Wars*. London: Cassel, 2000.

———. *Roman Warfare*. London: Cassel, 1999.

Haywood, Richard Mansfield. *Studies on Scipio Africanus*. Westport, CT:
      Greenwood, 1933.
Lazenby, J. F. *Hannibal's War*. Warminster: Aris and Phillips, 1978.
Liddell Hart, Basil. *Scipio Africanus: Greater than Napoleon*. Cambridge, MA:
      DaCapo Press, 1994 [1926].
Livy. *Hannibal's War, Books 21–30*, trans. J. C. Yardley. Oxford: Oxford University
      Press, 2006.
Meiklejohn, K. W. "Roman Strategy and Tactics from 509 to 202 B.C.," part 2.
      Greece and Rome 8, no. 22 (October 1938).
Montagu, John Drogo. *Greek and Roman Warfare: Battles, Tactics and Trickery*.
      London: Greenhill, 2006.
Polybius. *Histories*, trans. Evelyn Schuckberg. New York: Macmillan, 1962 [1889].
————. *The Rise of the Roman Empire*, trans. Ian Scott-Kilvert. London: Penguin,
      1979.
Scullard, H. H. *Scipio Africanus: Soldier and Politician*. Ithaca, NY: Cornell
      University Press, 1970.
Trevino, Rafael. *Rome's Enemies: Spanish Armies, 218 BC–19 BC*. London: Osprey,
      1986.
Wise, Terrence. *Armies of the Carthaginian Wars*. London: Osprey, 1982.
Zhmodikov, Alexander. "Roman Republican Heavy Infantrymen in Battle
      (IV–II Centuries BC)." *Historia* 49, no. 1 (2000).

Chapter 6

Anglim, Simon, Phyllis G. Jestice, Rob S. Rice, Scott M. Rusch, and John Serratt.
      Fighting Techniques of the Ancient World, 3000 BC–AD 500. New York:
      St. Martin's, 2002.
Appian. *The Roman History*, trans. Horace White. Cambridge, MA: Harvard
      University Press, 1912–13.
Baumgartner, Frederic J. *From Spear to Flintlock*. New York: Praeger, 1991.
Bianchini, Marie-Claude. *Vercingétorix et Alésia*. Paris: Editions de la Réunion des
      Musées Nationaux, 1994.
Bovie, Smith Palmer. "Perspectives." *Military History* 11, no. 3 (August 1994).
Caesar, Gaius Julius. *Caesar's Commentaries on the Gallic and Civil Wars: With
      the Supplementary Books Attributed to Hirtius; Including the Alexandrian,
      African and Spanish Wars*. trans. W. A. McDevitte and W. S. Bohn.
      New York: Harper & Brothers, 1869.
Caesar, Gaius Julius. *The Civil War: With the Anonymous Alexandrian, African, and
      Spanish Wars*, trans. John Palmer Carter. Oxford: Oxford University Press,
      1998.
Carey, Brian Todd, Joshua B. Allfree, and John Cairns. *Warfare in the Ancient
      World*. Barnsley, UK: Pen and Sword, 2005.
Cary, M., and H. H. Scullard. *A History of Rome*. 3rd ed. New York: Palgrave, 1975.
Cassius Dio. *Roman History*, trans. Earnest Cary. Cambridge, MA: Harvard
      University Press, 1914–27.

Dando-Collins, Stephen. *Caesar's Legion: The Epic Saga of Julius Caesar's Tenth Legion and the Armies of Rome.* New York: Wiley, 2002.

Delbrück, Hans. *Warfare in Antiquity*, trans. Walter J. Renfroe Jr. Lincoln: University of Nebraska Press, 1990.

Dodge, Theodore Ayrault. *Caesar, a History of the Art of War among the Romans down to the End of the Roman Empire with a Detailed Account of the Campaigns of Caius Julius Caesar.* Vol. 1. New York: Biblio and Tannen, 1963 [1892].

——. *The Great Captains.* New York: Barnes & Noble, 1995 [1889].

Fuller, J. F. C. *A Military History of the Western World.* Vol. 1. New York: Funk & Wagnalls, 1954.

Gabriel, Richard. *Great Armies of Antiquity.* Westport, CT: Greenwood, 2002.

Gabriel, Richard, and David Boose. *Great Battles of Antiquity.* Westport, CT: Greenwood, 1994.

Gilliver, Kate. *Caesar's Gallic Wars, 58–50 B.C.* New York: Routledge: 2003.

Gilliver, Kate, Adrian Goldsworthy, and Michael Whitby. *Rome at War: Caesar and His Legacy.* New York: Osprey, 2005.

Goldsworthy, Adrian. "Reassessing Caesar's Generalship." *Military History Quarterly* 15, no. 3 (Spring 2003).

——. *Roman Warfare.* New York: Harper Collins-Smithsonian, 2005 [2000].

Grant, Michael. *The Twelve Caesars.* New York: History Book Club, 2000 [1977].

Greenough, J. B., Benjamin L. D'Ooge, and M. Grant Danielle. *Caesar's Gallic War.* Boston: Ginn, 1898.

Gwatkin, William E., Jr. "Some Reflections on the Battle of Pharsalus." *Transactions and Proceedings of the American Philological Association* 87 (1956).

Herm, Gerhard. *The Celts.* New York: St. Martin's, 1977.

Jimenez, Ramon L. *Caesar against Rome: The Great Roman Civil War.* Westport, CT: Praeger, 2000.

Jones, Archer. *The Art of War in the Western World.* New York: Barnes & Noble, 1997 [1987].

Kahn, Arthur. *The Education of Julius Caesar.* NY: Schocken, 1986.

Keppie, Lawrence. *The Making of the Roman Army: From Republic to Empire.* London: Routledge, 1998.

——. "The Roman Army of the Later Republic." In Gen. Sir John Hackett, *Warfare in the Ancient World.* New York: Facts on File, 1989.

Lendon, J. E. *Soldiers and Ghosts.* New Haven, CT: Yale University Press, 2005.

Liddell Hart, Basil. *Strategy.* 2nd ed. New York: Praeger, 1968.

Maier, Ferdinand. "The Oppida of the Second and First Centuries B.C." In Sabatino Moscati, Otto Hermann Frey, Venceslas Kruta, Barry Raftery, and Miklós Szabó, eds., *The Celts.* New York: Rizzoli, 1991.

McCall, Jeremiah B. *The Cavalry of the Roman Republic: Cavalry Combat and Elite Reputations in the Middle and Late Republic.* New York: Routledge, 2002.

McCartney, Eugene. "On Aiming Weapons at the Face." *Classical Philology* 24, no. 2 (April 1929).

Meier, Christian. *Caesar*, trans. David Mclintock. New York: Harper Collins, 1995.

Morgan, John D. "Palaepharsalus—the Battle and the Town." *American Journal of Archaeology* 87, no. 1 (January 1983).

Nofi, Albert. "Pompey the Great and the Campaign of 49 B.C.: Analysis of a Military Blunder." Strategypage, *On War and Warfare*. http://www. strategypage.com/articles/default.asp?target'pompey.htm. Accessed 10 August 2007.

O'Reilly, Donald. "Besiegers Besieged." *Military History* 9, no. 6 (February 1993).

Peddie, John. *The Roman War Machine*. Conshohocken, PA: Combined Books, 1996.

Plutarch. *Parallel Lives*, trans. Bernadotte Perrin. Cambridge, MA: Harvard University Press, 1919.

Rankin, David. *Celts and the Classical World*. London: Routledge, 1996.

Reid, Matthew S. "Caesar's Counterinsurgency in Gaul," *Strategy and Tactics* 243 (June 2007).

Wagener, A. Plezner. "Aiming Weapons at the Face: A Sign of Valor." *Classical Philology* 24, no. 3 (July 1929).

Warry, John. *Warfare in the Classical World*. Norman: University of Oklahoma Press, 1995.

Chapter 7

Bacon, Peter Kirk. "A Critical Appraisal of Byzantine Military Strategy, 400–1000 AD." Master's thesis, Texas A&M University, 1998.

Barker, John W. *Justinian and the Later Roman Empire*. Madison: University of Wisconsin Press, 1977 [1966].

Brogna, Maj. Anthony. "The Generalship of Belisarius." Master's thesis, US Army Command and General Staff College, 1995.

Burns, Thomas S. *A History of the Ostrogoths*. Bloomington: Indiana University Press, 1984.

Bury, J. B. *History of the Later Roman Empire*. Vol. 2. New York: Dover, 1958.

Cameron, Averil. *Agathias*. Oxford: Clarendon Press, 1970.

———. *The Mediterranean World in Late Antiquity, AD 395–600*. New York: Routledge, 1993.

Christensen, A. *L'Iran sons les Sassanides*. Copenhague: Levin & Munksgaard, 1936.

Clausewitz, Karl von. *On War*. Princeton, NJ: Princeton University Press, 1976.

———. *Procopius and the Sixth Century*. London: Duckworth, 1985.

Delbruck, Hans. *The Barbarian Invasions*, trans. Walter J. Renfroe. Lincoln: University of Nebraska Press, 1990 [1980].

Dupuy, R. Ernest, and Trevor N. Dupuy, *The Encyclopedia of Military History*. New York: Harper & Row, 1977 [1970].

Elton, Hugh. "Army and Battle in the Age of Justinian (527–65)." In Paul Erdkamp, ed., *A Companion to the Roman Army*. Malden, MA: Blackwell, 2007.

Evans, J. A. S. *The Age of Justinian: The Circumstances of Imperial Power*. London: Routledge, 2000.

Farrokh, Kaveh. *Shadows in the Desert: Ancient Persia at War*. New York: Osprey, 2007.

Gabriel, Richard, and Donald Boose. *The Great Battles of Antiquity*. Westport, CT: Greenwood Press, 1994.

Gibbon, Edward. *Decline and Fall of the Roman Empire*. New York: Heritage Press, 1946 [1776–88].

Goldsworthy, Adrian. *In the Name of Rome*. London: Phoenix, 2004 [2003].

Greatrex, Geoffrey. "Byzantium and the East in the Sixth Century." In Michael Maas, ed., *The Cambridge Companion to the Age of Justinian*. New York: Cambridge University Press, 2005.

———. *Rome and Persia at War*. Leeds: Francis Cairns, 1998.

Greatrex, Geoffrey, and Samuel N. C. Lieu. *The Roman Eastern Frontier and the Persian Wars*. London: Routledge, 2002.

Haldon, John. *Warfare, State and Society in the Byzantine World, 565–1204*. London: UCI Press, 1999.

Jones, Archer. *The Art of War in the Western World*. New York: Barnes & Noble, 1997 [1987].

Lee, A. D. "The Empire at War." In Michael Maas, ed., *The Cambridge Companion to the Age of Justinian*. New York: Cambridge University Press, 2005.

Liddell Hart, Basil., *Strategy*. New York: Praeger, 1967.

Malalas, John. *The Chronicle of John Malalas*, trans. Elizabeth Jeffreys, Michael Jeffreys, Roger Scott, et al. Melbourne: Australian Association for Byzantine Studies, 1986.

Nicolle, David. *Medieval Warfare Source Book: Warfare in Western Christendom*. Vol. 1. London: Brockhampton Press 1999 [1995].

———. *Medieval Warfare Source Book: Christian Europe and its Neighbors*. Vol. 2. London: Brockhampton Press, 1998 [1996].

Oman, C. W. C. *The Art of War in the Middle Ages*, rev. and ed. John Beeler. Ithaca, NY: Cornell University Press, 1953 [1885].

Pohl, Walter. "Justinian and the Barbarian Kingdoms." In Michael Maas, ed., *The Cambridge Companion to the Age of Justinian*. New York: Cambridge University Press, 2005.

Procopius, *Secret History*, trans. Richard Atwater. New York: Dorset, 1992.

———. *History of the Wars*, trans. H. B. Dewing. Cambridge, MA: Harvard University Press, 2006 [1914].

Shahbazi, A. Sh. "History of Iran: Sassanian Army." *Iran Chamber Society*, 2001–8, http://www.iranchamber.com/history/sassanids/sassanian_army.php, 28 May 2008

Stanhope, Philip Henry (Lord Mahon). *The Life of Belisarius*. Yardley, PA: Westholme, 2006 [1829].

Treadgold, Warren, *Byzantium and Its Army, 284–1081*. Stanford, CA: Stanford University Press, 1995.

Whitby, Michael. *Rome at War, AD 293–696*. New York: Routledge, 2003.

Wilcox, Peter. *Rome's Enemies: Parthians and Sassanid Persians*. New York: Osprey, 2005 [1986].

Wolfram, Herwig. *History of the Goths*, trans. Thomas J. Dunlap. Berkeley: University of California Press, 1988 [1979].

Zachariah of Mitylene. *Syriac Chronicle*, trans. F. J. Hamilton and E. W. Brooks. London: Methuen, 1899.

Chapter 8

Alexander, Bevin. *How Great Generals Win*. New York: W. W. Norton, 2002 [1993].

———. *How Wars Are Won*. New York: Crown, 2002.

Allsen, Thomas. "The Rise of the Mongolian empire and Mongolian rule in north China." In Herbert Franke and Denis Twitchett, *The Cambridge History of China*, vol. 6. Cambridge: Cambridge University Press, 1994.

"Battle of the Kalka River 1223." from the Xenophon Group, no date, http://www. xenophon-mil.org/rushistory/battles/kalka.htm, 26 July 2008.

Biran, Michael, *Chinggis Khan*. Oxford: Oneworld, 2007.

Buell, P. D. "Subotei Ba'atur." In Igor de Ratchewiltz, Hok-lam Chan, Hsiao Ch'i-ch'ing, and Peter W Geier, eds., *In the Service of the Khan*. Wiesbaden: Harrossowitz, 1993.

Chambers, James. *The Devil's Horsemen*. New York: Atheneum, 1979.

Dalantai. "Menggu bingxue yanjiu: jian lun Chengjisiban yong bing zhi mi [Research into the Mongol art of war: The strategy of Chinggis Qahan]." Chengde: Junshi kexue chubanshe, 1990, trans. in Urunge Onon, *The Secret History of the Mongols*. Richmond, England: Curzon, 2001.

Dawson, Christopher, ed. *The Mongol Mission: Narratives and Letters of the Franciscan Missionaries in Mongolia and China in the Thirteenth and Fourteenth Centuries*. New York: Sheed & Ward, 1955.

De Hartog, Leo. *Genghis Khan: Conqueror of the World*. New York: Barnes & Noble, 1999 [1989].

Di Cosmo, Nicola. *Warfare in Inner Asian History: 500–1800*. Boston: Brill, 2002.

Gabriel, Richard. *Genghis Khan's Greatest General: Subotai the Valiant*. Norman: Oklahoma University Press, 2004.

———. "The Right Hand of Khan." *Military History*, May–June 2008.

Gabriel, Richard, and Donald Boose. *The Great Battles of Antiquity: A Strategic and Tactical Guide to Great Battles That Shaped the Development of War*. Westport, CT: Greenwood Press, 1994.

Gibbon, Edward. *The Decline and Fall of the Roman Empire*. New York: Heritage Press, 1946 [1776–88].

Hildinger, Erik. *Warriors of the Steppe*. New York: DaCapo, 2000 [1997].

Jackson, Peter. *The Mongols and the West, 1221–1410*. New York, Pearson Longman, 2005.

Javaini, Ata-malik. *Genghis Khan: The History of the World Conqueror,* trans. J. A. Boyle. Seattle, University of Washington Press, 1997 [1958].

Kahn, Paul. *The Secret History of the Mongols: The Origins of Chingis Khan*. San Francisco: North Point Press, 1984.

Kennedy, Hugh. *Mongols, Huns and Vikings at War*. London: Cassell, 2002.

Kosztolnyik, Z. J. *Hungary in the 13th Century*. New York: Columbia University Press, 1996.

Legg, Stuart. *The Barbarians of Asia: The Peoples of the Steppes from 1600 BC*. New York: Barnes & Noble, 1995 [1970].

Liddell Hart, Basil. *Great Captains Unveiled*. New York: DaCapo, 1996 [1927].

Lukinich, Imre. *A History of Hungary in Biographical Sketches*. Freeport, NY: Books for Libraries Press, 1968 [1937].

Man, John. *Genghis Khan: Life, Death, and Resurrection*. New York: St. Martin's, 2004.

Marshall, Robert. *Storm from the East*. Berkeley: University of California Press, 1993.

McCreight, Maj. Richard D. *The Mongol Warrior Epic: Masters of Thirteenth Century Maneuver Warfare*. Master's thesis, US Army Command and General Staff College, 1983.

Miranda, Joseph. "Khan: The Rise of the Mongol Empire in the 13th Century." *Strategy and Tactics* 229 (July–August 2005).

Mitchell, Robert, and Nevill Forbes, eds. *The Chronicle of Novgorod*. Hattiesburg, MS: Academic International Press, 1970.

Morgan, David. *The Mongols*. New York: Basil Blackwell, 1986.

Nicolle, David. *Medieval Warfare Source Book, Volume I: Warfare in Western Christendom*. London: Brockhampton Press, 1995.

———. *Medieval Warfare Source Book*. Vol. 2, *Christian Europe and Its Neighbors*. London: Brockhampton Press, 1996.

Nicolle, David, and Viacheslav Shpakovsky. *Kalka River, 1223*. Oxford: Osprey, 2001.

Onon, Urgunge. *The Secret History of the Mongols*. Richmond, England: Curzon, 2001.

Pittard, Maj. Dana J. H. *Thirteenth Century Mongol Warfare*. Research paper, Leavenworth, KS: US Army Command and General Staff College Press, 1994.

Prawdin, Michael. *The Mongol Empire*, trans. Eden Paul and Cedar Paul. London: George Allen and Unwin, 1967 [1938].

Ramirez, Lt. Col. Joe E. *Genghis Khan and Maneuver Warfare*. Student paper. Carlisle Barracks, PA: US Army War College, 2000.

Ratchnevsky, Paul. *Genghis Khan: His Life and Legacy*, trans. Thomas Haining. Malden, MA: Blackwell, 2000 [1983].

Sinor, Denis. "The Inner Asian Warriors." *Journal of the American Oriental Society* 101, no. 2 (April–June 1981): 133–44.

Spuler, Bertold. *The Mongol Period: History of the Muslim World*. Princeton, NJ: Markus Wiener, 1994 [1969].

Takemoto, Maj. Glenn H. *Back Azimuth Check: A Look at Mongol Operational Warfare*. Ft. Leavenworth, KS: US Army Command and General Staff College, 1992.

Trombetta, John J., and Steven C. Ippolito. "The Emergence of Sea Power in the Yuan Dynasty." 24 December 2007. www.militaryhistoryonline.com/ medieval/articles/mongolwarfighting.aspx. Accessed 21 July 2008.

Turnbull, Stephen. *Genghis Khan and the Mongol Conquests, 1190–1400*. Oxford: Osprey, 2003.

Weatherford, Jack. *Genghis Khan and the Making of the Modern World*. New York: Crown, 2004.

Chapter 9

Anderson, Perry. *Passages from Antiquity to Feudalism*. London: Humanities Press, 1974.

Ayton, Andrew. "Arms, Armour, and Horses." In Maurice Keen, ed., *Medieval Warfare: A History*. Oxford: Oxford University Press, 1999.

Baumgartner, Frederic J. *From Spear to Flintlock*. New York: Praeger, 1991.

Bennett, Matthew, et al. *Fighting Techniques of the Medieval World, AD 500–AD 1500*. New York: Thomas Dunne/St. Martin's, 2005.

Bloom, James. "The Hussites: 15th Century Armored Wagon Warfare." *Command* 35 (November 1995).

Contamine, Philippe. *War in the Middle Ages*, trans. Michael Jones. Oxford: Basil Blackwell, 1984 [1980].

Cornej, Petr. "The Hussite Art of Warfare." In *From the Hussite Wars to NATO Membership*. Prague: ELK, 2002.

Delbrück, Hans. *Medieval Warfare*, trans. Walter J. Renfroe Jr. Lincoln: University of Nebraska Press, 1982 [1923].

Dickie, Iain. "Vitkov, 1420." In Kelly Devries et al. eds., *Battles of the Medieval World, 1000–1500*. London: Amber Books, 2006.

Dupuy, Ernest, and Trevor N. Dupuy. *The Encyclopedia of Military History*. New York: Harper & Row, 1977 [1970].

Fudge, Thomas A. *The Magnificent Ride*. Brookfield, VT: Ashgate, 1998.

———. "'More Glory than Blood': Murder and Martyrdom in the Hussite Crusade." In *Bohemian Reformation and Religious Practices*, vol. 5, pt. 1. Prague: Philosophical Institute of the Academy of Sciences of the Czech Republic, 2004.

Gaillard, Philippe. "The Hussites," trans. Bob Gingel. *Claymore* 8 (1995).

Gillett, Ezra. *The Life and Times of John Huss*. Ann Arbor: Scholarly Publishing, University of Michigan Library, 2006 [1863–64].

Gravett, Christopher. *German Medieval Armies, 1300–1500*. Oxford: Osprey, 1985.

"Gunpowder Weapons of the Late Fifteenth Century." The Xenophon Group. 16 May 2001. http://xenophongroup.com/montjoie/gp_wpns.htm. Accessed 18 October 2008.

Hall, Bert S. *Weapons and Warfare in Renaissance Europe*. Baltimore: Johns Hopkins University Press, 1997.

Haywood, Matthew. "Hussite Battle Tactics and Organisation." *The Hussites of Bohemia*. 2002, http://myweb.tiscali.co.uk/matthaywood/main/Hussite_Tactics_and_Organisation.htm. Accessed 18 October 2008.

———. "Hussite Battles and Significant Events." *The Hussites of Bohemia*. 2002, http://myweb.tiscali.co.uk/matthaywood/main/Hussite_Battles_and_Significant_ events.htm. Accessed 18 October 2008.

———. "Jan Žižka." *The Hussites of Bohemia.* 2002, http://myweb.tiscali.co.uk/matthaywood/main/Jan_Žižka.htm. Accessed 18 October 2008.

———. "Medieval Germany." *The Hussites of Bohemia.* 2002, http://myweb.tiscali.co.uk/matthaywood/main/Medieval_Germany.htm. Accessed 3 July 2008.

———. "The Prelude to War" *The Hussites of Bohemia.* 2002, http://myweb.tiscali.co.uk/matthaywood/main/Hussites.htm#The%20Prelude%20to%20War. Accessed 3 July 2008.

———. "The Protagonists." *The Hussites of Bohemia.* 2002, http://myweb.tiscali.co.uk/matthaywood/main/Hussites.htm#The%20Hussite%20Wars%20 1419-1434, 3. Accessed July 3 2008.

———. "Warwagons." *The Hussites of Bohemia.* 2002, http://myweb.tiscali.co.uk/matthaywood/main/Warwagons.htm. Accessed 3 July 2008.

Hazard, Harry W., ed. *A History of the Crusades.* Vol. 3, *The Fourteenth and Fifteenth Centuries.* Madison: University of Wisconsin Press, 1975.

Heymann, Frederick Gotthold. *John Žižka and the Hussite Revolution.* Princeton, NJ: Princeton University Press, 1955.

Holmes, Richard, ed. *The Oxford Companion to Military History.* New York: Oxford University Press, 2001.

Housley, Norman. *The Later Crusades, 1274–1580: From Lyons to Alcazar.* New York: Oxford University Press, 1992.

Hughes, Phillip. *A History of the Catholic Church until the Eve of the Reformation.* Vol. 3, *1274–1520.* New York: Sheed & Ward, 1947.

Hutton, J. E. *History of the Moravian Church.* Charleston, SC: Bibliolife, 2008.

"John Žižka." *MacMillan's Magazine* 72 (May–October 1895).

Jorgensen, Christer. "Tannenberg, 1410." In Kelly Devries et al., *Battles of the Medieval World.* London: Amber Books, 2006.

Keen, Maurice. "The Changing Scene: Guns, Gunpowder, and Permanent Armies." In Maurice Keen, ed., *Medieval Warfare: A History.* Oxford: Oxford University Press, 1999.

Kej, Jirí. *The Hussite Revolution.* Prague: Orbis Press Agency, 1988.

Klassen, John, and Cynthia Paces. "Women in Hussite Wars." In Reina Pennington, ed., *Amazons to Fighter Pilots*, vol. 1. Westport, CT: Greenwood Press, 2003.

Lambert, Malcolm. *Medieval Heresy: Popular Movements from Bogomil to Hus.* New York: Holmes and Meier, 1977 [1976].

Lutzow, Count Francis. *The Hussite Wars.* New York: E.P. Dutton, 1914.

Macek, Josef. *The Hussite Movement in Bohemia.* London: Lawrence and Wishart, 1965.

McGuire, Michael. "Jan Žižka and the Hussite Wars, 1419–1434." In *Conflict: Historical Study #1.* San Diego: Simulation Design, 1976.

Nicholson, Helen. *Medieval Warfare.* New York: Palgrave Macmillan, 2004.

Nofi, Albert A., and Charles Dunnigan. *Medieval Life and the Hundred Years War.* 1997. http://www.hyw.com/books/history/1_Help_C.htm. Accessed 18 October 2008.

Nolan, Cathal J. *The Age of Wars of Religion, 1000–1650: An Encyclopedia of Global Warfare and Civilization*. Westport, CT: Greenwood Press, 2006.

Oman, C.W.C. *The Art of War in the Middle Ages, A.D. 378–1515*. Oxford: B. H. Blackwell, 1885.

Pribichevich, Stoyan. *World without End: The Saga of Southeastern Europe*. New York: Reynal & Hitchcock, 1939.

Riley-Smith, Jonathan, ed. *The Oxford History of the Crusades*. Oxford: Oxford University Press, 1999.

Sbeghen, Ken. "Heresy, Class, and Nationalism in the Bohemian Husssite Era." *Access: History* 1, no. 2 (2001).

Showalter, Dennis E. "Caste, Skill, and Training: The Evolution of Cohesion in European Armies from the Middle Ages to the Sixteenth Century." *Journal of Military History* 57, no. 3 (July 1993).

Swan, Jon. "Brother Jan Žižka's Wagon-fort Strategy." *Military History Quarterly* 5, no. 4 (Summer 1993).

Toman, Karel. *A Book of Military Uniforms and Weapons*, trans. Alice Denešová. London: Paul Hamlyn and Allan Wingate, 1964.

Turnbull, Stephen. *The Hussite Wars, 1419–36*. Oxford: Osprey, 2004.

Vybiral, Zdenik. "History of Tabor—A Look into the Mirror of Time." *Old Tabor*. 2002, http://old.tabor.cz/1ja/1historie/3.htm. Accessed 4 August 08.

Wilkinson, Stephan. "Žižkas' Zeal." *Military History* 24, no. 2 (April 2007).

Wylie, James A. *The History of Protestantism*. Vol. 1. New York: Cassel, 1878.

Chapter 10

Berry, Mary Elizabeth. *Hideyoshi*. Cambridge, MA: Harvard University Press, 1982.

Black, Jeremy. *War in the Early Modern World*. Boulder, CO: Westview Press. 1999.

Blomberg, Catharina. *The Heart of the Warrior: Origins and Religious Background of the Samurai System in Feudal Japan*. Sandgate, UK: Japan Library, 1994.

Brown, Delmer. "The Impact of Firearms on Japanese Warfare, 1543–98." *Far Eastern Quarterly* 7, no. 3 (May 1948).

Bryant, Anthony J. *Samurai, 1550–1600*. Oxford: Osprey, 1994.

Friday, Karl, and Seki Humitak., *Legacies of the Sword: The Kashima-Shinryu and Samurai Martial Culture*. Honolulu: University of Hawaii Press, 1997.

Hane, Mikiso. *Premodern Japan: A Historical Survey*. Boulder, CO: Westview Press, 1991.

Hilbert, Charles. "Samurai Slaughtered at Nagashino." *Military History* 13, no. 4 (1996).

Hooker, Richard. "Warring States Japan." 1996, *World Civilizations*. Washington State University, http://www.wsu.edu:8000/~dee/TOKJAPAN/WARRING.HTM. Accessed 30 January 2009.

Ion, A. Hamish, and Keith Neilson. *Elite Military Formations in War and Peace*. Westport, CT: Praeger, 1996.

Kure, Mitsuo. *Samurai: An Illustrated History*. Boston: Tuttle, 2001.

Lamers, Jeroen Pieter. *Japonius Tyrannus.* Leiden: Hotei, 2000.

Ledbetter, Nathan. "The Battle of Nagashino." Samurai Archives. N.d. http://www.samurai-archives.com/ban.html. Accessed 23 December 2008.

Lidin, Olof G. *Tanegashima: The Arrival of Europe in Japan.* London: Routledge, 2002.

McNab, Chris. "Nagashino." In Kelly DeVries et al., *Battles That Changed Warfare.* New York: Metro Books, 2008.

Morillo, Stephen. "Guns and Government: A Comparative Study of Europe and Japan." *Journal of World History* 6, no.1 (1995).

Parker, Geoffrey, *The Military Revolution* (New York: Cambridge University Press, 1996).

Perrin, Noel. *Giving up the Gun.* Boston: D. R. Godine, 1979.

Sadler, A. L. *The Maker of Modern Japan: The Life of Tokugawa Ieyasu.* London: George Allen & Unwin.1937.

Sansom, George. *A History of Japan, 1334–1615.* Stanford, CA: Stanford University Press, 1961.

Sato, Hiroaki. *Legends of the Samurai.* Woodstock, NY: Overlook Press, 1995.

Seal, F. W. "Oda Nobunaga." 2005, http://www.samurai-archives.com/nobunaga.html. Accessed 31 August 2008.

Sharpe, Michael. *Samurai Battles.* Edison, NJ: Chartwell Books, 2009.

Turnbull, Stephen. *The Book of the Samurai, the Warrior Class of Japan.* London: Arms and Armour Press, 1982.

———. *Japanese Warrior Monks, 949–1603.* Oxford: Osprey, 2003.

———. *Military History of the Samurai.* New York: Macmillan, 1977.

———. *Nagashino 1575.* Oxford: Osprey, 2000.

———. *The Samurai and the Sacred.* Oxford: Osprey, 2006.

———. *Samurai Commanders.* 2 vols. Oxford: Osprey, 2005.

———. *Samurai Warfare.* London: Arms and Armour, 1996.

———. *Samurai, World of the Warrior.* Oxford: Osprey, 2003.

———. "'Shorthand of the Samurai,' the Use of Heraldry in the Armies of the Sixteenth-Century Japan." In Harald Kleinschmidt, *Warfare in Japan.* Aldershot, UK: Ashgate, 2007.

Varley, Paul. "Oda Nobunaga, Guns, and Early Modern Warfare in Japan." In James C. Baxter and Joshua A. Fogel, *Writing Histories in Japan.* Kyoto: International Research Center for Japanese Studies, 2007.

Chapter 11

Addington, Larry H. *The Patterns of War through the Eighteenth Century.* Bloomington: Indiana University Press, 1990.

Ahnlund, Nils. *Gustavus Adolphus the Great*, trans. Michael Roberts. New York: History Book Club, 1999 [1940].

Alexander, Bevin. "How a Swedish King Created the Modern Army." *Armchair General* 3, no. 6 (January 2007).

———. *How Wars Are Won.* New York: Crown, 2002.

Asch, Ronald. *The Thirty Years War: The Holy Roman Empire and Europe, 1618–48*. New York: St. Martin's Press, 1997.

Ayton, Andrew, and J. L. Price. "The Military Revolution from a Medieval Perspective." In Ayton and Price, *The Medieval Military Revolution: State, Society and Military Change in Medieval and Early Modern Europe*. London: I. B. Tauris, 1989.

Baumgartner, Frederic J. *From Spear to Flintlock*. New York: Praeger, 1991.

Bobbit, Philip. *The Shield of Achilles*. New York: Random House Anchor Books, 2002.

Bonney, Richard. *The European Dynastic States, 1494–1660*. Oxford: Oxford University Press, 1991.

———. *The Thirty Years War, 1618–1648*. Oxford: Osprey, 2002.

Bowman, Francis J. "Sweden's Wars, 1611–32." *Journal of Modern History* 14, no. 3 (September 1942).

Britt, Albert Sidney III, et al. *The Dawn of Modern Warfare*. Wayne, NJ: Avery, 1984.

Brodie, Bernard, and Fawn Brodie. *From Crossbow to H-Bomb*. Bloomington: Indiana University Press, 1973 [1962].

Brumwell, Stephen. "Gustavus Adolphus." In Andrew Roberts, ed., *The Art of War: Great Commanders of the Modern World*. London: Quesrcus, 2009.

Brzezinski, Richard. *The Army of Gustavus Adolphus*. Vol. 1, *Infantry*. Oxford: Osprey, 2000 [1994].

———. *The Army of Gustavus Adolphus*. Vol. 2, *Cavalry*. Oxford: Osprey, 1999 [1993].

———. *Lützen, 1632*. Oxford: Osprey, 2001.

Chandler, David. *Atlas of Military Strategy*. London: Arms and Armour, 1998 [1980].

Childs, John. "Count Tilly." In Andrew Roberts, ed., *The Art of War: Great Commanders of the Modern World*. London: Quercus, 2009.

———. "Maurice of Nassau." In Andrew Roberts, ed., *The Art of War: Great Commanders of the Modern World*. London: Quercus, 2009.

———. *Warfare in the Seventeenth Century*. London: Cassel, 2001.

Connor, Maj. Robert E. "Gustavus Adolphus and the Crossing of the Lech." Essay in *Studies in Battle Command*. Ft. Leavenworth, KS: US Army Command and General Staff College, 2006). http://www-cgsc.army.mil/carl/resources/csi/battles/battles.asp. Accessed 31 August 2008.

Croxton, Derek. "A Territorial Imperative?" *War in History* 5 no. 3 (1998).

Cummins, Joseph. *The War Chronicles*. Beverly, MA: Fair Winds Press, 2008.

Delbruck, Hans. *The Dawn of Modern Warfare*, trans. Walter J. Renfroe. Lincoln: University of Nebraska Press, 1990 [1919].

DiPalma, Matthew. "Death of Gustavus Adolphus." *Military History* 15, no. 4 (October 1998).

Dodge, Theodore. *The Great Captains*. New York: Barnes & Noble, 1995 [1886].

Dupuy, R. Ernest, and Trevor N. Dupuy. *The Encyclopedia of Military History*. New York: Harper & Row, 1970.

Dupuy, Trevor, N. *The Evolution of Weapons and Warfare*. Indianapolis: Bobbs-Merrill, 1980.

Frye, Gordon. "From Lance to Pistol: The Evolution of Mounted Soldiers from 1550 to 1600." myArmory.com, http://www.myarmoury.com/feature_lancepistol.html. Accessed 18 June 2009.

Fuller, J. F. C. *A Military History of the Western World*. Vol. 2. New York: Funk & Wagnalls, 1955.

Gardiner, Samuel Rawson. *The Thirty Years War, 1618–1648*. New York: Greenwood Press, 1969 [1919].

Goodenough, Simon. *Tactical Genius in Battle*. London: Phaidon Press, 1979.

Guthrie, William P. *Battles of the Thirty Years War*. Westport, CT: Greenwood, 2002.

Hackett, John Winthrop. "The Profession of Arms." In *The Art and Practice of Military Strategy*. Washington, DC: National Defense University, 1984.

Haythornthwaite, Philip J. *Invincible Generals*. Poole, UK: Caxton, 2002 [1991].

Hollway, Don. "Triumph of Flexible Firepower." *Military History* 12, no. 6 (February 1996).

Howard, Michael. *War in European History*. Oxford: Oxford University Press, 1976.

Jones, Archer. *The Art of War in the Western World*. New York: Barnes & Noble 1997 [1987].

Jorgensen, Christer, et al. *Fighting Techniques of the Early Modern World, AD 1500–AD 1763*. New York: St. Martin's, 2005.

———. *Great Battles*. Bath: Paragon, 2007.

Kaiser, David. *Politics and War: European Conflict from Philip II to Hitler*. Cambridge, MA: Harvard University Press, 1990.

Laffin, John. *Links of Leadership*. New York: Abelard-Schuman, 1966.

Lee, Stephen. *The Thirty Years War*. New York: Routledge, 1991.

Liddell Hart, Basil. *Great Captains Unveiled*. New York: Da Capo Press, 1996 [1927].

———. *Strategy*. New York: Praeger, 1987 [1954].

Limm, Peter. *The Thirty Years War*. New York: Longman, 1994.

Livesey, Anthony. *Great Commanders and Their Battles*. Philadelphia: Running Press, 1987.

Maland, David. *Europe at War, 1600–1650*. Totowa, NJ: Rowman and Littlefield, 1980.

Malleson, G. B. *The Battlefields of Germany*. London: W. H. Allen, 1884.

McNeill, William H. *The Pursuit of Power*. Chicago: University of Chicago Press, 1982.

Parker, Geoffrey. *Europe in Crisis, 1598–1648*. Ithaca, NY: Cornell University Press, 1979.

———. *The Military Revolution*. Cambridge: Cambridge University Press, 1988.

———, ed. *The Thirty Years War*. New York: Routledge and Kegan Paul, 1987.

Piirimäe, Pärtel. "Just War in Theory and Practice: The Legitimation of Swedish Intervention in the Thirty Years War." *Historical Journal* 45, no. 3 (September 2002).

Rabb, Theodore K. *The Thirty Years War*. Lexington, MA: Heath, 1972.

Redmond, Lt. Col. Dennis K. "Gustavus Adolphus, Father of Combined Arms Warfare." Strategy Research Project, US Army War College, Carlisle Barracks, PA, 2000.

Roberts, Keith. *Matchlock Musketeer, 1588–1688*. Osford: Osprey, 2002.

Roberts, Michael. *Gustavus Adolphus*. New York: Longman, 1992 [1973].

Rothenberg, Gunther E. "Maurice of Nassau, Gustavus Adolphus, Raimondo Montecuccoli, and the 'Military Revolution' of the Seventeenth Century." In Peter Paret, ed., *Makers of Modern Strategy*. Princeton, NJ: Princeton University Press, 1989.

Showalter, Dennis E. "Gustavus' Greatest Victory." *MHQ: The Quarterly Journal of Military History* 16, no. 2 (Winter 2004).

Wedgewood, C. V. *The Thirty Years War*. New York: New York Review of Books, 2005 [1938].

Weigley, Russell F. *The Age of Battles*. Bloomington: Indiana University Press, 1991.

Wylie, James A. *A History of Protestantism*. Vol. 3, book 21, chs. 7–9. New York: Cassell, 1889). http://www.doctrine.org/history/HPv3b21.htm. Accessed 18 June 2009.

Chapter 12

Barnett, Correlli. *The First Churchill*. New York: Putman's Sons, 1974.

Barthorp, Chael. *Marlborough's Army, 1702–11*. Oxford: Osprey, 1980.

Baumgartner, Frank J. *From Spear to Flintlock: A History of War in Europe and the Middle East to the French Revolution*. New York: Praeger, 1991.

Berg, Richard. "The Classic Battles of the Duke of Marlborough." *Strategy and Tactics* 256 (May–June 2009).

Black, Jeremy. "1704: Blenheim, Gibraltar and the Making of a Great Power." *History Today* 54, no. 8 (August 2004).

——. *Britain as a Military Power, 1688–1815*. London: UCL Press, 1999.

——. *Warfare in the Eighteenth Century*. London: Cassell, 2002 [1999].

Britt, Albert Sydney III, Jerome A. O'Connell, Dave Richard Palmer, and Gerald P. Stadler. *The Dawn of Modern Warfare*. Wayne, NJ: Avery, 1984.

Chandler, David. *Atlas of Military Strategy*. London: Arms and Armour, 1998 [1980].

——. *Marlborough as Military Commander*. Staplehurst, UK: Spellmount, 2003 [1973].

——, ed. *Military Memoirs of Marlborough's Campaigns, 1702–1712*. London: Greenhill, 1998 [1968].

Chartrand, René. *Louis XIV's Army*. Oxford: Osprey, 1988.

Childs, John. *Warfare in the Seventeenth Century*. London: Cassell, 2003 [2001].

Churchill, Winston S. *Marlborough, His Life and Times*. Vols. 2–3, abr. Henry Steele Commager. New York: Scribner's Sons, 1968 [1934].

Coxe, William, and John Wade. *Memoirs of the Duke of Marlborough with His Original Correspondence: Collected from the Family Records at Blenheim, and Other Authentic Sources*. 2 vols. London: G. Bell and Sons, 1872.

Delbrück, Hans. *The Dawn of Modern Warfare*, trans. Walter J. Renfroe. Lincoln: University of Nebraska Press, 1985 [1919].

Dodge, Theodore A. *Gustavus Adolphus . . .* Boston: Houghton Mifflin, 1895.

Drew, Lt. Col. Dennis M. "Marlborough's Ghost: Eighteenth Century Warfare in the Nuclear Age." Report No. AU-ARI-CP-85-2. Maxwell AFB, AL: Air University Press, 1985.

Dupuy, Trevor N. *The Evolution of Weapons and Warfare*. Indianapolis, IN: Bobbs-Merrill, 1980.

Falkner, James. *Great and Glorious Days: Marlborough's Battles 1704–09*. Stroud, UK: Spellmount, 2007 [2002].

Falls, Cyril, ed. *Great Military Battles*. London: Spring Books, 1972 [1964].

Folkers, Maarten. *The Spanish Succession*. 2003–9. http://www.spanishsuccession. nl/. Accessed 17 July 2009.

Frey, Linda, and Marsha Frey. *The Treaties of the War of the Spanish Succession: An Historical and Critical Dictionary*. Westport, CT: Greenwood, 1995.

Fuller, J. F. C. *A Military History of the Western World*. Vol. 2. New York: Funk and Wagnalls, 1954.

Haythornthwaite, Philip J. *Invincible Generals*. London: Caxton, 2002 [1991].

Hussey, John. *Marlborough, Hero of Blenheim*. London: Weidenfeld & Nicolson, 2004.

Jones, Archer. *The Art of War in the Western World*. New York: Barnes & Noble, 1997 [1987].

Jones, J. R. *Marlborough*. Cambridge: Cambridge University Press, 1993.

Jorgenson, Christer, et al. *Fighting Techniques of the Early Modern World, AD 1500–AD 1763*. New York: St. Martin's, 2005.

Kaiser, David. *Politics and War: European Conflict from Philip II to Hitler*. Cambridge, MA: Harvard University Press, 1990.

Kennedy, Paul. *Grand Strategies in War and Peace*. New Haven, CT: Yale University Press, 1991.

Laffin, John. *Links of Leadership*. London: Abelard-Schuman, 1966.

Liddell Hart, Basil H. *Strategy*. New York: Praeger, 1967 [1954].

Livesey, Anthony. *Great Commanders and Their Battles*. Philadelphia: Courage Books, 1993 [1987].

"Eugene." In Frey and Frey, *Treaties of the War of the Spanish Succession*.

———. "Ramillies (Offus)." In Frey and Frey, *Treaties of the War of the Spanish Succession*.

Lynn, John. "The Ideals of Battle in an Age of Elegance." *Quarterly Journal of Military History* 15, no. 2 (Winter 2003).

Manning, Roger B. "Styles of Command in Seventeenth-Century English Armies." *Journal of Military History* 71, no. 3 (July 2007).

McKay, Derek, *Prince Eugene of Savoy*. London: Thames and Hudson, 1977.

McNeill, William H. *The Pursuit of Power*. Chicago: University of Chicago Press, 1982.

Meigs, Gen. Montgomery C. "Generalship: Qualities, Instincts, and Character." *Parameters* 31, no. 2 (2001): 4–17.

Morris, William O'Connor. "Villars." *English Historical Review* 8, no. 29 (January 1893).

Myers, Lt. Phillip E. "The Duke of Marlborough." *Artillery*, October–November 1973.

Ostwald, Jamel. "The 'Decisive' Battle of Ramillies, 1706: The Prerequisites for Decisiveness in Early Modern Warfare." *Journal of Military History* 64, no. 3 (July 2000).

Perret, Bryan. *The Changing Face of Battle*. London: Cassell, 2000.

Spencer, Charles. *Battle for Europe*. Hoboken, NJ: John Wiley, 2004.

Standford, Iain, Ian Crossall, and Col. Bill Gray. "The Schellenberg, 1704." *Strategy and Tactics* 243 (June 2007).

Storrs, Christopher. *War, Diplomacy and the Rise of Savoy 1690–1720*. Cambridge: Cambridge University Press, 1999.

Thackeray, Frank W., and John E. Findling. *Events That Changed the World in the Eighteenth Century*. Westport CT: Greenwood Press, 1998.

Tincey, John. *Blenheim, 1704*. Oxford: Osprey, 2004.

Treasure, Geoffrey. *The Making of Modern Europe, 1648–1780*. London: Routledge, 2003.

Weigley, Russell F. *The Age of Battles*. Bloomington: University of Indiana Press, 1991.

Williamson, Murray. "The Making of Marlborough." *Military History* 26, no. 1 (April 2009).

Wilson, Peter. "Warfare in the Old Regime 1648–1789." In Jeremy Black, ed., *European Warfare, 1453–1815*. New York: St. Martin's, 1999.

Wolf, John B. *The Emergence of the Great Powers, 1685–1715*. New York: Harper & Row, 1951.

Chapter 13

Addington, Larry H. *The Patterns of War through the Eighteenth Century*. Bloomington: University of Indiana Press, 1990.

Alexander, Bevin. *How Wars Are Won*. New York: Crown, 2002.

Alphin, Arthur. *West Point History of Small Arms*. West Point, NY: USMA Video Instruction Technology Division, n.d.

Asprey, Robert B. *Frederick the Great: The Magnificent Enigma*. New York: Ticknor & Fields, 1986.

Atkinson, Charles Francis. "Infantry: Linear Tactics." In *Encyclopedia Britannica*, 11th ed., 1910, vol. 14.

Baumgartner, Frank J. *From Spear to Flintlock: A History of War in Europe and the Middle East to the French Revolution*. New York: Praeger, 1991.

Black, Jeremy. *Warfare in the Eighteenth Century*. London: Cassell, 2002 [1999].

Britt, Albert Sydney III, Jerome O'Connell, Dave Richard Palmer, and Gerald P. Stadler. *The Dawn of Modern Warfare*. Wayne, NJ: Avery, 1984.

Browning, Reed. *The War of the Austrian Succession*. New York: St. Martin's, 1993.

Carlyle, Thomas. *History of Frederick the Second, called Frederick the Great*, 8 vols. New York: John B. Alden, 1885 [1858–65].

Chandler, David. *A Guide to the Battlefields of Europe*. Ware, UK: Wordsworth, 1998 [1965].

———. *Atlas of Military Strategy*. London: Arms and Armour, 1998 [1980].

———. *The Art of Warfare on Land*. London: Penguin, 2000 [1974].

Childs, John. *Armies and Warfare in Europe, 1648–1789*. New York: Homes and Meier, 1982.

Delbrück, Hans. *The Dawn of Modern Warfare*, trans. Walter J. Renfroe. Lincoln: University of Nebraska Press, 1985 [1919].

Dodge, Theodore A. *The Great Captains*. New York: Barnes and Noble, 1995 [1889].

Duffy, Christopher. *The Army of Frederick the Great*. New York: Hippocrene, 1974.

———. *Frederick the Great: A Military Life*. New York: Routledge, 1988 [1985].

———. "Rossbach, 1757." In Cyril Falls, *Great Military Battles*. London: Spring Books, 1969 [1964].

Dupuy, R. Ernest, and Trevor N. Dupuy. *The Encyclopedia of Military History*. New York: Harper & Row, 1977 [1970].

Dupuy, Trevor N. *The Evolution of Weapons and Warfare*. Indianapolis: Bobbs-Merrill, 1980.

Fraser, David. *Frederick the Great: King of Prussia*. New York: Fromm International, 2000.

Frederick II, King of Prussia. *The Confessions of Frederick the Great*, trans. Douglas Scaden. New York: Putnam's Sons, 1915.

Fuller, J. F. C. *A Military History of the Western World*. Vol. 2. New York: Funk and Wagnalls, 1954.

Goodenough, Simon. *Tactical Genius in Battle*. Oxford: Phaidon, 1979.

Haythornthwaite, Philip J. *Frederick the Great's Army*. Vol. 1, *Cavalry*. Oxford: Osprey, 1991.

———. *Frederick the Great's Army*, vol. 2, *Infantry*. Oxford: Osprey, 1991.

———. *Invincible Generals*. London: Caxton, 2002 [1991].

Jones, Archer. *The Art of War in the Western World*. New York: Barnes & Noble, 1997 [1987].

Jorgensen, Christer, et al. *Fighting Techniques of the Early Modern World, AD 1500–AD 1763*. New York: St. Martin's, 2005.

Kaiser, David. *Politics and War: European Conflict from Philip II to Hitler*. Cambridge, MA: Harvard University Press, 1990.

Kennedy, Paul. *Grand Strategies in War and Peace*. New Haven, CT: Yale University Press, 1991.

Kolenda, Christopher. *Leadership: The Warrior's Art*. Carlisle, PA: Army War College Foundation Press, 2001.

Laffin, John. *Links of Leadership*. London: Abelard-Schuman, 1966.

Lewis, Samuel J. "Frederick the Great and the Battle of Leuthen." Essay in *Studies in Battle Command*. Ft. Leavenworth, KS: US Army Command and General Staff College, 2006). http://www-cgsc.army.mil/carl/resources/csi/battles/battles.asp. Accessed 31 August 2008.

Liddell Hart, Basil H. *Strategy*. New York: Praeger, 1967 [1954].

Livesey, Anthony. *Great Commanders and Their Battles*. Philadelphia: Courage Books, 1993 [1987].

Marston, Daniel. *The Seven Years War*. Oxford: Osprey, 2001.

McDonough, Giles. "Frederick the Great, 1712–86." In Andrew Roberts, ed., *The Art of War*, vol 2. London: Quercus, 2009.

McNeill, William H. *The Pursuit of Power*. Chicago: University of Chicago Press, 1982.

Millar, Simon. *Rossbach and Leuthen: Prussia's Eagle Resurgent*. Oxford: Osprey, 2002.

Nosworthy, Brent. *The Anatomy of Victory*. New York: Hippocrene, 1990.

Palmer, R. R. "Frederick the Great, Guibert, Bülow: From Dynastic to National War." In Peter Paret, *Makers of Modern Strategy*. Princeton, NJ: Princeton University Press, 1986 [1943].

Parker, Geoffrey. *The Military Revolution*. Cambridge: Cambridge University Press, 1996.

Perret, Bryan. *The Changing Face of Battle*. London: Cassell & Co., 2000.

Phillips, Brig. Gen. Thomas R. *Roots of Strategy*. New York: MJF Books, 2005 [1940].

Pratt, Fletcher. *Battles That Changed History*. Garden City, NJ: Doubleday, 1956.

Ritter, Gerhard. *Frederick the Great,* trans. Peter Paret. Berkeley: University of California Press, 1974 [1954].

Seaton, Albert. *Frederick the Great's Army*. Oxford: Osprey, 1973.

Schieder, Theodor. *Frederick the Great*, trans. Sabina Berkeley and H. M. Scott. New York: Longmans, 2000.

Showalter, Dennis. "Calculation and Circumstance: The Leadership of Frederick the Great." In Christopher Kolenda, ed., *Leadership: The Warrior's Art*. Carlisle, PA: Army War College Foundation Press, 2001.

———. "Frederick II." *Military History* 24, no. 4 (June 2007).

———. *The Wars of Frederick the Great*. New York: Longman, 1996.

Sondahl, Birrion. "Frederick the Great's Masterpiece: The Battle of Leuthen." *Military History Online*. 15 December 2007. http://www.militaryhistoryonline. com/18thcentury/articles/battleofleuthen.aspx. Accessed 24 January 2008.

Stephenson, Lt. Col. Scott. "Old Fritz Stumbles: Frederick the Great, at Kunersdorf, 1759." Essay in *Studies in Battle Command*. Ft. Leavenworth, KS: US Army Command and General Staff College, 2006. http://www-cgsc.army.mil/ carl/resources/csi/battles/battles.asp. Accessed 31 August 2008.

Telp, Claus. *Evolution of the Operational Art, 1740–1813*. New York: Frank Cass, 2005.

Treitschke, Heinrich von. *The Confessions of Frederick the Great*, trans. Douglas Slayden. New York: Putnam's Sons, 1915.

Weigley, Russell F. *The Age of Battles*. Bloomington: University of Indiana Press, 1991.

Chapter 14

Alexander, Bevin. *How Great Generals Win*. New York: Norton, 2002 [1993].

———. *How Wars Are Won*. New York: Crown, 2002.

Arnold, James R. "Bold Gamble's Unexpected Crises." *Military History* 3, no. 2 (October 1986).

Black, Jeremy. *The Battle of Waterloo*. New York: Random House, 2010.

———. "Revolutionary and Napoleonic Warfare." In Jeremy Black, ed., *European Warfare, 1453–1815*. New York: St. Martin's, 1999.

Britt, Albert Sidney. *The Wars of Napoleon*. Wayne, NJ: Avery, 1985.

Bukhari, Emir. *Napoleon's Marshals*. London: Osprey, 1979.

Burbeck, James. "Napoleonic Artillery: Firepower Comes of Age." *War Times Journal*. 1996–2003 www.wtj.com/articles/napart/. Accessed 7 January 2009.

Castle, Ian. *Aspern and Wagram: Mighty Clash of Empires*. London: Osprey, 1994.

———. *Austerlitz 1805: The Fate of Empires*. London: Osprey, 2002.

———. "The Battle of Wagram." In *Zusammenfassung der Beiträge zum Napoleon Symposium "Feldzug 1809" im Heeresgeschichtlichen Museum*. 2009. Napoleon.org, 2009. http://195.154.144.20/en/reading_room/articles/files/474475.asp. Accessed 18 July 2010.

Chandler, David. *Atlas of Military Strategy*. London: Arms and Armour, 1998 [1980].

———. "Austerlitz." *Quarterly Journal of Military History* 5, no. 2 (Winter 1993).

———. *The Campaigns of Napoleon*. New York: Macmillan, 1966.

———, ed. *The Military Maxims of Napoleon*, trans. Lt. Gen. Sir George C. D'Aguilar. New York: Macmillan, 1987 [1901].

———. *On the Napoleonic Wars*. Mechanicsburg, PA: Stackpole, 1994.

———. "Perspectives." *Military History* 9, no. 1 (Summer 1998).

———. "The Right Man in the Right Place." *History Today* 49, no. 6 (1999).

———. "Toulon." *History Today* 49, no. 6 (1999).

Connelly, Owen. *The Wars of the French Revolution and Napoleon, 1792–1815*. New York: Routledge, 2006.

Conner, Susan P. *The Age of Napoleon*. Westport, CT: Greenwood, 2004.

Coutts, Maj. Ronnie L. "Deep Maneuver: Past Lessons Identified for Future Bold Commanders." Master's thesis, US Army Command and General Staff College, 2003.

Dean, Peter J. "Napoleon as Military Commander: The Limitations of Genius." *Napoleon Series*. 1995–2004. www.napoleon-series.org. Accessed 19 January 2010.

Dodge, Theodore A. *The Great Captains*. New York: Barnes & Noble, 1995 [1889].

———. *Napoleon*. Vol. 3. New York: AMS Press, 1970 [1906].

Dupuy, Trevor N. *The Evolution of Weapons and Warfare*. Indianapolis, IN: Bobbs-Merrill, 1980.

Dwyer, Philip. "Napoleon Takes Command." *Military History* 25, no. 3 (July 2008).

———. *Napoleon: The Path to Power*. New Haven, CT: Yale University Press, 2007.

Elting, John Robert. *Swords Around the Throne*. New York: Free Press, 1988.

Epstein, Robert M. "Patterns of Change and Continuity in Nineteenth-Century Warfare." *Journal of Military History* 56, no. 3 (July 1992).

Esdaile, Charles. *The French Wars, 1792–1815*. London: Routledge, 2001.

———. *Napoleon's Wars, an International History, 1803–1815*. New York: Viking, 2007.

Fisher, Todd. *The Napoleonic Wars*. Oxford: Osprey, 2001.

Fitzpatrick, Tim. "Napoleon's Final Triumph." *Military History* 25, no. 10 (March 2010).

Forczyk, Robert. *Toulon 1793: Napoleon's First Great Victory*. Oxford: Osprey, 2005.

Gibson, David J. "Napoleon and the Grande Armée: Military Innovations Leading to a Revolution in 19th Century Military Affairs." *Napoleon Series*. July 2000. www.napoleon-series.org. Accessed 19 January 2010.

Glover, Michael. *The Napoleonic Wars: An Illustrated History*. New York: Hippocrene, 1978.

Goetz, Robert. *1805: Austerlitz*. Mechanicsburg, PA: Stackpole, 2005.

Goodlad, Graham. "Napoleon at War: Secrets of Success, Seeds of Failure?" *History Review*, December (2009).

Grout, Lonny L. "Austerlitz: Napoleon Makes His Own Luck." *Military History Online*. 29 April 2007. http://www.militaryhistoryonline. com/19thcentury/articles/austerlitz.aspx. Accessed 21 May 07.

Harvey, Robert. *War of Wars*. New York: Basic Books, 2006.

Haythornthwaite, Philip J. *Austrian Army of the Napoleonic Wars*. Vol. 1, *Infantry*. London: Osprey: 1986.

———. *Austrian Army of the Napoleonic Wars*. Vol. 2, *Cavalry*. London: Osprey, 1986.

———. *Napoleon's Campaigns in Italy*. London: Osprey, 1993.

———. *Napoleon's Line Infantry*. London: Osprey, 1983.

———. *The Russian Army of the Napoleonic Wars*. Vol. 1, *Infantry, 1799–1814*. Oxford: Osprey, 1987.

———. *Weapons and Equipment of the Napoleonic Wars*. London: Cassel Arms & Armour, 1996 [1979].

Hollins, David. *Austrian Commanders of the Napoleonic Wars, 1792–1815*. Oxford: Osprey, 2004.

Horne, Alistair. *How Far from Austerlitz?* New York: St. Martin's, 1996.

Hyatt, A. M. J. "The Origins of Napoleonic Warfare: A Survey of Interpretations." *Military Affairs* 30, no. 4 (Winter 1966–67).

Ireland, Bernard. *The Fall of Toulon*. London: Cassell, 2005.

Jones, Archer. *The Art of War in the Western World*. New York: Barnes & Noble, 1997 [1987].

Kagan, Frederick W. *The End of the Old Order*. Philadelphia: Da Capo, 2006.

Kiley, Kevin. "The Eagle's Talons: Generalship in Le Grande Armee." *Napoleon Series*. 1995–2004. www.napoleon-series.org. Accessed 19 January 2010.

————. "ULTIMO RATIO REGUM: Organization, Tactics, and Employment of Artillery in the Grande Armee, 1800-1815." *Napoleon Series.* January 2001. http://www.napoleon-series.org/. Accessed 19 January 2010.

Laffin, John. *Links of Leadership.* London: Abelard-Schuman, 1966.

Leonard, Douglas W. "Napoleon, DeGaulle, and the Principles of War." Master's thesis, Florida State University, 2000.

Liaropoulos, Andrew N., "Revolutions in Warfare: Theoretical Paradigms and Historical Evidence: The Napoleonic and First World War Revolutions in Military Affairs." *Journal of Military History* 70, no. 2 (April 2006).

Liddell Hart, B. H. *Strategy.* New York: Praeger, 1968 [1954].

Livesey, Anthony. *Great Commanders and Their Battles.* Philadelphia: Running Press, 1993 [1987].

Luvaas, Jay. "Napoleon on Generalship." *Quarterly Journal of Military History* 12, no. 3 (Spring 2000).

————, ed. *Napoleon on the Art of War.* New York: Free Press, 1999.

Lynn, John A. "Toward an Army of Honor: The Moral Evolution of the French Army, 1789–1815." *French Historical Studies* 16, no. 1 (Spring 1989).

Maclachlan, Matthew. "Napoleon and Empire." *History Review* 59 (2007).

McConachy, Bruce. "The Roots of Artillery Doctrine: Napoleonic Artillery Tactics Reconsidered." *Journal of Military History* 65, no. 3 (July 2001).

McLynn, Frank. *Napoleon: A Biography.* London: Jonathan Cape, 1997.

Muir, Rory. *Tactics and the Experience of Battle in the Age of Napoleon.* New Haven, CT: Yale University Press, 1998.

Neillands, Robin. *Wellington and Napoleon.* New York: Barnes & Noble, 2004 [1994].

Obstfeld, Raymond, and Loretta Obstfeld. *Napoleon Bonaparte.* San Diego: Greenhaven, 2001.

Paret, Peter. "Napoleon and the Revolution in War." In Peter Paret, *Makers of Modern Strategy* Princeton, NJ: Princeton University Press, 1986.

Parker, Harold T. "The Formation of Napoleon's Personality: An Exploratory Essay." *French Historical Studies* 7, no. 1 (Spring 1971).

Paschall, Rod. "Napoleon's First Triumph." *Quarterly Journal of Military History* 12, no. 1 (Autumn 1999).

Riley, Jonathan. "How Good Was Napoleon?" *History Today* 57, no. 7 (July 2007).

————. *Napoleon as a General.* New York: Hambledon Continuum, 2007.

Roberts, Andrew. *Napoleon and Wellington.* New York: Simon & Schuster, 2001.

Ross, Stephen T. "Napoleon and Maneuver Warfare." US Air Force Academy Harmon Memorial Lecture #28, 1985.

Rothenberg, Gunther. *The Emperor's Last Victory.* London: Cassell, 2004.

————. *The Napoleonic Wars.* London: Cassell, 1999.

Seaton, Albert. *The Austro-Hungarian Army of the Napoleonic Wars.* Oxford: Osprey, 1973.

————. *The Russian Army of the Napoleonic Wars.* New York: Hippocrene, 1973.

Shoffner, Maj. Thomas A. "Napoleon's Cavalry: A Key Element to Decisive Victory." Master's thesis, US Army Command and General Staff College, 2002.

Shosenberg, James W. "Battle of Austerlitz." *Military History* 22, no. 9 (December 2005).

———. "Napoleon's Masterstroke at Rivoli." *Military History* 13, no. 5 (December 1996).

Van Creveld, Martin. *Command in War*. Cambridge, MA: Harvard University Press, 1985.

Wasson, Lt. Col. James N. "The Development of The Corps D'Armée and Its Impact on Napoleonic Warfare." *Napoleon Series*. 1995–2004. www.napoleon-series.org. Accessed 19 January 2010.

———. "Innovator or Imitator: Napoleon's Operational Concepts and the Legacies of Bourcet and Guibert." School of Advanced Military Studies, US Army Command and General Staff College, Fort Leavenworth, KS, 1998.

Weigley, Russell F. *The Age of Battles*. Bloomington: Indiana University Press, 1991.

Wilkinson-Latham, Robert. *Napoleon's Artillery*. London: Osprey, 1975.

Wood, William. "Forgotten Sword." *Military Affairs* 34, no. 3 (October 1970).

Chapter 15

Alexander, Bevin. *How Wars Are Won*. New York: Crown, 2002.

Austin, Paul Britten. *1815: The Return of Napoleon*. Mechanicsburg, PA: Stackpole Books, 2002.

Barbero, Allessandro. *The Battle: A New History of Waterloo*, trans. John Cullen. New York: Walker, 2006 [2003].

Barua, Pradeep P. "Military Developments in India, 1750–1850." *Journal of Military History* 58, no. 4 (October 1994).

———. *The State at War in South Asia*. Lincoln: University of Nebraska Press, 2005.

Bennell, Anthony S. *The Making of Arthur Wellesley*. Hyderabad: Orient Longman, 1997.

———, ed. *The Maratha War Papers of Arthur Wellesley, January to December 1803*. Phoenix Mill, UK: Sutton Publishing for the Army Records Society, 1998.

Black, Jeremy. *The Battle of Waterloo*. New York: Random House, 2010.

———. *Britain as a Military Power, 1688–1815*. London: UCL Press, 1999.

———. "Revolutionary and Napoleonic Warfare." In Jeremy Black, ed. *European Warfare, 1453–1815*. New York: St. Martin's, 1999.

Boot, Max. *War Made New*. New York: Gotham, 2006.

Boyce, D. George. "Assaye to the Assaye: Reflections on British Government, Force and Moral Authority in India." *Journal of Military History* 63, no. 3 (July 1999).

Bryant, J. G. "Asymmetric Warfare: The British Experience in Eighteenth-Century India." *Journal of Military History* 68, no. 2 (April 2004).

Chandler, David G. *The Art of Warfare on Land*. London: Penguin, 1974.

——. *The Campaigns of Napoleon*. New York: Macmillan, 1966.

——. *On the Napoleonic Wars*. Mechanicsburg, PA: Stackpole Books, 1994.

——. "Wellington and the Road to Waterloo." *MHQ: The Quarterly Journal of Military History* 12, no. 2 (Winter 2000).

Chartrand, Rene. *Spanish Army of the Napoleonic Wars (3)–1812–1815*. Oxford, Osprey, 1999.

Connelly, Owen. *The Gentle Bonaparte: A Biography of Joseph, Napoleon's Elder Brother*. New York: Macmillan, 1968.

Cooper, Randolf G. S. *The Anglo-Maratha Campaigns and the Contest for India*. Cambridge: Cambridge University Press, 2003.

Coote, Stephen. *Napoleon and the Hundred Days*. Cambridge, MA: DaCapo, 2005.

Corrigan, Gordon. *Wellington: A Military Life*. London: Hambledon and London, 2001.

Davies, Godfrey. *Wellington and His Army*. Oxford: Basil Blackwell, 1954.

Esdaile, Charles. *Napoleon's Wars, an International History, 1803–1815*. New York: Viking, 2007.

——. *The Peninsular War: A New History*. New York: Palgrave-Macmillan, 2003.

Fletcher, Ian. *Vittoria 1813*. Oxford: Osprey, 1998.

Fosten, Brian. *Wellington's Heavy Cavalry*. Oxford: Osprey, 1982.

——. *Wellington's Infantry*. Vol. 1. Oxford: Osprey, 1990.

——. *Wellington's Infantry*. Vol. 2. Oxford: Osprey, 1992.

Freudenberg, G. F. "The Qualities of a General." *Military Affairs* 45, no. 1 (February 1981).

Gates, David. *The Spanish Ulcer: A History of the Peninsular War*. New York: W.W. Norton, 1986.

Glover, Michael. *Warfare from Waterloo to Mons*. London: Cassell, 1980.

——. *Wellington as Military Commander*. London: B.T. Barsford, 1967.

——. *Wellington's Peninsular Victories*. London: Pan, 1963.

Griffith, Paddy. "Wellington—Commander." In Paddy Griffith, ed., *Wellington Commander*. Chichester, UK: Antony Bird, 1986.

Gurwood, Lt. Col., ed. *The Dispatches of Field Marshal the Duke of Wellington, during His Various Campaigns in India, Denmark, Portugal, Spain, the Low Countries, and France, 1799 to 1818*. Vol. 10. London: John Murray, 1838.

Hamilton-Williams, David. *Waterloo: New Perspectives*. New York: John Wiley & Sons, 1994.

Harvey, Robert. *War of Wars*. New York: Basic Books, 2006.

Haythornthwaite, Philip J. *British Cavalryman, 1792–1815*. Oxford: Osprey, 1994.

——. *British Napoleonic Infantry Tactics, 1792–1815*. Oxford: Osprey, 2008.

——. *Invincible Generals*. Poole, UK: Caxton, 2002.

——. *Wellington, the Iron Duke*. Washington, DC: Potomac Books, 2007.

Hendrick, Maj. J. Kevin. *A Campaign of Ropes: An Analysis of the Duke of Wellington's Practice of the Military Art during the Peninsular War, 1808 to 1814*. US Army Command and General Staff College, Ft. Leavenworth, KS, 1998.

Henry, Chris. *British Napoleonic Artillery, 1793–1815*. Oxford: Osprey, 2002.

Hibbert, Christopher. *Wellington: A Personal History*. Reading, MA: Perseus Books, 1997.

Hofschroer, Peter. "Did the Duke of Wellington Deceive His Prussian Allies in the Campaign of 1815?" *War in History* 5, no. 2 (April 1998).

———. "The Prussians and Wellington in Waterloo Campaign, 1815." *Napoleon: His Army and His Enemies*. N.d. http://napoleonistyka.atspace.com/Waterloo_myths_2.html. Accessed 16 June 2010.

Horne, Alistair. *How Far from Austerlitz?* New York: St. Martin's Press, 1996.

Howarth, David. "Waterloo: Wellington's Eye for the Ground." In Griffith, *Wellington Commander*.

Hussey, John. "Toward a Better Chronology for the Waterloo Campaign." *War in History* 7, no. 3 (2000).

Jones, Archer. *The Art of War in the Western World*. New York: Barnes & Noble, 1997 [1987].

Keegan, John. "Under Fire: Wellington at Waterloo." In Griffith, *Wellington Commander*.

Kohli, Jogindar Singh. *The Iron Duke of Wellington: Years of Indian Apprenticeship*. Lucknow, India: C. M. Bajaj, 1999.

Laffin, John. *Links of Leadership*. New York: Abelard-Schuman, 1970 [1966].

Lawford, James. *Wellington's Peninsular Army*. New York: Hippocrene [Osprey], 1973.

Longford, Elizabeth. *Wellington: The Years of the Sword*. London: Weidenfeld and Nicolson, 1969.

Mason, Philip. *A Matter of Honour*. New York: Penguin, 1976 [1974].

McNeill, William H. *The Pursuit of Power*. Chicago: University of Chicago Press, 1982.

Millar, Simon. *Assaye 1803*. Oxford: Osprey, 2006.

Moore, Richard. "Arthur Wellesley." *Napoleon Guide*. 1999. http://www.napoleonguide.com/leaders_welling.htm. Accessed 15 June 2010.

Muir, Rory. *Tactics and the Experience of Battle in the Age of Napoleon*. New Haven, CT: Yale University Press, 1998.

Neillands, Robin. *Wellington and Napoleon: Clash of Arms, 1807–1815*. New York: Barnes & Noble, 2002 [1994].

Niderost, Eric. "Seeds of Defeat Sown at Quatre Bras." *Military History* 13, no. 2 (June 1996).

Nofi, Albert. *The Waterloo Campaign*. Conshohocken, PA: Combined Books, 1993.

Pemble, John. "Resources and Techniques in the Second Maratha War." *Historical Journal* 19, no. 2 (June 1976).

Pitre, Brig. K. G. *The Second Anglo-Maratha War, 1802–1805*. Poona, India: Dastane Ramchandra, 1990.

Reid, Stuart. *British Redcoat*. vol. 2, *1793–1815*. London: Osprey, 1997.

———. *Wellington's Army in the Peninsula*. Oxford: Osprey, 2004.

Roberts, Andrew. *Napoleon and Wellington*. New York: Simon & Schuster, 2001.

———. *Waterloo: The Battle for Modern Europe*. New York: Harper Collins, 2005.

Roberts, P. E. *History of British India under the Company and the Crown*. 3rd ed. Oxford: Oxford University Press, 1952 [1921].

Roy, Kaushik. "Military Synthesis in South Asia: Armies, Warfare, and Indian Society, c. 1740–1849." *Journal of Military History* 69. no. 3 (July 2005).

Severn, John. *Architects of Empire: The Duke of Wellington and His Brothers*. Norman: University of Oklahoma Press, 2007.

Smith, Robert Barr. "'A Damned Nice Thing' at Waterloo." *Military History* 9, no. 1 (Summer 1998).

Strachan, Hew. *From Waterloo to Balaclava: Tactics, Technology and the British Army, 1815–1854*. New York: Cambridge University Press, 1985.

Strawson, John. *The Duke and the Emperor: Wellington and Napoleon*. London: Constable, 1994.

Uffindell, Andrew. *Great Generals of the Napoleonic Wars*. Stroud, UK: Spellmount, 2007 [2003].

Weigley, Russell F. *The Age of Battles*. Bloomington: Indiana University Press, 1991.

Weller, Jac. *Wellington at Waterloo*. London: Greenhill, 1992 [1967].

———. *Wellington in the Peninsula*. London: Greenhill, 1992 [1962].

Wootten, Geoffrey. *Waterloo 1815: The Birth of Modern Europe*. London: Osprey, 1992.

Young, Brig. Peter. *Blücher's Army, 1813–1815*. Oxford: Osprey, 1973.

Chapter 16

Carroll, Andrew. "A Sidelined Patton Shares His Philosophy on Leadership." *World War II Magazine*, May 2009.

Coram, Robert, *Boyd*. Boston: Little, Brown, 2002.

Fuller, J. F. C. *Generalship: Its Diseases and Their Cures*. Harrisburg, PA: Military Service, 1936.

Meigs, Montgomery. "Generalship: Qualities, Instinct, and Character." *Parameters* 31, no. 2 (2001).

INDEX